Our Children,
Their Children

**The John D. and Catherine T. MacArthur Foundation
Series on Mental Health and Development**

Research Network on Adolescent Development and Juvenile Justice

Also in the series:

The Changing Borders of Juvenile Justice
Transfer of Adolescents to the Criminal Court
Edited by Jeffrey Fagan and Franklin E. Zimring

Youth on Trial
A Developmental Perspective on Juvenile Justice
Edited by Thomas Grisso and Robert G. Schwartz

Edited by Darnell F. Hawkins
and Kimberly Kempf-Leonard

Our Children,

Their Children

*Confronting Racial
and Ethnic Differences
in American
Juvenile Justice*

The University of Chicago Press
Chicago and London

DARNELL F. HAWKINS is professor emeritus of African-American studies, sociology, and criminal justice at the University of Illinois at Chicago. He is the editor or author of several volumes including, most recently, *Violent Crimes: Assessing Race and Differences*. KIMBERLY KEMPF-LEONARD is professor of sociology, crime and justice studies, and political economy at the University of Texas at Dallas. She is the editor of the *Encyclopedia of Social Measurement*.

The University of Chicago Press, Chicago 60637
The University of Chicago Press, Ltd., London
© 2005 by The University of Chicago
All rights reserved. Published 2005
Printed in the United States of America

14 13 12 11 10 09 08 07 06 05   1 2 3 4 5

ISBN: 0-226-31988-1 (cloth)

Library of Congress Cataloging-in-Publication Data

Our children, their children : confronting racial and ethnic differences in American juvenile justice / edited by Darnell F. Hawkins and Kimberly Kempf-Leonard.
    p. cm. — (The John D. and Catherine T. MacArthur Foundation series on mental health and development. Research network on adolescent development and juvenile justice)
    Includes bibliographical references and index.
    ISBN 0-226-31988-1 (cloth : alk. paper)
    1. Juvenile justice, Administration of—United States.
2. Discrimination in juvenile justice administration—United States.   3. Crime and race—United States.   I. Hawkins, Darnell Felix, 1946–   II. Kempf Leonard, Kimberly.
III. Series.
HV9104.O97 2005
364.36′089′00973—dc22
                                                                                    2004030246

Contents

Foreword

Barry A. Krisberg

IN THE mid-1980s my colleagues and I analyzed data from the Children in Custody survey to document the enormous disparities in incarceration rates of white children and children of color. We also noted that the problem seemed to be getting worse. National policies to deinstitutionalize status offenders were reducing the numbers of white youths in out-of-home placements but were not having the same positive impact on minority youth incarceration. Further, policy shifts in the 1980s that were designed to stiffen penalties for more serious juvenile offenders were dramatically increasing rates of minority youths in correctional custody. There were other issues as well. We found that children of color were more likely than their white counterparts to be in public versus private programs, and these public programs were likely to be in higher-security facilities and subject to higher levels of institutional crowding.

The aggregate national data from Children in Custody were primarily descriptive and could not offer compelling explanations of the etiological forces behind these discrepancies. Interestingly, as late as the mid-1980s the research literature on race and juvenile justice was still limited to a few studies of police decision making. There were few empirical analyses of court and correctional practices as these relate to race. However, we concluded that the magnitude of the problem was so great that there needed to be a national policy debate about the causes and remedies of disproportionate minority confinement (DMC).

To some extent that national debate has been engaged. Amendments to the federal Juvenile Justice and Delinquency Prevention Act in 1992 mandated that states wishing to receive federal juvenile justice grants conduct analyses of DMC and make good faith efforts to respond to any identified issues. Despite several attempts to eliminate or water down the DMC amendment, Congress has kept this fairly minimum requirement in place. The net result has been a number of state and local analyses of the overrepresentation of minority youngsters in the juvenile justice system, as well as a series of training and program efforts designed to reduce the identified racial disparities. Progress towards the goal of actually reducing DMC has been less evident.

Alongside the federal effort, a few national foundations have identified the issue of DMC as a significant area of interest. For example, the Annie E. Casey Foundation incorporated reducing minority incarceration into its national effort to reduce the excessive use of juvenile detention facilities. The Casey Foundation has also funded the Heyward Burns Institute to work with local communities to reduce the numbers of minority youngsters in the juvenile justice system. Other philanthropic groups, including the Ford Foundation, the MacArthur Foundation, the Walter Johnson Foundation, the Rockefeller Foundation, and the Open Society Institute, have funded a national consortium, Building Blocks for Youth, to reduce the number of minority youths in correctional settings. This current volume is a further example of the commitment of the MacArthur Foundation to support high-quality research on the topic.

Despite the growing national concern over DMC, the research agenda has remained fairly restricted. This collection of research papers is an extremely valuable contribution to the advancement of serious scholarly inquiry on issues of race and juvenile justice. For example, some of the papers focus on the difficulties of unpacking the complex and interactive concepts of race, ethnicity, social class, and culture. Further, the authors worry about the adequacy of data sources and the particular biases that are introduced by those employing different research tools. Moreover, many of the contributors to this volume illustrate a subtle and historically informed comprehension of the issues of race and justice.

All in all, *Our Children, Their Children* is an important book about a serious subject. It moves us ahead along a road of knowledge development and social action that is insufficiently explored. While I would not endorse the views of each author in this volume, these disparate views need to be examined and fully debated. The overall quality of scholarship on race and justice evidenced in this book is well above the primitive and flawed scholarship on this topic that we have seen in the past from the likes of James Q. Wilson, Charles Murray, and John DiIulio. Professors Hawkins and Kempf-Leonard have resurrected the more sophisticated brand of criminological research that one associates with giants of the field such as Thorsten Sellin and Marvin Wolfgang.

Since I have been given the job of writing this foreword, I would like to use some of my space to advance two of my own complaints about research on race and juvenile justice, which are still exemplified in some of the papers in this volume. First, some authors in this volume continue to practice what C. Wright Mills referred to as "abstracted empiricism." They treat race as just another "variable" rather than try understand race as a profoundly important part of one's social and psychic existence from birth through death. One illustration of this is the traditional use of statistical controls to partial out the effects of all other factors to explain the relationships between race and juvenile justice outcomes. The authors appear to be telling us that if other factors appear to explain the observed empirical relationships, then race is not the "real" etiologic factor. But this position is sociologically naive. Unless you think that race is a purely genetic factor (an idea that biologists discredit), then race is expressed in other social, economic, cultural, and psychological factors. We know that race affects where one lives and how much education one receives. Race influences life expectancy and access to health care. Race and social class, and race and geography, are intertwined. So when analyses show that "other variables" reduce the variance explained by race, they are simply identifying the intervening variables through which race affects life outcomes. That the researchers find any residual race effect at all suggests to me that they have not measured all the pertinent intervening factors, or that they have inexactly measured another factor that I would call racism. Other examples of this problem are the studies of police-youth interactions that find that "demeanor" rather than race explains why minority youngsters are treated more harshly. Yet how can we possibly comprehend "demeanor," which is defined by social-psychological interactions, without reference to powerful cultural norms and behavioral expectations that are shaped by racial experiences?

My second concern is that the issue of race and juvenile justice must move past the traditional dialectic of black and white. In our increasingly multiracial and multicultural society the issues of DMC need to be looked at more broadly. Most of the available research is about the treatment of African American youths. There is scant knowledge about the disproportionate incarceration of Latino, Native American, Asian American, and Pacific Island youths. Yet in many locales in the West and Southwest, the incarcerated population is primarily Latino and Native American. Native Hawaiians are the most prevalent group in the juvenile justice system in Hawaii, and in California there is a growing presence in juvenile correctional facilities of Asian Americans, particularly youths whose families are from Vietnam, Cambodia, and Laos. Youngsters from Samoa, Guam, Micronesia, and the Philippines have very high rates of arrest and juvenile justice processing. While there are common forces that propel these various groups into the justice system, there are also distinctive cultural and group differences that must be understood. Put simply, the research agenda must go wider and deeper into the issues of race and juvenile justice.

The editors of this volume choose an apt title for this collection. Most of us would not tolerate existing juvenile justice policies (e.g., trying very young children in criminal courts or mandatory penalties) if these were directed at our own children. Most of us would seek a system that was compassionate, that tried to understand our child as an individual, and that sought to restore that youth to productive citizenship. We seem to tolerate a punitive, second-class justice system because we falsely believe that this social control apparatus is designed for other people's children. However, only when our communities embrace all young people as our own children can we even hope to achieve a reality of juvenile justice that is worthy of our nation's best ideals.

1

Introduction

Darnell F. Hawkins and
Kimberly Kempf-Leonard

Born in homes of comfort and surrounded by the protecting influences of the church and good society, we are slow to appreciate the immense difference between our favored fate and that of the child whose first breath is drawn in an atmosphere of moral impunity and in the midst of privation. (Letchworth 1886, 138–139)

What better education for a disorderly life can be found than that which the gang provides; inculcation of demoralizing personal habits, schooling in the technique of crime, the imparting of attitudes of irresponsibility, independence, and indifference to law, and the setting up of the philosophy of taking a chance and of fatalism. . . . Unsupervised gangs of older boys and young men continue this process of demoralization in the direction of more serious criminality. The end product is the slugger, the gunman, and the all-round gangster. (Thrasher 1927, 272–274)

The documents, as we see, corroborate our assumption that in studying the delinquency of children there is no need to ask what are the factors of demoralization, for there is no morality to start with. Except in the case of Ficki (a child whose delinquency career was profiled by the authors), all the cases show clearly that there is no constructive influence whatever in the families of the delinquent boys. In some cases (Falarski and Czalewski) the marriage-group is positively disorganized; . . . . But lack of positive constructive influences may very well coexist with apparently normal, *i.e.,* not abnormal family conditions. (Thomas and Znaniecki [1927] 1958, 1793)

Cornerville's problem is not lack of organization but failure of its own social organization to mesh with the structure of the society around it. This accounts for the development of the local political and racket organizations and also for the loyalty people bear toward their race and toward Italy. (Whyte [1943] 1981, 273)

The question has been asked many times: What is it, in modern city life, that produces delinquency? Why do relatively large numbers of boys from the inner urban areas appear in court with such striking regularity, year after year, regardless of changing population structure or the ups and downs of the business cycle? (Shaw and McKay [1942] 1969, 140)

In 1992, 3 in 10 juveniles living in central cities were black, and 2 in 10 were Hispanic. In 1992, 22% of all juveniles in the U.S. lived in poverty. Minority juveniles were more likely to live in poverty

1

than were nonminority juveniles. In 1992 the poverty rates for black juveniles (47%) and juveniles of Hispanic origin (40%) were far greater than the rate for white juveniles. (Snyder and Sickmund 1995, 6−7)

Overrepresentation of blacks, Hispanics, and American Indians in the juvenile justice system requires immediate attention. The existence of disproportionate racial representation in the juvenile justice system raises concerns about differential exposure to risks and the fairness and equal treatment of youth by the police, courts, and other players in the juvenile justice system. (McCord, Widom, and Crowell 2001, 258)

THE AIM of this collection of original papers is a state-of-the-science examination of the extent and causes and correlates of racial and ethnic differences in the processing of youths within the juvenile justice system. We have undertaken this effort during a period when the juvenile court and its assorted institutional appendages have come under increased scrutiny and criticism from both within and without. Much recent public discourse regarding how we care for and discipline our children appears quite reminiscent of debates occurring in the decades leading to the establishment of nation's first juvenile courts and correctional facilities (the 1880s through early 1900s). Public attitudes towards youths, juvenile law, and the administration of justice in the United States have always reflected a myriad of interacting and often competing social forces. Public perceptions of race, ethnic, social class, and place-of-birth differences and their relevance for criminal involvement have always figured prominently in that ideological, political and socioeconomic array of forces.

Much of the impetus for the most recent critical examination of juvenile justice can be traced to a decade of rapidly escalating rates of violent crime among juveniles between the early 1980s and the early 1990s (see Tonry and Moore 1998; Zimring 1998; McCord, Widom, and Crowell 2001). Though rates of juvenile violence have decreased in the decade since then, for many areas of the nation rates of youthful assault, battery, rape, and homicide remain at levels above those of decades earlier. The rise in youthful aggression was most pronounced in the nation's urban core and particularly among African Americans and some Latinos. On the other hand, the widely publicized school shootings in rural, small town, and suburban America during the 1990s, even as large city rates had begun to decline, served to dramatically increase the level and emotional intensity of public discourse regarding the causes of and solutions for youthful violence. In addition to serving as a stimulus for the "get tough" rhetoric that has accompanied criticisms of the juvenile justice system and its perceived failures, the spike in youthful violence was also the impetus for the unprecedented move in the 1980s by the federal Centers for Disease Control to declare interpersonal violence a "public health" problem (e.g., see Rosenberg and Fenley 1991; Fingerhut, Ingram, and Feldman 1992a, 1992b). That declaration has led to the establishment since then of an assortment of violence prevention initiatives, many of which are aimed primarily at racial and ethnic minority youths and their communities (e.g., see U.S. Department of Health and Human Services 2001).

As the series of quotations with which we began our introduction clearly illustrate, public and scholarly discussions of race, ethnic and social class inequities, and the pivotal role they may play in the etiology of antisocial conduct among juveniles and in shaping societal responses to such conduct have a very long history in the United States. Despite this legacy, our book is the first devoted in its entirety to a discussion of racial and ethnic differences within the context of the modern juvenile justice system. Much more attention has been paid to such differences among adults, but even in that arena, comprehensive discussions of race and ethnicity are often sorely lacking. A special issue of the journal *Crime and Delinquency* entitled "Minority Youth Incarceration and Crime" (Krisberg 1987) represents an earlier effort to review the growing literature on this topic; and in their book, *Minorities in Juvenile Justice,* Kempf Leonard, Pope, and Feyerherm (1995) summarize important findings from seven important state-level studies of differential processing. Apart from these efforts, there are no comprehensive treatments of the subject.[1] We do acknowledge the existence of governmental reports that have emerged from the federal Disproportionate Minority Confinement (DMC) initiative, which is discussed in several contributions to the present volume. As compared to the present volume, those studies and reports provide less discussion of racial and ethnic differences in the social conditions that contribute to differential rates of offending among youth; instead they focus primarily on the administration of justice.

This relative paucity of literature prompted contributors to the recent National Research Council report *Juvenile Crime, Juvenile Justice* to note the "scant research attention that has been paid to understanding the factors contributing to racial disparities in the juvenile justice system" (McCord, Widom, and Crowell. 2001, 258). Consistent with that observation, the report contains an informative and insightful chapter on race and ethnic disparity in juvenile crime and justice. Given the historical and contemporary salience of race and ethnicity in American society, our book aims at beginning to fill a rather unexpected and glaring void in the juvenile justice literature. We commence our discussion by probing the broader sociopolitical and historical contexts within which contemporary discourse on racial and ethnic difference is inevitably embedded. In an era characterized by rapid-fire media sound bites and a present-oriented culture, such attentiveness to the lessons of the past are increasingly uncommon, even within the world of academia. For those reasons, our discussion of the historical and ideological underpinnings of the problem of racial and ethnic disparity may, at first, seem somewhat misplaced. However, we believe that although a close reading of history always leaves unresolved questions as to what are the "facts" and what is the "truth," the past always informs the present. This is so even when the major lesson to be learned is that the lack of consensus we currently experience has its origins in the now seemingly distant past.

Our Children, Their Children: A Global and Historical Perspective

Much anthropological and historical evidence suggests that all societies, past and present, have viewed their children as heirs to their biological and cultural legacies. To this extent, a premium has been placed on the care and protection of infants and children, even though technological, cultural, and economic conditions inevitably affect the extent to which this goal can be actualized. For example, historians suggest that parental affection and efforts to socialize children in Western societies coincided with declines in infant mortality, first in the 1400s, then again in the early 1600s (Aries 1962; Berger and Luckmann 1967; Kett 1977). The sharp declines in rates of infant mortality were probably both a product of and a stimulus for a renewed societal commitment to give children the resources and attention needed to guarantee their physical and socioemotional growth and development. Included in this commitment to nurturance is the recognition that youth need to be both monitored and disciplined in order to assure their successful socialization into adulthood. Although the precise meanings of childhood, adolescence, and adulthood differ across societies and over time, the well-being of those perceived as our children is now seen as not only a matter of assuring biological and cultural survival, but also as a moral imperative.

For those living in modern, industrial societies the question of just who is included among the ranks of our children is hardly a rhetorical one. The rise of what social scientists label the nation-state, in both its modern and premodern forms, can be viewed as a global social experiment in which people were encouraged to adopt broader (than in the past) conceptions of group identity and belonging. People were encouraged to move beyond traditional notions of family, kin group, caste, and tribe to embrace more expansive notions of who is to be considered "my/our people," or in the case of the young, "my/our children." Some sociological theories have long held that the process of modernization itself is ideologically incompatible with the retention of individual and group divisions based solely on ascribed traits such as race, ethnicity, or family background.

It is clear that this global experiment has achieved its share of both successes and failures vis-à-vis that body of sociological theory. Notwithstanding the obvious success over the centuries in producing a sense of nationhood among diverse and often competing human groups in all parts of the globe, failings have also been quite evident. One of the defining features of social life in early modern societies, especially in the West, was the use of "race" and other dimensions of we-versus-they group identity to fuel a series of bloody, internecine wars and, later, acts of genocidal aggression within and across state boundaries. Clearly they served as "justification" for the atrocities committed before and during World War II in Europe. In other parts of the world, perceptions of what social scientists now label "ethnic" differences or religious schisms fueled similar we-versus-they conflicts, as they continue to do today.

Ruth Benedict ([1940] 1959) describes how these we-versus-they and us-versus-them conceptions also were used to justify the slave trade and the worst aspects of European colonialism and expansionism abroad. Even a cursory glance at world events reveals that many schisms linked to the perceived salience of race and ethnic difference persist in purportedly modern societies even at the turn of the twenty-first century. Today, as in the past, they serve to challenge and divide people's conceptions of what is considered the "common good" and "public interest," as well as views of who are considered to be "our people."

A primary theme underlying many of the contributions to this book is that long-standing patterns of socioeconomic, racial, and ethnic inequality in the United States today pose severe challenges to conceptions of how best to nurture, protect, and discipline the nation's children and youths. Contributors to this volume note that there are many well-documented precedents in the history of the United States, as a society, and of the history of juvenile crime and justice, in particular, which continue to shape modern law and policy.[2] Many of the challenges now facing the nation in the juvenile justice arena derive from the very nature of social life in all modern, urban, demographically and culturally heterogeneous societies. Others have their roots in the unique historical circumstances that have shaped the development of American society. Public opinion, laws, and social policies that convey distinctions between "our children" and "their children" may seem at odds with the very meaning of modernity, but are not at all at odds with well-entrenched patterns of group differentiation and inequality that have characterized much of American history.

Apart from the intergroup divisiveness that often characterizes contemporary societies, it is also clear that other aspects of life in modern industrial, urban societies pose risks for children and adolescents. Arguably, when compared to the past, many of the cultural, economic, and demographic changes associated with the rise of modern, urban societies have produced potentially greater obstacles to the successful personal and social development of youths of *all* ethnic, racial, and class backgrounds. There are potentially more threats to their safety and socioemotional well-being than were found in agrarian or preindustrial societies of the past or those that exist today. This is true despite the obvious benefits in terms of nutrition, health care, and overall economic well-being that have accompanied greater urbanization and modernization. Paul Goodman in *Growing Up Absurd* (1960) has eloquently chronicled the unique set of stressors and alienation faced by children as they grow up in urban, industrial society. The social and cultural dislocations and readjustments associated with the mass movement of populations from rural or small town settings to urban contexts have also been documented by other social scientists and historians. Many contributions to this volume, particularly those in the last two sections of the book, chronicle some of these stresses and strains and their impact on levels of racial and ethnic disparity within the juvenile justice system.

Having attempted to provide a broader, global context for the reading of the ensuing chapters, let us now consider the specific historical developments surrounding racial and ethnic disparities in American society and within the juvenile justice system at its inception.

The More Things Change . . .

Both before and after the inception of the nation's first juvenile court at the end of nineteenth century, and with it the gradual establishment of the assorted institutional appendages that are now labeled the "juvenile justice system," American society experienced periods of intense public debate regarding the causes of misconduct and crime among youths and what can be done to suppress such behavior. In his pioneering investigation of the origins of the nation's juvenile justice system, Platt (1969) noted that the "child savers" movement that led to the emergence of that system had its beginnings in deeply entrenched images of adult criminality and of delinquency among youths as a precursor to such crime.[3] As it is today, the juvenile justice system was seen as a means of preventing youths from becoming adult criminals. Images of the risks facing youth, and their negative impacts on healthy youth development, were evident in much scholarly, public, and jurisprudential discourse found in Europe and the United States between 1870 and 1900.

Schlossman (1974) reminds us, however, that the perceived linkages among class, ethnicity, race, moral turpitude, and inner-city location actually derive from the 1820s with the first influx of the Irish to American cities. He notes that these linkages were brought together as evocatively during the early 1850s as they would be later on. Schlossman further observes that the rhetoric of this period extended beyond matters of crime and justice. He cites such early commentators as Charles Loring Brace and Robert Hartley in New York, who extended the logic of that discourse to the successful campaigns of the period and later decades to establish tax-supported public schools. Such schools were touted as a means of both achieving the Americanization of the Irish and later-arriving ethnic immigrants and nonwhite migrants, and also as a means of saving them from lives of crime, depravity, and illiteracy.

Although the first official juvenile court originated in Illinois in 1899, Platt notes that in 1874 and 1892, Massachusetts and New York, respectively, passed laws providing for trials of minors apart from adults charged with crimes (Platt 1969, 9). Nevertheless, with the establishment in Illinois of the first court devoted solely to the processing of cases involving juvenile offenders, Chicago emerged, during the first decades of the twentieth century, as the site of not only the nation's first court but also much of the social science research and legal innovation that shaped that court and that continue to shape our views of adolescent crime and punishment at the beginning of the twenty-first century. Schlossman (1977), Krisberg and Austin (1978), Rothman (1980), and Bernard (1992) have all elaborated and extended Platt's observations in their own informative, and often critical (of each other) work on the history of American juvenile justice. Although the rise of the juvenile court at the start of the twentieth century is seen as the catalyst for public discourse about delinquency causation, the main impetus may have been the rapid expansion of public and private reformatories for children and youth in the mid- to late nineteenth century (Schlossman 1974, 1977).

Analysts who have documented the rise of the juvenile court and the juvenile justice system, including contributors to the present book, all report that attentiveness to ethnic, racial, and social class differences played a pivotal role in those late-nineteenth-century and early-twentieth-century developments. The quotations at the start of this chapter, some of which were made in the decades surrounding the turn of the twentieth century, clearly illustrate the concern for social inequality and group (racial, ethnic, and class) differences found among some of the earliest supporters of the juvenile court and its offshoots. They also illustrate the nature of the views during this period and later regarding the causes of delinquency among American youths and what could be done to prevent it. Despite their grounding in another era, even the earliest of these observations resonate with much contemporary thought, research findings, and public discourse. These include (1) questions of the social (as opposed to biological or what were sometimes called "constitutional" deficits) causes of delinquency, (2) why race and ethnic differences exist in delinquency involvement, and (3) what can or should be done to reduce the incidence of delinquency and its negative impact on the lives of children. Many of the chapters in this volume serve to highlight the contemporary salience of this pivotal socioetiological, jurisprudential, and public policy terrain, an ideological landscape whose contours were first sketched by these early observers.

Despite some areas of obvious contention, there is considerable agreement among the commentators we cite in their responses to questions regarding the causes of delinquency and remedies for it. Either explicitly or implicitly, many connect the causes of America's delinquency problem to life in the city. Platt (1969, chap. 2) describes this etiological impulse, which he labels "urban disenchantment," and notes the role it played in the "child savers" movement. Similarly, Bernard (1992) shows how urbanization, immigration, and rapid population growth in the period affected ideas about the causes of pauperism and delinquency. The earliest of the commentators cited above (Letchworth 1886; Thrasher 1927; and Thomas and Znaniecki [1927] 1958) contrast the perils of life in large cities with the less perilous lifestyles found in the small towns or rural areas from which most immigrants came. Of course, this urban-rural contrast was one of the preeminent themes found in the work of most sociologists of this period, especially those associated with the Chicago school of thought (e.g., see Park, Burgess, and McKenzie 1928).[4]

Platt (1969, 18–28) further notes, however, that the tenets of social Darwinism, including views of innate moral defects among the lower classes, also shaped views of both adult and juvenile criminal offenders during the late nineteenth century. Indeed, much of the earliest ideological debate found within the historiography of the juvenile justice system has centered on the question of to what extent biological determinism as manifested in the form of antipathy toward the lower social class among the middle and upper classes, has shaped views of delinquency and juvenile justice in the United States. In this regard it is important to note that during the past, much as they do today, biological determinist arguments and discourse took many forms. Apart from their grounding in the general tenets of social Darwinism, many were linked to the eugenics movement. While much of social Darwinist thought was decidedly "academic" in nature and designed to "explain" racial and ethnic differences, eugenicists introduced into the juvenile justice arena a more "applied" theory and along with it a problematic set of social policies said to be relevant for understanding individual and group differences in delinquent involvement. As such, it brought into the justice arena the basis for class-based efforts aimed at devising supposed remedial social policy aimed at the poor, as a group, and their overrepresentation among delinquents and criminals.

Indeed, while eugenics is frequently linked to such ominous practices as involuntary sterilization and lobotomies among older offenders (Lombroso 1876), it had perhaps a much greater impact on needy youths and their handling within the emerging juvenile justice system of the period than it did on the management and social control of adults, largely because of societal views of children and youths. Then, as today, the handling and control of youths were based on conceptions of their perceived "amenability," "malleability," and "moral flexibility." Most youths, unlike adults, were said to be capable of change and thereby capable of being saved from lives of crime. Then, as now, there were efforts, some more well intentioned than others, to use psychological and medical screening techniques to identify and isolate "defective delinquents" (e.g., see Haller 1963; and Rafter 1985). Schlossman (1974) notes that these views of lower-class and immigrant youths had seeped into the discourse about urban child welfare long before the end of the nineteenth century.

Because of the concentration of both white ethnic immigrants and non-white minorities and migrants in the nation's largest cities, the perceived causal associations among race/ethnicity, urban life, and crime and delinquency have been particularly pronounced in the United States. Such perceived associations have now existed for nearly two centuries. As we have noted, the notion of a broad-based "urban disenchantment" was used to depict the factors thought to lead to delinquency among immigrants. However, by the mid-twentieth century, analysts such as Shaw and McKay ([1942] 1969) would continue to stress the delinquency-producing effects of life in urban contexts but tend to focus largely on conditions in what were labeled the "inner," or "core," areas of the city. This reconceptualization of the causes of group differences in crime and delinquency was linked to the Chicago school of sociology, which sought to situate the study of ethnic, racial, and class differences in social behaviors within ecological contexts, as opposed to the exclusive focus of earlier etiological research and theory on the traits of individuals (e.g., see Park, Burgess, and McKenzie 1928). As recently as the late 1920s, these social scientists were actively engaged in a struggle to rebut purely "constitutional" theories of individual and group differences in social conduct.

The themes developed by Shaw and McKay continue to influence thinking about the causes of delinquency, as is evident in the excerpt cited from Snyder and Sickmund (1995), and as documented in various chapters of our book. Indeed, there has been a resurgence of interest in the importance of ecological contexts for understanding the linkages among race, ethnicity, and delinquency, a development we explore in our conclusion to this book. This trend has been prompted by recent innovative studies of the influence of neighborhoods on rates of crime and delinquency (Sampson and Groves 1989; Bursik and Grasmick 1993; Sampson and Wilson 1995; Krivo and Peterson 1996; Sampson 1997; Sampson, Morenoff, and Earls 1999; Morenoff, Sampson, and Raudenbush 2001). On the other hand, as many contributions to this book illustrate, more sophisticated, less ideologically grounded studies of individual traits have also come onto the delinquency research scene. This new generation of research aimed at unraveling the correlates of individual differences in rates of juvenile offending has shown that it has the potential to contribute much to our understanding of the determinants of class differences and, by extension, ethnic and racial differences as well.

That the very earliest debates about group differences in rates of delinquency were centered on white immigrant populations was largely due to the fact that the Great Migration of African Americans (and also Latinos) from the American South and Southwest was largely a twentieth-century phenomenon. With change in the "color" of the urban underclass came public and political discourse very similar to that associated with white ethnics, but at the same time American society witnessed the emergence of potentially more virulent and divisive public perceptions of the link between race/ethnicity and juvenile delinquency (Feld 1999). Several contributions to this book explore the increasing "racialization" of perceptions of juvenile delinquency and justice during this period. We will also return to this theme later in our introduction.

In sum, whether viewed as products of "urban disenchantment" or a more narrow "inner-city blight," several themes consistently emerge from both the historical and contemporary accounts of the causes of race and ethnic differences in rates of delinquency. First, poverty and the presumed social disorganization that results from it are widely accepted as important factors contributing to involvement in delinquency. Second, deficits in social learning and morality as a function of family life or deviant peers also are highlighted in most of these accounts. Third, life in disadvantaged ecological contexts, whether defined as disorganized white ethnic neighborhoods, black inner-city slums, Latino barrios, or Indian reservations, have all come to be associated with elevated levels of delinquency involvement. Various chapters in this book show that these remain prominent themes in contemporary scholarship on the etiology of delinquency but are much more vulnerable to critique and calls for clarification than they were in the past. These consistent themes notwithstanding, social science research has also revealed several areas of discord that have relevance for our understanding of race, ethnicity, and juvenile justice.

Particularly in response to questions of the causes of criminal and delinquent conduct, many analysts, past and present, have questioned the etiological significance of notions of "race" and "ethnicity." They ask whether, apart from the frequent association between racial/ethnic group membership and socioeconomic advantage or disadvantage, the designation of one's racial or ethnic status helps us predict who will offend, at what level they will offend, or what can be done to prevent violations of social norms. Inspired by the now long-standing critiques of notions of "race" within anthropology and other social sciences, such as those of Benedict ([1940] 1959) and Montagu ([1942] 1997), many recent commentators stress the fact that race is a "social construct" (Omi and Winant 1994). Within the criminal justice arena, this critique has raised serious questions about the link between race/ethnicity and differential rates of crime and violence (Hawkins 2003). Buttressing this line of research and theory, other researchers, inspired by Marxist and socialist conceptions of the primacy of economic and material well-being, ask whether race and ethnicity are perhaps less important for determining one's fate than is one's social class standing (see Wilson 1978 for a revival of the race-versus-class debate). That is, they propose that if one accounts for the effects of poverty and socioeconomic disadvantage on delinquent and criminal involvement, race/ethnicity labels explain very little, if any, of observed group differences. An early statement of this position within the context of juvenile crime and justice comes from the work of Shaw and McKay ([1942] 1969). They proposed that race differences in crime and delinquency are a function of socioeconomic variations in place, neighborhood, or community, as opposed to some other presumed difference between racial and ethnic groups such as native-born whites, white immigrants, or Americans of African or Mexican ancestry (see also Hawkins 1993, 1995). As several chapters in this book and our own conclusion reveal, this etiological puzzle remains an integral part of contemporary work on race, ethnicity, and juvenile justice.

Finally, while all seven of the observations with which our introduction began are attentive to the problem of ethnic or racial difference in rates of delinquency, they also remind us of the "ethnic succession" that has characterized life in American cities over the past century. For example, while white ethnic overrepresentation in delinquency is not an issue today, it was very much on the minds of the earliest observers of American juvenile crime and justice. Letchworth's contrasting of the lives of comfort and lives of deprivation during the 1880s alludes to the plight of the children of immigrants from eastern and southern Europe. As Schlossman (1974) has observed, several decades earlier, it was the Irish who were the target of such concern. In their classic ethnographic and sociological studies of urban America, Thomas and Znaniecki ([1927] 1958) and Whyte ([1943] 1981) turn their attention to the plight of those later immigrants. They attempt to account for high rates of delinquency among Polish and Italian immigrants in America's cities during the decades before and after the First World War. Similarly, Thrasher's pioneering study of gangs in Chicago (1927) chronicled the criminal involvement of a diverse array of European immigrant populations, including the American Irish. A similar concern for high rates of delinquency among these same white ethnic immigrants, as well as the children of persons of Mexican-American and African-American ancestry during the 1920s through 1940s, motivated the urban studies of Shaw (1929) and Shaw and McKay ([1942] 1969). Their work chronicled the arrival and gradual assimilation of many white ethnics into the American mainstream, as well as the internal migration of African Americans and Mexican Americans from the rural South and Southwest into cities of the urban North, and their even more gradual assimilation (or lack thereof) in those environments. Thus, reducing racial and ethnic differences in crime and justice may be tied to broader policy goals aimed at assuring socioeconomic and sociopolitical assimilation and accommodation.

As the twenty-first century begins, scholarly and public policy debates about overrepresentation among juvenile offenders involves primarily three racial/ethnic groupings: African Americans, Latinos/Hispanics, and Native Americans (McCord, Widom, and Crowell 2001). Though somewhat below the wider public's perceptual radar at this time, there is also a growing public concern for juvenile offending among some groups of south Asian immigrants[5] and a renewed interest in the plight of the "white underclass" residing in small town and rural America. Among those groups well above the radar, the work of Snyder and Sickmund (1995) and other contemporary research on delinquency have highlighted the disproportionate rates of offending and victimization now concentrated among those whom William Julius Wilson (1987) has labeled the "black, urban underclass." These are largely the descendants of African American migrants from the rural South who now live in the core areas (inner cities) of the nation's largest metropolitan areas.

As contributions to this volume will attest, the plight of African Americans has received much more notice and attention than that of Native or Mexican Americans. Such notice is a function of not only their disproportionate presence in the juvenile justice system, but also the way racial and ethnic groups are enumerated in the U.S. census and in crime statistics. As chapters in this volume reveal, the plight of racial and ethnic minorities in the American juvenile justice system has caught the attention of not only academic researchers and law enforcement, but also the U.S. Congress. Such interest has come in the form of federal mandates requiring scrutiny of the disproportionate confinement of minority youth (DMC). Before considering further the significant legal and public policy issues that have emerged from these concerns, let us examine yet another important dimension of the historical and contemporary debate regarding the nexus of race, ethnicity, and the youth crime problem in America.

Our Children, Their Children: Noblesse Oblige versus Repressive Social Control

Blake McKelvey has called the history of adult prisons in the United States a "history of good intentions" (1977). The many contradictions implied in McKelvey's descriptive label are borne out by the contents of his influential study. Much of his research suggests that despite good intentions, American penal reformers failed to achieve many of the lofty goals they set for themselves. Beginning with the model prisons for adults and late adolescents established by the Quakers in Pennsylvania at the end of the eighteenth century and continuing with the widespread adoption of that prototype all across the nation during the next century, the barbarity of actual practice often collided with the seemingly noble intentions of both the earliest and later reformers. In the delinquency arena, researchers have sometimes used McKelvey's label or its equivalent to describe the history of the American juvenile justice system. Even more than in the adult arena, the idea of "good intentions" appears to provide an apt description of the efforts of the earliest proponents of the establishment of the juvenile justice system. Both then and now, juvenile codes have included assertions that assuring "the best interests of the child" is the objective of, and justification for, legal or state intervention. The widely cited legal mechanism that facilitates this intervention is the *parens patriae* doctrine, by which the government can assume parental responsibilities. Given the perceived vulnerability of children and adolescents and professed societal obligations to protect and nurture them, that such efforts should be shaped by a concern for their best interests is fitting.

However, significant ethnic and racial disparity in both reported rates of juvenile offending and justice system processing over the past century has led to considerable debate regarding the actual nature of the "motives" that underlie efforts to "treat" and to "save" juvenile offenders. Work by McKelvey and others suggests that rehabilitation and penitence for adult criminals were part of the original motivation for the establishment of state-run prisons beginning at the end of the eighteenth century. Yet, by the time the first juvenile court was established, the trend toward viewing such "correctional" institutions as largely purveyors of retribution was well underway and would continue unabated over the next century. Norval Morris (1974) showed that by the end of the 1960s the rehabilitation ideal for adult prisons was almost completely a thing of the past. To the extent that juvenile justice is and has been greatly influenced by what happens in the adult arena, one would expect over time a similar erosion of rehabilitation principles in that system as well.

On the other hand, some observers of both the adult and juvenile justice systems have questioned the nature of the *initial* motivation of the nation's earliest reformers and architects of the juvenile justice system. Whether their intentions were indeed good or benevolent has been the subject of considerable debate. Indeed, this question has driven the historiography of crime and punishment in the United States for many decades. Some observers, such as McKelvey, are inclined to think of both adult and juvenile justice as exemplars of our failure to implement over time the well-intentioned goal of helping the less fortunate among us. Anthony Platt and David Rothman, among those described as critical, conflict-oriented analysts, offer a less charitable view of the earliest reformers. They attribute their motives largely to ethnic and racial animosities, fear and dislike of the poor, the relentless pursuit of group self-interest, and a penchant for repressive "law and order" policies.

Still other observers appear to be unwilling to declare a failure the efforts at social reform over the past century. They see much of value in both past and current efforts to "rehabilitate" both youthful and adult offenders. They bemoan the turn toward penal policies based on retribution for adults and staunchly resist the idea that the juvenile court has not been of benefit to American society. To the extent that "social control" based solely on ascriptive (biological) attributes such as race, ethnicity, or gender of both offenders and victims (as opposed to actual conduct) or consideration of one's social class status drive criminal justice practices, they seek an end to such bias. It is far beyond the scope of this introduction or this volume to address the merits of these competing positions. Any discussion of racial and ethnic differences must inevitably confront the tensions evident in these opposing views, and all of the contributors to this volume join in this debate in various ways.

Having acknowledged the impossibility of fully evaluating these positions, we do note that support for each of these seemingly opposing points of view can be found in the extant literature on crime, delinquency, and race/ethnicity in the United States. It is quite clear that much of the "social control" of both white ethnic immigrants and persons of color in the United States has been driven to some extent by the larger ethnic, racial, and class conflicts that have permeated this nation from its inception. The notion of the "dangerous classes" as applied to immigrant, white ethnic groups in the United States has been quite well documented (see Monkkonen 1975). The Irish may have had higher rates of criminality during the decades following their entry into the United States, and in later years; it is also true that they were targets of very aggressive policing, even as late as the turn of the twentieth century (Brown and Warner 1992; and Hawkins 1994, 1995). The same can be said for later-arriving immigrant groups from eastern and southern Europe. Since criminality in all ethnic groups tends to be concentrated among the young, surveillance of juvenile crime has been a major part of the extra scrutiny given immigrants in urban America, both during the past and today. Similarly, when viewed historically, the overrepresentation of African Americans, Native Americans, Mexican Americans, and during an earlier period, Chinese Americans is clearly the result of both differential rates of offending and now well-documented tactics of social control and repression. A reading of either the present volume or your daily newspaper shows that the question of how much of the current racial disparity is due to differential surveillance and social control based on race itself, is still the subject of considerable debate.

At the same time, the historiography of American juvenile and adult justice offers much evidence that while perhaps not well intentioned in every instance, some portion of the social reformers of the past were probably motivated by a genuine sense of noblesse oblige. They felt a genuine commitment to a life of helping their fellow citizens. Even some of the most critical analysts of the work of early and later criminal justice system "reformers" have acknowledged that their efforts were often driven by religious sincerity and charitable impulses derived from occupying positions of privilege. For example, the concern expressed by Letchworth in 1886 for the plight of "their children" as compared to "our children" probably reflected a genuine appreciation of the need to help those less fortunate than he. Today, the charitable impulses of America's elite are sometimes motivated by tax write-offs, but they are also motivated at times by a profound sense of obligation to help the "poor," even if driven sometimes by guilt. Finally, although many conflict theorists offer some plausible evidence to the contrary, many of the social reforms initiated by America's more privileged classes during the nineteenth and early twentieth centuries cannot easily be classified as purely in their self-interest. The enactment of child labor laws, mandatory and free public schools, and institutions designed to care for wayward, parentless youths at the expense of the state are all examples of such. Indeed, some recent accounts in the popular press have suggested that if America's current "power elite" were motivated by the same sorts of humanitarian concerns that drove the reform efforts of their nineteenth-century counterparts, many of the disparities documented in this volume would be less pronounced.

It is also true that the historical record does not support the argument that all efforts at social reform have been an unmitigated failure. Even at the start of the second century of juvenile justice, there is the potential for the adoption of social policies and laws than can build on the actual successes of the past while correcting many now obvious errors and flaws. We believe that contemporary and future efforts at reform will be unsuccessful to the extent that we do not confront honestly and forthrightly the continuing problem of racial, ethnic, and class inequality in American society at large and within those institutions charged with the administration of justice and the welfare of *our* children. As we will argue in our conclusion, there are many constructive things that can be done to begin to reduce the level of racial and ethnic disparity seen in the American juvenile justice system.

Caveat Emptor (of Sorts)

Despite our best efforts, this book, though pathbreaking in many respects, largely covers only the "criminal side" of the juvenile court. Earlier we mentioned the many appendages of the modern criminal justice system. In reality, many of these appendages might best be described as a part of the "civil side" of the juvenile court. Many others of these institutional appendages are entirely outside the juvenile justice system, as it is usually defined. Schlossman (1974, 1977) and many others have noted the extent to which the establishment of public schools in the United States was driven by the same social forces (and often persons) that led to the founding of the juvenile court and juvenile reformatories. Whether viewed as instruments of "social control" or "socialization," schools were an integral part of the institutional apparatuses designed to Americanize white immigrant and minority youths and save them from lives of crime. Today, as in years past, the "custody" and "protection" of children and youths are spread across a vast array of institutions. These include schools, hospitals, child welfare and protection agencies, law enforcement agencies, family and divorce courts, and a growing assortment of other specialized courts, health care providers, and private facilities. The juvenile court itself is inextricably linked to these other entities, and they play a vital role in helping the court do its job.

Important for the present discussion, all of these supporting agencies and institutions also experience problems related to racial, ethnic, and social class disparities within the clientele populations that they serve. Indeed, since many of these are "feeder" agencies for both the "criminal" and the "civil" sides of the juvenile court, racial and ethnic imbalances within them may actually drive the disparities seen in the juvenile court. Some of these institutional interactions are noted by the authors who have contributed to this volume; others are largely ignored. Consequently, it is clear that by focusing primarily on matters of crime and justice, we have not documented fully these linkages or probed the extent of racial and ethnic disparities in these other arenas, and their significance for understanding levels of disparity seen in our courts and juvenile correctional facilities. That task must await a future volume.

Notes

1. This is not so say that researchers during the past have completely ignored the problem of racial and ethnic disparity within the juvenile justice system. Numerous journal articles, governmental and nongovernmental research reports, chapters in academic books, and the like have all reported substantial disparity in rates of juvenile offending and system processing. However, findings from these widely varied and dispersed (across time and locale) studies have not been the object of a comprehensive effort at summarization or critique.

2. For example, though truly comprehensive nationwide data on system processing are not yet fully available, some preliminary findings suggest that one major policy response enacted in response to rising rates of youthful violence—namely, the transfer of youth from juvenile to adult courts—may be linked to considerations of race and ethnicity (Bortner, Zatz, and Hawkins 2000).

3. One of the consequences of the sharp rise in juvenile violence and the media hysteria that sometimes accompanied it is the view among many in the public that if a given juvenile offense is *serious* enough, it is ipso facto the equivalent of adult crime or criminality—the age of the offender does not matter. The juvenile court, which in its

earliest days was seen by many as a judicial vehicle designed to eliminate practices such as those that led to capital punishment for juveniles in England and the United States during earlier eras, now appears to face a return to the public sentiments that fueled such harsh practices in the past.

4. The fact that the earliest accounts of American delinquency explored life in urban contexts (largely in the East and Midwest) does not meant that delinquency in small town and rural contexts was not seen as a pervasive problem. Much of this tendency to focus of urban contexts has to do with (1) the tendency of immigrants such as the Irish and, later, southern and eastern European immigrants to choose to reside in opportunity-rich urban areas; (2) the economic "pull" that these contexts also exerted on the internal migration of African Americans, Mexican Americans, and, to a lesser degree, whites from the rural South and Southwest; and (3) the concentration of established and influential media outlets and the presence of socioeconomic and academic elites and social activists in those same urban contexts. The fact that rural delinquency was not completely ignored can be seen in the activities of the principal competitor of the Chicago School of Sociology at the turn of the twentieth century, namely, the sociology department at the University of North Carolina at Chapel Hill. Researchers in North Carolina and at other universities inspired by their lead tended to explored crime and delinquency in decidedly nonurban contexts.

5. Asian youths are by no means "below the radar" in many cities of California and Washington State in the West, and in some large cities of the East. But, for the nation as whole, their presence in the juvenile system and their involvement in acts of delinquency are not yet fully a part of public consciousness.

References

Aries, Phillippe. 1962. *Centuries of Childhood.* New York: Knopf.

Benedict, Ruth. [1940] 1959. *Race: Science and Politics.* New York: Viking Press.

Berger, Peter C., and Thomas Luckmann. 1967. *The Social Construction of Reality.* New York: Anchor.

Bernard, Thomas J. 1992. *The Cycle of Juvenile Justice.* New York: Oxford University Press.

Bortner, M. A., Marjorie S. Zatz, and Darnell F. Hawkins. 2000. "Race and Transfer: Empirical Research and Social Context." Pp. 277–320 in *The Changing Borders of Juvenile Justice: Transfer of Adolescents to the Criminal Court,* ed. Jeffrey Fagan and Franklin E. Zimring. Chicago: University of Chicago Press.

Brown, M. Craig, and Barbara D. Warner. 1992. "Immigrants, Urban Politics, and Policing in 1900." *American Sociological Review* 57:293–305.

Bursik, Robert J., Jr., and Harold G. Grasmick. 1993. *Neighborhoods and Crime: The Dimensions of Effective Community Control.* New York: Lexington.

Feld, Barry C. 1999. *Bad Kids: Race and the Transformation of the Juvenile Court.* New York: Oxford University Press.

Fingerhut, L. A., Ingram, D. D., and J. J. Feldman. 1992a. "Firearm and Nonfirearm Homicide among Persons 15 through 19 Years of Age: Differences by Level of Urbanization, United States, 1979–1989." *Journal of the American Medical Association* 267, no. 22:3048–3053.

———. 1992b. "Homicide among Black Teenage Males in Metropolitan Counties: Comparisons of Death Rates in Two Periods, 1983 through 1985 and 1987 through 1989." *Journal of the American Medical Association* 267, no. 223054–3058.

Goodman, Paul. 1960. *Growing Up Absurd: Problems of Youth in the Organized Society*. New York: Vintage Books.

Haller, Mark H. 1963. *Eugenics: Hereditarian Attitudes in American Thought*. New Brunswick, NJ: Rutgers University Press.

Hawkins, Darnell F. 1993. "Crime and Ethnicity." Pp. 89–120 in *The Socioeconomics of Crime and Justice*, ed. B. Forst. Armonk, NY: M. E. Sharpe.

———. 1994. "Ethnicity: The Forgotten Dimension of American Social Control." In *Inequality, Crime and Social Control*, ed. G. S. Bridges and M. A. Myers. Boulder, CO: Westview.

———, ed. 1995. *Ethnicity, Race, and Crime: Perspectives across Time and Place*. Albany, NY: State University of New York Press.

———. 2003. "Editor's Introduction." Pp. xiii–xxv in *Violent Crime: Assessing Race and Ethnic Differences*, ed. D. F. Hawkins. New York: Cambridge University Press.

Kempf Leonard, Kimberly, Carl E. Pope, and William H. Feyerherm, eds. 1995. *Minorities in Juvenile Justice*. Thousand Oaks, CA: Sage.

Kett, Joseph F. 1977. *Rites of Passage: Adolescence in America, 1790 to the Present*. New York: Basic.

Krisberg, Barry, ed. 1987. "Minority Youth Incarceration and Crime." Special issue, *Crime and Delinquency* 33, no. 2 (April).

Krisberg, Barry, and James Austin. 1978. *The Children of Ishmael: Critical Perspectives on Juvenile Justice*. Palo Alto, CA: Mayfield Publishing Co..

Krivo, Laura. J., and Ruth. D. Peterson. 1996. "Extremely Disadvantaged Neighborhoods and Urban Crime." *Social Forces* 75, no. 2 (December): 619–648.

Letchworth, William P. 1886. "Children of the State." Pp. 138–157 in *Proceedings of the National Conference of Charities and Corrections (PNCCC)*. St. Paul, MN.

Lombroso, Cesare. 1876. *L'Uomo Delinquente* [The Criminal Man]. Milan: Hoepli.

McCord, Joan, Cathy S. Widom, and Nancy A. Crowell. 2001. *Juvenile Crime, Juvenile Justice*. Washington, DC: National Academy Press.

McKelvey, Blake. 1977. *American Prisons: A History of Good Intentions*. Montclair, NJ: Patterson Smith.

Monkkonen, Eric. H. 1975. *The Dangerous Class: Crime and Poverty in Columbus, Ohio, 1860–1885*. Cambridge, MA: Harvard University Press.

Montagu, Ashley. [1942] 1997. *Man's Most Dangerous Myth: The Fallacy of Race*. 6th ed. Walnut Creek, CA: AltaMira Press.

Morenoff, J. D., R. J. Sampson, and S. W. Raudenbush. 2001. "Neighborhood Inequality, Collective Efficacy, and the Spatial Dynamics of Urban Violence." *Criminology* 39:517–560.

Morris, Norval. 1974. *The Future of Imprisonment*. Chicago: University of Chicago Press.

Omi, Michael, and Howard Winant. 1994. *Racial Formation in the United States*, 2nd ed. New York: Routledge.

Park, Robert, Edward W. Burgess, and R. D. McKenzie. 1928. *The City*. Chicago: University of Chicago Press.

Platt, Anthony M. 1969. *The Child Savers: The Invention of Delinquency*. Chicago: University of Chicago Press.

Rafter, Nicole Hahn. 1985. *Partial Justice: Women in State Prisons, 1800–1935*. Boston: Northeastern University Press.

Rosenberg, Mark L., and Mary A. Fenley, eds. 1991. *Violence in America: A Public Health Approach*. New York: Oxford University Press.

Rothman, David J. 1980. *Conscience and Convenience: The Asylum and Its Alternatives in Progressive America*. Boston: Little Brown and Co..

Sampson, R. J. 1997. "The Embeddedness of Child and Adolescent Development: A Community-Level Perspective on Urban Violence." Pp. 31–77 in Violence and Childhood in the Inner City, ed. J. McCord. New York: Cambridge University Press.

Sampson, R. J., and W. B. Groves. 1989. "Community Structure and Crime: Testing Social-Disorganization Theory." *American Journal of Sociology* 94:774–802.

Sampson, R. J., and W. J. Wilson. 1995. "Toward a Theory of Race, Crime and Urban Inequality." Pp. 37–54 in *Crime and Inequality,* ed. J. Hagan and R. D. Peterson. Stanford, CA: Stanford University Press.

Sampson, R. J., J. D. Morenoff, and F. Earls. 1999. "Beyond Social Capital: Spatial Dynamics of Collective Efficacy for Children." *American Sociological Review* 64:633–660.

Schlossman, Steve. 1974. "The 'Culture of Poverty' in Ante-bellum Social Thought." *Science and Society* 38, no. 2 (Summer): 150–166.

———. 1977. *Love and the American Delinquent: The Theory and Practice of "Progressive" Juvenile Justice, 1825–1920*. Chicago: University of Chicago Press.

Shaw, Clifford R. 1929. *Delinquency Areas: A Study of the Geographic Distribution of School Truants, Juvenile Delinquents, and Adult Offenders in Chicago*. Chicago: University of Chicago Press.

Shaw, Clifford R., and Henry D. McKay. [1942] 1969. *Juvenile Delinquency and Urban Areas: A Study of Rates of Delinquency in Relation to Differential Characteristics of Local Communities in American Cities*. Chicago: University of Chicago Press.

Snyder, Howard N., and Melissa Sickmund. 1995. *Juvenile Offenders and Victims: A National Report*. Washington, DC: Office of Juvenile Justice and Delinquency Prevention.

Thomas, William I., and Florian Znaniecki. [1927] 1958. *The Polish Peasant in Europe and America*. New York: Dover Publications.

Thrasher, Frederic M. 1927. *The Gang: A Study of 1,313 Gangs in Chicago*. Chicago: University of Chicago Press.

Tonry, Michael, and Mark H. Moore. 1998. *Youth Violence*. Chicago: University of Chicago Press.

U.S. Department of Health and Human Services. 2001. *Youth Violence: A Report of the Surgeon General*. Rockville, MD: U.S. Department of Health and Human Services.

Whyte, William Foote. [1943] 1981. *Street Corner Society: The Social Structure of an Italian Slum*. Chicago: University of Chicago Press.

Wilson, William Julius. 1978. *The Declining Significance of Race*. Chicago: University of Chicago Press.

———. 1987. *The Truly Disadvantaged: The Inner City, the Underclass, and Public Policy*. Chicago: University of Chicago Press.

Zimring, Franklin E. 1998. *American Youth Violence*. New York: Oxford University Press.

Racial and Ethnic Differences in Juvenile Crime and Punishment

Past and Present

2

The Role of Race and Ethnicity in Juvenile Justice Processing

Donna M. Bishop

Introduction

FEW FEATURES of the juvenile justice system are better documented than the long-standing and pronounced disparities in the processing of white and minority youths. Nationally, youths of color—especially African Americans and Hispanics[1]—are arrested in numbers greatly disproportionate to their representation in the general population. They are overrepresented among young people held in secure detention, petitioned to juvenile court, and adjudicated delinquent. Among those adjudicated delinquent, they are more often committed to the "deep end" of the juvenile system. When confined, they are more often housed in large public institutions rather than privately run group homes or specialized treatment facilities. And, at "the end of the line," prosecutors and judges are more apt to relinquish jurisdiction over them, transferring them to criminal court for prosecution and punishment as adults.

Despite decades of research, there is no clear consensus on why minority youths enter and penetrate the juvenile justice system at such disproportionate rates. Both public and academic discourse has tended to highlight two explanations. The first is that minority overrepresentation reflects race and ethnic differences in the incidence, seriousness, and persistence of delinquent involvement (the "differential offending" hypothesis). (For a review of the empirical literature on the nature and origins of racial and ethnic differences in offending, see Lauritsen 2005.) The second is that overrepresentation is attributable to inequities—intended or unintended—in juvenile justice practice (the "differential treatment" hypothesis). The purpose of this chapter is to review the research literature bearing on the second of these claims and, more specifically, to explore the mechanisms through which race and ethnicity influence juvenile justice system responses.

The presentation is organized into four sections. In section 1, I address basic definitional and interpretive issues and discuss deficiencies in the data sources relevant to the questions at hand. For background purposes, section 2 contains a brief overview of the extent of minority overrepresentation in the juvenile justice system for the nation as a whole and across states. The main body of the review is contained in section 3. Building on Pope and Feyerherm's (1990a, 1990b, 1992) comprehensive review of articles published in the 1970s and 1980s, I have updated the research and expanded the scope of the review to include more than 150 studies. They include quantitative analyses of individual-level case processing in police, court, and correctional settings; macrolevel or cross-jurisdictional studies of linkages between justice system responses and characteristics of organizations and the social environments in which they operate; and qualitative studies of organizations and decision makers, which are especially valuable in interpreting findings of the quantitative research. My overall assessment is that racial disparities in processing are attributable in part to differences in offending. Yet the evidence is incontrovertible that, in most jurisdictions studied, race differences in offending alone are insufficient to explain minority overrepresentation in the juvenile justice system (see also Pope and Feyerherm 1990a, 1990b, 1992; Tomkins et al. 1996; Feld 1999).[2] Moreover, while there is some truth to both the "differential offending" and "differential treatment" arguments, there is also truth that lies beyond and between these positions, in the politico-legal climate responsible for lawmaking and its enforcement, and in the conditions and circumstances that at once place youths at risk for delinquency and also provide the rationale for juvenile justice intervention. The issue is no longer simply *whether* whites and youths of color are treated differently. Instead, the preeminent challenge for scholars is to explain *how* these differences come about. Understanding the intervening mechanisms is essential if we are to replace "stab in the dark" efforts to reduce disproportionate minority confinement with strategic changes in policy and practice that hold more promise of success. Consistent with this objective, I examine the empirical research for what it has to say about the processes and conditions that engender racial disparities in justice system responses. In section 4, I summarize the state of our knowledge and discuss what I believe to be the most important implications for future research.

1. Preliminary Considerations

Disparity and Discrimination

The terms *disparity* and *discrimination* (or *bias*) in regard to race require discussion and clarification. Commonly, the term *disparity* is used to denote between-group differences in outcomes, irrespective of their origins. (Disparity might stem from differences in offending, from laws or policies that differentially impact minority youths, or from racism within the juvenile justice system.) *Discrimination* refers to "situations in which evidence suggests that extralegal or illegitimate factors are the cause of disparate justice system outcomes" (National Research Council and Institute of Medicine 2001, 230 – 231; for other variants, see Walker, Spohn, and DeLone 2000, 14 – 18). Although this definition of discrimination is one that is used commonly in the social science literature, it raises controversial and unresolved issues when applied to the juvenile court.

In studies of the effects of race[3] on processing in both the juvenile and adult systems, it is common for researchers to test multivariate models that include controls for legal factors (typically, offense severity and prior record) and to conclude that they have uncovered evidence of bias or discrimination if the race coefficient remains significant once these controls are introduced. In studies of the adult system, this conclusion is rather straightforward. In the criminal justice context, there is general agreement that offense-related variables are the only *legitimate* inputs into decision making: punishment is the primary goal, justice demands that like cases be treated alike, and the criteria that define "like" cases are clearly delimited by the principle of offense (Matza 1964; Feld 1987, 1988, 1993). However, studies of the juvenile court that draw inferences of discrimination after controlling only for legal factors ignore important distinctions between the juvenile and criminal justice systems.

Some would argue that a model that controls only for legal variables is greatly underspecified when applied to juvenile court processing. Traditionally, evaluation and treatment of young offenders have been understood as legitimate if not primary system goals. Rather than considering only offense and prior record, juvenile justice officials are expected at every point in the system except adjudication[4] to take account of the backgrounds and circumstances of youths brought before them and to individualize responses in light of youths' needs (Cicourel 1968; Emerson 1969; Matza 1964; Horwitz and Wasserman 1980a). This orientation is not simply a relic of a bygone era. Although juvenile justice philosophy and policy have shifted dramatically during the past thirty years to endorse and accommodate purposes of punishment, accountability, and community protection, treatment remains an explicit goal in the juvenile codes of nearly every state (Torbet and Szymanski 1998). Moreover, recent research indicates that juvenile court officials continue to embrace and to place a high priority on diagnostic and treatment objectives (e.g., Frazier and Bishop 1995; Sanborn 1996; Sanborn and Salerno 2004). From a treatment perspective, individual and social factors—for example, poor parental supervision, association with deviant peers, and poor school performance—are *legitimate* considerations in case processing, even if they are unevenly distributed by race. After all, inadequate family supervision (Gottfredson and Hirschi 1990; Loeber and Stouthamer-Loeber 1986;

McCord 1991; Patterson 1982; Patterson, Reid, and Dishion 1992; Sampson and Laub 1993b), school failure (Cernkovich and Giordano 1992; Empey and Lubeck 1971; Hirschi 1969; Liska and Reed 1985; Maguin and Loeber 1996), and exposure to delinquent peers (Akers 1998; Elliott and Menard 1996; Matsueda and Anderson 1998; Warr and Stafford 1991; Warr 1996) are among the strongest predictors of delinquency and are prominently linked to offending in most etiological theories. If extralegal factors that are causally linked to delinquency *should* prompt different responses to youths who are identical with respect to offense and prior record, then it is inappropriate to draw inferences of racial discrimination from studies that control only for legal factors (Dean, Hirschel, and Brame 1996).

On the other side, some argue that, regardless of its rehabilitative aims and claims, the juvenile court lacks the resources, expertise, and/or commitment to achieve treatment objectives. It administers punishment under the guise of treatment or treats only ineffectively (e.g., Feld 1999). Or they take the position that all coerced treatment—even if effective—constitutes punishment. Additionally, many maintain that, because the discretionary authority granted to justice officials who are expected to identify and respond to ill-defined needs is of necessity exceedingly broad, it is especially susceptible to abuse. Such authority too readily permits stereotypes of minority youths—as especially threatening, as especially needy, and so on—to influence decision making (Bortner, Zatz, and Hawkins 2000; Feld 1999; Hawes 1971; Platt 1977). Finally, they argue that the focus on youth "needs" deflects attention from broader social structural and cultural circumstances that contribute to disproportionate minority offending, serves as a convenient rationalization for the exercise of greater control over minority offenders, and insures the perpetuation of racial and ethnic inequalities. If the juvenile court is really in the business of punishment, if the ideal of "equality under the law" is impossible to achieve because racial stereotypes shape perceptions and assessments, and/or if the deck is stacked against minorities by virtue of "needs" that reflect social and economic disadvantage, then the principle of offense must control decision making (see, e.g., Feld 1999). By this view, decisions based on non-offense-related substantive considerations are as repugnant in the juvenile as in the criminal court. Consequently, evidence that race affects processing outcomes after only legal variables are controlled warrants an inference of discrimination in either setting.

While these issues are exceedingly important, I deliberately take no position on them here. My charge is a more simple one: to explore what we know about whether and how race and ethnicity influence juvenile justice processing. However, grappling with the "should" issues is imperative. As we will see below, analytic models that include variables that tap personal and social needs do a far better job of explaining processing outcomes than models that are limited to legal variables. Moreover, these extralegal factors are among those most responsible for the generation of racial disparities. In other words, race and ethnicity influence processing outcomes in no small way because the effects of social structural and cultural disadvantage may lawfully be considered. If we are to advance the discourse on racial justice, there must be further discussion and debate—in groups that include academics, justice officials, and policy makers—on whether and how extralegal factors should influence juvenile justice decision making.

Understanding How Race and Ethnicity Influence Juvenile Justice Decision Making

Race can influence processing outcomes in a variety of ways. The extant research contains much evidence of direct, indirect, contingent (interactive), and contextual effects operating at multiple stages, often in complex and subtle ways. Because each of these terms is often used imprecisely, they also require clarification.

A *direct effect* is said to exist when significant race differences in outcome persist after controlling for other variables. Consistent with what has just been said, a direct effect is compatible with, but does not necessarily support, an inference of bias or discrimination. If the model is underspecified, the addition of other variables (e.g., inadequate parental supervision, association with delinquent peers) might alter what appears to be a direct effect.

An *indirect effect* is one that operates through other variables. Consider family status. African American youths are more likely than white youths to reside in single-parent homes, and there is considerable evidence that youths from single-parent homes are more likely than those from two-parent homes to be referred for formal processing at intake. Racial disparities in referral outcomes are produced in part because race is correlated with family status, which in turn influences juvenile system responses. In other words, the effect of race is mediated by family status. Unfortunately, as Pope and Feyerherm (1992) have observed, some researchers erroneously conclude that race has no effect when a race coefficient is reduced to nonsignificance once variables such as family status are controlled.[5] Race does have an effect in these circumstances, but it operates through other variables. Moreover, it is essential that we identify the intervening mechanisms through which race and ethnicity influence official decision making if we are to reduce minority overrepresentation. In the example just given, the finding that family status mediates the effect of race could generate valuable discourse with juvenile justice decision makers about the importance of family structure versus family dynamics, about the desirability of considering both extended and nuclear families, and about the court's ability (or inability) to provide meaningful compensatory supervision where parental supervision is lacking.

A *conditional* or *interactive* effect is dependent on the level of other variables. Very commonly, researchers test only additive (main effects) models. These are premised on the assumption that the effect of race is the same across values of other variables, which may not be the case. For example, in their research on adult processing, Miethe and Moore (1986) found that an additive model showed little effect of race on judicial sentencing decisions. However, an interactive model revealed that "low-risk" African Americans were treated more leniently than "low-risk" whites, while "high-risk" African Americans were treated far more severely than "high-risk" whites. Failure to explore interactive effects can obscure substantial race differences in treatment (Miethe and Moore 1986; Zatz 1984).

Race effects also vary *contextually,* that is, across the environments, situations, and settings in which decisions are made. While researchers most often have explored the effects of individual-level characteristics on processing outcomes, increasingly scholars are attending to cross-jurisdictional variations in justice system responses. An instructive example is Sampson and Laub's (1993a) analysis of the effect of community social structure on rates of juvenile court petitioning, detention, and dispositional confinement across more than three hundred counties in twenty-one states. One of their most important findings was that placement rates for African American drug offenders were strongly related to concentrations of underclass poverty. In counties with high proportions of impoverished residents, African American drug offenders were much more likely to be incarcerated, while placement rates for white drug offenders were unaffected by poverty levels. These sorts of findings highlight the importance of exploring potential linkages among race, characteristics of the context in which decision making occurs (including variations in social structure, resource availability, organizational climate, and the like), and justice system responses. Racial discrimination may occur in some places with respect to some groups and at some stages in processing, and in different ways or not at all in others.

Weaknesses in the Data

Most studies of race and justice processing are limited to comparisons of either whites and African Americans or whites and nonwhites. The "nonwhite" category is especially problematic because it is unclear which racial groups are included or how are distributed. Separate data for Native Americans, Asians, and Pacific Islanders are frequently unavailable. More problematic still, most data sets fail to disaggregate race from ethnicity. Hispanic youths are usually coded "white." As a result, the extent of minority overrepresentation in the juvenile justice system, as well as the effect of race/ethnicity on processing decisions, is almost surely underestimated.

Measures of social class are seldom included in studies of juvenile case processing. Consequently, the effects of race and class are confounded. Without measures of social class, it is impossible for researchers to determine whether white and minority youths from the same socioeconomic backgrounds are treated similarly or differently by police, courts, and correctional agencies. Racial disparities in processing might be attributable to race per se, or to effects of social class that mediate the influence of race (e.g., differential access to resources, negative perceptions of the economically disadvantaged).

Many studies also fail to include information regarding individual and social factors that are likely to influence decision making in a justice system with a treatment orientation. These include considerations such as mental status, substance use, school attendance, school performance, level of parental supervision and support, and association with delinquent peers.

For a variety of reasons (e.g., lack of data, problems in operationalizing constructs), there is little research on some processing decisions. These include police decisions to initiate stops and to arrest, handle informally, or release suspects; prosecutorial decisions regarding whether to charge, the number and severity of charges to file, and whether to drop or reduce charges; and correctional agency decisions regarding placement, treatment, and release. Data and measurement problems frequently stymie efforts to study a number of critical issues, such as whether minority youths are differentially subject to prosecutorial overcharging. With these weaknesses in mind, we turn to a discussion of the research evidence on racial and ethnic disparities in the juvenile justice system.

2. Disproportionate Minority Representation in the Juvenile Justice System

The National Picture

As a backdrop for the discussion that follows, table 2.1 presents national data on the racial composition of the youth population at successive stages in the juvenile justice system.[6]

Arrest

In 1999, the *Uniform Crime Reports* (UCR) recorded 2.5 million juvenile arrests (National Center for Juvenile Justice 2003). White youths, who make up 79% of the population age 10–17, were underrepresented, accounting for 72% of arrests. African Americans were greatly overrepresented: they constitute 15% of the youth population, but accounted for 25% of arrests. Youths in the

Table 2.1: The Processing of Juveniles by Race, 1999

	White	African American	Other	Total
Population age 10–17[a]	24,730,541	4,833,800	1,695,899	31,260,240
	(79)	(15)	(05)	
Arrested[b]	1,812,180	630,254	72,953	2,515,387
	(72)	(25)	(03)	(100)
Arrest rate	7,328	12,905	4,302	
Relative risk, AA:W = 1.8:1				
Referred to court[c]	1,135,106	470,724	56,532	1,662,362
	(68)	(28)	(3)	(99)
Percentage of arrestees referred	63	75	77	
Referral rate	4,589	9,738	3,333	
Relative risk, AA:W = 2.1:1				
Detained[c]	206,871	118,866	12,968	338,705
	(61)	(35)	(4)	(100)
Percentage of referrals detained	18	25	23	
Detention rate	836	2,459	765	
Relative risk, AA:W = 2.9:1				
Formally charged[c]	612,102	305,626	29,567	947,295
	(64)	(32)	(3)	(100)
Percentage of referrals charged	54	65	52	
Charging rate	2,475	6,322	1,743	
Relative risk, AA:W = 2.6:1				
Adjudicated delinquent[c]	415,451	193,683	20,465	629,599
	(66)	(31)	(3)	(100)
Percentage of charged adjudicated	68	63	69	
Adjudication rate	1,680	4,007	1,207	
Relative risk, AA:W = 2.4:1				
Placed out of home[c]	98,642	56,281	5,002	159,949
	(62)	(35)	(3)	(100)
Percentage of adjudicated placed	24	29	24	
Placement rate	398	1,164	295	
Relative risk, AA:W = 2.9:1				

Note: Values in parentheses are percentages.

[a] Source: Puzzanchera et al. 2002.

[b] Source: National Center for Juvenile Justice 2003.

[c] Source: Stahl, Finnegan, and Kang 2002.

"other" category (Native American and Asian youths) contributed 3% of arrests. Relative to their proportions in the general population, youths in the "other" category were slightly underrepresented. However, within this group, state-level data (not shown) reveal significant differences in the probability of arrest for Native American and Asian youths. Overall, arrest rates are higher among Native Americans than among Asians. Individual data collection efforts at the state level also show wide variations in arrest rates *within* the Asian population: They are lowest among Chinese American, and highest among Cambodian American and Vietnamese American populations.

Overall racial disparities are perhaps best expressed in terms of arrest rates. Table 2.1 shows that the total arrest rate for African American juveniles in 1999 was 12,905, compared to 7,328 for whites, and 4,302 for youths of other races. There were also important differences by race in rates of arrest by offense type (data not shown). For example, African Americans were arrested for violent Index crimes at a rate of 893 per 100,000, while the arrest rate for these offenses among whites was 248 per 100,000 (National Center for Juvenile Justice 2003). Disparities of lesser magnitude were also found for rates of property Index crimes (3,091 for African Americans, 1,566 for whites). In all, African American youths were arrested at higher rates than whites in twenty-five of the twenty-nine UCR offense categories. Arrest rates for whites were higher than those for African Americans only for vandalism and offenses involving the use and abuse of alcohol (liquor law violations, drunkenness, and driving under the influence).

Court Referral

Table 2.1 shows that nearly 1.7 million youths were referred to the juvenile court in 1999 (Stahl, Finnegan, and Kang 2002). Approximately 63% of cases involving whites, 76% of those involving African Americans, and 77% of cases involving youth of other races were referred to court.[7] In other words, racial disparities were dramatic at this stage. Expressed in terms of youth at risk, African Americans were referred to court at a rate of 9,738 cases per 100,000. The comparable case rate for whites was 4,589, and, for other races, 3,333. Of the total youth population at risk, African Americans were 2.1 times as likely to be referred to court as whites.

Detention

In 1999, 338,705 cases resulted in detention. The overrepresentation of minorities was fairly pronounced at this stage: 25% of cases involving African Americans resulted in detention between referral and disposition, compared to 18% of cases involving whites, and 23% of cases involving youths of other races. As a result of these disparities, youths of color made up nearly 40% of the detention population.

African Americans and other minority youths were more likely to be detained than whites for each of the four offense categories recorded in the *Juvenile Court Statistics*. (See table 2.2.) However, racial disparities were more pronounced for some offense types than others. Disparities were most striking in the handling of drug offenses: among African Americans, 38% of drug cases resulted in detention, compared to only 17% among whites and 21%

Table 2.2: Juvenile Court Processing by Race and Offense Type, 1999

Offense Type	Detained[a] (%)			Formally Charged[b] (%)			Placed[c] (%)		
	White	African American	Other	White	African American	Other	White	African American	Other
Person	22	26	32	56	66	57	24	27	28
Property	15	20	17	52	60	47	21	25	24
Drugs	17	38	21	54	80	56	16	33	15
Public order	20	28	29	56	65	58	26	29	24
Total	18	25	23	54	65	52	22	28	24

Source: Stahl, Finnegan, and Kang 2002.

[a] Percentage detained among those referred.
[b] Percentage formally charged among those referred.
[c] Percentage placed among those adjudicated delinquent.

among youths of other races. It is also noteworthy that African Americans were more likely to be detained for drug offenses and (relatively minor) offenses against public order than for offenses against persons. This was not the case among whites or youths of other races, who were most likely to be detained for offenses against persons.

Formal Charging

Forty-three percent of the cases referred to the juvenile courts were dropped or diverted, while the remaining 57% were formally petitioned. The probability of formal charging was higher for African American youths than for whites or youths of other races. Sixty-five percent of referrals involving African Americans proceeded to formal charging, compared to 54% of referrals involving whites and 52% of referrals for other minorities. The composition of the population subject to formal prosecution was 32% African American, 64% white, and 3% other races. Table 2.2 shows that, as was true at detention, cases involving African Americans were more often petitioned than cases involving whites in all offense categories. But again, disparities were most pronounced for drug referrals: 80% of drug cases involving African Americans were formally charged, compared to 54% of drug cases involving whites, which represents a rather stunning 26-percentage-point difference.

Adjudication

Of all cases petitioned, two-thirds resulted in adjudications of delinquency. Table 2.1 shows that the pattern of racial disparity observed at previous stages is not evident at adjudication. In fact, the probability of being adjudicated delinquent among those petitioned was slightly *lower* for African Americans than for other youths. Sixty-three percent of the petitioned cases involving African Americans resulted in adjudications of delinquency, compared to 68% of cases involving whites and 69% of cases involving youths of other races. Nevertheless, due to the cumulative effect of minority overrepresentation at earlier decision points, the adjudicated population remained greatly overrepresentative of minorities. The racial composition of cases adjudicated was 66% white, 31% African American, and 3% other races. Expressed in terms of the total youth population at risk, African Americans were 2.4 times as likely to be adjudicated delinquent as whites.

Disposition

National juvenile court data for 1999 indicate that 25% of the cases that were adjudicated delinquent received out-of-home placements. Smaller racial disparities are apparent at disposition than at the front end of the system. Twenty-nine percent of cases involving African Americans were placed, compared to 24% for whites and other minorities. Although the risk of out-of-home placement for adjudicated African Americans was only modestly greater than for whites (1.2:1), the cumulative disadvantage, expressed as a proportion of the total population at risk, was substantial (2.9:1). Although African Americans were only slightly more likely to be placed than whites when adjudicated for a person, property, or public order offense, again disparities were pronounced for drug offenses. (See table 2.2.) While 16% of adjudicated drug cases resulted in placement when the defendant was white (and 15% when the case involved an "other" minority), 33% resulted in placement when the defendant was African American, a substantial 17% differential.

Youths in Juvenile Correctional Facilities

Correctional placement is one of the few points in the system for which data on both race and ethnicity are available. Table 2.3 presents race/ethnicity-specific custody rates for juvenile correctional facilities from the 1999 *Census of Juveniles in Residential Placement* (a one-day count). Because of the cumulative effect of disparities at earlier stages in processing, minorities were greatly overrepresented: they made up 62% of the institutional population (Sickmund, Sladky, and Kang 2004), nearly twice their proportion in the youth population.[8] The disparities across groups are striking: for every 100,000 African Americans in the juvenile population age 10–17, 958 were in residential placement on a single day in 1999. For Native Americans, the rate was 583, and for Hispanics, 440.[9] By comparison, the rates were low for whites (210) and Asian Americans (179). Stated somewhat differently, African Americans were nearly five times as likely to be incarcerated as whites, while Hispanic and Native American youths were incarcerated at rates two to three times greater than whites.

Table 2.3: One-Day Count of Juveniles in Correctional Placement by Race and Ethnicity, 1999

	Total	White	African American	Hispanic	American Indian	Asian	Other
N	108,391	41,246	42,963	19,922	2,013	2,137	609
Percent	100	38	39	18	2	2	1
Rate[a]	361	210	958	440	583	179	—[b]

Source: Sickmund, Sladky, and Kang 2004.

[a] Rate are calculated per 100,000 youths in the population age 10 to the upper age of juvenile court jurisdiction.

[b] No rate is shown because there is no comparable reference population.

State Variations

A 1992 amendment to the federal Juvenile Justice and Delinquency Prevention Act required states to identify, assess, and take steps to reduce disproportionate minority confinement (DMC) in order to be eligible for Formula Grant funds. In a report on the identification and assessment phases of the DMC initiative, Donna Hamparian and her colleagues gathered information on disproportionality at several processing points for those states that had completed assessments (Community Research Associates 1997). For each decision stage, they calculated an "index of disproportionality," which reflects the percentage of minority youths at that stage divided by the percentage of minorities in the state's population age 10–17. An index of 2.00, for example, indicates that minorities are represented at a rate twice their proportion in the at-risk population.

In twenty-five of twenty-six states reporting arrests of African Americans, they were overrepresented. The average index value was 2.25, but the value ranged from 0.6 to 3.9 (Community Research Associates 1997). In eight of thirteen states reporting arrests of Hispanic youths, they were also overrepresented, but with index values lower and less variable than those of African Americans. Only six of nineteen states where Native Americans make up at least 1% of the juvenile population had data on arrest, and they were often incomplete. Although limited, they showed overrepresentation in four of six states. Data on arrest were available in eight of fifteen states where Asians and Pacific Islanders constitute at least 1% of the juvenile population. In each case, these groups were underrepresented among arrestees.

In nearly all states reporting detention data, African American, Hispanic, and Native American youths were overrepresented. There was even greater variability across jurisdictions at detention than was the case at arrest. The overrepresentation of African American youths was greatest (average index value = 3.34), but across states index values varied greatly (from 0.7 to 10.7). Hispanics were overrepresented at a lesser rate (average index value = 1.45), with values ranging from 0.7 to 4.8. Due to incomplete data, indices of over-representation were not computed for Native Americans. However, in seven of nine states the data pointed toward overrepresentation.

In the vast majority of states reporting commitment data, African American, Hispanic, and Native American youths were overrepresented. Again, overrepresentation was greatest for African Americans (average index value = 3.46). In those nine states reporting commitment data for Native Americans, they were overrepresented at a rate higher than Hispanics. Asians and Pacific Islanders were underrepresented at commitment in every state reporting.

In sum, state-level data indicate that Asians and Pacific Islanders are most often underrepresented in the juvenile justice system, while overrepresentation is greatest for African Americans and somewhat less for Hispanics and Native Americans. Nevertheless, there is wide variation across jurisdictions, and across processing stages. Moreover, there appears to be no discernible pattern to the cross-jurisdictional variation. For example, the lowest levels of disparity in rates of white versus minority confinement were found in Florida, Idaho, Maine, Oregon, and Vermont, while the highest disparity levels were reported in Connecticut, New Jersey, Wisconsin, and Pennsylvania (Sickmund 2004). No regional patterns are apparent, nor do disparities seem to be linked to crime rates, size of the minority population, or other sociodemographic or economic indicators.

3. The Role of the Justice System in the Generation of Race and Ethnic Disparities

The review of research that follows is divided into two main sections, the first dealing with studies of police handling of juveniles, the second with studies of juvenile court processing and correctional placement.[10] Before turning to the literature on processing, it is essential to consider the broader politico-legal climate in which law enforcement and court processing take place. The analysis would be incomplete if we failed to appreciate that racial and ethnic disparities derive in part from laws that differentially target the behaviors, statuses, and life conditions associated with youths of color.

Enforcement of the law is constrained most obviously by the content of the law itself. At the national level, the "get tough," "law and order" climate of the past two decades has spawned legislation and strategic initiatives that have had a dramatic impact on racial disparities in the juvenile system. In some instances, the law reflects institutionalized racism by supporting policies and practices that, while perhaps not racist in intent, have nevertheless had a differential and sometimes profoundly negative impact on minority populations.

The "war on drugs" is perhaps the best recent example of a major initiative that has had a differential impact on minority youths. Although self-report studies showed little change in drug use from the mid-1980s into the 1990s, legislatures nevertheless targeted drug offenders for stepped-up enforcement and harsher punishments (Blumstein 1993, 1995; Tonry 1995). Arrest rates for drug offenses among white youths were higher than those for African American youths throughout the 1970s. However, after the initiation of the war on drugs, drug arrest rates for whites declined while arrests of African American youths skyrocketed.[11] By the early 1990s, arrest rates for drug offenses among African American youths were four to five times those for whites (Miller 1996, 85).

The National Criminal Justice Commission has concluded that racial disparities in drug arrests are attributable largely to enforcement strategies that focus almost exclusively on low-level dealers in minority neighborhoods. "Police found more drugs in minority communities because that is where they looked for them" (Donziger 1996, 115). That the war on drugs has been waged differentially against young minority offenders was undoubtedly influenced by the media, which promoted the notion that drug crime is exclusively an urban African American male phenomenon (Walker, Spohn, and DeLone 2000, 45). Also contributing to differential enforcement was the ease of making arrests in underclass neighborhoods, where drug sales more often take place on the street, dealers more often sell to strangers, and, because of high unemployment rates, a steady stream of young people is available to replace those who are arrested (Tonry 1994, 485–487; see also Horowitz and Pottieger 1991; Klein, Maxson, and Cunningham 1988).[12] Moreover, in some instances, legal reforms themselves seem to have encouraged the selective enforcement of drug laws in impoverished minority neighborhoods. For example, the Illinois legislature in the early 1990s passed a law mandating the transfer to criminal court of 15- and 16-year-olds charged with drug violations committed within 1,000 feet of public housing. A study of transfers in Cook County (Chicago) over a one-year period following the law's implementation revealed that *all* of the juveniles transferred under this provision were African American (Clarke 1996, 9).

Another illustration of how the politico-legal climate has exacerbated racial disparities involves the recent focus on juvenile gangs. Fueled by public fear of youth crime and by the perceived connection between drugs and gangs, legislatures provided monetary incentives for gang suppression activities and enhanced penalties for gang-related crimes, while "sweeps" and "crackdowns" on minority gangs became part of drug enforcement strategies (Walker, Spohn, and DeLone 2000; see also Bridges et al. 1993; Feeley and Simon 1992; Jackson 1992; Tonry 1994, 1995). Since 1995, the Office of Juvenile Justice and Delinquency Prevention (OJJDP) has sponsored the National

Youth Gang Survey, gathering information from law enforcement agencies on the scope of youth gangs and characteristics of gang members. On the 1996 survey, police officials estimated that 95% of youth gang members were nonwhite (primarily African American and Hispanic) and that gangs were responsible for nearly half of national drug sales (National Youth Gang Center 1999). These estimates, which other research suggests are inflated (Walker, Spohn, and DeLone 2000; Esbensen and Osgood 1999), provide a rationale for differential enforcement of antigang initiatives in minority communities.

Numerous additional examples could be cited (e.g., urban curfew laws, laws that mandate waiver of violent juvenile offenders regardless of age or prior record). The point is that in order to fully understand racial disparities in the juvenile justice system we must look beyond the operation of police, court, and correctional agencies to consider how politics, the media, and the law contribute to differential social control over minority youth populations.

Racial Disparities and Juvenile Processing

The material in this section is organized to correspond to the sequence of processing junctures in the juvenile justice system. This approach was selected because it reveals how disparities introduced at any single point reverberate through subsequent ones, and also because it underscores the potential linkages between racial disparities in processing and characteristics of the different actors and organizations responsible for decision making at different stages. Decisions at different points are made by individuals representing fairly autonomous organizations—for example, police, intake, prosecution, probation—which vary considerably in terms of goals, norms, functions, philosophies, external constituencies, and the like. These organizational features are likely to be reflected in the decisions of agency personnel.[13] Moreover, at different processing junctures, the nature of decisions varies, as does the degree to which discretion is constrained. So, for example, evidentiary considerations are likely to weigh heavily at adjudication, but not at judicial disposition. Conversely, assessments of offenders' needs and life circumstances presumably take on heightened significance at disposition but are largely irrelevant for purposes of adjudication.

The Police

There are strong theoretical grounds for believing that the impact of race and ethnicity on police handling of juveniles is potentially quite large. Although police officers' actions are constrained by statutes, regulations, directives, and the formal and informal norms of the departments in which they work, rules cannot cover all situations, and many situations are legally ambiguous (Lipsky 1980). In cases involving serious and violent crimes, discretion is limited.[14] But the vast majority of police-suspect encounters involve minor offenses, where arrests occur no more than 15% of the time, leaving a large margin for discretionary decision making (Black and Reiss 1970; Lundman, Sykes, and Clark 1978; Werthman and Piliavin 1967; Worden and Myers 1999; Engel, Sobol, and Worden 2000; Terrill 2001).

That there is little review of or accountability for many front-end decisions adds to the potential for bias. Most judgments are exercised in the field, free from oversight by superiors. Departmental policies generally require no record of encounters that do not result in arrest (Black and Reiss 1970; Worden and Myers 1999). If minority youths are more often arrested in situations where similar white youths are released or handled informally, these differentials will be almost impossible to detect. Moreover, external pressures for fairness and consistency in decisions to stop and arrest are fairly negligible. Adolescents—especially youths of color—constitute an especially weak and fragmented segment of American society, and they are unlikely to lodge complaints about harassment or discriminatory treatment. This means that officers who exercise their authority in ways that disadvantage minority youths frequently may do so with impunity. And, to the extent that racially discriminatory behaviors are believed to serve other important functions (e.g., efficient control of an especially threatening population), they are likely to be self-perpetuating.

That police decisions often must be made quickly based on very little information adds to the potential for bias. Officers draw on their personal backgrounds and experiences on the street to assess situations and make on-the-spot decisions (Smith and Visher 1981; see also Irwin 1985; Rubinstein 1973; Wilson 1968). Differentiation between dangerous and nondangerous places, and between suspicious and nonsuspicious persons, is essential to police work (Skolnick 1966), but, in the context of a society suffused with inequality, race- and class-linked features may become institutionalized as bases of differentiation (Lipsky 1980).

Despite the theoretical grounds for suspecting police bias, we know less about the influence of race on police handling of juveniles than about processing in other contexts. Because records of street encounters are seldom maintained, it is difficult to assess the factors that influence decisions to initiate contact or to arrest. It is also very difficult to measure discrepancies between "real" offenses and those recorded on arrest reports. The dearth of information is especially unfortunate because police are the primary gatekeepers of the juvenile court.[15] Selection bias introduced by the police is very likely to affect outcomes at later stages, even if no bias occurs at later stages (Farrell and Swigert 1978).

Moreover, bias introduced at the police stage is likely to be amplified at later stages and, more insidiously, to be subsumed under the cover of offense-related considerations whose legitimacy is unlikely to be challenged. If minority youths are systematically overcharged by police, the probability that they will penetrate deeper into the juvenile system is increased. Similarly, if police are more likely to arrest minorities in situations where white youths are released or handled informally, they will generate race differences in prior record. Seriousness of the offense and prior record are key predictors of outcomes at nearly every stage in court processing and their validity as proxies for actual behavior is seldom questioned. The dual problems of "bias amplification" (Dannefer and Schutt 1982; Farrell and Swigert 1978; Liska and Tausig 1979) and what might best be termed "offense contamination" are potentially critical consequences of racial bias in police decision making.

Research on Police-Juvenile Encounters and Arrests

Observational studies are the primary sources of information regarding police decisions to initiate encounters and to make arrests. Survey research, studies of police records, and comparisons of self-reported and official delinquency constitute other methodologies. All of these sources suggest that police-juvenile encounters and arrests are influenced not only by youths' offending but also by aspects of the police-juvenile encounter and the context in which it occurs. They also suggest that, in the main, racial and ethnic disparities in police decision making are not manifestations of intentional bias or prejudice. Instead, race effects are largely indirect: they reflect decisions based on considerations that, from the standpoint of the decision maker, appear to be race neutral and legitimate.

Organizational Factors Linked to Detection and Arrest: Racial disparities in police handling of juveniles are linked to at least three features of police administration and organization. One has to do with routine deployment decisions, that is, manpower allocations and their distribution across beats or sectors. In general, patrols are disproportionately distributed to geographic areas with the greatest numbers of calls for service and the highest rates of reported crime (Walker 1999), which tend to be areas characterized by higher concentrations of minorities and persons of lower socioeconomic status (SES) (Piliavin and Briar 1964; Conley 1994). While geographic assignment of officers based on need for police protection may be rational and defensible for some purposes, it has the effect of increasing police surveillance over minority populations, which in turn increases their likelihood of detection and arrest (Werthman and Piliavin 1967).

A second aspect of police administrative decision making that contributes to racial disparities has to do with strategic choices, such as whether to focus on "hot spots," to initiate "sweeps," to conduct "crackdowns" on certain kinds of crime, and the like. Recently, targeting "hot spots" and creating "drug-free zones" have become popular strategies that concentrate law enforcement resources in high-crime neighborhoods where minorities disproportionately reside.

A third aspect of police organization and administration that affects racial disparities in arrest has to do with characteristic styles of policing (Wilson 1968). There is some evidence that modern urban police departments tend to be "legalistic" in orientation: officers make arrests more often for minor offenses that in suburban or rural areas would be handled informally (Bridges et al. 1993). Again, the concentration of minority populations in urban areas produces racial disparities in arrest.

Neighborhood Context: Numerous researchers have suggested that neighborhood characteristics structure the exercise of officers' discretion in ways that make youths of color more vulnerable to stops and arrests (Robison 1936; Werthman and Piliavin 1967; Smith, Visher, and Davidson 1984; Smith 1986; Sampson 1986). In particular, they have proposed that typifications of neighborhoods based on considerations of race and class provide a heuristic for identifying "dangerous areas," "suspicious persons," and "unusual activity." Werthman and Piliavin (1967), Irwin (1985), and Smith (1986) report that officers characterize the territories they patrol and the people who reside within them into understandable categories, resulting in a process of "ecological contamination" that produces systematic variation in police conduct toward people in different neighborhoods. Irwin (1985) reports that officers tend to impute to persons who reside in "bad neighborhoods" the moral liability of the area itself, prompting a more aggressive orientation toward officer-initiated stops and arrests.

In an extensive observational study of twenty-four police departments in sixty neighborhoods, Smith (1986) found that, irrespective of neighborhood crime rates, police were more likely to initiate contacts with suspects in racially mixed and primarily African American neighborhoods. They were also more likely to use or threaten to use force in disadvantaged, racially mixed and primarily African American neighborhoods. (See also Terrill and Reisig 2003.) Neighborhood SES also had a direct effect on the probability of arrest, independent of characteristics of offenders or offenses. Citizens encountered in lower-class (disproportionately minority) neighborhoods were three times as likely to be arrested as persons in more affluent areas.

In a Seattle study that combined survey data and police records, Sampson (1986) found that neighborhood SES affected the likelihood of police-juvenile contacts independent of individual race, individual SES, or self-reported delinquent involvement. Delinquent involvement was the strongest predictor of police contact, followed by race (minorities were more likely to be arrested) and individual-level SES. But even when these variables were controlled, neighborhood SES had a significant effect, suggesting, consistent with Smith's findings, that officers intensify efforts at social control in economically depressed neighborhoods where minorities more often reside.

Other observational studies lend support to the "neighborhood bias" thesis. In their classic study of police-juvenile encounters, Piliavin and Briar (1964) found that juvenile bureau officers concentrated most of their attention on urban ghettos, where they indiscriminately harassed "suspicious" (especially minority) youths. More recently, Conley (1994) observed not only that communities of color were under heavier police surveillance but also that youths of color within these neighborhoods were more frequently stopped while walking or standing on the street. Chambliss (1994) reported that members of a rapid deployment unit differentially patrolled underclass African American neighborhoods. He claimed that investigative stops were racially motivated: young African American males driving in cars or standing in groups were routinely confronted, verbally harassed, and searched for weapons and drugs. (See also Boydston 1975; Massachusetts Attorney General 1990; Werthman and Piliavin 1967.)

The more public nature of activities in underclass neighborhoods also seems to contribute both opportunity and justification for racial disparities in police intervention. For example, Wordes and Bynum (1995) interviewed patrol officers in several Michigan jurisdictions regarding the initiation of contact with youths and found that officers regarded being in the "wrong neighborhood" and "hanging out" with no apparent purpose as suspicious behaviors that warranted investigative stops.

Citizen surveys also support the conclusion that people of color are more often watched, stopped, and questioned by police without legal justification (Browning et al. 1994; Friedman and Hott 1995; Bortner and Williams 1997; Anderson 1990, 1994). In a survey of Cincinnati residents, Browning and her colleagues (1994) found that 47% of African Americans, compared to 10% of whites, reported that they had been stopped or watched by the police when they had done nothing wrong. Racial disparities were especially pronounced among young people. The authors suggest that minority overrepresentation in police arrest data becomes a self-fulfilling prophecy, fostering the perception that differential police intervention is not racist but "good policing" (Browning et al. 1994, 9). That several appellate courts have condoned the use of race as one among other factors properly considered in making investigative stops only reinforces this view (Kennedy 1997, 136–167).

Situational Factors: Although studies of police-juvenile encounters are few, most suggest that, for minor offenses, race has an indirect effect on arrest that is mediated by youths' demeanor. In an early study, Piliavin and Briar (1964) observed officers in a single metropolitan department over a period of several months. About 10% of police-juvenile contacts involved serious offenses, which uniformly resulted in arrest and referral to court irrespective of other factors. Outcomes in the remaining cases were determined in large measure by the nature of the officer-suspect interaction.[16] Juveniles who appeared tough and disrespectful were more often arrested, while those who were polite and respectful were more often released. African American youths more often displayed a demeanor that prompted officers to view them as "potential troublemakers." In a clear example of racial stereotyping, officers recognized the potential prejudice involved in these attributions but justified them by pointing to departmental arrest data showing that African Americans committed more crimes than whites. Similar findings regarding the effects of demeanor have been reported by Black and Reiss (1970) and Lundman (1978). Most recently, Worden and Myers (1999), in a major observational study conducted in two states, reported that disrespect in an encounter significantly elevated the probability of arrest and that twice as many minority suspects as whites were described as disrespectful. In sum, there is strong evidence that demeanor plays a role in arrest in minor cases and that, in encounters with police, youths of color are (or are perceived to be) more belligerent and uncooperative (see also Ferdinand and Luchterhand 1970; Goldman 1963; Kurtz, Giddings, and Sutphen 1993; Wordes and Bynum 1995; Worden and Shepard 1996).[17]

Bittner (1990, 336) reported that officers frequently interpret hostile demeanor as an indicator of criminal propensity as well as a signal that the situation may get out of control. But demeanor can be misleading. Because most juvenile crime involves group offending (Zimring 1981), encounters with juveniles routinely occur in situations where youths are "on stage" before an audience of their peers. In such settings, "copping an attitude" of toughness or hostility may be a face-saving tactic rather than a harbinger of danger. A hostile attitude may also be a response to real or perceived police prejudice, especially if police concentrate surveillance on underclass areas and differentially stop minority youths. Such practices generate antagonism and perpetuate a vicious cycle (Anderson 1990; Winfree and Griffiths 1977; Griffiths and Winfree 1982).

The Complainant's Preference: Police responsiveness to the dispositional preferences of complainants also contributes to racial disparities in arrests for minor offenses (Black and Reiss 1970; Hohenstein 1969; Lundman, Sykes, and Clark 1978; Smith 1986). The vast majority of police-suspect encounters are citizen initiated (Black and Reiss 1970). Especially if the offense is not serious, the suspect is more likely to be released if the complainant does not support prosecution. Multiple studies have found that complainants more often urge arrest in cases involving African American suspects (Black and Reiss 1970; Lundman, Sykes, and Clark 1978; Smith and Visher 1981).

Postarrest Decisions: Charging

Testing for racial disparities in police charging decisions is extremely difficult. The measurement problems are nearly insurmountable.[18] Nevertheless, some studies germane to the issue have been conducted. Huizinga and Elliott (1987) compared self-reports of offending from the National Youth Survey (NYS) with FBI arrest data and found that the risk of arrest for an Index offense was substantially higher for minority youths than for whites who reported involvement in (grossly) comparable levels of offending. Among youths classified as Index offenders based on the NYS, minority youths were approximately twice as likely as whites to be charged with Index offenses. African Americans who were classified as less serious, non-Index offenders based on their self-reports were about seven times as likely as whites to be arrested for Index crimes.

In a study of police decision making in eight Georgia counties (Kurtz, Giddings, and Sutphen 1993), officers completed questionnaires following the arrest of male youths apprehended for non-traffic offenses. Officers were asked about the offense, the youth's demeanor, and the charges recorded at arrest. Kurtz and his colleagues assessed whether the charges recorded were the most serious that could have been made. In a multivariate analysis, they found that neither race nor SES was directly related to the severity of the charges. However, both race and class indirectly affected officers' charging decisions. African American and lower-SES youths were perceived to have a more hostile and uncooperative demeanor, which resulted in their being charged with more severe offenses.

Sutphen, Kurtz, and Giddings (1993) explored the same subject using a different methodology. They presented vignettes based on actual police-juvenile encounters to officers in several police departments. The nature of the incident and the race of the suspect varied across vignettes. For each incident, officers were asked whether they would make an arrest and what charges they would record. In vignettes involving theft, weapons, and drug cases, African American youths were more often arrested than whites and charged with more counts and more serious crimes. Only in a scenario involving alcohol possession were whites more likely to be arrested. Recall that the UCR data show that whites are overrepresented at arrest for alcohol-related crimes. That the alcohol offense scenario in Sutphen, Kurtz, and Giddings's research was the only one for which officers more often arrested whites is consistent with Piliavin and Briar's (1964) observation that official data about race and crime engender stereotypical expectations that influence officers' decisions.

Police Referral Decisions

In some jurisdictions, police officers are also responsible for deciding whether youths who have been taken into custody should be diverted from the system or referred to the court for formal processing.[19] Most of the research indicates that minority youths are more likely to be referred for formal processing than are legally similar whites (Bell and Lang 1985; Dannefer and Schutt 1982; Fagan, Slaughter, and Hartstone 1987; Ferdinand and Luchterhand 1970; Fisher and Doyle-Martin 1981; Goldman 1963; Kurtz, Giddings, and Sutphen 1993; Sealock and Simpson 1998; Thornberry 1973, 1979; Wilson 1968; Wordes and Bynum 1995; but see, contra, McEachern and Bauzer 1967; Sampson 1986; Terry 1967a, 1967b; Williams and Gold 1972). Interactions between race and offense type have also been reported. In serious cases, the offense itself becomes an overriding consideration. In more minor cases, extralegal considerations come into play, and redound to the disadvantage of youths of color (e.g., Fagan, Slaughter, and Hartstone 1987; Goldman 1963).

There is some evidence that the link between race and court referral is also mediated by youths' demeanor (Bell and Lang 1985; Kurtz, Giddings, and Sutphen 1993). In one of the few studies to include both African Americans and Hispanics, Bell and Lang (1985) compared outcomes in Los Angeles County for youths processed in sheriff's stations, where they were interviewed prior to decision making, and those processed in juvenile justice centers (JJCs), where decisions were made without benefit of interviews. No race or ethnic differences in processing were observed at the JJCs. At the sheriff's stations, however, youths' demeanor (rated by trained observers) influenced referral outcomes. Both African American and Hispanic youths were more often judged to have behaved in an aggressive or uncooperative manner during the interview, which significantly increased the likelihood of court referral.

Structural factors also may condition the impact of race. Dannefer and Schutt (1982) found that in urban counties, which had high proportions of minorities, police were significantly more likely to refer African American and Hispanic youths to court than their white counterparts. (In urban counties, race was a stronger predictor of referral even than severity of the offense.) By contrast, race had a much weaker effect in suburban counties with small minority populations. In interpreting these results, it may be useful to consider a thesis put forth by Tittle and Curran (1988, 52–53), who reported a similar result at the dispositional phase of processing in the juvenile court (see below). They suggested that responses to minority offenders are contingent upon white elites' perceptions of the level of threat posed by young minorities in the aggregate. In urban areas where minority populations tend to be concentrated and highly visible, youths of color are apt to be perceived as particularly threatening. It is not so much the objective threat that matters but, rather, symbolic aspects of threat: white adults perceive concentrations of nonwhite youths stereotypically (e.g., as aggressive, dangerous, lacking in impulse control), stirring fear and other negative emotions that in turn prompt intensified social control.

In sum, the literature indicates that, for a number of reasons, minority youths are more likely than whites to be arrested, referred to court, and detained by police. Because urban underclass neighborhoods have the highest rates of officially recorded crime, they are subject to higher levels of police surveillance. Concentrated surveillance in these areas results in more police-initiated encounters and arrests. The research also suggests that police are more suspicious of persons in low-SES neighborhoods with high minority concentrations, which tend to be typified as "bad" and "dangerous" areas. These typifications, which rest on race and class stereotypes, condone and even encourage a more aggressive posture with respect to stops, arrests, and use of coercive authority. At the level of the police-juvenile encounter, the extant research indicates that whites and minorities tend to be treated similarly when they are suspected of serious crimes. However, when the threat is less serious, extralegal factors—especially demeanor—influence police decision making. Youths who are perceived as hostile and uncooperative are more likely to be arrested, charged with more serious offenses, referred to court, and detained. Because African American and Hispanic youths tend to be (or are perceived to be) less cooperative, more gang involved, and more threatening, they are disadvantaged relative to whites. There is little evidence that other extra-legal considerations—for example, family structure, parental supervision, or school performance—affect police decision making, perhaps because police officers are unlikely to have information about these matters. At all stages of police processing, differential treatment of white and minority youths seems to be affected most by behavioral and attitudinal indicators of risk (danger and hostility) that are perceived to be linked to class and race. The overrepresentation of minorities in police arrest data, especially for violent offenses, reinforces racist expectancies.

Processing in the Juvenile Court

The philosophical foundations of the juvenile court have historically provided enormous potential for race and ethnicity to influence official decision making. Conceived in a social welfare model, the overriding goal of the court at its inception was to respond to the individual needs of the young people brought before it. Until the 1960s, when a radical reformation of the court took place, notions of "equality under the law" had little place in the juvenile court. In theory, at least, offenses were important only insofar as they were symptomatic of some underlying need or problem, which could as easily be signaled by a truancy or a shoplifting as by a robbery or aggravated assault. The potential for race and class to influence processing decisions was great given the enormous discretionary authority granted to justice officials, the lack of criteria to guide decision making, the informality and secrecy of court proceedings, the confidentiality of case records, and—laudatory though the goal might have seemed—the sheer arrogance embodied in the presumption that a cadre of predominantly white middle-class court personnel could diagnose impartially and treat effectively the problems of "other people's" (disproportionately poor and minority) children.

Beginning in the 1960s and 1970s and continuing to the present, juvenile court philosophy, policy, and practice have undergone a series of fundamental changes.[20] Although the court has not altogether abandoned its rehabilitative purpose, in most states the additional objectives of punishment and community protection have been conferred upon it (Sanborn and Salerno 2004). Today, it may be said that at multiple stages in processing, from intake to judicial disposition, court officials are guided to greater or lesser degrees by at least three "focal concerns" (Steffensmeier, Ulmer, and Kramer 1998). These include (1) punishment, or attention to matters of harm and culpability (the seriousness of the offense, the amount of injury or loss, the offender's role in the offense); (2) community protection, or the degree of danger posed by the offender (which directs the decision maker's attention to the seriousness of the current offense, the prior record, and the youth's moral character) (Emerson 1969); and (3) rehabilitation, which calls for identification of problems within the individual (e.g., drug and alcohol abuse, learning disabilities) and his or her social environment (e.g., problems relating to family, school, and peers) that may be alleviated through intervention. Unfortunately, court officials generally lack substantive criteria to assist them in determining what needs or problems should be considered or what weight they (individually or collectively) should be accorded. Moreover, many that may be considered (for example, family status) are not racially neutral.

Contributing to the potential for bias is the fact that, especially at the "front end" of the system, decisions to divert or refer for formal processing, and to release from custody or detain, often must be made within a matter of hours based on little information. In these circumstances, officials may rely on typifications—shorthand cues based on race and class stereotypes—in their attempts to differentiate between youths who pose a risk to the community and those who do not, and between those who are likely to respond to treatment and those who are not.

That there is little review of or accountability for decisions made at the front end of the system, that the process and records of the juvenile court are confidential and shielded from public view, and that juveniles most often proceed through the system without representation by counsel all add to the potential for discrimination.

All of the above mentioned characteristics of the juvenile court system differentiate it from its criminal court counterpart. It is somewhat telling that, after controlling for severity of the current offense and prior record, race effects are relatively rare in studies of processing in the criminal courts (Walker, Spohn, and DeLone 2000; Sampson and Lauritsen 1997),[21] yet they are common and often quite pronounced in research on juvenile court processing (e.g., Pope and Feyerherm 1992). Recent studies of the juvenile court process that have examined more than one decision point and that have employed multivariate models with controls for offense-related variables[22] consistently report significant race effects, usually at multiple processing stages (Austin, Dimas, and Steinhart 1991; Bishop and Frazier 1988, 1996; Bortner et al. 1993; Bridges et al. 1993; DeJong and Jackson 1998; Dunn et al. 1993; Johnson and Secret 1990; Kempf, Decker, and Bing 1990; Kurtz, Giddings, and Sutphen 1993; Leiber 1994, 1995; Leonard and Sontheimer 1995; McCarthy and Smith 1986; Wordes 1995; Wordes, Bynum, and Corley 1994; Wu and Fuentes 1998). The review that follows traces the sequence of court decision making, highlighting studies that point to sources of racial disparity independent of race differentials in offending.

Intake Decision Making

Intake is the first point of contact with the juvenile court, where initial decisions are made regarding formal processing and detention. Nationally, nearly half of all referrals are either closed or diverted at this stage, making intake a critical decision point. The intake function is typically carried out by probation officers or caseworkers, who most often review police arrest reports (or complaints from nonpolice sources), obtain information on prior offenses, and conduct interviews with youths and their parents or guardians. Perhaps because of differences in orientation and function between police organizations and juvenile court intake divisions, referral decisions made by intake personnel hinge to a lesser extent on offense and demeanor (the criteria most often used by police) and more on appraisals of youths' backgrounds and life circumstances.

Researchers have most often dichotomized intake referral outcomes, distinguishing between cases closed without action or handled informally and those referred for formal processing. The consensus of prior research is that legal variables are the strongest predictors: first offenders and those accused of lesser offenses are more often dropped or diverted (e.g., Bishop and Frazier 1988, 1996; Corley et al. 1996; Dean, Hirschel, and Brame 1996; DeJong and Jackson 1998; Kempf, Decker, and Bing 1990; Leonard and Sontheimer 1995; Leiber 1994, 1995; Leiber and Stairs 1999; McCarter 1997; Smith and Paternoster 1990). However, most studies also reveal racial and ethnic disparities in outcome that cannot be explained by legal factors (e.g., Arnold 1971; Bridges et al. 1993; Bishop and Frazier 1988, 1996; Dunn et al. 1993; DeJong and Jackson 1998; Frazier and Cochran 1986; Kempf, Decker, and Bing 1990 [rural areas]; Leiber 1994; Leonard and Sontheimer 1995; Poole and Regoli 1980; Smith and Paternoster 1990; Thomas and Sieverdes 1975; but see, contra, Dean, Hirschel, and Brame 1996; McCarter 1997; McCarthy and Smith 1986; Shelden and Horvath 1987). Studies that include both African Americans and Hispanics are few. They indicate that both minority groups are disadvantaged relative to whites, but that disparities in the treatment of Hispanic and white youths are not quite as marked as those between whites and African Americans (e.g., DeJong and Jackson 1998; Leonard and Sontheimer 1995).

Extending the analysis of intake options, some studies have trichotomized outcomes to differentiate between cases closed, those diverted, and those referred for formal processing. The most common finding is that, compared to whites with similar offenses and prior records, African American and Hispanic youths are less likely to be diverted but more likely both to be released outright and to be referred for formal processing (e.g., Bridges et al. 1993; Leiber 1994; Leiber and Jamieson 1995). In other words, youths of color differentially receive both the least severe and the most severe outcomes. A possible explanation for the higher rate at which cases involving minority youth are dropped is that intake officials correct for police bias when they recognize that youths have been arrested on weak evidence for which a conviction seems unlikely, or for marginal offenses for which a conviction seems unjust (see Corley et al. 1996).

Several factors have been identified that help explain why minority youths are less likely to be diverted from the system. One involves *failure to meet criteria for diversion*. Some organizational policies and regulations, although established with no intent to discriminate, nonetheless have a negative and differential impact on minority youths. As a matter of policy in many jurisdictions, juveniles are ineligible for diversion and must be automatically detained if their parents cannot be contacted and do not appear for a face-to-face interview. In a Florida study, Bishop and Frazier (1996) reported that minority families were less likely to have phones, access to transportation, access to child care, and the ability to take leave time from work without loss of pay, all of which made it more difficult for them to comply with official policy. Bond-Maupin, Chiago Lujan, and Bortner (1995) documented the devastating effects of a similar policy on Native American adolescents living on reservations, many of whose parents lacked phones and transportation.

In many jurisdictions, diversion to informal probation or other community-based sanctions or services also requires an admission of guilt (Snyder and Sickmund 1999). Leiber (1994) and Kempf, Decker, and Bing (1990) found that white youths more often admit guilt, which tends to be looked upon with favor by officials as a sign of openness to treatment. Of course, a higher proportion of arrested youths of color may be truly innocent. Even among those who are guilty, reluctance to admit guilt may say far more about their distrust of justice officials than about their amenability to treatment (Leiber 1994; Bishop and Frazier 1996). Nevertheless, the inference that youths of color lack remorse is one that tends to be drawn. As we will see below, the image of the "remorseless" minority offender extends well beyond the intake stage.

Disaggregation of data by *offense type* suggests another reason for racially disparate outcomes. Juveniles arrested for drug offenses are especially likely to be referred to court (Bell and Lang 1985; Kempf, Decker, and Bing 1990; Leonard and Sontheimer 1995). We have already seen that police more often target minority communities for enforcement of drug laws (Tonry 1994, 1995). That drug cases are disproportionately referred for formal processing at intake amplifies these racial disparities.

Family assessment also plays an important role in contributing to disparate outcomes. Evaluation of the family's ability to provide a wholesome environment for the socialization of children has traditionally been a dominant focus of juvenile court inquiry (Cicourel 1968; Emerson 1969; Feld 1999). While critics view these assessments as means by which elites rationalize extensions of control over minorities and the poor (Platt 1977; Schlossman 1977), defenders point to studies suggesting the centrality of family dysfunction (especially child-parent conflict and lack of parental supervision) in the etiology of delinquency (e.g., Hirschi 1969; McCord 1991; Patterson, Reid, and Dishion 1992; Sampson and Laub 1993b). Court officials view family support and intervention as proper functions of the juvenile court (e.g., Sanborn 1996).

In their study of juvenile courts in Missouri, Kempf, Decker, and Bing (1990) found that both family structure and judgments about the adequacy of parental supervision were strong predictors of intake referral decisions. Minority youths were less likely than white youths to reside in two-parent homes. In addition, case records reported that parents of minority youths were less willing to supervise their children and less capable of exercising proper control even when they expressed a willingness to do so. Although the basis for these judgments is unclear, the danger of racial stereotyping is unmistakable.

Kempf and her colleague's findings have been replicated in other jurisdictions. Austin (1995), Corley and his colleagues (1996), Frazier and Bishop (1995), Krisberg and Austin (1993), and Smith and Paternoster (1990) also found that intake decisions to handle cases formally were linked to broken homes, perceptions of inadequate parental supervision, and perceptions of parental unwillingness to work with court personnel. On all three dimensions, youths of color fared less well.

Some qualitative research suggests that officials' assessments of family life and parental supervision are affected by racial stereotypes. Frazier and Bishop (1995) interviewed juvenile court officials and found they generally viewed the families of African American youths in more negative terms than the families of whites. Even when two African American parents were in the home, they tended to be perceived as less capable of exercising control over their children than the parents of white youths. Negative attributes were presumed to be characteristic of minority families because African Americans as a group had higher rates of broken homes, poverty, and unemployment, and resided more often in neighborhoods where officials believed crime and drugs were prevalent.

Racial disparities have also been linked to *social class,* sometimes in terms of demeanor (Kurtz, Giddings, and Sutphen 1993) but most often in terms of differential access to resources. Bishop and Frazier (1996) reported that justice officials in Florida attributed racially disparate intake outcomes to the fact that middle-class families were able to purchase services privately (e.g., counseling, substance abuse treatment), while comparable services for poor youths could be obtained only by court order following an adjudication of delinquency (see also Cicourel 1968; Bortner et al. 1993). Officials generally defended the selective prosecution of poor (disproportionately minority) youths on the grounds that it enabled them to receive services they could not otherwise afford. In their analysis of processing in Arizona, Bortner and colleagues (1993, 73–74) concluded that "two tracks exist—one for those of families, largely middle- and upper-class Anglo, with means to afford private behavioral health treatment services, and a second for the children of low-income families, largely African American, Hispanic, and Native American children living in single-parent homes, perhaps surviving through public assistance."

School problems (attendance and performance) have also been found to predict intake decisions to refer youths for formal processing, independent of controls for legal and other social factors (Leiber 1995; Leonard and Sontheimer 1995). While difficulties in school are common among youths referred to intake, they are more common among African Americans, Native Americans, and Hispanics (e.g., Bridges et al. 1993; Dryfoos 1990; Jarjoura 1993; McCarter 1997). Thus, school problems become intervening variables through which race and ethnicity influence intake outcomes.

Detention

Like adults, juveniles may be detained if there is reason to believe that they will fail to appear at upcoming hearings. They are also eligible for "preventive detention" if they are predicted to commit further crimes. However, the standards that apply to the preventive detention of juveniles are much less restrictive than those that apply to adults. The Supreme Court has approved preventive detention of adults only when they are charged with one of a narrow range of offenses,[23] and only following a showing by clear and convincing evidence that no condition of release could assure the public safety (*United States v. Salerno,* 481 U.S. 739 [1987]). By contrast, the Court has approved the preventive detention of juveniles who pose a "serious risk" of committing *any* crime (*Schall v. Martin,* 467 U.S. 283 [1984]). In *Schall,* no restrictions were placed on the categories of juvenile defendants eligible for preventive detention, "serious risk" was not defined, and neither prediction criteria nor standards of proof were specified. As Feld (1999) has observed, the Court invited subjective decision making with enormous potential for misapplication.

Detention is one of the most frequently studied decision points in the juvenile system. It is also the point at which race effects unexplained by offense-related variables are most often found (e.g., Chused 1973; Pawlak 1977; Fenwick 1982; Bortner and Reed 1985; Frazier and Cochran 1986; McCarthy and Smith 1986; Fagan, Slaughter, and Hartstone 1987; Lockhart et al. 1991; Bishop and Frazier 1988, 1996; Kempf, Decker, and Bing 1990; Wordes, Bynum, and Corley 1994; Wordes 1995; Wordes and Bynum 1995; Johnson and Secret 1990; Bridges et al. 1993; Secret and Johnson 1997). In some studies, the effect of race is stronger than that of offense (Leonard and Sontheimer 1995) or prior record (Feld 1995). And, in many instances, the effect of race remains strong despite controls for a host of legal and social variables, including social class (Leonard and Sontheimer 1995; Wordes 1995; Wordes, Bynum, and Corley 1994). Studies that have included Native American and Hispanic youths report significant disadvantages to these groups as well (Corley et al. 1996; Krisberg and Austin 1993; Wordes, Bynum, and Corley 1994). Researchers have identified several factors that seem to contribute to racial disparities in detention outcomes:

Detention Criteria: Although some states have tried to regulate the use of detention by adopting risk assessment instruments and admissions screening criteria, drug offenders and gang members are sometimes targeted for presumptive detention (Orlando 1999). As we have already seen, drug enforcement tends to be heaviest in underclass, minority neighborhoods. Minority youths also have higher rates of gang membership than whites and are more often suspected of gang membership regardless of their involvement (Austin 1995; Bortner et al. 1993; Esbensen and Winfree 1998; Krisberg and Austin 1993; Miller 1996, 109).

Family, School, and Work: As was the case at referral, decisions to place youths in detention are apparently linked to judgments regarding whether they will receive adequate supervision and control during the predisposition period. Assessments of parental supervision play a prominent role in detention decisions (e.g., Fenwick 1982; Bridges et al. 1993; Corley et al. 1996; Kempf, Decker, and Bing 1990; Wu, Cernkovich, and Dunn 1997). Fenwick (1982) found that the strongest predictors of detention were not offense-related variables, but family structure, parents' expressed interest in the juvenile, and the quality of child-parent interaction. As noted above, there is considerable risk of racial stereotyping in assessments of parental attitudes and family dynamics.

School and work represent other sources of control and supervision. Whether youths are attending and/or performing well in school (Cohen and Kluegel 1979; Leonard and Sontheimer 1995; Wu, Cernkovich, and Dunn 1997) or are employed (Cohen and Kluegel 1979) have been linked to detention outcomes. As noted above, compared to whites, African American and Hispanic youths are more likely to have problems in school and are less likely to be employed.

Formal Charging

Relatively few studies have explored the influence of race/ethnicity on prosecutorial decisions to file formal charges, and they have produced mixed results. Bishop and Frazier (1988, 1996) found that race was only weakly related to formal charging once legal variables were controlled. However, race affected charging decisions indirectly: juveniles who were detained were more likely to be charged, and minority youths were considerably more likely to be detained than otherwise similar whites (See also Kempf, Decker, and Bing 1990). Other researchers report direct race effects at prosecutorial charging that disadvantage minority youths (MacDonald and Chesney-Lind 2001; Leonard and Sontheimer 1995 [African Americans but not Hispanics]), while still others report that minorities are less likely than legally similar whites to be formally charged (Bridges et al. 1993; Leiber 1994; Leiber and Jamieson 1995).

As noted earlier, there is a great need for further research on the connection between race and the number and level of charges filed and, relatedly, the nature of plea bargains offered. Unfortunately, this kind of research is hampered by the considerable difficulty in operationalizing key control variables, including the actual severity of the offense committed and the evidentiary strength of the case.

Adjudication

At the adjudicatory stage, judges decide whether to dismiss the case or make a finding of delinquency. Contrary to the results at virtually every other decision point, the most common finding is that, after controlling for offense and prior record, whites are considerably more likely than minority youths to be adjudicated delinquent (Dannefer and Schutt 1982 [urban counties only]; Dunn et al. 1993; Johnson and Secret 1990; Kempf, Decker, and Bing 1990 [rural areas]; Secret and Johnson 1997; Wu 1997; Wu, Cernkovich, and Dunn 1997; Wu and Fuentes 1998). A few studies report no race effect (Kempf, Decker, and Bing 1990 [urban areas]; Leiber 1994; Leiber and Jamieson 1995; Leonard and Sontheimer 1995), while findings of minority disadvantage are less common (Bishop and Frazier 1988; Bridges et al. 1993; MacDonald and Chesney-Lind 2001).

The mixed results for this stage probably reflect real jurisdictional differences. Nevertheless, the most common finding of minority advantage needs to be reconciled with the fairly consistent evidence of minority disadvantage at previous processing junctures. A plausible explanation is that different filtering processes are at work at adjudication. Because of the influence of extralegal variables at the arrest and referral stages, in some jurisdictions at least, minority defendants' cases may on the whole be weaker than whites' (see Dannefer and Schutt 1982; Fagan, Slaughter, and Hartstone 1987; Johnson and Secret 1990; Kurtz, Giddings, and Sutphen 1993). Judges may introduce a "correction" at adjudication because adjudicatory decisions call for a singular focus on proof of the offense, rather than on characteristics of youths and their social backgrounds.[24] Like tests of the effects of race on prosecutorial charging and plea negotiation, tests of the "correction" hypothesis require measures of evidentiary strength, which are difficult to construct.

Judicial Disposition

In theory, at least, court dispositions are guided by the three "focal concerns" noted at the outset of this discussion, that is, punishment, community protection, and treatment. At disposition, judges in most jurisdictions tend to rely heavily on predisposition reports prepared by probation officers for insight into factors relevant to these concerns. The report will generally address issues of harm and culpability relevant to punishment (e.g., the youth's statement regarding the offense, the probation officer's assessment of moral character, the victim's statement), issues of danger and risk relating to community protection (e.g., details of the prior record, the youth's behavior on probation or other previous dispositions), and matters relevant to treatment (e.g., alcohol and substance abuse; family, school, and peer influences that may have contributed to the offense; offender expressions of guilt or remorse; the number and type of prior dispositions that the youth has received).

The consensus of the extant research is that offense history is the strongest predictor of dispositional outcomes. Previous dispositions are also highly influential, much more so than current offense (e.g., Cohen 1975; Feld 1989; Henretta, Frazier, and Bishop 1986; Thornberry and Christenson 1984). That offense history and prior disposition are stronger predictors than current offense is consistent with the conclusion that judges at the disposition stage are more focused on community protection and treatment than punishment (see also Horwitz and Wasserman 1980b). Emerson (1969) suggests that judges at disposition are especially interested in assessing moral character. If a youth reappears in court multiple times, he or she is generally perceived as a hard-core delinquent with criminal values. Multiple previous (and, by definition, unsuccessful) dispositions ultimately lead to the conclusion that the youth is not amenable to treatment (Emerson 1969).

Unfortunately, prior record and previous dispositions, although *apparently* race neutral, are contaminated to unknown degrees. As we have seen, youths of color are more vulnerable to arrest and formal processing than otherwise similar whites. Compared to white youths engaged in the same behaviors, minorities more readily accumulate offense histories and dispositions from which inferences are drawn about character and capacity for reform.

The vast majority of studies indicate that race has a significant direct effect on dispositional outcomes after legal variables are controlled (e.g., Arnold 1971; Bazemore 1993; Bishop and Frazier 1988, 1992, 1996; Dean, Hirschel, and Brame 1996 [African Americans and Native Americans]; DeJong and Jackson 1998 [rural areas only]; Fagan, Slaughter, and Hartstone 1987; Jeffords, Lindsey, and McNitt 1993; Kempf, Decker, and Bing 1990 [rural areas only]; Krisberg and Austin 1993 [African Americans especially, Hispanics to a lesser extent]; Leiber and Jamieson 1995; Johnson and Secret 1990; Marshall and Thomas 1983; McCarter 1997; McCarthy and Smith 1986; Reed 1984; Thomas and Cage 1977; Thornberry 1973, 1979; but see, contra, Terry 1967b; Bailey and Peterson 1981; Phillips and Dinitz 1982; Cohen and Kluegel 1978). Moreover, researchers who have examined the effects of decisions made at earlier points in processing almost without exception report indirect effects of race operating through detention status. Two of the most consistent findings in the literature are that minority youths are more likely to be detained than otherwise similar whites, and that being detained strongly predicts harsher treatment at disposition (e.g., Bailey 1981; Bishop and Frazier 1988, 1992, 1996; Bortner 1982; Bortner and Reed 1985; Clarke and Koch 1980; Cohen and Kluegel 1979; Dunn et al. 1993; Feld 1989, 1995; Frazier and Bishop 1985; Frazier and Cochran 1986; Johnson and Secret 1990; Kempf, Decker, and Bing 1990; Leiber 1994; Leonard and Sontheimer 1995; Lockhart et al. 1991; McCarthy and Smith 1986; Secret and Johnson 1997; Wordes 1995; Wu 1997; Wu and Fuentes 1998). These findings highlight the importance of analyzing juvenile justice as a series of decision points. When research is restricted to a single, late-stage outcome, race effects can be obscured due to correlations between race and earlier processing decisions that predict these later outcomes. It is noteworthy that most of the studies reporting no race effect at disposition were single-stage analyses.

Prior research suggests that effects of race on judicial disposition may also be contingent on offense type. Several recent studies report that minority youths convicted of drug offenses are especially likely to receive more severe dispositions than whites (DeJong and Jackson 1998; Horowitz and Pottieger 1991; Leonard and Sontheimer 1995 [Hispanics but not African Americans]; Tittle and Curran 1988). Because the drug problem has become so thoroughly linked to minorities in the public view (Bortner, Zatz, and Hawkins 2000; Miller 1996; Tonry 1995), minority drug offenders may be perceived as more threatening than their white counterparts (Sampson and Laub 1993a).

As was the case at intake referral and detention, a not uncommon finding is that family considerations play a role at disposition in ways that work to the disadvantage of minority offenders. Youths from single-parent families and youths experiencing (or perceived to be experiencing) family problems receive more severe dispositions (e.g., Arnold 1971; DeJong and Jackson 1998; Horwitz and Wasserman 1980a; Kempf, Decker, and Bing 1990; Thomas and Cage 1977; but see, contra, Dannefer and Schutt 1982). Two studies conducted in the 1990s reported significant interactions between race and family variables that suggest discrimination based on racial stereotypes. Schissel's (1993) research in Canada showed that Aboriginal youths were treated more harshly if a parent did not appear in court while white juveniles whose parents did not appear were not so penalized. DeJong and Jackson (1998) found that living with two parents protected white youths against secure placement while African American youths were disadvantaged whether they lived with one or both parents.

Other evidence of the importance of the family—and of the intersection of race, class, and family—is provided by Sanborn (1996), who interviewed one hundred court officials in three eastern communities regarding factors that influence judicial disposition. Asked what they believed *should* be considered at disposition, officials identified family most often. Asked whether the juvenile court *in fact* discriminated against any particular youths, 87% of respondents answered positively. Those most often identified as the recipients of discriminatory treatment were African American males from dysfunctional families in lower-class neighborhoods.

Interactions between race and family disadvantage have also been reported by Leonard and Sontheimer (1995) and Wu and Fuentes (1998), who found that African American youths from very poor and welfare families were especially likely to be removed from their homes. Wu and Fuentes's interpretation of this result is that judges view minority youths as especially needy when they live in socially disorganized, underclass areas that weaken families and promote crime (see also Frazier and Bishop 1995). In other words, because minority youths are more likely to live in impoverished areas (due in no small part to racial prejudice, racial segregation, and lack of employment), they are more likely to be removed from their homes. The irony is that, however well intended court officials might be in taking this action, they are powerless to alter the neighborhood environments from which youths come and to which they will almost certainly return. Structural problems cannot be solved at the individual level.

An alternative explanation is suggested by conflict theory (Quinney 1977; Blalock 1967). From this perspective, minority youths from indigent families, especially if they are part of the urban underclass, are more often removed from their homes not because they are perceived to be particularly needy but because they are viewed as particularly threatening. This interpretation is consistent with findings of recent studies of sentencing in the criminal courts (where consideration of "needs" should not apply), which show that young, unemployed African American and Hispanic men face significantly higher odds of incarceration than either employed minority offenders or unemployed white offenders (Nobiling, Spohn, and DeLone 1998; Spohn and Holleran 2000). What both sets of results suggest is that the "economically dependent minority male" invokes a stereotype to which attributions of dangerousness and culpability are powerfully linked (see generally, Hawkins 1981, 230; Steffensmeier, Ulmer, and Kramer 1998, 767).

That race is an influential factor in perceptions and evaluations of - delinquent youths has recently been demonstrated by Bridges and Steen (1998). They examined predisposition reports prepared by juvenile probation officers in three counties in a western state and found pronounced differences in probation officers' assessments of the causes of offending among white versus minority offenders. Not unexpectedly, causal attributions were heavily influenced by prior record and current offense. However, race remained a significant predictor of probation officer assessments and recommendations even after legal factors were controlled.

Offending among African American youths, compared to whites, was more often attributed to enduring defects of character (as evidenced by lack of remorse, failure to accept responsibility for the offense, and the like) and less often to external features of their environments. In reports to the court, African Americans were described as less amenable to treatment and at greater risk of reoffending. In contrast, reports on white offenders significantly more often focused on the effects of family conflict, delinquent peers, poor school performance, and other *external* factors. By attributing whites' delinquency to *external* factors, probation officers portrayed them as fundamentally good kids who were victims of unfortunate circumstances. Consequently, they were perceived as less threatening and less likely to reoffend. Not surprisingly, then, probation officers recommended significantly more lenient sentences for whites than for African Americans. This study provides some of the most compelling evidence to date of racial stereotyping by juvenile justice officials and of the power of racial stereotypes to influence decision making.[25] More broadly, it shows how racist characterological and behavioral expectancies in the larger culture are insidiously and effectively reproduced in the juvenile courts.

Correctional Placement

Research has largely ignored decisions that take place after disposition. A host of important issues needs to be addressed. These include the influence of race on placement decisions, on the kinds of sanctions and services that offenders receive, on decisions to release offenders from correctional confinement, and on decisions to revoke probation and aftercare. The few studies that have examined placement and treatment decisions are discussed below.

The juvenile corrections system in most states includes a wide variety of facilities and programs, both public and private, ranging from large and generally very secure training schools to small, community-based group homes and halfway houses. Data from the 1997 *Census of Juveniles in Residential Placement* (Snyder and Sickmund 1999) showed that minority youths were more likely than whites to be housed in public rather than private facilities. Nationally, youths of color—including African Americans, Hispanics, Native Americans, Asians, and Pacific Islanders—made up 67% of the population in public commitment facilities and 55% of those housed in private facilities. Unfortunately, these data do not include information on facility type (e.g., training school, group home). They also do not speak to such important issues as whether racial disparities in placement correspond to differences in assessed risk or identified treatment needs.

In one of the few studies to include a focus on racial and ethnic differences in correctional placement, Leonard and Sontheimer (1995) found that, in Pennsylvania, committed Hispanics were more often sent to public residential facilities than were African Americans or whites, African Americans and Hispanics were more often placed in private residential facilities than were whites, and whites were more likely than African Americans or Hispanics to be sent to small privately run group homes, foster homes, and drug and alcohol treatment programs. The authors expressed concern that "perhaps de facto racial segregation occurs at placement" (1995, 120).

Kowalski and Rickicki (1982) included controls for offense, prior record, and "staff behavior ratings" in their analysis of placement decisions made at a diagnostic and evaluation (D&E) center to which youths were sent following commitment. Although youths of color were significantly more likely than whites to be placed in large institutions rather than group homes, race did not predict placement once controls were introduced. The strongest predictor of placement was the staff behavior rating, a composite measure that included demeanor, attitude toward authority, and behavior while at the center. Minority youths rated significantly more poorly than whites. The authors concluded that "the D&E Center avoided allowing race . . . to influence dispositions" (1982, 66). Such a conclusion ignores the very real possibility that staff assessments of youths' demeanor, attitudes, and behavior are shaped in important ways by the sorts of race-linked stereotypical expectations described by Bridges and Steen (see above).

Finally, an analysis of placements made by the Texas Youth Commission showed that while "high-risk" juveniles were placed in secure programs irrespective of race/ethnicity, among non-high-risk juveniles whites were significantly more likely than African Americans or Hispanics to be sent to programs providing specialized treatment (Jeffords, Lindsey, and McNitt 1993, 29). Jeffords and his colleagues also examined racial and ethnic differences in mental health diagnosis and in the placement of committed youths who had been diagnosed with mental health problems. They found that white youths were more likely to be diagnosed with emotional disturbances than African Americans or Hispanics, making them eligible for smaller, more specialized treatment programs. Moreover, among those diagnosed as emotionally disturbed and "in high need for treatment," white youths were significantly more likely to receive scarce treatment services (39%) than either African Americans (14%) or Hispanics (15%) (1993, 38). (For other evidence of racial disparities in access to mental health treatment, see Lewis et al. 1980; Kaplan and Busner 1992; Thomas, Stubbe, and Pearson 1999.)

Contextual Effects

The studies of juvenile court processing discussed thus far have focused on the connection between individual-level case characteristics and decision outcomes. While studies of this type constitute the bulk of the extant research, increasingly scholars are adopting a macrosociological perspective, inquiring whether racial and ethnic disparities in processing may be explained by or linked to the larger context in which processing occurs. Juvenile courts do not operate uniformly within the United States, or even within states (Feld 1991; Pope and Feyerherm 1992). Because courts are organized at the local level, practices vary greatly from one place to another. Variations in local practice may be influenced by such factors as community social structure, the availability of resources, and political, legal, and ideological features of courts and the communities in which they are located (e.g., Bridges et al.

1995; Feld 1991, 1999; Sampson and Laub 1993a; Secret and Johnson 1997). Although it is impossible given space constraints to review the research on all the nominated contextual sources of variation, major themes in the literature and their relevance to racial disparities in processing are briefly discussed below.

Urban-Rural Variations

Feld (1991, 1995, 1999) suggests that level of urbanization is linked to organizational characteristics of juvenile courts, which in turn have important implications for how cases are processed. He argues that because urban counties are more heterogeneous, diverse, and less stable than rural counties, with fewer mechanisms of informal social control, their juvenile courts tend to be more formal, bureaucratic, and due process oriented. They screen out fewer cases, process more cases formally, and make greater use of commitment. But they also handle cases more equitably than do rural courts: their legalistic orientation results in a focus on offense and prior record, rather than social characteristics of offenders. By contrast, in rural courts justice administration tends to be more informal. More cases are filtered out of the system at intake. Judges exercise more discretion and youths who have committed similar offenses may be treated very differently. "Equal treatment under the law" gives way to the traditional *parens patriae* mandate to provide individualized treatment based on juveniles' personal and social needs.

Some research supports this perspective. Feld (1990), Leonard and Sontheimer (1995), and Smith and Paternoster (1990) found that cases referred to courts in urban and suburban areas were more likely to progress beyond the initial referral stage (but see, contra, Johnson and Secret 1990). Processing in urban courts was more offense driven, social characteristics being less influential at intake than in rural areas (see also DeJong and Jackson 1998; Kempf, Decker, and Bing 1990).[26] Although urban courts were more evenhanded than rural ones in the referral and petitioning of cases, their propensity to move cases deeper into the system ultimately worked to the disadvantage of African Americans, who more often reside in urban areas.

Mixed results have been reported with respect to urban-rural differences in sentencing. Feld (1990) found that urban courts sentenced youths more severely than rural courts. By contrast, DeJong and Jackson (1998) and Kempf, Decker, and Bing (1990) reported more severe sentencing in rural courts, while Leonard and Sontheimer (1995) found that level of urbanization was unrelated to sentencing. Jeffords, Lindey, and McNitt (1993) reported that both urban and rural courts were equally likely to commit African American and Hispanic youths at higher rates than whites. Additionally, all of these studies report a great deal of variation in sentencing practice *across* urban counties.

Minority Composition, Poverty, and Racial Inequality

Racial disparities have been linked to other aspects of social structure. In their analysis of juvenile court disposition across thirty-one Florida counties, Tittle and Curran (1988) found that dispositional severity was predicted by the relative size of the nonwhite and youth populations. Irrespective of crime rates, significant racial disparities occurred only in communities with large percentages of nonwhites and young people, and especially for drug and sex offenses (see also Bridges et al. 1993; and Dannefer and Schutt 1982; but see, contra, Frazier, Bishop, and Henretta 1992). As discussed above, Tittle and Curran interpreted these results by proposing a variant of conflict theory, suggesting that it is not the objective level of threat posed by minority groups that impels efforts to control them but, rather, "symbolic" aspects of threat. When whites perceive that there are concentrated populations of minorities disproportionately engaged in behaviors that provoke fear, anger, and the like, they subject them to intensified social control (Tittle and Curran 1988, 52).

In a study of juvenile court processing in 322 counties in twenty-one states, Sampson and Laub (1993a) found that counties with greater underclass poverty and racial inequality detained youths and sentenced them to out-of-home placement at higher rates. The effects of structural context were more pronounced for African Americans than for whites. Particularly strong were the effects of concentrations of underclass poverty and levels of racial inequality on rates of African American out-of-home placement, especially for drug offenses.[27] Like Tittle and Curran, Sampson and Laub interpret their findings in terms of symbolic threat, proposing that economic elites in counties with high concentrations of the underclass, racial poverty, and inequality use the juvenile justice system to exert greater control over populations viewed as offensive and threatening (Sampson and Laub 1993a, 293).

Bridges and his colleagues (1995) explored the effects of several features of community social structure on racial disparities in juvenile confinement across counties in Washington State. They found that racial disparities in confinement were very unevenly distributed across counties and were unrelated to race differences in rates of arrest. Instead, low white confinement rates were found in urban communities and those with large minority concentrations, while high minority confinement rates were found in counties with high rates of violent crime. While the first two of these results are consistent with those of Sampson and Laub (1993a) and Tittle and Curran (1988), the link between violent crime rates and minority confinement rates has not been previously reported. Bridges and his colleagues also offer a threat interpretation, suggesting that stereotypical perceptions linking minorities to violence generate greater fear of minorities in communities with high levels of violent crime, which in turn prompts higher rates of minority incarceration.

Local Culture

Feld (1991) and Mahoney (1987) propose that cross-jurisdictional variations in juvenile justice processing are also related to the sociopolitical environments in which justice system agencies operate and upon which they rely for legitimation, resources, and clients. Mahoney conducted a two-year study of a single juvenile court and showed that case processing and outcomes were affected by local issues and events, including resource shifts, political infighting, personality characteristics of key players, and changing political climates. Hers is a revealing account of the ways in which courts are embedded in, dependent on, and interactive with the sociopolitical environment. Cross-jurisdictional variations in juvenile justice practice have also been linked to the idiosyncrasies of individual judges (e.g., Podkopacz and Feld 1996), to the bureaucratic structure of prosecutors' offices (Barnes and Franz 1989; Bishop and Frazier 1991), to methods of judicial appointment and levels of judicial specialization in juvenile justice matters (Hasenfeld and Cheung 1985; Kempf, Decker, and Bing 1990), and to organizational culture, reflected in the shared beliefs and expectations of juvenile court officials (Aday 1986; Stapleton, Aday, and Ito 1982; Smith and Paternoster 1990). Researchers have only begun to explore most of these issues, whose implications for understanding minority overrepresentation in the justice system are presently unclear.

4. Discussion and Conclusions

Although research on racial influences on juvenile justice processing is underdeveloped in many respects, the preponderance of the extant evidence supports the following conclusions. Race and ethnic differentials in processing are attributable in part to differential involvement in crime. Nevertheless, disparities that cannot be explained by race differences in offending are apparent at nearly every stage in the juvenile justice process. At the police level, decisions to deploy resources differentially to urban underclass neighborhoods put minority offenders at greater risk of detection and arrest. In lower-class and primarily nonwhite neighborhoods, police officers more often make proactive investigative stops, arrests, and use coercive authority, especially toward minority offenders. At the level of the police-juvenile encounter, race influences police decisions indirectly, at least with respect to minor offenses. Because minority youth suspects are more often perceived to be insolent and uncooperative, and because complainants more often request that they be arrested, officers more often choose to arrest, detain, and refer them to court than white youths involved in similar offenses.

Most individual-level studies of juvenile court processing have shown a substantial direct effect of race at multiples processing stages even after legal factors are controlled. Race differentials introduced by the police are com-pounded in the juvenile courts (especially at intake), eventually culminating in marked disparities in minority confinement. Although legal variables have the strongest effects on court processing from intake through final disposi-tion, they are contaminated to an unknown degree. Because minority youth are more likely to be arrested, charged with more serious offenses, and for-mally processed than their white counterparts, race bias is incorporated into and masked by the offense, prior record, and prior disposition variables that inform processing decisions.

The empirical record on individual-level case decision making in the ju-venile courts provides strong evidence that race has a substantial effect on de-cisions made at the "front end" of the system. Minority youths are less often diverted, more often referred for formal processing, and more often held in secure detention than white youths who are legally similar. By contrast, evi-dence of differential treatment at the prosecutorial charging stage is mixed. Contradictory results may reflect cross-jurisdictional differences in the ex-tent to which cases are prescreened for evidentiary sufficiency. At adjudica-tion, where evidentiary considerations presumably take precedence, there is little evidence of minority disadvantage. To the contrary, research suggests that judges may compensate at this stage for disparities introduced earlier in arrest, charging, and court referral decisions. At judicial disposition, evidence of race differentials in treatment is once again more pronounced. Many stud-ies report a direct race effect, and there is consensus that race influences ju-dicial disposition decisions indirectly: minority youth are considerably more likely than legally similar whites to be detained, and detainees receive more intrusive dispositions.

Recent cross-jurisdictional analyses also suggest that the structural context of juvenile courts influences justice system responses. There is evidence that courts in urban areas, areas characterized by racial inequality and underclass poverty, communities with high rates of violent crime, and communities with high proportions of minorities and the young process cases more formally, use detention more frequently, and impose harsher dispositions, especially for minority youths. Although the findings are far from conclusive, they hint that in impoverished high-crime areas where minorities are highly visible, youths of color are perceived by justice officials—and perhaps by the com-munity at large—as especially needy, especially threatening, or both.

Explaining Differential Treatment

There is little evidence of overt bias on the part of police officials. Instead, it appears that race and ethnic differentials in treatment are due in part to poli-cies and practices that appear to be race neutral but that are discriminatory in effect. Although it is rational to deploy scarce police resources in neighborhoods where crime rates are highest, these are areas in which minorities disproportionately reside. Subjecting poor, minority neighborhoods to differential surveillance and more police-initiated investigative stops may provoke antagonism among minority youth who perceive that they are being harassed, which in turn increases their likelihood of arrest, detention, and court processing.

Differential treatment by police may also be attributable to more subtle forms of bias related to the meanings officers attach to places and people. Because police officers seldom have sufficient information accurately to assess either the level of criminal activity or the dangers associated with the places they patrol and the people they encounter, they develop "typescripts" of the neighborhoods in which they work based on stereotypes and attributions that are linked to class and race: lower-class, racially mixed neighborhoods tend to be perceived as disreputable and dangerous, as are the people within them. That minorities are more likely to be stopped, arrested, and treated coercively in these neighborhoods may reflect this ecological bias (Smith 1986, 335).

Interpretations of differential treatment in the juvenile courts may benefit from consideration of two research findings. First, there is much more evidence of race effects in the juvenile than in the criminal courts (e.g., Sampson and Lauritsen 1997). Second, legal variables typically account for much less of the explained variance in juvenile than in criminal court outcomes. Taken together, these findings suggest that features of the juvenile court that distinguish it from its criminal counterpart are important in explaining racial disparities in processing. From its inception, the juvenile court has tried to balance the dual functions of social welfare and social control. The focus on individualized treatment is a unique feature of the juvenile court, calling for an assessment of youths' needs and life circumstances and the delivery of services to address their problems. Not surprisingly, then, studies that include controls for personal and social factors (e.g., family structure, willingness and ability of parents to provide control and supervision, school performance, employment status) report that these variables inform court referral, detention, and disposition decisions. From the perspective of juvenile court officials with a social welfare focus, these are legitimate considerations. That each of these factors tends also to be correlated with race makes it inevitable that minority youth will enter the juvenile court system more frequently and receive more intrusive dispositions. Race and ethnic differentials in treatment are built into the juvenile system as a result of its responsiveness to substantive factors that are correlated with race.

Also contributing to racially disparate outcomes are class differences in access to resources. Parents' ability to comply with requirements for diversion is affected by access to phones and transportation, resulting in greater formal processing of youths of color. At least equally important, socioeconomic status is linked to the availability of insurance to defray the costs of private mental health and substance abuse treatment; to financial resources to purchase services such as alternative education, legal assistance, and tutoring; and to knowledge about private service options and providers, and how to access them. Economically disadvantaged adolescents are often processed through the system in order that they might become eligible for treatment at state expense, while those from more affluent families can be diverted to purchase services on their own. Many justice officials view such practices as not only defensible but enlightened (Frazier and Bishop 1995, 32).

Insofar as the problems to which court officials respond are rooted in underlying social and economic conditions (e.g., poverty, racial inequality)—and there is considerable evidence that they are (Sampson 1987; Sampson and Groves 1989)—the same structural factors responsible for race differentials in offending also contribute to race disparities in justice system responses. In other words, differential offending and disparities in processing influence one another and are mutually affected by underlying structural conditions and the cultural contexts in which they occur (see also National Research Council and Institute of Medicine 2001, 228–260; Bortner, Zatz, and Hawkins 2000).

While racial disparities may be due in part to real differences in youths' backgrounds and circumstances and to differential access to resources, research suggests that these disparities also result from racial stereotyping in the filtering and processing of information. Because justice officials rarely have either the information or assessment tools on which to base reliable and valid assessments of an offender's dangerousness or amenability to treatment, they develop a "perceptual shorthand" (Hawkins 1981, 280; Steffensmeier, Ulmer, and Kramer 1998, 767) based on stereotypes and attributions that are linked to offender characteristics, including race and ethnicity. Because the unique substantive considerations of the juvenile court—that is, those related to diagnosing youth problems and providing appropriate treatments—tend to be especially vague and amorphous (e.g., what is a "dysfunctional" family?),[28] the juvenile court would appear to be an especially receptive host to these more subtle forms of discrimination.[29]

When decisions to process juveniles formally as opposed to informally, or harshly as opposed to leniently, hinge on evaluations of the social circumstances in which juveniles live, officials are in a precarious position. They must somehow evaluate comparatively perceived differences in family structure, neighborhood reputation, demeanor of juveniles and their families—indeed the culture of various groups from which juvenile defendants come. Almost invariably, there is a reliance on common stereotypes of the nonwhite community, family, and interpersonal styles to support differentials in dispositions received by whites and nonwhites. (Frazier and Bishop 1995, 35–36)

In addition to assessing the role that external factors play in contributing to a youth's delinquency, juvenile court officials (like their criminal court counterparts) are asked to make judgments about youths' culpability and their propensity for future offending. The risk that youths of color will be perceived differently from whites based on factors other than offense and prior record is particularly great: stereotypes of minority offenders as especially threatening and dangerous are deeply imbedded in popular culture. Nowhere is the evidence of racial stereotyping more apparent than in Bridges and Steen's (1998) research on probation officers' causal attributions, risk predictions, and sentencing recommendations. Environmental influences were downplayed in explanations of minority youth crime, while more permanent traits of character and personality were highlighted. Descriptions of minority youths as more culpable, more dangerous, and less treatable than their white counterparts legitimated more severe sentencing recommendations. Research in other contexts (e.g., simulated juror decision making) has also linked minority status to attributions of culpability (e.g., Bodenhausen and Wyer 1995; Gordon 1990; Lipton 1983; Pfeifer and Ogloff 1991). These studies corroborate the notion that race differentials in offending and arrest (especially for violence and drugs) engender and reinforce stereotypes of minority offenders as both more culpable and more dangerous than their white counterparts. This interpretation also fits the results of cross-jurisdictional studies showing higher levels of differential social control in counties with high concentrations of impoverished minority populations and in counties with high violent crime rates. In sum, at both the individual and community levels, it seems that the unique social welfare concerns of the juvenile court (based on real and perceived family, school, and other problems) combine with traditional social control concerns (focused on real and perceived culpability and danger to society) to produce greater minority involvement in the juvenile justice system.

Directions for Future Research

To understand more fully the sources of and dynamics underlying racial and ethnic disparities in juvenile justice processing, several avenues of research are likely to be productive. First, macrolevel analyses of social structural and organizational contexts offer an alternative line of inquiry that may be fruitful in explaining race and ethnic differentials in outcomes. Because race is correlated with ecological (and organizational) context, the association between race and processing outcomes may be confounded with the association between community (or organizational) context and processing outcomes. Suppose, for example, that juvenile courts nowhere treated minority youths any differently from whites, but that urban courts treated all cases more formally than rural ones. Racial disparities in outcome would appear in data aggregated across urban and rural areas simply by virtue of the geographic distribution of minorities. Moreover, case-level studies of data aggregated across jurisdictions would show significant direct effects of race on processing outcomes after legal variables were controlled, leading to false inferences about the influence of race on individual decision making. It is likely, of course, that both individual-level and macrolevel factors affect justice system outcomes. Multilevel research will be required to capture and sort out the complex processes at work.

Second, research should continue to focus on multiple processing stages. Race effects are more pronounced at some stages than others (e.g., intake vs. adjudication) and the mechanisms that mediate the effect of race vary across decision points (e.g., demeanor is important at arrest, while family considerations play a more predominant role at the intake referral and detention stages). In order to understand *how* race affects decision outcomes, researchers must examine decision stages separately rather than operationalizing dependent variables in ways that combine outcomes across stages.[30] Further, because decisions made at early decision points (e.g., detention) may affect subsequent processing outcomes, and because small race differences at early stages tend to compound as youths move further into the system, multiple decision points must be examined in order to capture the dynamics of the system.

Third, there are several critical decisions in processing that have been studied insufficiently. Compared to research on court processing, we have little information on police decisions, especially those that occur up to and including arrest. These data are typically difficult to obtain and require labor-intensive observational research. Similarly, we know little about correctional placement (e.g., type of facility), correctional programming (e.g., sanctions and services received), and release decisions. Finally, although many researchers have alluded to the possibility of differential overcharging of minority suspects, there is almost no research on this topic. To be sure, measurement issues present formidable challenges, but they can be overcome.

Fourth, most of the research has been limited to comparisons of whites and African Americans. In light of their growing numbers, the continued categorization of Hispanics as "white" in data and research is likely increasingly to obscure the experience of minority populations in the juvenile justice system and to minimize differences in the treatment of white and minority populations (Bortner, Zatz, and Hawkins 2000). While we have some descriptive data on African American, Native American, and Asian groups, few multivariate analyses have included these populations. It is important that Asian and Hispanic subgroups (e.g., Cambodian, Vietnamese, Mexican, Puerto Rican) be examined separately, especially in view of the growing diversity of the

Hispanic and Asian populations and the increasing ghettoization of some subgroups. Many of these subgroups share problems associated with urban African American populations, including poverty, unemployment, female-headed households, inferior education systems, and lack of access to health care and social services, as well as prejudice and negative stereotyping (Healey 1995; Portillos 1998).

Fifth, most models that explore the effects of race on juvenile court processing are flawed by specification error, as they fail to include controls for nonlegal substantive factors that appear to be quite influential in court referral, detention, and judicial disposition decisions. Researchers have only begun to incorporate into models of decision making variables that tap various aspects of family structure and dynamics, school attendance and performance, peer relations (including gang involvement), youths' personal problems (substance abuse, victimization, mental health status, learning disabilities), and neighborhood characteristics. Inclusion of these variables is likely to lead to a much more comprehensive understanding of the mechanisms through which race and ethnicity influence responses of the juvenile justice system. It is only by understanding the mechanisms through which race influences decision outcomes that we can begin to effect change. It is not enough, for example, to inform judges that African Americans are being referred more often at intake for formal prosecution than whites who have been arrested for similar crimes. They need to know that differential assessments of parental supervision contribute to these disparate outcomes. Only then can we begin to engage in fruitful dialogue regarding how these assessments are made, whether they are appropriately sensitive to cultural diversity, and, more broadly and importantly, whether such assessments are even relevant to the decision at hand (e.g., does the court have the resources to provide appropriate supervision where parental supervision is lacking?).

With the exception of studies that test for interactions between race and offense type and those that test for both main and interactive effects of social class, further analysis of models that include only legal and sociodemographic variables is unlikely to be productive, as we have pretty well exhausted this line of inquiry. Studies that include controls for personal and social variables are likely to advance our understanding, but they will be labor intensive. Because automated data sets generally exclude these variables, researchers will have to gather data from intake and court records in order to test more inclusive models.

Sixth, understanding race and ethnic differentials in processing would benefit from a directed research focus on racial stereotyping. Qualitative studies may be especially useful in this regard, although these kinds of studies need to be more systematic than they have been in the past. Many qualitative studies present anecdotal accounts which, while frequently insightful, are of limited scientific utility. Bridges and Steen's (1998) work represents a landmark quantitative study that should be replicated in other jurisdictions. Their research could be improved upon by including controls for substantive variables such as family structure, school attendance, employment status, and gang membership. An important unanswered question is whether court officials differentially minimize or ignore problems that would support external attributions of causation when assessing the backgrounds and life circumstances of minority youths. There is an enormous need for further research aimed at identifying the logic of explanation and evaluation that produces differential judgments about similar white and minority offenders. Although testing for evidence and effects of subtle forms of discrimination is difficult, it needs to become a major research priority.

Qualitative research is also needed to gain insight into the dynamics of decision making at all stages in the juvenile justice system. Though time consuming, systematic observational studies, like those conducted by Emerson (1969), Cicourel (1968), and Mahoney (1987), need to be undertaken. It will be helpful to explore the dynamics of interactions among youths, their parents, and the various court personnel with whom they come into contact. Given the especially strong evidence of race effects on referral and detention outcomes, ethnographic studies focused on the intake process are likely to be especially valuable in providing insight into the qualities and circumstances to which juvenile justice officials attend; the processes and criteria involved in the formation of evaluative judgments about youths' culpability, risk, and amenability to treatment; and the link between these and court officials' choices among alternative processing options.

Finally, research on minority overrepresentation in the juvenile justice system must continue to move beyond narrow questions relating to the organization and operation of juvenile justice agencies. Researchers have begun to explore connections between macrolevel community factors, especially those related to social and economic inequality, and juvenile justice system responses. Structural inequality has also been linked to race differentials in offending, to racial stereotyping, and to the politics of law making and enforcement. A major challenge before us is to develop and test theoretical linkages among (1) race differentials in offending; (2) the formation and reproduction of racial stereotypes of minority offenders, their families, and the neighborhoods in which they live; (3) law making that differentially affects minority youths; and (4) racial disparities in justice processing. All of these seem to be inextricably intertwined and mutually reinforcing. If they are, and if all are rooted in macrostructural factors, then none is likely to be reduced short of broad-scale social and economic change.

Notes

I thank James Alan Fox, Alex Piquero, Simon Singer, Cassia Spohn, and an anonymous reviewer for their helpful comments on earlier drafts of this chapter.

1. I use the term "Hispanic" rather than "Latino" and "Latina" in this paper, as it reflects current usage by the U.S. Bureau of the Census and governmental agencies (Steffensmeier and Demuth 2001).

2. In their review of research published in the 1970s and 1980s, Pope and Feyerherm (1992) found that race or ethnicity influenced decision making in two-thirds of the studies examined. Since that time, many additional studies have been conducted that provide even further evidence of race effects.

3. I use the term "race" rather than "race/ethnicity" throughout the remainder of the chapter because most of the available data and research do not include information on ethnicity.

4. At the adjudicatory hearing in both the juvenile and adult systems, the issue is fact-finding/determination of guilt. Extralegal factors clearly have no place in this determination.

5. Researchers also often fail to report associations between race and its covariates, making it impossible for readers to identify or assess the strength of mediating variables (Leiber 1994, 1995; Dean, Hirschel, and Brame 1996).

6. Because police, court, and corrections data are generated independently, it is not possible to track a cohort of individuals from arrest through correctional placement. The best we can do to approximate a cohort is to present data from a single year. I report figures for 1999 because, at the time of this writing, it is the most recent year for which data from all three sources are available.

7. There is some slippage here, as juvenile courts receive a small number of referrals from non-law-enforcement agencies.

8. With the inclusion of Hispanics, who make up 15% of youths age 10–17, minority youths constitute approximately 34% of the total juvenile population.

9. The much higher incarceration rate for Hispanics than whites corroborates the notion that levels of disparity are artificially reduced in studies where Hispanics are counted as "white."

10. Due to space constraints, I do not include a discussion of the differential impact of juvenile transfer laws on minority offenders. Instead, I refer the reader to Bortner, Zatz, and Hawkins's (2000) recent and comprehensive review of the literature on this topic.

11. African American youths reported levels of illicit drug use during this period similar to the levels in other racial and ethnic groups (National Institutes of Health 1995).

12. Horowitz and Pottieger (1991) compared self-reported delinquency and self-reported arrests in a population of heavily drug-involved youths living in Miami. They found strong racial differences in both users' and dealers' risk of arrest, which they attributed to the higher visibility of drug activity in African American communities. Along similar lines, a study of cocaine arrests in Los Angeles revealed that drug transactions in African American neighborhoods tended to occur in the streets while drug transactions in white communities more often took place in less visible places (Klein, Maxson, and Cunningham 1988).

13. For example, because intake units are typically staffed by caseworkers who are frequently treatment oriented, diversion/referral decisions may be influenced to a considerable degree by family dysfunction and other personal and social circumstances. By contrast, when cases are referred to prosecutors, who tend to be more punitive in orientation, offense and prior record are likely to take precedence.

14. Observational studies consistently show that when a felony is suspected, police make arrests more than 75% of the time.

15. Although parents, schools, and social agencies also refer cases to juvenile court, police are responsible for the vast majority (about 85%) of delinquency referrals (Puzzanchera et al. 2000, 7).

16. A plausible interpretation is that serious offenses are so threatening that they clearly demand a severe response. When the offense is minor, the threat is more ambiguous and extralegal considerations come into play.

17. Klinger (1994) argues that researchers may have overestimated the effects of demeanor by failing to distinguish between illegal (e.g., resisting arrest) and legally permissible suspect behavior. However, reanalyses of the data from earlier observational studies tend to confirm the original findings (Lundman 1994; Worden and Shepard 1996; Worden, Shepard, and Mastrofski 1996).

18. Ideally, researchers must first determine what knowledge the arresting officer possessed at the time charges were recorded. Then they must measure the severity of the offenses committed (based on circumstances known to police at the time) and compare these offenses to the severity of the statutory offenses recorded. In light of both the ambiguity in statutory offense definitions and the heterogeneity of behaviors that arguably fall within these definitions, the research challenges are enormous.

19. Detention decisions may also be made by police, although they tend more often to be a function of juvenile court intake. The few extant studies of police decisions to detain fairly consistently show either direct race effects that withstand controls for offense and prior record (Chused 1973; Wordes, Bynum, and Corley 1994; Wordes and Bynum 1995) or indirect effects operating through youths' demeanor (Bell and Lang 1985; Kurtz, Giddings, and Sutphen 1993; but see, contra, Fagan, Slaughter, and Hartstone 1987).

20. The U.S. Supreme Court initiated the transformation by extending to juveniles traditional criminal due process guarantees, applying procedural protections and standards of proof that would insure more accurate fact-finding at the adjudicatory stage in the process. These had the unintended effect of shifting the focus of the court system from the offender to the offense (Feld 1993, 1999). Subsequently, and for a variety of reasons (including disenchantment with rehabilitation following on the heels of a series of negative appraisals of treatment programs, fear generated by dramatic increases in juvenile gun violence in the 1980s and early 1990s, and media attention to alarmist claims regarding a new breed of juvenile "superpredators"), a "get tough" movement was born that continues to the present day.

21. When race effects have been observed in the criminal courts, they have most often been restricted to sentencing. There is some evidence that African American and Hispanic males, especially if young and unemployed, are more likely to be incarcerated than whites (e.g., Chiricos and Crawford 1995; Spohn 2000; Spohn and Holleran 2000; Steffensmeier and Demuth 2001).

22. Recall, however, that offense-related variables are hardly race neutral.

23. These include capital or life felonies, serious crimes of violence, and major drug and other felony crimes when the defendant has at least two prior convictions for the same offense.

24. Some research suggests that the correction at adjudication is more likely to take place in urban counties (Dannefer and Schutt 1982), which generally do less screening and diversion of cases at intake than rural counties (see below).

25. Although qualitative studies have long reported anecdotal accounts to the same effect (e.g., Bridges, Crutchfield, and Simpson 1987; Cicourel 1968; Tonry 1995), this study represents the first systematic empirical analysis of the influence of race on justice officials' assessments of juvenile offenders.

26. For example, Kempf, Decker, and Bing (1990) found that family structure was more consequential in intake decisions in rural than in urban courts.

27. Level of urbanization had no effect on rates of detention or placement once underclass poverty and racial inequality were controlled. This finding may help to explain the considerable variation in racial disparities in processing among urban jurisdictions observed in other studies. At the same time, it should be noted that Sampson and Laub's study was limited to counties with populations of forty thousand or more, so it does not speak to the issue of urban versus rural differences.

28. As noted above, qualitative studies suggest that single-parent minority families are perceived as somehow "more broken" that single-parent white homes and that, irrespective of family structure, parental supervision in minority families is perceived as less adequate.

29. Further, because the juvenile justice system legitimates the use of substantive extralegal considerations in the service of individualized justice, race-biased decision making is all the more likely to go undetected while officials retain images of themselves as unbiased (Tomkins et al. 1996).

30. Many studies obscure decision making at discrete junctures in the way that they operationalize processing outcomes. One illustration is the creation of an ordinal scale that includes release/dismissal, diversion, probation, and confinement. While this kind of scale captures levels of intrusiveness in dispositions, it combines outcomes that occur at juvenile court intake, prosecutorial charging, and judicial disposition.

References

Aday, David P., Jr. 1986. "Court Structure, Defense Attorney Use, and Juvenile Court Decisions." *Sociological Quarterly* 27:107–119.

Akers, Ronald L. 1998. *Social Learning and Social Structure.* Boston: Northeastern University Press.

Anderson, Elijah. 1990. *Street Wise: Race, Class, and Change in an Urban Community.* Chicago: University of Chicago Press.

———. 1994. "The Code of the Streets." *Atlantic Monthly* 273:81–94.

Arnold, William R. 1971. "Race and Ethnicity Relative to Other Factors in Juvenile Court Dispositions." *American Journal of Sociology* 77:211–227.

Austin, James. 1995. "The Overrepresentation of Minority Youths in the California Juvenile Justice System: Perceptions and Realities." Pp. 153–178 in *Minorities in Juvenile*

Justice, ed. Kimberly Kempf Leonard, Carl E. Pope, and William H. Feyerherm. Thousand Oaks, CA: Sage.

Austin, James, Juanita Dimas, and David Steinhart. 1991. *The Overrepresentation of Minority Youth in California's Secure Facilities.* San Francisco: National Council on Crime and Delinquency.

Bailey, William C. 1981. "Preadjudicatory Detention in a Large Metropolitan Juvenile Court." *Law and Human Behavior* 5:19–43.

Bailey, William C., and Ruth Peterson. 1981. "Legal versus Extralegal Determinants of Juvenile Court Dispositions." *Juvenile and Family Court Journal* 32:41–45.

Barnes, Carole Wolff, and Randal S. Franz. 1989. "Questionably Adult: Determinants and Effects of the Juvenile Waiver Decision." *Justice Quarterly* 6:117–135.

Bazemore, Gordon. 1993. "Washington Juvenile Law Reform: Problems in Implementation and Impact on Disparity." *Criminal Justice Newsletter* 14:1–3.

Bell, Duran, Jr., and Kevin Lang. 1985. "The Intake Dispositions of Juvenile Offenders." *Journal of Research in Crime and Delinquency* 22:309–328.

Bishop, Donna M., and Charles E. Frazier. 1988. "The Influence of Race in Juvenile Justice Processing." *Journal of Research in Crime and Delinquency* 25:242–263.

———. 1991. "Transfer of Juveniles to Criminal Court: A Case Study and Analysis of Prosecutorial Waiver." *Notre Dame Journal of Law, Ethics, and Public Policy* 5:281–302.

———. 1992. "Gender Bias in Juvenile Justice Processing: Implications of the JJDP Act." *Journal of Criminal Law and Criminology* 82:1162–1186.

———. 1996. "Race Effects in Juvenile Justice Decision-Making: Findings of a Statewide Analysis." *Journal of Criminal Law and Criminology* 86:392–414.

Bittner, Egon. 1990. "Policing Juveniles: The Social Context of Common Practices." Pp. 322–347 in *Aspects of Police Work,* ed. Egon Bittner. Boston: Northeastern University Press.

Black, Donald J., and Albert J. Reiss. 1970. "Police Control of Juveniles." *American Sociological Review* 35:63–77.

Blalock, Hubert M. 1967. *Toward a Theory of Minority-Group Relations.* New York: Wiley.

Blumstein, Alfred. 1993. "Making Rationality Relevant." *Criminology* 31:1–16.

———. 1995. "Youth Violence, Guns, and the Illicit-Drug Industry." *Journal of Criminal Law and Criminology* 86:10–36.

Bodenhausen, Galen V., and Robert S. Wyer, Jr. 1995. "Effects of Stereotypes on Decision Making and Information-Processing Strategies." *Journal of Personality and Social Psychology* 48:267–282.

Bond-Maupin, Lisa J., Carol Chiago Lujan, and M. A. Bortner. 1995. "Jailing of American-Indian Adolescents: The Legacy of Cultural Domination and Imposed Law." *Crime, Law, and Social Change* 23:1–16.

Bortner, M. A. 1982. *Inside a Juvenile Court.* New York: New York University Press.

Bortner, M. A., Carol Burgess, Anne Schneider, and Andy Hall. 1993. *Equitable Treatment of Minority Youth: A Report on the Overrepresentation of Minority Youth in Arizona's Juvenile Justice System.* Phoenix, AZ: Governor's Office for Children.

Bortner, M. A., and Wornie L. Reed. 1985. "The Preeminence of Process: An Example of Refocused Justice Research." *Social Science Quarterly* 66:413–425.

Bortner, M. A., and Linda M. Williams. 1997. *Youth in Prison: We The People of Unit Four.* New York: Routledge.

Bortner, M. A., Marjorie S. Zatz, and Darnell Hawkins. 2000. "Race and Transfer: Empirical Research and Social Context." Pp. 277–320 in *The Changing Borders or Juvenile Justice: Transfer of Adolescents to the Criminal Court,* ed. Jeffrey Fagan and Franklin E. Zimring. Chicago: University of Chicago Press.

Boydston, John. 1975. *San Diego Field Interrogation: Final Report.* Washington, DC: Police Foundation.

Bridges, George S., Darlene Conley, George Beretta, and Rodney L. Engen. 1993. *Racial Disproportionality in the Juvenile Justice System: Final Report.* Olympia, WA: State of Washington, Department of Social and Health Services.

Bridges, George S., Darlene Conley, Rodney L. Engen, and Townsend Price-Spratlen. 1995. "Racial Disparities in the Confinement of Juveniles: Effects of Crime and Community Social Structure on Punishment." Pp. 128–152 in *Minorities in Juvenile Justice,* ed. Kimberly Kempf Leonard, Carl Pope, and William H. Feyerherm. Thousand Oaks, CA: Sage.

Bridges, George S., Robert D. Crutchfield, and Edith Simpson. 1987. "Crime, Social Structure and Criminal Punishment: White and Nonwhite Rates of Imprisonment." *Social Problems* 34:345–361.

Bridges, George S., and Sara Steen. 1998. "Racial Disparities in Official Assessments of Juvenile Offenders: Attributional Stereotypes as Mediating Mechanisms." *American Sociological Review* 63:554–570.

Browning, Sandra Lee, Francis T. Cullen, Liqun Cao, Renee Kopache, and Thomas J. Stevenson. 1994. "Race and Getting Hassled by the Police: A Research Note." *Police Studies* 17:1–11.

Cernkovich, Steven A., and Peggy C. Giordano. 1992. "School Bonding, Race, and Delinquency." *Criminology* 30:261–291.

Chambliss, William J. 1994. "Policing the Ghetto Underclass: The Politics of Law and Law Enforcement." *Social Problems* 41:177–194.

Chiricos, Theodore G., and Charles Crawford. 1995. "Race and Imprisonment: A Contextual Assessment of the Evidence." Pp. 281–309 in *Ethnicity, Race, and Crime,* ed. Darnell F. Hawkins. Albany: State University of New York Press.

Chused, R. H. 1973. "The Juvenile Court Process: A Study of Three New Jersey Counties." *Rutgers Law Review* 26:488–539.

Cicourel, Aaron V. 1968. *The Social Organization of Juvenile Justice.* New York: Wiley.

Clarke, Elizabeth E. 1996. "A Case For Reinventing Juvenile Transfer." *Juvenile and Family Court Journal* 47:3–22.

Clarke, Stephen H., and Gary G. Koch. 1980. "Juvenile Court: Therapy or Crime Control, and Do Lawyers Make a Difference?" *Law and Society Review* 14:263–308.

Cohen, Lawrence. 1975. *Delinquency Dispositions: An Empirical Analysis of Processing Decisions in Three Juvenile Courts.* Analytic Report 9. Washington, DC: U.S. Government Printing Office.

Cohen, Lawrence E., and James R. Kluegel. 1978. "Determinants of Juvenile Court Dispositions: Ascriptive and Achieved Factors in Two Metropolitan Courts." *American Sociological Review* 27:162–176.

—. 1979. "The Detention Decision: A Study of the Impact of Social Characteristics and Legal Factors in Two Metropolitan Courts." *Social Forces* 58:146–161.

Community Research Associates. 1997. *Disproportionate Confinement of Minority Juveniles in Secure Facilities: 1996 National Report.* Washington, DC: Office of Juvenile Justice and Delinquency Prevention.

Conley, Dale J. 1994. "Adding Color to a Black and White Picture: Using Qualitative Data to Explain Racial Disproportionality in the Juvenile Justice System." *Journal of Research in Crime and Delinquency* 31:135–148.

Corley, Charles J., Timothy S. Bynum, Angel Prewitt, and Pamela Schram. 1996. "The Impact of Race on Juvenile Court Processes: Quantitative Analyses with Qualitative Insights." *Caribbean Journal of Criminology and Social Psychology* 1:1–23.

Dannefer, Dale, and Russell K. Schutt. 1982. "Race and Juvenile Justice Processing in Court and Police Agencies." *American Journal of Sociology* 87:1113–1132.

Dean, Charles W., J. David Hirschel, and Robert Brame. 1996. "Minorities and Juvenile Case Dispositions." *Justice System Journal* 18:267–285.

DeJong, Christina, and Kenneth C. Jackson. 1998. "Putting Race into Context: Race, Juvenile Justice Processing, and Urbanization." *Justice Quarterly* 15:487–504.

Donziger, Steven R., ed. 1996. *The Real War on Crime: The Report of the National Criminal Justice Commission.* New York: HarperCollins.

Dryfoos, Joy G. 1990. *Adolescents at Risk: Prevalence and Prevention.* New York: Oxford University Press.

Dunn, Christopher, Robert Perry, Stephen Cernkovich, and Jerry Wicks. 1993. *Race and Juvenile Justice in Ohio: The Overrepresentation and Disproportionate Confinement of African-American and Hispanic Youth.* Columbus, OH: Governor's Office of Criminal Justice.

Elliott, Delbert S., and Scott Menard. 1996. "Delinquent Friends and Delinquent Behavior: Temporal and Developmental Patterns." Pp. 28–67 in *Delinquency and Crime: Current Theories,* ed. J. David Hawkins. Cambridge: Cambridge University Press.

Emerson, Robert M. 1969. *Judging Delinquents: Context and Process in the Juvenile Court.* Chicago: Aldine.

Empey, Lamar T., and Steven G. Lubeck. 1971. *Explaining Delinquency.* Lexington, MA: D. C. Heath.

Engel, Robin Shepherd, James J. Sobol, and Robert E. Worden. 2000. "Further Exploration of the Demeanor Hypothesis: The Interaction Effects of Suspects' Characteristics and Demeanor on Police Behavior." *Justice Quarterly* 17:235–258.

Esbensen, Finn-Aage, and D. Wayne Osgood. 1999. "Gang Resistance Education and Training (GREAT): Results From the National Evaluation." *Journal of Research in Crime and Delinquency* 36:194–225.

Esbensen Finn-Aage, and L. Thomas Winfree. 1998. "Race and Gender Differences between Gang and Nongang Youths: Results from a Multisite Survey." *Justice Quarterly* 15:505–526.

Fagan, Jeffrey, Ellen Slaughter, and Eliot Hartstone. 1987. "Blind Justice? The Impact of Race on the Juvenile Justice Process." *Crime and Delinquency* 33:224–258.

Farrell, Ronald, and Victoria Swigert. 1978. "Prior Offense Record as a Self-Fulfilling Prophecy." *Law and Society Review* 12:437–453.

Feeley, Malcolm M., and Jonathan Simon. 1992. "The New Penology: Notes on the Emerging Strategy of Corrections and Its Implications." *Criminology* 30:449–474.

Feld, Barry C. 1987. "The Juvenile Court Meets the Principle of Offense: Legislative Changes in Juvenile Waiver Statutes." *Journal of Criminal Law and Criminology* 78:471–533.

————. 1988. "The Juvenile Court Meets the Principle of Offense: Punishment, Treatment, and the Difference It Makes." *Boston University Law Review* 68:821–915.

————. 1989. "The Right to Counsel in Juvenile Court: An Empirical Study of When Lawyers Appear and the Difference They Make." *Journal of Criminal Law and Criminology* 79:1185–1346.

————. 1990. "The Punitive Juvenile Court and the Quality of Procedural Justice: Distinctions between Rhetoric and Reality." *Crime and Delinquency* 36:443–466.

————. 1991. "Justice by Geography: Urban, Suburban, and Rural Variations in Juvenile Justice Administration." *Journal of Criminal Law and Criminology* 82:156–210.

————. 1993. "Criminalizing the American Juvenile Court." Pp. 197–280 in *Crime and Justice: A Review of Research,* vol. 17, ed. M. Tonry. Chicago: University of Chicago Press.

————. 1995. "The Social Context of Juvenile Justice Administration: Racial Disparities in an Urban Juvenile Court." Pp. 66- 97 in *Minorities in Juvenile Justice,* ed. Kimberly Kempf Leonard, Carl E. Pope, and William H. Feyerherm. Thousand Oaks, CA: Sage

————. 1999. *Bad Kids: Race and the Transformation of the Juvenile Court.* New York: Oxford University Press.

Fenwick, C. R. 1982. "Juvenile Court Intake Decision-Making: The Importance of Family Affiliation." *Journal of Criminal Justice* 10:443–53.

Ferdinand, Theodore, and Elmer Luchterhand. 1970. "Inner-City Youth, the Police, the Juvenile Court, and Justice." *Social Problems* 17:510–527.

Fisher, G. A., and S. M. Doyle-Martin. 1981. "The Effects of Ethnic Prejudice on Police Referrals to the Juvenile Court." *California Sociologist* 4:189–205.

Frazier, Charles E., and Donna M. Bishop. 1985. "The Pretrial Detention of Juveniles and Its Impact on Case Dispositions." *Journal of Criminal Law and Criminology* 76:1132–1152.

————. 1995. "Reflections on Race Effects in Juvenile Justice." Pp. 16–46 in *Minorities in Juvenile Justice,* ed. Kimberly Kempf Leonard, Carl E. Pope, and William H. Feyerherm. Thousand Oaks, CA: Sage.

Frazier, Charles E., Donna M. Bishop, and John C. Henretta. 1992. "The Social Context of Race Differentials in Juvenile Justice Dispositions." *Sociological Quarterly* 33:447–458.

Frazier, Charles E., and John K. Cochran. 1986. "Detention of Juveniles: Its Effects on Subsequent Juvenile Court Processing Decisions." *Youth and Society* 17:286–305.

Friedman, Warren, and Marsha Hott. 1995. *Young People and the Police: Respect, Fear and the Future of Community Policing.* Chicago: Chicago Alliance for Public Safety.

Goldman, Nathan. 1963. *The Differential Selection of Juvenile Offenders for Court Appearance.* Hackensack, NJ: National Council on Crime and Delinquency.

Gordon, Randall A. 1990. "Attributions for Blue-Collar and White-Collar Crime: The Effects of Subject and Defendant Race on Simulated Juror Decisions." *Journal of Applied Social Psychology* 20:971–983.

Gottfredson, Michael, and Travis Hirschi. 1990. *A General Theory of Crime.* Palo Alto, CA: Stanford University Press.

Griffiths, Curt T., and L. Thomas Winfree, Jr. 1982. "Attitudes toward the Police: A Comparison of Canadian and American Adolescents." *International Journal of Comparative and Applied Criminal Justice* 6:128–141.

Hasenfeld, Yeheskel, and Paul P. Cheung. 1985. "The Juvenile Court as a People-Processing Organization: A Political Economy Perspective." *American Journal of Sociology* 90:801–824.

Hawes, Joseph. 1971. *Children in Urban Society: Juvenile Delinquency in Nineteenth-Century America*. New York: Oxford University Press.

Hawkins, Darnell. 1981. "Causal Attribution and Punishment for Crime." *Deviant Behavior* 1:207–230.

Healey, Joseph. 1995. *Race, Ethnicity, Gender, and Class*. Thousand Oaks, CA: Pine Forge Press.

Henretta, John C., Charles E. Frazier, and Donna M. Bishop. 1986. "The Effect of Prior Case Outcomes on Juvenile Justice Decision-Making." *Social Forces* 65:554–562.

Hirschi, Travis. 1969. *Causes of Delinquency*. Berkeley: University of California Press.

Hohenstein, William F. 1969. "Factors Influencing the Police Disposition of Juvenile Offenders." Pp.138–149 in *Delinquency: Selected Studies*, ed. Thorsten Sellin and Marvin E. Wolfgang. New York: Wiley.

Horowitz, Ruth, and Anne E. Pottieger. 1991. "Gender Bias in Juvenile Justice Handling of Seriously Crime-Involved Youths." *Journal of Research in Crime and Delinquency* 28:75–100.

Horwitz, Alan, and Michael Wasserman. 1980a. "Formal Rationality, Substantive Justice, and Discrimination: A Study of a Juvenile Court." *Law and Human Behavior* 4:103–116.

———. 1980b. "Some Misleading Conceptions in Sentencing Research." *Criminology* 18:411–424.

Huizinga, David, and Delbert S. Elliott. 1987. "Juvenile Offenders: Prevalence, Offender Incidence, and Arrest Rates by Race." *Crime and Delinquency* 33:206–223.

Irwin, John. 1985. *The Jail: Managing the Underclass in American Society*. Berkeley: University of California Press.

Jackson, Pamela I. 1992. "Minority Group Threat, Social Context, and Policing." Pp. 89–102 in *Social Threat and Social Control*, ed. Allen E. Liska. Albany: State University of New York Press.

Jarjoura, G. Roger. 1993. "Does Dropping Out of School Enhance Delinquent Involvement? Results from a Large-Scale National Probability Sample." *Criminology* 31:149–171.

Jeffords, Charles, Jan Lindsey, and Scott McNitt. 1993. *Overrepresentation of Minorities in the Juvenile Justice System*. Austin: Department of Research and Planning, Texas Youth Commission.

Johnson, James B., and Phillip E. Secret. 1990. "Race and Juvenile Court Decision Making Revisited." *Criminal Justice Policy Research* 4:159–187.

Kaplan, Stuart L., and Joan Busner. 1992. "A Note on Racial Bias in the Admission of Children and Adolescents to State Mental Health Facilities versus Correctional Facilities in New York. *American Journal of Psychiatry* 149:768–772.

Kempf, Kimberly L., Scott H. Decker, and Robert L. Bing. 1990. *An Analysis of Apparent Disparities in the Handling of Black Youth within Missouri's Juvenile Justice Systems*. St. Louis: Department of Administration of Justice, University of Missouri—St. Louis.

Kennedy, Randall. 1997. *Race, Crime, and the Law*. New York: Pantheon Books.

Klein, Malcolm W., Cheryl L. Maxson, and Lea C. Cunningham. 1988. "Gang Involvement in Cocaine 'Rock' Trafficking." Unpublished report. Los Angeles: Social Science Research Institute, University of Southern California.

Klinger, David. 1994. "Demeanor or Crime? An Inquiry Into Why 'Hostile' Citizens Are More Likely to Be Arrested." *Criminology* 32:475–493.

Kowalski, Gregory S., and John P. Rickicki. 1982. "Determinants of Juvenile Postadjudication Dispositions." *Journal of Research in Crime and Delinquency* 19:66–83.

Krisberg, Barry, and James F. Austin. 1993. *Reinventing Juvenile Justice.* Newbury Park, CA: Sage.

Kurtz, P. David, Martha M. Giddings, and Richard Sutphen. 1993. "A Prospective Investigation of Racial Disparity in the Juvenile Justice System." *Juvenile and Family Court Journal* 44:43–59.

Lauritsen, Janet L. 2005. "Racial and Ethnic Differences in Juvenile Offending." In *Our Children, Their Children: Confronting Racial and Ethnic Differences in American Juvenile Justice,* ed. Darnell F. Hawkins and Kimberly Kempf-Leonard. Chicago: University of Chicago Press.

Leiber, Michael J. 1994. "A Comparison of Juvenile Court Outcomes for Native Americans, African Americans, and Whites." *Justice Quarterly* 11:257–279.

———. 1995. "Toward Clarification of the Concept of 'Minority' Status and Decision-Making in Juvenile Court Proceedings." *Journal of Crime and Justice* 18:79–108.

Leiber, Michael J., and Katherine M. Jamieson. 1995. "Race and Decisionmaking within Juvenile Justice: The Importance of Context." *Journal of Quantitative Criminology* 11:363–388.

Leiber, Michael J., and Jayne M. Stairs. 1999. "Race, Contexts, and the Use of Intake Diversion." *Journal of Research in Crime and Delinquency* 36:56–86.

Leonard, Kimberly Kempf, and Henry Sontheimer. 1995. "The Role of Race in Juvenile Justice in Pennsylvania." Pp. 98–127 in *Minorities in Juvenile Justice,* ed. Kimberly Kempf Leonard, Carl E. Pope, and William H. Feyerherm. Thousand Oaks, CA: Sage.

Lewis, D. O., S. S. Shanok, R. J. Cohen, M. Kligfeld, and G. Frisone. 1980. "Race Bias in the Diagnosis and Disposition of Violent Adolescents." *American Journal of Psychiatry* 137:1211–1216.

Lipsky, Michael. 1980. *Street-Level Bureaucracy.* New York: Russell Sage.

Lipton, Jack P. 1983. "Racism in the Jury Box: The Hispanic Defendant." *Hispanic Journal of Behavioral Science* 5:275–288.

Liska, Allen E., and Mark D. Reed. 1985. "Ties to Conventional Institutions and Delinquency: Estimating Reciprocal Effects." *American Sociological Review* 50:547–560.

Liska, Allen E., and Mark Tausig. 1979. "Theoretical Interpretations of Social Class and Racial Differentials in Legal Decision-Making for Juveniles." *Sociological Quarterly* 20:197–207.

Lockhart, Lettie L., P. David Kurtz, Richard D. Sutphen, and K. Gauger. 1991. *Georgia's Juvenile Justice System: A Retrospective Investigation of Racial Disparity.* Athens: University of Georgia Press.

Loeber, Rolf, and Magda Stouthamer-Loeber. 1986. "Family Factors as Correlates and Predictors of Juvenile Conduct Problems and Delinquency." Pp. 29–149 in *Crime and Justice: An Annual Review of Research,* vol. 7, ed. Michael Tonry and Norval Morris. Chicago: University of Chicago Press.

Lundman, Richard J. 1978. "Shoplifting and Police Referral: A Reexamination." *Journal of Criminal Law and Criminology* 69:395–401.

————. 1994. "Demeanor or Crime? The Midwest City Police-Citizen Encounters Study." *Criminology* 32:631–656.

Lundman, Richard J., R. E. Sykes, and John P. Clark. 1978. "Police Control of Juveniles: A Replication." *Journal of Research in Crime and Delinquency* 15:74–91.

MacDonald, John M., and Meda Chesney-Lind. 2001. "Gender Bias and Juvenile Justice Revisited: A Multiyear Analysis." *Crime and Delinquency* 47:173–195.

Maguin, Eugene, and Rolf Loeber. 1996. "Academic Performance and Delinquency." Pp. 145–264 in *Crime and Justice: A Review of Research,* vol. 20, ed. Michael Tonry. Chicago: University of Chicago Press.

Mahoney, Anne Rankin. 1987. *Juvenile Justice in Context.* Boston: Northeastern University Press.

Marshall, Ineke H., and Charles W. Thomas. 1983. "Discretionary Decision-Making and the Juvenile Court." *Juvenile and Family Court Journal* 34:47–60.

Massachusetts Attorney General. 1990. *Report of the Attorney General's Civil Rights Division on Boston Police Department Practices.* Boston: Office of the Attorney General.

Matsueda, Ross L., and Kathleen Anderson. 1998. "The Dynamics of Delinquent Peers and Delinquent Behavior." *Criminology* 36:269–308.

Matza, David. 1964. *Delinquency and Drift.* New York: Wiley.

McCarter, Susan. 1997. *Understanding the Overrepresentation of Minorities in Virginia's Juvenile Justice System.* Ann Arbor, MI: UMI Dissertation Services.

McCarthy, Belinda R., and Brent L. Smith. 1986. "The Conceptualization of Discrimination in the Juvenile Justice Process: The Impact of Administrative Factors and Screening Decisions on Juvenile Court Dispositions." *Criminology* 24:41–64.

McCord, Joan. 1991. "Family Relationships, Juvenile Delinquency, and Adult Criminality." *Criminology* 29:397–417.

McEachern, A. W., and Riva Bauzer. 1967. "Factors Related to Disposition in Juvenile Police Contacts." Pp. 148–160 in *Juvenile Gangs in Context,* ed. Malcolm Klein and Barbara Myerhoff. Englewood Cliffs, NJ: Prentice-Hall.

Miethe, Terance D., and Charles A. Moore. 1986. "Racial Differences in Criminal Processing: The Consequences of Model Selection on Conclusions about Differential Treatment." *Sociological Quarterly* 27:217–238.

Miller, Jerome. 1996. *Search and Destroy.* New York: Cambridge University Press.

National Center for Juvenile Justice. 2003. "Juvenile Arrest Rates by Offense, Sex, and Race." http://ojjdp.ncjrs.org.ojstatbb/excel/JAR_053103.xls.

National Institutes of Health. 1995. *Drug Use among Racial/Ethnic Minorities.* Report no. 95-3888. Washington, DC: National Institutes of Health.

National Research Council and Institute of Medicine. 2001. *Juvenile Crime, Juvenile Justice.* Panel on Juvenile Crime: Prevention, Treatment, and Control. Edited by Joan McCord, Cathy Spatz Widom, and Nancy Crowell, Committee on Law and Justice and Board on Children, Youth, and Families. Washington, DC: National Academy Press.

National Youth Gang Center. 1999. *1996 National Youth Gang Survey.* Washington, DC: Office of Juvenile Justice and Delinquency Prevention.

Nobiling, Tracy, Cassia Spohn, and Miriam DeLone. 1998. "A Tale of Two Counties: Unemployment and Sentence Severity." *Justice Quarterly* 15:401–427.

Orlando, Frank. 1999. *Controlling the Front Gates: Effective Admissions Policies and Practices.* Vol. 3 of *Pathways to Juvenile Detention Reform.* Baltimore: Annie E. Casey Foundation.

Patterson, Gerald R. 1982. *Coercive Family Process*. Eugene, OR: Castalia Press.

Patterson, Gerald R., John B. Reid, and Thomas J. Dishion. 1992. *Antisocial Boys*. Eugene, OR: Castalia Press.

Pawlak, Edward J. 1977. "Differential Selection of Juveniles for Detention." *Journal of Research in Crime and Delinquency* 14:152–165.

Pfeifer, Jeffrey E., and James R. Ogloff. 1991. "Ambiguity and Guilt Determinations: A Modern Racism Perspective." *Journal of Applied Social Psychology* 21:1713–1725.

Phillips C. D., and Simon Dinitz. 1982. "Labeling and Juvenile Court Dispositions: Official Responses to a Cohort of Violent Juveniles." *Sociological Quarterly* 23:267–278.

Piliavin, Irving, and Scott Briar. 1964. "Police Encounters with Juveniles." *American Journal of Sociology* 69:206–214.

Platt, Anthony M. 1977. *The Child Savers*. Chicago: University of Chicago Press.

Podkopacz, Marcy Rasmussen, and Barry C. Feld. 1996. "The End of the Line: An Empirical Study of Judicial Waiver." *Journal of Criminal Law and Criminology* 86:449–492.

Poole, Eric D., and Robert M. Regoli. 1980. "An Analysis of the Determinants of Juvenile Court Dispositions." *Juvenile and Family Court Journal* 31:21–32.

Pope, Carl E., and William H. Feyerherm. 1990a. "Minority Status and Juvenile Justice Processing: An Assessment of the Research Literature." Pt. 1. *Criminal Justice Abstracts* 22:327–335.

———. 1990b. "Minority Status and Juvenile Justice Processing: An Assessment of the Research Literature." Pt. 2. *Criminal Justice Abstracts* 22:527–542.

———. 1992. *Minorities and the Juvenile Justice System*. Washington, DC: Office of Juvenile Justice and Delinquency Prevention.

Portillos, Edwardo L. 1998. "Latinos, Gangs, and Drugs." Pp. 156–165 in *Images of Color, Images of Crime*, ed. Coramae Richey Mann and Marjorie S. Zatz. Los Angeles: Roxbury.

Puzzanchera, Charles, Anne L. Stahl, Terrence A. Finnegan, Howard N. Snyder, Rowen S. Poole, and Nancy Tierney. 2000. *Juvenile Court Statistics, 1997*. Washington, DC: Office of Juvenile Justice and Delinquency Prevention.

Puzzanchera, Charles, Wei Kang, Rowen S. Poole, and Y. Wan. 2002. *Easy Access to Juvenile Populations*. http://ojjdp.ncjrs.org/ojstatbb/ezapop.

Quinney, Richard. 1977. *Class, State and Crime: On the Theory and Practice of Criminal Justice*. New York: David McKay.

Reed, William. 1984. *Racial Differentials in Juvenile Court Decisions*. Baltimore: Institute of Urban Research.

Robison, Sophia. 1936. *Can Delinquency Be Measured?* New York: Columbia University Press.

Rubinstein, Jonathan. 1973. *City Police*. New York: Farrar, Straus and Giroux.

Sampson, Robert J. 1986. "Effects of Socioeconomic Context on Official Reaction to Juvenile Delinquency." *America Sociological Review* 51:876–885.

———. 1987. "Urban Black Violence: The Effect of Male Joblessness and Family Disruption." *American Sociological Review* 51:876–885.

Sampson, Robert J., and W. Byron Groves. 1989. "Community Structure and Crime: Testing Social Disorganization Theory." *American Journal of Sociology* 94:772–802.

Sampson, Robert J., and John H. Laub. 1993a. "Structural Variations in Juvenile Court Processing: Inequality, the Underclass, and Social Control." *Law and Society Review* 27:285–311.

———. 1993b. *Crime in the Making.* Cambridge, MA: Harvard University Press.

Sampson, Robert J., and Janet L. Lauritsen. 1997. "Racial and Ethnic Disparities in Crime and Criminal Justice in the United States." Pp. 311–374 in *Ethnicity, Crime, and Integration: Comparative and Cross-National Perspectives,* ed. Michael Tonry, Crime and Justice: A Review of Research, vol. 21. Chicago: University of Chicago Press.

Sanborn, Joseph B., Jr. 1996. "Factors Perceived to Affect Delinquent Dispositions in Juvenile Court: Putting the Sentencing Decision into Context." *Crime and Delinquency* 42:99–113.

Sanborn, Joseph B., Jr., and Anthony W. Salerno. 2004. *Juvenile Justice System.* Los Angeles: Roxbury.

Schissel, B. 1993. "A Sociolegal Analysis of Canadian Youth Justice: The Impact of Offender's Race on Judicial Decisions." *Journal of Criminal Justice* 21:522–552.

Schlossman, Steven. 1977. *Love and the American Delinquent: The Theory and Practice of "Progressive" Juvenile Justice.* Chicago: University of Chicago Press.

Sealock, Miriam D., and Sally S. Simpson. 1998. "Unraveling Bias in Arrest Decisions: The Role of Juvenile Offender Type-Scripts." *Justice Quarterly* 15:427–457.

Secret, Philip E., and James B. Johnson. 1997. "The Effect of Race on Juvenile Justice Decision Making in Nebraska: Detention, Adjudication, and Disposition, 1988–1993." *Justice Quarterly* 14:445–478.

Shelden, Randall G., and J. A. Horvath. 1987. "Intake Processing in a Juvenile Court: A Comparison of Legal and Nonlegal Variables." *Juvenile and Family Court Journal* 38:13–19.

Sickmund, Melissa. 2004. *Juveniles in Corrections.* Washington, DC: Office of Juvenile Justice and Delinquency Prevention.

Sickmund, Melissa, T. J. Sladky, and Wei Kang. 2004. "Census of Juveniles in Residential Placement Databook." http://www.ojjdp.ncjrs.org/ojstatbb/cjrp.

Skolnick, Jerome. 1966. *Justice without Trial: Law Enforcement in a Democratic Society.* New York: Wiley.

Smith, Douglas A. 1986. "The Neighborhood Context of Police Behavior." Pp. 313–342 in *Communities and Crime,* ed. Albert J. Reiss and Michael Tonry, Crime and Justice: A Review of Research, vol. 8. Chicago: University of Chicago Press.

Smith, Douglas A., and Raymond Paternoster. 1990. "Formal Processing and Future Delinquency: Deviance Amplification as Selection Artifact." *Law and Society Review* 24:1109–1131.

Smith, Douglas A., and Christy A. Visher. 1981. "Street-Level Justice: Situational Determinants of Police Arrest Decisions." *Social Problems* 29:167–177.

Smith, Douglas A., Christy A. Visher, and Laura A. Davidson. 1984. "Equity and Discretionary Justice: The Influence of Race on Police Arrest Decisions." *Journal of Criminal Law and Criminology* 75:234–249.

Snyder, Howard J., and Melissa Sickmund. 1999. *Juvenile Offenders and Victims: 1999 National Report.* Washington, DC: Office of Juvenile Justice and Delinquency Prevention.

Spohn, Cassia. 2000. *Thirty Years of Sentencing Reform: The Quest for a Racially-Neutral Sentencing Process.* Vol. 3 of *NIJ Criminal Justice 2000.* Washington, DC: United States Department of Justice.

Spohn, Cassia, and David Holleran. 2000. "The Imprisonment Penalty Paid by Young, Unemployed Black and Hispanic Male Offenders." *Criminology* 38:281–306.

Stahl, Anne L., Terrence A. Finnegan, and Wei Kang. 2002. *Easy Access to Juvenile Court Statistics: 1985–2000.* http://ojjdp.ncjrs.org/ojstatbb/ezajcs.

Stapleton, W. Vaughn, David P. Aday, Jr., and Jeanne A. Ito. 1982. "An Empirical Typology of American Metropolitan Juvenile Courts." *American Sociological Review* 88: 549–561.

Steffensmeier, Darrell, and Stephen Demuth. 2001. "Ethnicity and Judges' Sentencing Decisions: Hispanic-Black-White Comparisons." *Criminology* 39:145–178.

Steffensmeier, Darrell, Jeffrey Ulmer, and John Kramer. 1998. "The Interaction of Race, Gender, and Age in Criminal Sentencing: The Punishment Cost of Being Young, Black, and Male. *Criminology* 36:763–797.

Sutphen, Richard, P., David Kurtz, and Martha Giddings. 1993. "The Influence of Juveniles' Race on Police Decision-Making: An Exploratory Study." *Juvenile and Family Court Journal* 44:69–78.

Terrill, William. 2001. *Police Coercion: Application of the Force Continuum.* New York: LFB Publishing.

Terrill, William, and Michael D. Reisig. 2003. "Neighborhood Context and Police Use of Force." *Journal of Research in Crime and Delinquency* 40:291–321.

Terry, Robert M. 1967a. "The Screening of Juvenile Offenders." *Journal of Criminology, Criminal Law, and Police Science* 58:173–181.

———. 1967b. "Discrimination in the Handling of Juvenile Offenders by Social Control Agencies." *Journal of Research in Crime and Delinquency* 4:218–230.

Thomas, Charles W., and Robin J. Cage. 1977. "The Effects of Social Characteristics on Juvenile Court Dispositions." *Sociological Quarterly* 18:237–252.

Thomas, Charles W., and Christopher M. Sieverdes. 1975. "Juvenile Court Intake: An Analysis of Discretionary Decision-Making." *Criminology* 12:413–432.

Thomas, W. John, Dorothy E. Stubbe, and Geraldine Pearson. 1999. "Race, Juvenile Justice, and Mental Health: New Dimensions in Measuring Pervasive Bias." *Journal of Criminal Law and Criminology* 89:615–670.

Thornberry, Terence P. 1973. "Race, Socioeconomic Status and Sentencing in the Juvenile Justice System." *Journal of Criminology, Criminal Law, and Police Science* 64:90–98.

———. 1979. "Sentencing Disparities in the Juvenile Justice System." *Journal of Criminal Law and Criminology* 70:164–171.

Thornberry, Terence P., and R. L. Christenson. 1984. "Juvenile Justice Decision-Making as a Longitudinal Process." *Social Forces* 63:433–444.

Tittle, Charles R., and Debra A. Curran. 1988. "Contingencies for Dispositional Disparities in Juvenile Justice." *Social Forces* 67:23–58.

Tomkins, Alan J., Andrew J. Slain, Marianne N. Hallinan, and Cynthia E. Willis. 1996. "Subtle Discrimination in Juvenile Justice Decisionmaking: Social Scientific Perspectives and Explanations." *Creighton Law Review* 29:1619–1651.

Tonry, Michael. 1994. "Racial Politics, Racial Disparities, and the War on Crime." *Crime and Delinquency* 40:475–494.

———. 1995. *Malign Neglect: Race, Crime, and Punishment in America.* New York: Oxford.

Torbet, Patricia, and Linda Szymanski. 1998. *State Legislative Responses to Violent Juvenile Crime: 1996–1997 Update.* Washington, DC: Office of Juvenile Justice and Delinquency Prevention.

Walker, Samuel. 1999. *The Police in America.* Boston: McGraw-Hill.

Walker, Samuel, Cassia Spohn, and Miriam DeLone. 2000. *The Color of Justice: Race, Ethnicity, and Crime in America.* 2nd ed. Belmont, CA: Wadsworth.

Warr, Mark. 1996. "Organization and Instigation in Delinquent Groups." *Criminology* 34:11–37.

Warr, Mark, and Mark Stafford. 1991. "The Influence of Delinquent Peers: What They Think or What They Do?" *Criminology* 36:183–216.

Werthman, Carl, and Irving Piliavin. 1967. "Gang Members and the Police." In *The Police: Six Sociological Essays,* ed. David Bordua. New York: Wiley.

Williams, Jay R., and Martin Gold. 1972. "From Delinquent Behavior to Official Delinquency." *Social Problems* 20:209–229.

Wilson, James Q. 1968. "The Police and the Delinquent in Two Cities." Pp. 9–39 in *Controlling Delinquents,* ed. Stanton Wheeler. New York: Wiley.

Winfree, L. Thomas, Jr., and Curt T. Griffiths. 1977. "Adolescents' Attitudes toward the Police: A Survey of High School Students." Pp. 79–99 in *Juvenile Delinquency: Little Brother Grows Up,* ed. Theodore N. Ferdinand. Beverly Hills, CA: Sage.

Worden, Robert E., and Stephanie M. Myers. 1999. *"Police Encounters with Juvenile Subjects."* Unpublished paper commissioned by the Panel of Juvenile Crime: Prevention, Treatment, and Control, National Academy of Sciences.

Worden, Robert E., and Robin L. Shepard. 1996. "Demeanor, Crime, and Police Behavior: A Reexamination of the Police Services Study Data." *Criminology* 34:61–82.

Worden, Robert E., Robin L. Shepard, and Steven D. Mastrofski. 1996. "On the Meaning and Measurement of Suspects' Demeanor toward the Police: A Comment on 'Demeanor and Arrest.'" *Journal of Research in Crime and Delinquency* 34:83–105.

Wordes, Madeline. 1995. "Dimensions of Race Bias in the Juvenile Court: The Influence of Legal, Demographic, Social, and Community Characteristics on Detention and Disposition Decisions." Ph.D. diss., Michigan State University. Ann Arbor, MI: Dissertation Abstracts.

Wordes, Madeline, and Timothy S. Bynum. 1995. "Policing Juveniles: Is There Bias against Youths of Color?" Pp. 47-65 in *Minorities in Juvenile Justice,* ed. Kimberly Kempf Leonard, Carl E. Pope, and William H. Feyerherm. Thousand Oaks, CA: Sage.

Wordes, Madeline, Timothy S. Bynum, and Charles J. Corley. 1994. "Locking Up Youth: The Impact of Race on Detention Decisions." *Journal of Research in Crime and Delinquency* 31:149–165.

Wu, Bohsiu. 1997. "The Effect of Race on Juvenile Justice Processing." *Juvenile and Family Court Judges Journal* 48:43–51.

Wu, Bohsiu, Stephen Cernkovich, and Christopher S. Dunn. 1997. "Assessing the Effects of Race and Class on Juvenile Justice Processing in Ohio." *Journal of Criminal Justice* 25:265–277.

Wu, Bohsiu, and Angel Ilarraza Fuentes. 1998. "Juvenile Justice Processing: The Entangled Effects of Race and Urban Poverty." *Juvenile and Family Court Journal* 49:41–53.

Zatz, Marjorie. 1984. "Race, Ethnicity, and Determinate Sentencing: A New Dimension to an Old Controversy." *Criminology* 20:147–171.

Zimring, Franklin E. 1981. "Kids, Groups, and Crime: Some Implications of a Well-Known Secret." *Journal of Criminal Law and Criminology* 72:867–902.

3

Racial and Ethnic Differences in Juvenile Offending

Janet L. Lauritsen

Introduction

THE PREVIOUS chapter (Bishop 2005) makes it clear that minority youth are overrepresented in the juvenile justice system, and small differences in the handling of cases at early stages in the juvenile justice process can produce large differences in outcomes at the later stages. The fact that black and Latino youth constitute approximately 16% and 15% of the children under 18 years of age yet represent about 40% and 18% of youth held in residential placement facilities raises many questions about bias in the juvenile justice system (Snyder and Sickmund 1999). Not surprisingly, these discrepancies also prompt questions about the extent to which racial and ethnic groups vary in offense involvement and how such information is best obtained.

Social scientists use three major types of data to study group differences in offense involvement: arrest data generated by police departments, victim reports of offender characteristics from large random surveys, and self-reported offending data obtained through surveys of youth. Each source of information has strengths and weaknesses that will be discussed in detail below. Careful interpretation of all three sources of information makes it possible to assess whether the disproportionately higher rates of minorities in the juvenile residential facilities are a likely result of bias in the juvenile court system, a result of bias in law enforcement, or a function of differential rates of criminal activity.

Before describing what is known about racial and ethnic differences in juvenile offending, it is important to emphasize the complexity of this issue. Variations in the reliability and validity of data mean that more confidence is placed in knowledge about certain types of offending (e.g., homicide) than other types of crime (e.g., property and drug crimes). Limitations in the measurement and collection of data on race and ethnicity mean that many of our analyses lack much needed detail and fail to answer important questions about differences within and between minority and majority groups. In addition, conclusions about racial and ethnic differences, based largely on individual-level data, often remain incomplete. Analyses that also consider variations in community characteristics, broader socioeconomic conditions, and perceived injustices in the laws and the administration of those laws will provide a fuller understanding of the factors that account for observed racial and ethnic differences in juvenile offending. Those are beyond the scope of the research reviewed in this chapter.

This chapter is in five sections. The first describes how racial and ethnic data are gathered, and why current information is unable to address many important questions about group differences in offending. The second presents juvenile arrest data by race and discusses how these data can be compared to victims' reports and juveniles' self-reports as a way of cross-checking their validity. The third draws from all three data sources to summarize racial and ethnic differences in lethal and nonlethal violence, property crime, alcohol and drug violations, and weapons violations. An overview of the most prominent explanations of racial and ethnic differences in juvenile offending is presented in the fourth section. The final section concludes by summarizing the overall patterns and discussing where bias against juvenile minorities, rather than differences in criminal offense involvement, is evident.

Measuring Race and Ethnicity

Given the volume of American research on minorities and the criminal and juvenile justice systems, it would be reasonable to assume that the measurement of race and ethnicity is well established, reliable and valid, and without controversy. However, this is clearly not the case. The term "race" in the United States primarily refers to differences in skin color, even though biological research clearly shows that this conception is arbitrary and that there is no single set of traits that distinguishes one group from another. Rather, race definitions are socially constructed, and thus reflect the concerns and preoccupations of a given society (e.g., Hawkins 1995). In the United States, data collected on the race of juvenile offenders by federal agencies rely on the Census Bureau definition of race. Since 1977 this has included five broad, but mutually exclusive, categories—"white," "black," "American Indian, Eskimo, or Aleut," "Asian or Pacific Islander," and "other." Because most of the scientific research on racial differences in offending has been conducted during the past twenty-five years, and because the latter three racial groups constitute small proportions of the population, most empirical studies of juvenile offending have been restricted to comparisons of "whites" and "blacks."

It is also worth noting that no other country in the world uses this classification scheme for describing minority and majority groups, and only a handful of countries keep records on an offender's "race" (Tonry 1997).[1] According to Tonry (1997, 6–8), this is primarily for two reasons. First, many countries view race as irrelevant or fear that keeping such data would serve to create or reinforce stereotypes about minorities if they are reported to be disproportionately involved in certain types of crime. Second, in many countries the categories used in the United States (such as "black" versus "white") are seen as crude, overinclusive, and hence socially invalid. For example, in Canada, "black" citizens have originated from many different countries over the past century, including the United States, the West Indies, India, and Africa. By combining them into a single category, important cultural and socioeconomic differences among "blacks" are masked (Tonry 1997).

The concerns that other countries express about the definitions of racial categories as well as the use of such data are highly relevant here. Prompted by concerns that the existing categories did not capture many persons' sense of identity, the Census Bureau recently modified the definition of "race" following years of deliberation and community discussion. The new definition modifies the description of some of the racial categories and now allows persons to select one or more categories when they self-identify their race (U.S. Census Bureau 2001a). The current categories are: "white," "black or African American," "American Indian and Alaska Native," "Asian," "Native Hawaiian and other Pacific Islander," "some other race," and "two or more races." All federal agencies are required to use these new racial categories by January 1, 2003 (U.S. Census Bureau 2001b). However, since most data on juvenile offending are voluntarily submitted by state and local agencies, each jurisdiction ultimately retains the authority to collect such data as it sees fit.

The measurement of "ethnicity" also follows census guidelines, and it is treated as a characteristic separate from race. In the United States, ethnicity essentially refers to whether a person is "Hispanic" or "non-Hispanic," and the term is used to describe persons of Spanish-speaking origin who may identify themselves as belonging to any of the racial groups. There is great diversity in how Hispanics define themselves racially, and there are perhaps even greater cultural differences between, say, Puerto Ricans and Cubans than there are between racial groups. Not sharing a common culture, the myriad of groups classified as Hispanic often fail to meet the criteria we typically think of as constituting an ethnic group. For these and other reasons, the construct "Hispanic" has been criticized as a political definition that has little meaning (e.g., Mann 1993, 8–12). In light of such political disagreements, the government changed the "Hispanic" designation to "Hispanic or Latino," and the "black" designation to "black or African American" for the 2000 census. In the United States and abroad, it has become increasingly apparent that there may be greater differences within racial or ethnic groups than between groups.

The fact that there is growing awareness that race and ethnicity are sociopolitical terms subject to changes across time and differences across countries does not undermine the salience of race or ethnicity in the United States. As we saw in the previous chapter (Bishop 2005), there is significant racial and ethnic disproportionality in the juvenile justice system, and although definitions may vary, the conceptions of race used in the United States continue to have much legal, political, and social scientific salience. This is less true for the term "ethnicity," since public agreement as to whether someone is, for example, Hispanic or Latino, or some other ethnic heritage, is likely to be lower.[2] For the purpose of this chapter, the recent changes in the definitions should not be a significant source of error when describing cross-group differences. However, the interpretation of ethnic differences (for which data have not been so extensively collected) requires more caution.

Furthermore, while data aimed at describing racial and ethnic differences in juvenile offending have the potential to create or reinforce stereotypes, they also have the potential to eliminate stereotypes by showing whether, in fact, such differences do exist, and by providing insight into the causes of known group variations. For example, if we were to find that existing differences are the result of variations in economic status, then changes in economic conditions or the relationship between minority status and economic status would produce changes in racial and ethnic disproportionality. Given the legacy of race and the history of ethnic immigration in the United States, it seems clear that knowledge about the origins and consequences of disproportionality in the criminal and juvenile justice system is preferable to ignorance and uninformed debate.

It is also clear that the population of the United States is becoming increasingly diverse. While whites made up 83% and 80% of the population in 1980 and 1990, respectively, they constituted 75% of the population (reporting only one race) in 2000.[3] The remainder of the single-race population is 12.3% black or African American, 3.6% Asian, .9% American Indian or Alaska Native, and .1% Native Hawaiian or Pacific Islander. Nearly 6% of Americans do not see themselves as belonging to any of these groups, and instead report themselves as "some other race." Although not mutually exclusive groups, the number of persons reporting themselves as Hispanic or Latino is nearly equal to the number of blacks or African Americans. More detailed analysis shows that non-Latino whites now constitute just under 70% of the total population (U.S. Census Bureau 2001c).[4] This growing diversity in racial and ethnic identification will make group comparisons over time and place (in criminal offending or any other phenomenon) increasingly complex.

Measuring Juvenile Offending

Data for examining racial and ethnic differences in juvenile offending come from official data generated by police and juvenile justice agencies, and other sources such as self-reported delinquencies from surveys of youths, or victimization surveys in which victims describe the characteristics of their offenders. Although each source has strengths and weaknesses, they can be used together to create a useful assessment of patterns of offense involvement. The major data sources, and how they should and should not be used to study racial and ethnic differences in juvenile offending, are described below.

Arrest Data

Arrest data for persons under 18 years of age are typically used as the starting point for analyses of racial and ethnic differences in juvenile offending (see Snyder 2000 for a detailed discussion of arrest data). Arrest statistics represent the number of arrests reported by law enforcement agencies to the FBI's Uniform Crime Reporting (UCR) program. Juvenile arrest data for 2000 by racial categories are presented in table 3.1.

The percentages in this table can be compared to population percentages as a first step in approximating the extent to which racial groups are disproportionately arrested. Recall that about 16% of youth in the United States are black or African American and that less than 80% are white. Using population percentages it is easy to see that black youth are disproportionately arrested for violent index crimes and drug and weapons violations, and that property arrests are roughly proportionate to population size. Conversely, white youth are disproportionately arrested for alcohol violations, which include driving under the influence, liquor law violations, and drunkenness. What conclusions can be drawn from arrest data?

The most important limitation of arrest data is the fact that most crimes do not come to the attention of the police, and of those that do, most do not result in an arrest. If crimes committed by minorities are more likely to result in an arrest than crimes committed by whites, or if groups differ in the reporting of crime to the police, then estimates of racial and ethnic differences in offending rates based solely on arrest statistics are likely to be biased.

Comparing Arrest Data to Victims' Reports

It has been argued that arrest data can be used cautiously to assess race and ethnic differences in *violent* crime because national data on the racial makeup of arrestees can be compared with data derived from victims' reports of the perceived race of offenders using information available in the National Crime

Table 3.1: Arrests of Persons under 18 Years of Age by Offense Charged and Race, 2000

Offense Charged	White	Black	American Indian or Alaskan Native	Asian or Pacific Islander	Total
Total	1,120,383	389,876	18,881	25,662	1,554,802
	(72.1)	(25.1)	(1.2)	(1.7)	(100)
Offenses listed in	36,450	27,690	605	1,022	65,767
Violent Crime Index	(55.4)	(42.1)	(.9)	(1.6)	(100)
Homicide	377	399	4	21	801
	(47.1)	(49.8)	(.5)	(2.6)	(100)
Forcible rape	1,847	1,036	24	21	2,928
	(63.1)	(35.4)	(.8)	(.7)	(100)
Robbery	7,568	10,248	124	322	18,262
	(41.4)	(56.1)	(.7)	(1.8)	(100)
Aggravated assault	26,658	16,007	453	658	43,776
	(60.9)	(36.6)	(1.0)	(1.5)	(100)
Offenses listed in	238,988	94,018	4,615	6,985	344,606
Property Crime Index	(69.4)	(27.3)	(1.3)	(2.0)	(100)
Burglary	45,482	15,334	649	928	62,393
	(72.9)	(24.6)	(1.0)	(1.5)	(100)
Larceny-theft	170,386	63,723	3,479	5,290	242,878
	(70.2)	(26.2)	(1.4)	(2.2)	(100)
Motor vehicle theft	18,658	13,928	433	703	33,722
	(55.3)	(41.3)	(1.3)	(2.1)	(100)
Arson	4,462	1,033	54	64	5,613
	(79.5)	(18.4)	(1.0)	(1.1)	(100)
Alcohol violations	118,124	6,290	3,100	994	128,508
	(91.9)	(4.9)	(2.4)	(.8)	(100)
Drug abuse violations	573,288	320,895	4,561	6,142	904,886
	(63.4)	(35.5)	(.5)	(.7)	(100)
Weapons offenses	47,782	31,010	578	824	80,194
	(59.6)	(38.7)	(.7)	(1.0)	(100)

Source: adapted from U.S. Department of Justice, Federal Bureau of Investigation, 2001.

Note: Total arrests include numerous nonindex crimes not displayed here. The most commonly occurring nonindex crimes include simple assaults, disorderly conduct, curfew and loitering violations, and vandalism. Values in parentheses are percentages.

Victimization Survey (NCVS) (e.g., Hindelang 1978; Gove, Hughes, and Geerken 1985; Sampson and Lauritsen 1997). The NCVS is an ongoing sample survey conducted by the Bureau of Justice Statistics that measures the extent of personal and household victimization in the United States regardless of whether the incident was reported to the police. For crimes that involve face-to-face contact between the offender and the victim (i.e., violent crimes), the victim can typically report the sex, race, and approximate age of the offender. Comparisons of arrest and victim data have shown that the disproportionately high rate of robbery arrests among blacks is roughly equal to the level of involvement that is reported by victims. For cases of homicide, where victim reports are impossible, arrest data also are believed to accurately reflect racial differences because arrests are usually made on the basis of physical evidence and witness reports. Thus, for robbery and homicide it is believed that arrest data can be used to estimate black and white differences in offense involvement.[5]

Victim reports of the race of sexual and non-sexual-assault offenders might also be used to validate arrest data, but this is less often done because it has been found that victims are less likely to report these crimes to survey interviewers as well. In order to reduce this problem of underreporting, the methodology of the NCVS was changed in 1992, and the result was significantly higher rates of victim-reported assault and sexual assault victimization. Therefore, it is now useful to compare victims' reports of the race of rape offenders to information available in arrest data. Comparisons of rape arrest data and victim reports done for this report are roughly similar and suggest that arrest data may be used with caution to approximate race and ethnic differences in aggravated assault and sexual assault offending.[6]

The limitations of comparing the racial characteristics of offenders as reported by victims to differentials in arrest data are very important. First, it is impossible to use this method of verifying arrest data for the vast majority of crimes, because in most incidents, the victim does not see the offender. Second, the reliability of arrest data for making comparisons for groups other than blacks and whites cannot be assessed, because offenders that are nonwhite or nonblack are simply coded as "other" on the NCVS victim reports. Third, in nearly one-fourth of personal crimes there are multiple offenders (Bureau of Justice Statistics 1997), and juveniles are more likely to offend with others than are adults (Snyder 2000). Victim reports of crimes involving multiple offenders do not identify the characteristics of each offender, and thus, it is difficult to assess race and ethnic differentials for this substantial minority of crimes.

Not only is victim survey data limited to whether the offender was "black," "white," or "other," but also most arrest data do not consistently provide rates for Latinos relative to whites, blacks, Asians, or American Indians. This is because arrest data typically code race and ethnicity in the same way as the U.S. Bureau of the Census, and therefore it is very difficult to compare levels of Latino involvement in crime to levels of non-Latino whites or non-Latino blacks. Hence, the limitations of both arrest and victimization survey data have made it very difficult to study racial and ethnic differences in offense involvement beyond general comparisons of blacks with whites.

Even though, to a certain extent, black-versus-white arrest differentials for violent crime have been validated by victim reports, these assessments are useful only in the broadest sense (Crutchfield, Bridges, and Pitchford 1994).

Comparisons of arrest and victim data can be conducted only at the national level because reliable victimization survey data are not available for smaller areas such as states, cities, or counties. Black and white *levels* of offending vary considerably across different areas, and it is reasonable to assume that *differences* between the groups do as well. Thus, although black-versus-white differences in *national* arrest data approximate victims' reports about offenders, it cannot be concluded that disproportionality in *state or local* arrest statistics have been validated by victim reports.

Comparing Arrest Data to Juvenile Self-Reports of Offending

Self-report surveys provide another source of information about juvenile offending that bypasses some of the weaknesses inherent in arrest data and victimization reports. These surveys typically gather offending and other data directly from juveniles, via confidential interviews or written answers to a questionnaire. If the self-report data are gathered using random sampling techniques and reliable measures, they can be used to describe racial and ethnic patterns of juvenile offending, including differences for nonviolent crimes in which there is no face-to-face contact between the victim and offender.

While self-report data from juveniles have their strengths, they too have several disadvantages. First, there may be a difference in the validity of self-reports for different race and ethnic groups. For instance, early studies found that blacks were more likely than whites to fail to report serious misconduct in such surveys (Hindelang 1981; Hindelang, Hirschi, and Weis 1981; Huizinga and Elliott 1986), although a more recent study has found no racial differences in the validity of self-reports (Farrington et al. 1996). Second, very few self-report surveys use sample sizes that are large enough to describe racial and ethnic differences in serious violent offending. This is because violent behavior is relatively uncommon among the adolescent population, and reliable estimates of group differences for any rare event require very large sample sizes. Data from self-report surveys tend to be better suited to the study of more common delinquent behaviors such as minor theft and assault, alcohol use, and some forms of drug use. Finally, groups other than blacks and whites are rarely represented in these surveys in large enough numbers to provide a sufficient basis for comparison. Where available, racial patterns of juvenile offending as recorded in self-reports are discussed below.

In summary, each form of data has strengths and weaknesses, and the exclusive use of any one source of data can produce a biased picture of the relationship between race and ethnicity and juvenile offending. None of the data sources alone provides sufficient information about the characteristics of offenders and the nature of the behaviors committed. Nonetheless, by combining the findings from each of these sources of data, we can cautiously provide an assessment of racial and ethnic differences in juvenile offending.

Racial and Ethnic Differences in Juvenile Offending
Lethal Violence

Analyses of recent trends in youth homicide show that juvenile murder rates were relatively stable from 1980 through 1987, followed by a significant increase through the early 1990s and an equally significant decrease through 2000. Nearly all of the increase in youth homicide was due to increases in youth firearm deaths (Blumstein and Rosenfeld 1998). The juvenile arrest rate for murder more than doubled from 1987 to 1993 and declined equally from 1993 to 2000 (Snyder 2000; U.S. Department of Justice, Federal Bureau of Investigation 2001). The increase and subsequent decrease in juvenile homicide was composed primarily of increases in rates of juvenile murder committed by males, and their victims were primarily acquaintances and strangers, rather than family members (Snyder and Sickmund 1999). For the entire period of 1980 to 1997, young males constituted about 93% of the known juvenile homicide offenders, and blacks represented about 56% of offenders (Snyder and Sickmund 1999). Approximately eight hundred juveniles were arrested for homicide in 2000, and of these youths 50% were black, 47% were white, 1% were American Indian or Alaskan Native, and 3% were Asian or Pacific Islander (U.S. Department of Justice, Federal Bureau of Investigation 2001). Finally, it is also important to note that most homicide, including youth homicide, is intraracial. Over the past two decades, the risk of homicidal death for 14–17-year-old black youth has been between six and ten times greater than for white youth.

Racial and ethnic differences in homicide beyond black-versus-white comparisons can also be described. In 1997, the known juvenile homicide offending rates for racial groups (as classified in U.S. arrest data) were approximately 30 (per million youth ages 10–17) for whites, 34 for American Indians and Alaskan Natives, 44 for Asian and Pacific Islanders, and 194 for blacks (Snyder and Sickmund 1999). These national rates describe the average differences in youth homicide offending for these racial subgroups. However, it would be inaccurate to conclude that these same levels are found across all cities or states. National-level data cannot provide information about differences in offending for individuals living in various types of communities, nor can they provide us with information about Hispanic or Latino rates versus rates in these other groups. Knowing the extent of variation within racial and ethnic groups is an equally important concern, but it is also an issue that only a few studies have been able to address.

Martinez (2002) provides detailed descriptions of race and ethnic differences in juvenile (and adult) homicide offending across five ethnically diverse cities in the United States (Chicago, El Paso, Houston, Miami, and San Diego). His results demonstrate that young male Latino, black, and white homicide rates vary substantially across these cities. For instance, for the period of 1985 through 1995, the average Latino male (13–17-year-old) homicide offending rate ranged from a low of 1.5 (per 100,000) in San Diego to a high of 52.8 in Chicago. For the same time period, the average black male (13–17-year-old) homicide offending rate ranged from a low of 30.6 (per 100,000) in El Paso to a high of 255.5 in Chicago.[7] These results show how local patterns of offending can vary dramatically from national estimates. While white male youth generally commit homicide at lower average rates than Latino and black youth, the overall levels of homicide offending and the differences in lethal violence between these groups depend a great deal on the communities in which these youth reside.

Nonlethal Violence

Nonlethal violence incidents vastly outnumber homicides, and arrests for these incidents do as well. Of the more than sixty-five thousand juvenile arrests for violence in 2000, about eight hundred were for murder or manslaughter (U.S. Department of Justice, Federal Bureau of Investigation 2001). As noted above, it is possible to assess race differences in other forms of violent juvenile offending, but generalizations based on arrest data must be made more cautiously than those made possible by more detailed homicide records. Arrest reports for persons under 18 years of age show that in 2000, approximately 55% of violent crime arrestees were white, 42% were black, 1% were American Indian or Alaskan Native, and 2% were Asian or Pacific Islander. Compared to juvenile population proportions in the United States (79% white, 16% black, 1% American Indian or Alaskan Native, and 4% Asian or Pacific Islander), these figures suggest disproportionate involvement in nonlethal violence on the part of black youth, and lower-than-expected involvement on the part of Asian youth. When arrest data are restricted to specific forms of nonlethal violence, black youth appear to be most disproportionately involved in robbery (56%), aggravated assault (37%), and rape (35%) (U.S. Department of Justice, Federal Bureau of Investigation 2001).

Self-report data from juveniles also support the notion that black youth are involved in nonlethal violence at higher rates than white youth, with Latino youth involvement rates falling in between. For example, analyses of data from the National Youth Survey (NYS) found that black males were more likely to report involvement in these kinds of crimes (Elliott and Ageton 1980; Elliott 1994). In addition, data from the Office of Juvenile Justice and Delinquency Prevention's Program of Research on the Causes and Correlates of Delinquency find the same general pattern as well. In self-report data from random samples of high-risk youth in Pittsburgh, Denver, and Rochester, researchers found that white youth report involvement in violent street crimes at lower levels than black and Latino youth, with black males reporting the highest levels of involvement (Huizinga, Loeber, and Thornberry 1994). Additional analyses of these patterns have found that the differences in offending are confirmed by parent and teachers' reports as well (Farrington et al. 1996).

Finally, victim reports of racial and ethnic disparities for robbery and aggravated assaults by youth support the patterns found in official and non-official data (National Research Council and Institute of Medicine 2001). In the 1993–97 NCVS, victims of robbery who reported the offender to be under 18 years of age also reported that 27% of these offenders were white, 58% were black, and 12% were some other race. For these same years, juvenile arrest data indicated that 38% of the offenders were white, 60% were black, and 2% were some other race. For aggravated assault, victims' reports roughly match the arrest data. According to the victims, 51% of the offenders were white, 31% were black, and 15% were some other race, while the arrest statistics indicated that 57% were white, 41% were black, and 2% were other. Although there are some differences between the victim reports and the arrest statistics, the basic pattern suggests disproportionate involvement on the part of black youth in these crimes of nonlethal violence.

Property Offending

Property crime offending is much more common than violent offending, and despite the fact that violent crimes are more likely to be reported to the police, arrests of juveniles for property arrests outnumber those for violent crime by more than five to one (U.S. Department of Justice, Federal Bureau of Investigation 2001). For reasons noted earlier, arrest data for property crimes cannot be verified with victim's reports; thus, it is especially important to compare these patterns to findings based on juvenile self-report data. Generally speaking, juvenile property crime arrest data show that black youth are slightly more involved than white youth, although the level of disproportionality varies by type of property crime. Black youth are arrested for motor vehicle theft (41%) and stolen property violations (37%) at disproportionate levels, but there appear to be no differences in offending for the crimes of arson, vandalism, or forgery and counterfeiting (U.S. Department of Justice, Federal Bureau of Investigation 2001).

Self-report data confirm the generalization that there are few differences in property crime offending by juveniles of different racial or ethnic groups. Findings from the 1997 National Longitudinal Survey of Youth (NLSY) suggest that white juveniles (ages 12 – 16) are slightly more likely to have committed acts of vandalism, while no differences are found for motor vehicle thefts and thefts over fifty dollars (Snyder and Sickmund 1999). Earlier findings from the National Youth Survey report a similar lack of differences (Elliott and Ageton 1980). Thus, the arrest and self-report data suggest that racial and ethnic differences are minimal in juvenile property offending.

Alcohol Violations

In 2000, there were twice as many arrests of juveniles for alcohol violations than there were arrests of juveniles for violent crime (U.S. Department of Justice, Federal Bureau of Investigation 2001). The arrest data indicate that white youth are disproportionately involved in alcohol offenses, and that American Indian youth also are somewhat more likely than black or Asian youth to be arrested for these crimes. In 2000, white youth constituted 92% of arrests for driving under the influence, 92% of liquor law violations (e.g., underage possession), and 91% of drunkenness offenses. In contrast, black youth constituted 5%, 5%, and 8% of these arrests, respectively (U.S. Department of Justice, Federal Bureau of Investigation 2001).

Self-report data confirm the patterns found in arrest data. For example, white youth in the NLSY were more likely than minority youth to report ever drinking alcohol, and drinking alcohol within the past 30 days (Snyder and Sickmund 1999).[8] Data from another self-report survey (the National Household Survey on Drug Abuse) also confirm this finding: A greater proportion of non-Hispanic white youth (age 12 – 17) report drinking alcohol than non-Hispanic blacks, Hispanics, and other racial groups (Substance Abuse and Mental Health Services Administration 1998).

Drug Abuse Violations and Drug Use

In 2000, the number of juvenile arrests for drug abuse violations was nearly equal to the number of arrests for alcohol violations (U.S. Department of Justice, Federal Bureau of Investigation 2001); however, black youth were disproportionately arrested for these violations compared to white, American Indian, or Asian youth. Approximately 28% of juveniles arrested for the possession, sale, or manufacturing of illegal drugs were black, while 70% were white.

However, self-report data from juveniles on their own drug use and selling do *not* confirm the differences between black and white youth that are suggested by the arrest data. In the National Longitudinal Survey of Youth, white youth were somewhat *more* likely to report using marijuana (ever and in the past thirty days), selling any drugs, and selling marijuana, and there were *no* differences between the two groups in selling hard drugs (such as cocaine, LSD, or heroin) (Snyder and Sickmund 1999). Other national self-report surveys, such as the National Household Survey on Drug Abuse, also report higher levels of drug use among non-Hispanic white youth (Substance Abuse and Mental Health Services Administration 1998). Thus, unlike the arrest data for most other juvenile crimes, racial and ethnic patterns for drug arrests are *not* supported by self-report survey data.

Weapons Violations

The final category of offending examined here involves violations of weapons laws, including the illegal possession or carrying of a firearm. Following the upsurge in youth firearm homicides, many police departments began aggressive searches for handguns and other weapons, especially among youth. At the same time, a variety of surveys asked youth how often, if ever, they had carried a handgun or other weapon, and whether they had carried a gun to school.

The juvenile arrest data for weapons violations in 2000 report that about 67% of those arrested were white, 31% were black, and approximately 3% were either American Indian or Asian (U.S. Department of Justice, Federal Bureau of Investigation 2001). Thus, black youth were disproportionately likely to be arrested for a weapons violation. Recent self-report data confirm that black and Hispanic ninth- through twelfth-grade students are more likely than white youth to report carrying a weapon and carrying a gun. They are also more likely to report being threatened by a person with a gun or other weapon (Centers for Disease Control and Prevention 1998). These estimates suggest that approximately 10% of Hispanic and black students, and about 4% of white students, report carrying a gun within the past thirty days.

Summary

Table 3.2 summarizes the empirical evidence about racial and ethnic differences in juvenile offending by briefly noting the patterns found in the juvenile arrest data, and parallel evidence in other sources of information.

Explaining Racial and Ethnic Differences

Racial and ethnic differences in juvenile offending have been the topic of study for sociologists and criminologists for nearly a century. Nonetheless, no one theory has adequately explained why some racial or ethnic groups have higher or lower rates than others (Hawkins 1995). One of the reasons that racial and ethnic differences in juvenile offending are not well under-

Table 3.2: Summary of Racial and Ethnic Differences in Juvenile Offending by Crime Type

Pattern Found in Arrest Data	Source of Confirmation
Lethal violence:	
Black youth most disproportionately involved	Witness reports, case evidence
Latino youth disproportionately involved in some cities	
American Indian youth disproportionately involved	
Nonlethal violence:	
Black youth disproportionately involved	Victim reports, self-reports, parent and teacher reports
Property crime:	
White youth more involved for some offenses	Self-reports
Black youth more involved for some offenses	
Overall, minimal differences across groups	
Alcohol violations:	
White youth disproportionately involved	Self-reports (for white youth); no sufficient data for American Indian youth
American Indian youth disproportionately involved	
Drug abuse violations:	
Black youth disproportionately involved	Self-report data contrary to arrest data; white youth report higher levels in self-report data
Weapons violations:	
Black youth disproportionately involved	Self-reports (also show higher prevalence for Hispanic youth)

stood is that much research emphasizes individual-level factors (such as family structure, income, temperament, or school achievement) without considering the broader sociostructural characteristics that distinguish groups and individuals (Sampson and Lauritsen 1994; Hawkins et al. 2000). Research that explicitly incorporates community social and economic factors is most likely to help us understand racial and ethnic differences that do exist.

Rather than asking what attributes of individuals lead to criminal offending, community-level research asks what it is about community or group conditions that produces differential rates of crime across groups. Early research by Shaw and McKay ([1942] 1969) set the framework for these kinds of analyses. Using juvenile court data from the early to mid-twentieth century, Shaw and McKay found that high rates of juvenile delinquency persisted in core urban areas regardless of which racial or ethnic group inhabited the area.[9] They also found that the rates of delinquency for each of the racial or ethnic groups varied depending on the characteristics of the neighborhood in which they resided. This early observation was important because it showed that criminal behavior was not an inherent characteristic of a particular racial or ethnic group. If it were, groups would exhibit equally high rates of delinquency regardless of where they lived. Furthermore, we would not expect to see certain areas of the city sustain high rates of delinquency despite large-scale ethnic turnover.

The empirical findings reviewed earlier in this chapter have been based primarily on data gathered on individuals for the United States as a whole. Those data suggest disproportionate black and, to a lesser extent, Latino involvement in violent crimes, but much fewer differences in other types of crimes. In order to examine what factors might account for the differences in violence, we also need to know how these types of offending vary across communities. But arrest data can be limited for these purposes. The use of arrest data to assess levels of black, white, or Hispanic offending across communities requires us to assume that police departments and their practices (including resources, clearance rates, and the extent of bias and prejudice) are similar across each of the communities and/or jurisdictions. For crimes other than homicide, this is a highly questionable assumption. Moreover, arrest data do not typically include information about the community in which the crime occurred or the area in which the juvenile resides.

Nonetheless, there are studies that provide insight into racial and ethnic differences in juvenile violence by taking into account how these patterns vary across places. One such study was the homicide analysis by Martinez described earlier. His analyses showed that both the levels of and the differences between black, white, and Latino male juvenile homicide varied considerably across five U.S. cities. In some places, such as Miami, the gap between black youth and other groups (Latino and white) was very large, whereas in other areas, such as El Paso, the differences were much smaller. Comparisons of selected racial and ethnic groups across cities are illuminating as well. Black youth in Chicago were arrested for homicide at levels nearly nine times higher than in El Paso, while Latino males in these same cities were much more similar (homicide offending was 2.5 times greater in Chicago than in El Paso).

The findings from this kind of research are important, not only because they go beyond black-versus-white comparisons, but also because they pay attention to within-group differences that are rarely the focus in homicide or offending studies (Hawkins 1999). Martinez shows that there are important differences in juvenile homicide offending within groups depending on the city, and that these differences are larger than the differences between groups in those cities. Such findings reaffirm Shaw and McKay's assertion that race and ethnicity may serve as a weak *predictor* of violent offending, but that these factors are not direct *causes* in and of themselves. Indeed, it is clear that the importance of race or ethnicity depends a great deal on community context. Some cities have conditions that foster high rates of juvenile violence, while others may produce greater differences in violence between racial and ethnic groups.

It is also clear that broader social conditions are related both to levels of violent offending by youth and to racial and ethnic variation in these levels over time. In a recent study of how social and economic conditions are related to black and white youth homicide arrest rates from 1967 to 1998, Messner, Raffalovich, and McMillan (2001) found that increases in child poverty were associated with increased juvenile arrest rates for homicide, controlling for related factors such as unemployment and inequality. In other words, youth homicide rates rose during periods when youth poverty grew. This relationship was true for both white and black youth, which suggests that the causes of homicide offending are similar for both groups (see Sampson 1987 for similar conclusions about youth robbery). The difference in the levels of black and white homicide is due in part to the much greater likelihood that black youth are living under social and economic conditions in which violence is most likely.

In order to study how community conditions are related to nonviolent juvenile offending, we need to consider self-report data rather than arrest statistics. Recall that arrest data for nonviolent offenses have not been validated by victim reports, and that most self-reports and arrest data show few racial and ethnic differences in nonviolent juvenile offending. However, self-report data are often inadequate for studying juvenile offending across different types of communities, because many samples are designed to be nationally representative and therefore lack sufficient statistical power to study various types of areas. The three-city self-report study sponsored by Office of Juvenile Justice and Delinquency Prevention noted earlier is one of the few projects with the capacity to make assessments across cities (Denver, Pittsburgh, and Rochester). In analyses based on these data, researchers found greater involvement in violent street crimes for black and Latino males, and that some but not all of the differences were reduced once community and other conditions were taken into account (Huizinga, Loeber, and Thornberry 1994). Remaining differences are not completely understood. They may represent other individual or cultural differences, but more likely they represent the fact that the most deprived white youth live in areas that are much better off than the neighborhoods in which deprived black youth live (Sampson and Wilson 1995).

Although investigations of race, ethnicity, and youth violence show the importance of community conditions for understanding group differences in involvement, recent research in some of the nation's worst urban neighborhoods demonstrates the difficulties involved in finding potential solutions to this problem. A study of boys in three of the most violent areas of Washington, DC, found that most of the youths were "unsupervised and unsupported by families, schools, and community organizations that could teach them skills needed to lead productive lives" (Chaiken 2000, 2). Alienation from other youths also was common among the most seriously delinquent boys. Overcoming these issues is especially difficult in a climate of inadequate child and youth resources, and because of the fact that there are not sufficient numbers of adults who are able to work with youth in these dangerous areas.

Nonetheless, this report discusses the ways in which the problems of youth delinquency can begin to be remedied both in Washington, DC, and in similar kinds of areas. These include providing sufficient resources for early intervention programs and for supervision and structured activities during after-school hours (12–14). But this is only a first step. The researchers found that even when there were resources for the provision of these kinds of services, there were often major difficulties involved in the delivery of youth programs. These included inadequate support on the part of local businesses and government agencies, excessive numbers of unaffiliated agencies, and a lack of coordination and collaboration among youth service organizations. Although there were more than fifty youth service organizations in and around the three study neighborhoods, 80% of the boys in the study could not name a single local organization with programs for reducing youth violence. Only 24% of the boys reported ever participating in any of the activities of these community organizations.

These findings remind us that documenting the sources of juvenile offending is only the first step toward understanding what might work best to reduce that behavior. Moreover, it is certainly more difficult to alter root conditions of criminal behavior (such as neighborhood and family context) than to develop and assess programs that might reduce juvenile offending or racial and ethnic differences in that behavior. Of course, simply establishing such programs will be insufficient if they cannot reach their intended clients. As this research suggests, this problem is probably due to the high levels of alienation and the lack of social ties among youth most in need of assistance.

Conclusions

The empirical evidence reviewed here suggests that the relationship between race and ethnicity and juvenile involvement in crime is complex and contingent on the type of offense. The most commonly occurring crimes exhibited few group differences, while more rare and serious crimes of violence showed generally higher levels of black and Latino involvement. Equally important was the fact that group rates of homicide offending varied considerably across cities, indicating greater variation within racial and ethnic groups than between them.

It was also argued that more confidence is placed in the conclusions drawn from data that have been validated by other types of information. Arrest data were determined to be reasonable sources of information about differences in youth violence offending because the same general patterns have been found in self-reports and in victims' reports of their experiences. For the most serious but least common offenses we can be fairly confident in our assessments. Conclusions based on property crime arrest data and alcohol and weapons arrest violations also matched self-reports by youth. Black and Hispanic youth were more likely to carry a weapon, while white youth were more likely to engage in underage alcohol consumption and drinking and driving.

There was only one major class of offenses for which discrepancies between data sources were apparent—drug abuse violations. Self-report data indicate that white youth are more likely to use marijuana and other illicit drugs, and a greater proportion also report selling illegal drugs. These differences are small in magnitude but consistent enough across various samples and measures to raise serious concerns about bias in arrest data. If we assume that self-report data are valid for drug violations, as we assume for other types of offending, then the proportion of black youth arrested for these crimes is approximately twice as high as expected.

Although this gap in the drug arrest rates is very troubling, it is not immediately obvious how much of it is due to biased policing or enforcement, discriminatory laws, or inadequate data. What is clear is that there was a massive shift in drug enforcement activity, beginning in the 1970s, and escalating in the 1980s. The number of arrests for drug abuse violations by white juveniles declined 28% from 1980 to 1985, while the number of arrests for drug abuse violations by black juveniles increased 25% over the same time period (Sampson and Lauritsen 1997). Juvenile court data similarly show that the number of white youth referred to court for drug law violations declined by 6% between 1985 and 1986, while the number of referrals for black youth increased by 42% (Snyder 1990). The war on drugs in the 1980s was particularly punitive compared to earlier drug wars, leading many to charge the juvenile and criminal justice systems with racially discriminatory practices. It was also unprecedented in terms of resources: the U.S. federal drug control budget increased from approximately $2.4 billion in 1984 to more than $12.1 billion in 1994 (Executive Office of the President 1994).

It is possible, of course, to equally enforce the laws and still have an unfair legal system if the laws are created to have disproportionate impacts on specific groups. This is the argument made by Tonry (1995), who points out that the war on drugs was initiated at a time when national drug use patterns had already exhibited a considerable decline. Tonry further argues that the politically charged war on drugs, with its legislative and budgetary emphasis on the type of drug most likely to be used and detected in black disadvantaged urban areas (i.e., crack cocaine), could be viewed as racially discriminatory in intent and consequences.

While drug abuse violations do not constitute the majority of juvenile arrests, there were nearly twice as many of these arrests (145,000 in 1998; 128,000 in 1999) than arrests for all forms of juvenile violence combined (U.S. Department of Justice, Federal Bureau of Investigation 2001). Empirical studies have shown that formal sanctioning can produce cumulative disadvantages for youth as they move into adulthood. Such outcomes, and many of the other costs of punishments, obligate us to give careful thought to the purpose and fairness of our laws as well as the practices of law enforcement and the juvenile justice system.

In sum, only for violent crime do we find well documented gaps in offending between racial and ethnic groups, and many of these differences are smaller than the variations to be found among racial and ethnic groups living in different kinds of communities. One of the unintended consequences of having focused much of our research on violence is the possibility that those patterns will be incorrectly generalized to other types of offending, thus perpetuating false stereotypes about levels of minority involvement in crime. Hopefully, the issues discussed above will serve to challenge this tendency. Taking into account the full range of information on race, ethnicity, and youth crime shows us that the relationship between minority status and juvenile involvement in crime is complex, and contingent on the type of offense and the conditions of the communities in which children live.

Notes

1. These countries include England, Canada, Australia, and New Zealand. England keeps data that allow for comparisons between "white" and "Afro-Caribbean" in prison statistics. Canadian data permit "native" versus "non-native" comparisons, Australian data permit "Aborigine" versus "non-Aborigine" comparisons, and New Zealand data allow for comparisons between "Maori-Pacific Islanders" and "others" (Tonry 1997).

2. For instance, the Census Bureau defines ethnicity as the heritage of the person or the person's parents or ancestors before their arrival in the United States. Social disagreements are most likely to occur as the number of generations since arrival increases and as interethnic and interracial marriage increases.

3. Approximately 2.4% of the population reported that they were of two or more races.

4. The rate of growth from 1990 to 2000 was greatest for Asians (46%) and Hispanics or Latinos (58%), followed by American Indians and Alaska Natives (26%), blacks or African Americans (16%), and whites (6%). The percent change calculations for racial groups are based on those who identify themselves as belonging to one race only (98%), while the calculations of change in the Latino population are based on Hispanics or Latinos of any race.

5. Most violent crime is intraracial, and blacks experience significantly higher rates of homicide and robbery victimization.

6. Victim reports of the offender's race in lone-offender aggravated assault incidents suggest that approximately 60% of offenders are white, 28% are black, and 11% are other (Bureau of Justice Statistics 1997). Arrest data estimate that 62% of offenders are white, 36% are black, and 2% are Asian or American Indian (U.S. Department of Justice, Federal Bureau of Investigation 1998). For incidents of sexual assault, victims report that 69% of lone offenders are white, 25% are black, and 7% are other, while arrest data suggest that 60% are white, 37% are black, and 2% are Asian or American Indian.

7. Unlike the national homicide arrest data, homicide "offending" rates are calculated by Martinez to include the race of the arrestee plus the race of the suspect (not yet arrested) directly from homicide case reports in each of these city police departments. These rates however, are composed primarily of arrestees' race rather than suspects' race (personal communication, 2001).

8. White youth are also more likely than minority youth to smoke cigarettes.

9. In Chicago in the early twentieth century, various ethnic and racial groups were blamed for the city's juvenile delinquency problem, including Italians, Irish, Jews, Poles, Slavs, and later on, African-Americans and Latinos.

References

Bishop, Donna M. 2005. "The Role of Race and Ethnicity in Juvenile Justice Processing." In *Our Children, Their Children: Confronting Racial and Ethnic Differences in American Juvenile Justice,* ed. Darnell F. Hawkins and Kimberly Kempf-Leonard. Chicago: University of Chicago Press.

Blumstein, A., and R. Rosenfeld. 1998. "Explaining Recent Trends in U.S. Homicide Rates." *Journal of Criminal Law and Criminology* 88:1175–1216.

Bureau of Justice Statistics. 1997. *Criminal Victimization in the United States, 1995.* Washington, DC: U.S. Department of Justice, Office of Justice Programs.

Centers for Disease Control and Prevention. 1998. "Youth Risk Behavior Surveillance: United States, 1997." Morbidity and Mortality Weekly Report 47 (no. SS-3). Washington, DC: Government Printing Office.

Chaiken, M. 2000. *Violent Neighborhoods: Violent Kids.* Juvenile Justice Bulletin, March. Washington, DC: U.S. Department of Justice, Office of Justice Programs, Office of Juvenile Justice and Delinquency Prevention.

Crutchfield, R., G. Bridges, and S. Pitchford. 1994. "Analytical and Aggregation Biases in Analyses of Imprisonment: Reconciling Discrepancies in Studies of Racial Disparity." *Journal of Research in Crime and Delinquency* 31:166.

Elliott, D. 1994. "Serious Violent Offenders: Onset, Developmental Course, and Termination." *Criminology* 32:1–21.

Elliott, D. and S. Ageton. 1980. "Reconciling Race and Class Differences in Self-Reported and Official Estimates of Delinquency." *American Sociology Review* 45:95–110.

Executive Office of the President. 1994. "National Drug Control Strategy: Budget Summary." Washington DC: Office of National Drug Control Policy.

Farrington, D., R. Loeber, M. Stouthamer-Loeber, W. VanKammen, and L. Schmidt. 1996. "Self-Reported Delinquency and a Combined Delinquency Seriousness Scale Based on Boys, Mothers, and Teachers: Concurrent and Predictive Validity for African-Americans and Caucasians." *Criminology* 34:493–514.

Gove, W., M. Hughes, and M. Geerken. 1985. "Are the Uniform Crime Reports a Valid Indicator of the Index Crimes? An Affirmative Answer with Minor Qualifications." *Criminology* 23:451–501.

Hawkins, D. 1995. *Ethnicity, Race, and Crime.* Albany, NY: Suny Press.

———. 1999. "What Can We Learn from Data Disaggregation? The Case of Homicide and African Americans." Pp. 195–210 in *Homicide: A Sourcebook of Social Research,* ed. M. Smith and M. Zahn. Thousand Oaks, CA: Sage.

Hawkins, D., J. Laub, J. Lauritsen, and L. Cothern. 2000. *Race, Ethnicity, and Serious and Violent Juvenile Offending.* OJJDP Juvenile Justice Bulletin, June, NCJ 181202, U.S. Department of Justice.

Hindelang, M. 1978. "Race and Involvement in Common Law Personal Crimes." *American Sociological Review* 43:93–109.

———. 1981. "Variations in Sex-Race-Age-Specific Incidence Rates of Offending." *American Sociological Review* 46:461–474.

Hindelang, M., T. Hirschi, and J. Weis. 1981. *Measuring Delinquency.* Beverly Hills, CA: Sage.

Huizinga, D., and D. Elliott. 1986. "Reassessing the Reliability and Validity of Self-Report Delinquency Measures." *Journal of Quantitative Criminology* 2:293–327.

Huizinga, D., R. Loeber, and T. Thornberry. 1994. "Urban Delinquency and Substance Abuse: Initial Findings." Washington, DC: U.S. Department of Justice, Office of Justice Programs, Office of Juvenile Justice and Delinquency Prevention.

Mann, C. Richey. 1993. *Unequal Justice: A Question of Color.* Bloomington: Indiana University Press.

Martinez, R. 2002. *Latino Homicide: Immigration, Violence and Community.* New York: Routledge.

Messner, S., L. Raffalovich, and R. McMillan. 2001. "Economic Deprivation and Changes in Homicide Arrest Rates for White and Black Youths, 1967–1998: A National Time Series Analysis." *Criminology* 39:591–614.

National Research Council and Institute of Medicine. 2001. *Juvenile Crime, Juvenile Justice: Panel on Juvenile Crime: Prevention, Treatment, and Control..* Edited by J. McCord, C. Spatz Widom, and N. Crowell. Washington, DC: National Academy Press.

Sampson, R. J. 1987. "Urban Black Violence: The Effect of Male Joblessness and Family Disruption." *American Journal of Sociology* 93:348–382.

Sampson, R. J., and J. L. Lauritsen. 1994. "Violent Victimization and Offending: Individual-, Situational-, and Community-Level Risk Factors." In *Understanding and Preventing Violence,* vol. 3, *Social Influences.* Washington, DC: National Research Council, National Academy Press.

———. 1997. "Racial and Ethnic Disparities in Crime and Criminal Justice in the United States." In *Crime and Justice: An Annual Review of Research,* vol. 22, ed. M. Tonry. Chicago: University of Chicago Press.

Sampson, R. J., and W. J. Wilson. 1995. "Toward a Theory of Race, Crime, and Urban Inequality." In *Crime and Inequality,* ed. J. Hagan and R. Peterson. Stanford, CA: Stanford University Press.

Shaw, C., and H. McKay. [1942] 1969. *Juvenile Delinquency in Urban Areas.* Rev. ed. Chicago: University of Chicago Press.

Snyder, H. 1990. "Growth in Minority Detentions Attributed to Drug Law Violators." Washington, DC: U.S. Department of Justice, Office of Justice Programs, Office of Juvenile Justice and Delinquency Prevention.

———. 2000. *Juvenile Arrests 1999.* Juvenile Justice Bulletin, December. Washington, DC: U.S. Department of Justice, Office of Justice Programs, Office of Juvenile Justice and Delinquency Prevention.

Snyder, H., and M. Sickmund. 1999. *Juvenile Offenders and Victims: 1999 National Report.* Washington, DC: U.S. Department of Justice, Office of Justice Programs, Office of Juvenile Justice and Delinquency Prevention.

Substance Abuse and Mental Health Services Administration. 1998. "Risk and Protective Factors for Adolescent Drug Use: Findings from the 1997 National Household Survey on Drug Abuse." Office of Applied Studies, SAMHSA.

Tonry, M. 1995. *Malign Neglect: Race, Crime, and Punishment in America.* New York: Oxford University Press.

———, ed. 1997. "Ethnicity, Crime, and Immigration: Comparative and Cross-National Perspectives." Special issue, *Crime and Justice: A Review of Research,* vol. 21. Chicago: University of Chicago Press.

U.S. Census Bureau. 2001a. "Questions and Answers for Census 2000 Data on Race, March 14, 2001." *Census Bureau News* (www.census.gov/Press-Release).

———. 2001b. "Racial and Ethnic Classifications Used in Census 2000 and Beyond." www.census.gov/population/www/socdemo/race/racefactb.html.

———. 2001c. *Profile of General Demographic Characteristics: 2000.* Washington DC, U.S. Department of Commerce.

U.S. Department of Justice, Federal Bureau of Investigation. 1998. *Crime in the United States, 1997.* Washington, DC: Government Printing Office.

———. 2001. *Crime in the United States, 2000.* Washington, DC, Government Printing Office.

4

Degrees of Discretion

The First Juvenile Court and the Problem of Difference
in the Early Twentieth Century

David S. Tanenhaus

> The first impression made upon the observer by the children who
> appear before the bar of the [Chicago juvenile] court is that of their
> foreign appearance, the un-American air of the mother and father who
> accompany them, and the strangeness to them of all their
> surroundings.
>
> Sophonisba P. Breckinridge and Edith Abbott,
> *The Delinquent Child and the Home*, 1912

IN LIGHT of the nation's long and unfortunate history of discriminating against people of color in justice systems, it seems only natural to look at the American past in order to understand the continuing problem of the over-representation of minorities in juvenile justice (Friedman 1993; Miller 1996; Oshinsky 1996; Christianson 1998). Yet since the 1960s scholars have generally interpreted the development of American juvenile justice more in terms of class control than racial discrimination. This social or class control thesis posits that the inventors of the juvenile court harnessed the power of the state to mold poor and working-class children into disciplined workers for an industrial society (Platt [1969] 1977; Shelden and Osborne 1989; Schneider 1992). Although there have been some historical examinations of race and juvenile justice (Sanders [1933] 1968; Shelden 1979; Frey 1981; Pisciotta 1983; Young 1993, 1994; Trost 1996; Feld 1999; Wolcott 2000; Ward 2001), scholars tend to analyze either the treatment of white ethnics or African-Americans, but not the relationship between ethnicity and race in the evolution of juvenile justice.[1] This relationship is worth examining, since the juvenile court evolved during a transitional era for understandings of race, ethnicity, and "whiteness" (Jacobson 1998). We need to know what "race" meant to those who institutionalized it, and to the later generations who kept it in place.

As the populations of American cities exploded and became increasingly diverse in the late nineteenth and early twentieth centuries, progressive reformers campaigned to establish flexible, modern justice systems for the nation's urban areas (Willrich 2003). At the beginning of the twentieth century, for example, "60 percent of the residents of the nation's twelve largest urban centers were either foreign-born or of foreign parentage, and in many cities— Saint Louis, Cleveland, Detroit, Milwaukee, Chicago, New York—the figure approached and sometimes exceeded 80 percent" (Boyer 1978, 123–124). In addition, the first wave of sustained migration of African-Americans from the South to northern cities occurred shortly thereafter and raised concerns among progressive reformers (as well as the leaders of existing black communities) about how these transplanted, rural southerners and their children would adjust to their new surroundings (Spear 1967; Grossman 1989; Trotter 1991).

It was not an accident that Chicago, the nation's fastest-growing as well as one of its most "foreign"-populated cities at the turn of the twentieth century, served as the site for the establishment of the nation's first juvenile court in 1899. Illinois's model juvenile court act gave judges the authority to dispense with the legal principle of uniformity—the dictate that like cases should be treated in a uniform fashion—and to handle like cases in dissimilar manners (Sutherland 1924, 12–13). The founders of the juvenile court designed it partly to address the problems posed by difference in the modern world: How should the justice system handle the cases of children from different backgrounds and with different needs? What personal characteristics and environmental factors should courts take into consideration when processing an individual child's case? As a result, the founders of the juvenile court left future policy makers with the enduring issue of how to prevent officials from using their discretion in ways that institutionalized unacceptable forms of discrimination.

The chapter first analyzes the foundational principles of American juvenile justice. It examines how the court was created by child savers primarily to divert all juvenile offenders from the criminal justice system, but also to speed up the Americanization process for the "foreign" children, who were the vast majority of the court's early clientele. Concerns about Americanization, however, gradually diminished after Congress's passage of the Johnson-Reed Immigration Act of 1924, which limited immigration to 150,000 annually, established quotas for the number of "new immigrants" from southern and eastern Europe, and banned entirely the entrance into the country of persons who were ineligible for citizenship. This provision, in effect, banned Asians—half the world's population—from coming to America (Ngai 2004).

Ultimately, the principle of diversion, not Americanization, proved to be the court's more lasting contribution. The chapter then examines how the court responded to the increasing number of cases of black children in the early twentieth century. It concludes with an analysis of why an appreciation of the legal and social construction of race and an understanding of the original mission for juvenile justice may help practitioners and policy makers to address the continuing problem of overrepresentation of minorities in American juvenile justice (Bilchik 1999).

The Mission of Juvenile Justice: Diversion and Americanization

The historian Michael Grossberg has argued that American child welfare policy has vacillated between a fear for children and a fear of them (Grossberg 2002). The juvenile court movement certainly combined both of these fears. The progressive child savers, including prominent women reformers such as Julia Lathrop, a resident of Jane Addam's Hull House social settlement, who became the first chief of the United States Children's Bureau in 1912, were concerned that the criminal justice system severely harmed young people. They denounced it for transforming innocent children into hardened criminals and called for a more humane and constructive response to juvenile delinquency. As Judge Julian Mack famously asked, "Why is it not just and proper to treat these juvenile offenders, as we deal with the neglected children, as a wise and merciful father handles his own child whose errors are not discovered by the authorities? Why is it not the duty of the state, instead of asking merely whether a boy or girl has committed a specific offense, to find out what he is, physically, mentally, morally, and then if it learns that he is treading the path that leads to criminality, to take him in charge, not so much to punish as to reform, not to degrade but to uplift, not to crush but to develop, not make him a criminal but a worthy citizen?" (Mack 1909, 107).

The establishment of a juvenile court made it possible for legal actors to stop children from being held in jails, tried in adult courts, and imprisoned with adult offenders.[2] Richard S. Tuthill, the first judge of the Cook County Juvenile Court, explained: "the basic principle of the [juvenile court] law is this: That *no child under 16 years of age shall be considered or be treated as a criminal; that a child under that age shall not be arrested, indicted, convicted, imprisoned, or punished as a criminal*" (Tuthill 1904, 1; italics in original). The juvenile court would prevent the child from being "branded in the opening years of its life with an indelible stain of criminality" or to be placed "even temporarily, into the companionship of men and women whose lives are low, vicious, and criminal" (Tuthill 1904, 1). This diversionary rationale, as Franklin Zimring has shown, quickly became a universal principle of juvenile justice systems in almost every developed nation of the world and has remained so (Zimring 2000).

On the other hand, these same child savers who wanted to spare all children from being harmed by the criminal justice system were also fearful of what would happen to the nation if the boys and girls growing up in isolated "foreign colonies" in major urban areas remained "un-American"(Breckinridge and Abbott 1912, 66). Progressive reformers fervently believed that "the problem of integrating immigrants into American society could not simply be solved by giving them good jobs or distributing sufficient fruits from American capitalism, although these tasks were important. Immigrants had to be 'Americanized,' culturally and morally transformed from aliens into citizens, and given a sense of membership in and loyalty to the nation" (Gerstle 1994, 1050–1051). Supporters of the juvenile court believed that it had a role, even if a somewhat limited one, to play in the Americanization process of its wards.

In the Midwest during the early twentieth century, "foreign" children constituted the bulk of the caseloads for juvenile courts. In Milwaukee, for example, Steven Schlossman discovered that "over 90 percent of the children brought into court between 1907 and 1911 were the offspring of European immigrants. Of these, three out of four were either German or Polish" (Schlossman 1977, 144). Similarly, in Chicago, from 1899 to 1909, children with at least one immigrant parent accounted for over 72% of the delinquency cases heard by the court. Children with German (19.2%), Polish (12.4%), and Irish parents (9.7%) accounted for approximately 40% of the court's delinquency cases during its first decade of operations (Breckinridge and Abbott 1912, 61).

From the perspective of the child savers, these "foreign" children and their families, who were a majority of the population in the nation's largest cities, posed a real threat to social order. Unless these children were Americanized, they would not be able to preserve the nation's values and perpetuate its institutions. Obstructing the Americanization process, as the social investigators Breckinridge and Abbott pointed out, was the fact that "the foreign born residents of Chicago and of other large cities of the country, tend to segregate themselves in separate national groups where, in churches and schools, and in social, fraternal, and national organizations, the speech, the ideals, and to some extent the manner of life of the mother country are zealously preserved and guarded. In these large foreign colonies, which lead to a more or less isolated group life, there is therefore a problem of adaptation both difficult and complex; a problem which is especially perplexing in connection with the proper discipline of the American born children" (Breckinridge and Abbott 1912, 55). How, in other words, would these children be taught what it meant to be an American?

The progressive answer was to make the state into a parent (Rothman 1978). Through compulsory education laws and institutions such as the juvenile court, the state would exercise a parental role in this process of disciplining these children. As Timothy Hurley, the first chief probation officer of the Chicago Juvenile Court, declared, "the state is, after all, the first great father, and has a right, in the absence of proper care from the natural parents, to step in and take upon itself the work which the natural parents had proved themselves unable to do" (Hurley 1904, 10). And, as Breckinridge and Abbott noted, children who may "speak Polish, Hungarian, Russian, or Yiddish" at home had "to be trained for a civic life that has grown out of American experience and Anglo-Saxon tradition, and for an industrial life based on new world ideas of industrial organization and commercial justice" (Breckinridge and Abbott 1912, 56). In this regard, the solution to the problems posed by the influx of European immigrants was to use the state's power of *parens patriae* (the state as father or parent) to accelerate the process of Americanizing their offspring.

Significantly, in their classic study *The Delinquent Child and the Home,* Breckinridge and Abbott included "colored" children in their chapter entitled "The Child of the Immigrant." As they noted, "Nor is the problem of separateness of life and ideals limited to the so-called foreign groups. Difference of language is an effective barrier, but difference of color is a more effective and a more permanent one. It is necessary, therefore, for many purposes, to class with the various foreign colonies the 30,000 native colored citizens of Chicago, who although they do not suffer from lack of a common language, are barred from the complete enjoyment of many so-called common rights by a prejudice which manifests itself in many and subtle ways" (Breckinridge and Abbott 1912, 56). This inclusion of "colored" children with the "foreign" children demonstrates that the binary opposition of "white" and "black," which would dominate discussions of race relations by midcentury, had not yet taken firm hold among social scientists (Jacobson 1998). In addition, their suggestion that "color" might be a more permanent barrier than "language" was an ominous prediction.

In the paragraph following their discussion of "the colored citizens," Breckinridge and Abbott discussed "large national and racial groups which are maintaining a more or less independent community life" (Breckinridge and Abbott 1912, 56). Since this paragraph immediately followed the analysis of "colored" citizens, "racial groups" may be read to refer to blacks and whites. On the other hand, since this paragraph focused exclusively on European immigrants, this reference to "racial groups" can also be read to refer only to white races. This ambiguity captured the uncertain nature of "race" in this transitional era, a period when Americans still spoke about white races. From approximately the 1840s through the 1920s Americans used "race" not only to distinguish between "white" and "nonwhite" races, but also to classify the various "white" races, including Anglo-Saxons, Celts, Hebrews, Iberics, Latins, Mediterraneans, Slavs, and Teutons (Jacobson 1998). Fueled by concerns over white immigration, these discussions sought to ascertain which of these white races were "fit for self-government" in the American republic.

In *The Philadelphia Negro: A Social Study,* published the same year the Chicago Juvenile Court opened, the sociologist W. E. B. Du Bois commented on how Americans used race to structure citizenship. He explained, "We grant full citizenship in the World Commonwealth to the 'Anglo-Saxon' (whatever that may mean), the Teuton and the Latin; then with just a shade of reluctance we extend it to the Celt and Slav. We half deny it to the yellow races of Asia, admit the brown Indians to an anteroom only on the strength of an undeniable past; but with the Negroes of Africa we come to a full stop, and in its heart the civilized world with one accord denies that these come within the pale of nineteenth-century Humanity" (Du Bois [1899] 1996, 386–387). After the 1920s, however, Americans increasingly classified all whites as belonging to a single Caucasian race and used "ethnicity" to differentiate among white people, and thus minimize their differences from one another. As Matthew Jacobson has pointed out, "by the election of 1960 a Celt could become president, and though his religion might have been cause for concern in some quarters, his race never was" (Jacobson 1998, 92).

Thus, the initial mission of the juvenile court was not only to divert all children from the criminal justice system, but also to help Americanize the children growing up in "foreign colonies" who came before the court. Along with the public schools, the court sought to ensure that children acquired "at the earliest possible moment the use of the English language and an understanding of American institutions" before ultimately securing legitimate work in the new industrial economy (Breckinridge and Abbott 1912, 56). Yet in the early twentieth century many factors, including budgetary constraints and political opposition, limited the power of the juvenile court to Americanize "foreign" children. And, as fears about the "foreign" populations of American cities slowly dissipated,[3] the basic principle of the new court—diverting children from the harmful criminal justice system—turned out to be its most significant and enduring contribution, while the overrepresentation of minorities emerged as one of its most troubling and enduring problems (Bilchik 1999; Feld 1999).

The Limits of Early Juvenile Justice

Although juvenile court laws provided the legal flexibility to fashion individualized treatments in order to rehabilitate offenders, judges generally received minimal resources with which to exercise this discretion (Rothman

1980). A lack of funding prevented juvenile courts in American cities in the early twentieth century from developing the apparatus—especially adequately staffed probation departments—they would have required to become truly powerful forces for Americanizing children and their parents. As Julia Lathrop observed of Chicago, heavy caseloads that averaged between 50 and 150 children per officer made it unrealistic to expect a probation officer "to exercise much more than the somewhat humorously designated 'official parenthood' over most members of such a brood" (Lathrop 1905, 346). Chicago's overworked probation officers were representative; across the nation the majority of juvenile probation officers were overworked and underpaid (Tanenhaus 2004). Thus, it is more accurate to consider the juvenile court as one of many public and private institutions, such as schools and social settlements, which contributed to the process of Americanization in this period, while larger social forces such as the rise and spread of mass culture probably played a more significant role in the long run (Cohen 1990).

In Chicago, a privatized system of child welfare, religious tensions, and a developing color line all shaped the everyday practice of juvenile justice, including how the nation's model court processed the cases of many white Catholics and almost all "colored" children. The differential handling of these children's cases suggests that practitioners and policy makers should look carefully, when searching for bias in contemporary juvenile justice, at multiple decision-making points in the system at which children can be diverted, detained, or released.

Although the juvenile court was created in a spirit of religious harmony, within several years Catholic leaders, including the child saver Timothy Hurley, worried about the court's efforts to police their communities. Hurley, the president of the Visitation and Aid Society and editor of the *Juvenile Record*, had helped to draft the initial juvenile court legislation and had served as the first chief probation officer of the new court. In 1907 Hurley objected to the direction that Julian Mack, its presiding judge and a Jew, and Henry Thurston, its chief probation officer and a Protestant, were taking the court. The ensuing controversy revealed differential handling of children's cases, the blurry distinctions between juvenile "dependency" and "delinquency," the influential role of private institutions, and that juvenile courts in the early twentieth century operated in politically charged contexts.

The fact that a Jewish judge presided over a juvenile court with a heavily Catholic caseload was a potentially explosive situation. Judge Mack's supporters stressed that he understood the religious needs of Catholic children, and journalists often reported on his sensitive handling of Catholic cases. In one case, for example, a reporter described how the judge struggled with what to do with a boy who had stolen a bicycle but would not admit to his theft. "Suddenly he turns to the mother. 'Is the boy a Catholic? he asks. Yes.

'Has he made his first communion yet?' He is going to in three weeks. [To the boy] 'I'm going to give you another chance to tell me the truth four weeks from to-day,' says the Judge. 'This case is continued for four weeks. And I want you to try to learn to tell the truth at your first communion. You're to remember that; you're to try to learn to tell me the truth'" (Webster 1906, 399–400). Accounts like this demonstrated Mack's knowledge and appreciation of Catholicism.

Religious tensions and considerations had, in fact, contributed to the patchwork structure of child welfare in Illinois. Beginning in the 1870s, a largely privatized system of child welfare had evolved, in which private organizations managed institutions for dependent and delinquent children. These institutions, which generally had a religious affiliation, received monthly subsidies from the county based on the number of children cared for per month (Gittens 1994, 29–34). In 1899 the Illinois General Assembly had fitted the juvenile court into this preexisting system of child welfare. The lawmakers did not give the court jurisdiction over children already in private institutions or over any that the court might commit to these institutions in the future. In addition, to shore up support among Catholics, the juvenile court law required that the court commit children to "institutions controlled by persons who are of the same religious belief as the parents" (Pinckney 1912, 218). Thus, once a child was in an institution, the institution itself had control over the child and could release him or her without informing the juvenile court (*Report of a Committee* 1912, 16–17).

Judge Mack and Chief Probation Officer Thurston became frustrated with the practices of two Catholic institutions, St. Mary's Training School for Boys and the Chicago Industrial School for Girls, which released delinquent children without notifying the court. Although these institutions were nominally for dependent children, due to overcrowding in delinquent institutions the juvenile court had committed Catholic children involved in less serious offenses to these training schools (Breckinridge and Abbott 1912, 40). The court committed these juvenile offenders to these dependent institutions, instead of putting them on probation and allowing them to remain at home, because of the judge's reservations about the quality of the children's home life.

The institutions' release of these juvenile offenders without informing the court upset Judge Mack and Chief Probation Officer Thurston because they were worried about high recidivism rates. They believed that "persistent repeaters" diminished public support for the new court, which was still trying to establish its legitimacy as an institution that could help children and protect the public safety (Tanenhaus 2004). Not surprisingly, Mack and Thurston were angered when children whom the court had recently committed to St. Mary's or the Chicago Industrial School for Girls reappeared in court on new delinquency charges.

Although the court could not legally prevent the schools from releasing their wards, Mack used his judicial discretion to counter these releases. First, he placed more Catholic children on probation instead of committing them to these training schools. Second, he had Thurston assign probation officers to visit the homes of the children already discharged from these schools. Thus, the court extended its policing of Catholic children and their families.

Hurley was furious that the court was attempting to supervise these Catholics families so aggressively. He appealed to his political allies on the circuit court to remove Mack from the juvenile court. On June 27, 1907, the circuit court judges then met in a closed session to decide whether Mack should remain as the presiding judge of the juvenile court and, according to a local paper, "the vote was far from unanimous," but they decided to transfer Mack to the criminal court. After learning of Mack's removal from the juvenile court, Jane Addams declared that the judge's transfer was discouraging because "I considered him the greatest Juvenile Court judge in the United States" ("Removal of Jurist Brings Out Protest" 1907, 3). Although Mack was respected by the city's leading Protestant child savers, including the women of Addams's social settlement Hull House, he had angered influential Catholic reformers. And, as Hurley pointed out two months later at the grand opening ceremony for the city's first Juvenile Court and Detention Home building, "The poor may be indifferent at times and may be careless about their rights, but . . . where their children are concerned they will not be remiss in their duty and will not fail to remove any person who in any way misuses or abuses the power entrusted to him or her in regard to the administration of this juvenile court" (Anderson 1988, 1:219). Hurley had publicly warned the court and its staff to limit their policing of Catholic children and their families.

After Mack's removal, the practice of institutions' releasing children without notifying the juvenile court continued and provoked another political crisis. Mack's successor, Richard S. Tuthill, tried to stop these releases. Tuthill, who had also been Mack's predecessor, issued an order that declared: "No child shall be discharged from an institution until an order has been entered of record in said court. A probation officer shall be appointed to look after such discharged child in every instance, and make a report in writing to the chief probation officer—as often and as long as shall be by him deemed necessary" (Anderson 1988, 1:223). In response to this challenge to their authority, both Protestant and Catholic institutions hired attorneys. Faced with the prospects of a lawsuit, Judge Tuthill rescinded his bench order. As a result of these two controversies, the judicial attempts to extend the court's policing of children and families had been curtailed. Not only was the court's power to Americanize children further constrained, but the position of juvenile court judge had also become politicized.

These political struggles over the handling of children's cases reveal that despite the fact the juvenile justice was built upon the idea of judicial flexibility in the fashioning of individualized treatment plans for cases, discretion was actually dispersed throughout the system. The privatized structure of child welfare in Illinois led to Catholic and Protestant children from immigrant families having potentially very different experiences. Not only did the children receive different religious instruction in the various training schools, but the length of their commitments also depended upon an institution's release policy.

Even though Catholic and Protestant children's cases were processed differently, the children of European immigrants did benefit from their perceived "whiteness." As Chicago's black population substantially increased in the early twentieth century from less than 2% of the city's total population in 1900 to nearly 7% of it in 1930 and the city's South Side "Black Belt" was forged, most private child welfare institutions stopped accepting "colored" children. For instance, the Chicago Nursery and Half-Orphan Asylum (later Chapin Hall), which was founded in 1860, accepted black children until 1914 but then excluded them. As historian Kenneth Cmiel reported, "White hostility had risen after the race riots of the First World War. And migration from the South during 1917 and 1918 changed the racial composition of the city, hugely increasing the number of black children needing assistance. It was in this climate that Chapin Hall stopped serving African-Americans" (Cmiel 1995, 126). As the 1920s approached, private institutions, whether Catholic or Protestant, were accepting children based not only on their religion but also due to their "whiteness." By explicitly drawing the color line, private institutions limited the options that the juvenile court had in processing the cases of black children on the borderline of dependency and delinquency.

The Increasing Significance of Race in Early Juvenile Justice

Determining precisely how racial discrimination against blacks affected the operations of juvenile justice in Chicago (and elsewhere) during the early twentieth century requires at least two levels of analysis.[4] First, we need to know whether the juvenile justice system handled the cases of all black children. For if black children were excluded from the juvenile court based upon their race and had their cases prosecuted in the adult criminal justice system, then racial considerations shaped the very borders of juvenile justice. Second, we need to examine how the court processed the cases of black children *within* the juvenile justice system in order to see whether their cases were handled in a different fashion from those of white children. Since historians are only beginning to examine these related questions, the answers are more suggestive than definitive.

In the South, the region from which blacks migrated to Chicago, Geoffrey Ward has found that black children continued to be confined in adult jails, prisons, and workhouses well into the twentieth century (2001). Moreover, he discovered that many of them were also placed in the convict lease system and later chain gangs. These findings, coupled with correctional statistics about the number of youths in adult prisons in the Midwest during the early twentieth century (Cahalan 1986), suggest that race may have played a significant role in the prosecution of black children in the criminal justice system. However, addition research is needed to determine if and, if so, to what degree race played in the process of transferring children's cases in Chicago and elsewhere (Tanenhaus 2000).

Fortunately, there is some evidence about how the Chicago Juvenile Court processed the cases of black children in the early twentieth century. In describing the experiences of black southerners in general in this period, historian Jim Grossman has stated: "Migrants found a black community that seemed snobbish and condescending at times; but nevertheless the established community and the migrants shared one thing which set them all off from the rest of Chicago—race" (Grossman 1989, 160). Even though there were class divisions in the Black Belt, which narrowly stretched from the city's business district for more than thirty blocks south, as Grossman noted, race mattered more than class in the increasingly segregated city. The significance of race also became more apparent *within* the juvenile justice system. In 1903, the first year that data on race were available, the social scientist Earl Moses found that there were 56 cases of black delinquency—41 boys' cases and 15 girls' cases. In 1930, there were 657 cases; 503 involved boys and 154 involved girls. The percentage of black boys' cases had increased from 2.6% of the total of all boys' cases to 21.3%; the percentage of black girls' cases had increased from 6.5% to 20.9% of the total number of girls' cases. During this same period, the overall black population of Chicago had increased only from 1.8% to 6.9% (Moses 1936, 14).

In 1927, the percentage of cases of black children surpassed 20% for the first time in the court's history. During that year, 495 of the 2,197 cases heard by the Chicago juvenile court involved black children (Moses 1936, 14). And the court itself reported that it had to handle the cases of black children differently from those of "white" children. In the court's annual report Chief Probation Officer Harry Hill explained, "The difficulty of providing adequate care for the dependent and neglected colored children constitutes one of the greatest problems with which the court has to deal. The situation is complicated by a lack of resources in the community comparable with those available for white children in the same circumstances. Practically no institutions are to be found in the community to which this group of colored children may be admitted" (Hill 1927, 364). Due to this lack of facilities in Chicago's impoverished Black

Belt and the refusal of private institutions to accept "colored" children, the juvenile court committed black boys to the state-run St. Charles School for Boys—a reformatory for juvenile offenders—sooner than it would have in the cases of Jewish, Italian, or Polish children (Moses 1936, 16). In effect, the court processed the cases of dependent (i.e., abused or neglected) black boys as if they were serious juvenile offenders. This handling of these cases contrasted with the processing of the cases of delinquent "foreign" children who had committed minor offenses. In many of these cases, due to overcrowding in juvenile reformatories, the court had committed these white juvenile offenders to institutions for dependent children.

Committing dependent black children to a delinquent institution had several consequences. First, St. Charles delayed the parole of black children if they did not have suitable homes into which to be returned (Moses 1936, 17). As a result of early commitments and delayed releases, dependent black boys spent considerable amounts of time incarcerated in an institution for juvenile offenders. By the late 1920s, in fact, black boys comprised roughly a quarter of the inmates at St. Charles (Moses 1936, 17). Second, studies of recidivism from this period showed that "the chances of becoming a recidivist become greater as institutional commitments increase" (Moses 1936, 275). Thus, not only was the juvenile court treating dependent black boys as if they were juvenile delinquents; it may have also been helping them to become recidivists!

The juvenile court had even more limited options in the cases of black girls (Knupfer 2001). As Hill noted, the situation was "desperate," since "the State Training School for Girls at Geneva is the only institution to which they are admitted . . . [and] they accept but a small number of those who should be sent there." He added, "delinquent colored girls have frequently been held for periods as long as six months in the Juvenile Detention Home after commitment before they could be admitted to the school at Geneva" (Hill 1927, 364). Due to a lack of space, the court had to return many dependent and neglected "colored" children to "unfit homes where, under unfavorable circumstances, the court is forced to carry out treatment when only a small degree of success may be expected" (Hill 1927, 364). Therefore, delinquent black girls spent long periods in the detention home and neglected and dependent girls received few social services.

Thus, as the number of cases of black children appearing before the juvenile court grew over the course of the early twentieth century, the court's staff complained about the limited options in processing their cases. Whereas religion had been the most important consideration in the processing of the cases of children from "foreign" families at the turn of the century, as European immigrants were slowly becoming white Americans and more "colored" people migrated to American cities in the north and Midwest, the significance of race became more visible and tangible as the color line became more entrenched.

Historical Lessons for Practitioners and Policy Makers

This brief historical look at race, ethnicity and juvenile justice in the early twentieth century provides three lessons for today's juvenile justice practitioners and policy makers. First, it reveals that the concepts of "race," "ethnicity," and "whiteness" are legal and social constructions. They are not "natural" or immutable, even if they appear to be "common sense" (Harris 1993; Omi and Winant 1994; Ngai 2004). Thus, practitioners and policy makers should examine how unquestioned assumptions about these categories may affect the processing of juvenile cases in the twenty-first century. For instance, mid-twentieth-century efforts to address America's race problem focused attention on white-black relations but generally ignored other nonwhite minorities (Jacobson 1998). Moreover, the binary focus of these attempts to understand and improve the relations between the two races minimized the differences that existed among blacks and as well as the differences that existed among whites. This perspective often led to demeaning and nonproductive questions, such as "Why can't blacks be more like whites?"(Omi and Winant 1994, 20–23) This binary approach to the problem of difference not only stereotyped people, but also elided how European immigrants acquired "whiteness" and its accompanying privileges (Harris 1993). And, as we saw in the processing of juvenile cases in the early twentieth century, these privileges made a tremendous difference in a society increasingly divided along a color line.

The second lesson is about the mission of juvenile justice itself. Practitioners and policy makers should remember that the juvenile court was designed to divert children from the criminal justice system. Even though this chapter has revealed that there was differential processing of children's cases by the juvenile court, it is important to remember that at least these children's cases were being handled by the juvenile justice system, not the adult system. In addition, in future efforts to eliminate bias from the processing of juvenile cases, policy makers and practitioners should be careful about focusing exclusively on judicial discretion. Although judicial discretion was a foundational principle of juvenile justice, restraints on judicial discretion in the form of private institutions refusing to accept "colored" children forced judges in Chicago to process the cases of black children more harshly than those of white children. Thus, not only was discretion dispersed throughout the juvenile justice system, but racial bias at one major decision-making point also had ramifications for the entire system.

Finally, as this case study suggests, installing racism was a process that literally took time. That institutionalizing racial discrimination developed over time suggests that the removal of racial bias from modern justice systems is also a historical process. Thus, in order to fully understand the significance of race and juvenile justice, future scholarship must examine both the installation and removal of discriminatory practices from justice systems. When credible evidence suggests that racial bias is no longer part of a once discriminatory justice system, practitioners and policy makers should demand to know when and how it was eliminated, in order to determine whether this corrective process may be replicated elsewhere.

Notes

I would like to thank the editors, Darnell Hawkins and Kimberly Kempf Leonard; the reviewers, Steven Schlossman, Geoffrey Ward, and an anonymous one; as well as the members of the Faculty Research Seminar at UNLV (Andrew Bell, Gregory Brown, Maria Raquel Casas, Joseph A. Fry, Margo Lambert, Colin Loader, Michelle Tusan, Barbara Wallace, Mary Wammack, David Wrobel, and especially Paul Werth), for their insightful comments on drafts of this chapter.

    1. There are social scientific studies of race, ethnicity, and juvenile justice in the late twentieth century; however, see Bortner, Zatz, and Hawkins (2000) for a discussion of the methodological problems in this body of literature.

    2. By 1925, all the states, except Maine and Wyoming, had passed juvenile court laws (Lou 1927, 24).

    3. It is important to note that American cities continued to have large foreign populations well into the twentieth century (Gerstle 1994, 1060).

    4. I am indebted to Geoff K. Ward for suggesting this interpretative strategy, which also calls for further historical examination into participation of African-Americans as staff members of the court system and community organizers.

References

Anderson, Paul Gerard. 1988. "The Good to Be Done: A History of the Juvenile Protective Association of Chicago, 1898–1976." 2 vols. PhD diss., University of Chicago.

Bilchik, Shay. 1999. *Minorities in the Juvenile Justice System.* Washington, DC: U.S. Department of Justice.

Bortner, M. A., Marjorie S. Zatz, and Darnell F. Hawkins. 2000. "Race and Transfer: Empirical Research and Social Context." In *The Changing Borders of Juvenile Justice: Transfer of Adolescents to the Criminal Court,* ed. Jeffrey Fagan and Franklin E. Zimring. Chicago: University of Chicago Press.

Boyer, Paul. 1978. *Urban Masses and Moral Order in America, 1820–1920.* Cambridge, MA: Harvard University Press.

Breckinridge, Sophonisba P., and Edith Abbott. 1912. *The Delinquent Child and the Home.* New York: Charities Publication Committee.

Cahalan, M. W. 1986. *Historical Corrections Statistics in the United States, 1850–1984.* Rockville, MD: WeStat, Inc.

Christianson, Scott. 1998. *With Liberty for Some: 500 Years of Imprisonment in America.* Boston: Northeastern University Press.

Cmiel, Kenneth. 1995. *A Home of Another Kind: One Chicago Orphanage and the Tangle of Child Welfare.* Chicago: University of Chicago Press.

Cohen, Lizabeth. 1990. *Making a New Deal: Industrial Workers in Chicago, 1919–1939.* New York: Cambridge University Press.

Du Bois, W. E. B. [1899] 1996. *The Philadelphia Negro: A Social Study.* Philadelphia: University of Pennsylvania Press.

Feld, Barry C. 1999. *Bad Kids: Race and the Transformation of the Juvenile Court.* New York: Oxford University Press.

Frey, Cecil. 1981. "The House of Refuge for Colored Children." *Journal of Negro History* 66, no 1:10.

Friedman, Lawrence M. 1993. *Crime and Punishment in American History.* New York: BasicBooks.

Gerstle, Gary. 1994. "The Protean Character of American Liberalism. *American Historical Review* 99:1043.

Gittens, Joan. 1994. *Poor Relations: The Children of the State in Illinois, 1818–1990.* Urbana: University of Illinois Press.

Grossberg, Michael. 2002. "Changing Conceptions of Child Welfare in the United States, 1820–1935." In *A Century of Juvenile Justice,* ed. Margaret K. Rosenheim, Franklin E. Zimring, David S. Tanenhaus, and Bernardine Dohrn. Chicago: University of Chicago Press.

Grossman, James R. 1989. *Chicago, Black Southerners, and the Great Migration.* Chicago: University of Chicago Press.

Harris, Cheryl I. 1993. "Whiteness as Property." *Harvard Law Review* 106:1710.

Hill, Harry. 1927. "Annual Report of the Chief Probation Officer of the Juvenile Court." In *Charity Service Reports.* Cook County, IL.

Hurley, Timothy D. 1904. *Juvenile Courts and What They Have Accomplished.* Chicago: Visitation and Aid Society.

Jacobson, Matthew Frye. 1998. *Whiteness of a Different Color: European Immigrants and the Alchemy of Race.* Cambridge, MA: Harvard University Press.

Knupfer, Anne Meis. 2001. *Reform and Resistance: Gender, Delinquency and America's First Juvenile Court.* New York: Routledge.

Lathrop, Julia C. 1905. "The Development of the Probation System in a Large City." *Charities* 13 (January 7): 344.

Lou, Herbert H. 1927. *Juvenile Courts in the United States.* Chapel Hill: University of North Carolina Press.

Mack, Julian W. 1909. "The Juvenile Court." *Harvard Law Review* 23:104.

Miller, Jerome G. 1996. *Search and Destroy: African-American Males in the Criminal Justice System.* New York: Cambridge University Press.

Moses, Earl R. 1936. *The Negro Delinquent in Chicago.* Washington, DC: Social Science Research Council.

Ngai, Mae M. 2004. *Impossible Subjects: Illegal Aliens and the Making of Modern America.* Princeton, NJ: Princeton University Press.

Omi, Michael, and Howard Winant. 1994. *Racial Formation in the United States: From the 1960s to the 1990s*. New York: Routledge.

Oshinsky, David M. 1996. *Worse Than Slavery: Parchman Farm and the Ordeal of Jim Crow Justice*. New York: Free Press.

Pinckney, Merritt W. 1912. "Testimony of Judge Merritt W. Pinckney." In *The Delinquent Child and the Home*, ed. Sophonisba P. Breckinridge and Edith Abbott. New York: Charities Publications Committee.

Pisciotta, Alexander W. 1983. "Race, Sex, and Rehabilitation: A Study of Differential Treatment in the Juvenile Reformatory, 1825–1900." *Crime and Delinquency* 29:254.

Platt, Anthony M. [1969] 1977. *The Child Savers: The Invention of Delinquency*. 2nd ed. Chicago: University of Chicago Press.

"Removal of Jurist Brings Out Protest." 1907. *Chicago Evening Post*, 29 June.

Report of a Committee Appointed under Resolution of the Board of Commissioners of Cook County, Bearing the Date August 8, 1911. 1912. Chicago: Board of Commissioners of Cook County.

Rothman, David J. 1978. "The State as Parent: Social Policy in the Progressive Era." In *Doing Good: The Limits of Benevolence*, ed. Willard Gaylin et al. New York: Pantheon Books.

———. 1980. *Conscience and Convenience: The Asylum and Its Alternatives in Progressive America*. Boston: Little, Brown and Co.

Sanders, Wiley B. [1933] 1968. *Negro Child Welfare in North Carolina*. Montclair, NJ: Patterson Smith.

Schlossman, Steven L. 1977. *Love and the American Delinquent: The Theory and Practice of "Progressive" Juvenile Justice, 1825–1920*. Chicago: University of Chicago Press.

Schneider, Eric C. 1992. *In the Web of Class: Delinquents and Reformers in Boston, 1810s–1930s*. New York: New York University Press.

Shelden, Randall G. 1979. "From Slave to Caste Society: Penal Changes in Tennessee, 1830–1915." *Tennessee Historical Quarterly* 38:462.

Shelden, Randall G., and Lynn T. Osborne. 1989. "'For Their Own Good': Class Interests and the Child-Saving Movement in Memphis, Tennessee, 1900–1917." *Criminology* 27:747.

Spear, Allan H. 1967. *Black Chicago: The Making of a Negro Ghetto, 1890–1920*. Chicago: University of Chicago Press.

Sutherland, Edwin H. 1924. *Criminology*. Philadelphia: J. B. Lippincott.

Tanenhaus, David S. 2000. "The Evolution of Transfer out of Juvenile Court." In *The Changing Borders of Juvenile Justice: Transfer of Adolescents to the Criminal Court*, ed. Jeffrey Fagan and Franklin E. Zimring. Chicago: University of Chicago Press.

———. 2004. *Juvenile Justice in the Making*. New York: Oxford University Press.

Trost, Jennifer Ann. 1996. "Gateway to Justice: A Social History of Juvenile Court and Child Welfare in Memphis, Tennessee, 1910–1929." PhD diss., Carnegie-Mellon University.

Trotter, Joe William, ed. 1991. *The Great Migration in Historical Perspective: New Dimensions of Race, Class, and Gender*. Bloomington: Indiana University Press.

Tuthill, Richard S. 1904. "History of the Children's Court in Chicago." In *Children's Courts in the United States: Their Origin, Development, and Results*. Washington, DC: Government Printing Office.

Ward, Geoffrey K. 2001. "Color Lines of Social Control: Juvenile Justice Administration in a Racialized Social System, 1825–2000." PhD diss., University of Michigan.

Webster, Henry Kitchell. 1906. "The Square Deal with Children." *American Illustrated Magazine* 61:394.

Willrich, Michael. 2003. *City of Courts: Socializing Justice in Progressive Era Chicago.* Cambridge: Cambridge University Press.

Wolcott, David Bryan. 2000. "Cops and Kids: The Police and Juvenile Delinquency in Three American Cities, 1890–1940 (Detroit, Michigan, Chicago, Illinois, Los Angeles, California)." PhD diss., Carnegie-Mellon University.

Young, Vernetta D. 1993. "Punishment and Social Conditions: The Control of Black Juveniles in the 1800's in Maryland." In *History of Juvenile Delinquency: A Collection of Essays on Crime Committed by Young Offenders, in History and in Selected Countries,* ed. Albert G. Hess and Priscilla F. Clement. Aalen: Scientia Verlag.

———. 1994. "Race and Gender in the Establishment of Juvenile Institutions: The Case of the South." *Prison Journal* 73, no. 2:244.

Zimring, Franklin E. 2000. "The Common Thread: Diversion in Juvenile Justice." *California Law Review* 88:2477.

5

Race and the Jurisprudence of Juvenile Justice

A Tale in Two Parts, 1950–2000

Barry C. Feld

Introduction

A century ago, the processes of modernization and industrialization fostered a particular ideological conception of *childhood* and *positive criminality* and led Progressive reformers to create the juvenile court. The juvenile court combined the ideas of childhood innocence and vulnerability with new strategies of social control to create a judicial welfare alternative to the criminal justice system, to remove children from the adult process, and to enforce the newer conceptions of children's dependency. The juvenile court simultaneously affirmed the responsibility of families to raise their children and expanded the state's prerogative to act as *parens patriae,* or "superparent," and to exercise flexible control over young people in their "best interests." Because of some parents' perceived limitations, the social control of ethnic and racial minority offenders constituted one of juvenile courts' most important functions (Grubb and Lazerson 1982; Feld 1999). From its inception, the juvenile court sought to assimilate, integrate, "Americanize,"and control the children of the eastern European immigrants pouring into the cities of the East and Midwest (Sutton 1988; Platt 1977; Rothman 1980; Schlossman 1977).

Critical reexamination of juvenile courts' cultural and legal premises emerged only in the 1960s and culminated in the Supreme Court's *In re Gault* decision in 1967. By the time of *Gault* and the Warren Court's "due process revolution," the Progressives' consensus about state benevolence, the legitimacy of imposing certain values on others, and what rehabilitation entailed and when it occurred had become matters of intense dispute. Pluralism, racial diversity, and cultural conflicts challenged Progressives' consensus about the goals of rehabilitation. Empirical evaluations undermined Progressives' assumptions that correctional personnel possessed the technical ability to treat offenders effectively. Civil rights advocates questioned the benevolence of juvenile and criminal justice officials and criticized the invidious and discriminatory consequences of discretionary decision making. Increasingly, the Court emphasized procedural formality to regularize administrative decision making. In the decades since *Gault,* the Court's procedural decisions have provided the political and legislative impetus to transform the juvenile court from a nominally rehabilitative social welfare agency into a formal legal entity and fostered a convergence between juvenile and criminal justice systems.

This chapter analyzes the social structural and political context, the legal history, and the changing jurisprudence of juvenile justice over the past half-century through the prism of race. Race and race relations are socially constructed in a dynamic sociohistorical context and through political processes that interpret and explain variations associated with race and allocate power and resources along racial lines (Omi and Winant 1994). The first section focuses on the 1950s and 1960s and assays the macrostructural and racial changes and political forces that provided the initial impetus for the Supreme Court's juvenile justice due process decisions. The second section analyzes the sociological, criminological, and racial factors, media coverage, and political dynamics that led to the "get tough" reformulation of juvenile justice policies in the 1980s and 1990s. These sections contend that race has had two distinct and contradictory influences on the juvenile court during the second half of the twentieth century. The thesis of this chapter can be summarized succinctly—first the North went South, and then the South went North. During the 1950s and 1960s, the Supreme Court imposed national legal and equality norms on the southern states which still adhered strongly to a segregated and Jim Crow legal regime (Powe 2000). During the 1970s–1990s, conservative Republican politicians pursued a "southern strategy," used "crime" and "welfare" as code words for race for electoral advantage, and advocated "get tough" policies which ultimately have affected juvenile justice throughout the nation.

In the first period, during the 1950s and 1960s, social structural changes that began several decades earlier motivated the Supreme Court critically to reassess criminal and juvenile justice practices in response to broader concerns about racial discrimination and civil rights. The migration of African-Americans from the rural South to the industrial North and West in the decades before and after World War II increased the urbanization of Blacks and placed the issues of racial equality and civil rights on the national political agenda. The Warren Court's school desegregation, criminal procedure, and juvenile court decisions reflected a more fundamental shift in constitutional jurisprudence to protect individual civil rights and the rights of racial minorities. The second period of juvenile justice emerged in response to

Gault's formalization of court procedures and culminated in the "get tough" legislation of the early 1990s. Although protecting minorities' liberty interests provided the impetus for the Court's focus on juveniles' rights, during this period those procedural safeguards facilitated and legitimated the increased severity of delinquency sanctions that now fall disproportionately on minority offenders. *Gault* and the Court's due process revolution coincided with a synergy of campus disorders, escalating baby boom crime rates, and urban racial rebellions in the mid-1960s. National Republican politicians characterized these events as a crisis of "law and order," pursued an electoral strategy to appeal to White southern voters' racial antipathy and resistance to school integration, and engineered a conservative "backlash" to foster a political realignment around issues of race and public policy (Edsall and Edsall 1992). The increased punitiveness in juvenile justice, which began in the 1970s with the politicization of crime policies, peaked in the early 1990s as the surge in Black youth homicide rates provided further political incentive to "get tough" on youth crime through modification of juvenile court sentencing and transfer laws. During this period, media coverage put a Black face on youth crime and politicians exploited this perception.

I. The Warren Court and the Due Process Revolution

In the decades prior to and after World War II, Black migration from the rural South to the urban North increased minority concentrations in urban ghettos, made race a national rather than a regional issue, and provided the political and legal impetus for the civil rights movement (Lemann 1992). The civil rights movement challenged existing patterns of race relations and expanded the state's role in defining and responding to matters of race (Omi and Winant 1994). During the 1960s, the Warren Court's civil rights and criminal procedure decisions and the "constitutional domestication" of the juvenile court responded to structural and demographic changes taking place in American society, particularly those associated with race and youth crime. The constitutional and statutory recognition of Blacks' civil rights in the mid-1960s coincided with the baby boom escalation in youth crime and urban racial disorders, and by the end of the decade, Republican politicians began to exploit the issues of crime and race for electoral advantage.

Race and Social Structural Changes

More than three-quarters of a century ago, World War I curtailed European immigration and created a demand for Black southern laborers to work in northern factories (Trotter 1991). The outbreak of World War I simultaneously increased the demand for industrial production and reduced the availability of European immigrants to work in northern factories, and labor recruiters importuned rural southern Blacks to migrate (Trotter 1991; Gottlieb 1991). Between 1910 and 1920, more than a half-million Blacks migrated to nonsouthern states, followed by more than three-quarters of a million in the 1920s (Massey and Denton 1993). During the period between World Wars I and II, the devastation of the cotton crops by the Mexican boll weevil and the mechanization of cotton picking decreased southern demand for Black farmworkers and tenant sharecroppers (Trotter 1991). Worsening economic conditions during the Great Depression impelled an additional four hundred thousand Blacks to leave the South for northern cities. During this period, southern racial hostility, Jim Crow laws, Ku Klux Klan violence, outbreaks of lynching, poor segregated schools, and job discrimination provided additional incentives for Blacks to migrate (Lemann 1992). In the 1940s, opportunities to work in industries associated with war production during World War II induced more than one and one-half million Blacks to leave their rural homes. During World War II, twelve million men and women entered the armed forces, and fifteen million civilians relocated for new defense jobs. Between 1940 and 1944, wartime defense contractors integrated their workforces, and the Black population in urban areas increased dramatically.

When Blacks left the rural South, they moved primarily to cities. During the first half of the twentieth century, Blacks shifted from about three-quarters living in rural environments to about three-quarters residing in urban settings. In 1910, less than one-quarter of Blacks lived in cities. By 1940, half of Blacks lived in cities, and by 1960, more than three-quarters did. In 1870, 80% of Black Americans lived in the rural South; by 1970, 80% of Black Americans resided in urban locales, half in the North and West (Massey and Denton 1993).

When Blacks moved to cities, they lived almost exclusively in urban ghettos. Although African-Americans constituted only 2% of northerners in 1910, by 1960, they accounted for 7% of the northern population and 12% of urban residents (Gilens 1999). As racial diversity increased outside the South, northern Whites reacted to the flood of rural southern Black migrants with alarm and hostility (Hacker 1995). Threats, bombings, and violence reinforced racial discrimination and segregation in housing, education, and employment. Enforced residential segregation laid the foundation for the Black ghettos that now exist in virtually every major city (Trotter 1991). We will see in the next section that the ghettoization of African-Americans and the heavy concentration of violence and homicide within the urban, young Black male population provided politicians with an irresistibly attractive target of opportunity.

The post–World War II era also witnessed the suburbanization of America, as Whites began to move from cities to suburbs and isolated Blacks in blighted inner-city ghettos. In the period after 1945, federal housing, tax, and mortgage policies subsidized privately owned single-family homes (Katz 1989). The federal government simultaneously cut mortgage subsidies for the construction of rental units, and the Federal Housing Administration "redlined" sections of cities threatened by the "Negro invasion" and reduced the availability of mortgage and home improvement loans there (Gottlieb 1991). A massive federal road-building program and easy credit increased the number of automobiles and facilitated suburban growth (Gilens 1999). Even as federal highway policy subsidized White suburban dispersal, the location of interstate highways disrupted many Black urban communities and created physical barriers to contain their expansion (Katz 1989). Federal housing and highway policies contributed to and favored the development of predominantly White suburbs around the major cities and encircled urban poor and minority residents. Industry and employment opportunities began to move with the Whites on the highways to the suburbs.

Despite the postwar affluence and prosperity, the plight of Black Americans urgently demanded social and legal reforms. In 1948, the Democratic Party convention platform included a strong civil rights plank in response to northern Blacks' growing political influence and White liberals' opposition to segregation. In response, Strom Thurmond, then the Democratic governor of South Carolina, ran as a Dixiecrat in the 1948 presidential election, carried Alabama, Louisiana, Mississippi, and South Carolina, and demonstrated the power of race as a basis for political realignment (Edsall and Edsall 1992). Although Presidents Truman and Eisenhower took some important executive steps to address racial issues, such as integrating the military, Congress resisted antidiscrimination and civil rights laws, open housing laws, federal aid to education, and national health insurance. Even as the nation became more urbanized and racially diverse, conservative southern Democrats in Congress occupied key committee chairmanships and blocked legislative initiatives for racial equality, social justice, and urban programs.

During the cold war and McCarthy era, conservatives congressmen put advocates for civil rights and racial reform on the defensive. However, the legacy of Hitler's racist crimes and international competition between capitalism and communism for the allegiance of decolonizing nations of the third world required a national response to southern racial violence and apartheid (Kennedy 1997). During the 1950s and 1960s, the Warren Court's desegregation, civil rights, and criminal procedure decisions aimed to dismantle the southern system of White supremacy established by law and custom and to impose national legal norms on the region (Powe 2000).

Constitutional Jurisprudence and Protection of "Discrete and Insular" Minorities

Two decades earlier, the Supreme Court laid the jurisprudential foundation for the Warren Court's due process revolution. During the 1937–38 term, the Supreme Court distinguished between the scope of judicial review of economic legislation—where it gave the legislative branch broad authority—and its scrutiny of laws that affected personal and civil rights. While the Court granted legislatures broad authority to regulate economic matters, in the famous footnote 4 of *United States v. Carolene Products* (304 U.S. 144 [1938]), the Court announced that it would review more closely the electoral process to assure political fairness and would "strictly scrutinize" laws affecting racial and other "discrete and insular minorities" whose rights might suffer continually from majoritarian legal domination in the political process (Powe 2000; Cover 1982). The Court's emerging individual rights agenda recognized that racial minorities perpetually lost in the political process because of their vulnerability to scapegoating and race-baiting.

The great Black migration increased the visibility of the "American dilemma" and the plight of "discrete and insular" minorities and moved matters of race to the center of the nation's and the Warren Court's concerns about civil rights, crime policy, social welfare, and social justice (Myrdal 1972; Lemann 1992). The population shifts also altered the balance of political power and affected the characteristics of the justices whom Presidents Eisenhower, Kennedy, and Johnson appointed to the Supreme Court in the 1950s and 1960s (Powe 2000).

The Warren Court increased judicial activism to protect minority civil rights because "the questions associated with the Black experience in America raised, as no others could, the spectre of internal conflict between the values of a free and open political life . . . and of fair treatment of 'minorities'" (Cover 1982, 1300). In the South until the 1960s, law, custom, and whatever force was necessary combined to create a caste system of White supremacy. Southern Whites excluded Blacks from the political process, legally dominated them through duly enacted Jim Crow laws, and resorted to violent extralegal terrorism to enforce racial subordination. Terrorism flourished because southern law enforcement was almost exclusively local, political, and nonprofessional. Whites resorted to organized violence when the prospect of changes in prevailing racial mores threatened the lines between superiors and subordinates, between Whites and Blacks. In the absence of national legal intervention, private terror, legal discrimination, and political exclusion combined to disenfranchise and subordinate southern Blacks.

Race and Civil Rights

In the 1950s and 1960s, racial injustice and urban social problems presented volatile political issues that Congress was unable or unwilling to address because southern domination prevented adoption of remedial legislation. The task fell to the Supreme Court to fill the public policy void, to pursue racial equality, and to protect individual rights and civil liberties by dismantling the entrenched social and legal order of "separate but equal" deriving from *Plessy v. Feguson* (163 U.S. 537 [1896]; Powe 2000). Although the Legal Defense Fund of the National Association for the Advancement of Colored People attacked the doctrine of separate but equal in a variety of forums, the crucial battle in the struggle for racial justice and the dismantling of southern apartheid occurred in the effort to desegregate schools. In *Brown vs. Board of Education* (347 U.S. 483 [1954]), the Warren Court concluded separate was inherently unequal in public education. Although *Brown* ordered states to desegregate schools with "all deliberate speed," southern leaders challenged the constitutional legitimacy of the Court's decision and urged "massive resistance" to judicial imposition (Powe 2000). The modern civil rights movement drew on both national and indigenous southern groups such as the Black churches to create a constituency for racial change and included direct action and grassroots mobilization to augment the judicial and legislative activism of the movement's political elites (Omi and Winant 1994). Despite the successes of the civil rights movement, southern resistance to court-ordered desegregation in the 1950s, the Goldwater Republican presidential campaign of 1964, and the Wallace and Nixon campaigns of 1968 demonstrated the political power of racial appeals and "right-wing populism" (Edsall and Edsall 1992).

During the initial phases, the civil rights movement struggled to end segregation and to achieve equal rights and the right to vote. By 1964, political pressure generated by the civil rights movement and nationally televised violent southern reactions to Black protests led to passage of the Civil Rights Act of 1964, banning discrimination in schools and public accommodations, and the Voting Rights Act of 1965, prohibiting voting procedures designed to impede Black ability to vote. The Court's decisions, the passage of the Civil Rights and Voting Rights acts, and President Johnson's signing them into law created a national legal standard about race to which the executive branch, Congress, and the Court required the South to conform—during this period, the North went South.

The Due Process Revolution in Criminal Procedure

Beginning in the 1930s, the Supreme Court occasionally reviewed the administration of criminal justice to protect Blacks against southern injustice in cases like *Powell v. Alabama* (287 U.S. 42 [1932])—the case of the Scottsboro Boys—and *Brown v. Mississippi* (297 U.S. 278 [1936]). The early criminal procedure decisions involved egregious miscarriages of justice, race, and the death penalty (Kennedy 1997). Although the Court's oversight of state criminal procedures required it to depart from a century of legal tradition, precedent, and principles of federalism, the quality of southern "justice" made a mockery of the constitutional language of due process, with its mob-dominated trials, confessions extracted by torture, and appointment of defense counsel in capital cases on the morning of trial. The Supreme Court reviewed such cases because constitutional due process and national legal norms assumed that criminal trials should determine guilt or innocence based on admissible evidence. By contrast, southern state appellate courts often regarded any formalities of a criminal trial, however procedurally inadequate, as preferable to a lynch mob's summary execution. In many instances, southern criminal trials of Black defendants charged with the murder or rape of a White victim constituted little more than state-sponsored, formalized lynching (Klarman 2000; Kennedy 1997). Southern courts reacted especially defensively to criminal cases that challenged the Jim Crow legal regime, that threatened White supremacy, or that generated national criticism of southern treatment of Black defendants (Klarman 2000).

By the 1960s, the issue of race linked distrust of governmental benevolence, concern about criminal justice and social service personnel's discretionary decision making, rising youth crime rates, urban disorders, the crisis of "law and order," and the Supreme Court's due process jurisprudence. The Warren Court's criminal procedure decisions responded to the structural and racial demographic changes described earlier and attempted to protect minority citizens and to limit the authority of the state in the criminal justice arena. Beginning with *Brown v. Board of Education* and culminating in the civil rights movement in the 1960s, equality became the watchword of constitutional law reform. The feminist, gay and lesbian, and antiwar movements drew ideological support from Blacks' struggle for justice, adopted similar strategies, and shared a common critique of dominant cultural values and power arrangements (Edsall and Edsall 1992).

During the 1960s due process revolution, the Supreme Court resorted to adversarial procedural safeguards and judicial rules to limit states, to constrain law enforcement and administrative discretion, and to protect criminal defendants' rights. Several threads weave through the fabric of the Court's due process jurisprudence: an increased emphasis on individual liberty and equality, a distrust of state power, an unwillingness to rely solely on good intentions and benevolent motives, and skepticism about the exercises of discretion in the treatment of criminals and deviants. During the 1960s, the Warren Court's criminal and juvenile justice decisions interpreted the Fourteenth Amendment to the Constitution and the Bill of Rights to protect minorities from state officials; to impose the rule of law, administrative regularity, and procedural restraints on official discretion; and to infuse governmental services with greater equality (Graham 1970). The Court's criminal procedure decisions followed closely on its civil rights opinions, because those accused of crimes in the states consisted disproportionately of the poor, minorities, and the young. The Court's decisions redefined the relationship between individuals and the state, endorsed an adversarial, rather than a paternalistic, model to resolve disputes, and reflected the crucial linkage among race, civil rights, and criminal justice policies.

The Supreme Court used three interrelated constitutional strategies to decide criminal procedure cases: incorporation, reinterpretation, and equal protection (Graham 1970; Powe 2000). It incorporated provisions of the Bill of Rights into the Fourteenth Amendment's due process clause and applied those clauses to the states. In so doing, it redefined the relationship between federal constitutional authority and state police practices and criminal and juvenile justice administration. Second, it reinterpreted those provisions, expanded the meanings of those rights, exercised greater judicial oversight over local law enforcement officials, and extended constitutional safeguards to administrative officials previously immune from judicial scrutiny. Finally, the Court used equal protection to redress imbalances between White and non-White and rich and poor criminal defendants.

The Due Process Revolution in Juvenile Justice and In re Gault

During the 1960s, several forces combined to erode support for the "rehabilitative ideal" and encouraged the Supreme Court to require more procedural safeguards in juvenile justice administration. Left-wing critics of rehabilitation characterized penal programs as coercive and discriminatory instruments of social control through which the state oppressed the poor and minorities (American Friends Service Committee 1971). Liberals criticized the unequal treatment of similarly situated offenders that resulted from clinical personnel's exercise of discretion and contended that rehabilitation required a voluntary desire to change (Allen 1981; Mauer 1999). Evaluation studies questioned "what works," undermined the scientific bases of the treatment ideology, and further eroded support for rehabilitation (Garland 2001). Conservatives advocated "law and order" and favored repression over rehabilitation. During the turbulent 1960s, they perceived a fundamental breakdown of the moral and legal order in the rising crime rates, civil rights marches and civil disobedience, students' protests against the war in Vietnam, and urban and campus turmoil (Cullen and Gilbert 1982).

In the juvenile justice arena, the Supreme Court fired its first constitutional salvo in *Kent v. United States* (383 U.S. 541, 556 [1966]), in which Justice Abe Fortas observed that "the child receives the worst of both worlds: he gets neither the protections accorded to adults nor the solicitous care and regenerative treatment postulated for children." *Kent* required procedural due process in waiver proceedings that decided whether to transfer a youth from juvenile to criminal court for prosecution as an adult: assistance of counsel, access to the social reports on which the judge based her decision, written findings, and conclusions for appellate review.

The following year, in *In re Gault* (387 U.S. 1 [1967]), Fortas concluded that many features of juvenile justice system violated the Constitution and required a comprehensive overhaul. *Gault* identified fundamental contradictions between juvenile justice rhetoric and reality: the theory versus the practice of "rehabilitation" and the differences between the procedural safeguards afforded adult criminal defendants and those available to juvenile delinquents. *Gault* involved the delinquency adjudication and institutional confinement of a youth who allegedly made an obscene telephone call of the "irritatingly offensive, adolescent, sex variety" to a neighbor woman (387 U.S. at 4). Police took 15-year-old Gault into custody, detained him overnight without notifying his parents, and required him to appear at a juvenile court hearing the following day. A pro forma petition alleged simply that he was delinquent. The juvenile court judge heard no witnesses or sworn testimony, kept no record of the proceedings, and actively interrogated Gault about his involvement. After adjudicating him delinquent, the judge committed him to the state training school for the duration of his minority, that is, up to six years, even though an adult convicted of a similar offense could have received only a fifty-dollar fine or two months imprisonment.

Rather than accepting uncritically the Progressives' rehabilitative rhetoric, *Gault* examined the punitive realities of juvenile justice administration. The Court candidly appraised the realities of recidivism, failures of rehabilitation, the stigma of a delinquency label, breaches of confidentiality, conditions of confinement, and the arbitrariness of the process. As a matter of constitutional due process, *Gault* mandated that states provide some elementary procedural safeguards for delinquents charged with crimes and facing confinement: advanced notice of charges, a fair and impartial hearing, the right to counsel, the right to confront and cross examine witnesses, and the privilege against self-incrimination. Once *Gault* granted delinquents the privilege against self-incrimination, proponents of the juvenile court no longer could characterize delinquency proceedings either as "noncriminal" or as "nonadversarial." The Fifth Amendment privilege, more than any other provision of the Bill of Rights, serves as the guarantor of an adversarial process and the primary mechanism to maintain a balance between the state and the individual (Feld 1999). *Gault* represents a premier example of the Warren Court's expansion of constitutional rights and adversarial procedures to restrict the powers of the state, to assure the regularity of law enforcement, and thereby to reduce the need for continual judicial scrutiny.

The Court perceived a clear need for some procedures to protect delinquents and minority offenders. A survey conducted contemporaneously with *Gault* by the United States Children's Bureau for the President's Commission on Law Enforcement and Administration of Justice (1967) reported some limited data about the 207 larger juvenile courts serving populations of one hundred thousand or more. Three-quarters (74%) of those courts reporting the racial characteristics of delinquents disclosed that non-White juveniles constituted up to 40% of those against whom petitions were filed. Five percent of these largest urban courts reported that non-Whitesconstituted up to 60% of their delinquency populations. Virtually all of the juveniles who appeared in juvenile courts were not represented by counsel. Only 3% of the courts reported that lawyers accompanied delinquents in 40% or more of cases, and only one-tenth (10.8%) reported that counsel appeared in even 27% or more of delinquency cases (President's Commission on Law Enforcement and Administration of Justice 1967). Other analyses of juvenile justice administration from midcentury also provide evidence of racial biases in the handling of Black juveniles compared with Whites. A study of juvenile court disposition practices in 1964 reported that Black juveniles were more likely to be referred for formal processing and more likely to be committed to the state youth authority than were White juveniles with similar present offenses and prior records. Juvenile court practices appeared biased in favor of White, middle-class youths and skewed against lower-socioeconomic-status and minority youths (Arnold 1971). Another study compared the characteristics of Black and White delinquents committed to a state institution and found that the Black youths were younger, had fewer prior court appearances or institutional commitments, committed fewer and less serious offenses, and received fewer probationary sentences than did the confined White delinquents (Axelrad 1952). Although the confined Black youths appeared to be less seriously delinquent than their White counterparts, a lack of placement options other than state institutions accounted for the differences in patterns of commitments.

In subsequent decisions, the Supreme Court further amplified the criminal nature of delinquency proceedings. In *In re Winship* (397 U.S. 358 [1970]), the state charged Winship with stealing money from a teacher's purse. Although the juvenile court judge stated that he could not determine Winship's guilt beyond a reasonable doubt, the state statute allowed him to adjudicate him delinquent by the civil "preponderance of the evidence" standard. The Supreme Court reversed that decision and required the state to prove delinquency by the criminal standard of proof "beyond a reasonable doubt" rather than by a lower civil standard. The Court required the highest standard of proof to protect juveniles against unwarranted convictions, to guard against abuses of government power, and to assure public confidence in justice administration.

Five years after *Winship,* the Court in *Breed v. Jones* (421 U.S. 519 [1975]) held that the double jeopardy clause of the Fifth Amendment prohibits a state from criminally reprosecuting a youth as an adult after previously convicting him for the same crime in a delinquency proceeding. In *Jones,* the juvenile court initially adjudicated him delinquent for robbery, but after a presentence investigation concluded that he was not "amenable to treatment," the state then tried him as an adult. The Court framed the double jeopardy issue in terms of the applicability of a specific provision of the Bill of Rights to state proceedings and resolved the question by recognizing the identical interests of defendants in delinquency proceedings and criminal trials.

Despite their functional equivalence and similar purposes, the juvenile and criminal justice systems do not use identical, or even comparable, procedural safeguards. In *McKeiver v. Pennsylvania* (403 U.S. 528 [1971]), the Court declined to give juveniles all of the procedural safeguards of adult criminal prosecutions. *McKeiver* involved the fact-finding procedures used to determine the guilt of a youth charged with robbery, and a companion case involved the denial of a jury trial to Black children participating in a civil rights demonstration whom the state charged with the misdemeanor of "impeding traffic." *McKeiver* held that the Constitution does not guarantee a right to a jury trial in delinquency proceedings because due process and "fundamental fairness" require only accurate fact finding, which a judge could satisfy as well as a jury. Although *Gault* recognized that fundamental fairness required protection against governmental oppression as well as accurate fact-finding, *McKeiver* denied young offenders the right to a jury because it adhered to the ideal of *treatment* of children in a separate justice system. While the Court acknowledged the deficiencies and disappointments of the "rehabilitative ideal," it did not want to express its "ultimate disillusionment," abandon those concepts, and possibly return young offenders to the criminal justice system. *McKeiver* rejected the notion that delinquents required protection from the state, relied on the mythology of the paternalistic juvenile court judge, and minimized the threat to accurate fact-finding that closed delinquency trials posed. The absence of a jury affects the admissibility of evidence and the actual weight the fact finder gives to "proof beyond a reasonable doubt" and makes it easier to convict a youth in a delinquency proceeding than in a criminal trial (Feld 1999). The presumed differences between "treatment" and "punishment" also affect the delivery and quality of legal services in juvenile court. Decades after *Gault,* delinquents in many juvenile courts around the country still appear without the effective assistance of counsel (Feld 1993; ABA 1995; GAO 1995).

In the context of juvenile justice, however, *Gault* demonstrated the linkage between procedure and substance, because engrafting some procedural requirements at trial began to transform the court into a very different institution from the one Progressives contemplated. Progressive reformers focused on a child's social circumstances, environment and "real needs," intervened to rehabilitate rather than punish, and regarded proof of a specific offense as secondary. Although *McKeiver* denied juveniles a constitutional right to a jury trial, *Gault* and *Winship* imported the adversarial model, attorneys, the privilege against self-incrimination, the criminal standard of proof, and the primacy of legal guilt as a prerequisite to state intervention. By emphasizing some degree of criminal procedural regularity, the Court altered juvenile courts' focus from "real needs" to "criminal deeds" and effectively shifted delinquency proceedings from a social welfare inquiry into a criminal prosecution. By limiting the *parens patriae* theory and requiring procedural protections even when the state purported to act in delinquents' best interests, the Court provided the impetus to reexamine the underlying premises of juvenile courts and to shift them more explicitly toward traditional criminal law principles such as punishment and accountability. Formalizing the connections between criminal behavior and sanctions made clearer the criminal law foundations of juvenile courts that Progressives deliberately tried to obscure. By providing juveniles with most, but not all, criminal procedural safeguards, the Court legitimated the imposition of more punitive sentences. Once states grant even a semblance of procedural justice, however inadequate, juvenile courts more readily depart from a purely "rehabilitative" model. It is a historical irony that race provided the initial impetus for the Supreme Court to focus on procedural rights to protect minorities' liberty interests, those procedural rights permitted sanctions to escalate, and now those increasingly punitive penalties fall disproportionately heavily on minority offenders.

The Aftermath of the Due Process Revolution: Rights, Race Riots, and Conservative Reaction

Although complex structural, racial, and demographic changes in the 1960s contributed to the campus turmoil, rising baby boom crime rates, and urban racial disorders, critics of the Warren Court simplistically attributed them to the Court's criminal procedure decisions and to its moratorium on the death penalty (*Furman v. Georgia,* 408 U.S. 238 [1972]). By the early 1970s, this unfortunate confluence had important implications for race relations, domestic politics, and crime policy. Subsequent decades have witnessed a more conservative legal era and the Supreme Court's retrenchment of civil rights and criminal procedural safeguards.

During the second half of the 1960s, the focus of the civil rights movement shifted from ending apartheid and legal inequality to even more difficult issues of structural, economic, and social inequality. By the late 1960s, the Court and federal judges had begun to prescribe remedies to reduce racial inequality with far-reaching impacts on local schools, housing, and jobs. The Court's "rights revolution" also unleashed forces that would erode its political foundation by pitting the interests of traditionalists and liberals and of Blacks and working-class Whites against each other. In addition, the Court's decisions in the 1960s brought to the fore a host of other contentious social and moral issues—sexual privacy, contraception, school prayer, and the like—that further fueled a conservative backlash (Edsall and Edsall 1992). These opinions coincided with mounting opposition to the military draft and the war in Vietnam, and the claims for rights by gays, lesbians, feminists, and other groups. In the mid-1960s, under pressure of federal mandates, welfare rolls of the Aid to Families with Dependent Children program expanded, the proportion of Black welfare recipients increased, and politicians and the public increasingly associated poverty and welfare dependency with race (Gilens 1999). Among the political parties, the public increasingly identified Democrats with the new liberal and "rights" agenda and the interests of Blacks (Edsall and Edsall 1992).

A variety of structural factors—the *anomie,* stresses, and strains of urban life; the erosion of family and informal social controls; population density, anonymity, and heterogeneity; income inequality; and differences in family composition and community structures—all contribute to variations in urban crime rates (McCord 1997). In addition to the postwar processes of urbanization, the baby boom generation born after World War II created a demographic bulge, and rates of crime and delinquency began to escalate in the 1960s as the cohort moved through the age structure. Moreover, during the 1960s, urban riots rocked American cities as Blacks reacted violently to decades of segregation, deprivation, and alienation. In 1964, a White police officer in Harlem shot and killed a 15-year-old Black youth and set off the largest race riot since World War II. The following summer, Watts exploded in a riot. Thirty-eight riots erupted in 1966, and during the first nine months of 1967, 164 urban race riots occurred and augured the possibility of a national race war (Lemann 1992). The National Advisory Commission on Civil Disorders (1968), popularly known as the Kerner Commission, attributed the riots to a legacy of racial discrimination in employment, education, social services, and housing. Established in the aftermath of the riots, the Kerner Commission (National Advisory Commission on Civil Disorders 1968, 1) warned that the United States "was moving toward two societies, one Black, one White—separate and unequal." Recognizing the historical prevalence and persistence of segregation, discrimination, and poverty, the Kerner Commission cautioned that continuing current policies would "make permanent the division of our country into two societies; one, largely Negro and poor, located in the central cities; the other predominantly white and affluent, located in the suburbs" (National Advisory Commission on Civil Disorders 1968, 22). Finally, the commission noted the media's role in exacerbating racial divisions. "By failing to portray the Negro as a matter of routine and in the context of the total society, the news media have . . . contributed to the

Black-White schism in this country" (National Advisory Commission on Civil Disorders 1968, 383). The next section of this chapter examines some of the consequences of the trends the Kerner Commission foretold of Black urban poverty and White suburban affluence, and how media coverage of crime and race continue to distort White Americans' perceptions of race and crime and contribute to punitive justice system policies.

Although the Kerner Commission found that social structural forces strongly contributed to urban crime and racial disorder, crime and welfare emerged as potent political issues because the riots changed many Whites' perceptions of the legitimacy of Blacks' grievances, enabled many Whites to attribute crime and welfare dependency to individual choices rather than to structural forces, and provided the context of subsequent political appeals based on race in public policies. In addition, divisions within the civil rights movement between nonviolent, church-led moderate leaders and more radical "black power" advocates who espoused race-based nationalism, violent resistence, and separatism rather than integration produced a fragmentation of efforts and added a more ominous rhetoric to Blacks' claims for equality and justice (Omi and Winant 1994). In a matter of a few years between 1964 and 1968, urban riots, "black power" rhetoric, violent confrontations about civil rights and student protests against the Vietnam war, soaring rates of Black illegitimacy and welfare expenditures, and rising youth crime rates coalesced in the public mind, threatened middle-class traditions, and strengthened conservative opposition. Many Whites associated these social ills increasingly with Blacks who they felt had failed to take proper advantage of the equality of opportunity that the 1960s civil rights and voting laws afforded (Hacker 1995; Gilens 1999).

"Get Tough" Politics, Media Sensationalism, and the Second Revolution in Juvenile Justice

[C]onsiderations of race are now deeply imbedded in the strategy and tactics of politics, in competing concepts of the function and responsibility of government, and in each voter's conceptual structure of moral and partisan identity. Race helps define liberal and conservative ideologies, shapes the presidential coalitions of the Democratic and Republican parties, provides a harsh new dimension to concern over taxes and crime. . . . In terms of policy, race has played a critical role in the creation of a political system that has tolerated, if not supported, the growth of the disparity between rich and poor over the past fifteen years. Race-coded images and language changed the course of the 1980, 1984, and 1988 presidential elections. (Edsall and Edsall 1991, 53)

By the early 1970s, escalating rates of youth crime, dissatisfaction with the "treatment" model, and the emerging "politics of crime" prompted calls for a return to classical principles of criminal law (Garland 2001). During the 1970s, critics of rehabilitation and indeterminate sentences began to swing the penal policy pendulum toward proportionality, determinate sentences, and "just deserts" (von Hirsch 1976). The "just deserts" critique of rehabilitation produced strange philosophical and political bedfellows: liberals concerned about excessive discretion and discriminatory decisions, civil libertarians concerned about individual liberty and autonomy, and conservatives who denounced treatment as "soft on crime" and who advocated "law and order" and a reduced state welfare role (Garland 2001; Cullen and Gilbert 1982). Because liberals earlier had criticized rehabilitation and indeterminate sentences as arbitrary and discriminatory policies, they lacked a coherent crime policy alternative when conservatives proposed to "crack down" on criminals.

By the 1980s, the structural transformation of cities, increases in youth homicide and gun violence especially among urban Black males, and sensational news media depictions of violent Black youths fanned public anxieties and further fueled political calls to "get tough." Widespread misgivings about the ability of juvenile courts either to rehabilitate chronic and violent young offenders or simultaneously to protect public safety bolstered policies to crack down on youth crime and provided the impetus to prosecute larger numbers of youths as adults. Culminating in the late 1980s and early 1990s, virtually every state enacted tougher statutory changes either to simplify the transfer of young offenders to criminal courts and to subject them to substantial sentences as adults or to require juvenile court judges to impose determinate or mandatory minimum sentences on those youths who remained within an increasingly punitive juvenile system (Torbet et al. 1996; Feld 1998). Both strategies de-emphasize rehabilitation and the circumstances of the offender, stress personal and justice system accountability and punishment, and base sentencing decisions on the seriousness of the present offense and prior record. Cumulatively, these changes reflect a fundamental inversion of juvenile justice jurisprudence and sentencing policies—from rehabilitation to retribution, from an emphasis on the offender to the seriousness of the offense, from a focus on a youth's "amenability to treatment" or a child's "best interests" to public safety and punishment, and a transfer of sentencing discretion from the judicial to the legislative or executive branches.

Macrostructural Transformation of the Economy and Cities

The "get-tough" policies of the early 1990s reflect the confluences of macrostructural economic and racial demographic changes that occurred in cities during the 1970s and 1980s. One source was the deindustrialization of the urban core, the emergence of the urban Black underclass, the epidemic of "crack" cocaine, and the accompanying escalation in gun violence and Black youth homicides (Massey and Denton 1993; Blumstein 1995; Feld 1999).

A second factor was media coverage that disproportionately put a Black face on young criminals and reinforced the White public's fear and animus. Against this backdrop, conservative politicians politicized juvenile and criminal policies and used crime as a code word to make racial appeals for electoral advantage.

Between World War II and the early 1970s, semiskilled high school graduates could get good-paying union jobs in the automobile, steel, construction, and manufacturing industries. The mechanization of agriculture in the South coincided with increased opportunities in the northern industrial sectors, and during these three decades, five million Blacks migrated (Mauer 1999). Beginning in the 1970s, the transition from an industrial to an information and service economy reduced employment opportunities in the manufacturing sectors and bifurcated economic opportunities based on skills and education. Between 1969 and 1984, full-time employment in manufacturing decreased from 26% to 19% of the workforce, while employment in the service sectors increased from 13% to 28% (Katz 1989). In 1973, for the first time since the post–World War II period of sustained growth began, inflation-adjusted real hourly wages stagnated and then declined—by 2.8% in 1974 and 0.7% in 1975 (Edsall and Edsall 1992). Moreover, the globalized economy and the overseas challenges to the domestic automobile and steel industries constituted race-neutral developments with profound racial consequences as low-skill, entry-level jobs began to migrate overseas. Working-class Americans and unions previously had experienced their strongest gains in the auto and steel industries, and these sectors were among the primary victims of the economic deterioration of the late 1970s and 1980s. The postindustrial transition adversely affected blue-collar White workers, who saw their own wages, benefits, and middle-class status eroded. Despite being previous beneficiaries of trade union discrimination against minorities, White workers strongly resented affirmative action programs to expand apprenticeships, jobs, and seniority to Blacks, which they perceived to be at their expense when they already felt under stress.

The emerging information and service economy produced a widening earnings gap between high school and college graduates as the better educated got richer and the less well educated got poorer (Katz 1989). In less than twenty years, the gap between high school and college graduate's earnings widened both because the former earned less and the latter earned more. As recently as 1975, college graduates earned only about 25% more than did high school graduates (Wilson 1996). Two decades later, the average earning difference was almost 100%, as college graduates' earning capacity increased and high school graduates' real earning capacity declined about 25% (Jencks 1992; National Research Council 1993). Between 1975 and 1988, the average earnings of entry-level college-educated workers increased from 130% to

180% of those of high school graduates. However, as a result of historical differences in access to and funding for higher education, only 13.1% of Blacks aged 25–34 had college degrees compared with 24.5% of Whites, and the proportion of Blacks aged 18–24 enrolled in college declined during this period while that of Whites increased (Edsall and Edsall 1991).

Recall that during the post–World War II era, as Blacks migrated to larger, older cities, Whites simultaneously began to move from cities to suburbs. Government highway, housing, and mortgage policies encouraged suburban expansion around urban centers, spatially transformed many cities, and contributed to the growth of predominantly White suburbs surrounding increasingly poor and minority urban cores. Even after the war, restrictive housing covenants and Federal Housing Authority regulations discouraged racial integration and fostered separation between Blacks and Whites. Other public policies and private institutional decisions—federal highway, mortgage, and housing policies, real estate sales practices, bank mortgage loan practices, and insurance industry decisions—reinforced and sustained increased urban racial segregation. Government mortgage policies down-rated housing in areas where Blacks lived and made it more difficult to secure home improvement loans. Tax policies subsidized highway construction but not public transportation, facilitating suburban growth but not urban access. Zoning laws restricted the construction of new public housing projects to areas where such housing already existed. In the 1950s and 1960s, urban renewal and highway construction disrupted and destroyed many urban Black communities. Public policies and private institutional arrangements created and sustained racial segregation, amplified and exacerbated the harmful consequences of concentrated poverty, and adversely affected the economic and social welfare of Black Americans. Sampson and Lauritsen (1997, 338) argue that "even given the same objective socioeconomic status, blacks and whites face vastly different environments in which to live, work, and raise their children." They attribute the negative effects of concentrated poverty to deliberate public policies to contain and isolate minorities. For example, 70% of poor Whites live in nonpoverty areas compared with only 16% of poor Blacks. Conversely, fewer than 7% of poor Whites live in areas of concentrated poverty compared with 38% of poor Blacks (Mauer 1999). Racial segregation, cultural isolation, and concentration of poverty constitute the cumulative structural consequences of a host of disparate public policy decisions.

The migration of Whites to the suburbs, the growth of information and service sector jobs in the suburbs, the bifurcation of the economy based on education, and the deindustrialization of the urban core increased racial segregation and concentration of poverty among Blacks in the major cities and altered the political balance. Between 1970 and 1986, the suburban population, overwhelmingly White, grew from 40% to 45% of the nation's total, and it now constitutes a virtual electoral majority. Suburban Whites are able to satisfy most of their public service needs—schools, parks, police, and roads—through local and county tax expenditures. As a result, the divisions between urban and suburban municipalities has weakened Whites' ties to increasingly Black cities and reduced Whites' self-interest in state or federal programs which primarily benefit Blacks and the poor.

Deindustrialization and the Black Underclass

Macrostructural economic changes have had a cumulative, deleterious impact on urban minority residents (Wilson 1987, 1996). Job losses occurred primarily in those higher-paying, lower-skilled manufacturing industries to which urban minorities previously had greater access, and job growth occurred in the suburbs and in sectors of the economy that required levels of education beyond that possessed by many urban minority workers (Wilson 1987). As a result of the economic, spatial, and racial reorganization of cities, the past several decades have witnessed the emergence of a Black underclass living in concentrated poverty and in racial, social, and cultural isolation (Jencks and Peterson 1991; Katz 1993; Wilson 1987). The structural changes reduced young Black mens' employment prospects and the pool of marriageable males. Punitive drug sentencing policies, which disproportionately affect minority males, restrict subsequent employment opportunities and place unskilled Black males at a further economic disadvantage (Mauer 1999). As marriage to unemployed or unemployable Black males became less attractive, unwed childbearing and female-headed households increased among poor Black women (Wilson 1987, 1996). Since the mid-1960s, civil rights laws have enabled many middle-class Blacks to take advantage of economic opportunities to leave the ghettos. Their mobility has deprived minority communities of the human resources necessary for social stability and amplified the effects of concentrated poverty among the "truly disadvantaged" who remained behind (Wilson 1987).

Differences in Rates of Offending by Race: Crack Cocaine and Black Youth Homicide

In the mid-1980s, the introduction of crack cocaine into inner cities and the proliferation of guns among youth produced a sharp escalation in Black youth homicide rates (Blumstein 1995; Cook and Laub 1998; Zimring 1998). The increase in homicide among young Black males provided the immediate political impetus to "get tough" on youth crime generally. Because of real differences in rates of violent offending by race, "getting tough" effectively meant targeting young Black men. The mass media depict and the public perceive the juvenile courts' clientele primarily as poor, urban Black males.

Politicians manipulated and exploited these racially tinged perceptions with demagogic pledges to crack down on youth crime.

Over the past three decades, the Federal Bureau of Investigation's Index Crime rates, juvenile crime rates, and violent juvenile crime rates have followed roughly similar patterns—increasing from the mid-1960s until 1980, declining during the mid-1980s, and then rebounding to another peak in the early 1990s, since which time they have declined dramatically (Zimring 1998; Feld 1999; Snyder and Sickmund 1999). Between 1965 and 1980, the juvenile Index Violent Crime and homicide rates doubled, followed by a second, sharp upsurge between 1986 and 1994 (Cook and Laub 1998). The rapid escalation in juvenile violence in the late 1970s, and especially in the late 1980s, the arrests of increasingly younger juveniles for violence, and the dramatic rise in homicide provide the backdrop for public and political concerns about youth crime and the subsequent legal changes (Torbet et al. 1996; Feld 1999).

The role of race and guns has special relevance for understanding states' changes in waiver and sentencing laws in the early 1990s. Most of the dramatic changes in patterns of youth crime in the late 1980s reflect differences in arrest rates for violent crimes committed by juveniles of different races and the unique role of guns. Since the mid-1960s, police have arrested Black juveniles under 18 years of age for all violent offenses—murder, rape, robbery, and aggravated assault—at a rate about five times greater than that of White youths, and for homicide at a rate about seven times greater than that of White youths (Zimring 1998; Feld 1999). Beginning in 1986, when the youth homicide rates began to escalate sharply again, the arrest rates of Black and White juveniles diverged abruptly (Cook and Laub 1998). Between 1986 and 1993, arrests of White juveniles for homicide increased about 40% while those of Black youths jumped by 278% (Sickmund, Snyder, and Poe-Yamagata 1997; Snyder and Sickmund 1999).

Juveniles' use of guns constitutes the proximate cause of the sharp escalation of youth homicide that began in the mid-1980s. The number of homicide deaths that juveniles caused by means other than firearms averaged about 570 per year and fluctuated within a "normal range" of about 10% (Feld 1999). By contrast, between 1984 and 1994, the number of deaths caused by firearms increased more than fourfold (412%) (Zimring 1996; Zimring and Hawkins 1997; Feld 1999). Thus, in the span of a decade, arrests of adolescents for killing nearly tripled, and the use of firearms by juveniles accounted for almost the *entire* increase in youth homicide (Zimring 1996; Feld 1999). Because of the disproportionate involvement of Black youths in violence and homicide—as perpetrators and as victims—almost all of these "excess homicides" involving guns occurred within the urban Black male population (Cook and Laub 1998).

Analysts attribute the changes in age, gun use, and race in patterns of homicide to the crack cocaine drug industry that emerged in large cities during the mid- to late 1980s (Blumstein 1995). The low price of crack increased the numbers of buyers and weekly transactions, and thereby the number of sellers to accommodate the demand. Drug distribution attracted youths because juveniles faced less severe penalties than did adults, and it especially enticed young, urban, Black males who lacked alternative economic opportunities (Blumstein and Cork 1996). Youths in the drug industry take more risks than would adults and arm themselves for self-protection. The availability of guns contributed to the lethality of violence, because those involved in illegal markets cannot resolve their disputes through legal means (Reiss and Roth 1993). The diffusion of guns within the wider youth population for self-defense and status also contributed to the escalation of homicides (Blumstein and Cork 1996; Cook and Laub 1998). The lucrative and violent drug industry, in turn, further accelerated the deterioration of urban neighborhoods, hastened the exodus of stable families, undermined the authority of community leaders, weakened inhibitions against violence, and provided illicit role models to attract more adolescents into crime (National Research Council 1993).

Rationally, concentrations of poverty, crime and violence, disease, welfare dependency, and failing schools in certain communities might suggest the development of a variety of policy approaches to enhance public well-being, to ameliorate social problems, or to reallocate resources (Mauer 1999). Instead, the intersections of race, guns, and homicide fanned a public panic and political crackdown that, in turn, led to the "get tough" reformulation of juvenile justice policies. By the early 1990s, the prevalence of guns in the hands of children, the apparent randomness of gang violence and drive-by shootings, the disproportional racial minority involvement in homicides, and media depictions of callous youths' gratuitous violence had inflamed public fear. Politicians promoted and exploited those fears for electoral advantage, decried a coming generation of "superpredators" suffering from "moral poverty," and demonized young people to muster support for policies to transfer youths to criminal court and to incarcerate them (Miller 1996; Zimring 1998).

Media Coverage Puts a Black Face on Youth Crime

Media coverage of crime has contributed to the success of proponents of "get tough" juvenile justice policies (Mauer 1999). Reflecting housing patterns that began with the great migration nearly a century ago, most Black and White Americans live residentially segregated lives (Massey and Denton 1993; Kinder and Mendelberg 1995). Some Whites know about the Black underclass through direct exposure or indirectly from family or friends' reports of their experiences. However, most Whites' knowledge about Blacks comes from local television news reports about welfare, illegitimacy, drugs, crime, or unemployment, and this coverage tends to reinforce racial prejudices and stereotypes (Edsall and Edsall 1991; Dorfman and Schiraldi 2001).

Stereotypes enable people quickly to simplify and organize complex social experiences and to place people into categories that have meaning for them by focusing attention on information that is consistent with the stereotype and by ignoring or interpreting the information that contradicts it. The stereotypes that Whites hold of Blacks function as a perceptual screen that recognizes evidence that supports the stereotype and blocks information that contradicts it. The term "offender" itself elicits a predictable, negative stereotype—"an outsider, a young, lower-class male, physically unattractive, who has been convicted of a crime involving violence" with a clear racial coloration (Roberts 1992, 138). Media professionals who construct "news" unconsciously may cater to their White viewers' or readers' stereotypes and may use images, pictures, and stories with a racial content that their viewers more readily will recognize (Gilens 1999).

Crime is socially constructed, and "frames" represent alternative ways to interpret the phenomena and carry with them different policy implications (Beckett and Sasson 2000). The choice to get tough on youth crime reflects the ascendance of certain ways of understanding and framing crime in the political and media cultures and a decision to emphasize punishment and imprisonment policies over other, more humane policies (Mauer 1999). The intensification of punitiveness reflects the media's and politicians' representations and discussions of crime. Although news coverage may reflect public concerns, it far more often influences them by "priming" popular perceptions by the weight of coverage attached to an issue (Valentino 1999). Popular attitudes about crime typically follow political discourse and media portrayals (Roberts 1992). Public concerns, rather than responding to real changes in crime rates and dictating political reactions, appear to respond to political claims and media coverage (Beckett 1997).

News media coverage has systematically distorted reality by disproportionately overreporting violent crime and by overemphasizing the role of minority perpetrators in the commission of violent crime and thereby affected public perceptions (Dorfman and Schiraldi 2001). The overemphasis on violence and the involvement of racial minorities primes racial stereotypes and prejudice which, in turn, fuel harsher policies toward criminals. Crime news coverage amplifies, rather than challenges, claims of politicians about the severity of and need to get tough to suppress crime.

Media Coverage: Crime Is Violent

Most peoples' knowledge of the world around them comes from their local television news (Entman 1990; Roberts 1992; Oliver 1999). Local news programming favors an "action news" format to increase audience shares. Crime news focuses on the most frightening and sensational forms of violence because these stories are concrete, visual, and emotionally powerful. In standard crime news coverage, a news anchor announces a violent crime, a camera at the scene then follows with a firsthand account of the offense from victims, relatives, or bystanders, and a final scene focuses on the offender's identity and police efforts to apprehend the perpetrator. Local crime news coverage typically follows a standard script that consists of two principle elements (Gilliam et al. 1996; Gilliam and Iyengar 2000). The first element is that crime is violent—murder, rape, robbery, or gang violence. The second element features the "usual suspects"—minority perpetrators. The standard script's combining of images of violence and race exerts a pervasive and cumulative influence on popular opinion and public policy because viewers exposed to violent and racial imagery tend to support more punitive policies (Peffley, Shields, and Williams 1996; Gilliam et al. 1996).

News media depictions of crime do not reflect either rates of crime generally, the proportion of violent crime, or the proportion of crime committed by minorities, but instead systematically misrepresent reality (Dorfman and Schiraldi 2001). Local and network television news and television news magazines devote more coverage to crime, especially violence, than they do to any other subject . Local television news, in particular, disproportionately overreport the rarest types of crime, such as murder and rape: "if it bleeds, it leads" (Roberts 1992; Entman and Rojecki 2000). During the 1990s, overall violent crime decreased 20% while news coverage increased 83%, and homicides declined by one-third while network news coverage increased 473% (Dorfman and Schiraldi 2001). Although homicide accounts for less than 1% of all crime, it constitutes more than one-quarter of all crime coverage (Beckett and Sasson 2000; Gilliam and Iyengar 2000; Gilliam et al. 1996). Focusing so heavily on the most unusual crimes creates the misleading impression that they are typical. Moreover, violent crimes depicted in the media typically involve strangers, even though acquaintances or intimates commit most violent crimes and thereby reinforce a public perception of criminals as outsiders and predators.

Crime coverage also tends to be episodic rather than contextual and to focus on individual stories rather than to analyze crime trends or provide a broader perspective. Virtually all crime news lacks analyses of the larger social contexts, neighborhood conditions, or risk factors in a particular community associated with violence or rates of offending. Concrete examples and compelling anecdotes affect public perceptions more powerfully than do aggregate statistics. The absence of reporting about context or causation leaves the misleading impression that violent crime simply is inevitable and enables viewers to attribute it primarily to individual offenders' bad choices rather than to structural features. News coverage exacerbates the gap between reality—reflected in crime statistics and trends—and the public's misperception of reality and fails to provide sufficient bases and information for the public to make reasoned judgments or to evaluate politicians' claims about crime and justice policies (Roberts 1992; Dorfman and Schiraldi 2001). News media coverage of criminal justice administration typically emphasizes the system's failures—defendants freed on legal technicalities and lenient judges—and then presents advocates for more severe punishment as the remedy (Roberts 1992; Miller 1996).

Several organizational and structural factors skew local crime news coverage. Large metropolitan media markets span dozens of political jurisdictions and tend to focus on broad general coverage—sports, weather, crime, disasters, and human interest features—rather than the politics or policies of a particular municipality (Entman 1990). Crime fascinates the public and for-profit media seek increased market share through coverage of crime. News media working under the pressure of deadlines select subjects close at hand. Most news producers work and most Blacks live in urban areas, and this geographic proximity to minority offenders lends itself to their overrepresentation in crime stories (Gilens 1999; Valentino 1999). Media can produce crime stories regularly and efficiently by using official sources which lend an aura of veracity and credibility. Local police department are the main government agency open twenty-four hours a day for late-breaking news (Mauer 1999). News organizations' reliance on law enforcement agents as sources for information affects the depiction, coverage, and content of crime news reporting. Police may focus on violent crimes where they have higher clearance rates in order to portray themselves in a more favorable light. Journalists and editors consume the news they produce, and their systematic distortion of reality affects their own subjective perceptions, the editorial decisions they make, and the stories they subsequently present.

Media Coverage: Violent Criminals Are Black

The coverage bias toward overreporting violent crime further reinforces the public connection between race and crime. Although Blacks commit violent crimes at substantially higher rates than do Whites, news coverage portrays Blacks even more disproportionately involved in violent crimes than their actual commission rates (Gilliam et al. 1996; Hurwitz and Peffley 1997). Analyses of crime coverage report that over half of local television news crime stories explicitly refer to the race or ethnicity of the offender, 59% of violent crime stories implicate minority offenders, and Blacks constitute the largest identified group of minority offenders (Gilliam et al. 1996; Gilliam and Iyengar 2000). Stories with Black defendants are much more likely than those depicting White defendants to attribute responsibility to the individual rather than to the social context. Media reports more frequently portray Black defendants arrested for violent crimes anonymously, handcuffed, spread-eagled, or in police custody, and poorly dressed than they do violent White offenders (Entman 1992, 1994; Beckett and Sasson 2000; Peffley et al. 1996). Crime news stories' overemphases and portrayal of Blacks as threatening and menacing reinforces Whites' fears (Hurwitz and Peffley 1997; Peffley et al. 1996; Valentino 1999). Conversely, news media disproportionately depict crime victims as female, White, and affluent even though they experience less victimization than other demographic groups, especially Blacks. The "newsworthiness" of crime stories increases with White victims, decreases with Black victims, and is strongest when crime is interracial even though most crimes are intraracial (Dorfman and Schiraldi 2001).

The skewed emphasis on violence and the disproportionate overrepresentation of Blacks as perpetrators and underrepresentation as victims systematically mislead public understanding of crime and justice, reinforce Whites' negative perceptions of Blacks as dangerous, and promote pejorative stereotypes (Gilliam et al. 1996). Media framing, modern racism, and distorted public attitudes have led to a racialization of crime and public policy. Media depictions of crime in violent and racial terms activate White viewers' racial stereotypes about minorities, which then affect their views about crime and punishment and their susceptibility to political claims. The structure of coverage reinforces the explanation and interpretation that punishment is the most appropriate response to the crimes of bad individuals. These portrayals activate negative racial stereotypes, lend support to policies and practices of segregation and exclusion, sustain popular perceptions of Blacks as dangerous and undeserving, and foster more punitive policies (Kennedy 1997; Hurwitz and Peffley 1997; Gilens 1996; Gilliam and Iyengar 2000).

Experimental research reports that even brief exposure to a Black male in a televised crime story activates Whites' negative reactions based on global stereotypes about Black male violence. Experimental participants with anti-Black attitudes were more likely to misidentify and recall a Black subject of a crime news story than a White one (Oliver 1999). Such biased viewers also were more likely to believe a Black suspect was guilty, deserved more punishment, and was more likely to be violent in the future (Peffley et al. 1996). The negative and punitive perspectives of prejudiced individuals appeared impervious to contradictory information that refuted their racial stereotypes (Peffley, Hurwitz, and Sniderman 1997). Finally, public opinion appears to respond more strongly to images of race than to violence and to influence preferences for harsher crime policies. "The level of violence in news coverage of crime had no discernible effect on viewers' opinions. However, racial imagery in the news triggered fear of crime and a willingness to hold black people responsible for crime" (Gilliam et al. 1996, 19). Because racial biases tend to be stable, "cultural conservatives will find sympathetic audiences among this group, as long as they frame their antiwelfare and law-and-order policies as essential for the purpose of regulating undeserving and lawless minorities" (Peffley, Hurwitz, and Sniderman 1997, 52).

The Politics of Crime: Wedge Issues and Racial Appeals

The wide-spread adoption of policies to crack down on youth crime in the early 1990s are the culmination of the politicization of criminal and juvenile justice policies that began several decades earlier. Public officials may interpret social problems, such as crime, in different ways and respond to them with different policy prescriptions. "Claims makers," such as politicians, compete for public acceptance of the interpretations or frames they prefer and the policies they endorse. Over the past three decades, conservative politicians have successfully influenced public perceptions about the nature of crime, attributed the causes of crime to individual choices rather than to social structural forces, assigned responsibility to lenient justice agencies, and promoted policies to crack down on crime as part of a broader strategy for electoral advantage.

Civil rights activists used direct action and civil disobedience such as sit-ins to attempt to desegregate public facilities and in response to southerners' "massive resistance" to implementation of *Brown v. Board of Education*. Southern officials often reacted violently to protesters and characterized demonstrators as "criminals" and "mobs" fomented by "outside agitators" and Communists. Later, local and national politicians equated political dissent and crime, identified the civil rights movement's use of civil disobedience as a cause of crime, and urged its swift and severe suppression. Thus, early on, crime became a key element of political discourse about race.

Within the Democratic Party, divisions emerged in 1948 between northerners and southerners, and between racial and social policy liberals and conservatives over the adoption of a strong civil rights plank in the party platform. By the 1960s, the civil rights movement had heightened the visibility of Blacks in the South and forced the national Democratic party to choose between its White southern and Black northern constituencies. Although most Americans agreed in theory with principles of racial equality, many disagreed with the specific mechanisms that the courts and regulatory agencies developed to remedy inequality. The burden of integrating schools, housing, and employment fell more heavily on blue-collar and lower-middle-class White ethnic neighborhoods in the North and across the South. The expanding "rights revolution" and the associated social and cultural changes disturbed and angered many members of the White ethnic working and lower middle classes, who bore the brunt of these changes—civil rights for minorities, employment and reproductive rights for women, protection for criminal defendants, affirmative action and racial preferences in hiring for Blacks (Edsall and Edsall 1992).

During the turbulent 1960s, the sharp rise in youth crime and urban racial disorders evoked fears of "crime in the streets" and provoked cries for "law and order." Conservative political rhetoric framed the issue of crime in terms of dangerous and undeserving individuals who chose to commit crimes, rather than in terms of criminogenic social conditions that influenced their behavior. They promoted punitive criminal justice policies and undermined public support for social welfare measures. The Republican Party initiated a full-scale attack on liberal social policies and permissive Court decisions and ascribed the escalating baby boom crime, campus disorders, urban riots, welfare dependency, and social upheavals to the Warren Court and its liberal Democratic supporters.

Republican politicians seized crime control, affirmative action, and public welfare as racially tinged "wedge issues" with which to distinguish themselves from Democrats in order to woo southern White voters (Beckett 1997; Edsall and Edsall 1992). Crime policies for the first time became a central issue in partisan politics and acquired a distinctive racial coloration (Miller 1996; Gilens 1999). The polarization of the political parties on issues of race had its inception in the 1964 presidential confrontation between Lyndon Johnson, whose leadership led to the passage of the 1964 Civil Rights Act, and Barry Goldwater, a staunch conservative and opponent of the law (Edsall and Edsall 1991). That contest presaged the racial realignment of American politics as voters began to identify clear differences between the two parties on a host of race-related issues. Although the initial civil rights agenda focused on providing fundamental rights of citizenship for Blacks, such as the right to vote and equal access to public accommodations, the post-1964 civil rights agenda addressed broader goals of implementing rights and assuring equality of outcomes for Blacks, often through the use of racial preferences. Liberals identified social structural forces, racial inequality, and limited opportunity as root causes of crime and poverty, while conservatives attributed criminality and reliance on welfare to irresponsible individuals and argued that social programs only encouraged poor choices and fostered a culture of dependency. During the mid-1960s, the long-standing distinctions between the deserving and undeserving poor and the stereotypic belief that Blacks were lazy became intertwined when poor Blacks came to the media and public's attention (Gilens 1999). Conservatives strongly opposed governmental actions to redistribute public and private goods—jobs, education, housing, and the like—in pursuit of greater racial equality. Negative media coverage reinforced public perceptions and political depictions of Blacks as criminals and undeserving (Edsall and Edsall 1992; Gilens 1999).

[I]n the years following the civil rights legislation of the 1960s, racial attitudes became a central characteristic of both ideology and party identification, integral to voters' choices between Democrats and Republicans, and integral to choices between policy positions on a range of non-racial issues traditionally identified with liberalism and conservatism. At the same time, a wide range of social developments, including the emergence of a growing urban underclass and the associated problems of crime, joblessness, and urban school failure, were becoming, in the public mind, indelibly associated with race through the growing body of statistical information demonstrating disproportionate black involvement; through media coverage of crime, of declining labor-force participation among black males, and of a long-term (sometimes multi-generational) welfare clientele; and through increased public policy and academic interest in the intractable persistence of black and Hispanic poverty. (Edsall and Edsall 1992, 151)

The cause of civil rights changed the meanings of liberalism and conservatism and the perceptions of the Democratic and Republican parties. Many of the remedies instituted by the Warren Court to end discrimination and racial segregation and to grant legal and procedural rights to unpopular groups such as criminal defendants became associated in the public mind with the liberal agenda of the Democratic Party.

In 1968, Alabama Governor George Wallace's democratic presidential campaign helped to redefine the White backlash as right-wing populism against moral, racial, and cultural liberalism and elitisim. Similarly, Richard Nixon's 1968 republican presidential campaign attributed urban riots and rising crime rates to liberal "permissiveness" and criticized the Warren Court for "coddling criminals" and "handcuffing the forces of law and order." Nixon's strategy effectively straddled the conflict between general public support for the abstract principle of racial equality and growing public opposition to government-prescribed remedies for inequality. Nixon found a message that encompassed the position of the growing majority of White Americans who had come to believe that denying basic citizenship rights to Blacks was wrong, but who also opposed meaningful governmental remedies and court-enforced residential, employment, and educational integration (Edsall and Edsall 1991).

Republican political strategists concluded that they could find a receptive audience among White southerners, suburbanites, socially conservative ethnic Catholics and blue-collar workers and foster a political realignment through the use of racial issues and "coded" anti-Black rhetoric. Pursuing Kevin Phillips's "southern strategy" for electoral majority, Republicans courted the new constituencies with racially charged code words, such as "law and order," that indirectly evoked racial themes without explicitly challenging egalitarian ideals (Phillips 1969; Omi and Winant 1986). Since the 1960s, the national Republican Party has successfully converted criminal justice and social welfare "from subjects of policy to objects of politics" (Tonry 1995, 10).

Political reforms introduced in the Democratic Party after the 1968 convention proved more advantageous to the articulate and well-educated veterans of the civil rights, women's, and antiwar movements than to the traditional blue-collar and ward politicians in the competition for delegates. As the more liberal forces dominated the national Democratic party and worked to expand the rights of historically marginalized groups, Republicans courted many northern White blue-collar and lower-middle-class voters affected by legal remedies and redistributive national tax and welfare policies (Edsall and Edsall 1992). Moreover, because of the association between race, on the one hand, and violence, disorder, crime, and illegitimacy, on the other, liberals failed convincingly to address the increasingly conservative public attitudes spurred by rising crime and welfare rates and urban race riots. The inability of the left effectively to deal with these issues enabled "the political right to profit from explicit and covert manipulation of symbols and images relying upon assumptions about black poverty and crime—as in the Republican's 1988 campaign focus on the death penalty, Willie Horton, and the 'revolving prison door' television commercials" (Edsall and Edsall 1992, 114). Only in the early 1990s, under Bill Clinton, could national Democrats respond to the Republican's exploitation of the crime issue by embracing an equally tough rhetoric and fostering a bipartisan policy consensus for "law and order" (Kennedy 1997).

The increased racial polarization between Democrats and Republicans coincided with increased conservatism in public attitudes about other public policies related to issues of race. Americans value individualism and self-reliance—personal responsibility and individual choice—and these values tend to emphasize personal choices rather than social structural determinants of criminal behavior. The emphasis on individual responsibility and hard work also influences American attitudes toward welfare strongly to distinguish between the *deserving* and *undeserving* poor (Gilens 1999). Beginning in the mid-1960s, conservative Republicans advocated law and order, supported a war on crime, and favored repression over rehabilitation in response to rising crime rates, civil rights marches, students' protests against the war in Vietnam, and urban and campus turmoil. Evaluation research indicates that tougher penalties and increased use of imprisonment have relatively little effect on crime rates (Tonry 1995; Reiss and Roth 1993; Mauer 1999). Despite the absence of empirical justification for "get tough" policies, however, "sound-bite" politics, symbols, and rhetoric have shaped penal policies. Politicians fear being labeled "soft on crime" and avoid thoughtful discussions of complex crime policy issues in an era of 30-second commercials (Beckett 1997). Ideology, media coverage, and politics interact to produce ever harsher policies toward young offenders (Merlo 2000).

Political Rhetoric and Code Words to Appeal to Anti-Black Sentiments

Because it is "politically incorrect" to express overtly racist sentiments, research on "modern racism" attempts to identify closely intertwined, indirect indicators of racial animus such as anti-Black emotional affect, resistance to

Blacks' political demands, and a denial of the continued existence of racism or racial discrimination. Modern racism "is composed of a general and diffuse 'anti-black affect' combined with disaffection over the continuing claims of blacks on white resources and sympathies, rancor rooted in an attachment to traditional American, individualist values and in a conviction that racism has disappeared" (Entman 1990, 333). Modern racism perceives Blacks as overly demanding, undeserving, and threatening, and such attitudes emerge in media coverage and political discussion about welfare and crime policy.

Crime and welfare now widely serve as coded issues that enable politicians to play upon race—White Americans' negative views about Blacks—without explicitly playing the "race card" (Gilens 1996; Mendelberg 2001). Code words are symbols or phrases that indirectly implicate racial themes but do not directly challenge egalitarian ideals, which politicians can use to appeal to racist sentiments without providing clear evidence of racism or an intent to discriminate (Omi and Winant 1994; Dvorak 2000). By the 1970s, conservative politicians appreciated that they could deploy themes like "law and order" and "individual rights" to evoke racial understandings. By the 1980s, "welfare," "fairness," and "groups" had acquired implicit racial meanings as a backlash against liberal policies (Edsall and Edsall 1991; Dvorak 2000). The use of code phrases enables politicians to convey a well-known but implicit meaning—such as an appeal to Whites' racial hostilities—while being able to deny any racist interpretation (Miller 1996). Politicians manipulate and exploit these racially tinged words and perceptions for political advantage with demagogic pledges to get tough and crack down on "youth crime" which has become a code word for young Black males (Beckett 1997). "In the last quarter century especially, crime has become a coded way for politicians to talk about race, to signal to whites that they have their interests at heart. Capital punishment may be an especially effective venue for trafficking in racial fears and apprehensions. . . . [because] capital punishment for convicted murderers is extremely popular among white Americans" (Kinder and Mendelberg 1995, 413).

Race provides a focus for political conflicts over values, culture, and the allocation of material interests and implicates a host of policy issues—social welfare, neighborhood schools, the distribution of the tax burden, crime, drugs, and violence, family structure, and political allegiances (Edsall and Edsall 1992). As with violent crime, White American's hostility to public welfare reflects the majority's perception that most welfare recipients are Black, that Blacks evince less commitment to the work ethic, and that "welfare has become a 'code word' for race" (Gilens 1999, 3). Given the linkages in peoples' minds between race and other substantive issue, evocation of one issue, like welfare, also will activate other race-related issues, like crime (Valentino 1999).

In the past third of a century, conservative politicians and the mass media have pushed crime to the top of the political agenda by focusing on sensational and violent crime to promote "get tough" policies for political purposes. Since the late 1960s, Republican politicians in national elections have recognized the value of using anticrime rhetoric to appeal to White voters (Tonry 1994, 1995). Moreover, public officials constitute important sources of crime news. Politicians generate crime news stories to shape public attitudes and then purport to respond and promote particular criminal justice policies that they believe will provide them with a political advantage. For example, after Republican politicians declared a "war on drugs" during the 1980s and provided a steady stream of interviews, media coverage of drug stories increased sharply. These stories focused on crack rather than powder cocaine, increasingly depicted cocaine users and dealers as poor and non-White, participated in the creation of a "moral panic," reinforced "get tough" rhetoric, and abetted conservatives' advocacy of punitive laws (Tonry 1995; Beckett and Sasson 2000). An analysis of network coverage of the war on drugs between 1981 and 1988 reported that as the focus of law enforcement shifted from powder to crack cocaine, "the media frame shifted dramatically from white, suburban drug users in need of therapy to riveting images of violent black drug offenders in the inner city who were beyond the point of rehabilitation" (Hurwitz and Peffley 1997, 395). The 1980s war on drugs and the crack versus powder cocaine sentencing differentials under the federal guidelines produced a dramatically disproportionate impact on rates of conviction and incarceration of Blacks (Miller 1996; Tonry 1995; Kennedy 1997).

The 1988 Bush presidential campaign's focus on Willie Horton—a convicted Black murderer released on furlough who burglarized and stabbed a White middle-class man and raped a woman—tapped voter anger over criminal defendants' and prisoners' rights through the threatening archetype of the Black male rapist of a White woman (Anderson 1995; Mendelberg 2001). "Crime became a shorthand *signal,* to crucial numbers of white voters, of broader issues of social disorder, tapping powerful ideas about authority, status, morality, self-control and race" (Edsall and Edsall 1992, 224). Although the Bush campaign claimed at the time that Horton was about crime and Dukakis's "soft on crime" attitudes, rather than race, "By 1988, the assumption that black men were dangerous had soaked deeply into America's urban consciousness, powerfully reinforced by the steady flow of news coverage depicting black men under arrest, in court, in prison" (Anderson 1995, 217). Analysts of the Horton media campaign conclude that the appeal mobilized Whites' racial prejudices rather than their concerns about crime and that this, in turn, fostered great resistance to public policies to reduce racial inequality (Mendelberg 1997, 2001).

An association appears to exist between hostility toward Blacks and punitiveness in policy preferences; those who report great racial prejudice also tend to support more punitive crime control policies (Beckett and Sasson 2000). Conservatives' "law and order" rhetoric and veiled references toward race support and encourage such attitudes and policies. By the early 1990s, "youth crime" had acquired a coded meaning and juveniles had become another symbolic "Willie Horton"(Beckett 1997; Beckett and Sasson 2000).

Increased Punitiveness in Juvenile Waiver and Sentencing Policies

The politicization of crime policies and the connection in the public and political minds between race and youth crime has provided a powerful incentive to transform juvenile justice jurisprudence as well (Zimring 1998). Historically, a tension always has existed between social welfare and social control, between a concern with the best interests of the offender and with punishment and incapacitation for the offense, between safeguarding children and protecting society (Feld 1999; McCord, Widom, and Crowell 2001). In recent decades, the balance has shifted sharply from rehabilitation to retribution with the escalation of youth violence rates in the late 1970s and again in the early 1990s, and with public and political perception of youth crime primarily as an urban Black male phenomenon. The overarching jurisprudential themes of these legal changes include a shift from individualized justice to just deserts, from rehabilitation to retribution, from sentences based on the needs of the offender to the seriousness of the offense, from amenability to treatment and best interests to public safety and accountability, and a transfer of discretion from the judicial to the legislative or executive branches (Feld 1998, 1999).

Juvenile justice policies have become especially punitive toward youths charged with violent crimes, the offense category to which Black youths contribute disproportionately. Statutory changes make it easier for judges to transfer youths to criminal court, exclude certain serious offenses from juvenile court jurisdiction, and increase prosecutors' authority to file cases in adult court (Feld 1998, McCord, Widom, and Crowell 2001). The changes in waiver laws reflect a fundamental cultural and legal reconceptualization of youth from innocent and dependent children to responsible and autonomous adultlike offenders. "Get tough" politicians' sound bites—"adult crime, adult time" or "old enough to do the crime, old enough to do the time"—exemplify the reformulation of adolescence and represent crime policies that provide no formal recognition of youthfulness as a mitigating factor in sentencing (Feld 1997). State legislatures use offense criteria in waiver laws as dispositional guidelines to structure and limit judicial discretion, to guide prosecutorial charging decisions, or automatically to exclude certain youths from juvenile court jurisdiction (Torbet et al. 1996; Feld 1995, 1998). After controlling for the seriousness of the offense, juvenile court judges are more likely to transfer minority youths than White youths to criminal court, and the disparities are greatest for youths charged with violent and drug offenses (Poe-Yamagata and Jones 1999). Once youths make the transition to the adult system, criminal court judges sentence them as if they were adults, impose the same sentences, send them to the same prisons, and even execute them for the crimes they committed as children (Feld 1998; *Stanford v. Kentucky*, 492 U.S. 361 [1989]). Among those who have committed similar offenses and who have similar prior records, minority youths are disproportionately overrepresented among juveniles sentenced to adult prisons (Poe-Yamagata and Jones 1999; McCord, Widom, and Crowell 2001).

The jurisprudential shifts from offender to offense and from treatment to punishment that inspired changes in waiver policies increasingly affect the sentences that juvenile court judges impose on delinquent offenders as well. Progressive reformers envisioned a broader and more encompassing social welfare system for youths and did not circumscribe narrowly state power. Juvenile courts' *parens patriae* ideology combined social welfare with penal social control in one institution, minimized procedural safeguards, and maximized discretion to provide flexibility in diagnosis and treatment. Reformers focused primary attention on youths' social circumstances and accorded secondary significance either to procedural safeguards or to proof of guilt or the specific offense. More recently, however, the political impetus to waive the most serious young offenders to criminal courts also impels juvenile judges to "get tough" and punish more severely the remaining delinquents. As states' juvenile sentencing laws and policies increasingly "get tough," however, the distinctions between treatment and punishment and the Supreme Court's rationale in *McKeiver* to deny jury trials in delinquency proceedings become even more tenuous.

Several indicators reveal that juvenile court judges increasingly punish youths for their past offenses rather than treat them for their future welfare. Because Progressive reformers designed juvenile courts to discriminate and to distinguish between our children and "other peoples' children," these punitive practices fall disproportionately heavily on minority youths (Feld 1999; Poe-Yamagata and Jones 1999). Legislative preambles and court opinions explicitly endorse punishment as an appropriate component of juvenile sanctions. States' juvenile codes increasingly employ the rhetoric of accountability, responsibility, punishment, and public safety rather than a child's welfare or best interests (Feld 1988, 1998). States' juvenile sentencing laws increasingly emphasize individual responsibility and justice system accountability and provide for determinate or mandatory minimum sentences keyed to the seriousness of the offense (Torbet et al. 1996; Feld 1998). Currently, about half the states (22) use some type of "just deserts" determinate or mandatory minimum offense-based criteria to guide judicial sentencing discretion (Torbet et al. 1996; Sheffer 1995). Some states' legistaltures have enacted sentencing guidelines to impose presumptive, determinate, and proportional sentences based on a delinquent's age, the seriousness of the offense, and prior record (Feld 1988, 1998; Sheffer 1995). Other states' laws impose mandatory minimum sentences based on age and offenses that prescribe minimum terms of confinement or youths' level of security placement (Torbet et al. 1996; Sheffer 1995). Other states' departments of corrections administratively have adopted security classification and release guidelines that use offense criteria to specify proportional or mandatory minimum terms of confinement (Feld 1998). All of these de jure sentencing provisions—determinate and mandatory minimum laws and correctional and parole release guidelines—share the feature of offense-based dispositions that explicitly link the length of time delinquents serve to the seriousness of the crime they committed rather than to their "real needs." The recent report by the National Research Council, *Juvenile Crime, Juvenile Justice,* analyzed juvenile court sentencing practices and concluded that "State legislative changes in recent years have moved the court away from its rehabilitative goals and toward punishment and accountability. Laws have made some dispositions offense-based rather than offender-based. Offense-based sanctions are to be proportional to the offense and have retribution or deterrence as their goal. Strategies for imposing offense-based sentences in juvenile court include blended sentences, mandatory minimum sentences, and extended jurisdiction" (McCord, Widom, and Crowell 2001, 210). These statutory provisions use principles of proportionality and determinacy to rationalize sentencing decisions, to increase the penal bite of juvenile sanctions, and to allow legislators symbolically to demonstrate their toughness.

Empirical evaluations of juvenile court judges' sentencing practices consistently report two general findings. First, the "principle of offense"—present offense and prior record—accounts for most of the variance in juvenile court sentences that can be explained. Every methodologically rigorous study of juvenile court sentencing practices reports that judges focus primarily on the seriousness of the present offense and prior record when they sentence delinquents (Bishop and Frazier 1996; Feld 1999). Because juvenile court judges focus primarily on legal variables when they process youths, real differences in rates of criminal behavior by Black youths probably account for part of the disparities in justice administration. Various measures of delinquency— official arrest and conviction data, self-report surveys, and surveys of crime victims—all indicate higher rates of serious offending by Black youths than by Whites (McCord, Widom, and Crowell 2001). Part of these real differences in Black youths' rates of offending reflect their differential exposure to a host of risk factors associated with crime and violence—poverty, greater segregation and isolation in concentrated poverty neighborhoods than White youths, poor health care, and the like—as a result of the structural changes described earlier (McCord, Widom, and Crowell 2001).

Second, after researchers control for the effects of legal variables and differences in rates of offending by Black and White youths, it appears that the individualized justice of juvenile courts produces racial disparities in processing and sentencing minority offenders (Kempf-Leonard, Pope, and Feyerherm 1995; Miller 1996; Pope and Feyerherm 1992). To the extent that *parens patriae* ideology legitimizes individualization, it exposes disadvantaged youths to more extensive controls. In a society characterized by great inequality, those most in need are also those most at risk for juvenile court intervention. The structural context of juvenile justice administration also may adversely affect minority youths. Urban courts are more procedurally formal and sentence all delinquents more severely (Feld 1991). Urban courts also have greater access to detention facilities, and detained youths typically receive more severe sentences than those who remain at liberty. Because proportionally more minority youths live in urban environs, the geographic and structural context of juvenile justice administration may interact with race to produce minority overrepresentation in detention facilities and correctional institutions (Feld 1999; Snyder and Sickmund 1999).

The juvenile justice process entails a succession of decisions—intake, petition, detention, adjudication or waiver, and disposition—and the compound effects of even small disparities produces larger cumulative differences. In 1997, Black youths constituted about 15% of the population aged 10–17, 26% of juvenile arrests, 30% of delinquency referrals, one-third of the petitioned delinquency cases, and 40% of the inmates in public long-term institutions (McCord, Widom, and Crowell 2001). Minority youths, especially Blacks, are disproportionately overrepresented at each successive step of the decision-making process, with the greatest disparities occurring in the initial stages (Snyder and Sickmund 1999). A review of juvenile court sentencing studies found "[R]acial discrimination appears most widespread—minorities (and youth in predominantly minority jurisdictions) are more likely to be detained and receive out-of-home placements than whites regardless of 'legal' considerations. Because processing in the juvenile justice system is deeply implicated in the construction of a criminal (or 'prior') record, experiences as a juvenile serve as a major predictor of future processing" (Sampson and Lauritsen 1997, 362). Another recent analysis of the effects of discretionary decision making reported that "at almost every stage in the juvenile justice process the racial disparity is clear, but not extreme. However, because the system operates cumulatively the risk is compounded and the end result is that black juveniles are three times as likely as white juveniles to end up in residential placement" (McCord, Widom, and Crowell 2001, 257).

In 1988, Congress amended the Juvenile Justice and Delinquency Prevention (JJDP) Act to require states receiving federal funds to assure equitable treatment on the basis, inter alia, of race and to assess sources of minority overrepresentation in detention facilities and institutions (42 U.S.C. § 5633(a)(16) (1994)). In response to the JJDP Act mandate, many states examined and found racial disparities in their juvenile justice systems. A review of these studies reported that, after controlling for offense variables, minority youths were overrepresented in secure detention facilities in forty-one of forty-two states and in all thirteen states that analyzed other stages of decision making and institutional confinement (Pope 1994). When judges sentence delinquents, minority juveniles receive disproportionately more out-of-home placements than do White youths, while Whites receive disproportionately more probationary dispositions than do Black youths (Poe-Yamagata and Jones 1999). Black youths with no prior admission and with one or two prior admissions have much higher rates of commitment to state institutions than do White youths. Finally, Black youths confined in institutions serve longer periods in custody than do White youths committed for similar offenses (Poe-Yamagata and Jones 1999). The changes in sentencing laws associated with the crackdown on youth crime have had a substantial and cumulative impact on the proportion of minority youths in confinement. Examining the proportional changes in the racial composition of institutional populations for the 1985–95 period corresponding to the era of "get tough" legislative changes reveals that the overall numbers of youths in custody on any given day increased almost 40%, from 49,322 to 68,983 (Feld 1999). Despite the overall increase in daily custody populations, the percentage of White juveniles confined in public facilities actually *declined* 7%, while the percentage of confined Black juveniles *increased* almost 63%. The overall increases and proportional changes reflect the sharp growth in minority youth in confinement. Because of these changes in the numerical composition of confined delinquents, the proportion of White juveniles in custody declined from 44% to 32% of all youths, while the proportion of Blacks increased from 37% to 43% and that of Hispanics increased from 13% to 21% of confined youths (Feld 1999).

Conclusion

The issue of race has had two distinct and contradictory influences on juvenile justice theory and practice during the second half of the twentieth century. Initially, the Warren Court's due process revolution and *Gault* attempted to enhance civil rights, protect minority citizens, and limit the coercive powers of the state. But *Gault's* provision of procedural rights at trial legitimated punishment and fostered a procedural and substantive convergence with criminal courts. Three decades of judicial decision, legislative amendments, and administrative changes have converted the juvenile court into a scaled-down, second-class criminal court for young offenders that provides neither therapy nor justice.

The second phase of juvenile justice "reform" and the adoption of "get tough" policies in the early 1990s reflects the confluence of macrostructural, economic, and racial demographic changes that occurred in America's cities during the 1970s and 1980s, the emergence of a Black underclass living in concentrated poverty, and the rise in gun violence and youth homicides. Mass media portrayals and political rhetoric have firmly established in the public mind the connection between race and youth crime. Politicians exploit these racially tinged perceptions for political advantage with demagogic pledges to get tough on youth crime, which has become a code word for young Black males.

The transformation of the juvenile court and the crackdown on juveniles represent only one of several public policy responses to these social structural changes and to youth crime. A century ago, Progressive reformers had to choose between initiating social structural reforms that would ameliorate criminogenic forces or ministering to the individuals damaged by those adverse conditions. Driven by class and ethnic antagonisms, they ignored the structural implications of their delinquency theories and chose instead to "save children" and, incidentally, to preserve their own power and privilege. A century later, the same fundamental policy choices remain between controlling and punishing individuals and initiating social structural and policy changes. Unfortunately, contemporary public policy discourse about poverty, political economy, the allocation of societal resources and benefits, inequality, and crime all have become inextricably intertwined with questions of race. Poor Blacks living in concentrated poverty are effectively segregated from the social, economic, and political mainstream and engage in behaviors of which the dominant culture disapproves. The mass media convey biased and misleading images that incite White viewers' fear and indignation and activate stereotypes and prejudices. Conservative politicians exploit voters' sensitivities to matters of race with coded messages designed to sustain a right-wing coalition and promote racial animus. As a result, Americans engages in a subterranean discourse on race based on misleading images and potent symbols. As the public and politicians identify long-term poverty and its associated problems—unemployment, drug abuse, criminality, illegitimacy—as a Black condition separate from the mainstream of American society, policy makers can evade a sense of governmental responsibility or public obligation. The political, media, public, and cultural association of the image of the criminal with that of the urban Black male has fostered punitive policies rather than expanded employment or educational opportunities to prevent crime. For adult offenders, harsher policies over the past two decades, especially those associated with the war on drugs, have quadrupled rates of confinement, with a disproportionate impact on African-Americans (Mauer 1999; Tonry 1995). The transformation of the juvenile court into a punitive agency for the social control of "other people's children" provides another case study of the political exploitation of the connection in the public mind between race and youth crime (Feld 1999).

References

Allen, Francis A. 1981. *The Decline of the Rehabilitative Ideal: Penal Policy and Social Purpose.* New Haven, CT: Yale University Press.

American Bar Association. 1995. *A Call for Justice.* Washington, DC: American Bar Association.

American Friends Service Committee. 1971. *Struggle for Justice.* New York: Hill and Wang.

Anderson, David C. 1995. *Crime and the Politics of Hysteria: How the Willie Horton Story Changed American Justice.* New York: Random House.

Arnold, William R. 1971. "Race and Ethnicity Relative to Other Factors in Juvenile Court Dispositions." *American Journal of Sociology* 77:211–227.

Axelrad, Sidney. 1952. "Negro and White Male Institutionalized Delinquents." *American Journal of Sociology* 57:569–574.

Beckett, Katherine. 1997. *Making Crime Pay: Law and Order in Contemporary American Politics.* New York: Oxford University Press.

Beckett, Katherine, and Theodore Sasson. 2000. *The Politics of Injustice: Crime and Punishment in America.* Thousand Oaks, CA: Pine Forge Press.

Bishop, Donna M., and Charles S. Frazier. 1996. "Race Effects in Juvenile Justice Decision-Making: Findings of a Statewide Analysis." *Journal of Criminal Law and Criminology* 86:392–413.

Blumstein, Alfred. 1995. "Youth Violence, Guns, and the Illicit-Drug Industry." *Journal of Criminal Law and Criminology* 86:10–36.

Blumstein, Alfred, and Daniel Cork. 1996. "Linking Gun Availability to Youth Gun Violence." *Law and Contemporary Problems* 59:5–24.

Cook, Phillip J., and John H. Laub. 1998. "The Role of Youth in Violent Crime and Victimization." Pp. 27–64 in *Crime and Justice: A Review of Research,* vol. 24, ed. Michael Tonry and Mark H. Moore. Chicago: University of Chicago Press.

Cover, Robert M. 1982. "The Origins of Judicial Activism in the Protection of Minorities." *Yale Law Journal* 91:1287–1316.

Cullen, Francis T., and Karen E. Gilbert. 1982. *Reaffirming Rehabilitation.* Cincinnati: Anderson Publishing Co.

Dorfman, Lori, and Vincent Schiraldi. 2001. *Off Balance: Youth, Race and Crime in the News.* Washington, DC: Youth Law Center, Building Blocks for Youth.

Dvorak, Richard. 2000. "Cracking the Code: 'De-Coding' Color-blind Slurs During the Congressional Crack Cocaine Debates." *Michigan Journal of Race and Law* 5:611–663.

Edsall, Thomas Byrne, with Mary D. Edsall. 1991. "Race." *Atlantic Monthly* 267 (May): 53–86.

———. 1992. *Chain Reaction: The Impact of Race, Rights and Taxes on American Politics.* New York: W. W. Norton and Co.

Entman, Robert M. 1990. "Modern Racism and the Images of Blacks in Local Television News." *Critical Studies in Mass Communication* 7 : 332 – 345.

———. 1992. "Blacks in the New: Television, Modern Racism and Cultural Change." *Journalism Quarterly* 69 : 341 – 361.

———. 1994. "Representation and Reality in the Portrayal of Blacks on Network Television News." *Journalism Quarterly* 71 : 509 – 520.

Entman, Robert M., and Andrew Rojecki. 2000. *The Black Image in the White Mind: Media and Race in America.* Chicago: University of Chicago Press.

Feld, Barry C. 1988. "Juvenile Court Meets the Principle of Offense: Punishment, Treatment, and the Difference It Makes." *Boston University Law Review* 68 : 821 – 915.

———. 1991. "Justice by Geography: Urban, Suburban, and Rural Variations in Juvenile Justice Administration." *Journal of Criminal Law and Criminology* 82 : 156 – 210.

———. 1993. *Justice for Children: The Right to Counsel and the Juvenile Court.* Boston: Northeastern University Press.

———. 1995. "Violent Youth and Public Policy: A Case Study of Juvenile Justice Law Reform." *Minnesota Law Review* 79 : 965 – 1128.

———. 1997. "Abolish the Juvenile Court: Youthfulness, Criminal Responsibility, and Sentencing Policy." *Journal of Criminal Law and Criminology* 88 : 68 – 136.

———. 1998. "Juvenile and Criminal Justice Systems' Responses to Youth Violence." Pp. 189 – 261 in *Crime and Justice: An Annual Review,* vol. 24, ed. Michael Tonry and Mark H. Moore. Chicago: University of Chicago Press.

———. 1999. *Bad Kids: Race and the Transformation of the Juvenile Court.* New York: Oxford University Press.

Garland, David. 2001. *The Culture of Control: Crime and Social Order in Contemporary Society.* Chicago: University of Chicago Press.

General Accounting Office. 1995. *Juvenile Justice: Representation Rates Varied as Did Counsel's Impace on Court Outcomes.* Washington, DC: General Accounting Office.

Gilens, Martin. 1996. "'Race Coding' and White Opposition to Welfare." *American Political Science Review* 90 : 593 – 604.

———. 1999. *Why Americans Hate Welfare: Race, Media, and the Politics of Antipoverty Policy.* Chicago: University of Chicago Press.

Gilliam, Franklin D., Jr., and Shanto Iyengar. 2000. "Prime Suspects: The Influence of Local Television News on the Viewing Public." *American Journal of Political Science* 44 : 560 – 573.

Gilliam, Franklin D., Jr., Shanto Iyengar, Adam Simon, and Oliver Wright. 1996. "Crime in Black and White: The Violent, Scary World of Local News." *Harvard International Journal of Press/Politics* 1, no. 3 : 6 – 23

Gottlieb, Peter. 1991. "Rethinking the Great Migration: A Perspective from Pittsburgh." In *The Great Migration in Historical Perspective: New Dimensions of Race, Class and Gender,* ed. J. W. Trotter, Jr. Bloomington: Indiana University Press.

Graham, Fred P. 1970. *The Due Process Revolution: The Warren Court's Impact on Criminal Law.* New York: Hayden Books.

Grubb, W. Norton, and Marvin Lazerson. 1982. *Broken Promises: How Americans Fail Their Children.* New York: Basic Books.

Hacker, Andrew. 1995. *Two Nations: Black and White, Separate, Hostile and Unequal.* New York: MacMillan.

Hurwitz, John, and Mark Peffley. 1997. "Public Perceptions of Race and Crime: The Role of Racial Stereotypes." *American Journal of Political Science* 41:375–401.

Jencks, Christopher. 1992. *Rethinking Social Policy: Race, Poverty, and the Underclass.* New York: Harper Collins.

Jencks, Christopher, and Paul E. Peterson, eds. 1991. *The Urban Underclass.* Washington, DC: Brookings Institution.

Katz, Michael B. 1989. *The Undeserving Poor: From the War on Poverty to the War on Welfare.* New York: Pantheon Books.

———, ed. 1993. *The "Underclass" Debate: Views From History.* Princeton, NJ: Princeton University Press.

Kempf-Leonard, Kimberly, Carl Pope, and William Feyerherm. 1995. *Minorities in Juvenile Justice.* Thousand Oaks, CA: Sage.

Kennedy, Randall. 1997. *Race, Crime, and the Law.* New York: Random House.

Kinder, Donald R., and Tali Mendelberg. 1995. "Cracks in American Apartheid: The Political Impact of Prejudice among Desegregated Whites." *Journal of Politics* 57: 402–424.

Klarman, Michael J. 2000. "The Racial Origins of Modern Criminal Procedure." *Michigan Law Review* 99:48–97.

Lemann, Nicholas. 1992. *The Promised Land: The Great Black Migration and How It Changed America.* New York: Random House.

Massey, Douglas S., and Nancy A. Denton. 1993. *American Apartheid: Segregation and the Making of the Underclass.* Cambridge, MA: Harvard University Press.

Mauer, Marc. 1999. *Race to Incarcerate.* New York: New Press.

McCord, Joan. 1997. "Placing American Urban Violence in Context." In *Violence and Childhood in the Inner City,* ed. J. McCord. New York: Cambridge University Press.

McCord, Joan, Cathy Spatz Widom, and Nancy A. Crowell. 2001. *Juvenile Crime, Juvenile Justice.* Washington, DC: National Academy Press.

Mendelberg, Tali. 1997. "Executing Hortons: Racial Crime in the 1988 Presidential Campaign." *Public Opinion Quarterly* 61:134–157.

———. 2001. *The Race Card: Campaign Strategy, Implicit Messages, and the Norms of Equality.* Princeton, NJ: Princeton University Press.

Merlo, Alida V. 2000. "Juvenile Justice at the Crossroads: Presidential Address to the Academy of Criminal Justice Sciences." *Justice Quarterly* 17:639–661.

Miller, Jerome G. 1996. *Search and Destroy: African-American Males in the Criminal Justice System.* New York: Cambridge University Press.

Myrdal, Gunnar. 1972. *An American Dilemma.* 2 vols. New York: Pantheon Books.

National Advisory Commission on Civil Disorders (Kerner Commission). 1968. *Report.* Washington, DC: U.S. Government Printing Office.

National Research Council. 1993. *Losing Generations: Adolescents in High-Risk Settings.* Washington, DC: National Academy Press.

Oliver, Mary Beth. 1999. "Caucasian Viewers' Memory of Black and White Criminal Suspects in the News." *Journal of Communication* 49:46–60.

Omi, Michael, and Howard Winant. 1994. *Racial Formation in the United States: From the 1960s to the 1980s.* New York: Routledge.

Peffley, Mark, Jon Hurwitz, and Paul M. Sniderman. 1997. "Racial Stereotypes and Whites' Political Views of Blacks in the Context of Welfare and Crime." *American Journal of Political Science* 41:30–60.

Peffley, Mark, Todd Shields, and Bruce Williams. 1996. "The Intersection of Race and Crime in Television News Stories: An Experimental Study." *Political Communications* 13:309–327.

Phillips, Kevin. 1969. *The Emerging Republican Majority.* New Rochelle, NY: Arlington House.

Platt, Anthony. 1977. *The Child Savers: The Invention of Delinquency.* 2nd ed. Chicago: University of Chicago Press.

Poe-Yamagata, Eileen, and Michael A. Jones. 1999. *And Justice for Some.* Washington, DC: Building Blocks for Youth.

Pope, Carl E. 1994. "Racial Disparities in the Juvenile Justice System." *Overcrowded Times* 5:1–4.

Pope, Carl E., and William H. Feyerherm. 1992. *Minorities and the Juvenile Justice System.* Washington, DC: U.S. Department of Justice, Office of Juvenile Justice and Delinquency Prevention.

Powe, Lucas A., Jr. 2000. *The Warren Court and American Politics.* Cambridge, MA: Harvard University Press.

President's Commission on Law Enforcement and Administration of Justice. 1967. *Task Force Report: Juvenile Delinquency and Youth Crime.* Washington, DC: U.S. Government Printing Office.

Reiss, Albert J., Jr., and Jeffrey A. Roth, eds. 1993. *Understanding and Preventing Violence.* Washington DC: National Academy of Science.

Roberts, Julian V. 1992. "Public Opinion, Crime, and Criminal Justice." Pp. 99–164 in *Crime and Justice: A Review of Research,* vol. 16, ed. Michael Tonry. Chicago: University of Chicago Press.

Rothman, David J. 1980. *Conscience and Convenience: The Asylum and Its Alternative in Progressive America.* Boston: Little, Brown.

Sampson, Robert J., and Janet E. Lauritsen. 1997. "Racial and Ethnic Disparities in Crime and Criminal Justice in the United States." Pp. 311–374 in *Crime and Justice: A Review of Research,* ed. Michael Tonry. Chicago: University of Chicago Press.

Schlossman, Steven. 1977. *Love and the American Delinquent: The Theory and Practice of "Progressive" Juvenile Justice.* Chicago: University of Chicago Press.

Sheffer, Julianne P. 1995. "Serious and Habitual Juvenile Offender Statutes: Reconciling Punishment and Rehabilitation within the Juvenile Justice System." *Vanderbilt Law Review* 48:479–512.

Sickmund, Melissa, Howard N. Snyder, and Eileen Poe-Yamagata, E. 1997. *Juvenile Offenders and Victims: 1997 Update on Violence.* Washington, DC: U.S. Department of Justice, Office of Juvenile Justice and Delinquency Prevention.

Snyder, Howard N., and Melissa Sickmund. 1999. *Juvenile Offenders and Victims: A National Report.* Washington, DC: Office of Juvenile Justice and Delinquency Prevention.

Sutton, John. 1988. *Stubborn Children: Controlling Delinquency in the United States.* Berkeley: University of California Press.

Tonry, Michael. 1994. "Racial Politics, Racial Disparities, and the War on Drugs." *Crime and Delinquency* 40:475–494.

———. 1995. *Malign Neglect: Race, Crime, and Punishment in America.* New York: Oxford University Press.

Torbet, Patricia, Richard Gable, Hunter Hurst IV, Imogene Montgomery, Linda Szymanski, and Douglas Thomas. 1996. *State Responses to Serious and Violent Juvenile Crime: Research Report.* Washington, DC: Office of Juvenile Justice and Delinquency Prevention, National Center for Juvenile Justice.

Trotter, Joe William, Jr. 1991. "Black Migration in Historical Perspective: A Review of the Literature." In *The Great Migration in Historical Perspective: New Dimensions of Race, Class and Gender,* ed. J. W. Trotter, Jr. Bloomington: Indiana University Press.

Valentino, Nicholas A. 1999. "Crime News and the Priming of Racial Attitudes during Evaluations of the President." *Public Opinion Quarterly* 63 : 293 – 320.

von Hirsch, Andrew. 1976. *Doing Justice.* New York: Hill and Wang.

Wilson, William Julius. 1987. *The Truly Disadvantaged.* Chicago: University of Chicago Press.

———. 1996. *When Work Disappears: The World of the New Urban Poor.* New York: Alfred A. Knopf.

Zimring, Franklin. 1996. "Kids, Guns, and Homicide: Policy Notes on an Age-Specific Epidemic." *Law and Contemporary Problems* 59 : 25 – 37.

———. 1998. *American Youth Violence.* New York: Oxford University Press.

Zimring, Franklin, and Gordon Hawkins. 1997. *Crime Is Not the Problem: Lethal Violence in America.* New York: Oxford University Press.

2

Understanding Race Differences in Offending and the Administration of Justice

6

Suburban Sprawl, Race, and Juvenile Justice

Paul A. Jargowsky, Scott A. Desmond,
and Robert D. Crutchfield

I. Introduction

THROUGHOUT THE social sciences, there has been a renewed interest in understanding the social significance of geographic concentrations of poverty. After many years during which individualistic models dominated the literature, sociologists and economists have begun to ask once again how neighborhood characteristics affect fertility, marriage, and labor market outcomes. Criminologists have been ahead of the curve in that they have long appreciated the importance of neighborhood contexts in shaping adolescent behavior and criminal participation. In comparison to adults, adolescents not only have fewer connections to the world outside their own neighborhood and their local school, but are still in a developmental stage and may therefore be more susceptible than adults to peer groups and neighborhood conditions.

While criminologists and others interested in juvenile justice systems have long understood the vital role played by neighborhoods, they have often taken the existence of slums, ghettos, and barrios as a given. Yet there have been dramatic changes over time in the spatial organization of poverty, interacting with the spatial organization of racial and ethnic groups within the larger society. The United States has far more dangerous slums, where poor families and children are highly isolated from the social and economic mainstream, than many other developed nations with comparable or lower mean incomes. The decline of heavy manufacturing industries, which made use of low-skilled workers, in recent decades has multiplied the effects these forces have had on neighborhoods and on crime and delinquency. The prevalence of high-poverty zones in the United States, far from being a given, is the predictable result of the way in which urban areas have been developing since the end of World War II. The story involves both racial segregation and, increasingly, segregation by class. It also involves such issues as exclusionary zoning, governmental fragmentation, and suburban sprawl.

Discussion of development issues would normally be considered outside the scope of a book focused on issues of juvenile justice. We take the position, however, that criminologists have an important role to play in the debates concerning suburban sprawl, the concentration of poverty, and the connections between the two. More than most researchers, criminologists understand why the isolation of the poor in slums, ghettos, and barrios is deleterious to the larger society. Those who design and implement social interventions for youth in high-poverty central city neighborhoods also have a stake in these debates. The success or failure of such programs depends to a large extent on how neighborhood conditions change over time, which in turn is greatly affected by the overall metropolitan development paradigm. For all these reasons, we argue that spatial development processes, including suburban sprawl and racial and economic segregation, not only belong in this volume but are central to understanding the future prospects for juvenile crime and justice in the United States.

In this chapter, we begin by addressing the increasing concentration of poverty in the United States, a trend that leads to more and more children and young adults growing up in economically devastated and socially isolated neighborhoods, particularly African-American and Hispanic youth. A central cause of the increased isolation of the poor, greater concentration of poverty, and crime has been the growth of joblessness in many American cities. However, we also examine the metropolitan development process that contributes to the increasing concentration of poverty. In the course of this discussion, we go well beyond the normal scope of criminology literature into the areas of suburban sprawl, zoning, and growth management. Our contention, however, is that public policies in these areas have important implications for understanding the origins of juvenile criminal activity.

II. The Concentration of Poverty

Virtually anyone asked to talk about the meaning of poverty will start by talking about the lack of adequate resources to purchase goods and services, particularly those things considered to be necessities by contemporary standards. But, after that, most people will also add concerns about the fear of crime, gangs and drugs, ineffective schools, abandoned cars and vacant buildings, public housing projects, segregation, and other concerns about the physical environment of daily life. The latter set of issues pertains to characteristics of the neighborhoods in which poor families tend to live. The environmental, economic, and social characteristics of the neighborhood in which a poor child lives can have independent effects on the child's development, even after controlling for the parents' lack of resources. Together, these neighborhood characteristics constitute the spatial context of poverty.

Prior to the 1970s, poverty scholars nearly always considered poverty within its spatial context. For example, Michael Harrington's *The Other America* (1962) is organized for the most part geographically—considering Appalachia, the black ghetto, Skid Row, and so on—and pays careful attention to the local setting and how it interacts with and exacerbates the lack of family resources.[1] Elliot Liebow's *Talley's Corner* (1967), Gerald Suttles's *The Social Order of the Slum* (1968), and Lee Rainwater's *Behind Ghetto Walls* (1970) are entirely embedded within one neighborhood, as are many others of that genre. For Robert Park and the Chicago school of sociology, as for many of the earlier generation of poverty scholars, the connection between studying poverty and studying poor neighborhoods was so fundamental it was rarely necessary to spell it out explicitly. Moreover, given the high degree of segregation of American cities, talking about the spatial context of poverty also meant talking about racial and ethnic segregation.

A variety of factors came together to change the way poverty was studied in the United States. The first factor was the invention of the official federal poverty rate by Molly Orshansky in the 1960s. Despite its obvious flaws, which Orshansky readily admitted, the poverty rate was widely adopted and has been used ever since with little modification other than adjustments for inflation. Among other flaws, it is based solely on family-level variables—primarily income and family size (Ruggles 1990). It takes no account of the spatial context of poverty. Researchers, guided by the existence of a poverty standard, were led to the exploration of poverty as a family-level phenomenon. A second factor leading to individualistic models of poverty was the creation of the Current Population Survey (CPS), now the premier source of annual cross-sectional data on poverty, employment, and earnings. While the CPS was and is an excellent survey with a very large sample size—over 150,000 individuals in recent years—the publicly released data contain no identifiers for local neighborhoods. A third factor was the increasing influence of quantitative models drawn from economics that assume independence among observations, leading scholars to view individuals as autonomous actors and to underplay the role of neighborhood contexts.

As a result, models of poverty that largely ignored neighborhood and other spatial factors received greater prominence and more research funding. While the individual and family perspectives are obviously important in studying poverty, the spatial distribution of poverty is also fundamental to understanding trends in crime, the quality of life, and chances for socioeconomic mobility of those with low incomes. Neighborhoods provide the daily context of life, either ameliorating or exacerbating the problems faced by low-income families.

Fortunately, the issue of the spatial context of poverty has forcefully reemerged, inspired in large part by the publication of William Julius Wilson's *The Truly Disadvantaged* (1987). The body of work on this issue documents important changes in the spatial context of poverty, particularly as they affect members of minority groups living in central city areas. The socioeconomic maps of many metropolitan areas had been profoundly altered in the decades following the riots of the 1960s. Whites left the central city in large numbers, followed by middle-class blacks and Hispanics moving to middle-class enclaves, leaving the minority poor behind. High-poverty ghettos and barrios at the centers of large metropolitan areas expanded, and middle-class residential areas within the confines of the central city declined as peripheral suburbs grew rapidly. The central city poor were increasingly isolated in depopulated urban wastelands, coping simultaneously with a lack of resources within their families and destructive conditions within their neighborhoods and schools.

Between 1970 and 1990, there was a dramatic expansion in the concentration of poverty. Jargowsky (1997), examining 239 U.S. metropolitan areas, found that the number of poor persons residing in high-poverty ghettos and barrios nearly doubled, rising from 1.9 million in 1970 to 3.7 million in 1990. At the same time, the overall number of poor persons in these same metropolitan areas increased by 37%, due primarily to population growth and to a lesser extent due to a slight increase in the overall poverty rates of the metropolitan areas. As a result, a greater proportion of the poor lived in spatial contexts of extreme poverty: whereas 12.4% of the poor lived in high-poverty areas in 1970, by 1990 the figure was 17.9%.

The problem was particularly acute for members of minority groups. Whereas one-fourth of poor blacks in the 239 metropolitan areas resided in high-poverty neighborhoods in 1970, by 1990, the figure had risen to one-third. About one-fourth of the Hispanic poor lived in high-poverty areas in both 1970 and 1990, although the number of Hispanic residents of high-poverty areas increased dramatically due to the growth in this population. In contrast, poor non-Hispanic whites were far less likely to reside in high-poverty contexts. Only 2.9% of the white poor in 1970, and 6.3% in 1990, lived in neighborhoods of concentrated poverty.

Despite relatively little change in the overall poverty rates of these cities, there was a profound change in the spatial organization of poverty, leaving the poor substantially more socially and economically isolated from the mainstream of American society during this period. In the 1990s, there was a reversal of the trend, with a 24% reduction in the number of residents of high-poverty neighborhoods nationwide (Jargowsky 2003). Even after this decline, however, the concentration of poverty was still far greater in 2000 than in 1970, in terms of both the number of residents of high-poverty neighborhoods and the percentage of the poor living in such areas.

A number of factors have contributed to the increasing concentration of poverty. When the economy is particularly bad in a given metropolitan area, resulting in higher poverty rates in the general population, poverty tends to become more concentrated as well. But the overall national increase in the concentration of poverty cannot be attributed to the economy, since the economy was far stronger in 2000 than in 1970. The concentration of poverty will also be higher when minority groups, who have much higher poverty rates than the white majority, are clustered in segregated neighborhoods (Massey 1990; Massey and Denton 1993; Massey and Eggers 1990). Yet segregation by race and ethnicity has been on the decline since 1970 (Farley and Frey 1994; Harrison and Weinberg 1992). Other things being equal, the declines in racial and ethnic segregation since 1970 should have led to lower levels of concentrated poverty.

Since neither the economy nor segregation by race and ethnicity can explain the secular trend in concentration of poverty, another force must be at work. The prime suspect is the spatial reorganization of metropolitan areas, especially the continued depopulation of the core and the growth of economically homogeneous suburban rings. Inner-city neighborhoods are embedded in metropolitan housing markets in which the dominant trend since at least the end of World War II has been deconcentration (Berry and Gillard 1977). Suburbs at the far edges of metropolitan areas have grown explosively in recent decades; typically these new developments consist of large homes that are affordable only to higher-income families.

As the most advantaged group moves to the new developments from the slightly older suburban areas, middle-class families follow in their footsteps, moving from inner-ring suburbs or central city neighborhoods. This process of selective out-migration systematically reduces the income level of the residents left behind in the neighborhoods nearer the center of the metropolitan area. In the 1970–90 period, the result was a rapid increase in the number of high-poverty neighborhoods in the urban core (Jargowsky 1997). In the 1990s, many of these areas were redeveloped, housing projects were torn down, and gentrification was spurred by the strong economy. However, the out-migration pattern still led to consistent increases in poverty in the inner ring of suburbs as the outer ring continued its explosive growth (Jargowsky 2003).

III. Urban Sprawl and Central City Decline

The United States is unique among Western industrial nations in the extent of concentration of poverty.[2] The United States is also unique in that "affluent and middle-class Americans live in suburban areas that are far from their work places" (Jackson 1985, 6), a phenomenon referred to as "suburban sprawl." We will argue that the concentration of poverty and suburban sprawl are closely related; they are, in effect, two sides of the same coin of U.S. metropolitan development.[3]

There are many different and sometimes contradictory conceptions of the term "sprawl" in the literature. The current ambiguity regarding the meaning of sprawl is reminiscent of the discussion of the underclass in the mid-1980s. The latter term was brought to the fore by a series of widely read research papers by William Julius Wilson, culminating in the publication of *The Truly Disadvantaged* (1987). In Wilson's conception, the term "underclass" referred to persons residing in minority neighborhoods so socially isolated and economically disadvantaged that they became enveloped in a "tangle of pathology." However, the term was also adopted by social conservatives as a way to refer to persons caught up in a permissive cultural climate and who therefore acted irresponsibly and caused their own poverty (Magnet 1993). Liberals and urban advocates used the term as a loose synonym for the urban poor, one which placed an emphasis on their relationship to the larger class structure of American society. Further difficulties ensued when researchers attempted to operationalize the term for measurement purposes (Ricketts and Sawhill 1988; Abramson and Tobin 1994). Researchers, policy makers, and advocates adopted a trendy term and elided its meaning in convenient directions, ultimately destroying its usefulness.

The debate about sprawl has some of the same characteristics, and faces a similar danger. However, to understand the implications of sprawl for poverty and inequality, it is necessary to assign some concrete meaning to the term. Gregory Squires defines sprawl as "a pattern of urban and metropolitan growth that reflects low-density, automobile dependent, exclusionary, new development on the fringe of settled areas often surrounding a deteriorating city" (Squires 2002, 2). According to this definition, sprawl is not a fixed set of characteristics of a region's housing stock, but rather a characterization of the area's growth over time. The definition identifies several somewhat different characteristics that are said to comprise sprawl, each of which has different potential effects on the conditions that may contribute to juvenile crime and differential levels of offending among different racial and ethnic groups.

The first characteristic of sprawl, according to Squires's formulation, is low density. Density refers to the average number of persons per acre in new developments, but also to the discontinuous nature of the developments themselves. Transportation planners and environmentalists are particularly concerned with this aspect of sprawl. Low-density residential areas are inherently difficult to serve with public transportation in a cost-effective manner, resulting in nearly total reliance on individual automobiles for transportation. The resulting air pollution, traffic congestion, and land consumed by highway construction are negative externalities, the cost of which is not factored into either the developers' or home buyers' economic calculus. On the other hand, waves of suburban movers have shown a marked preference for lower density, indicating that there are benefits as well.

There is no question that the density of cities has been declining for decades, for a variety of reasons. For one thing, changes in transportation and communication have made lower density possible. For another, increasing real incomes have resulted in greater demand for space—both larger housing units and greater spacing between units. Thus, as far as sprawl is concerned, the question is not whether densities are declining but whether they are declining more rapidly than can be explained by the underlying economics.

Squires's definition also stresses that sprawl is rapid growth at the periphery of a city or metropolitan area. In the provocatively titled *The Dark Side of the American Dream,* the Sierra Club defined sprawl as "low-density development beyond the edge of service and employment" (Sierra Club 1998). On the other hand, growth at the periphery of existing developed areas is exactly what one would expect. Sprawl, in the sense of peripheral development, is certainly not a new phenomenon. By this definition, all cities and metropolitan areas have been sprawling throughout history. One can map the developed areas of London or Chicago or any major city over many decades or centuries, and, except for the occasional catastrophe, cities expand over time and the fastest rate of growth of the housing stock takes place in the fringe of the developed area. Between 1810 and 1820, the suburbs of New York grew faster than the central city, though at that time, well before New York's great consolidation, the "suburbs" included places like Brooklyn that we now consider the central city. Areas outside Philadelphia County grew faster than the county in that decade as well. The growth in Boston's suburbs first outpaced the growth of the city itself in the 1830s; Cleveland's and Saint Louis's in the 1840s (Jackson 1985, 316).

There is no necessary connection between urban sprawl, in the senses defined above, and poverty, inequality, or the concentration of poverty. If the new, low-density, peripheral suburbs developed with a complete menu of housing types, from gated communities to low- and moderate-income housing, segregation by income could actually decline as the city expanded. Low-density development could, in theory, provide a higher quality of life for low-income persons than dense, dangerous neighborhoods in central city housing projects. But in practice, U.S.-style sprawl creates a greater degree of separation between the rich and poor and therefore leads to vastly different experience for young persons from different income groups, with a disproportionate impact for minority youth. Thus, the key element of Squires's definition is that the new growth is "exclusionary." That is, new development—whether planned or unplanned, ugly or beautiful, high density or low density—that accentuates segregation of the rich and middle-class from the poor contributes to the concentration of poverty. Sprawl produces vast areas of concentrated wealth in the favored sectors of the city, while leaving the poor geographically and social isolated in the central city. While other aspects of sprawl have impacts on the poor as well, such as environmental degradation and low density, it is the pronounced tendency toward economic segregation that is the most likely to have implications for juvenile justice.

In fact, new housing construction in recent decades has contributed to the concentration of poverty. Recently developed neighborhoods, the vast majority of which are on the metropolitan periphery, have a substantially higher mean income than older neighborhoods, and suburban neighborhoods have a substantially higher mean income than central city neighborhoods, even controlling for year of construction (Jargowsky 2002). Perhaps more important, the variance in household mean incomes is lower among the newer neighborhoods in the suburbs, and this trend is particularly strong in suburban neighborhoods (Jargowsky 2002). Thus, the newer suburban neighborhoods are both wealthier and more homogeneous.

The newer neighborhoods are also more homogeneous in terms of race and ethnicity. Across all metropolitan areas in 1990, the oldest neighborhoods were about 60% non-Hispanic white, and therefore about 40% minority. As the neighborhood vintage becomes more recent, the proportion that is non-Hispanic white increases. The most recent neighborhoods—those in which the median housing unit was constructed in the 1980s—were 80% non-Hispanic white. However, when disaggregating by central city versus suburb, it turns out that all suburban neighborhoods, regardless of era of construction, are about 80% non-Hispanic white. Clearly, racial segregation in the suburbs is not a new pattern, and the older suburbs were constructed at a time when racial discrimination in housing was even stronger than it is today. Within central cities, the percentage that is non-Hispanic white varies from just about half in the older neighborhoods to 75% in the newest neighborhoods (Jargowsky 2002).

Suburbanization has been going on since cities were invented. At first suburbanization was limited by the transportation capacities of the foot and the horse. Once the transportation infrastructure made longer commutes possible, suburbs began to appear along streetcar lines (S. Warner 1962). The automobile and the construction of modern, high-speed roads opened up the suburbs even further. Suburbanization has always been about two different things. In the first place, people move to the suburbs to translate their economic success into desirable neighborhood amenities, such as single family homes, yards, and good schools (Gans 1967, 31–41). Second, as Park (1926) argued long ago, urban environments are shaped by the attempts of successful and mobile groups of persons to translate social distances between themselves and lower-status groups into physical distances that protect them from the real and perceived threats posed by the lower-status groups.

Suburbanization has, therefore, always involved both the "pull" of desirable suburban characteristics and the "push" of undesirable central city characteristics. This dual nature of suburbanization did not start with the riots of the 1960s, with the dramatic increases in crime in the central city in the 1970s, or with the emergence of the particular set of development patterns now called sprawl. To argue that sprawl is related to central city decline is not to argue that sprawl is what causes central city decline. It clearly does play a role, but it is just as valid to argue that central city decline is what causes sprawl. The "pull" of the suburbs is enhanced by the construction of large modern homes in ethnically and economically homogenous suburbs, perhaps with walls and a private security force. The "push" of central cities is exacerbated as higher-income families leave and the fiscal condition of the central cities worsens and the quality of public services, particularly education, declines.

The process is a spiral, and the relative balance of push and pull clearly varies over time. At the time of the riots, push clearly predominated, resulting in massive "white flight." In the late 1990s, as families moved from one distant suburb to an even more distant suburb, the pull of the amenities offered by the latest housing developments was probably relatively more important. It is pointless to argue about which of the two factors is the driving force in a fundamentally circular process of sprawl and decay.

Arguing that sprawl and central city decline are related does not imply that developers who construct housing units demanded by the market, or the families who choose suburban units with a wonderful complement of amenities, are evil people. Both groups are making decisions based on the incentives and the rules of the game as they exist in our metropolitan areas. Those incentives result from a complex set of tax rules, zoning rules, development subsidies, and governmental institutions (Squires 2002). These policy rules and mechanisms reflect both local preferences and the political power of development interests. They fundamentally shape the current pattern of development.

Sam Bass Warner (1972) argued that the decline of the central cities and the suburban explosion are part of a "chronic urban disease" that feeds on "a healthy body of everyday behavior and aspirations" (154). From the point of view of current suburbanites, the term "disease" may seem a bizarre description of a process that results in highly desirable housing developments. But the result of the process is the spatial separation of racial and income classes, the implications of which are addressed in the next section. The social, economic, and political costs of this development pattern, which accumulate slowly over many decades, need to be weighed and evaluated. If such costs are onerous, then a change in the rules and policies within which the development process occurs may well be justified.

IV. Implications for Urban Youth and the Juvenile Justice System

The processes just described have two important criminological conse-quences. First, they increase crime, and, in particular, because these processes differentially affect black and Hispanic inner-city communities, they increase minority crime. Second, they can exacerbate racially differential processing by the criminal justice system. This effect can be intended, as in the case of racial profiling in "dangerous neighborhoods," or unintended, which can hap-pen when urban police or courts have different policies, ostensibly because of "differences" in urban and suburban crime and delinquency problems. In some metropolitan areas completely different systems may emerge when the city is in one jurisdiction and some suburbs in another (Harris 2002).

Although the focus of this volume is juvenile delinquency, in this section we will discuss how these processes affect both juvenile and young adult crime. We will do this for two reasons. First, the processes that we are de-scribing affect both groups in similar ways, and the presence of marginalized young adults in proximity to marginalized juveniles can create the critical mass of potential law violators which increases both groups' crime and fur-ther destabilizes already troubled communities. Second, the criminal justice system is increasingly handling juveniles and young adults similarly, and some (Feld 1998, 1999) believe that this is especially so for inner-city minority juveniles.

In the remaining sections of this paper we will review some of the research that has focused on the connection between concentrated disadvantage and crime. Next, we will discuss one particular theoretical approach, social disor-ganization theory, which has been used to explain why communities differ in their rates of crime and disorder. After a brief description of contemporary so-cial disorganization theory, we discuss in more detail the effect that concen-trated disadvantage may have on the informal social control of crime in inner-city neighborhoods. After discussing poverty's effects upon several types of informal social controls, we move on to three important criminogenic forces plaguing many inner-city neighborhoods: oppositional cultures, joblessness, and inadequate schooling. Finally, we conclude with a brief discussion of how the concentration of poverty and suburbanization may influence the process-ing of delinquent youth.

V. Concentrated Disadvantage and Crime

Two studies by Peterson and Krivo (Krivo and Peterson 1996; Peterson and Krivo 1999) tested the hypothesis that concentrated disadvantage leads to more criminal activity, beyond the general effect of poverty. That is, if Wilson (1987) and others are correct, then as poverty increases the crime rate should also increase, but "extremely" disadvantaged neighborhoods, characterized by very high rates of poverty, joblessness, and family disruption, should have especially high rates of criminal behavior.

Using data from Columbus, Ohio, Krivo and Peterson (1996) characterized neighborhoods as having low (less than 20%), high (20%–39%), or extreme (more than 40%) rates of poverty, based on the percentage of the population in the neighborhood that is below the poverty line. The authors also included neighborhood (census tract) measures of family disruption, male joblessness, and occupational composition. When compared to neighborhoods with high levels of poverty, extremely impoverished neighborhoods did not have dramatically higher rates of property crime. Property crime rates in neighborhoods with extreme poverty were only 3.9% higher than the property crime rates in high-poverty neighborhoods. The patterns for violent crime, however, were quite different. "For all indicators except male joblessness, the difference in criminal violence between communities with high versus extreme disadvantage is substantially greater than the gap in violent crime between low and high disadvantage tracts" (Krivo and Peterson 1996, 630). The authors concluded that "Wilson is correct in arguing that extreme disadvantage provides a distinctly different structural context for crime" (Krivo and Peterson 1996, 631).

In a subsequent study, Peterson and Krivo (1999) examined the effect of racial segregation on concentrated disadvantage and homicide. The authors argued that racial residential segregation contributes to the concentration of disadvantage among African Americans, but not whites. Thus, segregation may cause higher homicide rates for African Americans indirectly through its effect on the concentration of disadvantage. The results of the study supported the authors' hypothesis. Segregation had a significant effect on the homicide rate for African Americans, but not whites, and the effect of segregation on the African-American homicide rate was explained by concentrated disadvantage.

The results of several studies by Barbara Warner (Warner and Pierce 1993; Warner 1997; Warner and Rountree 1997) support the notion that concentrated disadvantage is especially likely to lead to increases in crime. Warner's studies are not generally framed as a direct test of Wilson's (1987) theoretical arguments, but, nonetheless, they provide evidence that concentrated disadvantage leads to elevated crime rates. Warner and her colleagues examined the interaction between poverty and residential mobility and poverty and racial and ethnic heterogeneity. As nonwhite, middle-class residents have moved from inner-city neighborhoods to more affluent suburbs, inner-city neighborhoods have become more homogeneous in social class, and there is less mobility, because those who are able to leave the neighborhood already have. These neighborhoods are especially likely to have high rates of crime.

Referring to the results of Warner and Pierce (1993), Warner (1999) states that "findings suggest that poor *homogeneous* neighborhoods rather than poor heterogeneous neighborhoods have the highest crime rates, and similarly for robbery, poor *non-mobile* neighborhoods, rather than poor mobile neighborhoods have the highest crime rates" (104; emphasis in the original).

Although these studies do not highlight the role of suburban sprawl as a cause of crime, the connection should be apparent. Suburban sprawl and the concentration of poverty are closely related processes. Suburbanization has contributed to the creation of highly segregated inner-city neighborhoods with extremely high levels of poverty. In turn, criminological research strongly suggests that neighborhoods with extreme rates of poverty also have higher rates of criminal behavior. Thus, if suburbanization contributes to the concentration of poverty, then it also contributes indirectly to an increase in neighborhood crime rates.

VI. Explaining Crime in Poor Neighborhoods

We have long known that the social conditions described in the first section of this chapter are correlated with higher crime and delinquency rates. This observation led Chicago school sociologists to develop early versions of social disorganization theory to explain why inner-city neighborhoods have higher rates of many forms of "social pathology," but in particular crime (Shaw and McKay 1942). In recent decades studies have repeatedly demonstrated that crime and delinquency are higher in impoverished neighborhoods (Crutchfield, Geerken, and Gove 1982; Sampson and Castellano 1982; Bailey 1984; Loftin and Parker 1985; Patterson 1991).

Today, although some scholars debate which mechanisms are the most important causes of contemporary dislocations, they do agree that where there are concentrations of poverty within the city, crime rates are higher (Murray 1984; Wilson 1987; Massey and Denton 1993). What is less clear is how or why concentrated poverty leads to crime. Clearly, some crime and delinquency can be explained as a utilitarian reaction to deprivation (Becker 1968; Sullivan 1973). Those who lack legitimate opportunities can see burglary, larceny, and drug dealing as a rational alternative. Some seemingly less utilitarian crimes can also be explained with basic rational choice models. Homicide and assault, for example, can be a part of business for those marketing drugs. There is good evidence that a sizable portion of the increased homicides of the late 1980s and 1990s was a consequence of fierce competition over urban drug markets (Cork 1999; Blumstein, Rivara, and Rosenfeld 2000). Competitors were killed to protect or to take over territory. Drug dealers killed or were killed by those trying to rob them, since obviously there are no legitimate means of redress for those suffering losses as a result of criminal activity.

If we stop here in our explanation, however, we have a very incomplete picture. First, many crimes that occur disproportionately in very poor neighborhoods cannot be explained by referring to efforts to redress material needs or desires. Rape is a clear example, and the majority of homicides and assaults are not consequences of utilitarian moneymaking schemes (Wolfgang 1958; Luckenbill 1977). Furthermore, most burglaries and robberies yield very limited profits. Even drug dealing is not a financially winning proposition for most street-level dealers (MacCoun and Reuter 1992; Jacobs 1999). Second, crime-producing cultural patterns that are financially nonutilitarian clearly develop (Anderson 1999). Third, much urban crime, like crime elsewhere, is committed by teenagers during an age characterized more by bravado (not unique to urban youth) than by confrontation of the hard realities of providing in an unfair world. This is not to say, however, that urban youth do not recognize the fundamental unfairness of the social system that allows the middle class to flee problem-ridden cities, leaving them behind. A broader explanation than simply "rational calculus" resulting from economic deprivation is needed.

Social Disorganization

The concept "social disorganization" has been used by sociologists since the early twentieth century, but it has found new life in recent years. When Shaw and McKay (1942) wrote about social disorganization, the focus was on the negative effects of rapid and disruptive migration into neighborhoods. They recognized that with succeeding generations, urban residents would move in order to find better housing and, in general, a better life than could be experienced in crowded slums and ghettos. They could not have envisioned the sprawl that would result from post–World War II suburbanization. Nevertheless, urban sprawl has caused social dislocations not unlike those brought on by massive migrations to the cities of eastern and southern Europeans, and African-Americans from the rural South in the first half of the twentieth century. These dislocations inhibit community social control at the same time that they cause an increase in criminogenic forces.

Much of the recent work on neighborhoods and crime has focused on clarifying and extending the arguments of early social disorganization theorists (Bursik and Webb 1982; Bursik 1988; Sampson and Groves 1989). Sampson and Groves (1989) present and test a more formalized version of social disorganization theory. First, they define social disorganization as the inability of a community to maintain effective social controls (i.e., socially disorganized neighborhoods are unable to control the behavior of residents). Next, Sampson and Groves argue that elements of community structure, such as socioeconomic status, residential mobility, and racial and ethnic heterogeneity, have only weak direct effects on crime and delinquency. Instead, most of the effect of these elements of community structure on crime and delinquency is indirect through social disorganization (i.e., elements of social structure lead to social disorganization, which, in turn, leads to elevated crime rates). Socially disorganized neighborhoods lack informal friendship networks, participation in community organizations, and, most important, are unable to effectively supervise teenage peer groups. The results of Sampson and Groves's study supported their interpretation of the theory: elements of community social structure had weak direct effects on crime and delinquency, but the most important relationships were from social disorganization to crime and delinquency (unsupervised peer groups appeared to be especially important).

Bursik and Grasmick (1993) have also offered an elaborated "systemic model" of social disorganization that emphasizes "relational networks." Essentially, the model consists of four steps. First, the socioeconomic composition of a neighborhood is expected to affect residential stability and racial and ethnic heterogeneity. Second, residential stability and racial and ethnic heterogeneity affect the formation of primary and secondary relational networks. Third, the formation of relational networks affects the exercise of "private" and "parochial" control and effective socialization. Bursik and Grasmick (1993) explain: "whereas the private order of control refers to relationships among friends, the parochial order refers to relationships among neighbors who do not have the same sentimental attachment" (17). Thus, parochial control "represents the effects of the broader local interpersonal networks and the interlocking of local institutions, such as stores, schools, churches, and voluntary organizations" (17). They also point out that effective local organizations enable neighborhoods to solicit external resources, such as funds for neighborhood projects (traditionally, social disorganization theory has not fully recognized the importance of factors "outside" the immediate community). Finally, private control, parochial control, public control (which comes from the solicitation of external resources), and effective socialization are expected to have the strongest direct effects on the rate of crime in a neighborhood.

Poverty and Private Control (Social Ties)

The systemic model of social disorganization has been criticized for minimizing the role of poverty as a cause of neighborhood crime (Warner 1999), but, in general, according to the systemic model poverty leads to an increase in neighborhood crime rates indirectly because it leads to a decrease in "relational networks" (or "social ties"), which decreases a community's overall ability to exercise informal social control. As Warner (1999) explains: "communities with denser friendship ties . . . have greater potential for informal social control of group members (and their children) through increased possibilities for informal sanctions, such as loss of respect, isolation from the group, disapproval, or reprimand. In addition, these networks provide mechanisms for the articulation of common values that are necessary for informal surveillance of neighborhood activities and property" (Warner 1999, 101).

Research that has examined the effect of poverty on social ties and the informal social control of neighborhoods has generally not supported this hypothesis. Although at least one study (Bellair 1997) suggests that increasing levels of poverty lead to a reduction in the number of social ties between neighbors, the majority of the research suggests that there is no relationship between poverty or socioeconomic status and social ties (Sampson and Groves 1989; Warner and Rountree 1997; Bursik 1999; Rountree and Warner 1999; Veysey and Messner 1999). Given these results, it is difficult to argue that disadvantaged neighborhoods have higher rates of crime than their suburban counterparts because they have more limited social networks—there is considerable evidence that suggests that this is not the case.

Research on social ties has focused on the size of informal friendship networks or the frequency of interaction with friends and neighbors. Perhaps more important, however, is the "composition" or the quality of these networks. Although individuals living in impoverished, inner-city neighborhoods may have just as many ties as their middle-class, suburban counterparts, the quality of their social networks may be greatly diminished. Rankin and Quane (2000), for example, measured network composition using three questionnaire items that asked respondents how many of their close friends have steady jobs, were on public assistance, or were college graduates. Not surprisingly, neighborhood poverty significantly predicted all three measures of network composition, such that "the net effect of living in a high-poverty neighborhood is a reduction in the rates of employed and college-educated close friends by 22% and 29% . . . and an increase in the rate of close friends who are AFDC recipients by a factor of 1.8" (Rankin and Quane 2000, 151). Individuals living in extremely disadvantaged neighborhoods may have many social ties, but "lack contact with persons with the knowledge, experience, and most important, the valuable social connections to aid them in their efforts to improve their life circumstance" (Rankin and Quane 2000, 141).

Not only have researchers suggested that poverty may be unrelated to the density of social ties and friendship networks, but some have argued that thick networks, even if they do exist, may do little to reduce the level of crime in disadvantaged neighborhoods. Wilson (1996), for example, states that "what many impoverished and dangerous neighborhoods have in common is a relatively high degree of social integration (high levels of local neighboring while being relatively isolated from contacts in broader mainstream society) and low levels of informal social control (feelings that they have little control over their immediate environment, including the environment's negative influences on their children)" (63–64). Thus, social ties do not necessarily translate into effective social control.

Sampson, Raudenbush, and Earls (1997) have introduced a concept, "collective efficacy," that avoids the problems inherent in relying on friendship networks and social ties as a measure of informal social control. According to Sampson, Raudenbush, and Earls, collective efficacy combines neighborhood cohesion with a "willingness to intervene," or, as they state, "it is the linkage of mutual trust and the willingness to intervene for the common good that defines the neighborhood context of collective efficacy" (919). Social networks may, as Morenoff, Sampson, and Raudenbush (2001) state, "foster the conditions under which collective efficacy may flourish, but they are not sufficient for the exercise of control" (521). Furthermore, "distinguishing between the resource potential represented by personal ties, on the one hand, and the shared expectations among neighbors for engagement in social control represented by collective efficacy, on the other, may help clarify the systemic model" (521).

Collective efficacy may mediate the effect of concentrated disadvantage on criminal behavior. Sampson, Raudenbush, and Earls reported that "concentrated disadvantage," a measure that combined levels of poverty, extent of public assistance, percentage of households headed by females, unemployment, and the percentage of the population that is black, had a significant negative effect on collective efficacy. Concentrated disadvantage had a significant effect on crime, but this effect was significantly reduced when collective efficacy was introduced in their analysis. Although collective efficacy did not completely eliminate the effect of concentrated disadvantage on crime, it does appear that a significant amount of the effect of concentrated disadvantage is indirect, through collective efficacy.

Poverty and Parochial Control

Parochial control refers to more casual, less intimate relationships among neighbors who live in the same community, as well as the relationships and connections between local institutions. Criminologists have generally measured the level of parochial control in a community in one of two ways. Parochial control has been operationalized as the presence or absence of institutions or organizations, such as churches, libraries, or recreational centers, in a community (Peterson, Krivo, and Harris 2000; Rose 2000). The second approach has been to assess not the presence of such organizations, but the degree to which community members participate in local organizations.

If disadvantaged neighborhoods have fewer local organizations (a weaker institutional base), or people living in impoverished neighborhoods are less likely to participate in existing organizations, then parochial control could potentially be a mediator of the effect of disadvantage on crime.

Using the first of these approaches—a focus on the "institutional base" of communities—Rose (2000) examined the effect of social disorganization on the presence or absence of religious institutions (churches). The author argues that religious institutions are crucial to the health and well-being of communities because they serve many purposes. "In addition to ministering to their congregants . . . [religious institutions] support schools, community centers and offer services such as child care, after school programs, and food pantries. . . . These activities are the foundation of parochial control" (Rose 2000, 340). The results of Rose's (2000) study suggested a "curvilinear" relationship between poverty and the prevalence of religious institutions. As the level of poverty in a neighborhood increased, so did the prevalence of religious institutions, but only to a point. Further increases in the level of poverty brought a decrease in religious institutions. Rose argues that this pattern makes sense because "We expect to see the most organizations at the point where both need and resources are sufficient to sustain them" (354). The most disadvantaged neighborhoods may have the greatest need for the services provided by these organizations, but, because of their extreme disadvantage, they lack the resources that are needed to sustain such organizations.

Peterson, Krivo, and Harris (2000) also examined the effect of neighborhood disadvantage on local institutions and how the presence or absence of local institutions influences the level of violent crime in a community. Peterson and his colleagues considered the total number of four types of institutions present in a community (census tract): recreational centers, libraries, retail and other employment institutions (such as chain grocery stores and banks), and bars (the last of which were hypothesized to increase, rather than decrease, the level of crime in a community). They found that the number of libraries and retail and other employment institutions in a community had little effect on the violent crime rate and did not mediate the effect of economic deprivation and residential instability on violent crime. However, they did find some support for the crime-reducing capacity of recreation centers and the crime-producing effect of bars. These effects were particularly noticeable in the most economically disadvantaged areas. With regard to the effect of recreation centers, Peterson, Krivo, and Harris state, "our findings strongly suggest that rates of violence would be even higher in some of the most economically deprived areas if these tracts had fewer recreation centers" (Peterson, Krivo, and Harris 2000, 55). Unfortunately, just as recreation centers seemed to be particularly helpful in the most disadvantaged areas, bars in these same areas seemed to be especially detrimental.

For robbery and rape, "bars have stronger effects on violence in extremely deprived areas" (56).

Poverty and Public Control

Contemporary social disorganization proponents argue that the level of crime and disorder in a neighborhood is affected not only by the internal dynamics of the community itself, but also by external forces. Neighborhoods that have strong ties to local organizations, institutions, and public officials outside their immediate boundaries are more effectively able to solicit external resources that enable them to reduce crime and disorder within the neighborhood. Neighborhoods that are isolated from these external sources, however, are less able to control the undesirable behavior of community members and to deal with problems facing the neighborhood.

Within this framework, it can be argued that, compared to middle-class suburban neighborhoods, disadvantaged inner-city neighborhoods with high levels of poverty, joblessness, and family disruption will be less able to solicit external resources and establish ties with local officials and the police. Velez (2001) explored the impact of "disadvantage" (a combination of income, education, and family disruption) on public control and crime using survey items that asked respondents about their perceptions of public officials and the police (e.g., "The local government is concerned about your neighborhood" and "How would you rate the overall quality of police services in your neighborhood?"). When comparing neighborhoods with low, high, and extreme levels of disadvantage, Velez found that 88% of the neighborhoods with low disadvantage reported high levels of public control. In contrast, only 24% of the neighborhoods with high levels of disadvantage and 9% of the extremely disadvantaged neighborhoods reported high levels of public control. The results of Velez's study suggested that, controlling for other neighborhood characteristics, public control had a significant effect on the likelihood of being a victim of crime. Particularly relevant for our discussion here, Velez states that for "both household and personal victimization, public social control yields greater benefits for the reduction of victimization as neighborhood disadvantage increases" (855). Velez concluded that "the enhanced effect of public social control indicates that public social control is particularly important in disadvantaged neighborhoods—places where it is needed most. This suggests that a key component of neighborhood 'success' hinges on the ability of residents to work with more powerful outside institutions that are equipped to allocate much needed resources to disadvantaged neighborhoods" (856).

In summary, social disorganization theory and the criminological research on different forms of neighborhood-level social controls suggest a number of ways that suburban sprawl might lead indirectly to elevated crime rates. Because of suburbanization, many "better off" families have fled inner-city neighborhoods, resulting in neighborhoods that are highly segregated and extremely poor. This process reduces the overall level of social control in a neighborhood. First, residents of poor neighborhoods may have a lot of social ties, but they are most often tied to other people in the neighborhood who are equally marginalized, rather than to individuals who can help them gain access to educational and employment opportunities. Thus, private control is reduced and crime is more likely. Second, because disadvantaged neighborhoods lack the resources that are needed to sustain important institutions, parochial control is reduced and, again, criminal behavior is more likely. Finally, poverty-stricken neighborhoods have difficulty establishing ties with local officials and soliciting external resources, so public control is also reduced. Thus, suburban sprawl may theoretically contribute to an increase in criminal behavior indirectly through its effects on private, parochial, and /or public forms of social control.

Oppositional Cultures

Another set of alternatives for explaining the connection between poverty and elevated rates of crime, and not necessarily incompatible with social disorganization theory, is variations on the "culture of poverty" thesis. Banfield (1967) explained delinquency among the poor as a consequence of their inability to defer gratification. Critics of his point of view argue that Banfield's arguments are tautological—those with short time horizons (unable to defer gratification) are more likely to be poor and criminal and we know who has short time horizons because they live in poverty or commit crimes. More recently Murray (1984) has convinced many policy makers that growing poverty in America, with its accompanying social problems including crime, was caused by expansion of social welfare programs. Murray's arguments provided theoretical justifications for much of the "welfare reform" that was implemented between 1985 and the end of the twentieth century. His analysis, however, has been shown to be inconsistent with the evidence (Wilson 1987). Both Banfield and Murray mention social structural arrangements as a factor in the emergence of subcultures of poverty, but nearly all of their analyses, as well as their policy recommendations, focus on the values of poor people—in particular, the values of the poor that are thought to be inconsistent with the dominant middle-class values embraced by those living elsewhere in the city and in the suburbs.

A more promising variant of the oppositional culture thesis is elaborated by Anderson (1990, 1999) who explains crime in the disrupted communities produced by urban sprawl, economic dislocation, and class and racial segregation as in part a consequence of the development and maintenance of "the code of the streets." Anderson's analysis focuses on the differences between two urban neighborhoods which border each other, one in the process of gentrifying, the other blighted and poor. The processes he describes in the latter are applicable to other inner-city communities where the residents are isolated from the mainstream and where social processes have led to residential concentrations of poor people. These circumstances are similar to what happens when those who can leave depart the inner-city neighborhoods during suburbanization. Anderson (1999) describes a neighborhood where crime and violence are more likely because, in the face of little or no hope, young black men and boys adopt a hypermasculine code of conduct. What differentiates Anderson's perspective from others, such as Banfield and Murray, is that he clearly links the emergence of these codes to the social structural dislocations that have occurred because of racial segregation, job losses resulting from deindustrialization, and suburbanization. The behaviors of these young men are consequences of the circumstances in which they live, not the cause of the dislocations. To be clear, the crime and delinquency of these young men exacerbates the problems of their communities, because their illegal activity is another incentive for those who can move out to do so and a disincentive for others to move in.

In contrast to theoretical explanations that rely on social ties to explain elevated crime rates, an emphasis on oppositional cultures (or "cultural attenuation") argues that what is important is not the capacity to intervene when residents are engaging in undesirable behavior, but the perceived appropriateness of intervening. As Warner (1999) argues, "in impoverished neighborhoods when behaviors contradicting middle-class values arise, intervention may be less likely, *regardless* of the number of social ties" (110). Thus, a "cultural attenuation" model "explains the effects of poverty on crime rates through decreased community levels of intervention, rather than decreased social ties" (Warner 1999, 110).

As Warner argues, research that documents the existence of oppositional values in poor, inner-city neighborhoods is difficult to reconcile with the systemic model of social disorganization theory. According to Bursik and Grasmick (1993), the systemic model is based on the assumption that "consensus exists among the residents concerning the goal of living in an area relatively free from the threat of crime. If a widespread consensus cannot be shown to exist . . . then the framework is simply not viable" (20). In contrast, research on oppositional cultures suggests that there is little consensus of values in many impoverished, inner-city neighborhoods. Given that some scholars consider oppositional cultures to be inconsistent with the basic assumptions of the systemic model of social disorganiztion, more refined theoretical models that incorporate both structural and cultural explanations of crime are needed.

The renewed interest in developing explanations of crime that recognize the importance of culture, as well as the structural characteristics of neighborhoods, is very encouraging. While Anderson's description of the streets helps provide a fuller explanation, however, it does not explain what it is about urban dislocations that begins the criminogenic process. We believe that central to the process is joblessness and its effects on communities, families, and education.

Joblessness

Joblessness and marginal employment are significant predictors of criminal involvement of young adults (Crutchfield and Pitchford 1997). Cities with more joblessness have higher crime rates (White 1999), and neighborhoods with higher levels of unstable employment have higher crime rates (Crutchfield 1989; Crutchfield, Glusker, and Bridges 1999). There is growing evidence that joblessness in the urban core contributes to crime (Sampson 1987; Almgren et al. 1998). Urban job losses due to deindustrialization and the suburbanization of new employment then have an effect on criminality.

As we described above, a portion of this pattern is a consequence of a utilitarian calculus. We must recognize, however, that most workers who lost their jobs as a result of deindustrialization were past the age when most criminals are active in law-violating behavior. Crime is most frequently a young person's activity (Hirschi and Gottfredson 1983; Steffensmeier et al. 1989). It is unreasonable to expect that a middle-aged, laid-off steelworker or an auto industry assembly-line worker would turn to street crime after receiving a pink slip. So, how do job losses lead to crime?

First, it is the next generation of workers—disproportionately minority males between the ages of 18 and 25 that would be in the early years of their working lives—who are the potential participants in criminal behavior. Second, the most crime-prone segment of the population is adolescents who are between 15 and 17 years of age. Their primary roles are not as workers but as students. We must have an account of how the joblessness created by sprawl, the concentration of poverty, and income inequality affects the delinquency of this non-work-age population. Third, there is evidence that it is not just the employment circumstances of individuals that predicts their criminality, but also that of others who live in proximity to them. An explanation of how job losses lead to crime, minus the effects of utilitarian choices, must take these patterns into account.

In the classic *Talley's Corner* Leibow (1967) described how the days and lifestyles of black men in urban Washington, DC, were conditioned by their employment. To casual observers these men were idle near-do-wells who would rather "hang" on the corner than work, more interested in the friendship on that corner than taking on responsible adult roles in the work force or in their families. Leibow's ethnography documents that these men worked as day laborers and in the marginal secondary-sector jobs that were available to them. They only tangentially interacted with the women in their lives and their children because their employment did not pay sufficiently to permit them the luxury of assuming a "real man's" provider role.

Just as the lifestyles led by the men on Tally's corner were conditioned by their labor market experience, so too are the lives of the men and women left without jobs when the economy moves offshore or to the suburbs. Without work to structure their day, to give them hope and a reason to invest in the future, the circumstances described by Anderson (1990, 1999) can emerge. The code of the streets does not spring from nowhere, nor is it a part of blackness or Hispanicness. If it were simply a product of poverty, it would occur not just in inner-city neighborhoods, but elsewhere where the poor live. These crime-conducive codes are products of street corner lifestyles, which are themselves products of joblessness in inner-city neighborhoods, which isolate and concentrate poverty (Wilson 1987).

What has occurred in many core cities is that too few people have jobs and those who do are too frequently employed in marginal secondary-sector jobs. These jobs pay little, have few if any benefits, and provide limited opportunity for the future. These jobs neither pay sufficiently to dull the luster of what looks to be the fast, "easy" money of criminal enterprise nor provide the stakes in conformity that inhibit criminal behavior among young adults (Sampson and Laub 1993). Some are lured to crime because there are not attractive, or even reasonable, alternatives in the legitimate work world; others are not constrained to avoid "street lifestyles," the codes of the street, and behavior that makes crime not necessarily a calculated outcome, but certainly more likely (Crutchfield 1989). Criminal involvement is higher among those out of the labor force or employed in marginal jobs, and this effect is greatest where marginalized workers live in proximity to larger numbers of similarly situated others (Crutchfield and Pitchford 1997). This will occur more frequently with concentrations of the poor into central city neighborhoods resulting from suburbanization.

These problems are further exacerbated by the large increases in incarceration rates of recent decades (Beck 2000). Not surprisingly, a disproportionate number of those imprisoned have come from the same devastated inner-city neighborhoods that we have been describing. When released from prison they frequently return to those home neighborhoods.

Once they have been been imprisoned, the already compromised job competitiveness of these people is made more difficult by their status as ex-convicts (for a review, see Western, Kling, and Weiman 2001). Those who have served time have a considerably better chance of remaining on the street if they are fortunate enough to find gainful employment (Uggen 2000), but the spatial mismatch between jobs and potential inner-city workers means that low-skill, low-education workers, even those without felony records, struggle to find work, which means that many of those increased numbers of former prisoners will have even less success. Every indication is that without work they are more likely to reoffend, meaning that sentencing policies of recent decades will, in all likelihood, destabilize these communities even more because they both increase the proportion of the population not working and they are likely to increase crime rates.

Joblessness and Delinquency

The age distinction between "young adults" and "juveniles" in the inner city is meaningful only when they are charged with crimes, and as states increasingly broaden the conditions under which the juveniles can be sent to adult courts and into the adult penal system, even that distinction is blurring. More meaningful than the the age of 18 that we use to divide juveniles from adults is the answer to the question, Are they still in school or not? School is an important potential agent of social control for juveniles, just as sound employment is for adults (Wadsworth 2000). And, though school dropout rates have declined nationally, they remain high in the inner city (Jencks 1991). Although it is difficult to provide direct evidence that labor markets play a direct role in trends in dropout rates, there is some suggestive evidence that they may (Crane 1991).

Sprawl and its attendant isolations of poor neighborhoods lead job loss to increase crime in two ways. The first way is directly, through the processes described above. The second way is the effect that it has on juvenile delinquency through the effect of job losses on schooling. In isolated urban neighborhoods school-age children are less likely to have two important kinds of role models: adults who are regularly employed, who model conventional behavior and values (Wilson 1987), and adults whose career paths model the benefits of successful navigation from school to work (Crutchfield, Glusker, and Bridges 1999; Wadsworth 2000).

The argument here is that it is hard for children in deprived communities to internalize the belief that education is "a way out" when adults in the neighborhood have not benefited through conventional paths. A number of studies have found that school success is negatively related to delinquency (Ward and Tittle 1994; Voelkl, Welte, and Wieczorek 1999). While it is reasonable to expect that involvement in delinquency causes a decline in school performance, the causal direction is generally interpreted to work in the other direction. Children less successful in school are more likely to become involved in delinquency.

Table 6.1: Employment, School, and Juvenile Violent and Property Crime Involvement

	Violent Crime	Property Crime
Basic model variables:		
Age	−.092***	−.024
Sex	.276***	.181***
Race	.016	−.055***
Family income	.018	.046**
Parent's marital status	−.011	.117***
Central city resident	−.041**	−.045***
Macro variables:		
Population size	.012	.018
Percent black	.010	−.096***
Percent in poverty	−.077**	−.015
Median family income	−.075**	.039
Percent single mothers	.056*	.091***
Unemployment rate	.026*	.003
Unemployed/central city Interaction	.004	−.045***
Respondent's education and work variables:		
Been suspended from school	.165***	.161***
Out of school and work	.053***	.038**
Part-time employment	.005	.054***
Hours worked	.027	−.005
Amount of education experienced	−.047**	−.006
GPA	−.113***	−.116***
Parents' characteristics:		
Parents' job quality	.005	.024
Parents' education	.018	.093***
Father full-time	−.013	.104**
R^2	.179	.129

Source: Crutchfield, Rankin, and Pitchford 1993.

*$p < .05$.
**$p < .01$.
***$p < .001$.

Table 6.1 presents the results of analyses using data from the National Longitudinal Survey of Youth (Crutchfield, Rankin, and Pitchford 1993). The respondents included in these analyses are under the age of 18, the age when most nondropouts leave school. These tables show that a very important determinant of delinquent behavior is school performance. Those with higher grade point averages (GPA) are less involved in crime. Also, children who are neither in school nor working are the most likely to be involved in delinquency. Two things are important for our purposes here. First, juveniles' school success is partially explained by *adult* education and work experiences. This suggests that while older adults may not turn to crime when they are laid off or when they cannot find work, this circumstance could encourage the next generation to invest less in education, thereby weakening the crime-controlling influence of schools. Second, with fewer jobs available, one can reasonably conclude that school dropouts will be less likely to get even secondary-sector service jobs in isolated inner cities with high levels of poverty.

Wadsworth (2000) found that parent's employment is positively related to children's educational performance, which in turn negatively effects delinquency. Crutchfield, Rankin, and Pitchford found similar patterns. This pattern is exacerbated in cities affected by urban sprawl and suburbanization. In those places the loss of tax base is related to school decline. Thus, children lack both effective educational role models and are attending low-resource, less effective schools. We are not saying that parents in these communities do not value education. Perhaps the best way to illustrate this is to imagine that these parents believe in the value of education and try to convince their offspring that education is the ticket out of poor inner-city neighborhoods. It is not hard to imagine petulant adolescents responding by asking their parents, "If education is so important, what happened to you?"

In addition to the effects that job losses in the inner city have had on individuals' likelihood of becoming involved in criminal behavior, there are crime-causing impacts on communities as well. These impacts take two forms. There is the diminution of communities' capacity for social control, traditionally thought of as social disorganization, and independent of social control there appear to be increases in crime when there are concentrations of out-of-work or marginally employed people in a geographic area. With urban sprawl, increased concentration of poverty, and increased job losses, both occur.

Decades ago sociologists described the urban decay of the inner city in terms of social disorganization, the circumstance where effective social control was inhibited by a breakdown in norms and the fracturing of important institutions. Early in the twentieth century, disorganization was produced by rapid in-migration that disrupted the solidarity of neighborhoods. When people are not bonded and do not know their neighbors, the informal social control that is fundamental to communities is disrupted. Today, the problem is not in-migration, but the exodus of the most vital families from inner-city neighborhoods. Those that can move frequently do. This exodus is not limited to whites. Increasingly, blacks are populating suburbs. More often than not they move to predominantly black suburbs, but those with the capacity leave inner-city neighborhoods (South and Crowder 1997, 1998). As a consequence, social ties, which are as important to informal social control today as they were seventy years ago, have been broken. As they have for the past few decades, the initial reports of the 2000 U.S. census indicate that the urban cores of the big cities of the East and Midwest continue to lose population.

VII. School Funding

Above we described how the loss of jobs affects juvenile delinquency. Because this effect appears to occur where there are concentrations of unemployment and marginal jobs, it will disproportionately be a problem for inner-city populations left behind by suburbanization. In fact, one of the attractive features of suburbs for the families leaving the inner city is the leaving behind of neighborhoods with such concentrations. Another attractive feature of the suburbs is better schools. Much has been made of the unequal funding of schools and the negative consequences that result (Kozol 1991). We suggest that another consequence is that to the extent that school districts lose their tax base when more affluent families leave for the suburbs an already criminogenic environment, inner-city neighborhoods with concentrations of poor people become even more fertile ground for the spawning of delinquency when schools are underfunded. This problem is exacerbated by the special problems of children likely to populate many of these schools. Obviously, in many locations, they will be poorer, more likely to be nonnative English speakers, and come to schools with a host of other problems that are often discussed together as "ready to learn" issues. These factors make it more difficult for inner-city children to come to school prepared to behave, engage, and learn as well-fed, middle-class children do.

In simple terms, these underfunded schools will be more likely to foster higher delinquency rates because they will be less likely to develop important attachments to students. Students with these attachments are less likely to engage in delinquency (Hirschi 1969; Cernkovich and Giordano 1992). Such schools will be less likely to prepare children for either post-high-school education or the workplace. For example, Kirschenman and Neckerman (1991) found that employers outside Chicago reported that they were less likely to hire graduates of inner-city schools because they assumed they would be less prepared than students from suburban schools. While this pattern may be a convenient and apparently "nondiscriminating" way not to hire African-Americans, the job market prospects for these inner-city high school graduates remains weak. When young adults do not fare well in the labor market they are more likely to become involved in crime, especially when they are surrounded by similarly disadvantaged others (Crutchfield and Pitchford 1997).

To be sure, a host of government programs have been instituted to support school districts that have particular challenges such as poverty and the presence of students of English as a second language. Unfortunately, these programs do not make up for the shortfalls that exist when the funding of urban and suburban schools are compared (Parrish, Hikido, and Fowler 1998). Table 6.2 is a summary of a table that appears in a Department of Education

Table 6.2: General, Categorical, and Total Revenues per Student
by Metropolitan Status, 1991–92

Revenues by Metro Status Category	Percentage of all Students Enrolled	Revenue Type as a Percentage of Total Revenue	Actual Revenues per Student ($)	Cost- and Need-Adjusted Revenues per Student ($)
General revenues:				
Urban/central cities	26.9	77.4	4,476	3,563
Suburban/metropolitan	48.8	84.1	4,833	3,972
Rural	24.3	81.0	3,963	3,719
Categorical revenues:				
Urban/central cities	26.9	22.6	1,305	1,030
Suburban/metropolitan	48.8	15.9	914	758
Rural	24.3	19.0	932	878
Total revenues:				
Urban/central cities	26.9	100.0	5,781	4,593
Suburban/metropolitan	48.8	100.0	5,748	4,730
Rural	24.3	100.0	4,894	4,597

Source: Parrish, Hikido, and Fowler 1998, table II-6.

report on educational funding. This table compares per-student funding
for central city, suburban, and rural schools. The column labeled "Revenue
Type as a Percentage of Total Revenue" describes sources of funding for
three categories of school districts: urban and central city school districts,
suburban and metropolitan districts, and rural school districts. The "Categorical revenues" row describes the average percentage of each type of a district's funds that come from special, dedicated sources, such as funding for
students of English as a second language, or school lunch programs for poor
children. The complete table (not shown) includes actual expenditures, as
well as cost- and need-adjusted expenditures. The actual revenues per student
in central city and suburban schools are nearly the same, with the former
spending thirty-three more dollars than the latter. Both outspend rural districts. This apparent equity within metropolitan school districts masks important differences. Categorical funding, which includes support for particular needs such as school lunch programs, cannot be diverted for general
education. Central city schools have per-student funding comparable to suburban schools only when categorical funds are included. The final column
of table 6.2 shows the distribution of cost- and need-adjusted revenues per
student, which takes the demand for special funding into account for three
types of districts. Clearly, both central city and rural schools suffer in comparison to suburban schools (compare "Total revenues" for "Cost- and Need-
Adjusted Revenues per Student").

VIII. Criminal Justice and Racial Disparities

A great deal of research has been done in the past twenty-five years debating the existence of racial disparities in criminal and juvenile justice processing. Much of that research consists of arguments between those that contend that observed racial differences are nearly all a product of differentials in criminal involvement (Blumstein 1982; Langan 1985, Wilbanks 1987) and those arguing that in addition to those differences there is "unwarranted" racial disproportionality (see Bishop 2005). Some institutional causes for the latter have been explored (Crutchfield, Bridges, and Pitchford 1994). A largely unexplored example of such institutionally based racial disproportionality is suburbanization.

Although there is an ongoing shift of black and Latino populations to the suburbs, contemporary urban sprawl in America has been characterized disproportionately by white movement out of central cities, leaving a large number of cities populated by primarily black and brown people. To the extent that urban law enforcement practices differ from suburban practices, they can contribute to observed differences in the handling of both adult and juvenile criminal cases. To be sure, some of the differences in the way that police departments and courts act will be due to the higher crime rates of central cities. As metropolitan areas become increasingly sprawling, not only are urban and suburban populations subject to different police departments, but in the largest urban areas suburbanites live in different counties with completely separate criminal and juvenile justice systems. In these circumstances those setting and administering criminal justice policies—judges, prosecutors, and sheriffs (in some states)—are put into office and answer to a separate and predominately white electorate, while the core urban county's officials will be selected by a more integrated or primarily minority population. For our purposes, those being processed by the criminal justice system will be subject essentially to a different system. Harris (2002) found that juvenile courts in the largely minority inner city far more frequently sent juveniles to adult court for processing than did the juvenile court systems in the primarily white suburbs.

Police practices, too, may differ between urban and suburban departments. In a study of prosecutors' practices Crutchfield, Weis, Engen, and Gainey (1995) found that in one jurisdiction the city police department routinely filed all drug arrests as "expedite cases." Defendants in these cases were significantly less likely to be released before trial. Suburban departments routinely did not do this for similar cases because it would have required them to transport the arrested people to the county jail, located in the city. The suburban departments instituted a pragmatic policy to reduce the amount of time that officers were off patrol, transporting prisoners. Unfortunately, since the urban drug cases disproportionately involved minority defendants, this difference in policy had an unintended racially disproportionate effect, and cases where defendants were not released before trial were more likely to be convicted and to be sentenced more harshly.

One must also wonder if and how issues of racial profiling will differ between the predominately white suburbs and predominately minority inner cities. It is not immediately clear that the problem will necessarily be more likely in the one or the other setting. Where there are large minority populations, they might be viewed as threatening problem populations that are more likely to commit crime. Here police might profile to preempt this perceived heightened problem. On the other hand, where there are fewer people of color police might be more likely to take note and question minority people because they appeared out of place.

IX. Conclusion

The discussion in this chapter has covered a lot of ground. In a sense, it is a survey of surveys. Our purpose in tracing this circuitous route has been to suggest that criminologists ought to take a more acute interest in such seemingly unrelated issues as suburban sprawl. We argued that suburban sprawl and the concentration of poverty are related manifestations of the prevailing dynamic at work in U.S. metropolitan areas. This dynamic creates a residential pattern that is highly segregated by race and class and therefore gives rise to a host of social problems. The implications of the increasing spatial differentiation of our society has particularly important implications in the areas of juvenile justice and crime. Poverty and social disorganization provide a negative context for child development, especially among adolescents, who are more susceptible to the influences of crime and poverty in the neighborhood. Equally important, these segregated patterns steer the development of the juvenile justice system in certain directions, because police, judicial, and social service functions are implemented geographically. The resulting institutions tend to be less responsive to the needs of youth and more responsive to the need to maintain order in deeply troubled neighborhoods.

Criminologists and others interested in the juvenile justice system have done a great deal of research, much of it reviewed above, to document how poverty and social disorganization at the neighborhood level affects youth development and conditions the institutional response to juvenile crime. This research, as necessary and important as it is, takes for granted the existence of extremely disadvantaged neighborhoods. As long as metropolitan development proceeds along the lines of the past several decades, the continued existence and expansion of highly devastated neighborhoods is assured. In that context, neighborhood-level interventions, as important as they are in responding to the crisis on the ground, are like trying to sweep back the ocean with a broom. If the tide is coming in, failure is assured.

Criminologists must therefore pay greater attention to the process that creates criminogenic neighborhoods. Neighborhoods have effects, but they also have causes. Those who study juvenile justice issues have an important role to play in the suburban sprawl debate, because they are well positioned to point out the human, social, and economic costs of the status quo. Redirecting the enormous energies of the growth process toward more mixed-income, less segregated neighborhoods and communities can be achieved only if there is a greater appreciation of these costs in the research and policy-making communities.

Notes

1. The clearest exception to this pattern is the discussion of poverty among the elderly.

2. This claim is difficult to verify empirically, because neither the poverty rate nor the census tracts that serve as proxies for neighborhoods can be replicated in any consistent way across nations. Nevertheless, it seems clear that most European cities are not nearly as segregated by race and class as is common in the United States (Musterd and Ostendorf 1998; van der Wusten and Musterd 1998).

3. Parts of this section draw heavily on Jargowsky 2002.

References

Abramson, Alan J., and Mitchell S. Tobin. 1994. "The Changing Geography of Metropolitan Opportunity: The Segregation of the Poor in U.S. Metropolitan Areas, 1970 to 1990." In *Fannie Mae Annual Housing Conference, 1994*. Washington, DC: Fannie Mae Office of Housing Policy Research.

Almgren, Gunnar, Avery Guest, George Immerwahr, and Michael Spittel. 1998. "Joblessness, Family Disruption, and Violent Death in Chicago, 1970–90." *Social Forces* 76:1465–1493.

Anderson, Elijah. 1990. *Streetwise: Race, Class, and Change in an Urban Community*. Chicago: University of Chicago Press.

———. 1999. *Code of the Street: Decency, Violence, and the Moral Life of the Inner City*. New York: W. W. Norton.

Bailey, William C. 1984. "Poverty, Inequality and City Homicide Rates: Some Not So Unexpected Findings." *Criminology* 22:531–550.

Banfield, Edward C. 1967. *The Moral Basis of a Backward Society*. New York: Free Press.

Beck, Allen. 2000. *Prison and Jail Inmates at Midyear, 1999*. Washington, DC: U.S. Department of Justice.

Becker, Gary S. 1968. "Crime and Punishment: An Economic Approach." *Journal of Political Economy* 76:169–217.

Bellair, Paul E. 1997. "Social Interaction and Community Crime: Examining the Importance of Neighbor Networks." *Criminology* 35:677–703.

Berry, Brian L. J., and Quentin Gillard. 1977. *The Changing Shape of Metropolitan America: Commuting Patterns, Urban Fields, and Decentralization Processes, 1960–1970.* Cambridge, MA: Ballinger.

Bishop, Donna M. 2005. "The Role of Race and Ethnicity in Juvenile Justice Processing." In *Our Children, Their Children: Confronting Race and Ethnic Differences in American Juvenile Justice,* ed. Darnell F. Hawkins and Kimberly Kempf-Leonard. Chicago: University of Chicago Press.

Blumstein, Alfred. 1982. "On the Racial Disproportionality of the U.S. State Prison Populations." *Journal of Criminal Law and Criminology* 73:1259–1281.

Blumstein, Alfred, Fredrick P. Rivara, and Richard Rosenfeld. 2000. "The Rise and Decline of Homicide and Why." *Annual Review of Public Health* 21:505–541.

Bursik, Robert J., Jr. 1988. "Social Disorganization and Theories of Crime and Delinquency: Problems and Prospects." *Criminology* 26:519–551.

———. 1999. "The Informal Control of Crime through Neighborhood Networks." *Sociological Focus* 32:85–97.

Bursik, Robert J., Jr., and Harold G. Grasmick. 1993. *Communities and Crime.* New York: Lexington Books.

Bursik, Robert J., Jr., and Jim Webb. 1982. "Community Change and Patterns of Delinquency." *American Journal of Sociology* 88:24–42.

Cernkovich, Stephen A., and Peggy C. Giordano. 1992. "School Bonding, Race, and Delinquency." *Criminology* 30:261–291.

Cork, Daniel. 1999. "Examining Space-Time Interaction in City-Level Homicide Data: Crack Markets and the Diffusion of Guns among Youth." *Journal of Quantitative Criminology* 15:379–406.

Crane, Jonathan. 1991. "Effects of Neighborhoods on Dropping Out of School and Teenage Childbearing." In *The Urban Underclass,* ed. Christopher Jencks and Paul E. Peterson. Washington, DC: Brookings Institution.

Crutchfield, Robert D. 1989. "Labor Stratification and Violent Crime." *Social Forces* 68:489–512.

Crutchfield, Robert D., George S. Bridges, and Susan R. Pitchford. 1994. "Analytical and Aggregation Biases in Analyses of Imprisonment: Reconciling Discrepancies in Studies of Racial Disparity." *Journal of Research in Crime and Delinquency* 31:166–182.

Crutchfield, Robert D., Michael R. Geerken, and Walter R. Gove. 1982. "Crime Rate and Social Integration: The Impact of Metropolitan Mobility." *Criminology* 20:467–478.

Crutchfield, Robert D., Ann Glusker, and George S. Bridges. 1999. "A Tale of Three Cities: Labor Markets and Homicide." *Sociological Focus* 32:65–83.

Crutchfield, Robert D., and Susan R. Pitchford. 1997. "Work and Crime: The Effects of Labor Stratification." *Social Forces* 76:93–118.

Crutchfield, Robert D., Margo Rankin, and Susan R. Pitchford. 1993. "Inheriting Stakes in Conformity: Effects of Parents' Labor Market Experience on Juvenile Delinquency." Paper presented at the annual meetings of the American Society of Criminology, Phoenix.

Crutchfield, Robert D., Joseph G. Weis, Rodney L. Engen, and Randy R. Gainey. 1995.

A Study on Racial and Ethnic Disparities in the Prosecution of Criminal Cases in King County Washington: Final Report. Washington State Minority and Justice Commission.

Farley, Reynolds, and William H. Frey. 1994. "Changes in the Segregation of Whites and Blacks during the 1980s: Small Steps toward a More Integrated Society." *American Sociological Review* 59:23–45.

Feld, Barry C. 1998. "Juvenile and Criminal Justice Systems' Responses to Youth Violence." Pp. 189–261 in *Youth Violence,* ed. Michael Tonry and Mark H. Moore, Crime and Justice: A Review of Research, vol. 24. Chicago: University of Chicago Press.

———. 1999. "A Funny Thing Happened on the Way to the Centenary: Social Structure, Race and the Transformation of the Juvenile Court." *Punishment and Society* 1:187–214.

Gans, Herbert. 1967. *The Levittowners: How People Live and Politic in Suburbia.* New York: Pantheon Books.

Harrington, Michael. 1962. *The Other America: Poverty in the United States.* New York: MacMillan.

Harris, Alexes. 2002. "Sending 'Sophisticated' Children Upstairs: The Social, Legal, and Organizational Context of Contemporary Juvenile Waiver Proceeding." PhD diss., University of California, Los Angeles.

Harrison, Roderick J., and Daniel H. Weinberg. 1992. "Changes in Racial and Ethnic Residential Segregation, 1980–1990." Paper presented at the annual meetings of the American Statistical Association, Boston.

Hirschi, Travis. 1969. *Causes of Delinquency.* Berkeley: University of California Press.

Hirschi, Travis, and Michael Gottfredson. 1983. "Age and the Explanation of Crime." *American Journal of Sociology* 89:552–584.

Jackson, Kenneth T. 1985. *Crabgrass Frontier: The Suburbanization of the United States.* New York: Oxford University Press.

Jacobs, Bruce A. 1999. *Dealing Crack: The Social World of Streetcorner Selling.* Boston: Northeastern University Press.

Jargowsky, Paul A. 1997. *Poverty and Place: Ghettos, Barrios, and the American City.* New York: Russell Sage Foundation.

———. 2002. "Sprawl, Concentration of Poverty, and Urban Inequality." In *Urban Sprawl: Causes, Consequences, and Policy Responses,* ed. Gregory Squires. Washington, DC: Urban Institute Press.

———. 2003. *Stunning Progress, Hidden Problems: The Dramatic Decline of Concentrated Poverty in the 1990s.* Living Cities Census Series, Center on Urban and Metropolitan Studies. Washington, DC: Brookings Institution.

Jencks, Christopher. 1991. "Is the American Underclass Growing?" In *The Urban Underclass,* ed. Christopher Jencks and Paul E. Peterson. Washington, DC: Brookings Institution.

Kirschenman, Joleen, and Kathryn M. Neckerman. 1991. "'We'd Love to Hire Them, but . . .': The Meaning of Race for Employers." In *The Urban Underclass,* ed. Christopher Jencks and Paul E. Peterson. Washington, DC: Brookings Institution.

Kozol, Jonathan. 1991. *Savage Inequalities: Children in America's Schools.* New York: Crown Publishing.

Krivo, Lauren J., and Ruth D. Peterson. 1996. "Extremely Disadvantaged Neighborhoods and Urban Crime." *Social Forces* 75:619–650.

Langan, Patrick. 1985. "Racism on Trial: New Evidence to Explain the Racial Composition of Prisons in the United States." *Journal of Criminal Law and Criminology* 76:666–683.

Liebow, Elliot. 1967. *Tally's Corner*. Boston: Little, Brown.

Loftin, Colin, and Robert Nash Parker. 1985. "An Error-in-Variable Model of the Effect of Poverty on Urban Homicide Rates." *Criminology* 23:269–285.

Luckenbill, David F. 1977. "Criminal Homicide as a Situated Transaction." *Social Problems* 25:176–186.

MacCoun, Robert, and Peter Reuter. 1992. "Are the Wages of Sin $30 an Hour? Economic Aspects of Street-Level Drug Dealing." *Crime and Delinquency* 38:477–491.

Magnet, Myron. 1993. *The Dream and the Nightmare: The Sixties' Legacy to the Underclass*. New York: Morrow.

Massey, Douglas S. 1990. "American Apartheid: Segregation and the Making of the Underclass." *American Journal of Sociology* 96:329–357.

Massey, Douglas S., and Nancy A. Denton. 1993. *American Apartheid: Segregation and the Making of the Underclass*. Cambridge, MA: Harvard University Press.

Massey, Douglas S., and Mitchell L. Eggers. 1990. "The Ecology of Inequality: Minorities and the Concentration of Poverty, 1970–1980." *American Journal of Sociology* 95:1153–1188.

Morenoff, Jeffrey D., Robert J. Sampson, and Stephen W. Raudenbush. 2001. "Neighborhood Inequality, Collective Efficacy, and the Spatial Dynamics of Urban Violence." *Criminology* 39:517–559.

Murray, Charles. 1984. *Losing Ground: American Social Policy, 1950–1980*. New York: Basic Books.

Musterd, Sako, and Wim Ostendorf. 1998. "Segregation, Polarisation and Social Exclusion in Metropolitan Areas." In *Urban Segregation and the Welfare State: Inequality and Exclusion in Western Cities*, ed. Sako Musterd and Wim Ostendorf. New York: Routledge.

Park, Robert E. 1926. "The Urban Community as a Spatial Pattern and a Moral Order." In *The Urban Community*, ed. E. W. Burgess. Chicago: University of Chicago Press.

Parrish, Thomas B., Christine S. Hikido, and William J. Fowler, Jr. 1998. *Inequalities in Public School District Revenues*. Washington, DC: U.S. Department of Education, Office of Educational Research and Improvement.

Patterson, E. Britt. 1991. "Poverty, Income Inequality, and Community Crime Rates." *Criminology* 29:755–776.

Peterson, Ruth D., and Lauren J. Krivo. 1999. "Racial Segregation, the Concentration of Disadvantage, and Black and White Homicide Victimization." *Sociological Forum* 14:465–493.

Peterson, Ruth D., Lauren J. Krivo, and Mark A. Harris. 2000. "Disadvantage and Neighborhood Violent Crime: Do Local Institutions Matter?" *Journal of Research in Crime and Delinquency* 37:31–63.

Rainwater, Lee. 1970. *Behind Ghetto Walls*. Chicago: Aldine Publishing Co.

Rankin, Bruce H., and James M. Quane. 2000. "Neighborhood Poverty and the Social Isolation of Inner-City African American Families." *Social Forces* 79:139–164.

Ricketts, Erol R., and Isabel V. Sawhill. 1988. "Defining and Measuring the Underclass." *Journal of Policy Analysis and Management* 7:316–325.

Rose, Dina R. 2000. "Social Disorganization and Parochial Control: Religious Institutions and Their Communities." *Sociological Forum* 15:339–358.

Rountree, Pamela Wilcox, and Barbara D. Warner. 1999. "Social Ties and Crime: Is the Relationship Gendered?" *Criminology* 37:789–813.

Ruggles, Patricia. 1990. *Drawing the Line: Alternative Poverty Measures and Their Implications for Public Policy.* Washington, DC: Urban Institute Press.

Sampson, Robert J. 1987. "Urban Black Violence: The Effect of Male Joblessness and Family Disruption." *American Journal of Sociology* 93:348–382.

Sampson, Robert J., and Thomas C. Castellano. 1982. "Economic Inequality and Personal Victimization: An Areal Perspective." *British Journal of Criminology* 22:363–385.

Sampson, Robert J., and W. Byron Groves. 1989. "Community Structure and Crime: Testing Social Disorganization Theory." *American Journal of Sociology* 94:774–802.

Sampson, Robert J., and John Laub. 1993. *Crime in the Making: Pathways and Turning Points through Life.* Cambridge, MA: Harvard University Press.

Sampson, Robert J., Stephen W. Raudenbush, and Felton Earls. 1997. "Neighborhoods and Violent Crime: A Multilevel Study of Collective Efficacy." *Science* 277:918–924.

Shaw, Clifford R., and Henry D. McKay. 1942. *Juvenile Delinquency and Urban Areas.* Chicago: University of Chicago Press.

Sierra Club. 1998. *Sprawl: The Dark Side of the American Dream.* Washington, DC: Sierra Club. http://www.sierraclub.org/sprawl/report98/index.asp.

South, Scott J., and Kyle D. Crowder. 1997. "Escaping Distressed Neighborhoods: Individual, Community, and Metropolitan Influences." *American Journal of Sociology* 102:1040–1084.

———. 1998. "Leaving the 'Hood: Residential Mobility between Black, White, and Integrated Neighborhoods." *American Sociological Review* 63:17–26.

Squires, Gregory, ed. 2002. *Urban Sprawl: Causes, Consequences, and Policy Responses.* Washington, DC: Urban Institute Press.

Steffensmeier, Darrell J., Emilie A. Allan, Miles D. Harer, and Cathy Streifel. 1989. "Age and the Distribution of Crime." *American Journal of Sociology* 94:803–831.

Sullivan, Richard F. 1973. "The Economics of Crime: An Introduction to the Literature." *Crime and Delinquency* 19:138–149.

Suttles, Gerald D. 1968. *The Social Order of the Slum.* Chicago: University of Chicago Press.

Uggen, Christopher. 2000. "Work as a Turning Point in the Life Course of Criminals: A Duration Model of Age, Employment, and Recidivism." *American Sociological Review* 67:529–546.

van der Wusten, Herman, and Sako Musterd. 1998. "Welfare State Effects on Inequality and Segregation." In *Urban Segregation and the Welfare State: Inequality and Exclusion in Western Cities,* ed. Sako Musterd and Wim Ostendorf. New York: Routledge.

Velez, Maria B. 2001. "The Role of Public Social Control in Urban Neighborhoods: A Multilevel Analysis of Victimization Risk." *Criminology* 39:837–864.

Veysey, Bonita M., and Steven F. Messner. 1999. "Further Testing of Social Disorganization Theory: An Elaboration of Sampson and Groves's 'Community Structure and Crime.'" *Journal of Research in Crime and Delinquency* 36:156–174.

Voelkl, Kristin E., John W. Welte, and William F. Wieczorek. 1999. "Schooling and Delinquency among White and African American Adolescents." *Urban Education* 34:69–88.

Wadsworth, Tim. 2000. "Labor Markets, Delinquency, and Social Control Theory: An Empirical Assessment of the Mediating Process." *Social Forces* 78:1041–1066.

Ward, David A., and Charles R. Tittle. 1994. "IQ and Delinquency: A Test of Two Competing Explanations." *Journal of Quantitative Criminology* 10:189–212.

Warner, Barbara D. 1997. "Community Characteristics and the Recording of Crime: Police Recording of Citizens' Complaints of Burglary and Assault." *Justice Quarterly* 14:631–650.

———. 1999. "Whither Poverty? Social Disorganization Theory in an Era of Urban Transformation." *Sociological Focus* 32:99–113.

Warner, Barbara D., and Glenn L. Pierce. 1993. "Reexamining Social Disorganization Theory Using Calls to Police as a Measure of Crime." *Criminology* 31:493–517.

Warner, Barbara D., and Pamela Wilcox Rountree. 1997. "Local Social Ties in a Community and Crime Model: Questioning the Systemic Nature of Informal Social Control." *Social Problems* 44:520–536.

Warner, Sam Bass. 1962. *Streetcar Suburbs*. Cambridge, MA: Harvard University Press.

———. 1972. *The Urban Wilderness: A History of the American City*. New York: Harper and Row.

Western, Bruce, Jeffrey R. Kling, and David F. Weiman. 2001. "The Labor Market Consequences of Incarceration." *Crime and Delinquency* 47:410–427.

White, Garland. 1999. "Crime and the Decline of Manufacturing, 1970–1990." *Justice Quarterly* 16:81–97.

Wilbanks, William. 1987. *The Myth of a Racist Criminal Justice System*. Belmont, CA: Wadsworth.

Wilson, William Julius. 1987. *The Truly Disadvantaged: The Inner City, the Underclass, and Public Policy*. Chicago: University of Chicago Press.

———. 1996. *When Work Disappears*. New York: Alfred A. Knopf.

Wolfgang, Marvin E. 1958. *Patterns in Criminal Homicide*. Philadelphia: University of Pennsylvania.

7

Race and Crime

The Contribution of Individual, Familial,
and Neighborhood-Level Risk Factors to Life-Course-
Persistent Offending

Alex R. Piquero, Terrie E. Moffitt,
and Brian Lawton

1. Introduction

RECOGNIZING THAT antisocial behavior varies within neighborhoods, as well as across them, the study of how individuals and families find pathways out of "underclass" neighborhoods and away from crime has recently caught the eye of social scientists. A colorful description of life-course trajectories embarked upon by three African-American teenagers studied in Furstenberg and colleagues' (1999) *Managing to Make It* nicely illustrates the interrelated nature of individual, familial, and neighborhood influences on human behavior.

In the same deteriorating section of southwest Philadelphia, an area with above-average rates of crime and violence, there live three African-American adolescents, each of whom appears to be on a different life trajectory. JJ Newman and his family live in a dilapidated house on a block surrounded by abandoned structures. JJ had been caught on school grounds with a knife, had dropped out of school, had fathered a child, reported gambling at craps and pool, and had not sought employment. Just two blocks away from JJ in the same neighborhood, Robert James lives with his parents and siblings. Unlike JJ, Robert is doing well in school, is employed part-time, and aspires to be an accountant after college. In the same neighborhood, Lakisha Wilkenson, the youngest daughter of a single mother, is a resourceful young woman. She is doing well in school, is employed part-time, and is headed to college.

Several questions naturally arise from this vignette. For example, why are there "good" kids in bad neighborhoods and "bad" kids in good neighborhoods? The same may be asked about families. Why are there "good" families in bad neighborhoods and "bad" families in good neighborhoods?

Initially, several theoretical models may seem to offer some assistance in accounting for the different developmental trajectories among the three youths depicted above. One set of models points toward the concentration of poverty and family disruption in urban communities (Sampson and Wilson 1995). This concentration, which leads to the social isolation of residents, also has the effect of curtailing efforts to establish social organization and community culture; as a function of failed efforts in this regard, informal social control networks fail to develop, and patterns of criminal behavior and other negative sequelae ensue (Bursik and Grasmick 1993; Sampson, Raudenbush, and Earls 1997). Expanding on this view, Douglas Massey (1995) argues that high levels of poverty and segregation yield an ecological niche within which violent behavior becomes "a logical, rational adaptation" (1203). In other words, the violence exhibited by individuals residing in this ecological niche becomes a means of survival (Massey 1995, 1216). In sum, these models lead to the expectation that, to the extent that neighborhood pressures act as "strong, criminogenic situations" (see Mischel 1977; Anderson 1990), it follows that most (if not all) individuals living within them are expected to behave in a uniform way.

A second set of models seeks to account for individual heterogeneity in developmental trajectories via the role of individual and family factors. For example, several scholars have noted the importance of individual-level factors such as impulsivity, risk seeking, and aggressiveness in relating to antisocial and criminal behavior (see Hawkins, Laub, and Lauritsen 1998; Wilson and Herrnstein 1985). Similarly, family factors such as poor family management practices, family bonding, family and marital discord and conflict, stressful family events, residential mobility, and poor economic familial environment have all been linked to criminal and antisocial behavior of offspring (Hawkins, Laub, and Lauritsen 1998). Interestingly, researchers have also noted that these and other family-level factors have tended to influence individual characteristics that are proximately related to criminal and antisocial behavior. In sum, these models lead to the expectation that the presence of familial- and individual-level risk factors leads to a higher probability of criminal activity.

Unfortunately, the two models described above, structural level and familial or individual level, have tended to operate apart from one another; in other words, researchers and theorists interested in structural influences have tended to concentrate on structural factors to the neglect of familial- and individual-level factors, while researchers and theorists interested in familial- and individual-level influences have tended to concentrate on those sets of factors to the neglect of structural ones. This is not to say that researchers advocating one model over the other believe that the other neglected model is of little value; after all, evidence on the importance of structural (Sampson and Lauritsen 1994, 1997) as well as familial or individual (Loeber and Farrington 1998) influences on life-course trajectories is quite strong.

Recognizing the importance of both structural and familial or individual influences, several researchers have recently commented that an incorporation of these two theoretical models is likely to show that individual- and familial-level characteristics vary as a function of community variations (Magnusson 1988) or are context dependent (Wikstrom and Loeber 2000). In other words, the role that individual and family characteristics play in relating to criminal behavior may be different for individuals living in wealthy and socially well-integrated communities compared to individuals living in poor and socially disintegrated communities. This is likely to be the case for two reasons. First, resources for individual and familial functioning and management are likely to be better and more available in the former communities than in the latter. Second, individual- and familial-level risk factors tend to be exacerbated in disadvantaged communities.

At their core, models that incorporate individual, family, and community risk contend that individual-level factors modify children's vulnerability to risky environments such that individuals with certain attributes in particular contexts will be at risk for antisocial behavior (see Lynam et al. 2000). Therefore, interaction effects are expected to be observed when certain individual-level risk factors are met with in certain disadvantaged familial and community environments.

One such person-by-environment model has been advanced. This model is embedded in a theory guided by the realization that the aggregate depiction of the age-crime curve hides at least two distinct groups of offenders, composed of adolescent-limited and life-course-persistent offenders (Moffitt 1993). The former group of offenders is believed to engage in adultlike antisocial behavior throughout the teenage years as a result of the combined influences of the maturity gap and the peer social context of adolescence. For the most part, adolescent-limited offenders refrain from chronic and violent forms of antisocial behavior because, as adulthood ensues, they gain access to the very things they coveted as adolescents. Education, employment, marriage, and children all serve as constant reminders of things they have to lose should they return to their delinquent ways. The second group of offenders, life course persistent, follows a different pathway through life. As children, they exhibit cognitive deficits and difficulty in verbal functioning. These risk factors, which also take a toll on parental socialization, are difficult to overcome in stressed familial and neighborhood environs. As a result of the combined product of verbal disfunctioning and failed parental socialization efforts, life-course-persistent offenders exhibit failure in a variety of life domains, including education, employment, partners, and friendships. Another likely consequence is involvement in serious forms of antisocial and criminal behavior that is not only initiated early in the life course, but also continues to persist well into adulthood. A changed life path for these individuals is unlikely to appear.

Specifically, Moffitt (1993, 1994, 1997) contends that the importance of individual differences probably depends on the context in which they are embedded. Moffitt's characterization of life-course-persistent offenders suggests that individual differences in child neuropsychological health initiate a cumulative process of person-by-environment interactions that culminate in a pathological adult antisocial personality structure (Moffitt 1994, 3). Thus, life-course-persistent forms of antisocial behavior (e.g., early onset, frequency of arrest, chronicity, and violence) are likely to be observed among individuals experiencing a combination of child neurological vulnerability and parenting difficulties. In Moffitt's scheme, then, it takes more than cognitive deficits or school failure alone to lead to a life-course-persistent style of offending; instead, it is when these early life problems are met with in disadvantaged familial and neighborhood environments that patterns of antisocial behavior probably ensue. Several preliminary studies offer some support in this regard (Tibbetts and Piquero 1999; Raine, Brennan, and Mednick 1994; Raine et al. 1997; Piquero and Tibbetts 1999; Lynam et al. 2000).[1]

Although an integrated theoretical model composed of neighborhood-, familial-, and individual-level risk factors is promising, any discussion of urban inequality and crime must confront the issue of race. This is no small task, as the discussion of race and crime has been mired in an "unproductive mix of controversy and silence" (Sampson and Wilson 1995, 37). It should be no surprise then, that research has been slow to examine how individual and familial risk influence antisocial behavior across race and different neighborhood contexts. This is the case for two reasons. First, very few (if any) of the dominant criminological theories have adequately addressed the question of what accounts for race differences in criminal offending (Hawkins, Laub, and Lauritsen 1998, 39). Second, researchers studying criminal activity over the life course have tended not to employ or collect data for different races/ethnicities and neighborhood contexts. Herein, we attempt to provide some initial evidence that may be used as a starting point in studying the race-crime link.

The essay proceeds in the following manner. In section 2, we describe the theoretical framework within which we operate. In particular, we describe how contextual-, familial-, and individual-level models attempt to account for patterns of antisocial behavior in urban communities. In section 3, we outline our integration of the contextual-, familial-, and individual-level models for explaining antisocial behavior in general, and race differences in antisocial behavior in particular. The argument we advance is that individual and familial risk are exacerbated in the most disadvantaged communities, especially those disadvantaged communities in which African-Americans are over-represented. Our expectations are guided by extant research showing that African-Americans are differentially exposed to criminogenic conditions (Sampson and Wilson 1995), which typically center on poverty and family disruption (Sampson and Lauritsen 1994, 336). Moreover, we anticipate that the earlier in the life course these conditions are manifested, the more difficult it will be to overcome their negative consequences. In sum, our argument suggests that African-Americans in particular face ecological environments that are different from those faced by mainstream white populations, and it is these environments that influence family functioning and individual adaptation to difficult circumstances. Section 4 describes the data and variables employed in the analysis. Section 5 presents a series of hierarchical linear models that examine how the individual-, familial-, and neighborhood-level factors relate to criminal activity. Race-specific models are examined to determine if the constellation of contextual-, familial-, and individual-level risk factors predict antisocial behavior differently for whites and African-Americans as well as across distinct neighborhood contexts. Section 6 discusses the theoretical and policy implications of the results and outlines directions for future research.

2. Contextual, Familial, and Individual Models

Contextual Explanations

Research on communities and crime shows that neighborhoods with high rates of crime tend to be characterized by community structural characteristics such as concentrated poverty, high residential mobility, population heterogeneity, single-parent households, high rates of community change, and high family disruption (Bursik and Grasmick 1993; Shaw and McKay 1942). These effects have recently been shown to be mediated by community social processes such as socialization and informal social control patterns (Sampson, Raudenbush, and Earls 1997; Bellair 1997). That is, the factors listed above all undercut the capacity of a community to exercise informal social control, especially of teenage peer groups in public spaces (Sampson 1997, 36; Bursik and Grasmick 1993, 24). In sum, people who grow up and live in environments of concentrated poverty and social isolation are more likely to become teenage parents, drop out of school, achieve low educations, earn lower adult incomes, and become involved with crime, either as a perpetrator or as a victim (Massey 2001, 424).

Familial Explanations

The import of family structure, family management, and familial socialization has been of central concern for criminologists interested in explaining juvenile delinquency (Loeber and Stouthamer-Loeber 1986; Hirschi 1995). Although the literature regarding single-parent household effects at the individual level has produced mixed findings (Wells and Rankin 1991; Hirschi 1995), researchers have found that a mother's age at childbirth is related to the criminality of her offspring (Nagin, Pogarsky, and Farrington 1997). Researchers have also consistently documented that family management styles and familial socialization experiences are consistently related to antisocial behavior. In particular, in families where process (family climate, autonomy, discipline) and management (institutional connections, social networks, parental investments in children, private or magnet schooling) are suffering, the incidence of problem behavior among children is significantly high (Furstenberg et al. 1999). Similarly, researchers have found that when familial socialization processes (monitoring a child's behavior, recognition of a child's antisocial behavior, punishment of a child's antisocial behavior) are unsuccessful, delinquent and antisocial behavior is likely to ensue (Gottfredson and Hirschi 1990; Patterson 1980; Tremblay et al. 1992).

Individual Explanations

A large body of research has examined how individual-level risk factors are related to juvenile delinquency (Akers 1998; Gottfredson and Hirschi 1990; Loeber and Stouthamer-Loeber 1996). For example, scholars have attributed importance to individual dispositional characteristics such as impulsivity and guilt feelings (Loeber et al. 1998), IQ (Lynam, Mofitt, and Stouthamer-Loeber 1993), self-control (Gottfredson and Hirschi 1990), personality traits (Caspi et al. 1994), low birth weight and other prenatal and perinatal risk factors (Raine, Brennan, and Mednick 1994; Tibbetts and Piquero 1999), and biological and biosocial factors (Raine 1993). In general, the pattern of results from these studies shows that these and other individual differences are predictive of various manifestations of antisocial behavior over the life course (see Coie and Dodge 1998). And some research has shown that individual characteristics (i.e., individual-level factors such as cognitive functioning) are very strongly related to repeat or chronic offending (Denno 1986).

3. Integrating Contextual, Familial, and Individual Explanations

As we earlier noted, contextual, familial, and individual explanations have largely operated in isolation from one another, such that researchers interested in neighborhood influences have generally not adequately measured individual and family influences, just as researchers interested in individual and family influences have generally not adequately measured neighborhood influences (Farrington 1993, 30). The integration of these three levels of explanation is particularly important, because individuals grow up, live, and act in different kinds of social (i.e., familial and neighborhood) contexts (Wikstrom and Loeber 2000, 1114). Both Sampson (1997) and Moffitt (1997) have outlined the beginnings of a theoretical model that focuses on the embeddedness of families and children in the social context of local communities.

At the core of Sampson's theory is the notion that structural disadvantage and social disorganization combine to generate a community-level concentration of negative social ills, including low birth weight, cognitive impairment, and other adjustment problems, which in turn constitute major risk factors for later delinquency and violence. Importantly, Sampson also recognizes that parenting styles are an adaptation to considerations outside the household, especially the social organization of the community (Furstenberg 1993; Furstenberg et al. 1999). Communities that are characterized by an extensive set of social networks connecting adults are better able to facilitate the control and supervision of children. And since the quality of social capital available to families depends in large part on the stability of local communities, communities marked by social disorganization tend not to rank high on informal social controls, and therefore family functioning and "collective" familial socialization processes are compromised. Thus, in Sampson's view, disadvantaged communities tend to make it difficult for families to perform effective socialization. As a result, individual (and familial) risk factors are likely to be exacerbated in disadvantaged neighborhood environments.

Though Moffitt does not advance the argument based on informal social control and collective socialization that Sampson does, Moffitt locates a person by environment interaction in the most disadvantaged families and neighborhoods. In particular, she argues that individuals born with cognitive and nervous system deficits tend often to be born into familial environments that are ill equipped to help them overcome these deficits.[2] It is also likely that these individuals and families are located in disadvantaged neighborhoods in inner cities, which do not have the resources or opportunities available to aid such families and individuals. Taken together, these observations lead to the expectation that "family and neighborhood adversity mediate the relation between individual differences and antisocial outcomes" (Moffitt 1997, 155) such that "in disadvantaged homes . . . and neighborhoods, individual risk is exacerbated" (Moffitt 1993, 684). In other words, individual-level risk factors, such as cognitive deficits, tend to influence antisocial behavior more in disadvantaged familial and neighborhood contexts than they would in nondisadvantaged familial and neighborhood contexts, because disadvantaged environments are not equipped to counteract individual-level risk factors. Thus, such integration might be useful for explaining (1) differences across racial groups in crime and antisocial behavior, and (2) within-race differences in behavior.

Prior Research

To date, only a handful of studies have attempted to examine the types of multilevel expectations advanced by Sampson and Moffitt. Most of these studies have found that, at the individual level of analysis, neighborhood characteristics are significantly but weakly correlated with juvenile delinquency (Gottfredson, McNeil, and Gottfredson 1991; Lizotte et al. 1994; Peeples and Loeber 1994; Simcha-Fagan and Schwartz 1986) and academic competence (Elliott et al. 1996). Three of these studies in particular have attempted to examine how individual characteristics and offending vary as a function of neighborhood characteristics, and another study has sought to examine race-related issues.

Using cross-sectional data from Chicago and Denver, Elliott and his colleagues (1996) examined how organizational and cultural features of neighborhoods mediate the effects of ecological disadvantage on adolescent development and behavior. They found that the effect of neighborhood disadvantage on both aggregated rates and individual developmental outcomes was largely mediated by the level and form of neighborhood organization (i.e., informal social control). Lynam and colleagues (2000) used data from the Pittsburgh Youth Study to examine the relationship between impulsivity, neighborhood context, and juvenile offending. Their results showed that the effect of impulsivity on juvenile offending was stronger in poorer neighborhoods, and that poorer neighborhoods did not have a direct effect on juvenile delinquency. Wikstrom and Loeber (2000) also used data from the Pittsburgh Youth Study to examine how risk and protective factors related to antisocial behavior across different neighborhood contexts. Their results showed that while most boys with high risk factors offended regardless of neighborhood context, neighborhood effects on crime were greatest among those individuals with the most protective factors.

To the best of our knowledge, only one study has examined the extent to which individual factors and neighborhood context explain ethnic differences in juvenile delinquency. Using data for 506 boys from the Pittsburgh Youth Study, Peeples and Loeber (1994) uncovered a number of interesting results. First, they found that the relationship between race and offending was dependent on the type of neighborhood such that only in underclass neighborhoods was there a relationship between race and juvenile offending; in nonunderclass neighborhoods, no race effect was observed. Second, boys' hyperactivity and parental supervision were the strongest correlates of delinquency, while single-parent status and poverty or receipt of welfare assistance were not related to delinquency. Third, when individual-level risk factors were controlled, residence in underclass neighborhoods was significantly related to delinquency while ethnicity was not. Although Peeples and Loeber's effort provided important preliminary data on race differences in juvenile delinquency, their analysis is limited because they did not examine how individual risk was or was not exacerbated in adverse familial environments or explicate the multilevel nature of their data; that is, they did not employ methodological techniques that would allow them to better understand how individual- and familial-level factors operate across different neighborhood contexts.[3]

Although these collective efforts have been important in bringing evidence to bear on how contextual-, familial-, and individual-level factors relate to delinquency, an understanding of how individual risk is dependent on family and neighborhood context, and how this risk is then translated into antisocial behavior, remains limited (Wikstrom and Loeber 2000, 1110). This is especially the case because empirical research has not progressed very far toward understanding how the relationships between individual, familial, and neighborhood risk vary across races (Hawkins, Laub, and Lauritsen 1998). Yet research has identified important race differences in socialization processes across neighborhood and familial contexts (see Harrison et al. 1990).

Race Differences in Socialization Processes across Neighborhood and Family Contexts

Neighborhood Context

American communities differ considerably in the race and social class of families living within them (Massey and Denton 1993; Furstenberg et al. 1999), as well as how criminal behavior is distributed within and between such communities. Several years ago, Shaw and McKay (1942; 1949, 614) attempted to explain high rates of crime among white ethnics, including newly arrived immigrants and their offspring, and, in particular, recognized the interrelatedness of this point: "The important fact about rates of delinquents for Negro boys is that they too, vary by type of area. They are higher than the rates for white boys, but it cannot be said that they are higher than rates for white boys in comparable areas, since it is impossible to reproduce in white communities the circumstances under which Negro children live. Even if it were possible to parallel the low economic status and the inadequacy of institutions in the white community, it would not be possible to reproduce the effects of segregation and the barriers to upward mobility."

Elaborating on this fact, both Sampson and Wilson view the relationship between race and crime through contextual lenses that highlight the very different ecological contexts in which African-Americans and whites reside, "regardless of individual and family characteristics" (Sampson 1997, 32). Because the poorest of whites do not live in the kinds of ecologically concentrated, "truly disadvantaged" communities that the poorest of African-Americans live in (Massey 1995; Sampson and Wilson 1995; Wilson 1987), the structural barriers and cultural adaptations that undermine social organization are magnified for African-Americans. Massey (1995, 1206) further expands this concentration argument by pointing out the most salient "fact of black America [is] its high degree of residential segregation."

In sum, white neighborhoods and African-American neighborhoods offer a starked contrast in terms of the level of disadvantage. African-American neighborhoods, especially disadvantaged African-American neighborhoods, are likely to be geographically closer to poor and high-crime neighborhoods; the opposite is the case among white neighborhoods, even among disadvantaged white neighborhoods (see Pattillo 1998). Thus, the informal networks that provide the underlying social organization of these communities include long-term residents who are part of groups that actually contribute to or draw crime to their neighborhoods (Krivo and Peterson 2000, 557). In addition, because of the greater spatial clustering of disadvantage among African-American than among whites, the institutional and economic resources that diminish the likelihood of crime are fewer and father away for African-American communities than is the case for disadvantaged white neighborhoods (Krivo and Peterson 2000, 558). One likely result of this disadvantage is the toll it takes on collective efficacy.

Collective efficacy, which resembles mutual trust or cohesion and shared expectations for social control, has been found to be an inhibitor of violence (Sampson, Raudenbush, and Earls 1997). However, concentrated disadvantage, which strikes African-Americans more than whites, has been linked to lower collective efficacy, and research has shown collective efficacy to be related to homicide rates more strongly among African-American neighborhoods (Morenoff, Sampson, and Raudenbush 2001). Thus, neighborhood contexts influence individual behavior by means of community social organization, including the presence of adult role models, supervision, and monitoring, in addition to structure and routines. In sum, poor communities may lack informal control as well as the ability to regulate behavior of children and youth (Leventhal and Brooks-Gunn 2000).[4]

Familial Context

Important race differences in key measures of family structure have been identified. For example, historically, African-Americans have been disproportionately affected by single-parent heads of households and declining rates of marriage (Wilson 1996), conditions which have worsened in the inner city since the 1960s (Wilson 1987). Data from the 2000 census show that births to teenage mothers were two times greater for African-Americans (21.5%) than whites (11.1%). Similarly, births to unmarried mothers exhibited even larger race discrepancies; for African-Americans, the estimate was 69.1%, whereas the comparable figure for whites was 26.3%.

Race differences in live births also spill into the health care domain. For example, in 1998, over 84% of white women received prenatal care beginning in the first trimester, but only 73.3% of African-American women received such care. In fact, 7% of African-American women received late or no prenatal care, whereas the comparable figure among white women was 3.3%. Finally, low birth weight was a more significant problem among African-American women; in 1998, the percentage of births with low birth weight (less than 5 lbs., 8 oz.) was 13% among African-American women and 6.5% among white women.

In terms of family relations, research indicates that African-Americans in particular are less likely than whites to be married and more likely to experience marital separation (Wilson 1987, 68 – 69). Wilson (1987) notes that while African-American women are confronting a "shrinkage of "marriageable" (that is economically stable) men, white women are not experiencing this problem" (145). In fact, recent data from the Census Bureau (U.S. Census Bureau 2000, 43) indicate that 80.7% of whites were married, whereas 47.1% of African-Americans were married.

One by-product of these family structure differences across race is likely to be reduced supervision and, ultimately, failed socialization. In single-parent households, especially those headed by teenage mothers, there is likely to be less time to supervise and monitor the child's development and behavior. Furthermore, some evidence indicates that parents who reside in impoverished and dangerous neighborhoods may be less warm and more controlling with their children than parents in more advantaged and safe neighborhoods (Furstenberg 1993). Earls, McGuire, and Shay (1994) also found that parents who reported living in more dangerous neighborhoods also reported using more harsh control and verbal aggression with their children than did parents who resided in less dangerous neighborhoods. As a result of these distressed familial environments, socialization is no longer performed inside the household; instead, the socialization function is shifted outside the home and into nearby streets, where socialization is unlikely to evolve around education and employment, as is probably the case in households, but rather around a culture of honor and respect that is endemic to disadvantaged neighborhoods (see Anderson 1999; Ogbu 1991). This process is exacerbated among African-Americans in inner cities (Massey 1995).

Summary

Wilson's (1996) recent work perhaps best highlights the interactive nature of disadvantaged familial and neighborhood contexts. Specifically, he argues that since race is related to disadvantaged familial and neighborhood contexts, negative sequelae are magnified in inner cities, especially those areas populated largely by African-Americans. Therefore, African-American youth living in poor families and neighborhoods are likely not to be socialized into the disciplined habits associated with stable or steady employment that are of central importance to successful development (Wilson 1996, 106–107).

Moffitt takes Wilson's suppositions one step further. Specifically, Moffitt hypothesizes that, because institutionalized racism and poverty selectively afflict African-Americans, and these factors are associated with poor neurological health in childhood, difficulties in parenting children, and difficulty attaining roles of consequence and respect, life-course-persistent styles of offending might be elevated among ethnic minorities, particularly African-Americans in inner-city America:

Among poor blacks, prenatal care is less available, infant nutrition is poorer, and the incidence of fetal exposure to toxic and infectious agents is greater, placing infants at high risk for the nervous system problems that research has shown to interfere with prosocial child development. To the extent that family bonds have been loosened and poor black parents are under stress, high-risk infants should tend to develop the weak attachment bonds that research has shown to predispose to aggressive interpersonal behavior. To the extent that poor black children attend disadvantaged schools, there is less chance for correction of the learning difficulties that research has shown to contribute toward underemployment and recidivistic crime. Thus, for poor black children, the snowball of cumulative continuity is anticipated to begin rolling earlier, and it rolls faster downhill. (Moffitt 1994, 38–39)

As can be seen from the above discussion, relationships between contextual-, familial-, and individual-level risk factors will probably vary by race and, because of that, should be manifested in differences in successful development in general, and antisocial behavior in particular. Importantly, the theoretical models and expectations outlined above recognize the key point that, regardless of whether or not an African-American juvenile is raised in an intact or single-parent family, he or she is not likely to grow up in a community context similar to those of whites with regard to family structure and concentration of poverty (Sampson 1997, 65). Thus, a more complete understanding of child socialization and development should examine not only the familial environment, but also the community context in which families and children are embedded. And since socialization and learning begins early in the life course, researchers must seriously consider the social context of early childhood and its resultant effect on developmentally oriented outcomes (Brooks-Gunn, Duncan, and Aber 1997; Massey 2001).

This is especially important given that Loeber and Wikstrom (1993) found the effect of neighborhood residence on younger adolescents' problem behavior to be stronger than that found among older adolescents.[5]

Current Focus

Recognizing that individuals and families are only rarely studied in the context of their neighborhood, this chapter reports on an analysis of how individual- and familial-level variables relate to antisocial behavior across race as well as different types of neighborhood contexts. To examine this question, we follow a multilevel analytic approach that employs data from the Baltimore portion of the National Collaborative Perinatal Project (NCPP).

This study builds on prior efforts in a number of ways. First, we examine the long-term impacts of early-life individual, familial, and neighborhood disadvantage (measured between birth and age 10) on life-course-persistent styles of offending (measured at ages 27–33). Second, we examine the extent to which the interaction between individual risk and family adversity differentially relates to life-course-persistent offending across race as well as different types of neighborhood contexts. Third, given that multilevel studies across race are needed to differentiate individual and neighborhood effects (Hawkins, Laub, and Lauritsen 1998, 41), we employ multilevel modeling that explicates the "embeddedness" hypothesis advanced by both Sampson and Moffitt. This methodological approach allows us to examine how individual risk relates to criminal behavior across different familial contexts, as well as how the combined effect of individual and familial risk relates to criminal behavior across different neighborhood contexts. Such an approach is particularly important, since several prior efforts have failed to explicate the hierarchical structure of data sets (see Peeples and Loeber 1994; Wikstrom and Loeber 2000). Finally, our effort has the potential to document the importance of structural contexts in a certain time period (1960–65) because of the profound changes in the structure of urban minority communities in the 1970s (Sampson 1997, 69).

The current effort is particularly important in matters related to public policy, especially as they relate to individual-, familial-, and neighborhood-level risk factors. Knowledge of individual-level risk factors can help aid in prevention and intervention efforts geared toward reduction and/or cessation of risk factors. Research suggests that individual-level risk factors can be minimized and/or corrected if detected early in the life course (Olds et al. 1998; Tremblay and Craig 1995). Efforts aimed at curbing familial risk have also been found to be successful, especially as they relate to family functioning and process (Tremblay et al. 1992). Finally, many neighborhood-level variables (such as the concentration of poverty, family instability, and the lack of informal social control networks) are often determined by policy decisions made at local, state, and federal levels (Sampson and Lauritsen 1994). These decisions are far reaching and include those made in the real estate and banking industries (Yinger 1995), fire and health services (Wallace and Wallace 1990), and the location of public housing (Bursik 1989; Massey and Denton 1993). Knowledge of neighborhood-level correlates, either indirectly or directly related to antisocial behavior (see Bursik 1989; Skogan 1986), can help to identify points of intervention for policy officials.

4. Data

Data for this project come from the Baltimore site (at Johns Hopkins) of the NCPP, a survey of pregnant women seeking prenatal care. Located at several university-affiliated hospitals throughout the United States, the NCPP was a large-scale, multidisciplinary health and development study initiated by the National Institute of Neurologic and Communicative Disease and Stroke between 1959 and 1965 in which data were collected from fifty to sixty thousand pregnant women (Niswander and Gordon 1972). The women and their children were followed until the children reached 7 or 8 years of age (depending on the participating institution; 8 years at Johns Hopkins). The study population enrolled at each participating institution included either all available prenatal patients living within a defined geographic area or women randomly selected from those available in each prenatal clinic.

The Johns Hopkins sample consisted of pregnant women seeking prenatal care and delivery at the Johns Hopkins Hospital. The women were selected at random at the time of their first prenatal visit to the hospital's public obstetric clinic; most of the women lived in a lower socioeconomic enclave within a ten-block radius of the hospital (Hardy et al. 1997). They were selected on the basis of the last digit of their hospital history numbers. This number was assigned from a central hospital file at the point of first patient contact. The proportion of prenatal clinic registrants enrolled was increased by adding to the number of terminal digits selected from approximately 30% in 1960 until it reached about 70% in 1963 and 100% in 1964, the last year of NCPP enrollment. There were virtually no refusals to participate.[6] In Baltimore, data have been organized for over 2,300 women who gave birth to children participating in the study. The majority of sample members had all nine of the scheduled examinations throughout the first seven to eight years of their lives as part of their participation in the Johns Hopkins portion of the NCPP (Hardy et al. 1997). Detailed results from the NCPP appear in Nichols and Chen (1981) and Broman, Nichols, and Kennedy (1975), and empirical investigations of the criminal activity of cohort members have been conducted with data from both Philadelphia (Denno 1990; Piquero and Chung 2001;

Tibbetts and Piquero 1999; Piquero and Tibbetts 1999; Gibson, Piquero, and Tibbetts 2000, 2001; Piquero et al. 2002; Piquero 2000a, 2000b, 2001) and Providence (Lipsitt, Buka, and Lipsitt 1990; Piquero and Buka 2002).

Between 1992 and 1994, a research team from Johns Hopkins engaged in a retrospective follow-up study of both the mothers and children participating in the Baltimore NCPP. In order to qualify for the follow-up study, the children had to have been born between 1960 and 1965 and completed the assessments done at age 7 or 8. Of the 2,694 eligible children, 66% ($N = 1,758$) completed interviews (Hardy and Shapiro 1999). It is these 1,758 individuals who form the basis for the current study.

It is important to verify that the subjects who participated in the follow-up survey did not differ substantively from those not participating in the follow-up survey. Hardy and her colleagues (1997, 82) report that

Bias due to sample attrition [whether subjects who could not be interviewed at 27–33 years may have differed significantly from those who were interviewed] was considered by comparing the distributions of several JHCPS variables. Few differences were noted. [Subjects] not interviewed were born to mothers who were somewhat younger, had less educational attainment, and were more likely to be at or below the poverty level (47.9% vs. 43.1%) at the time of the [subjects'] birth than the mothers of the [subjects] interviewed. The proportion of [subjects] who were low birth weight did not differ between groups. At 7 to 8 years, differences in Wechsler Intelligence Scale for Children verbal IQ scores were not statistically significant, but those interviewed had somewhat greater skill in reading (46.3% vs. 36.9%) and fewer were neurologically suspect or abnormal (17.5% vs. 23.4%) than those not interviewed. Because of the relatively high proportions who were interviewed, the characteristics of the total sample (interviewed and not interviewed combined) were similar to those from whom interviews were obtained.

In an effort to determine if response rates differed across low-SES families compared to other SES families, we examined measures of the mother's SES at birth, with response rates for the subject interviewed between the ages of 27 and 33 in two ways. First, we calculated an ANOVA where we compared the mother's income at birth, her poverty index at birth, and whether she was receiving public assistance at birth across eight potential categories of subject follow-up at ages 27–33: (1) full subject interview ($N = 1,758$, 65.3%), (2) absent subject interview (2.6%), (3) deceased with data (2.6%), (4) refused (5.0%), (5) still in process at end of funding (5.8%), (6) not located (17.6%), (7) deceased with no data (.6%), and (8) unavailable (.4%) (total $N = 2,694$). All ANOVAs failed to uncover any significant differences on the three mother SES variables across the eight groups. Further, we undertook a difference-of-means test where we compared subjects with full follow-up interviews (group 1) and the not-located subjects (group 6) across all three mother SES variables. Once again, we failed to detect significant mother SES differences across subjects who completed the interview against subjects who could not be located.

Variables

Two different data sources were used. The first consisted of variables from the original Baltimore NCPP study that included information related to the birth, the first eight years of the child's life, and census-tract information. The second consisted of variables from the follow-up interviews with the children in the 1990s that included information related to peers and criminal behavior.

Dependent Variable

Two dependent variables are employed in the present study: prevalence and frequency of arrest. At the follow-up interview, subjects were asked whether they had been arrested (prevalence) and, if arrested, the number of times they had been arrested throughout their lives (frequency). Following Moffitt's suggestion that life-course-persistent styles of offending are statistically unusual and that the rate of life-course-persisters would constitute about 5% of the total sample, we identified those individuals from the follow-up interviews who ranked in the top 5% (84/1,758) of the arrest frequency distribution as "life-course-persistent" chronic offenders. The cutoff point (i.e., the top 5%) turned out to be seven arrests; consequently, the arrest frequency variable was recoded to 0 (one to six offenses) and 1 (seven or more offenses).[7]

Three other points concerning the self-reported arrest information must be made. First, although the designation of the top 5% as life course persistent is an approximation, it should not pose a problem because any imprecision would exert a conservative effect on our ability to obtain group differences. Second, researchers have shown that race differences exist for prevalence but not frequency (Blumstein et al. 1986, 41; Piquero, Farrington, and Blumstein 2003). Third, Moffitt hypothesizes that the biosocial interaction would not predict the prevalence of offending; instead, it would predict a "special sort of delinquency" and therefore be significantly related to the frequency of arrest (i.e., chronic offending), which is one marker for life-course-persistent offending (Moffitt 1994).

Still, some readers may observe that classification of offenders into distinct groups appears more art than science. For example, individuals who were arrested seven times in one year would be classified similarly to those individuals whose seven arrests were scattered over a number of years, and our approach would categorize both sets of individuals as life-course-persisters. Thus, it remains possible, though unlikely, that at age 30, some individuals may have said that they had seven arrests, but all of these could have been committed in a three-year period, say, from 13 to 15, with no more offending later on. To investigate this possibility, we performed a t-test between those individuals who had seven or more arrests and those individuals who did not (i.e., who had between one and six arrests). The self-reported age at first arrest for the "life-course-persisters" was 15.95, while the comparable figure among "adolescent-limiteds" was 20.85. This information provides some evidence of construct validity, because frequency of offending and earliness of onset are two important characteristics ascribed to life-course-persistent offenders (Moffitt 1994).[8]

In addition, we also used data from another birth cohort study, the second Philadelphia Birth Cohort (Tracy and Kempf-Leonard 1996), to examine the distribution of officially recorded arrests per individual, per year of observation. The data we used are drawn from the 6,674 persons who experienced at least one officially recorded arrest through age 26 in the 1958 cohort, as recorded by the Philadelphia Police Department (through age 17) and the Municipal and Court of Common Pleas of Philadelphia (from 18 to 26). For each arrest frequency, we subtracted the youngest arrest age in months from the oldest arrest age in months. This obviously produces missing values for individuals with an arrest frequency of 1, but for all the others it produces a distribution of the amount of time that lapses between the first and the last arrest in months. For individuals with seven or more arrests, we collapsed them to the same level in the data so that they are all in the same group. Our results showed that for those with two arrests, the mean time between the first and last arrest is 35 months, but this is a skewed distribution, so the median of 24 months is more representative. This compares to a mean and median of 104 months for those with seven or more arrests, implying that with increasing arrest frequency, the time between the first and last arrest is higher. Thus, among frequent offenders, arrests are more spread out than they are for relatively infrequent offenders, which suggests that it is relatively unlikely that those who experienced seven (or more) arrests were likely to commit them in a two- or three-year period. Given the importance of this issue, we return to it once again in the discussion section.

Independent Variables

Independent variables include individual-level risk, family adversity, peer delinquency, sex, race, and neighborhood disadvantage.

Peer Delinquency: We employ a two-item scale that asked respondents whether their teenaged friends were (1) involved with crime and (2) used drugs frequently. Originally, both items were scored on a three-point scale ranging from none to some to most. For purposes of the present study, each item was dichotomized as (0) none and (1) some/most, and then both items were summed.

Family Adversity: Designed to measure family adversity during the first few years of the child's life, the four items that make up the family adversity scale come from data collected about the mother during and after the pregnancy and closely resemble family adversity scales employed by other researchers (Rutter 1978; Stanton, McGee, and Silva 1989; Kolvin et al. 1988; Tibbetts and Piquero 1999; Piquero and Tibbetts 1999; Pryor and Woodward 1996). The items include (1) the age of the mother at childbirth (0 = 18 or greater; 1 = less than 18), (2) whether the mother was receiving public assistance at the time of childbirth (0 = no; 1 = yes), (3) the mother's educational attainment at childbirth (0 = at least high school graduate; 1 = less than high school), and (4) the mother's marital status at childbirth (0 = married; 1 = not married). Following Rutter's (1978) suggestion that the number of risk factors rather than the nature of the risk factors provides an appropriate measure of family adversity, the items were summed to form the family adversity scale.[9]

Individual Risk: Moffitt's developmental taxonomy identifies several different examples of compromised neuropsychological health. One of these is low birth weight (see Moffitt 1993, 1997). Low birth weight is a strong and consistent indicator reflecting increased risk for neuropsychological problems (McCormick 1985), and it has been linked to several adverse sequelae, including low cognition and attention, poor academic achievement, low intelligence, behavior problems, visual defects, cerebral palsy, and criminal behavior (see review in Tibbetts and Piquero 1999). Birth weight was measured at delivery by hospital staff and is coded 1 for low birth weight ($\leq$2,500g) and 0 for normal birth weight ($>$2,500g). This cutoff was originally adopted by the World Health Organization (1950) and has been consistently used in research (Coren 1993; Denno 1990; Paneth 1995; Shiono and Behrman 1995).

Biosocial Interaction: Moffitt's theory stresses the importance of a biosocial interaction between low birth weight and adverse familial environments. To compute this interaction, the raw scores of the component factors were mean centered in order to rid the measures of nonessential ill conditioning (the multicollinearity between the component variables produced by noncenteredness), which would inevitably cause multicollinearity between the component variables and their product terms (Aiken and West 1991; Jaccard, Turrisi, and Wan 1990).[10] High scores on the interaction are indicative of higher risk.

Neighborhood Disadvantage: Our measure of neighborhood disadvantage is modeled after those used in extant research (Elliott et al. 1996; Lynam et al. 2000; Moffitt 1997; Ross, Reynolds, and Geis 2000; Wikstrom and Loeber 2000), and most of the variables included in our index have been found to be directly related to criminal behavior (National Research Council 1993, 156). To create the neighborhood disadvantage scale, we use census tracts as the unit of analysis and employ data drawn from the 1970 census when subjects were between the ages of 5 and 10. There were a total of ninety-four census tracts, of which twenty-three (25%) were low disadvantage (not poor) and twenty-three (25%) were high disadvantage (very poor).

For the tracts in 1970, addresses provided by the mother and the subject as part of their follow-up interviews were hand coded by the Johns Hopkins research staff using the Baltimore City Health Department's *Census Tract Manual* (1973) and the 1970 Stewart CrissCross Directories for all other counties within the state of Maryland. Any partial, unknown, or nonexistent addresses were coded as missing, and data for subjects living outside Maryland were coded as missing ($N = 21$). We used principal components factor analysis to create a measure of neighborhood disadvantage with data from the 1970 census. The eleven variables (and their principal components loading) that form our measure were percent young adult dropout (.966), percent black (.987), percent female-headed household (.974), females 16 and older with kids, no husband and poverty status (.949), mean family income (.965), percent households with public assistance income (.994), percent persons below the poverty line (.971), percent families with public assistance income (.990), adult unemployment rate (.988), male unemployment rate (.987), and persons aged 18 to 24 (.977). All eleven items loaded onto a single-item factor.

The measurement of neighborhood disadvantage during early childhood is particularly important because it has been shown that neighborhoods influence individual development most powerfully in early childhood (Brooks-Gunn, Duncan, and Aber 1997; Massey 2001), and such effects appear to operate through peer networks and, more specifically, through their effect on parental behavior (Aber et al. 1997; Chase-Lansdale et al. 1997). Although this measure heavily weights minority status and does not directly assess social disorganization or community and/or informal social control, research indicates that communities experiencing high neighborhood disadvantage are unlikely to have or attract the resources necessary to develop and sustain high-quality institutions and organizations. Moreover, participation in local organization and development of informal social networks, such as friendship ties among community adults, is likely to be compromised. As a result, disadvantaged neighborhoods are likely to experience low collective supervision of youth and diminished resources for child care. In addition, residence in disadvantaged communities is likely to provide high exposure to physical danger, criminal activity, and drug use, which probably forces parents to keep youngsters indoors for physical protection. Two consequences of this feature of disadvantaged neighborhoods is that young children who stay indoors are likely to have fewer opportunities for interactions with a range of peers and adults and are also likely to "grow up quickly," with great responsibilities, concerns, and anxieties and with little time to devote to developmental tasks (Chase-Lansdale et al. 1997, 81).

Two methodological points regarding the neighborhood disadvantage scale are in order. First, we recognize that the social science community

Table 7.1: Descriptive Statistics

Variable	Nonoffenders (M (SD)) (N = 1,246)	Adolescent-Limited (M (SD)) (N = 428)	Life-Course-Persisters (M (SD)) (N = 84)	F Value
Race (1 = African-American; 2 = White)	1.839 (.367)	1.759 (.428)	1.797 (.404)	7.037*
Sex (1 = Male; 2 = Female)	1.657 (.474)	1.289 (.454)	1.095 (.295)	141.363*
Peer delinquency (0–2)	.794 (.837)	1.401 (.792)	1.780 (.521)	126.907*
Family adversity (0–4)	1.880 (.737)	2.035 (.744)	2.361 (.758)	20.885*
Mother's age at childbirth (0/1)	.141 (.348)	.189 (.392)	.321 (.469)	11.154*
Mother's public assistance (0/1)	.075 (.264)	.099 (.300)	.144 (.353)	3.168*
Mother's educational attainment (0/1)	.688 (.463)	.768 (.422)	.903 (.296)	12.463*
Mother's marital status at birth (0/1)	.266 (.442)	.305 (.460)	.421 (.496)	5.250*
Low birth weight (0/1)	.155 (.363)	.126 (.332)	.131 (.339)	1.218
Neighborhood disadvantage (−1.00/.48)	−.533 (.164)	−.515 (.178)	−.508 (.169)	2.530
Biosocial interaction (−1.66/1.76)	−.001 (.281)	.007 (.253)	.090 (.418)	4.097*

*$p < .05$.

has not come to agreement regarding the most appropriate measure of a neighborhood. Although local community areas, census tracts, and block groups are imperfect operational definitions of neighborhoods or local community in empirical research, such areas generally possess more ecological integrity (e.g., natural boundaries and social homogeneity) than cities or metropolitan areas, and they are more closely linked to the mechanisms assumed by social disorganization theory to underlie the etiology of crime (Bursik and Grasmick 1993; Sampson 1997, 35–36). Second, although we do not observe the mediating dimensions of social organization such as social participation and supervision of teenage peer groups, our measure does contain items that have been shown to be related to such mediating dimensions, which in turn predict variations in crime and delinquency (Sampson and Groves 1989). In effect, the majority of items in our measure are believed to index the attenuation of social and cultural neighborhood organization, which is effective for socialization within the neighborhood (Sampson 1997, 55). In sum, there is no reason we should not think that the link between community structural characteristics and community social processes established in other studies holds here (see also Wikstrom and Loeber 2000, 1119).

Sex of the Subject: Sex was coded 1 for males and 2 for females.

Race of the Subject: Race was coded 1 for African-Americans and 2 for whites.[11]

Descriptive statistics may be found in table 7.1. For ease of presentation, this information is broken down by offender category, including nonoffenders (N = 1,246), adolescent-limiteds (N = 428), and life-course-persisters

Table 7.2: Descriptive Statistics Presented by Race, Sex, and Neighborhood Disadvantage

Variable	White (N = 320)			African-American (N = 1,438)		
	Males	Females	Total	Males	Females	Total
High disadvantaged	37	37	74	346	416	762
Nonoffender	18	33		196	367	
Adolescence-limited	15	4		115	46	
Life-course-persistent	4	0		32	2	
Low disadvantaged	113	133	246	311	365	676
Nonoffender	49	100		158	318	
Adolescence-limited	52	32		122	42	
Life-course-persistent	12	1		28	5	
Total			320			1,438

($N = 84$).[12] Several comments regarding the pattern of association in this table are warranted. First, the distribution of race across offender categories reveals that, compared to whites, there are more African-Americans in the life-course-persistent category. In addition, males are overrepresented in the life-course-persistent offender category. Finally, those individuals in the life-course-persistent group appear to incur the most risk factors across all the individual, familial, and neighborhood measures.

Table 7.2 presents further descriptive information on the sample, by race and sex, so as to better describe the distribution of neighborhood disadvantage and offending. As can be seen, many more African-Americans than whites reside in disadvantaged neighborhoods. Further, with regard to offending, life-course-persistent status appears higher for males than females within race, with a higher number of life-course-persisters identified among African-Americans. Across race, life-course-persister membership was extremely rare for females.

A Note on Retrospective Data

The outcome variables and several independent variables are based on retrospective data, and some may question the ability of sample members to recall events that occurred in the past. These data collection techniques have fared well in methodological studies of the concordance between prospective and retrospective measures of similar variables. For example, Henry and others (1994, 98) found that agreement between prospective and retrospective measures of arrest were moderately good. And although the use of self-report measures of criminal behavior has been somewhat controversial (compare Huizinga and Elliott 1986; Hindelang, Hirschi, and Weis 1981; and Lauritsen 1998), the alternative to using self-report measures is the use of arrest and conviction records, which themselves may evidence other biases. We do not take the position that one method is inherently better than the other for two reasons. First, Farrington (1989, 418; see also Weis 1986, 44) has shown that self-reports and official conviction data produce "comparable and complementary results on such important topics as prevalence, continuity, versatility, and specialization in different types of offenses." Second, Moffitt and others (1994, 293) reported robust findings across self-reports, juvenile police records, and court convictions when studying the relationship between neuropsychological scores and delinquency.

Analysis Plan and Hypothesis

Generally, the framework within which we operate leads us to believe that neighborhood and family contexts shape the manner in which individual risk relates to antisocial behavior. In particular, extant theory predicts that these relationships will probably vary across race as well as neighborhood context. Thus, to the extent that individual-level characteristics modify children's vulnerability to disadvantaged environments, interaction effects should be observed such that individual risk factors would be more strongly related to offending in disadvantaged familial and neighborhood contexts than in more advantaged contexts, and these effects should be stronger for life-course-persistent offending among African-Americans than whites (Moffitt 1994). We employ hierarchical linear models to examine the theoretical model described above.

Before we turn to our results, we need to address the extent to which the potential race differences are a function of group average levels or developmental processes. That is, are developmental processes different across race (Ogbu 1993), or are they similar (Rowe, Vazsonyi, and Flannery 1994)? The former approach argues that being in a minority group necessitates different socialization strategies that, in turn, lead to different developmental pathways to antisocial behavior, while the latter approach argues that group average level differences result from different levels of developmental antecedents working through common developmental pathways. In sum, the crux of the issue is whether races differ in levels of risk factors and whether it is these mean differences in levels of risk exposure that explain mean differences in levels of outcomes such as crime (an explanation based on differences in degree) or whether race-specific developmental processes characterize life-course-persistent offending (an explanation based on differences in kind).

The next section attempts to work through these competing explanations as a way to answer the extent to which different pathways or different levels best characterize race differences in criminal offending.

5. Results

We begin the multivariate analysis by examining the additive relationships between individual, familial, and neighborhood risk as they relate to whether subjects reported an arrest by the follow-up interview. Coefficient estimates are presented in table 7.3. Among whites, sex (B $= -.142$) and knowledge of peer delinquency (B $= .911$) significantly predict arrest by the follow-up interview. Among African-Americans, both sex (B $= -1.495$) and knowledge of peer delinquency (B $= .651$) predicted arrest, as did adverse familial environments (B $= .362$). For both whites and African-Americans, neither low birth weight nor neighborhood disadvantage was related to arrest.

In table 7.4, we add Moffitt's biosocial interaction (low birth weight by family adversity) to the model. The patterns of estimates in the models containing the interaction are substantively the same in terms of coefficient size, strength, and significance. Among whites, both sex and peer delinquency

Table 7.3: HLM Analysis of Determinants of Arrest by Follow-Up Interview

Variable	Whites		African-Americans	
	B	SE	B	SE
Level-1 variables:				
Sex (1 = Female)	−.142***	.278	−1.495***	.158
Peer delinquency	.911***	.173	.651***	.130
Family adversity	.207	.358	.362***	.086
Low birth weight	.066	.539	−.060	.212
Level-2 variable:				
Neighborhood disadvantage	.265	.278	.620	.654

*$p < .05$.
**$p < .01$.
***$p < .001$.

Table 7.4: HLM Analysis of Determinants of Arrest by Follow-Up Interview (with Biosocial Interaction)

Variable	Whites		African-Americans	
	B	SE	B	SE
Level-1 variables:				
Sex (1 = Female)	−1.169***	.277	−1.496***	.159
Peer delinquency	.887***	.165	.654***	.132
Family adversity	.262	.359	.355***	.086
Low birth weight	−.001	.540	−.102	.229
Biosocial interaction	1.287	.965	.317	.246
Level-2 variable:				
Neighborhood disadvantage	.274	.450	.622	.657

*$p < .05$.
**$p < .01$.
***$p < .001$.

Table 7.5: HLM Analysis of Determinants of Frequency of Arrest by Follow-Up Interview

Variable	Whites		African-Americans	
	B	SE	B	SE
Level-1 variables:				
Sex (1 = Female)	−2.913*	1.100	−1.110**	.375
Peer delinquency	.718	.628	.453**	.167
Family adversity	−.188	.770	.507*	.228
Low birth weight	−.140	1.100	−.083	.301
Level-2 variable:				
Neighborhood disadvantage	−.095	.923	1.154	1.233

*$p < .05$.
**$p < .01$.
***$p < .001$.

significantly predicted arrest, while among African-Americans, significant effects were observed for sex, peer delinquency, and family adversity. Neither among whites nor among African-Americans did the biosocial interaction significantly predict arrest, nor did the additive effects of low birth weight and neighborhood disadvantage.

Since Moffitt's theory in particular argues for important etiological differences within the offending population, table 7.5 repeats the same analysis presented above with the exception that the outcome variable is based on life-course-persistent patterns of offending, measured by the frequency of self-reported arrests at the follow-up interview. Among whites, the only significant predictor of life-course-persistent offending was sex (B = −2.913), indicating that males were more likely than females to incur a higher frequency of arrests. Among African-Americans, the effects related to life-course-persistent offending were the same as they were for predicting arrest; namely, sex (B = −1.110), peer delinquency (B = .453), and family adversity (B = .507) served to increase the risk of life-course-persistent offending. As was the case for arrest among whites and African-Americans, both low birth weight and neighborhood disadvantage failed to significantly predict life-course-persistent offending.

In table 7.6, we introduce the biosocial interaction into the model. Among whites, sex (B = −2.915) is the only coefficient to significantly predict life-course-persistent offending. Importantly, the biosocial interaction fails to attain significance for whites. Among African-Americans, the findings are quite provocative. Although neighborhood disadvantage does not exert a significant effect on life-course-persistent offending, sex (B = −1.140), peer delinquency (B = .484), low birth weight (B = −1.230), and family adversity (B = .540), as well as the biosocial interaction (B = 1.731), significantly predict life-course-persistent offending. Of these findings, two deserve discussion. First, among African-Americans, the effect of low birth weight is negative, suggesting that the subjects born at low birth weight are less likely to incur life-

Table 7.6: HLM Analysis of Determinants of Frequency of Arrest by Follow-Up Interview (with Biosocial Interaction)

Variable	Whites		African-Americans	
	B	SE	B	SE
Level-1 variables:				
Sex (Female = 1)	−2.915*	1.113	−1.140**	.378
Peer delinquency	.709	.607	.484**	.166
Family adversity	−.203	.800	.540*	.216
Low birth weight	−.269	1.201	−1.230**	.447
Biosocial interaction	.505	1.305	1.731***	.457
Level-2 variable:				
Neighborhood disadvantage	−.121	.941	1.185	1.267

* $p < .05$.
** $p < .01$.
*** $p < .001$.

course-persistent styles of offending. Second, the positive effect of the biosocial interaction suggests that when low birth weight interacts with adverse familial environments, life-course-persistent offending patterns are likely to ensue. This is important insofar as it suggests that the deleterious consequences of low birth weight relate to life-course-persistent offending only when combined with adverse familial environments. Although the nature and sign of the biosocial interaction are in line with Moffitt's expectation that such interactions are predictive of life-course-persistent styles of offending, as well as the expectation that the interaction should be stronger among African-Americans than whites, the coefficients are not significantly different from one another.

Thus far, we have observed a pattern of results suggesting that individual and familial risk interact to relate to life-course-persistent styles of offending, and that such interactions are stronger among African-Americans. Although ruling out every possible rival causal factor is difficult, our results are in line with theoretical expectations. We next turn to an examination of how neighborhood risk plays a part in the genesis of life-course-persistent offending. (Note: Such a focus among the offending sample is important because the theoretical expectations proffered by Moffitt anticipate within-offender variation in how risk factors influence criminal offending.)

Given that African-Americans continue to live in communities strikingly different from those of whites, it is important to consider the interaction between individual (and familial) traits and neighborhood characteristics (Hawkins, Laub, and Lauritsen 1998, 42). To account for that, we next examine how the relation between individual and familial risk and life-course-persistent offending varies across race and neighborhood disadvantage.

To examine this issue, we partialed the offending sample into four groups characterized by race and neighborhood disadvantage, the latter split at the median. Splitting the continuous neighborhood disadvantage measure is im-

portant because it has been shown that highly disadvantaged structural characteristics will tend to generate social processes that produce a high risk
social context while neighborhoods with highly advantaged structural characteristics tend to generate social processes that produce a protective social
context (Wikstrom and Loeber 2000).

A chi-square test indicates that race and neighborhood disadvantage are
significantly related ($\chi^2_{(1)} = 56.913, p < .05, \phi = .332$). A few points are worthy of mention. First, within racial groupings, only 19.2% of whites live in disadvantaged neighborhoods, while 58.5% of African-Americans live in disadvantaged neighborhoods. Second, within disadvantaged neighborhoods, only
9.1% of whites live in disadvantaged neighborhoodswhile the comparable
figure among African-Americans is 90.9%. Finally, of the offending sample,
only 4.5% are composed of whites reared in disadvantaged neighborhoods,
while the comparable estimate among African-Americans is 44.9%. These
findings underscore the point that whites and African-Americans live in extremely different neighborhood environments (Sampson and Wilson 1995;
Massey 1995, 2001).

Because it is perhaps more meaningful to examine whether the social processes under study operate similarly across neighborhoods of differing racial
composition (see Morenoff et al. 2001), next we divided the offending sample
into four groups: (1) whites/nondisadvantaged neighborhoods ($n = 97$),
(2) whites/disadvantaged neighborhoods ($n = 23$), (3) African-Americans/
nondisadvantaged neighborhoods ($n = 163$), and (4) African-Americans/
disadvantaged neighborhoods ($n = 229$).[13] This division is illustrative and useful because it clearly shows the heterogeneity among sample members who
came from relatively poor sections of Baltimore and underscores two important features of the data. First, although the neighborhoods are very close to
one another, there remains substantial variation in disadvantage; that is, all
sample members are not "poor." Second, it shows that among whites, the majority do not reside in disadvantaged neighborhoods, whereas the opposite
pattern is the case among African-Americans.

Preliminary analysis revealed that the four groups did not differ significantly on the frequency of arrests at the follow-up interview ($F = .261$,
$p > .05$). On the face of it, this result suggests that disadvantaged neighborhoods do not necessarily sound a "siren call" for life-course-persistent offending, nor do whites and African-Americans reared in such environments
differ in their frequency of arrest. In order to examine if the covariates differed across each of the four race by neighborhood disadvantage groups, we
regressed life-course-persistent offending on sex, peer delinquency, family
adversity, low birth weight, and the biosocial interaction. The results may be
found in table 7.7.

The first pair of columns of table 7.7 show that, among whites in nondis-

Table 7.7: Logistic Regression of Determinants of Frequency of Arrest across Groups Defined by Race and Neighborhood Disadvantage

Variable	White Nondisadvantaged Neighborhood		White Disadvantaged Neighborhood		African-American Nondisadvantaged Neighborhood		African-American Disadvantaged Neighborhood	
	B	SE	B	SE	B	SE	B	SE
Sex	−1.821	1.085	−8.481	121.213	−.342	.566	−3.214*	1.303
Peer delinquency	.715	.564	4.843	59.325	.560	.396	.734*	.350
Family adversity	1.799	5.631	−.551	21.747	.523	.307	.821*	.287
Low birth weight	−.134	2.534	−9.592	215.121	−.894	1.005	−1.957	1.419
Biosocial interaction	7.738	38.184	.646	147.776	.622	1.217	2.698*	1.236
Constant	−1.041	1.658	−3.706	173.172	−2.128*	1.050	.323	1.441
χ^2 (df)	12.516 (5)		4.624 (5)		7.091 (5)		42.057 (5)	

*$p < .05$.

advantaged neighborhoods, none of the coefficients exert a significant effect on life-course-persistent offending, although males are slightly ($p < .10$) more likely than females to incur a higher number of arrests by the follow-up interview. Among whites in disadvantaged neighborhoods (shown in the second pair of columns), none of the coefficients significantly predicted life-course-persistent offending. The lack of significant effects observed among whites, regardless of the level of neighborhood disadvantage, may not necessarily be a failure of theoretical predictions; rather, it may be due to the fact that the sample sizes were quite low for the white sample, especially for those whites reared in disadvantaged neighborhoods.[14]

Among African-Americans in nondisadvantaged neighborhoods (the third pair of columns), none of the coefficients exerted a significant effect on life-course-persistent offending, though subjects reared in adverse familial environments were somewhat more likely than their counterparts to exhibit a higher frequency of arrest ($p < .09$). In the fourth pair of columns, the results for African-Americans reared in disadvantaged neighborhoods are presented. As can be seen, four of the five coefficients significantly predicted life-course-persistent offending. Although the additive effect of low birth weight was insignificant, sex (B $= -3.214$), knowledge of peer delinquency (B $= .734$), adverse familial environments (B $= .821$), and the biosocial interaction (B $= 2.698$) served to increase life-course-persistent styles of offending. Although the latter finding is important, because it indicates that the biosocial interaction of low birth weight and family adversity relates to life-course-persistent offending among African-Americans reared in disadvantaged neighborhood environments, the African-American biosocial coefficient was not significantly different from the other three coefficients, a finding that may be due to the relatively small sample sizes. Nevertheless, consistent with the theoretical predictions outlined earlier, this finding represents the first empirical observation, to the best of our knowledge, that among African-Americans, individual and familial risk are exacerbated in disadvantaged neighborhoods in such a way as to predict life-course-persistent styles of offending some twenty years later.[15]

6. Discussion

This essay began with a vignette of three teenagers, each residing in the same underclass neighborhood, whose developmental trajectories were unique. In an effort to present a more complete understanding of race, adolescent development, and antisocial behavior, we described several multilevel theoretical models that were designed to account for such divergent developmental trajectories.

Our analysis failed to uncover direct effects for individual and neighborhood risk. This is important insofar as it suggests that, in isolation, neither individual risk (measured as low birth weight) nor disadvantaged neighborhoods sound a "siren call" for life-course-persistent offending. Our results suggest that a model incorporating individual-, familial-, and neighborhood-level effects provides unique insights into antisocial behavior that may not otherwise be available. In particular, individual and familial risk combine to predict life-course-persistent styles of offending among African-Americans, and such a combination is magnified in disadvantaged neighborhoods among African-Americans. Thus, our results suggest that a more complete understanding of chronic antisocial behavior appears to necessitate a multilevel approach.

Regarding race, our results are somewhat mixed. On the one hand, the sources of life-course-persistent offending appeared to be more similar than different across race. In fact, none of the coefficients were significantly different across any of the group comparisons. This supports Rowe, Vazsonyi, and Flannery's (1994, 409) position that a common causal process underlies patterns of behavior across race, and that any differences that were observed were due to group average differences in common antecedents. On the other hand, the biosocial interaction between individual and familial risk was related to life-course-persistent offending *only* within African-American, disadvantaged neighborhoods. This result partially supports Sampson and Wilson's (1995) assertion that whites and African-Americans live in different ecological contexts, and it is within these contexts that race differences in antisocial behavior become pronounced. Although this effect could be due to the fact that very few whites were reared in disadvantaged neighborhoods, analyses of the biosocial interaction on life-course-persistent offending within the white sample failed to produce a significant effect. In sum, although the antecedents of life-course-persistent offending appear to be more similar than different across race, we continue to highlight the extremely different neighborhood contexts in which whites and African-Americans are reared.

To be sure, our data suffer from several limitations. First, our data come from Baltimore, and thus, generalization to other cities should be guarded, insofar as Baltimore, like many other East Coast cities in the latter half of the twentieth century, is racially segregated. In addition, Baltimore may be subject to different sorts of criminal and drug abuse patterns that may not be reflective of other cities in the United States. Second, we measured individual risk via low birth weight and familial risk via adverse familial environments. It may be that other types of individual risk factors (such as neuropsychological functioning) and familial risk factors (such as family functioning and disciplinary practices) relate to life-course-persistent offending in ways not observed in the present study. However, given the notorious difficulty in reproducing interactions, the fact that we replicated the biosocial interaction observed by Tibbetts and Piquero (1999) in Philadelphia using almost identical indicators in Baltimore leads us to believe that this finding warrants continued theoretical, research, and policy attention.[16] Third, our principal outcome measures were based on a self-report recall of the prevalence and frequency of arrest. Although recall measures based on arrest have fared well, future efforts should strive to obtain multimethod measures of criminal behavior. Fourth, because our measure of neighborhood disadvantage was static in nature, we could not assess the effect of changing neighborhood contexts. Although we heeded researchers' suggestions to measure neighborhood disadvantage early in life, it is quite possible that pathways to antisocial behavior are altered by changing neighborhood environs. The same limitation may be raised regarding our static family adversity measure. Fifth, our failure to detect a significant biosocial interaction effect among the whites in the Baltimore data may be, in part, a function of some restriction of variation in the variables constituting the biosocial interaction. Given that other researchers have documented significant biosocial interaction effects among whites (see review in Raine et al. 1997), future efforts should continue to further explore the nature of biosocial interactions across race.

With these limitations in hand, we envision a number of important future research directions. The first concerns the nature of neighborhood contexts. What would happen if individuals reared in disadvantaged neighborhoods were removed and placed in nondisadvantaged neighborhoods, or vice versa? For example, Shannon's (1988, 120) work with the Racine cohort showed that change in residence to crime-producing neighborhoods generated proportionately more increases in criminal activity than were generated among those individuals who moved to areas which were considered less likely to produce crime. Recent research tends to suggest that living among socially and economically advantaged neighbors can have positive influences on a range of behaviors and outcomes for children and youth (Leventhal and Brooks-Gunn 2000). Data from the Moving to Opportunity (MTO) studies have shown that when families living in public housing moved to lower-poverty neighborhoods, improvements were observed across several developmental outcomes, including (1) safety and child and parent physical mental health (Del Conte and Kling 2001), (2) self-sufficiency and parenting practices (Leventhal and Brooks-Gunn 2001), (3) achievement among elementary school children (Ludwig, Duncan, and Ladd 2001), (4) arrests for violent crimes and involvement in problem behavior (Del Conte and Kling 2001), and (5) social organization and psychological well-being (Rosenbaum 2001). Researchers with longitudinal data on neighborhood contexts should examine the extent to which early individual-level risk factors relate to antisocial behavior as neighborhood contexts change.

Second, the frameworks we explored focused on interactions between individuals, families, and neighborhoods. Clearly, other social contexts exist within which individual risk could differentially relate to antisocial behavior. Two of these include the school and the peer group. For example, individual-level risk could be magnified in poor and disadvantaged school environments which do not have capable resources that promote academic achievement and learning and/or contain a high prevalence of individuals who have similar risk factors for antisocial behavior (Brezina, Piquero, and Mazerolle 2001). Since disadvantaged schools often tend to be located in disadvantaged neighborhoods, it becomes exceedingly difficult to promote prosocial patterns of development and safety. Similarly, the peer social context is important for mediating the relationships between individual-level risk factors and antisocial behavior. As several researchers have shown (Caspi et al. 1993; Piquero and Brezina 2001), individual risk is exacerbated among peer social contexts that promote delinquency attitudes and behaviors.

Another related factor that may be relevant is the potential impact that incarceration and released offenders have on neighborhood life. For example, researchers have found that incarceration disrupts social networks by damaging familial, economic, and political sources of informal social control (Rose and Clear 1998; Rose et al. 2001). Moreover, as offenders return from incarceration stints, they are likely to challenge the community's capacity for self-regulation. As a result, the input/output incarceration process is likely to exhibit a toll on the community context in which individuals reside.

Third, our analysis failed to uncover an interaction effect between individual and familial risk among whites. Although we believed that this is probably due to the small number of whites in the sample and not necessarily to the lack of a true effect per se, it could be that poor whites in inner cities are simply not poor enough (when compared to poor inner-city African-Americans) to manifest risk for life-course-persistent offending. Perhaps a useful research direction would be to examine life-course-persistent offending among whites where very poor whites are likely to reside: in rural areas (Elder and Conger 2000).

Finally, although we followed the spirit of Moffitt's life-course-persistent designation, our offender group categories were still arbitrarily defined. As do other scholars (Nagin and Land 1993), we recognize that there may be several other methods for categorizing offenders into distinct criminal trajectories, and we encourage further research on this issue, as well as the manner in which the covariates studied in the current paper distinguish between trajectory memberships.

In the end, we believe that unique and important information is to be gained from a perspective that focuses on the social characteristics of communities that bear on the lives of children and families (Sampson 1997). Policy proscriptions must recognize that individual risk in and of itself may not be enough to culminate in a life-course-persistent pattern of antisocial behavior. Policy efforts therefore should attempt to target appropriate resources not only at individuals, but also at families and neighborhoods. Although this is a difficult task, research has shown that prevention efforts administered early in the life course have important developmental benefits. What is needed is an approach that is multifaceted and targeted at the appropriate levels. Several policy examples may be instructive here.

One prominent policy effort could be targeted at environmental contaminants, such as exposure to lead. High levels of lead have been linked to several different behavioral and developmental outcomes and have been found to cause permanent neurologic damage or death (McLoyd and Lozoff 2001, 316). Evidence suggests that racial and ethnic minorities are exposed to higher levels of environmental risks, including exposure to lead (Kington and Nickens 2001, 290). In fact, recent data from the U.S. Department of Health and Human Services (1988–94) showed that in poor African-American families, 22% of the children had elevated levels, which compares to much lower percentages among middle-income or high-income African-Americans. These racial differences have been linked to housing, with children living in houses built before the 1960s, and currently concentrated in older inner city areas, exhibiting the highest risk (Mahaffey et al. 1982).

It seems that lead exposure is one policy change that can be targeted by several different public agencies. For example, housing authorities could marshal resources to identify and remove lead-based paint in housing complexes, while at the same time inner-city families could be provided improved health care access as well as better health care quality in order to counteract early childhood exposure to lead. Since lead exposure detrimentally influences cognitive functioning, increased funding to city agencies and schools could help provide cognitive skills development classes to children differentially exposed.

Another policy effort concerns home visits by nurses. These types of visits can assist parents in developing effective parenting strategies, while behavioral and cognitive skills training efforts can help individuals overcome early cognitive deficits (e.g., Tremblay and Craig 1995; Olds et al. 1998). At the same time, municipality and state governments can help citizens improve neighborhood functioning by marshaling resources that can help overcome the plight of the urban poor. Although employment is a priority among these efforts (Wilson 1996), research has shown that improvements in this regard appear to trickle down to the familial and individual level of functioning.

Perhaps one area that has been implicated in several developmental outcomes including academic and employment success, psychological well-being, and antisocial behavior is general health and health care. Health is socially embedded in the larger conditions in which individuals live and work

(Williams 2001, 388). Given that "health care is the sine qua non of adult and child development [and that] access to the health care system . . . is contingent on the community in which one lives" (Bronfenbrenner, Moen, and Garbarino 1984, 299), it is even more important that policy officials focus their efforts to make health care a top priority to individuals and families early in the life course. This is especially so among poor African-Americans in urban areas, who, by the very nature of their residential location, do not have ready access to opportunities to adequate and affordable health care (Kington and Nickens 2001, 259). Since health influences every facet of life, including one's ability to work, to socialize, to think, to learn, to communicate, and to reproduce (Kington and Nickens 2001, 253), efforts along these lines have the ability to pay long-term dividends.

This is especially the case with one apparently preventable health concern: low birth weight. The high proportion of low-birth-weight infants among African-American women remains one of the most important puzzles to be solved (Foster 1997). Given that it is likely that environmental and behavioral factors are adversely affecting the pregnancies of African-American women (McLoyd and Lozoff 2001, 340), prevention efforts aimed at addressing low-birth-weight appear important. An outcome evaluation of the Vermont Intervention Project found that an intervention designed to enhance the skill and confidence of mothers with low-birth-weight children significantly improved the cognitive development of low-birth-weight children (Achenbach, Phares, and Howell 1990). And since cognitive abilities are implicated in academic achievement, antisocial behavior, and other developmental outcomes, a policy on improving the health of low birth weight children appears relevant. As our results have shown, low birth weight interacts with adverse familial and neighborhood environments among African-Americans in such a way as to produce life-course-persistent patterns of offending some twenty years later. Continued theoretical, empirical, and policy attention in this regard appears warranted.

Notes

1. Some research has provided results somewhat contradictory to Moffitt's typology (Aguilar et al. 2000). In particular, empirical research using advanced statistical models designed to isolate relatively homogeneous categories of offenders has uncovered several additional groups of offenders (Nagin, Farrington, and Moffitt 1995). The most prominent of these is the "low-level chronic" group. Because of their particular pattern of offending, persistent but low-level offending from childhood to adolescence and/or from adolescence to adulthood, this group does not map onto either of Moffitt's two offender groups.

2. This is not to say that individuals born with cognitive deficits are not born into

affluent environments. Although this scenario is unlikely in Moffitt's scheme, affluent environments tend to be able to provide the resources necessary for children to overcome their early deficits.

3. This latter point is important because it speaks to the developmental context that is shaping much of the landscape in the social sciences. This perspective emphasizes "viewing lives in context and the need for researchers to examine the multiple contexts that influence children and families (e.g., schools/child care, peers, communities), as well as the relations among these contexts" (Leventhal and Brooks-Gunn 2000, 310).

4. Leventhal and Brooks-Gunn (2000, 330) note that, even when African-American children and youth reside in affluent neighborhoods, these neighborhoods may lack adequate resources or may have lower-quality resources than those available to their white peers in affluent neighborhoods. Nevertheless, African-American children residing in poor neighborhoods may be less likely to benefit from enriching home environments (Klebanov et al. 1997).

5. Although the focus of the current presentation is on the influence of early childhood socialization agents and individual-level risk factors, this does not imply that change over time across different contexts is irrelevant. In fact, children and adolescents are likely to be susceptible to particular forms of influence at different ages, and the interplay among individual characteristics as well as family and neighborhood context may shift across different developmental periods (Aber et al. 1997). For example, the influence of family context may be stronger when the child is younger, and this influence may be affected by neighborhood context in a different way with a younger child than with an older one (e.g., parenting practices regarding discipline or where a child is allowed to go in the neighborhood might be operating with younger children, and informal social contacts of the family members to provide opportunities for work might be operating with older adolescents). An examination of how these and other changing contexts influence behavior is beyond the scope of this presentation but appears important for matters at hand.

6. To be sure, there may be some self-selection bias of women who sought services, and they may differ from the other disadvantaged mothers who did not seek prenatal care. Still, as our results will show, there are different levels of risk factors and offspring outcomes among the mothers who chose to be in the project.

7. We also conducted a sensitivity analysis where we set the life-course-persistent offending cutoff to six arrests. The results revealed conclusions substantively similar to those presented herein.

8. The actual ages at first arrest for these groups is likely to be lower, because of memory telescoping in retrospective reports of offending onset (Henry et al. 1994), and because the first offense tends to antedate the first arrest by two to four years (Moffitt et al. 2001).

9. To be sure, our measure of family adversity, though similar to those used in extant research, does not directly measure familial socialization or familial interaction. Still, the major family factors included in this measure are all well correlated with the extent of parental concern for the child or are conditions that affect the ability of the parent to monitor and correct the child's behavior (Gottfredson and Hirschi 1990, 91).

10. The major threat of multicollinearity in interactive models is not substantive, but rather practical (Jaccard, Turissi, and Wan 1990, 31). High correlations between predictors can cause computational errors on standard programs. Centering the variables

(prior to forming the multiplicative term) is a means of addressing the problem. Such a transformation will tend to yield low correlations between the product term (the biosocial interaction) and the component parts of the term (i.e., low birth weight and family adversity). When we examined the zero-order correlations, multicollinearity did not appear to be a problem.

11. There were only four subjects who reported an "other" race/ethnicity affiliation. These individuals were recoded into the African-American grouping.

12. Of the 1,758, there were 4 cases which had missing data on the arrest prevalence measure, so we could not place these 4 individuals into a group. Further, there were a total of 515 individuals who reported being arrested at least once. Unfortunately, 3 of these individuals (all African-American) did not have valid information on the frequency of their arrests (i.e., they reported "Don't know" on the frequency question); hence, they were removed from further analysis, leaving a sample of 512 offenders available for analyses.

13. As noted earlier, three cases had missing data on arrest frequency. Two of these cases came from African-Americans living in nondisadvantaged neighborhoods, while the other came from an African-American living in a disadvantaged neighborhood. The following analyses, then, are based on 512 offenders.

14. The low sample size for whites in disadvantaged neighborhoods may create a statistical power problem. Statistical power questions how often one would fail to identify a relationship that in fact exists in the population. At the same time, the failure to identify a large number of whites in disadvantaged neighborhoods is not endemic to our data set. In fact, in other data sets, analyses are not performed on whites because none of them live in neighborhoods that experience the same level of disadvantage experienced by African-Americans. For example, Moffitt (1997, 155–156) could not locate white boys residing in disadvantaged neighborhoods in the Pittsburgh Youth Study (see also Sampson and Wilson 1995).

15. Recall that the analyses reported in table 7.6 were based on the original life-course-persistent designation (i.e., seven or more arrests signified membership in the life-course-persistent group). As was the case in previous supplemental analysis, we lowered the life-course-persistent threshold to six or more arrests and reestimated the models across races and neighborhood designation. We arrived at the same substantive conclusions as before. In addition, it is also important to note here that lowering the threshold for life-course-persistent membership from seven or more arrests to six or more arrests resulted in adding only two white individuals to the life-course-persistent group. For example, of the eighty-four life-course-persistent offenders, defined as those with seven or more arrests, seventeen were white and sixty-seven were African-American. When the life-course-persistent threshold was lowered to six or more offenses, the life-course-persistent group increased to ninety-six individuals, of which nineteen were white and seventy-seven were African-American. Thus, lowering the life-course-persistent threshold has the effect of including more African-American than white individuals.

16. It should be noted that it is relatively easy to get interactions in experiments because the researcher randomly assigns the subjects to cells that are equal sizes. But in "real life," if most vulnerable children are born into poor environments, then there are seldom enough subjects in the interaction cells (i.e., vulnerable + rich, or invulnerable + poor) to have statistical power.

References

Aber, J. L., M. Gephart, J. Brooks-Gunn, J. Connell, and M. B. Spencer. 1997. "Neighborhood, Family, and Individual Processes as They Influence Child and Adolescent Outcomes." In *Neighborhood Poverty,* vol. 1, *Context and Consequences for Children,* ed. J. Brooks-Gunn, G. J. Duncan, and J. L. Aber. New York: Russell Sage Foundation.

Achenbach, T. M., V. Phares, and C. T. Howell. 1990. "Seven-Year Outcome of the Vermont Intervention Program for Low-Birthweight Infants." *Child Development* 61: 1672 – 1681.

Aguilar, B., L. A. Sroufe, B. Egeland, and E. Carlson. 2000. "Distinguishing the Early-Onset-Persistent and Adolescent-Onset Antisocial Behavior Types: From Birth to 16 Years." *Development and Psychopathology* 12: 109 –132.

Aiken, L. S., and S. G. West. 1991. *Multiple Regression: Testing and Interpreting Interactions.* London: Sage.

Akers, R. L. 1998. *Social Learning and Social Structure: A General Theory of Crime and Deviance.* Boston: Northeastern University Press.

Anderson, E. 1990. *Streetwise: Race, Class, and Change in an Urban Community.* Chicago: University of Chicago Press.

———. 1999. "The Social Ecology of Youth." In *Youth Violence,* ed. M. Tonry and M. H. Moore, Crime and Justice: An Annual Review of Research, vol. 24. Chicago: University of Chicago Press.

Baltimore City Health Department. 1973. *Census Tract Manual.* Baltimore: Baltimore City Health Department.

Bellair, P. E. 1997. "Social Interaction and Community Crime: Examining the Importance of Neighbor Networks." *Criminology* 35: 677–703.

Blumstein, A., J. Cohen, J. A. Roth, and C. A. Visher, eds. 1986. *Criminal Careers and "Career Criminals."* Washington, DC: National Academy Press.

Brezina, T., A. R. Piquero, and P. Mazerolle. 2001. "An Empirical Test of Agnew's Macro-strain Theory." *Journal of Research in Crime and Delinquency* 38: 362–386.

Broman, S. H., P. L. Nichols, and W. A. Kennedy. 1975. *Preschool IQ: Prenatal and Early Developmental Correlates.* New York: Wiley.

Bronfenbrenner, U., P. Moen, and J. Garbarino. 1984. "Child, Family, and Community. In *Review of Child Development Research,* ed. R. Parke. Chicago: University of Chicago Press.

Brooks-Gunn, J., G. Duncan, and J. L. Aber, eds. 1997. *Neighborhood Poverty: Context and Consequences for Children.* Vol. 1. New York: Russell Sage Foundation.

Bursik, R. J., Jr. 1989. "Political Decision-Making and Ecological Models of Delinquency: Conflict and Consensus." In *Theoretical Integration in the Study of Deviance and Crime,* ed. S. Messner, M. Krohn, and A. Liska. Albany, NY: SUNY Press.

Bursik, R. J., Jr., and H. G. Grasmick. 1993. *Neighborhoods and Crime.* New York: Lexington.

Caspi, A., D. Lynam, T. E. Moffitt, and P. A. Silva. 1993. "Unraveling Girls' Delinquency: Biological, Dispositional, and Contextual Contributions to Adolescent Misbehavior." *Developmental Psychology* 29: 19 –30.

Caspi, A., B. T. E. Moffitt, P. A. Silva, M. Stouthamer-Loeber, R. Krueger, and P. Schmutte. 1994. "Are Some People Crime-Prone? Replications of the Personality-Crime Relationship across Countries, Genders, Races, and Methods." *Criminology* 32: 163 –196.

Chase-Lansdale, P. L., R. A. Gordon, J. Brooks-Gunn, and P. K. Klebanov. 1997. "Neighborhood and Family Influences on the Intellectual and Behavioral Competence of Preschool and Early School-Age Children." In *Neighborhood Poverty* vol. 1, *Context and Consequences for Children*, ed. J. Brooks-Gunn, G. J. Duncan, and J. L. Aber. New York: Russell Sage Foundation.

Coie, J. D., and K. A. Dodge. 1998. "Aggression and Antisocial Behavior." In *Handbook of Child Psychology*, vol. 3, *Social, Emotional, and Personality Development*, ed. N. Eisenberg. New York: John Wiley and Sons.

Coren, S. 1993. *The Left-Hander Syndrome.* New York: Vantage Books.

Del Conte, A., and J. King. 2001. "A Synthesis of MTO Research on Self-Sufficiency, Safety and Health, and Behavior and Delinquency." *Poverty Research News (Joint Center for Poverty Research)* 5:3–6.

Denno, D. W. 1986. "Victim, Offender, and Situational Characteristics of Violent Crime." *Journal of Criminal Law and Criminology* 77:1142–1158.

———. 1990. *Biology and Violence: From Birth to Adulthood.* Cambridge: Cambridge University Press.

Earls, F., J. McGuire, and S. Shay. 1994. "Evaluating a Community Intervention to Reduce the Risk of Child Abuse: Methodological Strategies in Conducting Neighborhood Surveys." *Child Abuse and Neglect* 18:473–485.

Elder, G. H., Jr., and R. D. Conger. 2000. *Children of the Land: Adversity and Success in Rural America.* Chicago: University of Chicago Press.

Elliott, D. S., W. J. Wilson, D. Huizinga, R. J. Sampson, A. Elliott, B. Rankin. 1996. "The Effects of Neighborhood Disadvantage on Adolescent Development." *Journal of Research in Crime and Delinquency* 33:389–426.

Farrington, D. P. 1989. "Self-Reported and Official Offending from Adolescence to Adulthood." In *Cross-National Research in Self-Reported Crime and Delinquency*, ed. M. Klein. Dordrecht: Kluwer.

———. 1993. "Have Any Individual, Family, or Neighborhood Influences on Offending Been Demonstrated Conclusively?" In *Integrating Individual and Ecological Aspects of Crime*, ed. D. P. Farrington, R. J. Sampson, and P. O. H. Wikstrom. Stockholm: Swedish National Council for Crime Prevention.

Foster, H. 1997. "The Enigma of Low Birth Weight and Race." *New England Journal of Medicine* 337:1232–1233.

Furstenberg, F. F., Jr. 1993. "How Families Manage Risk and Opportunities in Dangerous Neighborhoods." In *Sociology and the Public Agenda*, ed. W. J. Wilson. Newbury Park, CA: Sage.

Furstenberg, F. F., Jr., T. D. Cook, J. Eccles, G. H. Elder, Jr., and A. Sameroff. 1999. *Managing to Make It: Urban Families and Adolescent Success.* Chicago: University of Chicago Press.

Gibson, C. L., A. R. Piquero, and S. G. Tibbetts. 2000. "Assessing the Relationship between Maternal Cigarette Smoking during Pregnancy and Age at First Police Contact." *Justice Quarterly* 17:519–542.

———. 2001. "The Contribution of Family Adversity and Verbal IQ to Criminal Behavior." *International Journal of Offender Therapy and Comparative Criminology* 45:574–592.

Gottfredson, M., and T. Hirschi. 1990. *A General Theory of Crime.* Stanford, CA: Stanford University Press.

Gottfredson, D. C., R. J. McNeil, and G. C. Gottfredson. 1991. "Social Area Influences on Delinquency: A Multi-level Analysis." *Journal of Research in Crime and Delinquency* 28:197–226.

Hardy, J. B., and S. Shapiro. 1999. *Pathways to Adulthood: A Three-Generation Urban Study, 1960–1994: Baltimore, Maryland.* Codebook. . Ann Arbor, MI: Inter-university Consortium for Political and Social Research.

Hardy, J. B., S. Shapiro, D. Mellits, E. A. Skinner, N. M. Astone, M. Ensminger, T. LaVeist, R. A. Baumgardner, and B. H. Starfield. 1997. "Self-Sufficiency at Ages 27 to 33 Years: Factors Present between Birth and 18 Years that Predict Educational Attainment among Children Born to Inner-City Families." *Pediatrics* 99:80–87.

Harrison, A. O., M. N. Wilson, C. J. Pine, S. Q. Chan, and R. Buriel. 1990. "Family Ecologies of Ethnic Minority Children." *Child Development* 61:347–362.

Hawkins, D. F., J. H. Laub, and J. L. Lauritsen. 1998. "Race, Ethnicity, and Serious Juvenile Offending." In *Serious and Violent Juvenile Offenders: Risk Factors and Successful Interventions,* ed. R. Loeber and D. P. Farrington. Newbury Park, CA: Sage.

Henry, B., T. E. Moffitt, A. Caspi, J. Langley, and P. A. Silva. 1994. "On the 'Remembrance of Things Past': A Longitudinal Evaluation of the Retrospective Method." *Psychological Assessment* 6:92–101.

Hindelang, M., T. Hirschi, and J. Weis. 1981. *Measuring Delinquency.* Beverly Hills, CA: Sage.

Hirschi, T. 1995. "The Family." In *Crime,* ed. J. Q. Wilson and J. Petersilia. San Francisco: ICS Press.

Huizinga, D., and D. S. Elliott. 1986. "Reassessing the Reliability and Validity of Self-Report Delinquent Measures." *Journal of Quantitative Criminology* 2:293–327.

Jaccard, J., R. Turrisi, and C. K. Wan. 1990. *Interaction Effects in Multiple Regression.* Newbury Park, CA: Sage.

Klebanov, P. K., J. Brooks-Gunn, P. L. Chase-Lansdale, and R. A. Gordon. 1997. "Are Neighborhood Effects on Young Children Mediated by the Home Environment?" In *Neighborhood Poverty,* vol. 1, *Contexts and Consequences for Children,* ed. J. Brooks-Gunn and J. L. Aber. New York: Russell Sage Foundation.

Kington, R. S., and H. W. Nickens. 2001. "Racial and Ethnic Differences in Health: Recent Trends, Current Patterns, Future Directions." In *America Becoming: Racial Trends and Their Consequences,* ed. N. J. Smelser, W. J. Wilson, and F. Mitchell. Washington, DC: National Academy Press.

Kolvin, I., F. Miller, M. Fleeting, and P. Kolvin. 1988. "Social and Parenting Factors Affecting Criminal-Offense Rates." *British Journal of Psychiatry* 152:80–90.

Krivo, L. J., and R. D. Peterson. 2000. "The Structural Context of Homicide: Accounting for Racial Differences in Process." *American Sociological Review* 65:547–559.

Lauritsen, J. L. 1998. "The Age-Crime Debate: Assessing the Limits of Longitudinal Self-Report Data." *Social Forces* 76:1–29.

Leventhal, T., and J. Brooks-Gunn. 2000. "The Neighborhoods They Live In: The Effects of Neighborhood Residence on Child and Adolescent Outcomes." *Psychological Bulletin* 126:309–337.

———. 2001. "Moving to Better Neighborhoods Improves Health and Family Life among New York Families." *Poverty Research News (Joint Center for Poverty Research)* 5:11–12.

Lipsitt, P. D., S. L. Buka, and L. P. Lipsitt. 1990. "Early Intelligence Scores and Subsequent Delinquency: A Prospective Study." *American Journal of Family Therapy* 18: 197–208.

Lizotte, A. J., T. P. Thornberry, M. D. Krohn, D. Chard-Wierschem, and D. McDowall. 1994. "Neighborhood Context and Delinquency: A Longitudinal Analysis." In *Cross-National Longitudinal Research on Human Development and Criminal Behavior*, ed. E. G. M. Weitekamp and H. J. Kerner. Netherlands: Kluwer Academic Publishers.

Loeber, R., and D. P. Farrington. 1998. *Serious and Violent Juvenile Offendersw*. Newbury Park, CA: Sage.

Loeber, R., D. P. Farrington, M. Stouthamer-Loeber, T. E. Moffitt, and A. Caspi. 1998. "The Development of Male Offending: Key Findings from the First Decade of the Pittsburgh Youth Study." *Studies on Crime and Crime Prevention* 7: 141–172.

Loeber, R., and M. Stouthamer-Loeber. 1986. "Family Factors as Correlates and Predictors of Juvenile Conduct Problems and Delinquency." In *Crime and Justice: An Annual Review of Research*, vol. 7, ed. M. Tonry and N. Morris. Chicago: University of Chicago Press.

Loeber, R., and P. O. Wikstrom. 1993. "Individual Pathways to Crime in Different Types of Neighborhoods." In *Integrating Individual and Ecological Aspects of Crime*, ed. D. P. Farrington, R. J. Sampson, and P. O. H. Wikstrom. Stockholm: National Council for Crime Prevention.

Ludwig, J., G. Duncan, and H. Ladd. 2001. "The Effect of MTO on Baltimore Children's Educational Outcomes." *Poverty Research News (Joint Center for Poverty Research)* 5: 13–15.

Lynam, D. R., A. Caspi, T. E. Moffitt, P. O. H. Wikstrom, R. Loeber, and S. Novak. 2000. "The Interaction between Impulsivity and Neighborhood Context on Offending: The Effects of Impulsivity Are Stronger in Poorer Neighborhoods." *Journal of Abnormal Psychology* 109: 563–574.

Lynam, D., T. E. Moffitt, and M. Stouthamer-Loeber. 1993. "Explaining the Relation between IQ and Delinquency: Class, Race, Test Motivation, School Failure, or Self-Control." *Journal of Abnormal Psychology* 102: 187–196.

Magnusson, D. 1988. *Individual Development from an Interactional Perspective: A Longitudinal Study*. Hillsdale, NJ: Lawrence Erlbaum.

Mahaffey, K., J. Annest, J. Roberts, and R. Murphy. 1982. National Estimates of Blood Lead Levels: United States, 1976–1980: Association with Selected Demographic and Socioeconomic Factors." *New England Journal of Medicine* 307: 573–579.

Massey, D. S. 1995. "Getting Away with Murder: Segregation and Violent Crime in Urban America." *University of Pennsylvania Law Review* 143: 1203–1232.

———. 2001. "Residential Segregation and Neighborhood Conditions in U.S. Metropolitan Areas." In *America Becoming: Racial Trends and Their Consequences*, vol. 1, ed. N. J. Smelser, W. J. Wilson, and F. Mitchell. Washington, DC: National Academy Press.

Massey, D. S., and N. A. Denton. 1993. *American Apartheid: Segregation and the Making of the Underclass*. Cambridge, MA: Harvard University Press.

McCormick, M. C. 1985. "The Contribution of Low Birth Weight to Infant Mortality and Childhood Morbidity." *New England Journal of Medicine* 312: 82–90.

McLoyd, V. C., and B. Lozoff. 2001. "Racial and Ethnic Trends in Childrens' and Adolescents' Behavior and Development." In *America Becoming: Racial Trends and Their Consequences,* vol. 2, ed. N. J. Smelser, W. J. Wilson, and F. Mitchell. Washington, DC: National Academy Press.

Mischel, W. 1977. "The Interaction of Person and Situation." In *Personality at the Crossroads: Current Issues in Interactional Psychology,* ed. D. Magnusson. Hillsdale, NJ: Lawrence Erlbaum.

Moffitt, T. E. 1993. "Adolescence-Limited and Life-Course Persistent Antisocial Behavior: A Developmental Taxonomy." *Psychological Review* 100:674–701.

———. 1994. "Natural Histories of Delinquency." In *Cross-National Longitudinal Research on Human Development and Criminal Behavior,* ed. E. G. M. Weitekamp and H.-J. Kerner. Dordrecht: Kluwer Academic Publishers.

———. 1997. "Neuropsychology, Antisocial Behavior, and Neighborhood Context." In *Violence and Childhood in the Inner City,* ed. J. McCord. New York: Cambridge University Press.

Moffitt, T. E., A. Caspi, M. Rutter, and P. A. Silva. 2001. *Sex Differences in Antisocial Behaviour.* Cambridge: Cambridge University Press.

Moffitt, T. E., D. R. Lynam, and P. A. Silva. 1994. "Neuropsychological Tests Predicting Persistent Male Delinquency." *Criminology* 32:277–300.

Morenoff, J. F., R. J. Sampson, and S. W. Raudenbush. 2001. Neighborhood Inequality, Collective Efficacy, and the Spatial Dynamics of Urban Violence." *Criminology* 39:517–560.

Nagin, D. S., D. P. Farrington, and T. E. Moffitt. 1995. "Life-Course Trajectories of Different Types of Offenders." *Criminology* 33:111–139.

Nagin, D. S., and K. C. Land. 1993. "Age, Criminal Careers, and Population Heterogeneity: Specification and Estimation of a Nonparametric, Mixed Poisson Model." *Criminology* 31:327–362.

Nagin, D. S., G. Pogarsky, and D. P. Farrington. 1997. "Adolescence Mothers and the Criminal Behavior of Their Children." *Law and Society Review* 31:137–162.

National Research Council. 1993. *Losing Generations.* Washington: National Academy Press.

Nichols, P. L., and T. Chen. 1981. *Minimal Brain Dysfunction: A Prospective Study.* Hillsdale, NJ: Erlbaum.

Niswander, K., and M. Gordon. 1972. *The Women and Their Pregnancies.* Washington, DC: U.S. Department of Health, Education, and Welfare.

Ogbu, J. U. 1991. "Immigrant and Involuntary Minorities in Comparative Perspective." In *Minority Status and Schooling: A Comparative Study of Immigrant and Involuntary Minorities,* ed. M. A. Gibson and J. U. Ogbu. New York: Garland Publishing.

———. 1993. "Differences in Cultural Frame of Reference." *International Journal of Behavioral Development* 16:483–506.

Olds, D., C. R. Henderson, Jr., R. Cole, J. Eckenrode, H. Kitzman, D. Luckey, L. Petit, K. Sidora, P. Morris, and J. Powers. 1998. "Long-Term Effects of Nurse Home Visitation on Children's Criminal and Antisocial Behavior: 15-Year Follow-Up of a Randomized Controlled Trial." *Journal of the American Medical Association* 280:1238–1244.

Paneth, N. S. 1995. "The Problem of Low Birth Weight." *Future of Children: Low Birth Weight (Center for the Future of Children)* 5:19–34.

Patterson, G. R. 1980. "Children Who Steal." In *Understanding Crime,* ed. T. Hirschi and M. R. Gottfredson. Beverly Hills, CA: Sage.

Pattillo, M. E. 1998. "Sweet Mothers and Gangbangers: Managing Crime in a Black Middle-Class Neighborhood." *Social Forces* 76:747–774.

Peeples, F., and R. Loeber. 1994. "Do Individual Factors and Neighborhood Context Explain Ethnic Differences in Juvenile Delinquency." *Journal of Quantitative Criminology* 10:141–158.

Piquero, A. R. 2000a. "Assessing the Relationships between Gender, Chronicity, Seriousness, and Offense Skewness in Criminal Offending." *Journal of Criminal Justice* 28:103–117.

———. 2000b. "Frequency, Specialization, and Violence in Offending Careers." *Journal of Research in Crime and Delinquency* 37:392–418.

———. 2001. "Testing Moffitt's Neuropsychological Variation Hypothesis for the Prediction of Life-Course Persistent Offending." *Psychology, Crime, and Law* 7:193–215.

Piquero, A. R., and T. Brezina. 2001. "Testing Moffitt's Account of Adolescence-Limited Delinquency." *Criminology* 39:353–370.

Piquero, A. R., and S. L. Buka. 2002. "Linking Juvenile and Adult Patterns of Criminal Activity in the Providence Cohort of the National Collaborative Perinatal Project." *Journal of Criminal Justice* 30:259–272.

Piquero, A. R., and H. L. Chung. 2001. "On the Relationships between Gender, Early Onset, and the Seriousness of Offending." *Journal of Criminal Justice* 29:189–206.

Piquero, A. R., D. P. Farrington, and A. Blumstein. 2003. "The Criminal Career Paradigm." In *Crime and Justice: A Review of Research,* vol. 30, ed. M. Tonry. Chicago: University of Chicago Press.

Piquero, A. R., C. Gibson, S. Tibbetts, M. Turner, and S. Katz. 2002. "Maternal Cigarette Smoking during Pregnancy and Life-Course-Persistent Offending." *International Journal of Offender Therapy and Comparative Criminology* 46:231–248.

Piquero, A. R., and S. G. Tibbetts. 1999. "The Impact of Pre/Perinatal Disturbances and Disadvantaged Familial Environments in Predicting Criminal Offending." *Studies on Crime and Crime Prevention* 8:52–70.

Pryor, J., and L. Woodward. 1996. "Families and Parenting." In *From Child to Adult: The Dunedin Multidisciplinary Health and Development Study,* ed. P. A. Silva and W. R. Stanton. Oxford: Oxford University Press.

Raine, A. 1993. *The Psychopathology of Crime.* San Diego: Academic Press.

Raine, A., P. Brennan, D. P. Farrington, and S. Mednick. 1997. *Biosocial Bases of Violence.* New York: Plenum Press.

Raine, A., P. Brennan, and S. Mednick. 1994. "Birth Complications Combined with Early Maternal Rejection at Age 1 Year Predispose to Violent Crime at Age 18 Years." *Archives of General Psychiatry* 51:984–988.

Rose, D. R., and T. R. Clear 1998. "Incarceration, Social Capital, and Crime: Implications for Social Disorganization Theory." *Criminology* 36:441–480.

Rose, D. R., T. R. Clear, E. Waring, and K. Scully. 2001. "Coercive Mobility and Crime: Incarceration and Social Disorganization." *Justice Quarterly* 20:33–64.

Rosenbaum, E. 2001. "The Social Context of New Neighborhoods among MTO Chicago Families." *Poverty Research News (Joint Center for Poverty Research)* 5:16–19.

Ross, C. E., J. R. Reynolds, and K. J. Geis. 2000. "The Contingent Meaning of Neighborhood Stability for Residents' Psychological Well Being." *American Sociological Review* 65:581–597.

Rowe, D. C., A. T. Vazsonyi, and D. J. Flannery. 1994. "No More Than Skin Deep: Ethnic and Racial Similarity in Developmental Process." *Psychological Review* 101:396–413.

Rutter, M. 1978. "Family, Area and School Influences in the Genesis of Conduct Disorders." In *Aggression and Antisocial Behavior in Childhood and Adolescence,* ed. L. A. Hersov, M. Berger, and D. Shaffer. Oxford: Pergamon Press.

Sampson, R. J. 1997. "The Embeddedness of Child and Adolescent Development: A Community-Level Perspective on Urban Violence." In *Violence and Childhood in the Inner City,* ed. J. McCord. New York: Cambridge University Press.

Sampson, R. J., and W. B. Groves. 1989. "Community Structure and Crime: Testing Social Disorganization Theory." *American Journal of Sociology* 94:774–802.

Sampson, R. J., and J. L. Lauritsen. 1994. "Violent Victimization and Offending: Individual, Situational, and Community-Level Risk Factors." In *Understanding and Prevention Violence,* vol. 3, ed. A. J. Reiss and J. Roth. Washington, DC: National Academy Press.

———. 1997. "Racial and Ethnic Disparities in Crime and Criminal Justice in the United States." In *Ethnicity, Crime, and Immigration: Comparative and Cross-National Perspectives,* ed. M. Tonry, Crime and Justice: An Annual Review of Research, vol. 21. Chicago: University of Chicago Press.

Sampson, R. J., S. W. Raudenbush, and F. Earls. 1997. "Neighborhoods and Violent Crime: A Multilevel Study of Collective Efficacy." *Science* 277:918–924.

Sampson, R. J., and W. J. Wilson. 1995. "Toward a Theory of Race, Crime, and Urban Inequality." In *Crime and Inequality,* ed. J. Hagan and R. D. Peterson. Stanford, CA: Stanford University Press.

Shannon, L. W. 1988. *Criminal Career Continuity: Its Social Context.* New York: Human Sciences Press.

Shaw, C. R., and H. D. McKay. 1942. *Juvenile Delinquency in Urban Areas.* Chicago: University of Chicago Press.

———. 1949. *Juvenile Delinquency in Urban Areas.* Revised ed. Chicago: University of Chicago Press.

Shiono, P. H., and R. E. Behrman. 1995. "Low Birth Weight: Analysis and Recommendations." *Future of Children: Low Birth Weight (Center for the Future of Children)* 5:14–18.

Simcha-Fagan, O., and J. E. Schwartz. 1986. "Neighborhood and Delinquency: An Assessment of Contextual Effects." *Criminology* 24:667–697.

Skogan, W. 1986. "Fear of Crime and Neighborhood Change." In *Communities and Crime,* ed. A. J. Reiss, Jr., and M. Tonry. Chicago: University of Chicago Press.

Stanton, W. R., R. McGee, and P. A. Silva. 1989. A Longitudinal Study of the Interactive Effects of Perinatal Complications and Early Family Adversity on Cognitive Ability." *Australian Paediatric Journal* 25:130–133.

Tibbetts, S. G., and A. R. Piquero. 1999. "The Influence of Gender, Low Birth Weight, and Disadvantaged Environment in Predicting Early Onset of Offending: A Test of Moffitt's Interactional Hypothesis." *Criminology* 37:843–877.

Tracy, P. E., and K. Kempf-Leonard. 1996. *Continuity and Discontinuity in Criminal Careers.* New York: Plenum.

Tremblay, R. E., and W. Craig. 1995. "Developmental Crime Prevention." In *Building a Safer Society,* ed. M. Tonry and D. P. Farrington. Chicago: University of Chicago Press.

Tremblay, R. E., F. Vitaro., L. Bertrand, M. LeBlanc, H. Beauchesne, H. Boileau, and L. David. 1992. "Parent and Child Training to Prevent Early Onset of Delinquency: The

Montreal Longitudinal-Experimental Study." In *Preventing Antisocial Behavior: Interventions from Birth through Adolescence,* ed. J. McCord. New York: Guilford Press.

U.S. Census Bureau. 2000. *Statistical Abstract of the United States.* Washington, DC: U.S. Census Bureau.

Wallace, R., and D. Wallace. 1990. "Origins of Public Health Collapse in New York City: The Dynamics of Planned Shrinkage, Contagious Urban Decay and Social Disintegration." *Bulletin of the New York Academy of Medicine* 66:391–434.

Weis, J. G. 1986. "Issues in the Measurement of Criminal Careers." In *Criminal Careers and "Career Criminals,"* ed. A. Blumstein, J. Cohen, J. A. Roth, and C. Visher. Washington, DC: National Academy Press.

Wells, L. E., and J. H. Rankin. 1991. "Families and Delinquency: A Meta-analysis of the Impact of Broken Homes." *Social Problems* 38:71–93.

Wikstrom, P. O. H., and R. Loeber. 2000. "Do Disadvantaged Neighborhoods Cause Well-Adjusted Children to Become Adolescent Delinquents? A Study of Male Juvenile Serious Offending, Individual Risk, and Protective Factors and Neighborhood Context." *Criminology* 38:1109–1142.

Williams, D. R. 2001. "Racial Variations in Adult Health Status: Patterns, Paradoxes, and Prospects." In *America Becoming: Racial Trends and Their Consequences,* vol. 2, ed. N. J. Smelser, W. J. Wilson, and F. Mitchell. Washington, DC: National Academy Press.

Wilson, J. Q., and R. J. Herrnstein. 1985. *Crime and Human Nature.* New York: Simon and Schuster.

Wilson, W. J. 1987. *The Truly Disadvantaged.* Chicago: University of Chicago Press.

———. 1996. *When Work Disappears.* New York: Knopf.

World Health Organization. 1950. *Public Health Aspect of Low Birthweight.* WHO Technical Report Series, no. 27. Geneva: WHO.

Yinger, J. 1995. *Closed Doors, Lost Opportunities: The Continuing Costs of Housing Discrimination.* New York: Russell Sage Foundation.

8

Explaining Assessments of Future Risk

Race and Attributions of Juvenile Offenders
in Presentencing Reports

Sara Steen, Christine E. W. Bond,
George S. Bridges, and Charis E. Kubrin

SOCIOLOGICAL THEORIES of law and social control often explain the legal process, and specifically the disposition of criminal cases, in terms of the reactions of court officials to the perceived behavioral and status characteristics of defendants. These theories argue that court officials acquire and employ mental images of defendants and their behaviors, such as "dangerous," "reformable," or a "typical offender." In distinguishing among defendants and their crimes, court officials make evaluations about the character, motivations, and background of defendants. Based on these evaluations, some defendants are perceived as more excusable than others, while others are viewed as more blameworthy and deserving of punishment. Officials' perceptions, then, are a critical theoretical link in explaining the relationship between defendant characteristics and case dispositions.

Ethnographies of courts have often shown that the perceptions of court officials shape punishment outcomes (e.g., Cicourel 1968; Emerson 1969; Sudnow 1965). However, quantitative analyses of legal decision making have tended to focus on the influence of groups of characteristics (such as legal variables vs. extralegal variables) on criminal case outcomes. As a result, the role of perceptual factors in legal decision making has often been inferred from the presence of a statistically significant difference in outcomes between groups of defendants. Recent studies have shifted toward a concern with specifying the perceptual processes that might link defendant characteristics to punishment outcomes (e.g., Albonetti 1991; Albonetti and Hepburn 1996; Bridges and Steen 1998; Farrell and Holmes 1991). Nonetheless, only a few studies have included direct measures of these perceptual processes or have attempted to estimate the relationship between defendants' characteristics, officials' perceptions, and punishment (Bridges and Steen 1998; Drass and Spencer 1987; Swigert and Farrell 1977). Consequently, our understanding of the perceptual processes involved in legal decision making remains limited.

Perceptual processes may be particularly important for understanding decision making in the juvenile justice system. Traditionally, juvenile courts have been characterized by an orientation toward rehabilitation and the doctrine of *parens patriae*. Despite current trends shifting juvenile courts away from these early precepts (Kempf-Leonard and Peterson 2001), these conceptualizations of the court's role remain part of the ideological context for making decisions about juvenile offenders. These traditional orientations toward treatment and child welfare compel court officials to make judgments about the character of youth coming before them, rather than simply imposing punishments. The central tasks involved in this process include judgments of blameworthiness and reformability. As pointed out by Emerson (1969), the very nature of the decision of what to do about a youth is intimately tied to questions about his or her character and motivations: "the juvenile court is largely guided by its judgments and inferences regarding the nature of the delinquent actor involved. That is, the solution to the problem—what can and must we do with this case?—generally depends on the answer to: what kind of youth are we dealing with here? This involves a process of inquiry into the youth's *moral character*" (89–90; italics in the original). Thus, the traditional parental role of the court blurs the distinction between legal and nonlegal (or social) factors. In order to make decisions about treatment, a juvenile's social circumstances, as well as his or her case characteristics, need to be considered. The context of the juvenile court highlights the need for scholars to move away from framing court decision making in terms of legal and extralegal factors and to focus on the *processes* that link defendant and case characteristics to dispositional outcomes. Particularly in thinking about the juvenile court, understanding these "processes of inquiry"—that is, identifying the elements officials consider in forming character judgments and specifying the paths by which these judgments influence case outcomes—is absolutely essential.

An important task for researchers, therefore, is to explore the types of perceptions and attributions used by court officials. Our knowledge about these perceptual processes has been largely restricted to broad stereotypes based on defendant characteristics, particularly race. If we are to improve our theoretical understanding of how defendants are processed by the courts, we need to pay attention to the *process*, and not just the outcomes. In this chapter, we focus on presentencing reports compiled by probation officers to account for their recommendations for the treatment of black and white juvenile offenders. Our concern is largely descriptive, examining how probation officers assess and explain the risk of reoffending for black and white juvenile offenders. Two key questions structure our analysis. First, are there distinct clusters of attributions about behavior and character that officials use in the presentencing reports? Second, does their use of these typifications vary between black and white offenders?

Classifying Offenders: The Work of Court Officials

The work of court officials involves more than simply obtaining information about defendants, their cases and their backgrounds. This work also involves a search for meaning about the character of defendants, the causes of their behavior, and its likely reoccurrence. Central to this search for meaning is the development of typifications or "diagnostic stereotypes" (Kelly 1996) about defendants and their offenses, into which defendants can be slotted and their punishment justified. These typifications are clusters of social characteristics, environmental and motivational factors. By drawing on typifications, officials are concerned with whether defendants and their cases reflect sufficient features to be classified within these accepted explanations for offending behavior (e.g., Emerson 1969; Farrell and Holmes 1991; Kelly 1996; Piliavin and Briar 1964; Steffensmeier and Terry 1973; Sudnow 1965; Swigert and Farrell 1977; Wiseman 1970).

Organizational demands to process large number of cases in a timely manner promote an organizational need to classify or evaluate defendants quickly. Through formal and informal socialization experiences, officials learn how to identify and classify defendants (Kelly 1996), and what characteristics and explanations are salient. This set of rules and protocols linking types of defendants to suitable outcomes has been called a "working ideology" (Kelly 1996) or a "theory of office" (Drass and Spencer 1987; Rubington and Weinberg 1973). These shared classification processes allow officials to routinize their decision making (Farrell and Holmes 1991; Rubington and Weinberg 1973), and promote the timely handling of cases (Kelly 1996; Scheff 1966; Sudnow 1965). Thus, these typifications reflect larger organizational goals and interests (Drass and Spencer 1987; Emerson 1983).

Typifications are also important in the justification and rationalization of recommendations and decisions by court officials. The organizational need to account for the decision-making process through documentation further embeds the use of typifications (Margolin 1992). As the decisions of court officials are open to review, officials must be prepared to "justify their decisions by providing accounts which render their decisions reasonable and rational" (Drass and Spencer 1987, 279). In producing these documents, officials rely on a set of commonly shared perceptions of what offenders are like. For instance, in a study of how social workers classify child abusers, Margolin (1992) found that social workers routinely perceived "suspects" as "perpetrators," which in turn made their testimony "discreditable." Put differently, these typifications "provide institutionally relevant means for 'explaining' or 'accounting for' the patterns of behavior that led to the identification of 'trouble'" (Emerson 1969, 91).

Recently, theories of social cognition, and in particular causal attributions, have provided theoretical insights into how court officials classify and describe defendants (Albonetti 1991; Bridges and Steen 1998). Attribution theory has traditionally been concerned with the process by which individuals construct explanations for particular events (Fiske and Taylor 1991). Criminological research in this tradition suggests that court officials make inferences about the causes of criminal behavior in particular cases, and that, over time, these develop into shared causal explanations for the criminal behavior of defendants. Early studies suggested that officials attribute meanings to past and future behavior based on stereotypes associated with membership in particular social categories (Fountaine and Emily 1978). More recent work has found that officials distinguish between offenses they perceive to have been caused by internal (personality) factors and those caused by external (environmental) factors. Defendants whose behavior is perceived to have external causes are judged to be less culpable for their behavior, a judgment that results in more lenient treatment by the court (Bridges and Steen 1998).

Race and the Evaluation of Defendants

Numerous scholars have argued that racial disparity in legal decision making is a result of dominant groups' perceiving racial minorities as a threat to their interests and the existing social order (Bridges, Crutchfield, and Simpson 1987; Hawkins 1987; Liska 1992; Spitzer 1975; Tittle and Curran 1988). Courts may punish minority defendants more severely than whites because they are perceived as more threatening, and therefore more deserving of punishment. More important, as we are interested in assessments of threat and risk of reoffending, our theories of racial discrimination in legal decision making argue that perceived threat produces racial differences in perceptions of offenders and their crimes.

When making assessments and decisions, court officials rely in part on perceptions of, and attributions about, a defendant's dangerousness, blameworthiness, and future behavior. There are several ways that these attributions may be race based. For instance, officials may attribute different motivations to minority defendants from the ones they attribute to white defendants, leading to different attributions about the causes of the criminal behavior. Alternatively, they may perceive minority defendants as having different attitudes from those of white defendants, leading to different attributions about blameworthiness. Finally, different excuses for defendants' behaviors may be more salient and acceptable for white defendants than minority defendants. These racial differences in perceptions may lead to different diagnoses and, in turn, different punishment outcomes (Bridges and Steen 1998; Heimer and Staffen 1995). If minority defendants are classified as more culpable for their behavior, they are likely to be seen as "deserving of more severe penalties" (Peterson and Hagan 1984, 67).

Although there is some empirical support for the argument that court officials perceive minority defendants differently from the way they perceive white defendants (Bridges and Conley 1995; Bridges, Crutchfield, and Simpson 1987; Peterson and Hagan 1984; Tonry 1995), few studies clearly identify racial differences in the way officials classify offenders. Of those studies that examine different typifications of defendants, the results suggest a more complicated story than the application of simple stereotypes. For instance, Cicourel's study (1968) found that minorities were more likely than whites to be perceived as disrespectful of authority and, in particular, disrespectful of court officials. More recently, Bridges and Steen (1998) found that probation officers more frequently attributed black youths' offending to negative attitudes and personality traits, while stressing environmental explanations for the offending of white youths.

Study Questions

In this chapter, we explore court officials' use of attributions about the behavior and characteristics of juvenile offenders, as reflected in their written accounts of cases. We are interested in describing the perceptual processes used by officials to explain their recommendations and decisions. First, we examine whether there is evidence that court officials rely on different explanations and descriptions of defendants in their assessments of risk of reoffending. Based on past research, we anticipate that court officials will refer to different explanations for the behavior and motivations of juvenile offenders in their assessments. We expect that the *types* of arguments used to explain an assessment that a youth is at a low risk of reoffending will be qualitatively different from the types of arguments used in high-risk assessments. Although some of the explanations may be overlapping, we expect that, overall, low-risk offenders will be described as having different problems and attitudes from those of high-risk offenders. Second, we consider whether there are racial differences in the attributions and explanations used by court officials. Within each risk assessment category, we postulate that there will be a strong association between the offender's race and the type of explanation used. Our prior research leads us to expect that officials will be more likely to perceive minority offenders as less reformable than white offenders, and to attribute their delinquent behavior to attitudinal and personality characteristics rather than environmental factors.

Study Design
Data and Sample

The data for this study come from presentencing reports written by juvenile court probation officers (for more description, see Bridges and Steen 1998). Probation officers prepare the narrative reports to support their assessments of the youth's likelihood of future offending and amenability to treatment, and their sentencing recommendations. The narratives play a pivotal role in juvenile justice decision making, as judges rely on the reports to make judgments about the appropriate court response to a particular offender. The reports contain summary information about a youth's social history, an assessment of the likelihood of reoffending, and recommendations for sentencing. In each case, the reports are based upon the probation officer's interviews with the youth, with his or her family, and from written reports such as school records. While the overall length of the reports ranges from two to ten pages, the summary assessments of risk that we use for the present analyses range from two sentences to one page.

An important part of these narrative reports is the assessment made by probation officers about a youth's likelihood of reoffending. Such assessments are the culmination of the probation officer's experience with the youth and, along with the sentencing recommendation, they constitute the central element of the summary section of the reports. Assessments of the risk of reoffending—the perceived threat of future crime—act as a bridge between a probation officer's personal interaction with the youth and his or her sentencing recommendation. By translating the social and legal information about a youth into a judgment about her or his likelihood of reoffending, probation officers frame recommendations in probabilistic terms. In the final section of each narrative report, the probation officer classifies the youth as having a "low," "moderate," or "high" risk of reoffending. This study examines how probation officers generate these classifications.

Probation officers' written descriptions of youth are, in part, provided to support the recommendations and decisions they make about youth and their cases (Scott and Lyman 1968). Thus, in using these narratives, we must consider whether the characterizations and attributions documented by probation officers actually reflect their perceptions and "diagnoses" of offenders or, alternatively, are simply established legal rationales routinely offered by officials and accepted by juvenile court judges for justifying classification decisions. If the former is true, then the attributions are a critical link in the causal sequence of factors influencing assessments, recommendations and other decisions. If the latter is correct, and the attributions follow from classification decisions rather than precede them, then the attributions may play a less important causal role in treatment decisions. Two aspects of the present study suggest that the probation officers' characterizations typically preceded rather than followed classification and treatment decisions (Bridges and Steen 1998). The first is that state laws require presumptive sentencing of juveniles and thereby focus the attention of court officials on the characteristics of the offense and offender in formulating assessments and recommendations. These laws establish a formal logic and order to the assessment process that limit the extent to which classification (or sentencing) may precede evaluation. A second aspect of the study suggesting that attribution precedes classification and treatment are observations and interviews of probation officers who completed the narrative reports on many cases analyzed in this study. While it is possible that some may have reached treatment decisions without careful assessment of offenders, observations and interviews with probation officers revealed the opposite. Typically, classification decisions were made following careful consideration of the youth, his or her crimes, and the youth's risk of future criminal activity. None of the interviews or any aspect of the observations provided a reason to believe that rationales were developed following decisions about offenders or that probation officers' gave great weight to individual judges' expectations about case outcomes in formulating their descriptions of offenders and their crimes.[1]

We analyze a subsample of 277 reports drawn from juvenile court cases processed through three courts in Washington State between 1990 and 1991 (Bridges et al. 1993).[2] Washington has been a forerunner in the move toward formalizing juvenile justice; in 1994, researchers called the Washington system "the most structured in the country, placing the greatest authority with the state legislature in determining appropriate penalties" (Lieb, Fish, and Crosby 1994, iii). Specifically, the state introduced sentencing guidelines into the juvenile justice system in 1977, removing some of the broad discretion traditionally granted juvenile court judges. The guidelines require judges to follow sentencing ranges derived from an offender's prior record and the seriousness of the presenting offense. Part of the goal of such reforms was to reduce the introduction of extralegal factors (including race) into the decision-making process, making Washington a particularly interesting site for studying the effects of race on risk assessments.

The present study compares cases involving black youth with those of white youth; youth of other races and ethnicities were excluded from the analyses due to insufficient numbers (44 cases were other or unknown racial groups). In addition, explanations and assessment information was missing in 72 reports. Thus, our sample was reduced to 161 cases. Of the cases in the

Table 8.1: Description of Sample

	Full Sample	White Offenders	Black Offenders
Female (%)	13	13	13
Mean age (years)	15.7	15.7	15.8
Mean number of prior convictions	3.57	3.33	4.13
Mean offense seriousness[a]	4.65	4.70	4.50
Mean assessment of risk[b]	2.30	2.22	2.47
Number of cases	161	112	49

[a] Statutory seriousness level for the most serious presenting offense. Range from 1–8 in this sample (with high values indicating the least serious offenses).
[b] Range 1–3, where 1 = low risk, 2 = moderate risk, and 3 = high risk.

final sample, 49 reports are for black offenders and 112 are for white offenders. (Basic descriptives for the study sample are provided in table 8.1.)

Demographic information and legal histories for all juvenile offenders were obtained from case files. Our analyses are restricted to the race of the offender. Legal information collected from case files included the severity of the presenting offense (statutorily defined offense seriousness levels) and the offender's prior offense record (number of prior convictions).

Analytic Strategy

To analyze the narrative data, we grouped individual cases by risk level to identify the emergent patterns of explanations within each level. Specifically, we looked for *clusters* of factors that probation officers consistently used in explaining their risk assessments.[3] For example, at the moderate risk level, the following descriptions frequently appeared together: the offender has some serious risk factors (e.g., dysfunctional family, poor school performance); the offender recognizes that he or she has problems; the offender is eager to cooperate with the court; and the offender has "potential." We categorized narratives in which these characteristics clustered as "the offender making a 'cry for help.'" These are youth who have serious problems but are willing to cooperate and are capable of reform.

To aid in this process, we used *Atlas-ti,* a qualitative data analysis program that allows the user to mark certain segments of text with various codes (identified by the user), and at later stages to retrieve various segments marked with the same codes. The program also enables researchers to group both documents (in this case, individual reports) and codes. We used this feature at various stages of the analysis to group cases by individual factors, by types of explanations, by risk level, and by race. Thus, after sifting through the reports and identifying each individual factor used to explain risk assessments, we were able to identify factors that regularly appeared together, and to identify different sets of factors (or kinds of explanations) that appeared at different

Table 8.2: Impact of Legal Variables on Risk Assessment by Race

Legal Variables	Risk Assessment	Black Offenders		White Offenders	
		N	%	N	%
No priors	Low risk	1	14	6	24
	Moderate risk	1	14	7	28
	High risk	5	71	12	48
1–5 priors	Low risk	6	20	16	27
	Moderate risk	6	20	20	33
	High risk	18	60	24	40
6 or more priors	Low risk	3	25	4	15
	Moderate risk	1	8	8	30
	High risk	8	67	15	56
Offense seriousness levels 1–4	Low risk	9	31	11	18
(most serious)[a]	Moderate risk	3	10	20	32
	High risk	17	59	31	50
Offense seriousness levels 5–7	Low risk	1	7	11	31
	Moderate risk	3	21	11	31
	High risk	10	71	13	37
Offense seriousness levels 8–9	Low risk	0		3	33
(least serious)	Moderate risk	1	20	2	22
	High risk	4	80	4	44

Note: Information on prior offense history was missing for two white offenders, and information on offense seriousness was missing for one black offender and six white offenders.

[a] Statutory seriousness level for the most serious presenting offense. Range 1–8 in this sample.

levels of risk. These grouping features allowed us to see patterns in the data that we may not otherwise have noticed.

In the present study, we do not control for the role of legal factors on the assessment of risk of reoffending. However, data presented in table 8.2 suggests that risk assessments are not strongly influenced by legal factors such as prior record and offense seriousness. Although the numbers in each category are small, we can cautiously conclude that neither a youth's prior record of offending nor the seriousness of a youth's presenting offense drives the race differences we find in risk assessments. Most notably, in every legal category, a larger percentage of black offenders are categorized as "high risk" than white offenders. Furthermore, a majority of black offenders (more than 50%) in *every legal category* are categorized as "high risk." In contrast, a majority of white offenders are categorized as "low" or "moderate risk" in every legal category, with two exceptions: those offenders with six or more prior convictions (56% are categorized as "high risk") and those committing the most serious offenses (50% are categorized as "high risk"). These patterns provide support for the argument that, rather than relying on a youth's offending behavior, probation officers draw from a repertoire of identifiable explanations in justifying assessments of risk.

To explore racial differences in probation officers' characterizations of offenders, we compared the percentage of cases in which particular justifications appear for black offenders to the percentage in which those justifications appear for white offenders. Due to the small number of cases and the exploratory nature of these analyses, we did not test for statistically significant differences between these groups. We note those comparisons where the small number of cases limits our conclusions.

Results of Analysis

While the present analysis is largely descriptive, it provides some interesting insights into the different ways probation officers think about black and white offenders. To interpret the results presented in table 8.3 (below), we

Table 8.3: Explanations for Risk Assessments by Risk Level and Race

Risk Level	Explanation for Assessment	Black Offenders		White Offenders	
		N	%	N	%
Low	Total low-risk offenders	10		26	
	Out of character	5	50	14	54
	Poor decision making	0	0	10	38
	Past problems	6	60	5	19
Moderate	Total moderate-risk offenders	8		35	
	Needs treatment:				
	Cry for help	2	25	9	26
	Fixable	2	25	9	26
	Needs to be removed from current environment:				
	Drifting	2	25	5	14
	Family life is chaotic	0	0	9	26
	Needs to be held accountable	3	38	2	6
High	Total high-risk offenders	31		51	
	Poor lifestyle choices:				
	Criminal lifestyle	10	32	8	16
	Lack of constructive activities	2	6	10	20
	Egocentric value system:				
	Doesn't take offense seriously	6	19	4	8
	Lack of concern for others	6	19	10	20
	Uncooperative/defiant:				
	No desire to change	12	39	12	24
	Manipulative	2	6	9	18
	Out of control:				
	Lacks internal controls	6	19	14	27
	Lacks external controls	13	42	20	39

Note: As more than one justification could be used, the percentages within each risk group may total more than 100.

must begin with a few observations. First, the percentages of offenders in each risk category are quite different for black and white offenders. Of the 49 black offenders in the sample, 20% (10 offenders) fall in the low-risk category, 16% (8 offenders) in the moderate-risk category, and 64% (31 offenders) in the high-risk category. Of the 112 white offenders, 23% (26 offenders) are assessed as low risk, 31% (35 offenders) as moderate risk, and 46% (51 offenders) as high risk. These numbers are important for two reasons. First, twice as many white offenders fall in the moderate-risk category as black offenders. This may point to a tendency on the part of probation officers to assess black offenders as either low risk (i.e., victims) or high risk (i.e., hardened offenders), with little middle ground. In contrast, almost a third of the white offenders in the sample fall in the moderate-risk category, suggesting that probation officers make greater use of middle ground (arguing that an offender could go either way—away from or deeper into criminality) for this group. Second, the absolute number of black offenders in the low- and moderate-risk categories is too small to draw definitive conclusions about differences between black and white offenders.

The percentages in table 8.3 represent the percentage of offenders in a particular risk category for whom the given justification or attribution is used. For example, of ten black low-risk offenders, five (50%) fall into the "out of character" group. Probation officers sometimes use more than one kind of explanation for an offender (this is especially true for high-risk offenders), which means that the percentages within each risk group will sum to more than 100%.

Low-Risk Offenders

In classifying an offender as having a low risk of reoffending, probation officers are generally attempting to support a recommendation for little or no intervention by the court. We identify below three kinds of claims used by probation officers in low-risk assessments.

1. The Offense Was out of Character

The first way to explain a low-risk assessment is to attribute the offense as being out of character for the youth. As can be seen in Jake's case,[4] probation officers draw on a series of indicators to claim that the offending behavior was not characteristic of the youth, and therefore the court does not need to intervene to stop the behavior:

This is a bright, capable boy from a good, responsible, intact family. After the offense, Jake immediately personally apologized to the schools. Further court involvement is not necessary and would serve no purpose. Jake is a good boy who is not delinquently oriented and has already had sanctions at home and by the school for this one time incident. He will not be in further trouble with the law.

Virtually all of the offenders described in this way come from "stable families" which provide sufficient support and structure to prevent future offending. These youth are often described as doing well in school, holding realistic goals for the future, and having prosocial peers. A positive attitude is also a consistent factor in these cases, with probation officers describing the youth as "genuinely remorseful," "knowing what she did was wrong," or "willing to accept the consequences for his actions." The combination of external controls within the family and internal controls in the offender leads probation officers to conclude that a brief involvement with the court has had the necessary impact in terms of deterring future offending behavior (the offender has "learned his or her lesson"), and that continued involvement is unnecessary (and may in fact be harmful).

If probation officers tend to view minority defendants as less reformable, then we would expect that fewer black offenders would be characterized as committing an offense that was out of character than white offenders. This, however, does not appear to be the case. At least in this low-risk category, there does not seem to be a greater tendency to characterize white youth as having a noncriminal character and black youth as having a criminal character. The offense was described as being out of character in similar proportions of cases for black and white offenders (50% of low-risk black youth, 54% of low-risk white youth).

2. The Offense Was a Result of Poor Decision Making

Probation officers characterize a second group of low-risk offenders as poor decision makers. In these cases, the offender is described as having low self-control, often due to low self-esteem. These offenders are drawn into crime by peers, and are portrayed as unsophisticated offenders:

Jim is not a criminally oriented youth, but is easily led and often impulsive in his actions. He finds it difficult to say no to friends, even when he knows the actions are wrong. It is my opinion that Jim has a low opinion of himself and tries to raise his status in the eyes of his peers by being cool.

As with the previous low-risk group, attitude often contributes to an assessment that a youth engaged in poor decision making:

Ricky is not criminally oriented nor is he arrogant, obstinate or disagreeable like many other juveniles. He has made a serious mistake and realizes it.

Unlike youth for whom the offense was out of character, probation officers did not always mention attitude for this group of low-risk offenders. While none of the low-risk offenders were described as having a bad attitude, several of the reports in this category contained no mention of the youth's attitude.

Thus, this lack of emphasis on the youth's potential and his or her positive attitude is the key distinction between poor decision makers and offenders for whom the delinquent act was seen as out of character.

While more than a third (38%) of white low-risk offenders are characterized as poor decision makers, no black low-risk offenders appear in this category. The absence of black offenders as poor decision makers may reflect a perception on the part of probation officers that arguments of impulsivity are not sufficient in explaining a low-risk assessment for black offenders. Rather, probation officers may be countering assumptions of a criminal character by describing in some detail the positive elements of a black youth's character. In particular, probation officers may feel pressure to emphasize a positive attitude in the case of a black youth (this would be consistent with our expectation that attributions about black youth are likely to include a negative attitude).

3. The Offense Was a Result of Past Problems

The third explanation for low-risk assessments is that the causes of an offender's behavior are problems that are either no longer relevant or, more often, that the offender is currently dealing with successfully. Many of these youth have had serious problems in the past (e.g., family neglect, physical or emotional abuse, or anger management problems), problems that are viewed as risk factors for future offending. To explain a low-risk assessment, probation officers often portray this group of offenders as having experienced tremendous tragedies in their lives, and as being actively engaged in overcoming these experiences:

Hannah is currently performing at a relatively high standard. She has been in treatment for a few weeks, but is making substantial progress. Given what she has suffered and been exposed to, she is a very courageous young lady to be so honest and giving in her treatment. . . . We believe she is sincere. She has a very strong support system in place to see her through it for the next several years. Hannah opted for treatment. She IS involved in her own salvation.

These are youth who have made serious progress toward dealing with their problems, either by moving into another environment or through counseling. Their willingness to cooperate with the court and work on their problems places them in the low-risk group.

In contrast to poor decision makers, a group populated entirely by white offenders, black offenders are much more likely than white offenders to fall into the past problems category of low-risk offenders (60% of black offenders compared to 19% of white offenders). When these particular results are read together, they seem to reflect a perception that negative external influences on white low-risk offenders are more likely to be peers (contributing to poor decision making), while for black low-risk offenders they are more likely to be serious traumas. Similarly for the "out of character" group, one might argue that probation officers emphasize the inner strength of black low-risk offenders (in this case, their desire to change and efforts to work through their problems) to discourage assumptions of criminal character.

Moderate-Risk Offenders

By placing youth in the moderate-risk category, probation officers see an offender who could go either way—with appropriate intervention by the court, the youth could stop offending; without such intervention, the youth will be likely to continue offending. Generally, the probation officers' explanations point to recommendations that a particular *type* of intervention is needed to prevent these youth from continuing with their delinquent behavior. These explanations are therefore qualitatively different from those for offenders at either a low or high risk of reoffending. Three types of characterizations of offenders and their behavior (described below) are relied on in moderate-risk assessments.

1. The Youth Needs, and Is Amenable to, Treatment

Some of the youth that fall into the category of moderate risk are youth who need help and who have demonstrated either the desire or the ability to be helped. The first group in this category includes offenders who have serious problems but also have potential and recognize the need for help. These youth might be described as making a "cry for help." Matt is typical of such cases:

Matt is a very intelligent, yet very confused young man. When one combines his early childhood problems with his ongoing battle for identity it is fairly easy to see why Matt is in trouble with the juvenile court.... While this may seem like an unusual time to become somewhat optimistic about Matt's chances, based on our last conversation, he may have finally had the right combination of circumstances to focus him in the right direction.... He talked about his need to change and grow internally and acknowledged that he had to stop looking externally for anything that promised a quick fix.

Probation officers invariably describe these youth with both a positive attribute (e.g., nice, honest, respectful, pleasant) and a somewhat negative attribute (e.g., confused, hurt, angry, depressed). The latter is seen as a result of their life problems, while the former is seen as evidence of their future potential. These youth have all had contact with the court previously, have generally done well under the court's supervision, but have slipped when returned to their chaotic home environments. In these cases, probation officers often appear to characterize these offenders as benefiting from further court involvement: these are offenders who may have serious risk factors, but where the probation officer sees potential and the youth is eager to cooperate with the court in getting the necessary help. Similar percentages of black (25%) and white (26%) offenders fall into this group.

A second group in the category of offenders who can be helped are simply characterized as fixable. These offenders have done well in treatment in the past, and have made some progress toward solving their problems. They are therefore assumed to be amenable to the services provided by the court. This group differs from the "cry for help" group because this is generally the only thing mentioned in the report; little is said about a youth's potential or his or her serious problems. Again, there are no substantive differences between black and white offenders: 25% of black offenders and 26% of white offenders fall into this category.

2. The Youth Needs to Be Removed from Current Environment

Another type of explanation found in the narratives is that offenders need to be removed from their current environment because they lack internal and/or external controls on their behavior. In these cases, probation officers do not seem to be arguing for the need for a particular type of intervention (i.e., treatment or punishment), but rather for any intervention at all that would take the youth away from his or her present situation.

The first group of offenders in this group might be categorized as drifters. Probation officers perceive these youth as lacking direction in life and, in part because of this, easily influenced by delinquent peers. These are youth who could go either way; they need to be reined in before they become serious criminals:

Leroy appears to be drifting. He has dropped out of school and remains unemployed. He talks about finishing school and claims he has goals to become employed. He does not appear to be focused. . . . He is not the kind of youngster that needs commitment to DJR but he is slowly moving in that direction.

Many of these youth have minimal external controls on their behavior (i.e., their families do not provide sufficient structure), and many also have weak internal controls due to low self-esteem and a lack of clear direction. These youth are unfocused, but not yet hardened criminals. Black offenders are somewhat more likely to fall into this category than white offenders (25% vs. 14%). However, given the extremely small numbers in this category (two blacks and five whites), any conclusions may be premature.

The second group of offenders who need to be removed from their current environment includes youth whose family life is chaotic. There is generally some kind of pattern of behavior in these families that the probation officers describe as harmful. In some cases, this pattern is related to family interaction characterized by conflict, while in others the pattern is based on parental behavior that involves drug use and/or criminal activity. Probation officers argue that the families of these offenders cannot provide sufficient structure and control to keep the youth out of trouble:

Sean is a young man who is a vulnerable target to negative influences due to his dependent personality needs. His parents do not seem to be able to provide adequate control for Sean at this point in time. Leaving Sean at home may enhance the future recurrence of the crime. Sean needs to be removed from the community and be placed in a structured environment.

Probation officers often frame these offenders as victims (in Sean's case, as a "vulnerable target"). They argue that these youth need structure and that the only way for them to get it is for the court to remove them from their current environment. While 26% of white moderate-risk offenders fall into this category, no black offenders do (this finding is discussed below).

3. The Youth Needs to Be Held Accountable

The last type of explanation supporting an assessment of moderate risk is that an offender needs to be held accountable. These are youth who do not recognize the consequences of their behavior, either due to immaturity (as in Allan's case below) or, more often, due to a negative attitude:

This writer is inclined to believe that Allan has not been involved in selling drugs for a long period of time, primarily because he appears to be unsophisticated, immature, and naive. Nonetheless, he needs to be held accountable, and punished. He is a youngster in need of immediate impacting to lessen his risk of reoffending.

In these cases, the probation officers proffer the hope that, by punishing these offenders, they will come to appreciate that there are serious consequences to their behavior, and that this awareness will deter future delinquent activity.

The most interesting race differences in the moderate-risk category are between youth whose family life is chaotic and those who need to be held accountable. While 26% of white offenders are described as having a chaotic family life, no black offenders are described in this way. In contrast, probation officers characterize 38% of black offenders as needing to be held accountable, compared to only 6% of white offenders. This difference is consistent with the distinction of internal and external, where whites are more likely to be described as having external problems (e.g., family life), and blacks are more likely to be described as having internal problems (e.g., making bad decisions and needing to be punished). Again, however, because of the total number of moderate-risk black youth (eight), any interpretation must be made with caution.

High-Risk Offenders

High-risk offenders are generally youth with a combination of the kinds of risk factors described thus far. While negative attitudes and difficult circumstances are seen as surmountable for lower-risk offenders, they tend to be seen as personality traits or permanent conditions for high-risk offenders. We identify below four categories of risk factors used in high-risk assessments.

1. The Youth Makes Poor Lifestyle Choices

The first kind of explanation used by probation officers in high-risk assessments relates to offenders' poor lifestyle choices. Probation officers seem to characterize youth who make these choices in two ways: as youth who are engaged in a pattern of destructive behavior, and as youth who choose not to engage in constructive behavior. The first category contains youth who are often described as having a criminal lifestyle. Indicators of entrenchment in a criminal lifestyle include descriptions of behavior that is "patterned" or "escalating," and involvement in a drug or crime culture or a gang.

Luis is entrenched in the gang and drug cultures. He has been a Crip for some time. He has been supporting himself by selling drugs. He stressed how selling drugs was an easy and quick way to make large sums of money. In talking with Luis, what was evident was the relaxed and open way he discussed his life style.

It is interesting to note that affiliation with gangs arises exclusively in reports of high-risk offenders. Probation officers clearly have little hope that youth who are gang members or have close ties to gangs will be able to remove themselves from their peers and thereby have a chance at interrupting their criminal careers.

The second category consists of youth who lack constructive activities and have few structured goals. In comparison to the moderate-risk drifters, this lack of direction is seen as a more permanent condition among high-risk offenders:

Peter lacks a great deal of motivation and self discipline toward any life goals. He has an escalating pattern about following directions. He is virtually marking time.

While similar percentages of black (38%) and white (36%) offenders are described as making poor lifestyle choices, their choices are characterized differently. Probation officers are much more likely to describe black offenders as having a criminal lifestyle (32%, compared to 16% of white offenders), while they are more likely to describe white offenders as having a lack of constructive activities (20%, compared to 6% of black offenders). This difference may reflect in part a greater tendency to mention gang membership for black offenders. However, it may also reflect a characterization of blacks as actively making destructive choices, compared to whites, who are characterized as not making constructive choices.

2. The Youth Displays an Egocentric Value System

A second group of high-risk offenders includes those who have what probation officers describe as an egocentric value system. The first category of offenders in this group are youth who do not take the offense seriously.

Offenders who are unwilling to accept responsibility for their offending and/
or fail to consider the consequences of their behavior are often categorized as
high risk. Probation officers generally attribute these attitudes to an egocentric personality:

Will is here because of drug dependence and a personality pattern that is highlighted by rigid thinking, inability to assume responsibility for his behavior, and a self-centered manner of operating.

Anjie's behavior seems to be very impetuous with no consideration for potential consequences.
She appears to have a tremendously skewed value system.

As with the two offenders described above, the values of high-risk youth in
this category often center on immediate satisfaction and fulfillment of personal desires, values which prevent offenders from taking responsibility for
their actions. Black offenders are somewhat more likely than white offenders
to be described in this way (19% of blacks compared to 8% of whites).

Another manifestation of an egocentric value system is a lack of concern
for others and, particularly, for victims. This lack of empathy is generally tied
to the youth's personality, rather than to specific circumstances (as with lower-
risk offenders). Probation officers describe many high-risk offenders as "unable" to understand that their behavior is harmful to others:

Robert seems to show no remorse for his victims. It is possible that this juvenile does not have
the ability to comprehend the cause and effect of his delinquent behavior.

Lloyd looks and acts like an immature adolescent, however, his actions are that of a streetwise,
sophisticated youth who is interfacing with other youth who don't see anything wrong with vic-
timizing a person. His behavior is deteriorating. He doesn't appear to be remorseful for his participation in the offenses.

Both of these cases illustrate what might be described as an emotional void.
Neither of these offenders has a value system that includes concern for others
or an understanding of the difference between right and wrong. Equal percentages of black and white offenders (19% and 20%, respectively) fall into
this category.

3. The Youth Is Uncooperative or Defiant

A third set of factors characterizing high-risk offenders relates to the youth's
attitude and behavior toward the court. One category of offenders in this
group are youth who have established, through their behavior and/or their
attitude, no desire to change. The majority of these youth have had prior involvement with the court and have failed to comply with court orders:

William has done little while on supervision to improve his situation. William has been given the
opportunity to avail himself of resources in the community, but has not taken advantage of these
opportunities.

In describing these cases, probation officers argue that, because the court "has done everything it can" for these youth, there is nothing left but punishment. Attitude is clearly important here, and many youth are portrayed as uncooperative or, in some cases, actively defiant:

Joseph has shown himself to be unwilling to submit to authority. There is an inability or unwillingness to cooperate with treatment.

The assumption about offenders like Joseph is that they are working against the court rather than with it, and should be treated accordingly.

Related to cooperation with the court, some youth are described as always trying to get around the rules and manipulate the system. These are youth who try to manipulate situations to their advantage, often distancing themselves from responsibility for their behavior:

Leonard has used his good looks and somewhat charming personality to manipulate his way through school, home and his dealings in the community. Leonard can easily be described as a smooth talker and he doesn't worry about much of anything.

Manipulative offenders are assumed to be unworkable, as they are perceived as dishonest and calculating. To be successful at manipulation, a youth must have some positive traits to draw on, such as a charming personality (as with Leonard) or intelligence. In some ways, these youth might be seen as worse than other high-risk offenders because they have the potential to be productive, yet they use this potential to cheat both their victims and the court system.

While similar percentages of black and white offenders are described as uncooperative, they fall into different categories within this larger characterization. Black offenders are more likely than white offenders to be described as having no desire to change (39% compared to 24%). White offenders, in contrast, are more likely to be described as manipulative (18% compared to 6% of black offenders). This difference might represent a perception that white offenders have greater potential (potential is a necessary element in manipulation), while black offenders are more likely to be defiant and uncooperative with court processes.

4. The Youth Is Out of Control

The final characterization of high-risk offenders includes youth whom probation officers see as out of control. This includes both offenders with low internal controls and those with few external controls. Offenders who lack internal controls appear at every risk level. In the case of high-risk offenders, however, lacking internal controls tends to be seen as a personality trait rather than a momentary lapse in judgment:

Billy has been opportunistic and pragmatic about getting what he wants. He is not adequately restrained by a need to use rules or impose value judgments voluntarily on his own behavior.

External controls are also important in preventing offending behavior. In describing an offender who lacks external controls, probation officers invariably discuss the youth's family situation. The families of high-risk offenders are often described in great detail, with the parents described as "enablers," "in denial," providing "inconsistent discipline" or "not enough structure." The family is seen as a major obstacle to the youth's potential for rehabilitation:

> Family members tend to make excuses for Chad's behavior and to enable him to avoid taking responsibility and facing consequences. As a result, Chad is impulsive, immature, and seeks immediate gratification without regard to the requirements of the situation.

Black and white offenders are described as out of control in fairly similar proportions. Forty-two percent of black offenders and 39% of white offenders are described as lacking external controls, while whites are slightly more likely to be described as lacking internal controls (27% compared to 19% of black offenders).

Discussion and Conclusions

In our exploratory analyses of how probation officers explain and assess the future risk of offending, we found that probation officers use qualitatively different kinds of attributions and explanations. Probation officers relied on explanations about the immediate causes of the present offense, and why these causes would not lead to future offending, in their assessments of low-risk youth. For instance, the current offense was described as resulting from poor decision making, being out of character, or due to past problems. In contrast, probation officers were more likely to make attributions about their *general* character and problems in assessing moderate- or high-risk offenders. Explanations emphasizing a youth's attitude and the court's ability to intervene in particular ways were typical for moderate-risk youth; while in high-risk cases, explanations focused on a youth's character, values, or persistent life problems.

Interestingly, this study adds complexity to the dichotomy of internal versus external attributions about the causes of offending behavior that previous research has suggested. In earlier work, Bridges and Steen (1998) argued that probation officers were more likely to use negative internal attributions to explain the delinquent behavior of black offenders and negative external attributions to explain white offenders' delinquency.

Our current analysis presents three striking results. First, in the assessments of low-risk youth, there is no evidence that the internal/external dichotomy of attributions explains racial differences in officers' perceptions of offenders. Probation officers were *not* more likely to draw on internal attributions (the offense was "out of character") for black youth, or external attributions (the offense was due to "past problems") for white youth. Indeed, equal proportions of black and white offenders are described as committing "out of character" offenses, and a somewhat larger proportion of black offenses were attributed to "serious past problems." These results raise the possibility that probation officers may feel the need to counter assumptions of weak moral character for black youth in order to explain a low-risk assessment for these youth. This possibility is strengthened by the fact that probation officers never relied on attributions of "poor decision making" in low-risk assessments of black offenders. This is the only explanation for a low-risk assessment that does not include a description of the youth's positive attitude, and its use characterizes more than one-third of the low-risk assessments for white youth. Probation officers simply did not categorize black youth as low-risk offenders without emphasizing their desire to change, willingness to cooperate with the court, and/or feelings of remorse.

Second, explanations mirroring the internal/external distinction between black and white youth were much more likely to be seen in assessments of moderate-risk youth. Evaluations of the future offending behavior of black youth were most likely to be attributed to internal characteristics, such as drifting, lacking meaningful life goals, or needing to be held accountable. Indeed, the only explanation for moderate-risk assessments that is based entirely on an offender's attitude ("needs to be held accountable") was invoked solely for black offenders. In contrast, explanations for risk assessments at this level for white youth were more likely to be based on external characteristics such as a chaotic family life. In assessments of moderate-risk youth, one of the most common external attributions ("behavior exacerbated by the youth's family") was used exclusively to describe white offending.

Finally, the characterizations that probation officers used in high-risk assessments are not easily categorized into theoretical framework of internal and external attributions. Perhaps the most interesting racial difference at this level—the use of attributions of "poor lifestyle choices"—implies a different way of thinking about the attribution process that does not rely directly on the internal/external distinction. Specifically, while equal proportions of black and white high-risk offenders had their offending behavior attributed to "poor lifestyle choices," probation officers were more likely to describe black offenders as actively making destructive choices (such as remaining in a gang) while describing white offenders as failing to make constructive choices (such as developing meaningful goals). This suggests that black youth are more likely to be perceived as making active choices to maintain a criminal lifestyle, while white youth are more likely to be perceived as not making active choices to move away from such a lifestyle (a more passive view of decision making).

Overall, these results indicate that, although there were some clear racial differences in the types of typifications and attributions that probation officers used to explain risk assessments, these differences could not always be explained by the internal/external dichotomy. Probation officers often drew on both internal and external factors to justify a particular risk assessment. These findings suggest that the internal/external conceptualization of the attribution process is only the first step in constructing theories to explain legal decision making.

There are two important limitations on our findings. First, the small number of black offenders in some categories (particularly the moderate-risk offenders) means that our conclusions remain somewhat tentative. Second, given the exploratory nature of this research, we were unable to control for factors other than race (such as offense type and prior record) that may have important effects on the assessment of risk. However, as our preliminary analyses suggested that legal factors might not be the strongest predictors of risk assessments, research should examine the particular circumstances of individual cases (i.e., looking at offense descriptions rather than relying on offense seriousness levels). This could provide fascinating insights into the ways that probation officers work with both offender and offense characteristics to form judgments and recommendations. In particular, studies examining "exceptional" or unexpected cases—cases where the seriousness of the offense and/or the offender's prior record would not easily predict the risk assessment (e.g., an offender committing a serious offense who is categorized as low risk)—could be particularly useful.

This research demonstrates that we cannot continue to overlook the role of officials' perceptions and attributions in the classification and treatment of offenders. Court officials appear to have different explanations and views about the causes and motivations of behavior that vary by the race of the defendant. We argue that the crucial link in understanding differential treatment and punishment outcomes is the translation of offender status characteristics to attributions about character and motivations. This chapter has identified some of the elements of this "perceptual logic of explanation" (Bridges and Steen 1998, 568), and how these elements are shaped by the race of the offender.

Future research on race and legal decision making needs to consider the *subjective* aspects of decision making. We need to better understand how court officials perceive, define, and classify offenders—in short, our theories need to focus on *process,* and not just outcomes. This requires the integration of perceptual processes—the social psychology of decision making—into theories of law and social control (Albonetti 1991; Albonetti and Hepburn 1996; Bridges and Steen 1998).

Our findings also point to the importance of considering the risk assessment process in developing interventions to reduce racial disproportionality within juvenile justice. Future policies on the disproportionate confinement of minority youth must focus on court procedures for evaluating the risk of reoffending. One approach, which is being or has been implemented in some jurisdictions, entails uniform risk assessments—a standard set of criteria for evaluating youth and the likelihood of recidivism. This approach mitigates the effects of differential attributions about youth made by judges or probation officers, relying on standard criteria to structure risk assessments. In this approach, courts can reduce differential assessments of minority and white youth with similar offense histories and backgrounds and thereby reduce racial disparities in court dispositions. Of course, standardized risk assessment may prove difficult to implement in some courts. Contradicting the rehabilitative ideal and ideology that pervade many juvenile justice programs, standardized assessments reduce the exercise of discretion by court officials in evaluating the individual circumstances of youth adjudicated for crimes. A further concern is the extent to which any standardized criteria are differentially associated with particular racial and ethnic groups (e.g., criteria related to family structure and dynamics may not recognize cultural differences in family organization or parenting practices).

A related and perhaps less controversial approach to minimizing differential attributions and assessments is training curricula for judges and court personnel that identify critical criteria that are race neutral for assessing risk. While not relying on uniform procedures for officials to follow in evaluating each individual case, this approach reduces differential attributions and assessments by establishing court norms and/or policies for screening that focus on patterns of prior criminal behavior (e.g., chronic assaults or other violent offenses, drug abuse, or serious delinquency) rather than personal or social background characteristics of defendants. Rigorous training in these norms and policies, coupled with endorsement by senior justice officials, will institutionalize their use in juvenile justice decision making.

At the heart these approaches to future policy is the idea that court reforms for reducing disproportionate minority confinement must alter the process of decision making in juvenile justice. While no single set of policies will necessarily alter (or should alter) how individual court officials perceive juvenile offenders and the crimes they commit, courts must implement policies that mitigate the effects of differential perceptions of youth on their assessment and treatment by court personnel. And as future research more clearly specifies the mechanisms by which perceptions shape court decisions, reforms in policy must address the social psychological processes that foster invidious and unfair treatment of minority youth by juvenile justice programs.

Notes

1. We recognize, however, that officials in some regions within the state and those in other states may subscribe to other, less formal approaches in classifying and assessing delinquent youth.

2. The original study sample for the three counties or courts was 1,300 cases (400, 400, and 500 cases in the three counties). The subsample used in the present study was drawn as an interval sample: every fourth case from the larger sample for two counties and every fifth case from the third. The final subsample of reports was 277 cases (23 cases were not available for review because they were in use by probation staff at the time of sampling). The subsample overrepresents youth with case files that include written documentation about the youth and their families. These cases tend to have higher proportions of minorities and offenders with more extensive criminal histories than occur in the population of all youth processed through the courts.

3. Note that the term "factor" is used here not as part of a quantitative analytic strategy (i.e., factor analysis), but rather to indicate one element decision makers consider in developing risk assessments. We were interested in the factors that emerged from our narratives: thus, we did not code for predetermined factors, but rather looked for factors that regularly appeared in our narratives.

4. Pseudonyms have been used to preserve confidentiality.

References

Albonetti, Celesta A. 1991. "The Integration of Theories to Explain Judicial Discretion." *Social Problems* 38:247–266.

Albonetti, Celesta A., and John R. Hepburn. 1996. "Prosecutorial Discretion to Defer Criminalization: The Effects of Defendant's Ascribed and Achieved Status Characteristics." *Journal of Quantitative Criminology* 12:63–81.

Bridges, George S., and Darlene Conley. 1995. *Racial Disproportionality in County Juvenile Facilities.* Olympia, WA: Department of Social and Health Services, State of Washington.

Bridges, George S., Darlene Conley, Gina Beretta, and Rodney Engen. 1993. *Racial Disproportionality in the Juvenile Justice System.* Olympia, WA: Department of Social and Health Services, State of Washington.

Bridges, George S., Robert D. Crutchfield, and Edith Simpson. 1987. "Crime and Social Structure and Criminal Punishment: White and Nonwhite Rates of Imprisonment." *Social Problems* 34:345–361.

Bridges, George S., and Sara Steen. 1998. "Racial Disparities in Official Assessments of Juvenile Offenders: Attributional Stereotypes as Mediating Mechanisms." *American Sociological Review* 63:554–570.

Cicourel, Aaron. 1968. *The Social Organization of Juvenile Justice.* New York: John Wiley.

Drass, Kriss A., and J. William Spencer. 1987. "Accounting for Pre-sentencing Recommendations: Typologies and Probation Officers' Theory of Office." *Social Problems* 34:277–293.

Emerson, Robert M. 1969. *Judging Delinquents: Context and Process in Juvenile Court.* Chicago: Aldine.

———. 1983. "Holistic Effects in Social Control Decision-Making." *Law and Society Review* 17:425–455.

Farrell, Ronald A., and Malcolm D. Holmes. 1991. "The Social and Cognitive Structure of Legal Decision-Making." *Sociological Quarterly* 32:514–529.

Fiske, Susan T., and Shelley E. Taylor. 1991. *Social Cognition*. New York: McGraw-Hill.

Fountaine, Gary, and Catherine Emily. 1978. "Casual Attribution and Judicial Discretion." *Law and Human Behavior* 2:323–337.

Hawkins, Darnell F. 1987. "Beyond Anomalies: Rethinking the Conflict Perspective on Race and Criminal Punishment." *Social Forces* 65:719–745.

Heimer, Carol A., and Lisa R. Staffen. 1995. "Interdependence and Reintegrative Social Control: Labeling and Reforming 'Inappropriate' Parents in Neonatal Intensive Care Units." *American Sociological Review* 60:635–654.

Kelly, Delos H. 1996. "General Introduction." Pp. 1–9 in *Deviant Behavior: A Text-Reader in the Sociology of Deviance*, 5th ed., ed. Delos H. Kelly. New York: St Martin's Press.

Kempf-Leonard, Kimberly, and Elicka S. L. Peterson. 2001. "Expanding Realms of the New Penology: The Advent of Actuarial Justice for Juveniles." *Punishment and Society* 2:66–97.

Lieb, Roxanne, Lee Fish, and Todd Crosby. 1994. *A Summary of State Trends in Juvenile Justice*. Olympia, WA: Washington State Institute for Public Policy.

Liska, Allen E. 1992. *Social Threat and Social Control*. Albany: State University of New York Press.

Margolin, Leslie. 1992. "Deviance on the Record: Techniques for Labeling Child Abusers in Official Documents." *Social Problems* 39:58–70.

Peterson, Ruth D., and John Hagan. 1984. "Changing Conceptions of Race: Towards an Account of Anomalous Findings of Sentencing Research." *American Sociological Review* 49:56–70.

Piliavin, Irving, and Scott Briar. 1964. "Police Encounters with Juveniles." *American Journal of Sociology* 70:206–214.

Rubington, Earl, and Martin S. Weinberg. 1973. "The Public Regulation of Deviance." Pp. 117–123 in *Deviance: The Interactionist Perspective*, 2nd ed., ed. Earl Rubington and Martin S. Weinberg. New York: Macmillan.

Scheff, Thomas J. 1966. "Typification in the Diagnostic Practices of Rehabilitation Agencies." In *Sociology and Rehabilitation*, ed. Marvin B. Sussman. Washington, DC: American Sociological Association.

Scott, Marvin B., and Stanford M. Lyman. 1968. "Accounts." *American Sociological Review* 22:664–670.

Spitzer, Steven. 1975. "Toward a Marxian Theory of Deviance." *Social Problems* 22:638–651.

Steffensmeier, Darrell, and Robert M. Terry. 1973. "Deviance and Respectability: An Observational Study of Reactions to Shoplifting." *Social Forces* 51:417–426.

Sudnow, David. 1965. "Normal Crimes: Sociological Features of the Penal Code in a Public Defender Office." *Social Problems* 12:255–275.

Swigert, Victoria, and Ronald Farrell. 1977. "Normal Homicides and the Law." *American Sociological Review* 42:16–32.

Tittle, Charles R., and Debra A. Curran. 1988. "Contingencies for Dispositional Disparities in Juvenile Justice." *Social Forces* 67:23–58.

Tonry, Michael H. 1995. *Malign Neglect: Race, Crime, and Punishment in America*. New York: Oxford University Press.

Wiseman, Jacqueline P. 1970. *Stations of the Lost*. Chicago: University of Chicago Press.

9

"Justice by Geography"

Racial Disparity and Juvenile Courts

Timothy M. Bray, Lisa L. Sample,
and Kimberly Kempf-Leonard

FOR DECADES criminologists have tried to understand whether and why racial disparity exists in juvenile justice by looking at characteristics of youths and controlling for the nature of their cases. There is now wide consensus that differential treatment exists, but, despite increasing sophistication and rigor of the empirical research, we have not adequately explained the reasons for it. There has been some speculation but almost no research on race effects due to location or other traits specific to the court. In this chapter we argue not only that understanding case-processing differences by race and ethnicity requires multilevel theory and data, but also that traditional analytical techniques are not adequate to the task. We first review what is known about "justice by geography" and racial disparity in juvenile justice. We then present findings based on juvenile court data from Missouri to show how multilevel statistical techniques are needed to convey more clearly the patterns of case processing and racial disparity.[1]

Several years ago Abraham Blumberg (1967) commented that efforts to understand disparities in case-processing and court decisions had focused too narrowly on race, ethnicity, and social class. In admonishing researchers, he said: "Largely overlooked is the variable of the court organization itself, which possesses a thrust, purpose, and direction of its own. It is grounded in pragmatic values, bureaucratic priorities, and administrative instruments" (15).

More recently, while explaining how courts work, George Cole and Marc Gertz (1998) noted as follows: "The customs and traditions of each jurisdiction vary because local practices are influenced by factors such as size, politics, and demographics. Among these, differences between urban and rural areas are a major factor" (293). Cole and Gertz also identify the function of "local legal culture" as helping to define the boundaries for protocol and distinguish between "us" and how "they" do things elsewhere. Important elements of court protocol include "the going rate" for case processing, and the relative merit accorded specific factors of a case (292). Their argument that court processing varies according to locale is presented chiefly through excerpts from three widely cited studies of individual criminal courts (Eisenstein, Flemming, and Nardulli 1988; Feeley 1979; and Levin 1975).

Similar arguments are applied to juvenile court processing. Local culture, ethnocentrism, and particularly the "us" versus "them" clash, are the basis of several studies of the origins of the juvenile court and criticism of the "child savers" (Odem 1995; Odem and Schlossman 1991; Platt 1969; Schlossman 1977; Shelden 1981; see also Tanenhaus 2005). These arguments form part of the basis on which Feld (1999) challenges current practices with racial bias and argues for the abolition of juvenile courts. Several scholars suggest practical or bureaucratic explanations for regional variation across juvenile courts (Bortner 1982; Cicourel 1968; Emerson 1969, 1983; Matza 1964; Tepperman 1973). The notion that reality is something akin to justice by geography for juveniles is not surprising given the traditional *parens patriae* orientation in which court officers have unparalleled discretion and are encouraged to address the individualized needs of each youth, perhaps irrespective of his or her behavior (Rothman 1980). It is understandable if, in the absence of guidance from state legal codes, protocol for case processing develops based on other local factors. However, to be of value in efforts to improve upon our legal response to juvenile offenders and to reduce racial disparities in particular, we need to know whether racial disparity is related to court disparity and, if so, how and why these jurisdictional differences exist.

The answer may be as simple as size, with large courts more likely to standardize case processing with formal policies and expediency while small courts use more informal negotiations between acquaintances (Tepperman 1973). Alternatively, the difference may be due to the nature of routine caseloads. Emerson (1983) suggested that as otherwise heinous offenses become more common place in court processing, and staff members become more desensitized, they are less likely to define such cases as serious. To the extent that offense seriousness is a factor in court decision making, disparities may reflect the types of cases court officials regularly encounter.

However, justice by geography may exist for more complex reasons. The best effort at demarcation thus far is a typology that classified 150 metropolitan juvenile courts along a three-part continuum as "traditional," "transitional," or "due process" in their orientation (Stapleton, Aday, and Ito 1982). Ignoring the metropolitan court foundation and omitting the middle type, "transitional," several scholars have adapted the typology loosely to interpret rural and urban differences (Bishop, Frazier, and Henretta 1989; Bishop and

Frazier 1991; Burruss and Kempf-Leonard 2002; Fagan and Deschenes 1990; Feld 1991; Heuser 1985; Kempf, Decker, and Bing 1990; Lockhart et al. 1991; McNulty 1996; Poulos and Orchowsky 1994; Schneider and Schram 1983).

Although urban and rural differences might support the simple size explanation, the dichotomy of traditional and due process orientations does appear to have face validity. Rural courts seem intuitively to fit the label "traditional," or "pre-Gault," in that they more often operate informally, have routine cases that involve minor offenses or nonoffenders, and serve a more homogenous residential population. In contrast, urban courts get labeled "due process," or "post-Gault," because they more often use formal procedures and specialized staff—including a growing number of attorneys—to impose sanctions and treatment on serious delinquents but provide minimal attention to minor offenders or nonoffenders. Using this dichotomy to speculate about racial disparities in juvenile court outcomes, Feld offered this racial threat hypothesis: "In cities characterized by greater racial inequality, segregation, and concentrated poverty, politicians and the public may perceive young black males as especially threatening and use the juvenile justice system to impose more punitive sanctions to control these ominous 'underclass' youths. . . . Urban juvenile courts appear to process youths more formally and sentence them more severely than do their rural counterparts. Because proportionally more black youths now reside in urban areas, they experience greater risk of exposure to these harsher juvenile court sanctions" (113).

In order better to understand racial disparity, therefore, it is important that we also work to understand what it is about cross-court differences that give rise to that disparity. We next examine prior research on cross-court variation to determine how best to proceed with our own investigation of justice by geography as it may relate to racial disparities.

Prior Research on Race and Justice by Geography

Barry Krisberg and his colleagues (Krisberg, Litsky, and Schwartz 1984) examined interstate variations in juvenile confinement in youth facilities, jails, and adult prisons. Using data from three sources for 1979, they observed "glaring differences" and "disparities" in admission rates, lengths and conditions of confinement, expenditures per youth, and facility crowding. In concluding "[I]t may not be too harsh a judgment to characterize our juvenile corrections practices as 'justice by geography'" (177), they appear to be the first to coin this phrase. In a subsequent article with other authors, they identified racial disparity in state incarceration rates (Krisberg et al. 1987). To explain these "interjurisdictional differences," they recommended that future research examine (1) different crime patterns, (2) differing incarceration policies, (3) the use of private facilities, and (4) different resources of community-based programs for minority youths (190).

Although Krisberg and his colleagues may have been the first actually to call it such, the issue of justice by geography has been a focus of several studies. Indeed, in our search of past research from which our study could benefit, we located twenty-eight studies with geographic comparisons of court sanctioning (shown in table 9.1). There may be others we failed to find. Regrettably, there appears to be no prior exemplary study. Five of these studies examine adult sentencing (Austin 1981; Hagan 1977; Kempf and Austin 1986; Myers and Talarico 1986; Pope 1976) and one uses measures of local policing and confinement as independent variables (Sampson 1986), so they are less relevant for our purposes. Most of the studies of juvenile justice systems do not examine race or ethnicity. Among those that do include race, three include only descriptive analyses (Hamparian et al. 1982; Krisberg, Litsky, and Schwartz 1987; McGarrell 1991). In the remaining three studies (Kempf, Decker, and Bing 1990; Leonard and Sontheimer 1995; Lockhart et al. 1991) nonwhite youths are more apt than comparable white youths to be confined or placed out of home in nonrural courts, and particularly so in urban courts. There may be measurement error in each of these three studies, however, because a single court-level measure of urbanization is included among other individual case-level measures.

Compared to race, evidence of disparity in waiver processing is much more consistent among studies that have examined location or justice by geography (Bishop et al. 1989; Bishop and Frazier 1991; Fagan and Deschenes 1990; Feld 1987, 1990, 1995; Hamparian et al. 1982; Heuser 1985; McNulty 1996; Poulos and Orchowsky 1994). Of course, residential locations of minority youths may make it difficult to disentangle the effects of race and geography on judicial waiver practices (see Bishop 2005). According to Bishop and her colleagues, "[T]he difference in the criminal court handling of juveniles in the two counties is largely attributable to differences in bureaucratic practices rather than to differences in the seriousness or perceived prosecutorial merit of transfer cases" (1989, 191). Subsequently, Bishop and Frazier contended that "juvenile offenders in the two counties were at different levels of risk for criminal prosecution largely because of idiosyncrasies in the organization of the prosecutors' offices" (Bishop and Frazier 1991, 295). Similarly, Feld (1987) argued that "[I]diosyncratic differences in judicial philosophies and the locale of a waiver hearing are far more significant for the ultimate adulthood decision than is any inherent quality of the criminal act or characteristics of the offending youth" (494). A later study argued that waiver outcomes depend largely on the individual judge presiding over the court (Podkopacz and Feld 1996, 479). Beyond idiosyncrasies of decision makers, Poulos and Orchowsky (1994) speculated thus about the rural and urban differences they found: "[B]ecause [judges

Table 9.1: Overview of Prior Research on Justice by Geography

Study	Subjects	Juvenile or Adult	Location and Time	Type of Analysis	Justice-by-Geography Finding	Harsher
Aday 1986	500 cases	Juvenile	2 courts, 1978–79	Regression	Yes	Traditional less "patterned"
Austin 1981	1,664 cases	Adult	IA, 1976	Discriminant	Yes, sentencing	Rural and suburban
Bishop and Frazier 1991	583 cases	Juvenile	FL, 1981–84	Tabular	Yes	Larger, bureaucratic
Bridges et al. 1995	Rates	Juvenile	31 WA counties, 1990–91	Regression	Yes, confinement	Less urban, more crime
Cohen and Kluegel 1978	6,894 males	Juvenile	Denver and Memphis, 1972	Likelihood ratios	Yes, disposition	Traditional
Crank 1990	Arrest statistics		IL, 1986	Regression	Yes, policing styles	NA
Dannefer and Schutt 1982	1,225 cases	Juvenile	2 NJ counties, 1973–75	Regression	Yes	Hispanics
Dean et al. 1996	2,348 cases	Juvenile	10 NC counties, 1993	Regression	No	More densely less densely populated
DeJong and Jackson 1998	4,683 cases	Juvenile	PA, 1990	Probit	Yes, referral placement	
Fagan and Deschenes 1990	201 cases	Juvenile	4 cities, 1981–84	Discriminant	Yes, waiver	NA
Feld 1991	17,195 cases	Juvenile	MN, 1986	Regression	Yes, placement, secure	Urban
Frazier et al. 1992	32 FL counties	Juvenile		Regression	Yes, multiple outcomes	Nonwhites

Study	Data	Type	Location/Year	Path	Effect	Finding
Hagan 1977	974 inmates 507 surveys	Adult	Canada		Yes, sentencing	Rural
Hamparian et al. 1982	Waiver	Juvenile	U.S. states	Descriptive	Yes, waiver	Elected judges rural less due process
Hasenfeld and Cheung 1985	216 staff surveys, court statistics		U.S., 1974	Regression	Yes, commitment rate	
Johnson and Scheuble 1991	36,680 cases	Juvenile	1 state, 1975–83	Odds ratios	Yes, disposition	Rural
Johnson and Secret 1995	22,707 cases	Juvenile	NE, 1982–87	Regression	Yes, adjudication; no, disposition	Rural
Kempf and Austin 1986	Cases	Adult	PA, 1980	Regression	Yes, in/out and Length	
Kempf et al. 1990	2,620 cases	Juvenile	MO, 1987–88	Regression	Yes	Urban race bias rural and urban
Krisberg et al. 1984	Custody rates	Juvenile	U.S. states, 1979	Descriptive	Yes, admissions, lengths, expenditures, conditions, crowding	
Krisberg et al. 1987	Custody rates	Juvenile	U.S. states, 1982	Descriptive	Yes, incarceration rates	Nonwhite (public > private)
Leonard and Sontheimer 1995	1,797 cases	Juvenile	PA, 1989	Regression	Yes, multiple outcomes	Suburban and urban
Lockhart et al. 1991	3,277 cases	Juvenile males	GA, 1988	Regression	Yes, multiple outcomes	Decentralized, urban (black)
McGarrell 1991	Custody rates	Juvenile	U.S. states, 1973 and 1987	Regression	Yes, and over time	Diverse population less privatization

(continued)

Table 9.1 (*Continued*)

Study	Subjects	Juvenile or Adult	Location and Time	Type of Analysis	Justice-by-Geography Finding	Harsher
McGarrell 1993	159 referral rates	Juvenile	Counties in 17 states, 1985 and 1989	% change	Yes, rate of referral	NA
Myers and Talarico 1986	18,884 sentences	Adult	GA, 1976–82	Regression	Yes, confinement	Urban
Pope 1976	32,694 arrests	Adult	CA, 1969–71	Tabular	Yes, confinement	Rural
Poulous and Orchowsky 1994	727 cases	Juvenile	VA, 1988–90	Regression	Yes, waiver	Urban/metropolitan
Sampson 1986	171 robbery and homicide rates		171 cities, 1980	Regression	Yes	Less police aggressiveness more jail confinement
Sampson and Laub 1993	Custody rates	Juvenile	322 counties, 1985	Regression	No	
Stapleton et al. 1982	150 staff surveys	Juvenile	150 metro areas, 1979–80	Factor	Yes	Traditional
Tepperman 1973	72 courts	Juvenile	MA, 1970	Path	Yes, disposition	Urban
Tittle and Curran 1988	5,669 cases	Juvenile	31 FL counties	Regression	Yes	Diverse population

serving metropolitan areas] see so many serious offenders, their threshold for defining an offense as serious enough to warrant transfer may be higher than that of their rural counterparts. On the other hand, metropolitan judges may have at their disposal more options at the juvenile court level than their rural counterparts and thus rely less heavily on the last resort of transfer" (14).

Although not commenting specifically on geographic differences, a related concern expressed by Barnes and Franz (1989) is that "organizational policies are almost as important as the offender's behavior in explaining the waiver decision" (126). One organizational concern may be self-preservation. Bortner argued that "portraying these juveniles as the most intractable and the greatest threat to public safety, the juvenile justice system not only creates an effective symbolic gesture regarding protection of the public but it also advances its territorial interest in maintaining jurisdiction over the vast majority of juveniles and deflecting more encompassing criticisms of the entire system" (Bortner 1986, 69–70). More recently, Feld (1999) echoed her concerns as follows: "[J]uvenile court judges may transfer some youths to safeguard the jurisdiction of their courts, and organizational or political concerns may explain as much about waiver decisions as the dangerousness or treatability of a youth" (217–218).

Although our review of past research has identified concern about justice by geography, there is no consensus about the cause of this geographic disparity. Indeed, most past inquiries have not set out to test hypotheses about courts but have attempted ad hoc theorizing to speculate about statistically significant findings associated with an "urban/rural" variable. In addition, no research on this topic has addressed concerns about the need to pursue multilevel data (Sampson 1986; Hawkins, Laub, and Lauritsen 1998, 2000), although obviously any differential treatment by race would occur within the court environment. We consider research using multilevel statistical techniques next.

Prior Research with Multilevel Techniques

The nexus of race and justice by geography should be investigated using techniques that take into account the multilevel nature of the court-offender relationship. Hierarchical linear modeling (HLM) is such a technique (Griffin 1997; Hofman 1997; Raudenbush and Sampson 1999; Wang 1999), but its application to justice system questions is relatively new. A criticism of traditional modeling techniques (e.g., ordinary least squares regression and logistic regression) when applied to multilevel problems is that they are capable of addressing only "one layer." Specifically, to understand racial disparity in juvenile court outcomes, we need information about two layers: (1) individual or case-level data about particular cases (e.g., offense and youth's prior record) and (2) court-level data (e.g., urban versus rural and nature of case-loads). If we use traditional techniques, we can merely add the court-level measures to the model with case-level measures.

This "tacking on" introduces some measurement problems. Essentially, though, errors arise because these models distort the true variation by distributing information for the smaller number of courts (forty-five in our data) across the much larger number of individual cases (4,243 in our data). In the case of a variable called "urban/rural," the math behind traditional analytical techniques assumes that variable to be as free to vary across cases as is the race of youth, when in fact it is not. All juveniles in any given court will have the same value for "urban/rural." The implication of these issues will be discussed in more detail later; for now suffice it to say that HLM techniques represent an attempt to control for these issues and present findings that are more true to reality.

Relatively new to the field of criminology, HLM is found most often in etiology-based research (Cattarello 2000; Sung 1999; Welsh, Greene, and Jenkins 1999). Examples exist in research from other fields, such as psychology (Boyle and Willms 2001; Ross 2000; Waugh 2001), education (Goddard, Sweetland, and Hoy 2000; Lee 2000; Teitler and Weiss 2000), and business (de Jonge et al. 1999; Hardy and Hazelrigg 1999; Vancouver 1997; VanYperen, van den Berg, and Willering 1999). We could locate only two studies in which HLM was used to investigate some phenomenon related to the administration of justice.

Michael Reisig and Roger Parks (2000) used HLM techniques to explain the racial variation in attitudes toward, and satisfaction with, the police. They regressed individual-level variables (race, age, gender, whether the subject was a homeowner, perceived safety, incivility, neighborhood crime rate, and the familiarity of the officer) and neighborhood-level predictors (concentrated disadvantage and homicide rate) on satisfaction with the police. Their measure for concentrated disadvantage was a weighted factor score based on the percentages of the population that were poor, in the labor force, unemployed, in female-headed families, and black. They found that a cluster of "quality of life" variables contributed most to explaining the racial variation in attitudes.

John Woolredge and his colleagues (Woolredge, Griffin, and Pratt 2001) compared the results of pooled logistic regression and hierarchical linear models to explain the variation in prison inmate misconduct. They discussed four problems that occur using pooled logistic regression with multilevel data. First, collinearity between individual and aggregate-level measures may exist, because people are often *not* randomly distributed across environments. Second, correlated error within aggregates at the individual level occurs, because there are differences in selection probabilities for individuals across aggregates. Third, heteroscedasticity may exist, because different numbers of individuals exist within the aggregates in the sample. Fourth, tests of aggregate-level null hypotheses may be biased, because the tests are based on the number of individuals, not the number of aggregates, in the model. Fortunately, HLM techniques can adjust statistically for these problems.

Woolredge, Griffin, and Pratt (2001) found that the two types of techniques yielded different results. This difference occurs because pooled logistic regression models spread the values of prison crowding (their aggregate measure) across all inmates within a prison, thereby reducing the total variance to be explained because the number of inmates varies across facilities. In contrast, all values of prison crowding have equal weight in the calculation of total variance in the HLM analysis (222). They conclude, "models including both individual- and aggregate-level predictors can increase the understanding of inmate deviance beyond models including only individual-level or only aggregate-level influences" (227). Also, "the hierarchical models revealed much more consistency in prediction . . . we recommend the use of hierarchical modeling over pooled regression in related research" (228).

Data and Research Methods

We examine data from all juvenile court cases processed in Missouri between 1992 and 1997. Our primary unit of analysis is the juvenile referral, or court case, not the juvenile. It is possible that, as a result, some juveniles appear in the data more than once (e.g., a child referred for auto theft in 1992 is later referred for burglary in 1995). Due to privacy restrictions, however, the juveniles are not individually identifiable in the data and therefore cannot be removed. This is not necessarily a problem. First, we are interested in modeling the impact of individual-level and court-level variables on court decisions, so court decisions would seem to be the logical unit of analysis. Second, in line with previous researchers, we include for each case the juvenile's prior referral count as a predictor of case outcome.

Though data were routinely collected for every juvenile referral from each of the forty-five circuit courts, we are restricting our analyses to adjudicated cases of felony theft, vehicle theft, burglary, and arson that involved either white or black males. These restrictions better enable us to have sufficient numbers of cases of comparable severity to examine even quite rural jurisdictions. We want only adjudicated cases including offenders that were eligible for commitment to a juvenile facility so that we can compare formal judicial dispositions. These case-level data enable us to examine race and justice by geography, while controlling for "similarly situated" cases on several important dimensions.

In addition to race (black = 1; white = 0) and placement disposition (yes = 1; no = 0), we measure youth's age in years (a continuous variable measuring the difference in date of referral and date of birth), the number of prior juvenile court referrals (including law violations, status offenses, and abuse or neglect victimization) at the time of the hearing, and prehearing custody status (yes $= 1$; no $= 0$).

In addition to those case-level variables, we also make use of information at the circuit court level. When labeling court circuits urban (1) or rural (0), we use the U.S. Census Bureau's following definition of an urbanized area: "a continuously built-up area with a population of 50,000 or more. It comprises one or more places—central place(s)—and the adjacent densely settled surrounding area—urban fringe—consisting of other places and non-place territory" (United States Bureau of the Census 1994, 12-1).

Eleven circuits are thereby classified as urban (5, 6, 7, 11, 16, 21, 22, 23, 29, 31, 40), and thirty-four circuits are rural. We identify court caseload as the total number of adjudicated cases from 1992 to 1997. We capture the extent to which these felony property crimes were routine cases to the court by examining the percentage of all adjudicated cases represented by our four types of property crimes. Initially, we describe the case-level data with tabular analysis and the court-level data with thematic maps.

Multivariate statistical techniques are necessary to examine racial disparity related to justice by geography. Because we use two techniques and multiple stages with each, it is perhaps easiest to view our analyses as a series of equations. In the interest of clarity and brevity, we will discuss our analytical techniques here and reserve our presentation of equations for the discussion of results.

We use two regression frameworks to model the relationship between geography and racial disparity. First, following an often-used approach in this research, we test the relationship using a series of logistic regression equations. Essentially, these logistic regressions predict the natural log of the odds of placement based on the given predictors; exponentiating the predicted log odds will provide the predicted odds of out-of-home placement. Traditionally, the variables included in the regression are attributes of a given child (e.g., race, age, and prior arrests) and the offense at issue. To model the effects of geography, court-level variables (such as caseload and urban or rural location) are attributed to the kids within those courts and included in the typical logistic regression equation.

Current methodological understanding raises issues with this traditional approach. A key assumption underlying logistic regression is one of independence. This means we assume that each case is no more likely than any other case to have a particular value on a given variable. It is fair to make this assumption with regard to those case-level variables, such as offense seriousness, detention, and age. When we begin adding court-level variables into this traditional model, however, we begin to violate this assumption. In any one court, *all* cases are assigned the same value on the "urban/rural" variable. Cases are not explicitly free to vary. As Jan de Leeuw notes in the introduction to the Bryk and Raudenbush textbook on hierarchical linear modeling, "individuals in the same group are closer or more similar than individuals in different groups" (1992, xiv). Thus, when court-level measures are included in case-level logistic regression models, the values for those court attributes are spread across all cases included in the model. The unequal distribution of these values, due to differences in the number of cases across circuits, reduces the variance in placement outcomes (Wooldredge, Griffin, and Pratt 2001, 222). The results from such techniques are inefficient and may misstate the actual significance of the relationship between two variables.

For that reason, we rely on hierarchical modeling techniques to augment our analyses. Specifically, we use hierarchical nonlinear modeling to estimate the effects of child-level and court-circuit-level predictors on the log odds of a child's receiving out-of-home placement. Hierarchical modeling techniques recognize the inherent multilevel, or hierarchical, structure of the phenomenon we are studying (i.e., case decisions are made within courts). We can therefore more explicitly examine the *two* questions that are of interest to us. What characteristics of cases lead to judicial decisions to place juveniles outside the home, *and* what is it about juvenile courts that lead to placement decisions?

With hierarchical modeling, we specify two models that are later combined. The level-1, or case-level, model incorporates characteristics such as the race of the adjudicated youth. The level-2, or court-level, model combines court-level characteristics and specifies how they are expected to interact with characteristics of the cases. These models are then combined for a maximum likelihood estimation. In the following results section, this analytical approach will be made clearer.

Results

Map 9.1 shows the total number of adjudicated cases by circuit. The metropolitan areas of Kansas City and St. Louis understandably have caseloads that exceed by far those of more rural circuits that encompass multiple counties. Map 9.2 shows the rate of placement among adjudicated cases, and it is clear that size is not directly related to formal disposition. The range of court placement rates is 7.7%–82.6%, and courts with the highest rates are the darkest shade on the map. Some of the highest placement rates occur in circuits toward the less sparsely populated center of the state.

Table 9.2 shows the percentage of adjudicated cases in which youths were detained in custody and had dispositions with out-of-home placement. Among all cases adjudicated in the state between 1992 and 1997, 34.1% were

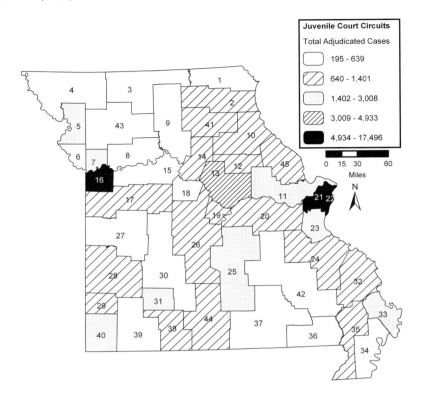

Map 9.1. Total cases adjudicated in Missouri juvenile court systems, 1992–97.

held in prehearing detention and 28.3% were committed to a youth facility. A higher proportion of black youths than white youths received each type of custody, but the disparity was greater earlier at detention (46.4% black, 29.5% white) than at placement (32.5% black, 26.8% white). Detention and placement increased with age, then declined beginning at age 16. Detention and placement also were directly related to the number of prior referrals to court, although having a lengthy prior record was common among the adjudicated cases. Four was the average number of prior referrals, and the range extended from zero (28.1% of adjudicated cases) to forty-nine. Urban courts detained 37.1% of the cases that were subsequently adjudicated, compared to only 30.2% of the cases in rural courts. Rural and urban courts placed similar proportions of their adjudicated cases.

Next, we present three logistic regression models of the likelihood of out-of-home placement among the adjudicated cases (results shown in table 9.3).

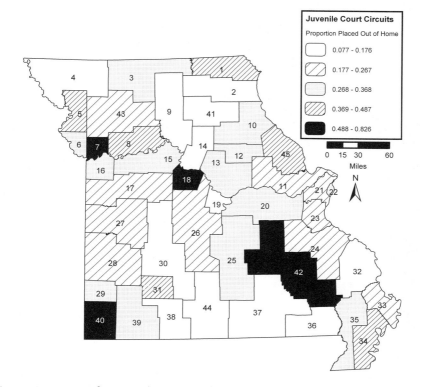

Map 9.2. Proportion of cases resulting in out-of-home placement in Missouri juvenile court systems, 1992–97.

First, we predict the statewide log odds of placement based only on race (eq. A). This race model provides the initial quantitative picture of disparity. The race of the youth is a statistically significant predictor of the likelihood that an adjudicated case resulted in an out-of-home placement. Whereas odds of placement were 0.395 overall, among white youths the odds were 0.365 and among black youths the odds were 0.481. As the column labeled "Exponentiated β" indicates, black youths were roughly 1.316 times more likely than white youths to receive out-of-home placement.

To the race model, we then add variables to compare cases similarly situated according to prehearing detention status, number of prior referrals, and age of the youth (individual case-level criteria often found to be related to racial disparity; see eq. B). In the presence of these controls, the impact of race on placement diminishes and actually reverses slightly, failing to achieve statistical significance. Third, in equation C we add or "tack on" a traditional

Table 9.2: Distribution of Detention and Placement by Youth's Race, Age, Prior Record, and Court Type: Missouri's Adjudicated Cases, 1992–97

	Percentage Detained	Percentage Placed	N
Youth's race:			
Black	46.4	32.5	1,164
White	29.5	26.8	3,079
Youth's age at referral:			
≤10	14.6	12.2	41
11	21.5	18.5	65
12	28.7	20.4	181
13	32.9	26.5	486
14	34.0	27.6	888
15	37.1	30.6	1,270
16	34.0	29.7	1,248
≥17	25.5	21.6	51
Number of prior referrals:			
≤6	32.8	23.9	3,379
7–19	38.5	44.7	742
≥20	44.3	52.5	122
Court urbanization:			
Urban	37.1	28.7	2,414
Rural	30.2	27.8	1,829
Court familiarity with property felonies (% of caseload):			
<5%	35.9	27.2	2,013
>5%–<9%	32.7	29.3	1,716
≥9%	31.9	29.4	514
Total	34.1	28.3	4,243

court-level predictor, urban or rural location. Race remains insignificant when the court-level dichotomy is added, although the risk of placement among adjudicated cases appears to be higher in rural than urban courts. The fully specified case-level logistic regression model with the urban/rural court dichotomy correctly predicts an out-of-home placement decision for 73.8% of the adjudicated cases. On the surface, the last two logistic regression results suggest that there is no racial disparity in juvenile processing with regard to out-of-home placement. The significant race effect in the initial model might be considered an artifact—a misleading result—obtained because we did not fully specify the other predictors, as we did for the results of equation C. Recalling our earlier caution, however, one must recognize that racial disparity at earlier stages of the court process (e.g., at the decision to refer), in combination with the fully specified case-level model, may mask the existence of disparity at the sentencing stage.

Table 9.3: Logistic Regression Models for Out-of-Home Placement

	Coefficient (β)	Standard Error	Exponentiated β
Estimates for equation A (race only):[a]			
Black	0.275*	0.075	1.316
Constant	−1.007	0.041	0.365
Estimates for equation B (all case-level variables):[b]			
Black	−0.058[n.s.]	0.083	0.943
Detained	1.116*	0.074	3.054
Prior referrals	0.078*	0.006	1.081
Age	0.074*	0.028	1.077
Constant	−2.818	0.437	0.060
Estimates for equation C (with court-level urban/rural variable):[c]			
Black	−0.015[n.s.]	0.085	0.985
Detained	1.122*	0.074	3.072
Prior referrals	0.080*	0.006	1.083
Age	0.075*	0.028	1.077
Urban court	−0.185*	0.076	0.831
Constant	−2.747	0.438	0.064

Note: n.s. = not significant.
[a] $N = 4{,}243$; $\chi^2 = 13.352$ (1 df; $p \leq .05$); -2 log likelihood = 5,044.592; percentage correct = 71.7.
[b] $N = 4{,}230$; $\chi^2 = 438.513$ (4 df; $p \leq .05$); -2 log likelihood = 4,605.201; percentage correct = 73.8.
[c] $N = 4{,}230$; $\chi^2 = 444.446$ (5 df; $p \leq .05$); -2 log likelihood = 4,599.268; percentage correct = 73.8.
*$p \leq .05$.

Basic Logistic Regression Models of Out-of-Home Placement

Equation A: race only

$$\eta_i = \beta_0 + \beta_1 \text{Race}$$

Equation B: all case-level variables

$$\eta_i = \beta_0 + \beta_1 \text{Race} + \beta_2 \text{Detention} + \beta_3 \text{Priors} + \beta_4 \text{Age}$$

Equation C: with court-level urban/rural variable

$$\eta_i = \beta_0 + \beta_1 \text{Race} + \beta_2 \text{Detention} + \beta_3 \text{Priors} + \beta_4 \text{Age} + \beta_5 \text{Urban}$$

The difficulty with equation C is a bit complicated, but it can be shown mathematically that combining the case-level and court-level measures in a logistic regression model may yield misleading results. As we stated earlier, one statistical method of overcoming those shortcomings is HLM. We apply hierarchical nonlinear models to pick up where we left off with equation C, attempting to identify court-level characteristics that may contribute to the observed geographic disparity in placement rates. We specify a model that predicts the odds of placement based on characteristics of cases and courts in such a way that correctly addresses issues of independence.

We begin with what is called a "fully unspecified model." In such a model, we assess the statewide odds of placement (i.e., the average likelihood across courts) and the degree to which this statewide average varies from court to court. As equation D shows, we are specifying a given youth's odds of placement as a function of the statewide average odds of placement (γ_{00}) and some court-level variation above or below that average (v_{0j}). If that variation is statistically distinguishable from zero, then there is evidence that the chance that an adjudicated case will result in placement differs among all courts in the state. Reflecting on the results shown in table 9.4, we see that, statewide, the average odds of placement for an adjudicated case are 0.405. Notice that this is slightly higher than overall odds derived by logistic regression— 0.405 compared to 0.395. This slightly higher estimate of odds occurs because the model makes use of information not used in logistic regression—the court in which the adjudication occurred. Additionally, we see that the variance component (v_{0j}) is statistically significant, indicating that the odds of placement do vary significantly across Missouri's juvenile courts. In a nutshell, these results reveal that, on average, any given case is more likely not to result in out-of-home placement, but these odds vary significantly from circuit to circuit.

This analysis proceeds along two paths. First, we must fully specify our case-level model by including those case characteristics we believe influence the likelihood that the case will result in placement, assess the magnitude and significance of their effect, and assess the degree to which their effects vary across Missouri's juvenile courts (see eq. E and eq. F). Once the level-1 model is fully specified, we turn our attention to understanding the court-level (level-2) processes that might explain this cross-court variation (eqq. G–J).

We begin in equation E, where we expect that the odds of placement are a function of some statewide average odds of placement (γ_{00}), the statewide effect of prior referrals (γ_{10}), the statewide effect of prehearing detention (γ_{20}), the statewide effect of race (γ_{30}), and the statewide effect of age (γ_{40}). To ease interpretation of zeroed coefficients, we recenter age on 15 by subtracting 15 years from each youth's age. Our new variable tells us how much older or younger than 15 each youth is. In addition, we will inspect for significant cross-court variation from the statewide effects of prior referrals (v_{1j}), prehearing detention (v_{2j}), race (v_{3j}), and age (v_{4j}), and variation from the average statewide odds not attributable to these predictors (v_{0j}).

The results (shown in table 9.4) indicate that the overall odds (γ_{00}) are against out-of-home placement, but the likelihood of placement increases for cases involving youths with prior referrals (γ_{10}) or who have been detained

Table 9.4: Case-Level Hierarchical Models for Out-of-Home Placement

	Coefficient	Standard Error
Estimates for equation D (fully unspecified hierarchical model):		
Fixed effects (statewide effects):		
Mean log odds of placement (γ_{00})	-0.903*	0.115

	Variance Component	χ^2(df)
Random effects (cross-circuit variations):		
Mean log odds (v_{0j})	0.471*	297.390 (44)

	Coefficient	Standard Error
Estimates for equation E (model with case-level predictors):		
Fixed effects (statewide effects):		
Mean log odds of placement (γ_{00})	-2.107*	0.152
Prior referrals (γ_{10})	0.229*	0.020
Detained (γ_{20})	1.278*	0.140
Black (γ_{30})	0.261 n.s.	0.156
Age (γ_{40})	0.084 n.s.	0.036

	Variance Component	χ^2(df)
Random effects (cross-circuit variations):		
Mean log odds of placement (v_{0j})	0.666*	90.137 (25)
Prior referrals (v_{1j})	0.006*	323.854 (25)
Detained (v_{2j})	0.305*	53.863 (25)
Black (v_{3j})	0.166 n.s.	25.590 (25)
Age (v_{4j})	0.008 n.s.	35.407 (25)

	Coefficient	Standard Error
Estimates for equation F (case-level predictors without court-level variation in race and age):		
Fixed effects (statewide effects):		
Mean log odds of placement (γ_{00})	-2.111*	0.153
Prior referrals (γ_{10})	0.229*	0.020
Detained (γ_{20})	1.286*	0.139
Black (γ_{30})	0.289*	0.107
Age (γ_{40})	0.066*	0.031

	Variance Component	χ^2(df)
Random effects (cross-circuit variations):		
Circuit mean (v_{0j})	0.676*	171.277 (41)
Prior referrals (v_{1j})	0.006*	359.297 (41)
Detained (v_{2j})	0.293*	74.390 (41)

Note: n.s. = not significant.

*$p \leq .05$.

(γ_{20}). The statistically significant variance components indicate that the additive effect of prior referrals and prehearing detention (v_{1j} and v_{2j}) vary significantly from court to court, and we continue to see significant variation in the overall odds of placement (v_{0j}) from court to court.

These results also show that race (γ_{30}) and age (γ_{40}) are not significant predictors of placement, suggesting that the difference between the odds of placement for black youth and white youth is not statistically different from 0. The model further reveals that the variance components for these variables (v_{3j} and v_{4j}) fail to achieve statistical significance—meaning no departure from the statewide average effect is detectable. The failure of both the statewide average effect and court-level departures from that effect, coupled with the lower reliability coefficients (not shown) for the race and age variables, suggest that the statewide average effects may not be achieving statistical significance due to overspecification (we are trying to partition too little information into too many pieces).

To more efficiently explore the effects of race and age, we next specify the equation to exclude cross-court variation for those variables (eq. F, results in table 9.4). Like our logistic regression results, these results show that, overall, the more likely case outcome is not placement, and that prior referrals (γ_{10}), detention (γ_{20}), and age (γ_{40}) all increase the likelihood of placement across all courts. Unlike the logistic regression results, however, these findings indicate that *race (γ_{30}) matters.* The odds of placement are increased when the youth is black.

We also begin to decode the cross-court variation in odds of placement. Recall that the results of equation D tell us that the odds of placement vary significantly across courts: at the margin, the odds that a case will result in placement differ from circuit to circuit. In equation F, we partial out that cross-court variation across the predictors of placement. We see that the effect of prior referrals (γ_{10}) is significant, and it varies significantly from court to court (v_{1j}). Likewise, the effect of detention (γ_{20}) is significant, and it varies significantly from court to court (v_{2j}). The effects of race (γ_{30}) and age (γ_{40}) are also significant, but there is no evidence that these effects are different in any one court than they are in any other (again, see eq. E). We still see significant variation across courts in their overall odds of placement (v_{0j}), even after accounting for differences between courts in prior referrals and detention.

Case-Level Hierarchical Models of Out-of-Home Placement

Equation D: fully unspecified hierarchical model

$$\eta_{ij} = \gamma_{00} + v_{0j}$$

Equation E: model with case-level predictors

$$\eta_{ij} = \gamma_{00} + \gamma_{10}\text{Priors} + \gamma_{20}\text{Detained} + \gamma_{30}\text{Race} + \gamma_{40}\text{Age}$$
$$+ v_{1j}\text{Priors} + v_{2j}\text{Detained} + v_{3j}\text{Race} + v_{4j}\text{Age} + v_{0j}$$

Equation F: case-level predictors without court-level variation in race and age

$$\eta_{ij} = \gamma_{00} + \gamma_{10}\text{Priors} + \gamma_{20}\text{Detained} + \gamma_{30}\text{Race} + \gamma_{40}\text{Age}$$
$$+ v_{1j}\text{Priors} + v_{2j}\text{Detained} + v_{0j}$$

Having fully specified our case-level (level-1) model in hierarchical terms, we have identified the presence of cross-court variation in the overall odds of placement and the effects on placement of prior referrals and prehearing detention. We have yet to explore the potential explanations for that variation. For that, we examine the court-level variables.

Equation G estimates the effects of those previously detailed case-level variables and includes an estimate of the impact on deviation from statewide average odds due to court caseload. Specifically, our caseload variable measures the difference between the number of true finding cases (the juvenile equivalent of a "guilty" finding) for each circuit and the cross-court average (γ_{01}, hereafter referred to as the grand-centered mean). As speculated earlier, the differences between courts in their odds of placement may be due simply to differences in the volume of cases they process. Because we are dealing with placement decisions that occur after true findings, the total caseload refers to the total number of true findings in the court during the time period studied. As with equation F, we continue to find that the statewide odds of placement favor a decision not to place, and that those odds are increased for youths with prior referrals or prehearing detention, or youths who are black or older (see results in table 9.5). Again, there remains significant cross-court variation in the overall odds of placement, and caseload fails to achieve significance as a predictor of this cross-court variation.

Equation H replaces the caseload variable with a court's urban or rural location (again, γ_{01}). Across courts, adjudicated cases are still more likely not to result in placement (γ_{00}), and the odds of placement increase when the youth has had prior referrals (γ_{10}), has been held in detention (γ_{20}), is black (γ_{30}), or is older (γ_{40}). As the results in table 9.5 suggest, the court's rural or urban location does not significantly contribute to the overall variation in the odds of placement statewide (γ_{01}), and significant variation remains about the statewide average odds of placement (v_{0j}). We still observe significant variation across courts in the effects of prior referrals and prehearing detention (v_{1j} and v_{2j}). In short, we find that a court's urban or rural setting does not significantly account for the court-to-court variation in odds of placement.

In equation I, we replace the urban or rural distinction with our measure of court familiarity with, or routine processing of, felony property crimes on

Table 9.5: Hierarchical Model for Out-of-Home Placement—Court Characteristics

	Coefficient	Standard Error
Estimates for equation G (using caseload to explain cross-court variation):		
Fixed effects (statewide effects):		
Mean log odds of placement (γ_{00})	−2.114*	0.159
Caseload (γ_{01})	0.000[n.s.]	0.000
Prior referrals (γ_{10})	0.229*	0.001
Detained (γ_{20})	1.294*	0.142
Black (γ_{30})	0.292*	0.108
Age (γ_{40})	0.066*	0.031

	Variance Component	χ^2(df)
Random effects (cross-court variations):		
Court Mean (υ_{0j})	0.737*	167.815 (40)
Prior Referrals (υ_{1j})	0.081*	361.054 (41)
Detained (υ_{2j})	0.558*	74.615 (41)

	Coefficient	Standard Error
Estimates for equation H (using urban or rural location urban to explain cross-court variation):		
Fixed effects (statewide effects):		
Mean long odds of placement (γ_{00})	−2.238*	0.171
Urban Circuit (γ_{01})	0.447[n.s.]	0.280
Prior Referrals (γ_{10})	0.231*	0.020
Detained (γ_{20})	1.274*	0.140
Black (γ_{30})	0.284*	0.107
Age (γ_{40})	0.066*	0.031

	Variance Component	χ^2(df)
Random effects (cross-court variations):		
Court Mean (υ_{0j})	0.620*	172.986 (40)
Prior Referrals (υ_{1j})	0.006*	369.814 (41)
Detained (υ_{2j})	0.293*	74.806 (41)

	Coefficient	Standard Error
Estimates for equation I (using routine caseload to explain cross-court variation):		
Fixed effects (statewide effects):		
Mean log odds of placement (γ_{00})	−2.124*	0.159
Court familiarity (γ_{01})	2.194[n.s.]	4.297
Prior referrals (γ_{10})	0.230*	0.021
Detained (γ_{20})	1.292*	0.141
Black (γ_{30})	0.290*	0.107
Age (γ_{40})	0.066*	0.031

	Variance Component	χ^2(df)
Random effects (cross-court variations):		
Court mean (υ_{0j})	0.744*	172.901 (40)
Prior referrals (υ_{1j})	0.006*	365.387 (41)
Detained (υ_{2j})	0.313*	74.718 (41)

Note: n.s. = not significant.

*$p \leq .05$.

individual odds (again, γ_{01}). Court familiarity is defined as the percentage of a court's adjudicated caseload represented by the four property crimes chosen for this analysis. In theory, courts in which these cases represent a larger proportion of the total cases may treat these cases differently from courts in which these cases are less common. The results presented in table 9.5 indicate no significant effects of court familiarity on the overall average odds of placement. The effects of the case-level predictors are largely unchanged from other models, and there remains significant variation about the state average likelihood of placement across circuits.

Court-Level Hierarchical Models of Out-of-Home Placement

Equation G: using caseload to explain cross-court variation

$$\eta_{ij} = \gamma_{00} + \gamma_{01}\text{Caseload} + \gamma_{10}\text{Priors} + \gamma_{20}\text{Detained} + \gamma_{30}\text{Race} \\ + \gamma_{40}\text{Age} + v_{1j}\text{Priors} + v_{2j}\text{Detained} + v_{0j}$$

Equation H: using urban or rural location to explain cross-court variation

$$\eta_{ij} = \gamma_{00} + \gamma_{01}\text{Urban} + \gamma_{10}\text{Priors} + \gamma_{20}\text{Detained} + \gamma_{30}\text{Race} \\ + \gamma_{40}\text{Age} + v_{1j}\text{Priors} + v_{2j}\text{Detained} + v_{0j}$$

Equation I: case-level with routine caseload to explain cross-court variation

$$\eta_{ij} = \gamma_{00} + \gamma_{01}\text{Specialization} + \gamma_{10}\text{Priors} + \gamma_{20}\text{Detained} \\ + \gamma_{30}\text{Race} + \gamma_{40}\text{Age} + v_{1j}\text{Priors} + v_{2j}\text{Detained} + v_{0j}$$

Finally, in equation J we remove the circuit court characteristic predictors and inspect for an impact of circuit demographics. Loosely following the racial threat hypothesis, we specify a model in which levels of racial isolation within the circuit affect deviation from the statewide odds of placement. Racial isolation is assessed using the racial isolation index (xP^*x). In their catalog of racial segregation measures, Massey and Denton define the isolation index as an index "which measures the extent to which minority members are exposed only to one another, rather than to majority members" (1988, 288). If the threat hypothesis paints an accurate picture of the processes that underlie the racial disparity in placement decisions, we would expect our racial isolation index to make a significant contribution to the court-to-court variation in overall odds of placement.

Table 9.6 presents the results of equation J, which specifies a court circuit's racial isolation score as a predictor of its variation from the statewide mean odds of placement. As with our previous attempts to model cross-court variation, we find no significant effect of racial isolation, and no significant change in the observed coefficients for our traditional predictors: across the state, odds still favor a no-placement decision, and odds of placement are

Table 9.6: Hierarchical Model for Out-of-Home Placement—Circuit Demographics

	Coefficient	Standard Error
Estimates for equation J (using racial isolation index to explain cross-court variation):		
Fixed effects (statewide effects):		
Mean log odds of placement (γ_{00})	-2.113	0.159
Racial isolation (γ_{01})	-0.422[n.s.]	0.659
Prior referrals (γ_{10})	$0.229^{\star}$	0.021
Detained (γ_{20})	$1.294^{\star}$	0.141
Black (γ_{30})	$0.299^{\star}$	0.109
Age (γ_{40})	$0.066^{\star}$	0.031

	Variance Component	$\chi^{2}(\text{df})$
Random effects (cross-court variations):		
Court mean (υ_{0j})	$0.745^{\star}$	173.460 (40)
Prior referrals (υ_{1j})	$0.007^{\star}$	360.436 (41)
Detained (υ_{2j})	$0.554^{\star}$	74.576 (41)

Note: n.s. = not significant.
$^{\star}p \leq .05$.

increased by a youth's prior violations, increased age, prehearing detention, or black race.

Circuit Demographic Hierarchical Model of Out-of-Home Placement

Equation J: using racial isolation index to explain cross-court variation

$$\eta_{ij} = \gamma_{00} + \gamma_{01}\text{Racial Isolation} + \gamma_{10}\text{Priors} + \gamma_{20}\text{Detained} \\ + \gamma_{30}\text{Race} + \gamma_{40}\text{Age} + \upsilon_{1j}\text{Priors} + \upsilon_{2j}\text{Detained} + \upsilon_{0j}$$

Summary and Conclusions

Initially, we presented a picture of geographic disparity in the overrepresentation of black youth in court cases resulting in decisions for out-of-home placement. We further suggested that, given no further explanation, we might cite these observations as evidence that the disparity in race is a case of "justice by geography."

Closer inspection confirms that, as we suggested, there is more here than meets the eye. Overall, odds of placement vary from circuit to circuit in Missouri's juvenile court system. At the margin, the likelihood that a youth's hearing will result in out-of-home placement is different depending on court location. Using advanced hierarchical modeling techniques that recognize the nested nature of these placement decisions, we are able to "partial out" this cross-court variation and ask where, specifically, this variation occurs.

We began by modeling, with traditional logistic regression models, several predictors of placement decisions often cited in the literature: prior juvenile court referrals, prehearing detention, race, and age. While logistic models that include only race as a predictor revealed a significant contribution of race, the race of the youth did not matter once priors, age, and detention were taken into account. To this model, we added a traditional court-level predictor, finding with logistic regression that a court's rural or urban location was a significant predictor of placement decisions. One might conclude from these findings that geography matters more than race. From the order in which these results have been presented, one might even conclude that some combination of prior referrals, detention, and urban or rural setting accounts for the increased likelihood that a case involving a black youth will result in out-of-home placement. Logistic regression, however, makes some assumptions about statistical independence that our data (and many others') do not merit.

With hierarchical modeling techniques, which provide redress to this assumption of statistical independence, a different story is told. First, we find that, indeed, geography matters—the likelihood of placement varies significantly across juvenile courts—confirming what a simple map might suggest to the naked eye. Second, we see that the odds of placement increase for older youths, black youths, those youths who have a history of prior referrals, and those who have been held in detention. This contradicts the results from the logistic regression analyses, which showed no significant influence for race when prior record, detention, and age were controlled.

Where the hierarchical techniques make their most significant contribution, however, is in their ability to more accurately portray the observed court-to-court variation in placement odds. While the overall odds of placement vary across courts, this is due to cross-court variation in the effects of prior referrals and prehearing detention. The effects of age and race do not vary across circuits. Thus, the fact that a case involves a black youth will increase the chance of out-of-home placement *regardless* of the court in which the case is processed. The fact that this same youth was detained prior to his hearing also improve his chances of placement, but courts vary in how heavily this detention influences decisions to place.

Finally, we attempted to account for the remaining cross-court variation using frequently cited court characteristics and demographic factors, distinguishing between urban and rural jurisdictions, a dichotomy frequently mentioned as important in past research. We first employed court caseload, urban versus rural setting, and court familiarity as potential explanatory factors for the remaining cross-court variation in overall odds. None of these effects appeared statistically significant. Following up on the racial threat hypothesis, we employed the racial isolation index as a potential predictor, and also found no significant effect. In sum, although we found cross-court variation with regard to the odds of placement, we were not able to discern the factors at the court level that explain this variation. If nothing else, this finding shows the current state of ignorance regarding the larger context in which case outcome decisions are made. Our results suggest that the individual attributes of youths and offenses cannot alone explain the dispositions of their cases. More attention must be paid to the aggregate-level factors that interact with judicial decision making, so we can better understand the dynamics of juvenile processing as they relate to the personal characteristics of youths.

A methodological note also arises from this chapter and speaks to the utility of advanced multilevel modeling techniques in understanding the complexities of courtroom decision making. Where logistic regression techniques suggest that urban or rural settings make a difference while race does not, hierarchical modeling techniques, which appropriately incorporate the nested, multilevel nature of the data, show the opposite. The selection of the appropriate modeling technique is important. This chapter illustrates how choosing one over another can drastically change the story the data tell.

We conclude that justice is not blind to race, at least for the cases, youths, and locations we have studied. While at the surface it appears that justice may be less blind to race in some areas than in others, closer inspection reveals this not to be the case. A policy maker might look at a map and conclude that targeted interventions and special programs are required to reduce the differential treatment by race evident in certain areas of the state. We suggest that, using the right techniques and armed with the right information, that policy maker would see that, at least in this case, the problems of racial disparity are equally distributed across courts. Regardless of the circuit in which a black male was adjudicated, he was more likely to be placed outside the home than similarly situated white males. Targeted interventions may address the most egregious of violations but may fail to affect the underlying processes that result in statewide disparity. Correctly modeling the problem is the key to understanding it, and therefore the key to fixing it. In this case, understanding that the effects of race are the same for all court circuits, and are not a part of the court-to-court variation in odds of placement, shapes the potential system responses.

Notes

We thank the Missouri Juvenile Justice Advisory Group and the Department of Public Safety for their support of an earlier project on which these data are based.

1. We describe the statistical procedures in detail for research methodologists, and the findings are summarized less technically for readers primarily interested in implications of this study.

References

Aday, David P., Jr. 1986. "Court Structure, Defense Attorney Use, and Juvenile Court Decisions." *Sociological Quarterly* 27 : 107–119.

Austin, Thomas L. 1981. "The Influence of Court Location on Type of Criminal Sentence: The Rural-Urban Factor." *Journal of Criminal Justice* 9 : 302–316.

Barnes, Carol Wolfe, and Randal S. Franz. 1989. "Questionably Adult: Determinants and Effects of the Juvenile Waiver Decision." *Justice Quarterly* 6, no. 1 : 117–135.

Bishop, Donna M. 2005. "The Role of Race and Ethnicity in Juvenile Justice Processing." In *Our Children, Their Children: Confronting Racial and Ethnic Differences in American Juvenile Justice,* ed. Darnell F. Hawkins and Kimberly Kempf-Leonard. Chicago: University of Chicago Press.

Bishop, Donna M., and Charles E. Frazier. 1991. "Transfer of Juveniles to Criminal Court: A Case Study and Analysis of Prosecutorial Waiver." *Notre Dame Journal of Law, Ethics and Public Policy* 5 : 281–302.

Bishop, Donna M., Charles E. Frazier, and John C. Henretta. 1989. "Prosecutorial Waiver: Case-Study of a Questionable Reform." *Crime and Delinquency* 35, no. 2 : 179–201.

Blumberg, Abraham S. 1967. "The Practice of Law as a Confidence Game." *Law and Society Review* 1 : 15–39.

Bortner, Margaret A. 1982. *Inside a Juvenile Court: The Tarnished Ideal of Individualized Justice.* New York: NYU Press.

—. 1986. "Traditional Rhetoric, Organizational Realities: Remand of Juveniles to Adult Court." *Crime and Delinquency* 32, no. 1 : 53–73.

Boyle, Michael H., and J. Douglas Willms. 2001. "Multilevel Modeling of Hierarchical Data in Developmental Studies." *Journal of Child Psychology and Psychiatry and Allied Disciplines* 42, no. 1 : 141–162.

Bridges, George S., Darlene J. Conley, Rodney L. Engen, and Townsand Price-Spratlen. 1995. "Racial Disparities in the Confinement of Juveniles: Effects of Crime and Community Social Structure on Punishment." Pp. 128–152 in *Minorities in Juvenile Justice,* ed. K. Kempf Leonard, C. E. Pope, and W. H. Feyerherm. Thousand Oaks, CA: Sage.

Bryk, Anthony S., and Stephen W. Raudenbush. 1992. *Hierarchical Linear Models.* London: Sage.

Burruss, George, and Kimberly Kempf-Leonard. 2002. "The Questionable Advantage of Defense Counsel in Juvenile Court." *Justice Quarterly* 19, no. 1 : 37–68.

Cattarello, Anne M. 2000. "Community-Level Influences on Individuals' Social Bonds, Peer Associations, and Delinquency: A Multilevel Analysis." *Justice Quarterly* 17, no. 1 : 33–60.

Cicourel, A. V. 1968. *The Social Organization of Juvenile Justice.* New York: John Wiley.

Cohen, Lawrence E., and James R. Kluegel. 1978. "Determinants of Juvenile Court Dispositions: Ascriptive and Achieved Factors in Two Metropolitan Courts." *American Sociological Review* 43 : 162–176.

Cole, George F., and Marc G. Gertz. 1998. *The Criminal Justice System: Politics and Policies.* 7th ed. Belmont, CA: Wadsworth.

Crank, John P. 1990. "The Influence of Environmental and Organizational Factors on Police Style in Urban and Rural Environments." *Journal of Research in Crime and Delinquency* 27, no. 2 : 166–189.

Dannefer, Dale, and Russel K. Schutt. 1982. "Race and Juvenile Justice Processing in Court and Police Agencies." *American Journal of Sociology* 87:1113–1132.

Dean, Charles W., J. David Hirschel, and Robert Brame. 1996. "Minorities and Juvenile Case Dispositions." *Justice System Journal* 15:487–504.

DeJong, Christina, and Kenneth C. Jackson. 1998. "Putting Race into Context: Race, Juvenile Justice Processing, and Urbanization." *Justice Quarterly* 15:487–504.

de Jonge, Jan, Gerard J. P. van Breukelen, Jan A. Landeweerd, and Frans J. N Nijhuis. 1999. "Comparing Group and Individual Level Assessments of Job Characteristics in Testing the Job Demand-Control Model: A Multilevel Approach." *Human Relations* 52, no. 1:95–122.

Eisenstein, James, Roy B. Flemming, and Peter F. Nardulli. 1988. *The Contours of Justice: Communities and Their Courts.* Boston: Little, Brown.

Emerson, Robert M. 1969. *Judging Delinquents: Context and Process in Juvenile Court.* Chicago: Aldine.

———. 1983. "Holistic Effects of Social Control Decision-Making." *Law and Society Review* 17, no. 3:425–455.

Fagan, Jeffrey, and Elizabeth Piper Deschenes. 1990. "Determinants of Judicial Waiver Decisions for Violent Juvenile Offenders." *Journal of Criminal Law and Criminology* 81, no. 2:314–347.

Feeley, Malcolm M. 1979. *The Process Is the Punishment: Handling Cases in a Lower Criminal Court.* New York: Russell Sage Foundation.

Feld, Barry C. 1987. "The Juvenile Court Meets the Principle of the Offense: Legislative Changes in Juvenile Justice Statutes." *Journal of Criminal Law and Criminology* 78, no. 3:471–533.

———. 1990. "The Punitive Juvenile Court and the Quality of Procedural Justice: Disjunctions between Rhetoric and Reality." *Crime and Delinquency* 36, no. 4:443–466.

———. 1991. "Justice by Geography: Urban, Suburban, and Rural Variations in Juvenile Justice Administration." *Journal of Criminal Law and Criminology* 82:156–210.

———. 1995. "Violent Youth and Public Policy: A Case Study of Juvenile Justice Law Reform." *Minnesota Law Review* 79, no. 5:965–1128.

———. 1999. *Bad Kids: Race and the Transformation of the Juvenile Court.* New York: Oxford University Press.

Frazier, Charles E., Donna M. Bishop, and John C. Henretta. 1992. "The Social Context of Race Differentials in Juvenile Justice Dispositions." *Sociological Quarterly* 33:447–458.

Goddard, Roger D., Scott R. Sweetland, and Wayne K. Hoy. 2000. "Academic Emphasis of Urban Elementary Schools and Student Achievement in Reading and Mathematics: A Multilevel Analysis." *Educational Administration Quarterly* 36, no. 5:683–702.

Griffin, Mark A. 1997. "Interaction between Individuals and Situations: Using HLM Procedures to Estimate Reciprocal Relationships." *Journal of Management* 23, no. 6:759–773.

Hagan, John. 1977 "Criminal Justice in Rural and Urban Communities: A Study of the Bureaucratization of Justice." *Social Forces* 55, no. 3:597–612.

Hamparian, Donna, Linda Estep, Susan Muntean, Ramon Priestino, Robert Swisher, Paul Wallace, and Joslyn White. 1982. *Youth in Adult Courts: Between Two Worlds.* Washington, DC: U.S. Department of Justice, Office of Juvenile Justice and Delinquency Prevention.

Hardy, Melissa A., and Lawrence Hazelrigg. 1999. "A Multilevel Model of Early Retirement Decisions among Autoworkers in Plants with Different Futures." *Research on Aging* 21, no. 2 : 275 – 303.

Hasenfeld, Yeheskel, and Paul P. L. Cheung. 1985. "The Juvenile Court as a People-Processing Organization: A Political Economy Perspective." *American Journal of Sociology* 90 : 801 – 824.

Hawkins, Darnell, John H. Laub, and Janet L. Lauritsen. 1998. "Race, Ethnicity, and Serious Juvenile Offenders." In *Serious and Violent Juvenile Offenders: Risk Factors and Successful Interventions*, ed. Rolf Loeber and David Farrington. Thousand Oaks, CA: Sage.

Hawkins, Darnell F., John H. Laub, Janet L. Lauritsen, and Lynn Cothern. 2000. *Race, Ethnicity, and Serious and Violent Juvenile Offending*. Washington, DC: U.S. Office of Juvenile Justice and Delinquency Prevention.

Heuser, James P. 1985. *Juveniles Arrested for Serious Felony Crimes in Oregon and "Remanded" to Adult Criminal Courts: A Statistical Study*. Salem, OR: Oregon Department of Justice, Crime Analysis Center.

Hofmann, David A. 1997. "An Overview of the Logic and Rationale of Hierarchical Linear Models." *Journal of Management* 23, no. 6 : 723 – 744.

Johnson, David R., and Laurie K. Scheuble. 1991. "Gender Bias in the Disposition of Juvenile Court Referrals: The Effects of Time and Location." *Criminology* 29, no. 4 : 677 – 698.

Johnson, James B., and Philip E. Secret. 1995. "The Effects of Court Structure on Juvenile Court Decisionmaking." *Journal of Criminal Justice* 23 : 63 – 82.

Kempf, Kimberly L., and Roy L. Austin. 1986. "Older and More Recent Evidence on Racial Discrimination in Sentencing." *Journal of Quantitative Criminology* 2, no. 1 : 29 – 47.

Kempf, Kimberly L., Scott Decker, and Robert Bing. 1990. *An Analysis of Apparent Disparities in the Handling of Black Youth within Missouri's Juvenile Justice Systems*. Jefferson City: Missouri Department of Public Safety.

Krisberg, Barry, Paul Litsky, and Ira Schwartz. 1984. "Youth in Confinement: Justice by Geography." *Journal of Research in Crime and Delinquency* 21 : 153 – 181.

Krisberg, B., I. Schwartz, G. Fishman, Z. Eisikovits, E. Guttman, and K. Joe. 1987. "The Incarceration of Minority Youth." *Crime and Delinquency* 33, no. 2 : 173 – 205.

Lee, Valerie E. 2000. "Using Hierarchical Linear Modeling to Study Social Contexts: The Case of School Effects." *Educational Psychologist* 35, no. 2 : 125 – 141.

Leonard, Kimberly, and Henry Sontheimer. 1995. "The Role of Race in Juvenile Justice in Pennsylvania." Pp. 98 – 127 in *Minorities in Juvenile Justice*, ed. K. Kempf Leonard, C. E. Pope, and W. H. Feyerherm. Thousand Oaks, CA: Sage.

Levin, Martin A. 1975. "Delay in Five Criminal Courts." *Journal of Legal Studies* 4, no. 1 : 83 – 131.

Lockhart, Lettie L., P. David Kurtz, Richard Sutphen, and Kenneth Gauger. 1991. "Georgia's Juvenile Justice System: A Retrospective Investigation of Racial Disparity." Athens: School of Social Work, University of Georgia.

Massey, Douglas S., and Nancy A. Denton. 1988. "The Dimensions of Residential Segregation." *Social Forces* 67 : 281 – 315.

Matza, David. 1964. *Delinquency and Drift*. New York: Wiley.

McGarrell, Edmund F. 1991. "Differential Effects of Juvenile Justice Reform on Incarceration Rates of the States." *Crime and Delinquency* 37 : 262 – 280.

————. 1993. "Trends in Racial Disproportionality in Juvenile Court Processing, 1985–1989." *Crime and Delinquency* 39:29–48.

McNulty, Elizabeth. 1996. *Arizona Juvenile Transfer Study: Juveniles Transferred to Adult Court, 1994.* Phoenix: Administrative Office of the Courts, Arizona Supreme Court.

Myers, Martha, and Susan Talarico. 1986. "Urban Justice, Rural Injustice? Urbanization and Its Effect on Sentencing." *Criminology* 24:367–391.

Odem, Mary E. 1995. *Delinquent Daughters.* Chapel Hill: University of North Carolina Press.

Odem, Mary E., and Steve Schlossman. 1991. "Guardians of Virtue: The Juvenile Court and Female Delinquency in Early 20th Century Los Angeles." *Crime and Delinquency* 37:186–203.

Platt, Anthony M. 1969. *The Child Savers: The Invention of Delinquency.* Chicago: University of Chicago Press.

Podkopacz, Marcy R., and Barry C. Feld. 1996. "The End of the Line: An Empirical Study of Judicial Waiver." *Journal of Law and Criminology* 86, no. 2:449–492.

Pope, Carl E. 1976. "The Influence of Social and Legal Factors on Sentencing Dispositions: A Preliminary Analysis of Offender Based Transaction Statistics." *Journal of Criminal Justice* 4:203–221.

Poulous, Tammy Meredith, and Stan Orchowsky. 1994. "Serious Juvenile Offenders: Predicting the Probability of Transfer to Criminal Court." *Crime and Delinquency* 40:3–17.

Raudenbush, Stephen W., and Robert Sampson. 1999. "Assessing Direct and Indirect Effects in Multilevel Designs with Latent Variables." *Sociological Methods and Research* 28, no. 2:123–153.

Reisig, Michael D., and Roger B. Parks. 2000. "Experience, Quality of Life, and Neighborhood Context: A Hierarchical Analysis of Satisfaction with the Police." *Justice Quarterly* 17, no. 3:607–630.

Ross, Catherine E. 2000. "Neighborhood Disadvantage and Adult Depression." *Journal of Health and Social Behavior* 41, no. 2:177–187.

Sampson, Robert J. 1986. "Crime in Cities: The Effects of Formal and Informal Social Control." Pp. 271–311 in *Crime and Justice: A Review of Research,* vol. 8, ed. A. Reiss, Jr., and M. Tonry. Chicago: University of Chicago Press.

Sampson, Robert J., and John H. Laub. 1993. *Crime in the Making: Pathways and Turning Points through Life.* Cambridge, MA: Harvard University Press.

Schlossman, Steve. 1977. *Love and the American Delinquent: The Theory and Practice of "Progressive" Juvenile Justice.* Chicago: University of Chicago Press.

Sheldon, Randall G. 1981. "Sex Discrimination in the Juvenile Justice System: Memphis, Tennessee, 1900–1917." In *Comparing Male and Female Offenders,* ed. M. Q. Warren. Newbury Park, CA: Sage.

Stapleton, Vaughan, David P. Aday, Jr., and Jeanne A. Ito. 1982. "An Empirical Typology of American Metropolitan Juvenile Courts." *American Journal of Sociology* 88:549–564.

Sung, Joon Jang. 1999. "Age-Varying Effects on Family, Alcohol, and Peers on Delinquency: A Multilevel Modeling Test of Interactional Theory." *Criminology* 37, no. 3:643–685.

Tanenhaus, David S. 2005. "Degrees of Discretion: The First Juvenile Court and the Problem of Difference in the Early Twentieth Century." In *Our Children, Their Children:*

Confronting Racial and Ethnic Differences in American Juvenile Justice, ed. Darnell F. Hawkins and Kimberly Kempf-Leonard. Chicago: University of Chicago Press.

Teitler, Julien O., and Christopher C. Weiss. 2000. "Effects of Neighborhood and School Environments on Transition to First Sexual Intercourse." *Sociology of Education* 73, no. 2:112–132.

Tepperman, Lorne. 1973. "The Effect of Court Size on Organization and Procedure." *Canadian Review of Sociology and Anthropology* 10, no. 4:346–365.

Tittle, Charles R., and Debra A. Curran. 1988. "Contingencies for Dispositional Disparities in Juvenile Justice." *Social Forces* 67, no. 1:23–58.

United States Bureau of the Census. 1994. *Geographic Areas Reference Manual.* Washington, DC: U.S. Government Printing Office.

Vancouver, Jeffery B. 1997. "The Application of HLM to the Analysis of the Dynamic Interaction of Environment, Person and Behavior." *Journal of Management* 23, no. 6:795–818.

VanYperen, Nico W., Agnes van den Berg, and Martijn C. Willering. 1999. "Toward a Better Understanding of the Link between Participation in Decision-Making and Organizational Citizenship Behaviour: A Multilevel Analysis." *Journal of Occupational and Organizational Psychology* 73:377–392.

Wang, Jianjun. 1999. "Reasons for Hierarchical Linear Modeling: A Reminder." *Journal of Experimental Education* 68, no. 1:89–93.

Waugh, Russell F. 2001. "Measuring Ideal and Real Self-Concept on the Same Scale, Based on Multifaceted Hierarchical Model of Self-Concept." *Educational and Psychological Measurement* 61, no. 1:85–101.

Welsh, Wayne N., Jack R. Greene, and Patricia H. Jenkins. 1999. "School Disorder: The Influence of Individual, Institutional, and Community Factors." *Criminology* 37, no. 1: 73–115.

Woolredge, John, Timothy Griffin, and Travis Pratt. 2001. "Considering Hierarchical Models for Research on Inmate Behavior: Predicting Misconduct with Multilevel Data." *Justice Quarterly* 18, no. 1:203–231.

10

Race, Ethnicity, and Juvenile Justice

Is There Bias in Postarrest Decision Making?

Paul E. Tracy

Introduction

THIS RESEARCH investigates the issue of disproportionate minority confinement (DMC) in the Texas juvenile justice system. Investigations of the extent
to which minorities are disproportionately represented in the juvenile justice
system, given their underlying percentage distribution in the youth population, are an important area of scholarly inquiry. The essence of the issue is
whether members of certain race or ethnic groups receive differential (biased)
handling across the various stages of the juvenile justice system. In many
ways, the DMC issue is reminiscent of the debate that began in the 1960s concerning the "dark figure of crime" and the "real" relationship surrounding race
and involvement in delinquency (see, e.g., Hindelang 1978; Tracy 1978, 1987;
and Elliott and Ageton 1980). However, the DMC issue, and inquiry into its
possible causes, is more complicated than should be the case because of the
highly politicized, and often ideological, manner, by which the issue arose
and has been pursued. That is, most research in criminology is conducted by
independent scholars and is guided by one or more theories or conceptualizations of the phenomenon with subsequent tests of attendant hypotheses.
The issue of DMC in the juvenile justice system, however, has been affected
by federal mandates, and possibly influenced by the political interests which
often accompany such mandates.

Thus, unlike the issues treated in the vast majority of criminological research, DMC has been actively raised and publicized by the federal government, which has also mandated that if states wish to participate in certain formula funding programs, then the issue must be studied and assessed as part
of the qualification process. Further, federal mandates have even prescribed
the manner in which the problem should be identified and assessed, and

subsequent interventions initiated. It is argued here that these federal mandates have diminished the quality of research undertaken concerning DMC. Most important, although the available research has yielded inconclusive findings, and does not provide strong and reliable evidence of systematic racism or discrimination, numerous government publications portray the results to the contrary. This only further complicates, distorts, and politicizes the issue.

The federal mandates surrounding DMC arise because the federal government makes funding available to the states for juvenile justice initiatives and programs. The federal agency which provides formula funding to the states with respect to juvenile delinquency, juvenile justice, and related issues is the Office of Juvenile Justice and Delinquency Prevention (OJJDP). The enabling legislation under which OJJDP functions is the Juvenile Justice and Delinquency Prevention Act of 1974 , as amended. OJJDP has mandated various requirements under which the states receive federal funds under the act. One of these requirements concerns the issue of DMC in the juvenile justice system which may be found in title II, section 223 (a) (23), of the act, as amended in 1988. This section of the act provides that states should address efforts to reduce the proportion of juveniles detained or confined in secure detention facilities, secure correctional facilities, jails, and lockups who are members of minority groups, if such proportion exceeds the proportion that such groups represent in the general population. In order that states would approach the determination of DMC in a focused, comprehensive and systematic manner, OJJDP published in the *Federal Register* of August 8, 1989, a set of rules or requirements for implementing title II, section 223 (a) (23). The OJJDP guidelines call for a two-stage process: (1) states must document whether minority juveniles are disproportionately detained or confined in secure detention or correctional facilities, jails, or lockups, in relation to their proportion of the youth population; and (2) if documentation on these issues is unavailable, or alternatively, if it is available and demonstrates that minorities are disproportionately detained or confined in relation to their proportion in the youth population, states must provide a strategy for addressing DMC in the juvenile justice system.

OJJDP subsequently decided that the original guidelines were insufficient and promulgated another set of regulations. The revised guidelines (*Federal Register,* May 31, 1995) require that (1) states must provide a completed assessment of DMC including the identification and explanation of differences in arrest, diversion, and adjudication rates; court dispositions other than incarceration; the rates and periods of prehearing detention in and commitments to secure facilities; and transfers to adult court; and (2) when DMC is found, the state must provide a time-limited plan for reducing disproportionate confinement. In essence, the new OJJDP guidelines assume that the mere presence of DMC represents evidence that such overrepresentation is illegitimate and, therefore, discriminatory. Alternatively, DMC in the juvenile justice system, including both disproportionate detention and postadjudication confinement rates, may be quite legitimate, explainable, and justified owing to legally permissible factors. Simply, there are two alternative scenarios. There is a "differential selection" or bias thesis which argues that minority youth are *more likely* than white youth to be arrested, detained, adjudicated, and incarcerated regardless of the nature, extent, and quality of their delinquent acts and prior criminal history. Alternatively there is also a "differential involvement" thesis which posits that minority youth are differentially handled by the system owing to a variety of factors such as a more serious current offense (e.g., personal violence or drug violations), a more extensive prior record, accelerating recidivism, or even a history of previous lenient dispositions which have failed. Unlike the differential selection thesis, which posits racial bias or the stereotyping of minorities as more dangerous, the differential involvement approach posits legitimate, legally permissible factors which result in the harsher handling of certain cases.

It is noteworthy that OJJDP adopted the differential selection thesis, despite the absence of evidence supporting such a conclusion, and by so doing diminishes what could have been a significant policy initiative. That is, investigation of DMC is desirable, as it might lead to remedying system biases where such biases are exist. But, by adopting a presumptive stance that DMC is caused by racial bias (i.e., differential selection), less attention is paid to differential involvement and the investigation of the factors responsibility for the more frequent delinquency of minority youth. How did such a presumptive stance on DMC become part of a federal legislative mandate? Two notable commentators on the history of OJJDP, Feyerherm (1995) and Howell (1997), have maintained that the origins of DMC relate to specific developments in the late 1980s. Feyerherm (1995) has pointed out that the first reference to the DMC issue in legislative annals was the testimony of Ira Schwartz in 1986 before the Subcommittee on Human Resources of the United States House of Representatives. Feyerherm notes that Schwartz informed Congress that "Minority youth now comprise more than half of all the juveniles incarcerated in public detention and correctional facilities in the United States and that despite widely held perceptions to the contrary, there is recent research showing that minority youth do not account for a substantially disproportionate amount of serious crime. However, minority youth stand a much greater chance of being arrested than white youth, and once arrested, appear to be at great risk of being charged with more serious offenses than whites who are involved in comparable levels of delinquency" (Schwartz 1986, 5; as cited in Feyerherm 1995, 7–8). Schwartz and others also suggested that minority overrepresentation in detention centers *does not seem to be a function of greater minority involvement in serious juvenile crime* (Schwartz et al. 1987, 233; emphasis added).

Of course, it is more than arguable whether the observations of Schwartz and his colleagues about the relative criminality of minority as opposed to white youth, and about the comparability of levels of offending, are valid. Indeed, there was available, both prior to and about the same time as his congressional testimony, substantial evidence which disputes these observations. This evidence was available with respect to (1) racial overrepresentation in arrest and prison data (see, for example, Blumstein 1982), (2) studies of official delinquency (see, for example Wolfgang, Figlio, and Sellin 1972; Hindelang 1978; Hamparian et al. 1978, 1985; Shannon 1980; and, particularly, Tracy, Wolfgang, and Figlio 1985), and (3) self-report studies of delinquency (Tracy 1978; Hindelang, Hirschi, and Weis 1979, 1981; and Elliott and Ageton 1980). In fact, the research by Tracy, Wolfgang, and Figlio (1985) with the 1958 Philadelphia birth cohort was funded by OJJDP, and the findings were well publicized and distributed by OJJDP itself prior to the Schwartz testimony.

Feyerherm (1995) and Howell (1997), the former director of the National Institute of Juvenile Justice and Delinquency Prevention and deputy director of OJJDP, are in agreement that another crucial development in the origin of DMC mandates was the lobbying efforts of the National Coalition of State Juvenile Justice Advisory Groups (now called the Coalition for Juvenile Justice). Feyerherm (1995, 9) has indicated that the coalition began raising the problem of DMC in two annual reports (National Coalition of State Juvenile Justice Advisory Groups 1987, 1989) to Congress, and as a featured topic during its 1988 meeting. Howell has shown that the coalition informed Congress in the 1989 annual report that 55% of incarcerated youth were minorities and the percentage had been increasing since 1979 (Howell 1997, 37). Howell has even suggested that one of the coalition's most important accomplishments was convincing Congress to amend the JJDP Act by adding the DMC mandate (1997, 37).

A Contemporary Federal View of DMC

OJJDP exerts a strong influence over the states by its power to withhold formula funding if DMC is not investigated and documented in accord with the guidelines, and then subsequently resolved to OJJDP's satisfaction. Even though a particular state's DMC data may be entirely legitimate and explainable, the state must nonetheless develop plans for reducing DMC or else sacrifice its formula funds. In addition to the legal mandates and the threat of frozen formula funds, OJJDP promulgates reports and bulletins which provide a distorted picture of DMC nationally. These reports serve to reinforce the notion that minorities are experiencing differential or selective processing for their delinquent behavior. The message which is conveyed, whether actually intended or not, is that this harsher, more severe, or selective treatment represents racial bias on the part of the various agents of the juvenile justice system. By so doing, OJJDP perpetuates a climate which makes it difficult and burdensome for a state to defend itself and successfully demonstrate that DMC results from valid and appropriate decision making concerning real differences in offending and are not evidence of a selection bias and do not represent biased handling of minority youth.

Examples abound of such highly questionable, if not accusatory, OJJDP reporting concerning DMC. There is the widely distributed bulletin series Juvenile Justice Bulletin, including the volume *Minorities in the Juvenile Justice System* (Bilchik 1999). In his report, Shay Bilchik (the OJJDP administrator until February 2000) draws upon a national study of descriptive data concerning juvenile offenders, victims, and juvenile justice system parameters that was conducted on behalf of OJJDP (*Juvenile Offenders and Victims* [Snyder and Sickmund 1999]). Bilchik notes that "The most recent statistics available reveal significant racial and ethnic *disparity* in the confinement of juvenile offenders. In 1997, minorities made up about one-third of the juvenile population nationwide but accounted for nearly two-thirds of the detained and committed population in secure facilities. For black juveniles, the disparities were most evident. While black juveniles ages 10 to 17 made up about 15% of the juvenile population, they accounted for 26% of the juveniles arrested and 45% of delinquency cases involving detention. About one-third of adjudicated cases involved black youth, yet 40% of juveniles in secure residential placements were black. *These are numbers that cannot be ignored*" (1999, 1; emphasis added).

Bilchik (by way of Snyder and Sickmund 1999, 192), does distinguish among disparity, overrepresentation, and discrimination, and appropriately notes that these terms have different meanings and that overrepresentation is not necessarily a result of discrimination (1999, 2). Yet the bulletin (like the national report) is filled with descriptive data which nonetheless send a message that discrimination may be a significant causal factor. That is, the report details the disparities which exist, especially for black youth, at all the stages of the juvenile justice system. Of course, reaching the conclusion that minority youth are treated differently just because they are African American or Hispanic, requires statistically rigorous analyses of the data, not just descriptive tables and charts. Bilchik (1999) and Snyder and Sickmund (1999) admit that detailed causal analysis is necessary to resolve whether minority disparity in juvenile justice has its origins in discrimination as opposed to behavioral and legal factors. Bilchik (1999, 3) and Snyder and Sickmund (1999, 193) further argue that, "on a national level, such detailed analysis is not possible with the data that are available." Yet, although the requisite data are not available, Bilchik (1999) and Snyder and Sickmund (1999) make inferences which are not supported by the OJJDP data that are used in the report, or by citations to other literature. For example, Bilchik (1999, 3) and Snyder and Sickmund (1999, 193) readily admit that research findings on DMC are not consistent but still stress that data available for most jurisdictions across the country indicate that minorities are overrepresented in the juvenile justice system, especially in secure facilities. More importantly, despite not presenting any obviously necessary data to support their point, or providing citations or references to published studies which would substantiate the claims, these authors declare that "Some research also suggests that differences in the offending rates of white and minority youth cannot explain the minority over representation in arrest, conviction, and incarceration counts" (Bilchik 1999, 3; Snyder and Sickmund 1999, 193). Further, after referring to a literature review previously conducted for OJJDP (Pope and Feyerherm 1990a, 1990b, 1992, 1993) that was nine years old, the authors indicate, again with no apparent citations, that "Since that research, a rather large body of research has accumulated across numerous geographic regions that reinforces these earlier findings. Thus, existing research suggests that race/ethnicity does make a difference in juvenile justice decisions in some jurisdictions at least some of the time" (Bilchik 1999, 3; Snyder and Sickmund 1999, 193). Surely, a few references to this accumulating literature are necessary to support the opinions being offered, especially since the literature has been typified as a rather "large body of research." Yet no such citations are provided. Unsupported claims of what the research literature suggests about DMC are unacceptable in such a high-profile report especially when the right kinds of data or analysis are unavailable to determine the "real" situation surrounding DMC. The fundamental question then is, Why base such an important national-level report on only aggregate-level descriptive data? Why not use a detailed analysis of high-quality, individual-level case data that are available for a particular jurisdiction so that a proper test of causal factors could be done? If such data or such detailed causal studies do not exist, then OJJDP could have devoted some of its considerable resources to funding such a study. One has to wonder why OJJDP continues to propagate the view that "questions regarding the causes of the observed disparity and over representation remain unanswered" (Bilchik 1999, 3; Snyder and Sickmund 1999, 193) when Snyder has noted elsewhere that "A part of this differential handling can be attributed to the findings that *nonwhite youth were more likely to have prior court referrals and were more likely to be referred to court for more serious offenses*" (1990, 2–3; emphasis added).

Prior Research

Contrary to characterizations in widely disseminated federal reports, the most striking aspect of the research concerning DMC is not that it has provided substantial evidence of differential race or ethnicity-based handling, but, rather, that it is inconclusive and provides consensus on one issue, and one issue only—that the proportion of minorities processed through the various decision stages exceeds the proportion that minority youth represent in the youth population. Simply, prior research indicates minorities are overrepresented in cases handled by juvenile justice agencies, but DMC research is inconclusive in all other respects. Prior research has provided neither methodologically nor statistically adequate documentation that the DMC disparity is due to racial bias. There are crucial questions which remain unanswered. Are minorities overrepresented because they commit a disproportionate amount of juvenile delinquency? Alternatively, are minorities overrepresented because the juvenile justice system accords minority youth differential handling which selects them for processing, in the first place, and continues to expose them to harsher treatment at successive stages, because and simply because, they are racial or ethnic minorities?

A well-publicized assessment (Pope and Feyerherm 1990a, 1990b, 1992, 1993) of the DMC literature has played a significant role in the creation of a distorted image of the findings from research on minorities and juvenile justice. The Pope and Feyerherm study is singularly important because it is frequently cited as providing strong evidence that minorities are treated differently (i.e., more harshly). The study is almost always cited in OJJDP publications concerning DMC, and the citations are usually employed to bolster an argument that there is substantial and widespread evidence of significant bias against minorities. A few examples will suffice to demonstrate this. In a widely publicized and extensively distributed OJJDP report entitled *Juvenile Offenders and Victims* (and its companion piece, *Minorities in the Juvenile Justice System* [Bilchik 1999]), Snyder and Sickmund (1999) offer the following: "Further, there is *substantial* evidence that minority youth are often treated differently from majority youth within the juvenile justice system. In a review by Pope and Feyerherm of existing literature, approximately two-thirds of the studies examined showed that racial and/or ethnic status did influence decision-making within the juvenile justice system" (Snyder and Sickmund 1999, 193; emphasis added).

Similarly, in another of OJJDP's DMC bulletins, Devine, Coolbaugh, and Jenkins (1998) use only one research citation (to Pope and Feyerherm 1990a, 1990b, 1993) to justify the following appraisal: "A growing body of literature has focused on the problem of selection bias in juvenile justice systems. Much of this literature suggests that processing decisions in many State and local juvenile justice systems *are not racially or culturally neutral*. Minority juveniles are more likely than other juveniles to become involved in the system. The over representation is apparent at various decision points in the juvenile justice system (arrest, detention, prosecution, and so forth) and may intensify as juveniles continue through the system" (Devine, Coolbaugh, and Jenkins 1998, 2; emphasis added).

Pope and Feyerherm have indicated that it is critically important to examine this body of literature so that strengths and weaknesses can be determined and gaps in our knowledge be identified (1993, 1). Unfortunately, Pope and Feyerherm's fifteen-month study conducted for OJJDP does not deliver the promised rigorous assessment and does not provide sufficiently definitive findings that would permit claims as definitive as the selections offered above by Snyder and Sickmund, Bilchik, and Devine, Coolbaugh, and Jenkins. Despite what appears to be a comprehensive content analysis of the research literature, including the coding of crucial design and statistical analysis features of the studies, the Pope and Feyerherm study is basically descriptive, is practically devoid of analysis (at least it reports no analytical results), and thus provides little more than a cataloging of prior research. The specific deficiencies of the study are as follows. First, Pope and Feyerherm could have guarded against "selection bias" by providing a more detailed discussion of the exclusion process by which the original pool of 250 studies was reduced to the subsample of 46. Second, despite the coding of highly useful and analytically valuable information about the studies, there is no assessment of the connection between such information about the study and the results that were or were not obtained. Pope and Feyerherm do not appear to have utilized the characteristics of the studies in any rigorous fashion to assess the quality of the underlying research. It is questionable, therefore, for anyone to claim, as we have reported above, that the Pope and Feyerherm results provide *substantial evidence* of differential handling of minority youth, or that the study has shown that cases in urban jurisdictions are more likely to receive severe outcomes at various stages of processing than are cases in nonurban areas. Simply, there is no statistically meaningful way in which such characterizations can be validly gleaned from the Pope and Feyerherm study.

Findings from the DMC Literature

Despite federal government publications which portray a very different view of the literature, the minority processing research is inconclusive and has established no consistent body of findings. While some research suggests that race/ethnicity is a significant factor in how dispositions are administered (see, e.g., Bishop and Frazier 1988a, 1996; Bortner, Sunderland, and Winn 1985; Fagan, Slaughter, and Hartstone 1987; Feyerherm 1981; Johnson and Secret 1992), other research examining the influence of race/ethnicity on dispositions has shown little or no race/ethnicity effect (Bailey and Peterson 1981; Bortner and Reed 1985; Cohen and Kluegel 1978, 1979; Horwitz and Wasserman 1980; Kowalski and Rickicki 1982).

There are, however, a few commonalities which have emerged concerning possible explanations for the inconclusiveness of previous research efforts

(Feyerherm 1995; Kempf, Decker, and Bing 1990; Bridges et al. 1993; Kempf-Leonard, Pope, and Feyerherm 1995). One reason suggested for the variability of the findings is that many of the early studies of disproportionality focused on only one specific stage of the juvenile justice decision making process. Restricting the scope to include only one decision point limits the capacity to detect differential handling at different stages of the system (Pope 1984; Pope and Feyerherm 1990a, 1990b; Kempf-Leonard and Sontheimer 1995). Few of the early studies have examined the treatment of youth at multiple process points. Recent research has attempted to overcome this major deficiency and has focused on four general decision points within the juvenile justice system where racial bias may occur: (1) police decision to refer, (2) decision to detain at intake, (3) prosecutor's decision, and (4) court dispositions.

Detention at Intake

The decision to detain a juvenile at intake can have significant implications for subsequent stages of the decision-making process (Bridges et al. 1993). Consequently, it is one of the most important junctures in the process. Youth who are detained are more likely than youth who are not detained to have their cases forwarded for prosecution. A number of studies have found that a juvenile's race/ethnicity is a significant predictor of the decision to detain. Although many of these studies are unpublished reports of research conducted for state juvenile justice commissions, some are nonetheless rigorous assessments. For example, Kempf, Decker, and Bing (1990) studied youth processed in the juvenile justice system in Missouri. They used a sophisticated stratified sampling design and covered both urban and rural court jurisdictions. They found that African Americans in rural areas were significantly less likely than whites to be detained, while in urban courts, white youth were significantly less likely than African American youth to be detained. However, Kempf, Decker, and Bing found that juveniles' prior referrals and the presence of legal counsel were the strongest predictors of detention, followed by the absence of parents in court, felony referrals, violence, race/ethnicity, status offenses, and nonpolice referrals. Kempf (1992; see also, Kempf-Leonard and Sontheimer 1995) conducted a similar study in Pennsylvania. A stratified sample of 1,797 cases was drawn from urban, suburban, and rural courts. The results showed that detention was more common for Latino and African American youth.

In their study of juvenile justice processing in Washington State, which included 1,777 juvenile justice cases, Bridges and colleagues (1993) reported that older non-Anglo youth were more likely than Anglo youth to be detained, even when researchers controlled for a number of differences between cases and personal characteristics of the youth. This study also suggested that youth with irregular school attendance and from single-parent households were significantly more likely to be detained than youth with good attendance and from two-parent households. To the extent that minorities are more likely than Anglos to come from single-parent families and are more likely to have irregular school attendance, they are at greater risk than Anglos for being detained for committing similar offenses.

A juvenile's criminal history can (and legally should be allowed to) influence the manner in which subsequent offenses are handled. A number of studies provide evidence that findings of racial discrimination at various processing stages have been confounded by the effects of a juvenile's previous detention (Bishop and Frazier 1988a; Johnson and Secret 1992; Kempf, Decker, and Bing 1990; Lockhart et al. 1991; Leiber 1992). This research suggests that, as youth with multiple prior offenses typically receive harsher treatment than first-time offenders, studies of racial disparity must take into account the number and severity of past offense for each juvenile record examined. Bortner and Reed (1985) found that the two strongest predictors of the assignment of youth to detention at intake were the number of prior referrals that a juvenile had accumulated and his or her access to legal counsel. Youth with prior referrals were more likely to be detained for the current offense than were youth without prior referrals. Other research confirms the importance of prior referrals and the presence of counsel in the decision to detain (Frazier and Bishop 1995).

Bishop and Frazier (1988b) examined the disposition of 161, 369 juvenile justice cases in Florida between 1985 and 1987 and found that race/ethnicity was predictive of being held in secure detention, even after researchers controlled for prior record, offense severity, and other important background variables. The typical non-Anglo juvenile in this study had a 16% probability of being placed in detention, compared to a 12% probability for Anglo youth. Like other researchers, they also found that the presence of a prior record was one of the leading predictors of detention. Other researchers, however, have found little evidence that race/ethnicity affects how youth are assigned to detention. Using case records from Alabama (Jefferson County), McCarthy (1985) found that juveniles' prior offenses and the severity of the current offense explained detention status, whereas race/ethnicity was not a significant predictor. McCarthy and Smith (1986) have also conducted a path analysis (more sophisticated than the usual analyses in DMC) of juvenile justice decision making, including detention and disposition. Unfortunately, the authors used "days of detention" rather than detention status, and an ordinal "disposition scale" rather than discrete dispositions. The results, which do indicate some race differentials, are not comparable to other studies, and the design suffers from "omitted variable bias," as the severity of prior offenses was not included in the analysis.

Prosecutor's Decision

Further penetration in the juvenile justice system is achieved when petitions are filed by the prosecuting attorney. The decision to file petitions with the juvenile court for adjudication of youth is generally made by the prosecuting attorney. The most consistent finding at this decision point is that, regardless of their race/ethnicity, youth who are detained prior to adjudication are much more likely to be subsequently charged with offenses and confront court hearings than youth who are not detained (Bridges et al. 1993; Kempf 1992). However, prior research has not documented a consistent association between race/ethnicity and the decision to file court petitions. Kempf, Decker, and Bing (1990) did not find a relationship between race and the petition decision in Missouri. Yet Kempf (1992) found that, in both urban and rural juvenile justice jurisdictions in Pennsylvania, petitions were filed more often for African American youth than for Anglo youth. In addition, youth from single-parent households or youth with alcohol abuse problems were more likely to have petitions filed against them. Bridges and colleagues (1993) examined factors associated with court referrals of felonies and violent offenses and found that non-Anglo youth were more likely than their Anglo peers to be charged with an offense, even when controls for case-specific differences were taken into account. However, other findings in this same study suggested that, in some instances, non-Anglo youth were less likely to have petitions filed against them. Non-Anglo youth, especially Hispanics with prior records of being diverted (away from prosecution), were more likely than Anglo youth to be diverted for subsequent offenses. The petition-stage results are clouded even further by the Leiber (1992) study in Iowa which found that in County A there was no race effect, while in County B minority youth were significantly less likely to be petitioned to court than whites.

Bishop and Frazier's (1996) examination of juvenile cases in Florida indicates that, like the decision to detain, prosecutorial decision making is significantly influenced by the seriousness of the offense and by prior records for a given juvenile case, yet it is only slightly influenced by race/ethnicity. They report that in relation to its impact on detention status, "The impact of race is very modest: the typical white youth has a 32% chance of being referred to court, compared to a 34% chance for the typical nonwhite youth" (404). They also find that gender and age influence the probability of court referrals.

Disposition

A review of the literature suggests, but not very conclusively, that the disposition of juvenile court hearings disfavor minority youth and that sentences resulting in confinement are disproportionately higher for minority youth than for Anglo youth. Researchers have found that, when compared with Anglo youth, African American youth are more likely to have their cases adjudicated (Huizinga and Elliot 1987; Fagan, Slaughter, and Hartstone 1987) and are less likely to have their cases dismissed (Kempf, Decker, and Bing 1990). Among a sample of juvenile cases examined by Fagan, Slaughter, and Hartstone (1987), African Americans were less likely than Anglos to have their cases dismissed, except in more serious offenses. Kempf, Decker, and Bing (1990) suggest that the differential treatment of youth might be explained by the type of counsel they have access to, and that "there is evidence that black youths who commit serious offenses are more likely to admit their guilt, while their white counterparts may plead to lesser charges with a private attorney" (1990, 17).

Race/ethnicity has been found to be a predictor of dispositions, even with controls for relevant legal criteria such as prior record, severity of the offense, and the type and level of injury or damage (Bishop and Frazier 1988a, 1988b, 1996; Bortner, Sunderland, and Winn 1985; Fagan Slaughter, and Hartstone 1987). Bridges and colleagues (1993) found that race/ethnicity was directly related to confinement sentences, a pattern that persisted even after adjustments were made in the seriousness of offenses, prior record, juvenile's age, and other legally relevant characteristics. Other research concerning the likelihood of an adjudication or a disposition which imposes confinement has not found consistent racial differentials. Kempf, Decker, and Bing (1990) did not find significant race effects in Missouri for either dispositions or sentences. Similarly, in Kempf's (1992; Kempf-Leonard and Sontheimer 1995) research in Pennsylvania, African American youth were significantly less likely than whites to receive unfavorable court adjudications. The absence of race effects at adjudication and sentencing has also been reported by Leiber (1992).

Yet higher rates of detention among minority youth may increase the likelihood of their being sentenced to confinement following adjudication. Bridges, Conley, Engen, and Price-Spratlen (1995) found that minority youth in their sample were, on average, prosecuted at substantially higher rates than Anglos. They attributed this finding to the significantly increased likelihood of prosecution for minority youth with prior records of juvenile court referral, and for youth detained prior to adjudication. As minority youth are much more likely than their Anglo counterparts to be detained prior to adjudication, they are at greater risk for more serious punitive measures, including confinement, within the juvenile justice system. Besides prior offenses and the seriousness of the current offense(s), other personal and demographic characteristics can influence outcomes. The location of the juvenile court (Kempf-Leonard and Sontheimer 1995) can make a difference. In some cases, urban courts have been found to be more evenhanded in their processing of minorities than are rural courts (Bridges et al. 1993; Kempf-Leonard and Sontheimer 1995).

Limitations of Prior Research

It is clear that research investigating differential minority processing across various stages of the juvenile justice system has not produced a consistent body of findings, and certainly has not yielded consistent evidence that minority youth are handled differently as a major consequence of race or ethnicity. Some studies find differential handling at certain stages but not at others. Some studies find urban versus rural differentials, while other studies find the reverse. Still other research finds no racial differentials at all and, instead, has determined that youth (regardless of race or ethnicity) proceed further and further through the various stages of the system and receive unfavorable decisions at these stages because of the severity of their present conduct and/or the frequency and severity of their prior delinquent conduct. Despite the view maintained in OJJDP publications to the contrary, "substantial" evidence of systematic racial discrimination is simply not available.

Of course, there may be numerous explanations for the inconsistency of prior research. A few of the more obvious possibilities are offered below. First, the inconclusiveness of earlier research may be a function of the research design and statistical methodology used. A great deal of the previous research has relied primarily on bivariate statistical techniques and has thereby been restricted to examining associations between race/ethnicity and other variables one by one. Furthermore, the findings of differential handling from these studies are very probably confounded by the uncontrolled variance of other key variables. For instance, while researchers could empirically verify racial differences among youth in court dispositions, they were unable to determine whether (1) these differences were attributed to racial bias within the courts, (2) they were due to differences in the severity or the types of offenses that Anglo and non-Anglo youth committed, or (3) they collectively represented an artifact of disparities during earlier stages in juvenile justice processing.

In order to address these and other questions, recent research has incorporated more rigorous statistical techniques, such as regression analysis, and these more rigorous techniques have allowed researchers to control for a number of critical variables and to examine and explain outcomes at individual decision points. However, even though more recent studies have utilized rigorous techniques, such as logistic regression, multivariate models have not always been used correctly. Two studies widely noted in support of DMC demonstrate this. First, an analysis by Feld (1989, 1995) demonstrates the dangers of using advanced statistical techniques incorrectly. Feld used statewide data for Minnesota from 1986 and selected all cases from the largest

county, Hennepin (containing Minneapolis), as it also had the highest proportion of minority youth according to census data. After presenting a series of
all-too-familiar bivariate analyses, Feld reports regression analyses of factors
influencing (1) appointment of counsel, (2) detention decision, and (3) out-of-
home or secure placement. The problem with Feld's analyses is simply that
he used ordinary least squares (OLS) regression analysis with binary dependent variables. Ordinary least squares statistical analysis procedures are totally inappropriate under such circumstances. There is every reason to believe, therefore, that Feld's findings are meaningless and are merely an artifact
of using inappropriate statistical analyses. Second, a paper by Austin (1995)
analyzes aggregate data on arrests, dispositions, and confinement data for
California and case-level data covering the point of arrest through final court
disposition. Austin's aggregate data findings indicated that minorities, especially African Americans, are overrepresented in California's juvenile justice
system (1995, tables 7.1–7.5). However, the assessment of whether such overrepresentation was legitimate was reported through the use of cell percentage comparisons based on contingency table analysis without any accompanying significance tests or measures of association to assess the quality and
strength of the results. Using only these rudimentary analyses, Austin concluded that African American youth were disadvantaged at both stages of
juvenile processing. We learn only in a footnote (n. 4) that a logistic analysis
was conducted and showed a "residual ethnic effect," but one for which "the
effects of race were clearly diminished." How small was the residual effect?
How diminished was the race factor after using a powerful technique (logistic analysis) compared to the much more limited technique of contingency
tables? Which background factors were significant predictors of the processing decisions? Austin provides no answer to these crucial questions.

Second, previous research has analyzed the administration of juvenile justice only in selected jurisdictions in a particular area (e.g., Kempf, Decker,
and Bing 1990), revealing considerable variation among jurisdictions regarding how juvenile justice is administered to minorities. By overlooking important regional and area differences in how juvenile justice cases are processed, the generalizability of these studies has been severely constrained
(Bridges et al. 1995).

Last, the focus of most prior research has been almost exclusively on the
characteristics of cases and their outcomes, without consideration of the
views and perceptions of juvenile justice practitioners (Kempf 1992; Kempf-
Leonard, Pope, and Feyerherm 1995; Bridges et al. 1995). Because such views
may affect the processing of youth accused of offenses, not accounting for
this information in their analyses limits previous studies to only partially addressing the issue of racial disparity. Bridges and Steen (1998) have recently
provided a very persuasive argument in this regard. They note: "A critical but

overlooked concern is how court officials' perceptions of juvenile offenders contribute to racial differences in legal dispositions. Differing perceptions of youth and their crimes may legitimate racial disparities in official assessments of a youth's dangerousness and risks of future criminal behavior. They also may foster the differential treatment of minority and white offenders in the disposition of criminal cases" (1998, 554). Although the Bridges and Steen study did not find significant racial differentials, and in fact found that case characteristics mediated the relationship between race and perceived risk, the study is important for developing such an innovative approach to DMC research—including practitioner judgments as part of the analysis of outcomes. Further research should endeavor to follow this example.

The Present Study

The present study covers three Texas counties. The research relied on a combination of data: aggregate arrests, juvenile referral data compiled by state agencies, and survey data, to provide a comprehensive picture of juvenile processing in Texas. In attending to many of the suggestions and limitations of previous studies, this study takes these concerns seriously. First, juvenile processing at various stages (detention at intake, referral to the prosecutor, prosecutor's decision, and court disposition) are examined. Second, the research focuses on Anglo, African American, and Hispanic youth and females, thus ensuring that the study covers as wide a rage of possible disparity as possible across two urban counties and one rural county. Last, multivariate statistical techniques were used to test for correlates of juvenile processing.

Methods

Sample Selection

In Texas, because juvenile cases are processed at the county level, as juvenile probation departments and courts are organized along county lines, we selected three Texas counties: two urban, referred to as County 1 and County 2, and one rural, referred to as County 3. The counties were chosen because they reflect very different environments (very large urban, large urban, and small rural) and thus constitute very different contexts for the occurrence of delinquent acts in the first place, and different local cultures for the processing of delinquency cases. The first step was to determine the number of overall referrals and youth (a juvenile could have multiple referrals) for the specified time period. The most serious offense was always listed as the reason for referral. The next step involved selecting youth whose last referrals fell within the indicated time period. This restriction was necessary for two important reasons. First, the sociodemographic data available were accurate only for the most recent referral. This sampling strategy also precluded the sampling of youth who were in the system during the 1993–94 period but who had referrals after 1994. By sampling in this way, all of the final dispositions for cases processed during 1993–94 were available by the time data collection efforts began in 1995. In County 3, researchers had to access all cases processed during 1990–95 to obtain a large enough sample. Second, to avoid any bias created by the presence of a few multiple offenders, researchers allowed only one referral per juvenile in this sample. If a juvenile had multiple referrals during the specified time period, only the last was selected.

For County 1, 62,101 referrals were accessed from 35,583 youth, representing 1.8 referrals per juvenile. Researchers identified 27,591 individuals whose last referral occurred between 1993 and 1994. In other words, at the time the study was initiated in 1995, none of these youth had any subsequent referrals, and the most recent referral in 1993 or 1994 appeared as the last entry in the database. From this pool of individuals, 2,000 nonduplicate cases involving felonies and misdemeanors were randomly selected (see table 10.1). Another 2,000 nonduplicate cases involving status offenses were also selected. Details on the racial/ethnic and gender composition are provided in table 10.1. Generally, for misdemeanors and felonies, each racial/ethnic group represented approximately one-third of all juvenile referrals. The majority of cases involved males. For status offenses, however, Anglo youth accounted for about 50% of the cases in the data set. Similar breakdowns are presented for County 2 and County 3.

For County 2, 15,142 referrals were accessed from 7,089 youth, representing 2.1 referrals per juvenile. Researchers identified 4,857 individuals whose last referral occurred between 1993 and 1994. In other words, at the time the study was initiated in 1995, none of these youth had any subsequent referrals, and the most recent referral in 1993 or 1994 appeared as the last entry in the database. From this pool of individuals, 2,000 nonduplicate cases involving felonies and misdemeanors were randomly selected (see table 10.1). Also, as in County 1, 2,000 nonduplicate cases referred for status offenses were selected. For County 3, 763 referrals were accessed pertaining to 386 youth, representing 2.0 referrals per juvenile. Due to the much lower number of referrals, all cases in the County 3 database were included.

Measurement of Variables

Dependent Variables: The following outcome variables were analyzed: (1) the juvenile was detained at intake; (2) the case was informally adjusted by the intake juvenile probation officer or was sent to the district attorney (DA) for possible prosecution; (3) the case was referred to court; and (4) the case resulted in secure placement in a Texas Youth Commission (TYC) secure facility or some other alternative (e.g., probation or acquittal and dismissal).

Table 10.1: Referral Data from the Targeted Counties (1993–94)

	County 1	County 2	County 3
Number of referrals:	62,101	15,142	763
Percent African American	33.6	30.4	55.6
Percent Anglo	30.5	25.7	27.1
Percent Hispanic	34.1	42.7	17.0
Percent female	28.9	24.0	12.5
Percent male	71.1	76.0	53.5
Number of juveniles:	35,583	7,089	386
Percent African American	31.2	25.6	43.8
Percent Anglo	33.9	31.8	33.7
Percent Hispanic	32.9	40.8	22.0
Percent female	34.2	31.6	17.9
Percent male	65.8	68.3	82.1
Last Referral Data:			
Juveniles	27,591	4,857	381
Percent African American	29.3	24.3	43.6
Percent Anglo	35.8	35.8	33.6
Percent Hispanic	32.7	37.8	22.3
Percent female	36.7	34.6	18.1
Percent male	70.1	67.8	82.2
Sample of misdemeanors and felonies:			
Juveniles	2,000	2,000	371
Percent African American	34.3	26.5	44.2
Percent Anglo	31.3	36.5	33.7
Percent Hispanic	34.5	37.0	22.1
Percent Female	30.0	32.3	17.8
Percent Male	70.1	67.8	82.2
Sample of status offenses:			
Juveniles	2,000	506	6
Percent African American	22.0	13.0	16.7
Percent Anglo	52.8	48.6	50.0
Percent Hispanic	25.3	38.3	33.3
Percent female	66.9	71.3	50.0
Percent male	33.2	28.7	50.0

Independent Variables: In addition to basic demographic variables, we focused on a set of independent variables present in all three counties. A description of the independent variables present in all three data sets follows, as well as how they were defined and operationalized. Descriptive statistics for the three counties are presented in table 10.2.

Severity of the Last Offense: Following Frazier and Bishop (1995), a six-point scale of the severity of the offense was used. Because a juvenile can have multiple referrals, each of which can, in turn, involve multiple offenses, only the

Table 10.2: Descriptive Statistics of Samples from Targeted Counties
(Felonies and Misdemeanors)

	County 1	County 2	County 3
Percent African American	34.0	26.5	44.2
Percent Anglo	31.0	36.5	22.1
Percent Hispanic	35.0	37.0	33.7
Percent male	70.0	67.8	82.2
Percent in school	45.0	32.2	87.1
Percent parents married	11.0	9.4	NA
Percent living with two parents	12.2	NA	27.5
Percent in gangs	NA	10.5	9.4
Mean age	15.3	15.3	14.9
(Standard deviation)	(1.6)	(1.7)	(1.6)
Mean severity of current offense	2.4	2.8	3.3
(Standard deviation)	(1.6)	(1.7)	(1.8)
Average severity of past offenses	0.9	1.1	1.3
(Standard deviation)	(1.7)	(1.8)	(2.2)
Average number of previous referrals	1.3	1.5	1.4
(Standard deviation)	(3.1)	(3.2)	(3.2)
N	2,000	2,000	371

most severe offense of the referral was included in the analysis. If the offense was a felony committed against a person, it was given a value of 6. If the offense was a felony committed against property, it was given a value of 5. If the offense was a felony of any other type (involving, for example, drugs or public order), it was given a value of 4. If the offense was a misdemeanor committed against a person, it was coded 3. If the offense was a misdemeanor committed against property, it was coded 2. If the offense was a misdemeanor of any other type (involving, for example, drugs or public order), or a status offense, it was coded 1.

Criminal History: Two variables were constructed to capture prior criminal history. First, the frequency of previous offenses was used to capture the extent of prior delinquency. Second, in order to capture the nature of prior delinquency, all prior delinquent offenses were coded for severity using the six-point scale described above. The severity scores across all prior offenses were summed and the total divided by the number of referrals (scores ranged from 1 to 15). This measure is thus the average severity of past delinquent offenses. The average severity score had a correlation of .60 with the frequency of past offenses in County 1. In County 2 and County 3, the correlation was .50.

Measurement Problems: Sample Selection Bias

The juvenile justice system has a series of distinct stages in a sequential process. In the first stage, some youth are arrested, while others are not. There are at least three other stages in the juvenile justice process within the three counties: (1) informal adjustment, (2) case sent to the DA and case subsequently prosecuted, and (3) court adjudication with a disposition of secure placement. At each of these four stages (arrest, informal adjustment, prosecution, and secure placement), the characteristics of the juvenile population are significantly and qualitatively different from those in the preceding stage. This often leads to a situation called "sample selection bias." Some researchers have argued that the sample selection bias imposed on the data by this multistage process should be corrected with an econometric method called the Heckman (1979) procedure (Kempf-Leonard and Sontheimer 1995). Heckman developed the procedure to correct for the sample selection bias inherent in two-stage data sets. His sample was composed of two groups: (1) women who were working and (2) women who were not working. The two categories of his model were women who chose to work and women who did not, two qualitatively distinct groups. Heckman could make statements about women who worked and those who did not. He could predict the wages of working women, but he could not predict how much a nonworking woman would earn. In order to do this, Heckman needed to correct for the sample selection bias.

In theory, Heckman's technique is applicable only to two-stage processes. However, Kempf-Leonard and Sontheimer (1995) argue that even though the juvenile justice process entails more than two stages, the Heckman procedure is necessary to correct for the selection bias inherent in decision making. In the current study, researchers have data to model three distinct stages. Furthermore, we could not make the kind of corrections necessary to generalize the findings to the entire population of juveniles, because we did not have data for the first stage (i.e., juveniles who were not arrested). It would seem highly unlikely that any study of juvenile justice would have available a comparable sample of youth who had been criminally active yet who had not been arrested for these activities. Also, in order for the procedure to work correctly, two assumptions must be made about selection bias. The first is that there were some juveniles who did not get prosecuted (or detained or placed in TYC), but who could (or should) have been. Since the current study examined the possibility of race/ethnicity effects in the prosecution of juveniles, among other things, researchers recognized the distinct possibility that juveniles of one race/ethnicity may be less likely to be prosecuted (or experience other outcomes) than are juveniles of another race/ethnicity. The second key assumption is that only those juveniles who should have been prosecuted were, in fact, prosecuted. We could not make the assumption that if a juvenile was prosecuted in court, there was no alternative outcome for that juvenile. Our inability to meet these two fundamental assumptions underlies our reluctance to use Heckman's correction in this study.

Results

Case Flow

This study investigated four stages within the juvenile system and the decision to handle cases one way or another: (1) decision to detain at intake, (2) decision to refer a case to the DA for possible prosecution, (3) decision to file a court petition, and (4) decision to place a juvenile in secure custody. The flow of cases across these decision points is shown in figures 10.1–10.3.

County 1

The descriptive counts of the 2,000 delinquency cases in County 1 are shown in figure 10.1, as is the attrition of cases as they move from stage to stage. Figure 10.1 indicates that at intake, the race/ethnic breakdown of the cases was almost perfectly even: 34.3% African American, 34.5% Hispanic, and 31.3% Anglo. About 68% of the cases were handled at the initial intake stage with no further processing. Of the 2,000 cases, only 641 (32%) were referred to the DA. There is an indication that African Americans were slightly more likely to have their cases referred to the DA, as opposed to being handled informally, as African Americans constituted a slightly higher percentage of the referred cases compared to intake (37.1% vs. 34.3%). On the other hand, the

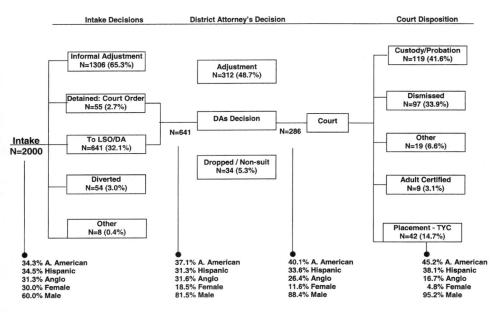

Figure 10.1. The juvenile justice process in County 1

percentage of Hispanics declined (31.3 vs. 34.5), and the concentration of Anglos was almost identical (31.6% vs. 31.3%). Of the 641 cases referred to the DA for further processing, 286 (44.6%) had petitions filed against them by the DA. At this stage, African Americans (40.1% vs. 34.3% at intake) were slightly overrepresented, while Hispanics (33.6% vs. 34.5% at intake) and Anglos (26.4% vs. 31.3% at intake) were slightly underrepresented. Among the 286 youth petitioned to court, 97 (34%) of the cases were dismissed or the individuals were found not guilty; another 9 individuals (3.1%) were certified as adults; 19 cases (3.1%) received some other type of court disposition; and 42 (14.7%) were sent to TYC for secure placement. The racial/ethnic profile of the cases which received a secure disposition indicates that, compared to their initial percentage at intake, African Americans (45.2%) and Hispanic youth (38.1%) were overrepresented, while Anglos (16.7%) were substantially underrepresented. Thus, the demographic profile at intake and at subsequent stages reflects that African Americans are overrepresented, Anglos are consistently underrepresented, and Hispanics vary between these positions. The fundamental question, however, is whether these differences are legitimate and can be explained by permissible legal criteria, or whether, in the absence of such criteria, the race/ethnic differentials represent differential selection of minority youth for "harsher" handling.

County 2

Figure 10.2 shows the various stages of juvenile justice processing in County 2 and the case flow characteristics by race/ethnicity and gender. At the intake stage, the gender characteristics of the youth show that about two-thirds of the juveniles were male, while a little less than one-third were female. In terms of the race/ethnicity of the youth, 26.6% were African Americans, 37% were Hispanic, and 36.5% were Anglo delinquents. About 36% of the cases were resolved at intake with no further processing. Of the 2,000 cases, 1,286 (64.3%) youth were referred to the DA. Compared to County 1, the referral rate in County 2 is approximately twice as high (64.3% vs. 32.1%). The profile of the cases referred to the DA is almost exactly the same as the profile at the starting point (27.1% African American, 37.2% Hispanic, and 35.7% Anglo). Of the 1,286 cases referred to the DA, in turn, 128 (9.9%) had petitions filed by the DA for subsequent court processing. At this processing point, we find that the percentage of African Americans has increased by about 5.5 percentage points from the initial intake stage(26.5%) compared to court stage (32.0%), Hispanics have slightly increased (from 37.9% to 38.8%), and Anglos have become underrepresented (decreasing from 36.5% to 29.7%).

Of the 128 youth who were petitioned to court, 6 (4.6%) of the cases were dismissed or the individuals were found not guilty, 9 (7%) were certified as adults, and 8 (6.3%) were sent to TYC. The remainder received some kind of

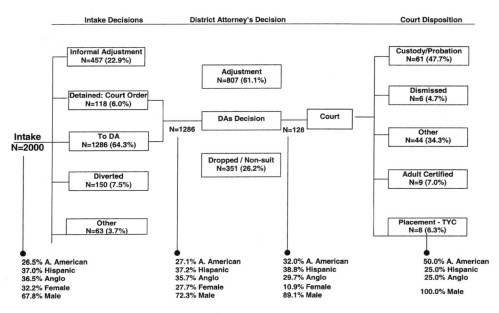

Figure 10.2. The juvenile justice process in County 2

disposition, such as probation (61, or 47.7%), or other disposition categories that were clearly not probation or TYC placements (34%). Because there were just 8 cases where the court ordered a placement in TYC, the relative percentages by race/ethnicity should be viewed with caution, as they represent just .4% of the original cases at intake. Nevertheless, African Americans had twice as many of the referrals (4, or 50%) as both Hispanics and Anglos (2, or 25%). Although the confinement cases are not sufficiently numerous to permit as rigorous (and reliable) an analysis as was possible with County 1, the analyses of the other three decision points will still determine if differences due to race/ethnicity and gender are apparent among youth at the other decision points in the juvenile justice process in County 2.

County 3

In County 3, fewer cases were available and a slightly longer baseline period was used (1990–95 compared to 1993–1994). The longer period for the rural county was necessary owing to the lower base rate of referrals, as was expected in a rural area. In County 3, researchers had to access all cases processed during 1990–95 to obtain a large enough sample. This produced 371 cases processed through the juvenile justice system. Figure 10.3 displays data con-

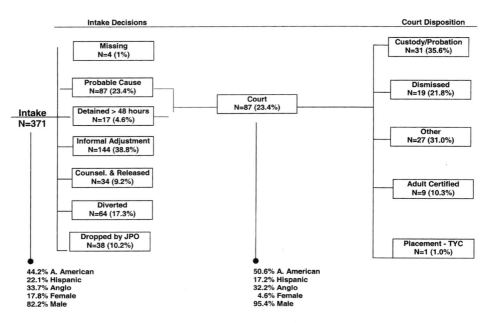

Figure 10.3. The juvenile justice process in County 3

cerning the various stages of juvenile justice processing in County 3. Because of constraints in the computerized data fields, it was not possible to highlight the DA stage in County 3. Thus, we focus on the intake stage, referral to court, and court disposition.

Of the 371 youth in the sample, individuals in few cases—only 17 (4.6%)—were detained for more than two days. The vast majority of cases, about 77%, were handled at intake. Informal dispositions predominated at the intake stage as 242 cases, or 65.2%, were disposed of at intake. The informal processing involved adjustment—144 cases (38.8%); diversion—64 cases (17.3%); and counseling—34 cases (9.2%). About 10% of the cases were dropped, and another 23.4% were referred to court. At the intake stage, 44.2% of the juveniles were African American, 22.1% were Hispanic, and 33.7% were Anglo. At the court hearing stage, the 87 cases were handled as follows. First, 19 cases (21.8%) were dismissed, while another 27 (31.0%) received an unspecified, informal disposition. The modal disposition was probation, for which there were 31 cases, or 35.6% of all court dispositions. Nine cases were referred to adult court, and only one juvenile was sent to TYC. At the court hearing stage, we find overrepresentation for African Americans (50.6%), underrepresentation for Hispanics, and parity for Anglos (32.2%).

Stage One: Detention

In Texas, a juvenile may be held in detention (preadjudication incarceration) after intake for up to two working days before being brought before a judge. If a child is brought before the court or delivered to a detention facility as authorized by sections 51.12(a) (3) and (4) of the Texas Family Code (*Texas Family Code* 1995), the intake officer shall immediately investigate and shall release the child unless detention is warranted under subsection (b). When a child is brought before an intake worker, a judge or some other referee, at least one of five statutory criteria must be met to detain him or her for a longer period of time. According to section 53.02, subsection (b), of the Texas Family Code, a child taken into custody may be detained prior to hearing on the petition only if (1) he or she is likely to abscond or be removed from the jurisdiction of the court; (2) suitable supervision, care, or protection for him or her is not being provided by a parent, guardian, custodian, or other person; (3) he or she has no parent, guardian, custodian, or other person able to return him or her to the court when required; (4) he or she may be dangerous to himself or may threaten the safety of the public if released; or (5) he or she has previously been found to be a delinquent child or has previously been convicted of a penal offense punishable by a term in jail or prison and is likely to commit an offense if released.

In County 1, detention data were measured in three ways: (1) ever detained, (2) detained for longer than two days, and (3) detained by order of a judge or referee. Two hundred forty-four youth (12.2%) were detained at intake. Of these youth, 101 (5.1%) were detained for more than two days. Fifty-six youth (2.8%) were detained after a court hearing. The last measurement of detention turned out to be the most accurate. The variable "detained for more than two days" corresponds to court-ordered detention approximately 75% of the time. The reasons for detention were not available on computer records in County 1; therefore, researchers conducted a separate analysis of the reasons for detention. In County 2, detention status was also measured in three ways: (1) ever detained, (2) detained for more than two days, and (3) detained after a hearing. Two hundred and thirty-five youth (11.8%) were ever detained at intake, 120 (6.0%) were detained for more than two days, and 117 (5.9%) of these youth were detained after a hearing. The correlation between the latter two measurements of detention is .85. Computerized records of court-ordered detentions were unavailable in County 3. Therefore, detention status could be measured in only two ways: (1) ever detained and (2) detained longer than two days. Table 10.3 provides the logistic regression results for court-ordered detention status and the predictor variables for the three counties.

In County 1, the strongest correlate of court-ordered detention status is

Table 10.3: Factors in the Decision to Prosecute a Case

	County 1		County 2			County 3	
	All Cases (Unstandardized Coefficient) (SE)	Males (Unstandardized Coefficient) (SE)	All Cases (Unstandardized Coefficient) (SE)	Males (Unstandardized Coefficient) (SE)	Females (Unstandardized Coefficient) (SE)	All Cases (Unstandardized Coefficient) (SE)	Males (Unstandardized Coefficient) (SE)
African American	.35 (.46)	.44 (.49)	.40 (.27)	.93** (.32)	−1.89** (.70)	.06 (.59)	.26 (.64)
Hispanic	.90 (.46)	1.03* (.48)	.09 (.27)	.43 (.32)	−1.93** (.73)	−.13 (.75)	.02 (.78)
Female	−1.3 (.74)		−.24 (.26)			−.34 (.79)	
Age	.10 (.12)	.08 (.12)	.15 (.08)	−.25** (.09)	−.49** (.20)		
School enrollment	.15 (.35)	.04 (.37)	−.66** (.25)	−.46 (.29)	−1.61** (.59)		
Parental marital status	.08 (.24)	.09 (.24)	−.67 (.49)	−.85 (.61)	−.31 (.99)		
Live with both parents	.08 (.22)	.08 (.23)					
Offense severity	.87** (.12)	.90** (.13)	.39** (.06)	.37* (.07)	.45** (.15)	.09 (.15)	.12 (.15)
Severity of past offenses	.13* (.07)	.14* (.07)	.10* (.05)	.09 (.04)	.47** (.16)	.21** (.10)	.15 (.10)
Number of past offenses	.12* (.02)	.12** (.03)	.14** (.02)	.12** (.02)	.26** (.07)	.02 (.06)	.02 (.06)
Intercept	−9.6 (.20)	−9.5 (.21)	6.54 (.13)	8.4 (1.5)	3.7 (.31)	3.8 (.71)	−3.8 (.77)
N	1,992	1,394	1,835	1,242	595	371	305
−2log L	189.7	161.9	195.6	154.4	62.4	8.44	4.4
(df)	(10)	(9)	(9)	(8)	(8)	(6)	(5)

*p < .05.
**p < .01.

the "severity of the alleged criminal offense." In addition to the severity of the presenting offense, significant coefficients were obtained for (1) number of past offenses, (2) severity of past offenses, and (3) being Hispanic. Each of these factors has a positive and significant impact on detention status. None of the other factors were significantly related to court-ordered detention. In the male-only model, two of the three offense-related measures (severity of the presenting offense and number of past offenses) have the strongest predictive power concerning whether the juvenile was detained. In addition, two other variables have significant (but at a less significant level) effects on detention status. These measures are (1) severity of past offenses and (2) being a Hispanic offender. In the female data, only two females were detained with a court order—too few to conduct multivariate analyses.

In County 2, the factors associated with the decision to detain a juvenile are as follows: (1) severity of the alleged criminal offense, (2) number of previous offenses, (3) being enrolled in school, and (4) severity of past offenses. Excluding school enrollment, each component is positively correlated with detention. As was the case for County 1, the regression results do not indicate that either race or ethnicity was significantly associated with a decision to detain the delinquent prior to the delinquency hearing. In the male-only model, the variables that are correlated with detention are (1) severity of the alleged criminal offense, (2) age, (3) being African American, and (4) number of previous offenses. Each component is positively correlated with male juveniles' detention status. A statistical control for gang membership does not substantially mitigate the effect of being African American: African American youth are still 21% more likely to be detained than are their Anglo peers. Various interaction terms were included in alternate models, but these effects were not significant. In the female-only data, just twenty-one females were detained. The logistic model did converge. However, due to the small sample size, caution must be exercised in interpreting the results. That is, because of small numbers of detainees, the coefficients are relatively unstable, and a small change in numbers could change the size and direction of the coefficients. Factors associated with the detention decision are (1) age, (2) being Hispanic, (3) being African American, (4) severity of the alleged criminal offense, (5) severity of past offenses, (6) number of previous offenses, and (7) being enrolled in school. It is noteworthy, that African American and Hispanic females are less likely than Anglo females to be detained at intake. The severity of the alleged offense and the number and severity of past offenses are positively associated with the decision to detain females.

Computerized records of court-ordered detentions were unavailable in County 3. Therefore, detention status could be measured in only two ways: (1) ever detained and (2) detained longer than two days. Due to the fact that fewer cases were processed in County 3, a smaller number of independent variables were included in the model. Only seventeen offenders (fifteen males and two females) were detained for more than two days. Although the logistic regression model did converge, interpretation should be made with caution. Only one predictor variable made a significant impact on detention: the severity of past offenses. Thus, an offender with relatively serious past offenses is more likely to be detained at the intake stage. There were no significant race or ethnicity effects surrounding the detention decision. Thus, DMC was not evident in County 3. A similar regression model was applied with the male-only data. Only fifteen males were detained for more than two days. Again, interpretations should be made with caution. There were no significant effects associated significantly with the detention decision. Only four females were ever detained, and just two females were detained for more than two days. Thus, no multivariate analyses were conducted.

Stage One: Summary

In County 1, three legally permissible offense measures—(1) severity of the current alleged offense, (2) number of prior delinquent acts, and (3) severity of prior delinquent acts—are significant correlates of detention decisions. All of these factors meet the detention eligibility criteria shown above. In addition, after offense conduct measures are controlled, Hispanic males are significantly more likely than Anglo males to be detained. It must be noted, in addition, that African American status was not significant in either the total case or male-only regression models. This signifies that African American youth, when the severity of past and current conduct and the number of prior referrals are controlled in the equation, do not receive detention merely as a consequence of their minority status. Parenthetically (and only speculatively, of course), we strongly suspect that gang membership or activity is a likely candidate for the significant effect of Hispanic status. County 1 has a significant delinquent gang problem, of which Hispanic gangs are a very active part. However, we were unable to control for gang membership in the County 1 analysis, due to the lack of reliable gang information in the data base. In County 2, two predictors reflecting offense-related conduct, the severity of the alleged criminal offense and the number of past offenses, are the strongest predictors of the detention decision. However, all other factors being equal, African American males are more likely than their Anglo peers to be detained. Similarly, but in the opposite way, minority females are less likely than Anglo females to be detained at intake. It also appears that age and school enrollment have a significant influence on the decision to detain girls. In County 3, only the legally permissible measure pertaining to the severity of past offenses was associated with detention status. The race/ethnicity of the juvenile has no effect on detention decisions made at intake in County 3.

Stage Two: Referring of a Case to the DA

An informal adjustment is a means of resolving a juvenile's case through community service, counseling, or release under parental supervision, among other possibilities. Some delinquency cases are not accorded an informal adjustment and are forwarded to the prosecutors. We examined the role of the same predictor variables as in stage 1. The results for Counties 1 and 2 are presented in table 10.4.

In County 1, several factors are associated correlated with the decision to forward a case to the DA for possible prosecution: (1) severity of the alleged offense, (2) living with two parents, (3) number of previous offenses, (4) being enrolled in school, and (5) being female. All these variables, except for gender, increase the likelihood of the case's being sent to the DA. Females are less likely to have their cases sent to the DA. The coefficients for African American and Hispanic youth were not significant. Thus, neither race nor ethnicity was associated with a decision to forego informal proceedings and send the case to the DA for further processing. It might be surprising, and even counterintuitive, that school enrollment would have a positive impact on the odds that the case would be referred to the D.A. However, this variable was coded "1" if any of the following was true: the juvenile was (1) attending school, (2) enrolled but not attending, (3) had been held back, or (4) had irregular attendance. Since the file was available to the intake workers, it would be likely that criteria 2, 3, and 4, if present, would lead to a referral decision. In the male-only model, the factors that are correlated with the decision to forward a case to the DA for possible prosecution, as opposed to obtaining an informal adjustment at intake, are these: (1) severity of the alleged offense, (2) number of previous offenses, and (3) being enrolled in school. Each of these components is positively correlated with the decision to refer a case to the DA for possible prosecution. Again, neither race nor ethnicity is significantly associated with this decision. In the female-only model, the factors that are correlated with the decision to refer a juvenile's case to the DA for possible prosecution, as opposed to obtaining an informal adjustment at intake, are these: (1) severity of the alleged criminal offense, (2) being Hispanic, and (3) number of prior offenses. Being Hispanic, as opposed to being Anglo, has a negative influence. In other words, Hispanic females are less likely than Anglo females to be referred to the DA's office. Youth who have committed relatively serious offenses and who have prior referrals are more likely to have their cases sent to the DA. Interaction terms were not significant for this model.

In County 2, the factors associated with sending a case to the DA for possible prosecution, as opposed to obtaining an informal adjustment at the intake screening stage, are as follows: (1) severity of the alleged criminal offense, (2) parents' marital status, (3) number of previous offenses, and (4) being

Table 10.4: Factors in the Decision to Refer a Case to the DA

	County 1			County 2		
	All Cases (Unstandardized Coefficient) (SE)	Males (Unstandardized Coefficient) (SE)	Females (Unstandardized Coefficient) (SE)	All Cases (Unstandardized Coefficient) (SE)	Males (Unstandardized Coefficient) (SE)	Females (Unstandardized Coefficient) (SE)
African American	.03 (.16)	.19 (.19)	.35 (.29)	−.02 (.16)	.15 (.21)	−.12 (.25)
Hispanic	−.16 (.16)	.21 (.19)	−1.2 (.33)	−.02 (.14)	−.18 (.17)	.45 (.25)
Female	−.30** (.15)			−.51** (.12)		
Age	−.06 (.04)	.06 (.05)	.08 (.09)	.03 (.04)	−.003 (.05)	.18** (.06)
School enrollment	.40** (.13)	.48** (.16)	.34 (.27)	.07 (.19)	.05 (.23)	.17 (.33)
Parental marital status	.19 (.11)	.20 (.12)	.05 (.99)	.74** (.23)	.69* (.28)	.92** (.42)
Live with both parents	.28 (.11)	.24 (.12)	.19 (.12)			
Offense severity	.94** (.04)	.98** (.05)	.83** (.10)	.55** (.05)	.47** (.05)	.84** (.15)
Severity of past offenses	.06 (.05)	.08* (.02)	−.06 (.13)	.08 (.03)	.06 (.05)	.21** (.12)
Number of past offenses	.08** (.02)	.07* (.02)	.22** (.10)	.09** (.02)	.05 (.04)	.19** (.09)
Intercept	−4.5 (.67)	−4.7 (.76)	4.5 (.15)	−.93 (.62)	−.14 (.77)	−4.6 (.12)
N	1,921	1,348	573	1,666	1,102	530
−2log L	854.4	700.9	143.0	254.3	123.7	125.9
(df)	(10)	(9)	(9)	(9)	(8)	(8)

*$p < .05$.
**$p < .01$.

female. Except for the last factor, "being female," each of the components is positively correlated with the decision to refer a case to the DA for possible prosecution. Females were 12% less likely to have their cases forwarded to the DA. There were no significant racial or ethnic differences in the decision to refer. In the male-only data, the factors that are correlated with sending a juvenile's case to the DA for possible prosecution, as opposed to obtaining an informal adjustment, are (1) severity of the alleged criminal offense and (2) parents' marital status. Each of these factors is significantly and positively associated with the decision to refer a case to the DA for possible prosecution. If a male juvenile is alleged to have committed a relatively serious offense and has parents who are married, his case will probably be referred to the DA for possible prosecution. As with the models for all delinquents, there were no significant race or ethnicity effects. In the female-only model, the variables that are correlated with sending a juvenile's case to the DA for possible prosecution, as opposed to obtaining an informal adjustment, are these: (1) severity of the alleged criminal offense, (2) number of previous offenses, (3) age, and (4) having married parents. Without exception, all of these components are positively correlated with the decision to refer a case to the DA for possible prosecution. There were no race or ethnicity effects.

Stage Two: Summary

The severity of the current offense is a factor that it is not only legally permissible to take into consideration, but also is obviously highly determinative of the need to refer a case for prosecution and is the most important factor in all three models in both counties. In addition, the number of prior offenses, the severity of past offenses, and school enrollment also play significant roles at this decision point. Generally, females, particularly Hispanic females, are less likely to have their cases referred to the DA. Most important, there is no evidence, whatsoever, that minority youth receive unfavorable referral decisions. African American and Hispanic offenders are treated the same as Anglo delinquents, unless the youth is a female and Hispanic, for which the decision is significantly more favorable (i.e., fewer cases are referred for prosecution). Race/ethnicity does not significantly affect decisions made at this stage of the process in either county.

Stage Three: Decision to Prosecute a Case

The DA's decision to prosecute a case was modeled as a simple yes/no. The DA chooses to prosecute a case, or to follow another course of action, such as deferring prosecution and authorizing an informal adjustment, or even dropping the case altogether. The results for the three counties are given in table 10.5.

Table 10.5: Factors in the Decision to Refer a Case to Court

	County 1		County 2			County 3	
	All Cases (Unstandardized Coefficient) (SE)	Males (Unstandardized Coefficient) (SE)	All Cases (Unstandardized Coefficient) (SE)	Males (Unstandardized Coefficient) (SE)	Females (Unstandardized Coefficient) (SE)	All Cases (Unstandardized Coefficient) (SE)	Males (Unstandardized Coefficient) (SE)
African American	.41 (.22)	.52* (.24)	.08 (.12)	.17 (.27)	.33 (.82)	.16 (.35)	.04 (.37)
Hispanic	.36 (.22)	.51* (.25)	-.02 (.26)	-.02 (.26)	.05 (.80)	-.09 (.42)	-.18 (.43)
Female	-1.60** (.24)		-.99** (.30)			-1.08** (.58)	
Age	.07 (.06)	.05 (.06)	.10 (.07)	.10 (.08)	.16 (.26)		
School enrollment	.70** (.19)	.66** (.21)	.04 (.28)	-.07 (.30)	.22 (.97)		
Parental marital status	.23 (.11)	.20 (.13)	.07 (.33)	.08 (.36)	.17 (.87)		
Live with both parents	.001 (.11)	.04 (.12)					
Offense severity	.20** (.05)	.19** (.05)	.38** (.06)	.38** (.07)	.47** (.19)	-.04 (.09)	-.03 (.09)
Severity of past offenses	.04 (.05)	.04 (.03)	.17** (.06)	.14** (.04)	.44** (.16)	.13 (.09)	.14 (.09)
Number of past offenses	.01 (.02)	.007 (.03)	.08** (.03)	.06* (.03)	.20** (.08)	.24** (.11)	.25** (.12)
Intercept	-2.8 (.94)	-2.6 (.99)	-5.43 (1.2)	-5.23 (1.3)	.06 (.02)	-.77 (.40)	-.73 (.42)
N	616	502	1,284	846	338	222	182
-2log L	78.5	49.8	117.2	73.8	29.0	46.4	27.3
(df)	(9)	(9)	(9)	(8)	(8)	(6)	(5)

*$p < .05$.

Table 10.5 indicates that in County 1, the following factors are significantly associated with the DA's decision to prosecute a case, rather than to defer prosecution: (1) severity of the alleged offense, (2) being enrolled in school, and (3) being male. In the male-only model, the factors that are significantly associated with the DA's decision to prosecute a case, rather than to defer prosecution, are (1) severity of the offense, (2) being enrolled in school, (3) being African American, and (4) being Hispanic. All of these factors are positively correlated with the DA's decision to prosecute. Compared to similarly situated Anglo males, African American and Hispanic youth are more likely to be prosecuted. In the female-only data, only thirty-one cases were prosecuted. The logistic model did converge. However, due to the small sample size, the results should be interpreted with caution. The only factor that is correlated with the DA's decision to prosecute a case, rather than to defer prosecution, is the severity of the alleged criminal offense. Race/ethnicity is not correlated with the decision to file a petition or to prosecute the case.

In County 2, the factors that are correlated with the DA's decision to prosecute a case, rather than to defer prosecution, are (1) severity of the alleged criminal offense, (2) number of previous offenses, (3) severity of past offenses, and (4) being female. All of these components are significantly associated with increased odds that the DA will decide to prosecute. However, being female has a negative correlation with the DA's decision. If a juvenile is alleged to have committed a relatively severe offense, has committed previous offenses, has comparatively serious past offenses, and is male, that juvenile has significantly greater chances of being prosecuted. All factors being constant, females are 26% less likely to be prosecuted; however, only fourteen females in the sample were prosecuted. There were no significant race or ethnicity effects. In the male-only data, the only factors that are correlated with the DA's decision to prosecute a case, rather than to defer prosecution, are the legally permissible offense-related measures: (1) severity of the alleged criminal offense, (2) severity of past offenses, and (3) number of previous offenses. All of these components are positively correlated with the DA's decision to prosecute. There were no significant race or ethnicity effects. In the female-only model, only fourteen cases were forwarded for prosecution. The logistic model did converge. However, due to the small sample size, interpretation of the results must be made with great caution. The factors predicting the filing of a petition are, as with males, the legal factors: (1) severity of the alleged criminal offense, (2) severity of past offenses, and (3) number of previous offenses. All three are positively correlated to the DA's decision to file a petition. There were no significant race or ethnicity effects.

In County 3, it was not possible to distinguish intake decisions made by a probation officer from those made by a prosecutor. Once a juvenile has been brought in by police or other agencies, does he or she receive an informal adjustment at intake, or is his or her case referred to court? The factors that are correlated with the decision to forward a juvenile's case to the next level of processing, as opposed to being informally adjusted, are these (in order of importance): (1) number of previous offenses and (2) being female. If a juvenile is has had numerous previous offenses, his case is more likely to be referred for prosecution, but, if the offender is female, she is less likely to be prosecuted. The race/ethnicity of the juvenile is not correlated with this decision. In the male-only data, there was but one factor correlated with the decision to send a case to court as opposed to an informal adjustment: the number of previous offenses. Race/ethnicity is not correlated with this decision. In the female-only data, only four females were prosecuted in County 3 preventing multivariate analysis.

Stage Three: Summary

In County 1, the severity of the offense and school status are the strongest correlates of the decision to file a petition. When all the variables in the model are taken into account, there is a correlation between being an African American or Hispanic male and the decision to prosecute in the male-only model. This relationship between race/ethnicity and the decision to prosecute appears to be conditioned by the number of prior referrals. As noted previously, the absence of a gang variable may also be a critical factor, since it may mitigate the race/ethnicity effect reported here. In County 2, the severity of the offense, the severity of prior offenses, the frequency of past offenses, and gender are the most significant predictors of the decision to file a petition. Race/ethnicity is not correlated with the decision to file a petition or to prosecute the case. In County 3, the number of previous offenses and gender are important correlates of the decision to send a case to the DA or court. Race/ethnicity is not a factor in the decision.

Stage Four: Placement by the Court

Of course, the ultimate issue which confronts us in this research concerns whether, upon adjudication, minority youth are disproportionately (and selectively) sentenced to a secure placement in a juvenile facility. Given the range of options available to the court, secure placement would represent the harshest possible disposition. In this study, placement was generally considered to be any kind of court-ordered relocation of a juvenile to a "new" environment. In the context of this report, placement means being sentenced to TYC. The decision for court-ordered placement is modeled as an either-or decision (two alternatives). Thus, either the juvenile is placed in the custody

Table 10.6: Court Placement in the Texas Youth Commission in County 1

	All Cases (Unstandardized Coefficient) (SE)	Males (Unstandardized Coefficient) (SE)
African American	.13	.26
	(.53)	(.57)
Hispanic	−.07	.11
	(.57)	(.60)
Female	.63	N/A
	(.81)	
Age	.20	.21
	(.18)	(.19)
School enrollment	−.10	.02
	(.46)	(.48)
Parental marital status	.19	.24
	(.25)	(.26)
Live with both parents	−.12	−.14
	(.25)	(.25)
Offense severity	.38**	.43**
	(.14)	(.15)
Severity of past offenses	.07	.08
	(.10)	(.10)
Number of past offenses	.25**	.24**
	(.06)	(.06)
Intercept	−7.6	−8.3
	(3.0)	(3.1)
N	271	240
−2log L	55.9	50.8
(df)	(10)	(9)

*$p < .05$.
**$p < .01$.

of TYC or another disposition is handed out. The latter possibility includes probation, community service, acquittal, dismissal, or an administrative order. Only County 1 had a sufficient number of placement cases for analysis. The results are presented in table 10.6.

The factors that are a statistically significant component when the court orders placement are two: (1) number of previous offenses and (2) severity of the alleged criminal offense. Each of these components of the judicial decision has a substantial positive impact on the odds that the youth will be incarcerated. A juvenile with more past offenses who has committed a serious current offense is likely to be committed to a TYC facility. Moreover, each of these two factors is not only legally permissible as a criterion for judgment, but is also exactly the type of delinquency factor that a court would be expected to utilize in its decision making. Further, and most important, neither of the race/ethnicity factors was associated with secure confinement decisions; neither African American nor Hispanic status, compared to Anglo delinquent status, significantly influenced the court in making an out-of-home placement. Likewise, in the male-only data, the variables that were significant correlates of the decision to order placement were (1) number of previous offenses and (2) severity of the alleged criminal offense. The findings are identical to those for all cases. In County 1, there is no racial impact at this confinement stage of juvenile processing. In the female-only data, only two females were sent to TYC, consequently, no multivariate analyses could be conducted.

Stage Four: Summary

In County 1, it is readily apparent that the severity of the current offense is consistently the strongest factor in the various juvenile justice stages for all cases, for males, and for females. In addition, in most instances, other criminal history variables, such as the severity of the prior record and/or the number of prior offenses, were also found to be significant correlates of processing decisions. There are five instances where race/ethnicity is a significant correlate in the outcome decision; four of the instances disfavor minority males, while one instance favors minority females. Otherwise, race/ethnicity does not play a significant role in any of the other stages in County 1. First, Hispanic youth, both overall and for males, are significantly *more likely* than their Anglo peers to be detained at intake. Here, being Hispanic is the second strongest correlate of the detention decision, after the severity of the offense. Second, Hispanic females are significantly *less likely* than Anglo females to have their cases referred to the DA. Here, being Hispanic is the second strongest correlate of this decision, after the severity of the offense. Third, African American and Hispanic males are significantly more likely than Anglo males to have their case referred by the DA to court for adjudication. However, the relationship between race/ethnicity and the prosecutor's decision is conditioned by another predictor variable—the number of prior referrals.

These analyses suggest that race/ethnicity matters at two decision points in the male-only case data. However, researchers feel that the race/ethnicity effect for Hispanic and African American males may be mitigated by controlling for gang membership; however, no reliable data on gang membership were available in the County 1 data for the 1993–94 period. Moreover, statewide survey respondents report that other factors, such as the juvenile's demeanor or attitude at his or her hearing, are correlated with outcomes or decisions. Survey findings also indicate that there are significant communication-related issues between juvenile justice staff and parents of minority youth that could explain actions taken against minority youth, particularly at the intake detention stage. Finally, females receive less severe dispositions at two of the decision points. However, changes in the Texas Family Code, introduced in January 1996, are likely to have resulted in recent decisions that are more gender neutral. That is, a system of progressive sanction guidelines is now in place, which requires the judiciary to follow recommended sanctions or provide on the record the rationale for any departure from the recommended sanctions.

In County 2, with respect to the decision to detain, the only race/ethnicity-related finding is that African American males are significantly more likely than Anglo males to be detained at intake. However, being African American is the third strongest correlate of the detention decision, after the severity of the current offense and age of the juvenile. Minority females are also less likely to be detained. It is noteworthy, that African American and Hispanic females are less likely than Anglo females to be detained at intake. These analyses indicate quite strongly that race/ethnicity is generally not a factor in decisions made at later stages of juvenile processing. Thus, there appears to be no persistent race/ethnicity effect in County 2. Gender is an important correlate of many outcomes in County 2, where female youth receive less severe outcomes at two of the decision points. While this may have been true during the 1993–94 time period, County 2 staff and others contacted through our survey indicate that the implementation of the new Texas Family Code provisions, effective January 1, 1996, has resulted in more equal treatment of female and male youth.

Overall, the results for County 2 indicate, unequivocally, that legally permissible and substantively meaningful factors represent the operative criteria upon which juvenile justice officials make their decisions. Consistently, severity of current offense, severity of prior offenses, and number of prior delinquent acts emerged as significant correlates of decision making for all cases and for males and females separately.

In County 3, the most important finding concerns the fact that neither race nor ethnicity was a significant factor for the two decision points: detention and case referral to the court. Females were less likely to be prosecuted, but since only a few females were involved, the impact of gender preferences in favor of girls is not a substantial problem.

Implications

The focus of this study was whether certain racial or ethnic groups were processed selectively and differently across the various stages of the juvenile justice system compared to majority youth. In particular, the research problem involved whether African American and Hispanic youth, compared to their Anglo peers, were processed in a biased way at four decision-making stages— (1) detention at the preadjudication stage, (2) referral to the DA for prosecution, (3) referral to court for adjudication, and (4) sentencing to secure confinement—because of their minority status as opposed to legally relevant criteria which would explain and justify the differential treatment.

It was noted at the outset of this volume that the DMC issue is reminiscent of the criminological debate which began in the 1960s concerning the "dark figure of crime" and the nature of the "real" relationship surrounding race and involvement in delinquency, in contradistinction to the "image" of crime prevalent in official crime data. On one hand, the DMC processing debate was shown to involve a "differential selection" thesis which maintains that minority youth are arrested, detained, adjudicated, and incarcerated because of their minority status and regardless of the nature, extent, and quality of their delinquent acts and prior criminal history. Alternatively, the DMC processing issue also concerns a "differential involvement" thesis which argues that minority youth are differentially handled by the system not because of their race or ethnic status, but, rather, because of a variety of legal factors such as a more serious current offense (e.g., delinquency involving personal violence or drug violations which the system may be trying to crack down on), a more extensive prior record of delinquency, accelerating recidivism, or even a history of previous lenient dispositions which have failed. Thus, unlike the differential selection thesis, which posits racial bias or the stereotyping of minorities as more dangerous, the differential involvement approach posits legitimate and legally permissible factors which result in the handling of certain cases more selectively (i.e., harshly) than others. It was also shown that the DMC research literature is inconsistent and equivocal and hardly provides a consistent body of research showing conclusively that the overrepresentation of minorities has been caused by selective and racially-biased decision making. Last, it was also argued that the research literature has been mischaracterized, further complicating and politicizing the issue. Ultimately, the implication is that the suspicion of racism where none has been found deflects attention away from the real issue which cries out for attention and solutions—the reasons for differential involvement on the part of minority youth in the first place.

This study collected and analyzed case-level data for three Texas counties pertaining to four distinct decision points in the juvenile justice system. In theory, there were a total of thirty-six distinct possibilities for the differential handling of minority youth (i.e., 4 system stages × 3 counties × 3 offender groups [all, males, and females]). Only eight occurrences were found for which differential handling of minorities occurred, but not all such occurrences were unfavorable, as three occurrences represented differential handling which favored the minority youth compared to Anglos. Thus, the present study found only five instances out of a possible thirty-six for which minority youth received unfavorable system processing.

County 1

County 1 is one of the largest counties in Texas, with a population in excess of several million people. Generally, decisions in County 1 were based on three legally permissible offense measures: (1) severity of the current alleged offense, (2) number of prior delinquent acts, and (3) severity of prior delinquent acts. However, County 1 exhibited five of the eight differential minority handling occurrences and four of the five that represented unfavorable situations. First, Hispanics overall and, second, Hispanic males were significantly more likely than Anglo males to be detained. Third, Hispanic and African American males were significantly more likely to be referred to court, compared to similarly situated Anglo males. Fourth, however, Hispanic females were significantly less likely than Anglo females to be referred to the DA's office for prosecution.

While only speculation, it is possible that gang membership might be responsible for the two significant and unfavorable effects for Hispanics and the one for African Americans. County 1 had a significant gang problem, in which Hispanic and African American youth were very involved. It was not possible to control for gang membership in the County 1 analysis. However, if it had been possible to include gang membership in the models, it would probably have mitigated the impact of being Hispanic or African American. From all indications, and at the crucial final disposition stage in particular (secure confinement), there is little evidence indicating that minority youth in County 1 receive differential (i.e., much harsher) handling from authorities than their Anglo peers.

County 2

County 2 had eleven possible occurrences for the differential handling of minorities, as there were no females who received a final disposition of incarceration. Like the results for County 1, the results for County 2 indicate that, with two exceptions (out of eleven), juvenile justice authorities utilize legally permissible factors in making decisions on how to handle cases. This was the finding for "all cases" for all four decision points. County 2 did have two differential occurrences; one unfavorable and one favorable. African American males were significantly more likely to be detained than their Anglo counterparts. However, both Hispanic and African American females were significantly less likely to be detained than Anglo girls. The results indicate that, almost always, legally permissible and meaningful factors represent the operative criteria upon which juvenile justice officials make their decisions. Consistently, severity of current offense, severity of prior offenses, and number of prior delinquent acts emerged as significant correlates of decision making for all cases and for males and females separately.

County 3

The single most important finding was that neither race nor ethnicity was a significant factor for the two decision points in County 3 (detention and case referral to the court). Females were less likely to be prosecuted, but since only a few females were involved, the impact of gender preferences in favor of girls is not a substantial problem.

Race and Delinquency Involvement

The most important implication of this research concerns research and theory development into the connection between race/ethnicity and involvement in delinquency. The findings suggest that criminology can ill afford to continue a research agenda that so adamantly refuses to acknowledge the existence of racial and ethnic differentials in the prevalence, incidence, and severity of delinquency that it is unable to explain the causes of such differences. The results show an absence of strong and consistent race and ethnic differentials in juvenile processing in Texas. In fact, the findings indicate that even when such differentials occur, they do not affect the most important stage of juvenile justice decision making: the final disposition stage. Thus, the DMC issue, with its presumptive stance of racial and ethnic bias, must be reexamined, as it has for too long deflected proper attention away from the fundamental issue. That issue is the extent to which race, and to a lesser extent ethnicity, is significantly associated with a more pronounced involvement in delinquency generally, and serious acts of delinquent behavior in particular. Yet the literature continues to sidestep the issue, and offers instead observations which obfuscate the key problem and continually propose the wrong research agenda. For example, Pope and Feyerherm have suggested that "Thus, differential involvement in youth crime may, in part, account for the increasing number of minorities coming into contact with the juvenile justice system. However, differential involvement in crime is a different issue from what happens to youthful offenders once they enter the juvenile justice system" (1993, 1).

I must strongly disagree with Pope and Feyerherm. Differential involvement in youth crime is not a different issue; in fact, it is the real essence of the DMC problem. In effect, if minority youth commit more offenses, then there will be more such youth available for processing at each point of the juvenile justice process than Anglo youth. Moreover, if minority youth do in fact commit more serious delinquent acts, have longer and more serious prior records, and have even more recent court contacts than majority offenders, then they face a much greater risk of receiving "unfavorable" decisions at each and every stage of the process. This risk of what the DMC advocates call harsh treatment will be greater for minority youth, not because they are members of a racial or ethnic minority, but, rather, because the nature and severity of their delinquency careers warrant decisions such as detention, referral for prosecution, and even confinement upon adjudication. The consequence is that minority youth will be disproportionately represented at each and every stage of the juvenile justice process owing to legitimate legal criteria. It is simply incorrect, as Pope and Feyerherm have done, to separate the issue of differential involvement from the issue of differential processing. It is this artificial and unjustified separation which perpetuates the OJJDP mandates. As we have noted previously, these mandates assert that any evidence whatsoever of DMC is immediately suspect and requires further assessment in order to avoid funding problems under the formula grant program. It would appear, therefore, that valuable resources are being wasted on juvenile justice processing issues rather than devoting the vast majority of such resources to the problem of delinquency proneness and the associated risk factors which place minority youth in a complex of social and environmental factors pushing them towards delinquent conduct. Thus, the problem is almost surely one of societal inequities rather than practitioner racism, and, equally surely, the juvenile justice system cannot be expected to overcome the societal disadvantages that place minority youth at much greater risk of starting a delinquency career, continuing it through their youth, and ultimately, making the transition to a life of adult crime (see, e.g., Tracy and Kempf-Leonard 1996).

There appears to be a substantial and ill-advised reluctance among criminologists to confront the race and crime issue. Sampson and Wilson, in commenting on the available data pertaining to race and violent crime, have recently suggested the following: "Despite these facts, the discussion of race and crime is mired in an unproductive mix of controversy and silence. At the same time that articles on age and gender abound, criminologists are loath to speak openly on race and crime for fear of being misunderstood or labeled racist" (2000, 126). They have also argued, quite convincingly, that "Still others engage in subterfuge, denying race-related differentials in violence and focusing instead on police bias and the alleged invalidity of official crime statistics; this in spite of evidence not only from death records but also from survey reports showing that blacks are disproportionately victimized by, and involved in, criminal violence. . . . criminologists have, with few exceptions, abdicated serious scholarly debate on race and crime" (2000, 126–127).

I agree completely. In fact, I would also suggest that, in an effort to subscribe to the tenets of political correctness, criminologists have avoided confronting the overwhelming evidence surrounding race and involvement in crime, particularly violent crimes against the person, drug-related offenses, and weapons offenses. Researchers have focused instead on the alleged system biases and discrimination in the processing of offenders like those that are subsumed in the DMC initiative. The consequence, unfortunately, is that this diverts scholarly attention away from the crucial questions surround race/ethnicity and crime, and fosters instead the study of highly peripheral issues that bring us further and further away from the "right stuff."

There is sufficient evidence available over the past thirty years, and even longer (see LaFree 1995), that there is a significant association between race and criminality. The following represent the conclusions reached by a few of the researchers who felt compelled to stimulate the research community to confront the issue of race and crime. Perhaps at this time the discipline will muster the fortitude to confront the results surrounding race and involvement in crime, however unpleasant, and develop a research agenda competent to investigate the causes and correlates of the race effects that have so often been found, rather than focus on collateral issues (such as racially biased decision making) which are given greater primacy.

In their classic work on the subculture of violence, Wolfgang and Ferracuti noted thirty years ago that "Statistics on homicide and other assaultive crimes in the Unites States consistently show that Negroes have rates between four and ten times higher than whites. Aside from a critique of official arrest statistics that raises serious questions about the rate of Negro crime, there is no real evidence to deny the greater involvement that Negroes have in assaultive crimes" (1969, 264). Similarly, in a work that specifically focused on explicating the race and crime relationship, Wolfgang and Cohen have shown that "With monotonous regularity in methodologically well designed studies of delinquency, from Shaw and McKay in Chicago to Lander in Baltimore, and in many less capably performed analyses, the disparity between white and Negro rates of juvenile violence has been duly spread before scholars and citizens. It should be kept in mind, however, that none of these figures demonstrates that Negroes as a race are more prone to crime. They do demonstrate that the average black citizen is more likely than the average white citizen to be exposed to a plethora of conditions that result in his being arrested, convicted and imprisoned. Most of these conditions are inherent in the social structure and are not subject to control by an individual" (1970, 34).

Twenty years after Wolfgang and Ferracuti first developed their thesis on a subculture of violence, a subculture which they believed might disproportionately recruit or affect minority populations, Curtis (1989) argued for the development of a more informed social policy concerning violence, especially concerning the poverty, unemployment, and other social ills suffered by the underclass in America. Curtis observed that "Violent crime is too complex for any brief statement to be entirely accurate in explaining disproportionate minority involvement in violent and related crimes. But no explanation since the Violence and Kerner Commissions better explain the available statistics on levels of violence, trends in violence, the role of relative economic deprivation, and the independent determinant of race" (1989, 141). A similar concern about race and violence was raised by Prothrow-Stith (1991) within the context of public health issues surrounding homicide in the African American community. Prothrow-Stith, then the assistant dean at Harvard University's School of Public Health, noted that "Black men are far more likely than whites to be the victims and the perpetrators of violent acts. This racial correlation is not new. Since 1929, when the FBI began keeping racially segregated homicide statistics, black males have run a 6 to 12 times greater risk of dying the victim of homicide. While blacks are approximately 12 percent of the population, they generally comprise half of all those arrested for murder and non-negligent homicide and half of the homicide victims" (1991, 65).

As was noted in the introduction, the evidence of disproportionate minority involvement in crime is strong and cuts across multiple data sources. The evidence is available with respect to (1) arrest and prison data (see, for example Blumstein 1982), (2) studies of official delinquency (see, for example Wolfgang, Figlio, and Sellin 1972; Hindelang 1978; Hamparian et al. 1978, 1985; Shannon 1980; and particularly Tracy 1990; and Tracy, Wolfgang, and Figlio 1990), and (3) self-report studies of delinquency (see, for example Hindelang, Hirschi, and Weis 1979, 1981; and Elliott and Ageton 1980). A recent assessment of the literature by Hawkins, Laub, and Lauritsen (1998) confirms that the predominance of African Americans cuts across the major sources data on crime and offenders: (1) official crime data, (2) self-report studies, and (3) victimization surveys. The findings with respect to official delinquency are especially pronounced. For example, Tracy (1990) has reported evidence from the analysis of delinquency careers in the 1958 birth cohort study in Philadelphia: that nonwhite males in the cohort compared to white males (1) were twice as likely to be recorded as delinquent and (2) had offense rates that were 2.6 times higher for overall offenses, 3.7 times higher for Uniform Crime Reports index offenses, and 8.3 times higher for UCR violent crimes. These results come from a delinquency-career-based analysis using longitudinal data and do not suffer from the generalizability problems of cross-sectional research.

Similarly, recent results from three longitudinal studies being conducted in Rochester, Denver, and Pittsburgh on behalf of the Causes and Correlates Program of OJJDP would seem to confirm the validity of official crime research (Kelley et al. 1997). That is, the researchers constructed a measure of self-reported serious violence that incorporated aggravated assault, robbery, rape, and gang fights, and the questions were asked at each interview session and examined differences in serious violence prevalence rates across ethnic groups. The results indicated that a greater proportion of minorities were involved in self-reported violence: with the single exception of 18-year-olds in Rochester, the violence prevalence rates were higher among minority groups than among Caucasians at each age and site, and the differences were often substantial (Kelley et al. 1997, 5).

Alternatively, an often cited study in support of a discrepancy between official and unofficial data is Elliott's (1994) more recent analyses of the National Youth Survey. Elliott has noted that at the peak age of offending (i.e., age 17), 36% of black males and 25% of white males reported that they had committed one or more serious violent offenses (1994, 5). The supposedly significant point about this finding is that it represents a smaller differential than is usually found in studies that employ official delinquency records, thus leading to a question about the validity of the official data. Further, Elliott also found that nearly twice as many blacks as whites continued violent offending into early adulthood, and that the male race differential up to age 30 is close to that observed in official data (1994, 7–8). Thus, Elliott's results are more useful to explain the white-versus-minority differentials for adult crime than for the juvenile venue of such activity.

The promise of self-report research is yet to be achieved, and some of the reasons are clear. First, although the self-report technique is generally believed to provide more complete data on an offender's delinquency career, owing to the absence of the possible selection effects present in official data, it is quite clear that retrospective self-reports from respondents are affected by other effects such as recall errors and the general inability of respondents to provide a precise sequencing of the illegal acts reported, especially when the subject reports many offenses per year per offense type. This raises the issue of the validity of self-reports, especially across race groups (see Hindelang, Hirschi, and Weis 1981, 1979). Second, the usually small sample sizes and the absence of sufficient numbers of high-rate offenders preclude the generalization of results to offender groups that represent the most meaningful study subjects for research on juvenile and criminal careers (Cernkovich, Giordano, and Pugh 1985).

At this point it is difficult to conclude that self-report and official measures are or are not congruent, particularly in terms of the correlates of delinquency, because of the lack of concurrent official and self-report data (on sufficient sample sizes) in prior research. It is obvious that this knowledge gap strongly suggests the use of multiple measures of illegal behavior. The use of such data allows a cross-validation check of official delinquency measures and provides for the analysis of a host of research issues that would not be possible with only one kind of offense data. Yet, at this time, it must be concluded, as it has been in a recent assessment of the literature by Hawkins, Laub, and Lauritsen (1998), that the predominant involvement of African Americans in delinquency and crime cuts across the major sources of data on crime and offenders: (1) official crime data, (2) self-report studies, and (3) victimization surveys (see also, Hawkins et al. 2000).

I hope that future research will be less concerned with whether the extensive race differences in criminality are real or represent society's biased response to delinquency. Future research must devote more attention, and more focused attention, to delinquency where it is located most often, and on the conditions which foster the differences that have been observed time and time again. Sampson and Wilson (1995) have suggested that criminology must develop a macrosocial or community-level focus which investigates structural and cultural correlates of crime. A recent paper by Hawkins, Laub, and Lauritsen (1998) endorses and extends the suggestions of Sampson and Wilson, and offers valuable insights as to what a community-level research agenda might look like and how it might elucidate previously elusive aspects of crime. The suggestions of all these researchers are important, and we strongly urge the field to embrace this research agenda, which acknowledges race effects, then proposes a worthwhile strategy to understand and explain the effects, and then attempts to provide a basis to remedy the conditions that give rise to differential crime in the first place.

Of course, it is one thing to search for the societal correlates of delinquency and crime; it is quite another thing to convince government authorities and marshal support for the principle that the most effective crime-fighting strategy is one which addresses the underlying social conditions and factors that facilitate or predispose some people to commit crimes. Ira Schwartz, who has devoted his professional life to the juvenile justice system, has noted that "it is sheer folly to think that we will be able to tackle the juvenile crime problem effectively without addressing some of the country's broader domestic issues" (1987, 177). I agree with this view. It is abundantly clear that the most crucial problem to be addressed in the near future, and one basic to society, is the amelioration of those circumstances which lead to poverty and diminished social and economic opportunities and to poor school achievement, which in turn are all strongly related to early involvement as juveniles with the police and juvenile courts. Prevention and intervention strategies that uncover and eliminate the social, psychological, physiological, and other, as yet to be determined, influences which produce these unacceptable social and moral faults in the development of our youth must be discovered and implemented. This posture must take the form of a national policy which is given the highest possible priority and which enjoys the allocation of substantial and sustained resources.

References

Austin, J. 1995. "The Over Representation of Minority Youth in the California Juvenile Justice System: Perceptions and Realities." Pp. 153–178 in *Minorities in Juvenile Justice,* ed. K. Kempf-Leonard, C. E. Pope, and W. H. Feyerherm. Thousand Oaks, CA: Sage.

Baily, W., and R. Peterson. 1981. "Legal versus Extra-legal Determinants of Juvenile Court Dispositions." *Juvenile and Family Court Journal* 32:41–59.

Bilchik, S. 1999. *Minorities in the Juvenile Justice System.* Juvenile Justice Bulletin: 1999 National Report Series. Washington, DC: Office of Juvenile Justice and Delinquency Prevention.

Bishop, D. M., and C. E. Frazier. 1988a. "The Influence of Race in Juvenile Justice Processing." *Journal of Research in Crime and Delinquency* 25:242–263.

———. 1988b. "A Study of Race and Juvenile Justice Processing in Florida." Unpublished report, University of Florida.

———. 1996. "Race Effects in Juvenile Justice Decision Making: Findings of a Statewide Analysis." *Journal of Criminal Law and Criminology* 86:393–414.

Blumstein, A. 1982. "On the Racial Disproportionality in the United States' Prison Populations." *Journal of Criminal Law and Criminology* 73:1259–1281.

Bortner, M., and W. Reed. 1985. "The Preeminence of Process: An Example of Refocused Justice Research." *Social Science Quarterly* 66:413–425.

Bortner, M., M. Sunderland, and R. Winn. 1985. "Race and the Impact of Juvenile Deinstitutionalization." *Crime and Delinquency* 31:35–46.

Bridges, G. S., D. J. Conley, G. Beretta, and R. L. Engen. 1993. "Racial Disproportionality in the Juvenile Justice System: Final Report." Olympia: State of Washington, Department of Social and Health Services.

Bridges, G. S., D. J. Conley, R. L. Engen, and T. Price-Spratlen. 1995. "Racial Disparities in the Confinement of Juveniles: Effects of Crime and Community Social Structure on Punishment." Pp. 128–152 in *Minorities in Juvenile Justice,* ed. K. Kempf-Leonard, C. E. Pope, and W. H. Feyerherm. Thousand Oaks, CA: Sage.

Bridges, G. S., and S. Steen. 1998. "Racial Disparities in Official Assessments of Juvenile Offenders: Attributional Stereotypes as Mediating Mechanisms." *American Sociological Review* 63:554–570.

Cernkovich, S. A.; P. C. Giordano; and M. D. Pugh. 1985. "Chronic Offenders: The Missing Cases in Self-Report Delinquency Research." *Journal of Criminal Law and Criminology* 76:705–732.

Cohen, L. E., and J. R. Kluegel. 1978. "Determinants of Juvenile Court Dispositions: Ascriptive and Achieved Factors in Two Metropolitan Courts." *American Sociological Review* 43:162–176.

———. 1979. "Selecting Delinquents for Adjudication." *Journal of Research in Crime and Delinquency* 16:143–163.

Curtis, L. A. 1989. "Race and Violent Crime: Toward a New Policy." Pp. 139–170 in *Violent Crime, Violent Criminals,* ed. N. A. Weiner and M. E. Wolfgang. Newbury Park, CA: Sage Publications.

Devine, P., K. Coolbaugh, and S. Jenkins. 1998. *Disproportionate Minority Confinement: Lessons Learned from Five States.* Juvenile Justice Bulletin. Washington, DC: Office of Juvenile Justice and Delinquency Prevention.

Elliott, D. S. 1994. "Serious Violent Offenders: Onset, Developmental Course, and Termination." *Criminology* 32 : 1–21.

Elliott, D. S., and S. S. Ageton. 1980. "Reconciling Race and Class Differences in Self-Reported and Official Estimates of Delinquency." *American Sociological Review* 45 : 95–100.

Fagan, J., E. Slaughter, and E. Hartstone. 1987. "Blind Justice? The Impact of Race on the Juvenile Justice Process." *Crime and Delinquency* 33 : 224–258.

Feld, B. C. 1989. "The Right to Counsel in Juvenile Court: An Empirical Study of When Lawyers Appear and the Difference They Make." *Journal of Criminal Law and Criminology* 79 : 1185–1346.

———. 1995. "The Social Context of Juvenile Justice Administration: Racial Disparities in an Urban Juvenile Court." Pp. 66–97 in *Minorities in Juvenile Justice*, ed. K. Kempf-Leonard, C. E. Pope, and W. H. Feyerherm. Thousand Oaks, CA: Sage.

Feyerherm, W. 1981. "Juvenile Court Dispositions of Status Offenders: An Analysis of Case Dispositions." Pp. 127–144 in *Race, crime and criminal justice*, ed. R. L. McNeely and C. E. Pope. Thousand Oaks, CA: Sage.

———. 1995. "The DMC Initiative: The Convergence of Policy and Research Themes." Pp. 1–15 in *Minorities in Juvenile Justice*, ed. K. Kempf-Leonard, C. E. Pope, and W. H. Feyerherm. Thousand Oaks, CA: Sage.

Frazier, C. E., and D. M. Bishop. 1995. "Reflections on Race Effects in Juvenile Justice." Pp. 16–46 in *Minorities in Juvenile Justice*, ed. K. Kempf-Leonard, C. E. Pope, and W. H. Feyerherm. Thousand Oaks, CA: Sage.

Hamparian, D. M., J. M. Davis, J. M. Jacobson, and R. T. McGraw. 1985. "The Young Criminal Years of the Violent Few." Washington, DC: U.S. Government Printing Office.

Hamparian, D. M., R. S. Schuster, S. Dinitz, and J. P. Conrad. 1978. *The Violent Few: A Study of Dangerous Juvenile Offenders*. Lexington, MA: D. C. Heath.

Hawkins, D. F., J. H. Laub, and J. I. Lauritsen. 1998. "Race, Ethncity and Serious Juvenile Offending." Pp. 30–46 in *Serious and Violent Juvenile Offenders*, ed. R. Loeber and D. P. Farrington. Thousand Oaks, CA: Sage.

Hawkins, D. F., J. H. Laub, J. L. Lauritsen, and L. Cothern. 2000. *Race, Ethnicity, and Serious Violent Juvenile Offending*. Juvenile Justice Bulletin. Washington, DC: Office of Juvenile Justice and Delinquency Prevention.

Heckman, J. 1979. "Sample Selection Bias as a Specification Error." *Econometrica* 47 : 153–161.

Hindelang, M. J. 1978. "Race and Involvement in Crime." *American Sociological Review* 43 : 93–109.

Hindelang, M. J., T. Hirschi, and J. G. Weis. 1979. "Correlates of Delinquency: The Illusion of Discrepancy between Self-Report and Official Measures." *American Sociological Review* 44 : 995–1014.

———. 1981. *Measuring Delinquency*. Beverly Hills, CA: Sage Publications.

Horwitz, A., and M. Wasserman. 1980. "Some Misleading Conceptions in Sentencing Research." *Criminology* 19 : 411–424.

Howell, J. C. 1997. *Juvenile Justice and Youth Violence*. Thousand Oaks, CA: Sage.

Huizinga, D., and D. S. Elliott. 1987. "Juvenile Offenders: Prevalence, Offender Incidence, and Arrest Rates by Race." *Crime and Delinquency* 33 : 206–223.

Johnson, J., and P. Secret. 1992. "Race and Juvenile Court Decision Making Revisited." *Criminal Justice Policy Review* 4:124–139.

Kelley, B. T., D. Huizinga, T. P. Thornberry, and R. Loeber. 1997. *Epidemiology of Serious Violence.* Juvenile Justice Bulletin. Washington, DC: Office of Juvenile Justice and Delinquency Prevention.

Kempf, K. L. 1992. "The Role of Race in Juvenile Justice in Pennsylvania." Shippensburg, PA: Center for Juvenile Justice Training and Research.

Kempf, K. L., S. H. Decker, and R. Bing. 1990. *An Analysis of Apparent Disparities in the Handling of Black Youth: Technical Report.* St. Louis: University of Missouri—St. Louis, Department of Administration of Justice, Center for Metropolitan Studies.

Kempf-Leonard, K. L., C. E. Pope, and W. H. Feyerherm, eds. 1995. *Minorities in Juvenile Justice.* Thousand Oaks, CA: Sage.

Kempf-Leonard, K. L., and H. Sontheimer. 1995. "The Role of Race in Juvenile Justice in Pennsylvania." Pp. 98–127 in *Minorities in Juvenile Justice,* ed. K. L. Kempf-Leonard, C. E. Pope, and W. H. Feyerherm. Thousand Oaks, CA: Sage.

Kowalski, G., and J. Rickicki. 1982. "Determinants of Juvenile Post-adjudication Dispositions." *Journal of Research in Crime and Delinquency* 19:66–83.

LaFree, G. 1995. "Race and Crime Trends in the United States, 1946–1990." Pp. 169–193 in *Ethnicity, Race, and Crime: Perspectives across Time and Place,* ed. D. F. Hawkins. Albany: State University of New York Press.

Leiber, M. J. 1992. "Juvenile Justice Decision Making in Iowa: An Analysis of the Influences of Race on Case Processing in Three Counties." Cedar Falls: University of Northern Iowa.

Lockhart, L., P. Kurtz, R. Stutphen, and K. Gauger. 1991. "Georgia's Juvenile Justice System: A Retrospective Investigation of Racial Disparity." Athens: University of Georgia Press.

McCarthy, B. R. 1985. "An Analysis of Detention." *Juvenile and Family Court Journal* 36:49–50.

McCarthy, B. R., and B. L. Smith. 1986. "The Conceptualization of Discrimination in the Juvenile Justice Process: The Impact of Administrative Factors and Screening Decisions on Juvenile Court Dispositions." *Criminology* 24:41–64.

National Coalition of State Juvenile Justice Advisory Groups. 1987. *An Act of Empowerment.* Bethesda, MD: National Coalition of State Juvenile Justice Advisory Groups.

———. 1989. *A Report on the Delicate Balance.* Bethesda, MD: National Coalition of State Juvenile Justice Advisory Groups.

Pope, C. E. 1984. "Blacks and Juvenile Crime: A Review." In *The Criminal Justice System and Blacks,* ed. D. E. Georges-Abeyie. New York: Clark Boardman.

Pope, C. E., and W. H. Feyerherm. 1990a. "Minority Status and Juvenile Justice Processing: An Assessment of the Research Literature." Pt. 1. *Criminal Justice Abstracts* 22:327–335.

———. 1990b. "Minority Status and Juvenile Justice Processing: An Assessment of the Research Literature." Pt. 2. *Criminal Justice Abstracts* 22:527–542.

———. 1992. "Minorities and the Juvenile Justice System." Washington, DC: Office of Juvenile Justice and Delinquency Prevention.

———. 1993. "Minorities and the Juvenile Justice System: Research Summary." Washington, DC: Office of Juvenile Justice and Delinquency Prevention.

Prothrow-Stith, D., with M. Weissman. 1991. *Deadly Consequences*. New York: Harper Collins Publishers.

Sampson, R. J., and W. J. Wilson. 1995. "Toward a Theory of Race, Crime, and Urban Inequality." Pp. 37–54 in *Crime and Inequality,* ed. J. D. Hagan and R. D. Peterson. Stanford, CA: Stanford University Press.

———. 2000. "Toward a Theory of Race, Crime, and Urban Inequality." Pp. 126–137 in *Crime,* ed. R. D. Crutchfield, G. S. Bridges, J. G. Weiss, and C. Kubrin. Stanford, CA: Stanford University Press.

Schwartz, I. M. 1986. Testimony before the House Subcommittee on Human Resources, June 19.

———. 1987. *(In)Justice for Juveniles*. Lexington, MA: Lexington Books.

Schwartz, I. M., G. Fishman, R. R. Hatfield, B. A. Krisberg, and Z. Eisikovits. 1987. "Juvenile Detention: The Hidden Closets Revisited." *Justice Quarterly* 4:219–235.

Shannon, L. W. 1980. "Assessing the Relationship of Adult Criminal Careers to Juvenile Careers." Washington, DC: Office of Juvenile Justice and Delinquency Prevention.

Snyder, H. S. 1990. *Growth in Minority Detentions Attributed to Drug Law Violators*. OJJDP Update on Statistics. Washington, DC: Office of Juvenile Justice and Delinquency Prevention.

Snyder, H. S., and M. Sickmund. 1999. *Juvenile Offenders and Victims: 1999 National Report*. Pittsburgh: National Center for Juvenile Justice.

Texas Family Code. 1995. Vol. 3. St. Paul, MN: West Publishers.

Tracy, P. E. 1978. "An Analysis of the Prevalence and Incidence of Self-Reported Delinquency and Crime." PhD diss., Center for Studies in Criminology and Criminal Law, University of Pennsylvania.

———. 1987. "Race and Class Differences in Official and Self-Reported Delinquency." Pp. 87–121 in *From Boy to Man, from Delinquency to Crime,* ed. M. E. Wolfgang, T. P. Thornberry, and R. M. Figlio. Chicago: University of Chicago Press.

———. 1990. "Prevalence, Incidence, Rates, Other Descriptive Measures." Pp. 51–77 in *Measurement Issues in Criminology,* K. L. Kempf. New York: Springer-Verlag.

Tracy, P. E., and K. Kempf-Leonard. 1996. *Continuity and Discontinuity in Criminal Careers: The Transition from Delinquency to Crime*. New York: Plenum Press.

Tracy, P. E., M. E. Wolfgang, and R. M. Figlio. 1985. *Delinquency in Two Birth Cohorts, Executive Summary*. Washington, DC: Office of Juvenile Justice and Delinquency Prevention.

———. 1990. *Delinquency Careers in Two Birth Cohorts*. New York: Plenum Press.

Wolfgang, M. E., and B. Cohen. 1970. *Crime and Race: Conceptions and Misconceptions*. New York: Institute of Human Relations Press.

Wolfgang, M. E., and F. Ferracuti. 1969. *The Subculture of Violence*. London: Tavistock Publications.

Wolfgang, M. E., R. M. Figlio, and T. Sellin. 1972. *Delinquency in a Birth Cohort*. Chicago: University of Chicago Press.

3

Toward
Remedial
Social Policy

11

Disproportionate Minority Confinement/Contact (DMC)

The Federal Initiative

Carl E. Pope and Michael J. Leiber

Concerns about the impact of race on juvenile justice decision making have long been noted, and much research has been devoted to this issue. It is only within the past decade or so, however, that national attention has been directed to this area. In the 1988 amendments to the Juvenile Justice and Delinquency Prevention (JJDP) Act of 1974 (Pub. L. 93-415, 42 U.S.C. 5061 *et seq*). Congress required that states participating in the Formula Grants Program demonstrate specific efforts to reduce the proportion of juveniles detained or confined in secure detention facilities, secure confinement facilities, jails, and lockups who are members of minority groups if such proportion exceeds the proportion such groups represent in the general population. For purposes of the JJDP Act, the Office of Juvenile Justice and Delinquency Prevention (OJJDP) defined minority populations as African-Americans, American Indians, Asians, Pacific Islanders, and Hispanics (OJJDP Regulations, 28 CFR Part 31).

In the 1992 amendments to the JJDP Act, the attempt to reduce disproportionate minority confinement (DMC) was elevated to a core requirement, with future funding eligibility tied to state compliance. The JJDP Act was modified in 2002 to address "juvenile delinquency prevention efforts and system improvement efforts designed to reduce, without establishing or requiring numerical standards or quotas, the disproportionate number of juvenile members of minority groups, who come into contact with the juvenile justice system." This change broadened the DMC initiative from "disproportionate minority confinement" to "disproportionate minority contact," requiring an examination of possible disproportionate representation of minority youth at all decision points in the juvenile justice continuum.

Addressing the DMC requirement still involves four phases of activities: identification (identifying the extent to which DMC exists), assessment (assessing the reasons for DMC if it exists), intervention (developing an intervention plan to address these identified reasons), and, more recently, evaluation and monitoring (evaluating the effectiveness of the strategies and continuing to examine the juvenile justice decision-making process and monitor disproportionality trends over time).

To implement efforts to address disproportionate minority contact, formerly confinement, states have sponsored numerous studies at the state and local levels and published reports of their findings. There are now four national reports which summarize states' efforts at each phase since the enactment of the amendment (Feyerherm 1993; Hamparian and Leiber 1997; Hsia and Hamparian 1998; and Hsia, Bridges, and McHale 2004). Also available are the *Disproportionate Minority Confinement Technical Assistance Manual* (2000), a DMC Web site that contains tools (e.g., a video PowerPoint presentation—"Proposed Methods for Measuring Disproportionate Minority Contact [DMC]" as required by the 2002 Juvenile Justice and Delinquency Prevention Act §223(a)(22)), and other resources (e.g., a listing of and access to state assessment studies). The OJJDP Web site is ojjdp.ncjrs.org/dmc/index.html.

Additionally, major reports published include lessons learned from five OJJDP-sponsored disproportionate minority confinement pilot states Devine, Coolbaugh, and Jenkins 1998), race and arrest data (Pope and Snyder 2003), updated disproportionate minority confinement national data (Snyder and Sickmund 1999; Poe-Yamagata and Jones 2000; Villarruel and Walker 2002), and data on the transfer of juvenile offenders to adult court Juszkiewicz 2000; Males and Macallair 2000; Justice Policy Institute 2001). There is also an article on the DMC requirements (Leiber 2002), an OJJDP bulletin which provides a synthesis of the research literature on racial and ethnic disparity (Pope, Lovell, and Hsia 2002), and three books that deal specifically with the DMC initiative (Kempf-Leonard, Pope, and Feyerherm 1995; Leiber 2003; Tracy 2002).

The objective of this chapter is to provide a historical overview of the activities employed to address disproportionate minority youth confinement/contact. More specifically, we examine in detail the initial research assessments on the search for the causes of disproportionality. A general summary of state attempts to implement each phase of the DMC requirement is also provided. The discussion concludes with directions for future research and policy development.

Background on Disproportionate Minority Confinement/Contact

The traditional explanations for understanding disproportionate minority confinement/contact in both the criminal and juvenile justice system emphasize differential offending and/or selection bias (e.g., Hindelang 1978; Tonry 1995; Miller 1996; Hawkins et al. 2000; see also Bishop 2005). The term "selection bias" generally refers to disparate treatment, discrimination, and the like. The sponsors of the DMC initiative and the intent of the requirement focus on selection bias with a specific emphasis on the inequitable treatment of minority youth relative to white youth within the juvenile justice system. In this section, we provide a historical background for the systems approach to the disproportionate confinement of minority youth. We do this by discussing the intentions of those involved in bringing the issue to the attention of Congress and their reliance on (1) statistics indicating increasing minority youth confinement, (2) findings from self-report surveys suggesting few differences in delinquent behavior,[1] and (3) studies reporting the presence of racial bias within juvenile court proceedings.

As discussed by Feyerherm (1995), Congress, the Coalition for Juvenile Justice, the National Council of Juvenile and Family Court Judges, and concerned individuals (e.g., Ira Schwartz of the Center for the Study of Youth Policy and Barry Krisberg of the National Council on Crime and Delinquency) pushed for the disproportionate minority youth confinement as an issue within a justice systems approach at both the national and the state levels. For example, in 1987 Congressman Thomas Tauke, at a hearing before the House Subcommittee on Human Resources, stated that "minority juveniles are disproportionately incarcerated and we need to determine if a dual juvenile justice system is emerging" (Tauke 1987, 3).

In their third and fourth annual reports, *An Act of Empowerment* (1987) and *A Delicate Balance* (1989), as well as at their spring conference held in 1988, the Coalition for Juvenile Justice focused on issues of minority youth in confinement and the differential processing of children of color. The theme of selection bias is also found in the title of the coalition's ninth annual report, *Pursuing the Promise: Equal Justice for All Juveniles* (1993), and in the text, as in the statement "Consistent with the mandates of the Juvenile Justice and Delinquency Prevention Act, the Coalition is primarily concerned with problems directly related to the juvenile justice system itself and, in this case, its potential for 'selection bias'" (Coalition for Juvenile Justice 1993, 9).

The adoption of a systems perspective appeared to be the result of a reliance on the information provided by the Children in Custody Census of juvenile detention, correctional, and shelter facilities (Krisberg et al. 1987; see also Snyder and Sickmund 1995). Data from the Children in Custody Census revealed the presence of minority youth overrepresentation and increased reliance on confinement that had been occurring since the late 1970s. Krisberg and his colleagues (1987), for example, were among the first to show that the proportion of minority youth in public correctional facilities increased by 26% from 1979 to 1982 even though the number of minority youth arrested declined during these same years. Krisberg and his colleagues

(1987, 184) also found that African American males were almost four times more likely than white males to be incarcerated in detention centers and training schools during this time. Between 1985 and 1989, increases in minority youth overrepresentation were also quite pronounced in delinquency referrals to juvenile court, petitioned cases, adjudicated delinquency cases, and delinquency cases resulting in placement outside the home (e.g., McGarrell 1993). One must keep in mind that minority youth made up 30% of the general juvenile population age 10–17 between 1985 and 1989. Of minority youth, African Americans represented 15%, Hispanics 12%, Native Americans 1.2%, and Asians 3.3%.

A review of the literature also suggests that research by Huizinga and Elliott (1987) and Pope and Feyerherm (1990a, 1990b) was influential in shaping the direction of the DMC requirement. Huizinga and Elliott (1987) used six waves of data from the National Youth Survey covering the years 1976–83 and information from arrest records to assess the relationship among race, offending patterns, and the likelihood of arrest.

With the exception of one year, Huizinga and Elliott (1987) found few consistent differences across racial groups in their rates of self-reported delinquency for the years 1977–80. Furthermore, Huizinga and Elliott (1987) reported that African Americans were apprehended and charged with more serious crimes than whites involved in the same kinds of offenses. In their conclusion, the authors stated that "further investigation of the relationship of race to arrest and juvenile justice system processing is required if reasons underlying the differences in incarceration rates are to be more fully understood" (Huizinga and Elliott 1987, 221). Both Schwartz (1986) and Krisberg (1988) referred to these findings in their testimony before Congress prior to the passage of the DMC mandate in 1988.

The first OJJDP-funded research effort dealing with the juvenile processing of minority youth, which predates the DMC initiative, was conducted by Pope and Feyerherm (1990a, 1990b). This project involved three phases, the first of which included an examination of the existent research literature examining race/ethnicity and juvenile justice processing. The results of this examination showed that, overall, minority youth, especially youth of color, did receive the most severe outcomes, thus raising a major concern with regard to the equity of juvenile processing within some jurisdictions. The second phase involved an identification of programs across the country that addressed equity concerns within juvenile justice systems—in other words, programs that would ensure that similarly situated youthful offenders were treated in a similar manner regardless of racial and ethnic status. The results of this effort was disappointing, in that few such programs were found to exist, at least in those jurisdictions which reported the information.

The final phase of the Pope and Feyerherm study involved the development of an analytical model that would be capable of identifying racial/ethnic disparities across juvenile justice systems. In order to develop this model, two data sets were obtained from the National Juvenile Court Center for the year 1985. These data sets contained computerized juvenile justice data for the states of California and Florida. Utilizing a "branching probabilities" technique, this analysis revealed marked differences in juvenile processing within both states, with minority youth more at risk than white youth. It should be noted that this analysis did not establish a pattern of discrimination. The purpose was to identify patterns with regard to race/ethnic disparities within both state systems. Further analysis would then have to be undertaken in order to account for racial and ethnic disparities. Indeed, this was the focus of later research projects that addressed the disproportionate confinement of minority youth and will be discussed in this chapter.

In summary, increases in the number of minority youth in the juvenile justice system and the research by Huizinga and Elliott and by Pope and Feyerherm set the stage and agenda for addressing disproportionality within the context of the equitable usage of secure confinement for minority youth. Although the DMC requirement centered on confinement in secure settings, the intent of the requirement was to focus on decision making at all stages in the system leading to confinement (Feyerherm 1995). Thus, the recent change from confinement to contact really formalized what was emphasized in principle. Overall, the emphasis on fairness in case processing and outcomes for minority youth lessened the concern over why minority youth get into the system and, therefore, made the issue of differential offending an unnecessary controversy (Feyerherm 1996).

The DMC Initiative and State Compliance

As of the fall of 2003, most states that participate in the Formula Grants Program have completed the identification and assessment phases of the DMC requirement and are now implementing programs and policies within the context of the intervention phase. Only a small number of states are in the process of an evaluation of the intervention activities, and even fewer are at the monitoring stage (Devine, Coolbaugh, and Jenkins 1998). Until recently, the states of Alaska, California, Kentucky, Massachusetts, New Mexico, South Carolina, and Tennessee received intensive technical assistance from OJJDP to continue efforts in each of the four phases to address DMC. Connecticut has also just conducted a second study into the causes of minority youth overrepresentation in its juvenile justice system (Hartstone and Richetelli 2001). In the section that follows, a general overview is provided of each state's efforts to comply with each phase of the DMC requirement.

Implementation of the DMC Requirement

The discussion that follows is a summary of efforts nationwide and is based on a review of state identification matrices, assessment studies, reports, and state three-year plans. Additional reviews of the DMC requirement can be found elsewhere (e.g., *Disproportionate Minority Confinement Technical Assistance Manual* 2000; Hamparian and Leiber 1997; Kempf-Leonard, Pope, and Feyerherm 1995; Leiber 2002; Hsia, Bridges, and McHale 2004). Recall that state-specific research reports can located at OJJDP's Web page (ojjdp.ncjrs.org/dmc/index.html) under "tools."

The Identification Phase: Minority Overrepresentation Exists Nationwide

For the identification stage, documentation initially was required in the form of two matrices that indicate the extent to which minority youth are disproportionately arrested, confined in secure detention or correctional facilities, jails or lockups, or transferred to criminal court. Information is provided in the form of indices that represent the under- and overrepresentation of minorities relative to their representation in the population of youth.[2] The matrices should contain information on these decision points for each minority youth group and for at least three counties where minority representation is most prevalent. A review of the identification matrices (not shown here, but see Hamparian and Leiber 1997; Leiber 2002) reveals that states often failed to meet these requirements.

States, for example, aggregated the information into one category of minority youth and reported data for the state as a whole. The collapsing of all minorities into one group can obscure or mask the specific overrepresentation of one minority group relative to another minority group. Similarly, the failure to differentiate by county makes it difficult for states to identify areas and focus resources where minority overrepresentation is most problematic. Despite these shortcomings, the identification data indicate that minority youth are disproportionately overrepresented in the juvenile justice system and the extent of the problem exists to varying degrees nationwide. The data also confirm trends reported in aggregate form from the Children in Custody series (e.g., Krisberg et al. 1987; Snyder and Sickmund 1995) and to some extent arrest statistics as reported by the FBI's Uniform Crime Reports (e.g., Bilchick 1999) and the FBI's National Incident-Based Reporting System (Pope and Snyder 2003).

Minority youth overrepresentation is evident in every state, and while its extent is not restricted to any specific region of the country, there is quite a bit of variability between the states concerning the amount of overrepresentation. For example, Arizona reported slight overrepresentation of minorities for arrests, secure detention, secure corrections, and transfer to adult court, while in Maryland minority youth are significantly overrepresented at each outcome.

Although minority youth overrepresentation, for the most part, exists at all of the decision points, the greatest overrepresentation is for secure corrections, secure detention, and transfers to adult court. Minorities make up on average between two and two and a half times their percentage of the at-risk youth population. On average the lowest minority youth overrepresentation is at the stage of arrest.

The decision point where minority youth overrepresentation is greatest varies by state. In Kansas, the index values are highest for secure detention and secure corrections, whereas in Massachusetts the greatest overrepresentation is for minority youth transferred to adult court and those placed in adult jails. In Tennessee, the highest index values are for waivers of jurisdiction and secure detention.

When minority groups are distinguished, overrepresentation is greatest for African Americans, followed by Hispanics and Native Americans. Typically, states that report indices for Asian American youth indicate under-representation.

In summary, minority youth overrepresentation exists nationwide and at each point in the system. The stage with the greatest overrepresentation appears to vary by the state, but, on average, the greatest overrepresentation seems to be at secure detention and secure corrections, followed by transfer to adult court. African American youth are overrepresented in the system more than are other minority youth.

The information reported in the matrices representing the identification of the extent of overrepresentation do not generally involve the use of controls for the factors that might explain these occurrences (i.e., those related to explaining differences in offending and legal and extralegal considerations). Next, a general discussion on the second phase of the DMC requirement, the assessment of the causes of minority youth overrepresentation in arrests and the juvenile justice system, is provided.

The Assessment Phase: Race Appears to Influence Juvenile Justice Decision Making

If a determination has been made from the identification phase that disproportionate minority representation exists, the state is required to conduct an assessment that investigates the specific reasons for this situation. Because the causes of disproportionate minority confinement may vary by state and locality, the OJJDP initially did not provide many specific instructions on how to conduct the assessment. Assessments were expected to, at a minimum, explain differences between whites and minorities in arrest and other outcomes in juvenile justice proceedings, including the waiver of youth to adult court. The assessment was also to have included information for at least three counties where minorities were most represented and when relevant, separate data when multiple minority groups were present. A summary of state efforts to assess the causes of disproportionate minority youth confinement is presented in table 11.1.

Since, for all intents and purposes, there was no standard procedure for conducting the assessment, individual states varied in their research strategies and, in some instances, their ability to comply with the stated minimum requirements. States often failed to (1) differentiate among minority youth, often focusing only on African Americans; (2) include legal and extralegal considerations that might influence decision making; (3) examine decision making as a process that spans multiple stages; and (4) employ multivariate statistically procedures and tests for race interaction relationships (e.g., see Alabama, Delaware, North Dakota, South Carolina). Some state assessments also focused only on aggregate data at the state level or only counties consisting largely of white youth to arrive at conclusions concerning race and juvenile justice outcomes (e.g., Nebraska). Last and unfortunately, few state assessments involved the examination of encounters between police and youth. Of those few studies, police decision making was found to contribute to minority overrepresentation (Bynum, Wordes, and Corley 1993; cf. Harris et al. 1998). In Connecticut, for example, racial disparity was found at several police decision-making points (length of time held at the police station, use of secure holding, and placement in detention) (Hartstone and Richitelli 1995).

Consequently, more insight is needed into the disproportionate confinement of minority youth at the local level, the extent to which being a minority other than an African American influences decision making, and what role the police play in the process. These shortcomings of some of the assessment studies parallel those that often characterize research conducted on race and juvenile justice in general (e.g., Bishop 2005; Bishop and Frazier 1988; Engen, Steen, and Bridges 2002; Hagan 1974; Leiber 1994; Leiber and Stairs 1999; Leiber and Mack 2003a; Pope and Feyerherm 1992; Pope, Lovell, and Hsia 2002).

Despite the limitations of some state assessment studies, a majority of the research not only addressed these issues but yielded information that increased our understanding of disproportionate minority confinement and possibly laid the groundwork for the development and implementation of strategies to reduce minority youth overrepresentation in the juvenile justice system. A review of the findings from forty-four state assessments reveals that most studies ($n = 32$) found evidence of race differences in juvenile justice outcomes that are not totally accounted for by differential involvement

Table 11.1: Summary of State Assessment Studies

State	Study Sites	Racial/Ethnic Groups Involved	Decision-Making Points Investigated	Analytical Procedures Used	Research Results	Race Effect(s)[a]
Alabama	Statewide and 6 counties	White/Caucasian, African American	Arrest, detention, court appearance, adjudication, probation, and commitment to DYS, secure facility, or adult jail	Bivariate; surveys with judges	African Americans overrepresented at all points but jail; extent of overrepresentation varied by locality	No; overrepresentation due to legal factors
Alaska[b]	Statewide	White/Caucasian, Alaskan Native, African American, Asian, other	Referral, Preadjudication detention, intake, court proceedings, supervision	Bivariate	Race differences at all decision points; Alaskan Natives underrepresented in informal probation	No; overrepresentation due to legal factors
Arizona	Pima and Maricopa counties	White/Caucasian, African American, Native American, Hispanic, minority	Detention, adjustment, petition, judicial dismissal, commitment	Regression interviews with range of individuals; public forums	Race differences at 10 of 15 decision points; extent of differences varied by group, point, and locality	Yes
Arkansas[b]	Statewide and Jefferson, Sebastion, and Washington counties	White/Caucasian, African American, other	Arrest, detention, commitment, waiver	Descriptive; bivariate	Race differences at all points statewide; minority overrepresentation at diversion; extent of differences varied by group and locality	No; overrepresentation due to legal factors

(continued)

Table 11.1: (*Continued*)

State	Study Sites	Racial/Ethnic Groups Involved	Decision-Making Points Investigated	Analytical Procedures Used	Research Results	Race Effect(s)[a]
California	Statewide and Los Angeles, San Francisco, and Sacramento counties	White/Caucasian, African American, Hispanic/Latino, Asian	Detention, disposition, commitment to CYA, length of stay	Bivariate; multivariate analytic models; some controls	Race differences at detention and sentencing; extent of differences varied by group and locality, but greatest for African Americans	Yes
Colorado	City and County of Denver, El Paso County, city of Lakewood, and Mesa County	White/Caucasian, African American, Hispanic, other	Arrest, detention	Comparison of juvenile detention, screening, and assessment as guide to actual decision and placement; cluster profiles; focus groups; surveys of police; descriptive	Race differences varied by group and locality; gender findings noted	Yes
Connecticut	Statewide and 26 police departments, 5 state police barracks, and 14 juvenile matters offices	White/Caucasian, African American, Hispanic, Asian	Police decisions, petition, detention, official vs. unofficial, service needs, probation officer recommendation, disposition, length of commitment	Regression; interviews with delinquent offenders; public forums	Differences in African American and Hispanic juveniles at placement in secure confinement; extent of race differences varied by group and locality, but greatest for African Americans	Yes

State	Sample	Groups	Decision points	Analysis	Findings	Overrepresentation explained?
Delaware	(1) New Castle County	White/black, Hispanic	Adjudication	Descriptive; multivariate analysis; some controls	Minority overrepresentation due to crime	No; overrepresentation due to legal factors
	(2) Statewide and 14 police jurisdictions	White/black	No. of charges for felonies at arrest	Descriptive	Minority overrepresentation due to crime	No; evidence of harsher police charging patterns
Florida	(1) Statewide, districts, and Hillsborough County	White/Caucasian, African American, Hispanic	Referral, detention, prosecution, dispositions, transfer to adult court	Descriptive; events associated with decisions	Nonwhite differences at all stages; extent of differences varied by point and locality; overrepresentation greatest for African Americans	Yes
	(2) Statewide	White/Caucasian, nonwhite	Petition, detention, commitment, transfer to adult court	Analysis; bivariate; regression; phone survey with juvenile justice personnel	Nonwhite differences at all points	Yes
Georgia	(1) 16 police departments and 8 juvenile courts in 8 counties	White/Caucasian, African American	Arrest, intake adjudication, court disposition, commitment, placement	Interviews; regression model; path model	Perceptions of race differences at arrest, disposition, and commitment; crime severity, demeanor, SES, and presence of attorney influences decisions; race has indirect effects through these factors	Yes

(continued)

Table 11.1: (Continued)

State	Study Sites	Racial/Ethnic Groups Involved	Decision-Making Points Investigated	Analytical Procedures Used	Research Results	Race Effect(s)[a]
Georgia (continued)	(2) 4 urban and 12 rural counties	White/Caucasian, African American	Adjudication, disposition	Archival analysis; scenario with judges and probation officers; bivariate analysis; regression	African Americans overrepresented at both points; youth treated more severely in rural locality	No; overrepresentation due to legal factors
	(3) Statewide	White/Caucasian, African American	Intake, detention, petition, adjudication, disposition, commitments	Regression	African Americans more likely to receive commitments	Yes
Hawaii	Statewide, Family court for First Circuit, and city and County of Honolulu	White/Caucasian, Samoan/African American, Filipino	Delinquent status, delinquent adjusted, petition, adjudication	Regression; focus groups	Minority overrepresentation at counsel, release, and probation; extent of overrepresentation varied by group	No; overrepresentation due to legal factors
Idaho	6 counties	White/Caucasian, Native American, Asian	Arrest, diversion, detention, adult court, adjudication, disposition, commitment	Descriptive; regression; interviews	Minority overrepresentation; data problems	Unknown
Illinois[b]	26 counties, aggregate data, and case-level data	White/Caucasian, African American, Hispanic	Police custody, detention, adult jail, lockups, waivers, corrections	Descriptive; bivariate; semistructured interviews with youth	Minority overrepresentation at most points and for most localities; African Americans' overrepresentation greater than Hispanics'	Yes

State	Geographic scope	Racial/ethnic groups	Decision points	Methodology	Findings	Overrepresentation due to legal factors
Indiana[b]	Statewide and 11 counties	White/Caucasian, African American, other	Arrest, pretrial detention, petition, adjudication, sentencing, posttrial treatment	Descriptive; bivariate	Minority overrepresentation in length of detention, likelihood of petition, and placement at sentencing	No; overrepresentation due to legal factors
Iowa	4 counties	White/Caucasian, African American, Asian, Hispanic, Native American	Intake petition, adjudication, initial appearance, disposition	Regression; interviews with delinquent youth and decision makers' public forums	Racial/ethnic disparity at intake, petition, and disposition	Yes
Maryland	Statewide, breaking counties into 6 areas	White/Caucasian, African American	Intake/referral, formalization, probation, detention, residential, secure confinement, waiver	Regression	African Americans overrepresented at all points; extent of overrepresentation varied by point and locality; gender findings noted	Yes
Massachusetts	(1) Statewide and 4 counties	White/Caucasian, African American, Hispanic, Asian	Arrest, adjudication, detention, commitment	Regression; surveys with personnel; interviews with youth	African Americans' overrepresentation greater than other minorities' and present at all points and localities; other minority overrepresentation differed by locality	No; overrepresentation due to legal factors
	(2) Statewide	White/Caucasian, Hispanic, Asian	Arrest	Census block	Minorities overrepresented	No; overrepresentation due to legal factors

(continued)

Table 11.1: (Continued)

State	Study Sites	Racial/Ethnic Groups Involved	Decision-Making Points Investigated	Analytical Procedures Used	Research Results	Race Effect(s)[a]
Michigan	Police departments and juvenile courts in 7 counties	White/Caucasian, African American, Native American, Hispanic	Police decisions, detention, intake, disposition at formal hearing	Regression; probit scenario and protocol analysis; interview with officers and juveniles in detention; Observation	Race differences at all points; African American indirect effects with family; extent of overrepresentation varied by locality; gender findings noted	Yes
Minnesota	16 counties	White/Caucasian, African American, Native American	Arrest, detention, out-of-home placement, waiver	Bivariate; regression; survey of public hearings	Race differences at pretrial detention and out of home; race differences varied by group and locality; presence of counsel important; data problems	Yes
Mississippi	1990 Mississippi youth court data files focusing on county and urban courts	White/Caucasian, African American, nonwhite	Pretrial detention, final disposition, delinquency	Bivariate; Some controls; Vignettes; Self-report of youth; surveys of police, prosecutors, and judges	Race differences at pretrial detention and final dispositions	Yes
Missouri	8 circuits focusing on court files	White/Caucasian, African American	Intake, informal supervision, detention, petition, adjudication, disposition out of home, recidivism	Regression	African Americans overrepresented at detention, petition, and out of home placements; race differences varied by locality; gender findings noted	Yes

State	Jurisdiction	Racial groups	Decision points	Methods	Findings	
Nebraska	(1) 2 counties	White/Caucasian, African American, Hispanic, Native American, Asian	Detention, petition, arraignment, adjudication, disposition	Regression; survey; interviews	Race differences at detention and final disposition; race differences varied by locality; gender findings noted; data problems	Yes
	(2) 4 counties	White/Caucasian, African American, Hispanic, Native American, other	Predetention, petition, secure confinement	Descriptive; regression; interviews; survey	Race differences at each stage; extent of race differences differed by group, point, and locality	Yes
New Jersey[c]	Unknown number of counties	White/Caucasian, African American, Hispanic	Committed	Bivariate; some controls	Race differences to commit, indirect effects with family makeup	Yes
New Mexico[b]	Statewide in unknown number of counties	White/Caucasian, Native American, Hispanic	Detention, secure corrections	Unknown	Race difference at both decision points; extent of race differences varied by point, groups, and locality	Yes
New York	(1) New York City	White/Caucasian, African American, Hispanic	Probation referral, petition, arraignment	Regression with hierarchical strategy; interview with focus groups	Race differences at probation referral, arraignment, and sentencing; few differences between African Americans and Hispanics; data problems	Yes

(continued)

Table 11.1: (Continued)

State	Study Sites	Racial/Ethnic Groups Involved	Decision-Making Points Investigated	Analytical Procedures Used	Research Results	Race Effect(s)[a]
	(2) Eric and Monroe counties			Structural interviews with juvenile personnel and practitioners; focus groups, workshops	Perceived police response is different to African Americans; gender discrepancies noted	No; overrepresentation due to legal factors
North Carolina	10 counties	White/Caucasian, African American, Native American	Intake, commitment	Regression; focus groups	Race differences at intake and commitment; race differences varied by group and locality	Yes
North Dakota	Statewide and 4 reservations	White/Caucasian, African American, Native American, other	Arrest, referral, detention, adjudication, disposition	Descriptive; bivariate	Race differences at all points; extent of differences varied by group and locality; Overrepresentation greatest for Native Americans; gender findings noted	Yes
Ohio	Statewide and 17 counties	White/Caucasian, African American, minority	Official referral, detention, adjudication	Descriptive; probabilities; regression; interviews with youth; decision-making simulation	Race differences at detention; Race/determinants; indirect effects with secure confinement; extent of race differences varied by locality	Yes

Oklahoma	Statewide	White/Caucasian, African American, Native American, Hispanic, Asian	Arrest, detention, placement, confinement	Descriptive; bivariate; survey of system personnel	Race differences at every point but adjudication; differences greatest for African Americans; differences varied by group and locality	Yes
Oregon	3 counties	White/Caucasian, African American	Unknown	Some controls	Race differences varied by point and locality; race differences at secure confinement especially strong	Yes
Pennsylvania	14 counties	White/Caucasian, African American, Hispanic	Intake, petition, detention, adjudication, disposition	Descriptive; bivariate; regression; interviews with decision makers	Race differences at every point but adjudication; race differences varied by group; case processing and race differences varied by locality	Yes
Rhode Island	Statewide	White/Caucasian, African American, Hispanic, Native American, Asian	Amount of serious crime committed; lack of funds for attorney; background of youths	Individual and group interviews with juvenile justice personnel and community representatives	Minority over-representation	No; overrepresentation due to legal factors
South Carolina	Chester, Florence, and Richland counties	White/Caucasian, African American	Secure confinement	Descriptive; regression; interviews with focus groups	Race differences at secure confinement	Yes

(continued)

Table 11.1: *(Continued)*

State	Study Sites	Racial/Ethnic Groups Involved	Decision-Making Points Investigated	Analytical Procedures Used	Research Results	Race Effect(s) [a]
South Dakota	Statewide and 3 largest counties	White/Caucasian, minority	Diversion, adjudication, disposition	Regression	Race differences at points; race interaction effects; race difference by locality; gender findings noted; data problems	Yes
Tennessee [b]	3 rural counties and 6 MSAs	White/Caucasian, African American, minority	Confinement, probation, waiver, diversion	Descriptive; bivariate	Race differences at most points; extent of race differences varied by point and locality	Unknown
Texas	3 localities	White/Caucasian, African American, Hispanic, Asian	Detention at intake, referral to prosecutor, prosecutor's decision, disposition	Logistic regression; survey of practitioners; case scenario evaluation; Regression; ANOVA	African American and Hispanic differences at detention and prosecutor's decision; interaction effect with prior referral and later decision point; extent of differences varied by point and locality; gender findings noted; criminal history strongest determinant of case scenario evaluations	Yes

Utah	Statewide	White/Caucasian African American Asian	Arrest, detention, juvenile court referral, disposition, length of placement	Bivariate variance tests; comparative with youths and professionals	Race differences at all points; extent of race differences varied by group and locality	Yes
Virginia[c]	6 court service units	White/Caucasian, African American, Asian, minority	Diversion/petition, detention/release, adjudication/disposition, commitment	Series of studies; bivariate; regression; path analysis; youth survey; focus group	Race differences at diversion/petition and length of detention; race indirectly related to intake through source of complaint; race differences by locality	Yes
Washington	Statewide, and 6 counties	White/Caucasian, African America, North American, Hispanic, Asian	Arrest, referral detention, diversion, prosecution, adjudication, confinement	Regression; observation; interviews with officials and youth	Race differences varied by point and locality; race indirect effects varied with prior referral and detention on adjudication and confinement; levels of minority concentration, degree of urbanization, and levels of violent crime are key explanatory factors	Yes

Table 11.1: (*Continued*)

State	Study Sites	Racial/Ethnic Groups Involved	Decision-Making Points Investigated	Analytical Procedures Used	Research Results	Race Effect(s)[a]
West Virginia	33 counties	White/Caucasian, African American, other	Referral, arrest, detention, commitment, placement out of state	Bivariate; some controls	Race differences at detention, commitment, and out-of-state placement; race differences varied by locality; data problems	Yes
Wisconsin	Brown, Fond du Lac, Milwaukee, Rock, and Waukesha counties	White/Caucasian, African American, Native American, Hispanic, minority	Intake, petition, consent decree, waiver, adjudication, secure confinement	Descriptive; bivariate; multiple; classification analysis	Race differences at some points; extent of race differences at case processing varied by group and locality	No; over-representation due to legal factors

Source: Leiber 2002 and updated Hamparian and Leiber 1997.

[a]Race effect is defined as either the presence of a statistically significant race relationship with a case outcome that remains once controls for legal factors have been considered. The race effect is considered a "yes" if the effect is present at *any* decision point and the outcome could be lenient and/or severe.
[b]Report could be identification or assessment.
[c]Information taken from state plan update or summary report.

in crime. Research in Florida and Maryland, for example, indicated overrepresentation of minority youth throughout the system (Bishop and Frazier 1990; Iyengar 1995).

More specifically, Bishop and Frazier (1990) used statewide data over a three-year period to examine case processing through Florida's juvenile justice system and found that race (being nonwhite) did make a difference with regard to outcome decisions. According to Bishop and Frazier (1990, 3), "Nonwhite juveniles processed for delinquency offenses in 1987 received more severe (i.e., more formal and/or more restrictive) dispositions than their white counterparts at several stages of juvenile processing. Specifically, we found that when juvenile offenders were alike in terms of age, gender, seriousness of the offense which prompted the current referral, and seriousness of their prior records, the probability of receiving the harshest disposition available at each of several processing stages was higher for nonwhite than for white youth." These disparities were found to exist for petition, secure detention, commitment to an institution, and transfer to adult court. Likewise, minority overrepresentation was found at ten of the fifteen decision points examined in Arizona (Bortner et al. 1993), while in Pennsylvania race effects were evident at all stages except adjudication (Kempf-Leonard 1992). In Iowa, race effects varied by jurisdiction, stage in the proceedings, and racial group (Leiber 1992a, 1992b; see also Leiber 1995; Leiber and Jamieson 1995; Leiber and Stairs 1999; Leiber 2003; Leiber and Mack 2003b; Leiber and Fox 2005).

In Ohio, race had a direct effect on detention decisions, and detention status, in turn, affected decisions to commit juveniles to correctional facilities (Dunn et al. 1993). A similar indirect race effect through detention was found in Washington (Bridges et al. 1993). Several studies have also discovered that many legal and extralegal variables may be racially tainted and work to the disadvantage of minority youth.

Lockhart and others (1990), for example, examined racial disparity in 159 counties within Georgia's juvenile justice system. With 1988 as the base year, this study revealed that a major determinant of outcome was the severity of the current charge and the extent of prior contact with the juvenile justice system. Compared to white youth, African American youth tended to have more prior contact and to be arrested for more severe offenses. As the authors note, "Thus, gross racial disparities do exist in Georgia's juvenile justice system. The fact that law enforcement officials have considerable discretion in the determination of how many and what types of charges to place against an alleged offender complicates the interpretation of such disparities. Black youth either are committing more serious crimes at younger ages than are white youth, or they are being charged with more serious crimes at younger ages than are white youth. In the former instance, we have understandably disparity. The second scenario constitutes racial discrimination" (Lockhart et al.

1990, 10). These results point to the possibility that offense and prior record are not legally neutral factors. If bias influences these decisions, then race differences may be augmented throughout the system (see also Miller 1996).

Race was also found to interact with a number of extralegal variables. For example, being African American and from a single-parent family influenced decision makers in Michigan (Bynum et al. 1993). In Missouri, being African American and female increased the likelihood of being detained. This relationship was conditioned by locality: African Americans females were more likely to be detained in urban localities, while in rural settings white females were more likely to receive informal supervision than any males or African American females with similar characteristics (Kempf-Leonard, Pope, and Feyerherm 1990). As Kempf, Decker, and Bing state (1990, 18), "As shown in this study, race and gender biases do exist within juvenile justice processing in Missouri. They are less obvious than the glaring rural and urban differences, but they are no less important. Evidence exists that decision processes are systematically disadvantaging youths who are either Black, female or both. They receive harsher treatment at detention, have more petitions filed 'on their behalf,' and are more often removed from their family and friends at disposition."

Perhaps one of the major findings of the Missouri study is the difference between the urban and rural courts. In essence, two different types of juvenile courts operate in Missouri—a legalistic court in urban areas and a traditional pre-Gault model in rural areas—each of which provides different treatment that places African American youth at greater risk.

Although not addressed in great detail by most assessment studies, the locality of the court appears to aid in providing a fuller understanding of disproportionate minority confinement and the contexts of decision making. In Ohio, race was not found initially to be predictive of confinement disposition (Dunn et al. 1993). When community characteristics were controlled for in the analysis, however, minority youth were more likely to be given a harsher disposition than white youth. In Washington, county characteristics most associated with disproportionality were the concentration and growth of minorities in the counties, the degree of urbanization, and levels of violent crime and chronic juvenile offending. These contexts affected decision making directly and indirectly (Bridges et al. 1993).

States also used surveys, interviews of decision makers, and focus groups as parts of the assessment phase. Some states employed these techniques in conjunction with multivariate analyses (e.g., Hawaii) and/or bivariate analyses (e.g., Illinois). A wide range of responses were offered to explain the causes of minority youth overrepresentation. A few states reported responses that emphasized discriminatory policies and procedures, racial stereotyping, and cultural and language barriers as explanations for disproportionality (e.g., Arizona, California, Oklahoma). The most common explanations for this occurrence focused on minority criminality and the factors associated with delinquency, such as poverty and the family (e.g., Alabama, Delaware, Nebraska, Texas, Utah).

In some states, the use of semistructured interviews with juvenile justice personnel showed that race bias was often indirectly operating through decision makers' perceptions of minority youth and their families—in particular, African Americans—that were fostered by stereotyping (e.g., Frazier and Bishop 1995; Leiber 1993). In Florida, for example, the respondents indicated that assessments about single-parent homes are made when handling youth and include inquiries into the ability of the family to provide supervision and to have the youth adhere to possible court stipulations. Those interviewed indicated that a single-parent home is seen as more dysfunctional and affects minorities more harshly since they are more likely to come from such households. In addition, Frazier and Bishop (1995) point out further that decision makers see nonwhite families as less adequate than white families even when both families are broken. The broken minority family was perceived as "more broken" than similar families of whites (1995, 35).

Summary

The findings of race differences that cannot be totally explained away by legal factors and questions concerning the extent to which legal and extralegal factors may work to the disadvantage of African Americans relative to whites support prior research. For example, for the years 1970–88, Pope and Feyerherm (1990a, 1990b) found that roughly two-thirds of the studies reported minority youth, primarily African Americans, received more severe outcomes than white youth. In addition, prior record and assessments about the family were found not to be racially neutral. Subsequent analysis of the research literature for the period 1989–99 revealed similar findings (Pope, Lovell, and Hsia 2002; Bishop 2005).

Furthermore, findings and explanations for overrepresentation centered on the indirect effects of race with both legal (i.e., prior record) and extralegal factors (i.e., assessments about the family) that reflect more often subtle than direct, overt racial bias. The effects may be small or not as strong as the influence of legal factors, but the cumulative effect across decision-making stages works to the disadvantage of minority youth. The characteristics of the community and/or the court can also provide a greater sense of the contexts of decision making than solely legal and extralegal factors.

The Intervention Phase: Direct Services, Training and Education, and System Change

Recall that the intervention phase of the DMC requirement should focus ideally on strategies to address the causes of minority overrepresentation in the system as identified by the assessment study. Most states are currently implementing interventions to reduce minority youth confinement. It is important to note that although some states link the intervention method(s) to the results from the identification and assessment phases of the DMC requirement, many have not clearly linked research findings to their plans or the implementation of these strategies (e.g., Iowa; see also Hamparian and Leiber 1997). To illustrate the varied approaches to address racial and ethnic disproportionality, table 11.2 details the efforts to comply with each of the four phases for four states: Iowa, Oregon, Pennsylvania, and Washington.

The discussion that follows is primarily based on information provided by two sources: the *Disproportionate Minority Confinement Technical Assistance Manual* (2000) and *Disproportionate Confinement of Minority Juveniles in Secure Facilities: 1996 National Report* (Hamparian and Leiber 1997). For more information on intervention strategies aimed at detention reform see Hoyt, Schiraldi, Smith, and Ziedenberg (1999) (www.aecf.org/initiatives/jdai/pdf/overview.pdf). The proposed and actual intervention initiatives can be classified into the categories of direct services, training and education, and system change(s).[3]

Direct Services

Direct services involve reducing disproportionate confinement through efforts that deal with the causes of delinquent behavior among minority youth and youth in general in the form of prevention and intervention programs. These programs include, among other things, services to address the negative effects of living in impoverishment, poor academic attendance and performance, faulty social skills, and unhealthy relationships with family, other adults, and peers. Information on these kinds of direct services can be found in a number of publications (e.g., Montgomery et al. 1994; Milhalic et al. 2004; Sherman et al. 1997).

Direct services also involve the use of community-based alternatives to secure confinement and secure detention, diversion, and/or assistance to minority youth and their families in the form of advocacy. The Bethesda Day Treatment program, for example, is a community-based alternative that operates during weekdays, after school, in the evenings, and on the weekends and offers an array of services that include individualized academic counseling, drug and alcohol abuse counseling, life skills development, and employment opportunities. The Civil Citation Program used in Hillsborough County, Florida, is a diversion initiative that allows police officers to issue a sanction of up to forty hours of community service for youth involved with a nonserious crime instead of executing an arrest. An example of an advocacy program is Baltimore's Detention Response Unit. The advocacy program uses assessment criteria to screen each youth referred to detention and attorneys to attend to the legal aspects of the case. The ultimate objective is to divert youth away from detention and shorten the length of stay for those detained.

Training and Education

Training and education are other examples of intervention methods that attempt to make people aware of racial bias, the DMC requirement, and how to provide services to meet the needs of a variety of racial/ethnic groups. These efforts have been typically delivered in the form of cultural and gender sensitivity training of police officers and juvenile court personnel (e.g., North Carolina). Other methods include holding DMC conferences or summits (e.g., Wisconsin) and distributing brochures (e.g., Hawaii).

System Change

System change as an intervention to address disproportionate minority confinement entails the diversification of personnel, the use of detention screening criteria and intake screening criteria, and legislative reform. In Washington, for example, three pieces of legislation have been passed to bring about system change. In 1993, counties receiving state funds are required to address minority overrepresentation in detention and other juvenile facilities; create a work group to develop criteria for the prosecution of juvenile offenders for the purpose of guiding and restricting discretion on the part of prosecutors; review disproportionality in diversion, and examine the use of detention as a contributing mechanism to DMC.

In 1994, legislation was passed that mandated annual reporting requirements on minority representation by state agencies overseeing delinquent youth. Local juvenile justice advisory committees were also established to monitor and report on disproportionate minority confinement and review and report citizen complaints concerning bias within local juvenile justice systems. In 1996, two pilot counties were selected to implement prosecutor guidelines to reduce racial inequality (Sayan, McHale, and Bridges 2000; Juvenile Justice Racial Disproportionality Work Group 1994).

State and county programs have focused on a number of things that include cultural diversity training, improved dissemination of information, alternatives to detention, recruitment of minority volunteers and increased efforts to diversify staff, conflict resolution training, standardized risk assessment tools, and the adoption of prosecutor guidelines. Research and evaluation have also been encouraged and funded. Some jurisdictions also advocate the use of community liaisons to the juvenile court and the hiring of more minorities and bilingual staff (e.g., Colorado).

Although not a system change intervention per se, many states also cite the need to improve the quality of data available on minority overrepresentation (e.g., Arizona). Underlying this system change is the need to provide

Table 11.2: History of DMC Differentiated by State

Phase or Activity	Iowa	Oregon	Pennsylvania	Washington
Identification (extent of DMC)	Overrepresentation of minorities; minorities are 4.8% of population, but 37% of jail/lockups, 32% of detention, and 28% of Boys State Training school are minorities	Overrepresentation of minorities; 2–4 times as many minorities in secure correction facilities as represented in the general public; minorities are overrepresented at each of the decision stages in court system	Overrepresentation of minorities in arrests, secure detention, secure correctional facilities, and adult transfers; minorities are 12% of population, but 70% of secure placement and transfer to adult court in 1988 were minorities	Overrepresentation of minorities; minorities are 11% of population, but 31% of referrals, 30% of adjudicated, and 37% of committed to DJR facilities are minorities
Assessment(s) (cause(s))	Quantitative analysis of 7,000 juvenile offenders from 4 counties; qualitative analysis of 84 officers and 609 youth from the same 4 counties; data analyzed legal and extralegal factors	A number of studies using descriptive analysis with controls for crime severity; qualitative focus groups with juvenile justice personnel from 3 counties	Quantitative analysis of a survey of 604 juvenile court officials and analysis of 1797 juvenile court files in 14 counties; data analyzed race, gender, prior record, family income, family problems, circumstance of the offense, type of delinquency, and the locality of the court; qualitative analysis entailing interview responses of juvenile justice personal	Quantitative analysis of 1,777 cases in 6 counties; qualitative analysis in which 177 respondents were interviewed; a number of studies conducted by Bridges at University of Washington

Interventions	Grant funds to aid agencies and communities to develop programs that emphasize life skills, school-based liaisons; formation of the Jane Boyd House, which provides counseling, mentoring, and access to social services; DMC coordinator; DMC resource center; DMC subcommittee—chair researcher at the University of Northern Iowa; DMC conferences; pilot project—alternatives to detention—site; technical assistance to 6 communities	Referral to program, which advocates responsibilities including, needs assessments, referrals, and maintaining contact with family; assessment of the cultural competency of the agency and staff; programs and services for juveniles provided after they leave the state training school; detention diversion project; governor summits	Community-based programs were implemented to slow down the overrepresentation in the system; a number programs target life skills, work skills, physical, social, educational, and vocational initiatives, and conflict resolution; DMC coordinator; DMC subcommittee; DMC conferences	Legislative changes mandating funding of programs focusing on cultural diversity, improved dissemination of information, alternatives to detention, recruitment, standardized risk assessment tools, and adoption of prosecutor guidelines; DMC work group committee; continuous research
Evaluation and monitoring	No outcome evaluations; minority overrepresentation still evident	Evaluations conducted by individual counties, some by interviews while others looked through court and case files for outcomes; reduction in youth held in detention	Process at outcomes evaluations conducted by counties and researchers associated with Temple University; reduction in minority overrepresentation	Evaluation conducted individual counties and research at University of Washington; monitoring of DMC in place; reduction in minority overrepresentation

more useful information on the extent of disproportionate minority confinement, where disproportionality is occurring, the kinds of interventions that may be needed to reduce it, and the effects of efforts over time (*Disproportionate Minority Confinement Technical Assistance Manual* 2000, 47).

Summary

Most states use or advocate the employment of direct services, training and education, and system change. Because of the complexity and the multiple causes of disproportionality, multiple approaches are needed to reduce minority youth confinement. However, the most common strategies adopted by states involve community-based prevention and intervention programs to reduce delinquency among youth and programs to increase cultural and gender sensitivity competency training (Hamparian and Leiber 1997). For example, in Pennsylvania, a number of prevention and intervention programs were implemented in three targeted areas (see Hsia and Hamparian 1998).

Common threads run through each of the programs. The community-based initiatives in each targeted area focused to varying degrees on the enhancement of work and life skills of young minority females; targeting at-risk minority youth to participate in educational, physical, social, and vocational initiatives; tutoring and improving school attendance; and conflict resolution and impulse control (Hsia and Hamparian 1998; Pennsylvania Commission on Crime and Delinquency 1996).

The primary strategies that Iowa initiated to address DMC involved the use of Formula Grant Funds to aid agencies and communities in the development of programs to deal with a wide range of issues that included DMC (Division of Criminal and Juvenile Justice Planning and Statistics 2000). The practice of awarding of community grants in this manner began in 1991 and continued until 2000. The projects funded through the discretionary grant process have included community crime prevention programs such as those that emphasize life skills, school-based liaisons, day treatment, tracking and monitoring, and "rights of passage" programs. Rights-of-passage programs are culturally based, serve African American youth, and among other things involve recognition of phases into adulthood. In late 2001, money from the Formula Grant Funds was used to fund a pilot detention diversion program and establish a DMC resource center (www.uiowa.edu/~nrcfcp/dmcrc) with the holding of a statewide DMC conference as one of its responsibilities.

In Marion, Oregon, the County Commission on Families and Children implemented a program that allows for the assessment of the cultural competency of agencies and staff to provide and meet the needs of diverse youth. The project emphasizes not only cultural sensitivity assessments, but also evaluations, corrective action, the diversity training of personnel, and the development of bilingual and bicultural foster homes (Brown-Kline 1994).

For the past decade, the Annie E. Casey Foundation's Juvenile Detention Alternatives Initiative (JDAI) has worked with Multnomah County, Oregon, and others across the nation to combine strategies to make detention more efficient in detaining only youth that truly represent a risk to public safety and moving youth quickly through the system to other kinds of treatment and punishment. To make detention more efficient and to detain fewer youth, four core strategies were recommended and implemented in Multnomah County. These are (1) objective admissions screening instruments, (2) new or enhanced alternatives to detention programs, (3) expediting case processing to reduce lengths of stay, and (4) new policies and practices for probation violations, warrants, and "awaiting placement" cases (Justice Policy Institute 2002). It is important to note that in the implementation of the first core strategy the objective instruments were based on criteria that are more race neutral. For example, instead of criteria like "good family structure," which might be biased toward intact, nuclear families and, therefore, against minority youth, the instruments asks whether there is an adult willing to be responsible for assuring the youth's appearance in court (Justice Policy Institute 2002). Sponsored by the governor's office, a statewide summit on crime that includes an emphasis on the disproportionate confinement of minorities is also held in Oregon.

The Evaluation and Monitoring Phase: A Lack of Research and Data

The fourth and final phase of the DMC requirement is the evaluation of the interventions implemented to reduce DMC. At this time, little information exists that provides us with a comprehensive picture of the success states had in meeting this phase nationwide. Many states are still in the process of implementing interventions and have not yet conducted evaluations. Unfortunately, there are also some states that have interventions in place but lack an evaluation component (*Disproportionate Minority Confinement Technical Assistance Manual* 2000; Hamparian and Leiber 1997).

The results from evaluations of interventions from a few states show some promise for dealing with minority youth confinement. For example, an evaluation of the Civil Citation Program in Hillsborough County, Florida, previously discussed in the section on intervention, indicates a 5% reduction in the number of African American youth handled officially by police and an increase of 30% in the number of African Americans handled nonjudicially. Similarly, an evaluation of a program in Waterloo, Iowa, designed to reduce further delinquent behavior among youth, especially African Americans, facing incarceration in the state training school yielded evidence of a reduction in the severity of delinquency among reoffenders (Leiber and Mawhorr 1995). The Second Chance Program is a community-based intervention program for delinquent youth placed on probation and emphasizes the improvement of social skills, preemployment training, and work experience.

The State of Oregon's Commission on Children and Families contracted with a private research agency in the early 1990s to conduct a process evaluation of the intervention programs in Lane, Marion, and Multnomah counties (Brown-Kline 1994). The process evaluation began with a meeting with the representatives from the three pilot counties and staff from the Oregon Commission on Children and Families and other service providers. The objectives of the meeting were to familiarize the counties with the evaluation and share information that included identifying problems and challenges, factors that should be considered when conducting the evaluation, methods of collecting data, and what the counties wanted to receive from the process evaluation (Brown-Kline 1994, 8). Brown-Kline used the input from this meeting to conduct the process evaluation.

The methodology used to conduct the process evaluation varied by county. In Lane County, group interviews were conducted with youth participating in the program, staff, and the Multicultural Committee within the Department of Youth Services (DYS). Case files, evaluation reports, and client-tracking data were also included in the review process. In Marion County, surveys were completed by sixteen funded agencies and five diversity trainers. Group interviews were also performed with key stakeholders: the Marion County Commission on Families and Children's Diversity Committee and the Juvenile Justice Task Force. As in Lane County, the process evaluation included a review of program data and quarterly reports. Group interviews were conducted with community-based providers, paroled youth, parole officers, and a family member support group in Multnomah County. Juvenile court personnel and staff from the training school were also interviewed.

The results from the process evaluation indicate some shortcomings and challenges (e.g., taking longer to begin the program than anticipated, and a need for the development of outcome measures), but progress in meeting most of the stated objectives of the interventions was evident (Brown-Kline 1994). In fact, the Cultural Competency Model implemented in Marion County received honorable mention for the 1995 Multicultural Diversity Award (Oregon Youth Authority 1999).

In Pennsylvania, a major criterion for the initial funding of programs was an evaluation component. Shippensburg University conducted the first-year evaluation of the programs in Dauphin County. A follow-up evaluation of the five programs in Dauphin County and four projects in Philadelphia was conducted by a team of researchers from Temple University (Welsh, Jenkins, and Harris 1999; Welsh, Harris, and Jenkins 1996; Harris et al. 1995). The evaluations consisted of three parts and were viewed as part of an ongoing process. The first part of the evaluation consisted of community assessments of each targeted area, which included an examination of social, economic, and crime indicators and interviews with individuals to identify needs and resources. Among other things, a process evaluation made up the second component of the evaluation. The third part focused on program effectiveness in terms of recidivism and retention in school and academic performance.

Results from the process evaluation indicate some program implementation issues, which included suggestions to employ hands-on directors to monitor the interventions (Harris et al. 1995; Welsh, Harris and Jenkins 1996). Findings from the outcome evaluation of programs in Dauphin County report a positive effect on recidivism. The rate of recidivism over a three-year period for a high-attendance group was 25.8%—a figure that is impressive considering nearly half of the youth had an arrest prior to their referral. In comparison, the control group had a recidivism rate of 53% (Welsh, Jenkins, and Harris 1999). Welsh and colleagues, however, found that the effects of the programs on academic performance, dropout rates, and truancy were weak.

Pennsylvania has made significant efforts to educate the public, juvenile justice personnel, and relevant agencies about disproportionate minority youth confinement (Hsia and Hamparian 1998). For example, as previously noted, a DMC subcommittee has played an essential role in encouraging support for the assessment research, the implementation of the community-based intervention and prevention programs, and the evaluation of those efforts. Since 1990, the DMC subcommittee has met at least four times a year, and nine of the ten members are minorities. In addition to a strong DCM subcommittee, the Juvenile Court Judges' Commission has worked to promote the DMC initiative. The commission, for example, offers cultural diversity training for judges and other juvenile justice personnel and has sought to employ of minorities. At least three conferences have been held in the state to disseminate and promote awareness of the extent of disproportionality in the state, the activities the state is using to address it, and the results of research on the topic.

The DMC subcommittee and the Juvenile Court Judges' Commission, as well as the Juvenile Advisory Council and Pennsylvania's Commission on Crime and Delinquency, have effectively worked with the governor of the state to incorporate the disproportionate confinement issue within the larger scope of concerns related to juvenile justice. Support for this claim comes from the nearly four million dollars of support provided to address racial and ethnic disproportionality and the creation of a delinquency prevention specialist position that entails as one of its responsibilities the DMC initiative (Hsia and Hamparian 1998). Hsia and Hamparian report that data for 1995 show that state efforts have resulted in reductions in minority youth arrests and confinement in secure detention and correctional facilities (1998, 8).

Reductions in the presence of minority youth at some points in the system have also been reported in Washington (McHale 2001) and Connecticut (Harstone and Richetelli 2001). In Connecticut, for example, for African American youth held in detention the index value was 4.52 in 1990–91 compared to 3.91 in 1998. For secure corrections for the same years, the index value for African Americans was 4.31 compared to 3.32. Results from an evaluation of the previously discussed detention project in Multnomah County, Oregon, indicate that only 12% of African Americans, 11% of Latinos, and 9% of whites brought to intake ended up being detained, and the average daily population of the detention center dropped from sixty in 1995 to thirty-three in 2000 (Justice Policy Institute 2002, 12; www.co.multnomah.or.mulnomah.or.us/dcj/jcdet/reform.shtml).

Directions for Research and Policy

Analysis of the DMC initiative and research findings demonstrate that concerns regarding disparity and possible bias with regard to the juvenile processing of minority youth are not misplaced. Clearly, there is substantial evidence to suggest that minority youth (principally youth of color) are at risk of receiving more severe dispositions across a number of jurisdictions. Moreover, these inequities occur across a variety of decision points (arrest, intake, detention, adjudication, and disposition) and are more pronounced at some decision points than at others. However, it should also be noted that a body of research exists showing no race effects. In other words, when legal factors are considered (e.g., seriousness of the offense, prior contact with the system, and the like), race differences disappear or become minimal in some jurisdictions. Nonetheless, the weight of the evidence does suggest that inequalities within the preponderance of juvenile justice systems are real and, therefore, cause for concern.

Perhaps the greatest contribution of the DMC requirement and the efforts of OJJDP to date is actually having attempted to identify the nature of disproportionate minority confinement, support research in order to understand it, and assist in developing policies and procedures to attempt to overcome it. At least it demonstrates progress in the right direction, in that the overall goal should be to make the juvenile justice system "just." If minority youth are unduly at risk than something needs to be done about it. Unfortunately, as discussed above, research and policy implementation has not been perfect. For example, evaluation and monitoring of efforts have been less than adequate, in that most jurisdictions have not done this in an effective and timely manner. While many states have established goals for implementation of policies and programs, available evidence suggests that very few are actually carrying them out. Currently, there is no mechanism for determining whether states are actually implementing and accomplishing these goals. This should be addressed in future programming efforts.

Research should continue to be supported especially in those states that have not as yet adequately addressed this issue. As noted elsewhere (Pope and Feyerherm 1990a, 1990b; Hamparian and Leiber 1997; Pope, Lovell, and Hsia 2002; Leiber 2002) research should be attentive to a number of issues. For example, researchers should examine processing data as finely as possible to avoid masking effects and variation (aggregation and disaggregation). While more studies employing combinations of methods have been in evidence, it is still important to emphasize the need for qualitative components. It is clear that increasing precision in identifying causes and mechanisms leading to disparities requires more qualitative research. Interviews, focus groups, town hall meetings, and/or other techniques are necessary to develop an explanation of why officials in one jurisdiction focus on formal processing of youth while officials in another use informal alternatives to deal with similarly situated youth.

Researchers need to recognize the importance of targeting racial groups other than African Americans (e.g., American Indians and Asian Americans) especially because these populations may be clustered in geographic areas where research efforts have been sparse. In addition, there continue to be gaps in the knowledge base concerning the extent to which and/or the manner in which attitudes of minority youth (especially in police encounters) and background or family characteristics may be mechanisms through which race affects racially and ethnically disproportionate confinement (Leiber, Nalla, and Farnworth 1998; Leiber 2003).

A national strategy for research should emphasize a more comprehensive representation of the United States and the populations of direct interest. This strategy should encourage greater reach, at least by geographic area, by type of jurisdiction, and by racial groups under study. The national agenda should also include and emphasize the development of local partnerships at jurisdiction and community levels. The primary focus for examining the existence of disproportionate minority confinement, factors contributing to it, and subsequent planning and implementing of specific strategies and actions to address related issues must be the local jurisdiction and the local community. Therefore, suggested mechanisms for local planning and action should be developed. Disproportionate minority confinement is a complex problem that cannot be examined and remedied in a piecemeal approach. The contributing factors need to be studied comprehensively, and the intervention strategies must be multifaceted in nature and implemented and evaluated over an extended period of time.

Notes

1. Self-report studies have also revealed that African Americans commit more crimes and more serious crimes than whites (e.g., Hindelang 1978; Hawkins et al. 2000), and these differentials may be accounted for by structural factors, such as the economic makeup of a community (e.g., Farrington et al. 1996).

2. The index value of disproportionality for each decision point is calculated by dividing the percentage of minority juveniles represented at each point in the system by the percentage of minority juveniles in the state's at-risk population. For example, if 60% of the youth in a state's juvenile detention facilities were African American and 30% of the state's at-risk population was African American, the index value would be 2.0. A value greater than 1.0 indicates that minorities are disproportionately represented, while an index value under 1.0 indicates underrepresentation. Thus, an index of 2.0 would mean that minority juveniles are represented at a rate twice their representation in the general at-risk population. This calculation of difference in *proportion* ratios has recently been changed to a difference in *rate* ratios. For more information on the calculation of the rate ratio refer to the OJJDP DMC Web site: ojjdp.ncjrs.org/dmc/index.html.

3. The focus of this chapter is on the DMC mandate and how states have attempted to comply with the federal requirements of the mandate. It is important to note that the federal government (OJJDP) has not been the only agency to address the DMC issue (others include, e.g., the Annie Casey Foundation, Building Blocks for Youth, and the W. Haywood Burns Institute for Juvenile Justice Fairness and Equity).

References

Bilchik, S. 1999. *Minorities in the Juvenile Justice System*. 1999. National Report Series, Juvenile Justice Bulletin. Washington, DC: Office of Juvenile Justice and Delinquency Prevention.

Bishop, Donna M. 2005. "The Role of Race and Ethnicity in Juvenile Justice Processing." In *Our Children, Their Children: Confronting Racial and Ethnic Differences in American Juvenile Justice,* ed. Darnell F. Hawkins and Kimberly Kempf-Leonard. Chicago: University of Chicago Press.

Bishop, D., and C. Frazier. 1988. "The Influence of Race in Juvenile Justice Processing." *Journal of Research in Crime and Delinquency* 22:309–328.

———. 1990. *A Study of Race and Juvenile Processing in Florida*. Report submitted to the Florida Court Racial and Ethnic Bias Study Commission.

Bortner, P., C. Burgess, A. Schneider, and A. Hall. 1993. *Equitable Treatment of Minority Youth: A Report on the Overrepresentation of Minority Youth in Arizona's Juvenile Justice System*. Prepared for the Governor's Office for Children. Phoeniz, AZ.

Bridges, G., D. Conley, G.Beretta, and R. Engen. 1993. *Racial Disproportionality in the Juvenile Justice System*. Report to the Commission on African American Affairs and Management Services Division/Department of Social and Health Service. Olympia: State of Washington.

Brown-Kline, Joan. 1994. Disproportionate Minority Confinement Program. Prepared for the County Commission on Families and Children. Marion, OR.

Bynum, T., M. Wordes, and C. Corley. 1993. *Disproportionate Representation in Juvenile Justice in Michigan*. Technical report prepared for the Michigan Committee on Juvenile Justice.

Coalition for Juvenile Justice. 1987. *An Act of Empowerment*. Washington, DC: Coalition for Juvenile Justice.

———. 1989. *A Delicate Balance*. Washington, DC: Coalition for Juvenile Justice.

———. 1993. *Pursuing the Promise: Equal Justice for All Juveniles*. Washington, DC: Coalition for Juvenile Justice.

Devine, P., K. Coolbaugh, and S. Jenkins. 1998. *Disproportionate Minority Confinement: Lessons Learned from Five States*. Juvenile Justice Bulletin. Washington, DC: Office of Juvenile Justice and Delinquency Prevention.

Disproportionate Minority Confinement Technical Assistance Manual. 2000. Washington, DC: U.S. Department Of Justice, Office of Juvenile Justice and Delinquency Prevention.

Division of Criminal and Juvenile Planning and Statistics. 2000. *Youth Development Approach for Iowa's Children and Families: Formula Grant Application and Three-Year Comprehensive Plan*. Des Moines, IA.

Dunn, C., S. Cernkovich, R. Perry, and J. Wicks, 1993. *Race and Juvenile Justice in Ohio: The Overrepresentation and Disproportionate Confinement of African American and Hisanic Youth*. Report prepared for the Governor's Office of Criminal Justice, Colum-bus, OH.

Engen, R., S. Steen, and G. Bridges. 2002. "Racial Disparities in the Punishment of Youth: A Theoretical and Empirical Assessment of the Literature." *Social Problems* 49, no. 2: 194–220.

Farrington, D., R. Loeber, M. Stouthamer-Loeber, W. Van Kammen and L. Schmidt. 1996. "Self-Reported Delinquency and a Combined Delinquency Seriousness Scale Based on Boys, Mothers, and Teachers: Concurrent and Predictive Validity for African Americans and Caucasians." *Criminology* 34:493–518.

Feyerherm, W. 1993. *The Status of the States: A Review of State Materials Regarding Overrepresentation of Minority Youth in the Juvenile Justice System*. Washington, DC: U.S. Department of Justice, Office of Juvenile Justice and Delinquency Prevention.

——— 1995. "The DMC Initiative: The Convergence of Policy and Research Themes." pp. 1–15 in *Minorities in Juvenile Justice,* ed. Kimberly Kempf-Leonard, Carl E. Pope, and William Feyerherm. Thousand Oaks, CA: Sage Publications.

———. 1996. *Disproportionate Minority Confinement: Lessons Learned for the Pilot State Experiences*. Portland, OR: Portland State University.

Frazier, C., and D. Bishop. 1995. "Reflections on Race Effects in Juvenile Justice." pp. 16–46 in *Minorities in Juvenile Justice,* ed. K. Kempf-Leonard, C. E. Pope, and W. Feyerherm. Thousand Oaks, CA: Sage.

Hagan, J. 1974. "Extra-legal Attributes and Criminal Sentencing: An Assessment of a Sociological Viewpoint." *Law and Society Review,* pp. 357–393.

Hamparian, D., and M. J. Leiber. 1997. *Disproportionate Confinement of Minority Juveniles in Secure Facilities: 1996 National Report*. Report prepared for the Office of Juvenile Justice and Delinquency Prevention. Champaign, IL: Community Research Associates.

Harris, P., W. Welsh, P. Jenkins, J. Mullen, and E. Becton, Jr. 1995. *Evaluation of Minority Overrepresentation Programs*. Philadelphia: Temple University.

Harris, R., C. Huenke, J. Rodriguez-Labarca, and J. O'Connell. 1998. *Disproportionate*

Representation of Minority Juveniles at Arrest: An Examination of 1994 Charging Patterns by Race. Dover: DE: Delaware Statistical Analysis Center.

Hartstone, E., and D. Richetelli. 1995. *An Assessment of Minority Overrepresentation in Connecticut's Juvenile Justice System.* Report prepared for the State of Connecticut, Office of Policy and Management Policy Development and Planning Division. Hartford, CT: Spectrum Associates.

————. 2001. *A Reassessment of Minority Overrepresentation in Connecticut's Juvenile Justice System.* Report prepared for the State of Connecticut, Office of Policy and Management Policy Developemnt and Planning Division. Hartford, CT: Spectrum Associates.

Hawkins, D., J. Laub, J. Lauritsen, and L. Cothern. 2000. *Race, Ethnicity, and Serious and Violent Juvenile Offending.* Juvenile Justice Bulletin. Washington, DC: Office of Juvenile Justice and Delinquency Prevention.

Hindelang, M. 1978. "Race and Involvement in Common Law Personal Crimes." *American Sociological Review* 43:93–109.

Hoyt, E., V. Schiraldi, B. Smith, and J. Ziedenberg. 1999. *Pathways to Juvenile Detention Reform: Reducing Racial Disparities in Juvenile Detention.* Pathways to Juvenile Detention Reform, vol. 8. Baltimore, MD: Annie E. Casey Foundation.

Hsia, H., G. Bridges, and R. McHale. 2004. *Disproportionate Minority Confinement 2002 Update.* Washington, DC: Office of Juvenile Justice and Delinquency Prevention.

Hsia, H., and D. Hamparian. 1998. *Disproportionate Minority Confinement: 1997 Update.* Juvenile Justice Bulletin. Washington, DC: Office of Juvenile Justice and Delinquency Prevention.

Huizinga, D., and D. Elliot. 1987. "Juvenile Offenders: Prevalence, Offender Incidence, and Arrest Rates by Race." *Crime and Delinquency* 33:206–223.

Iyengar, L. 1995. *The Disproportionate Representation of African-American Youth at Various Decision Points in the State of Maryland.* Summary report prepared for the Maryland Department of Juvenile Justice. Baltimore.

Justice Policy Institute. 2001. *Drugs and Disparity: The Racial Impact of Illinois' Practice of Transferring Young Drug Offenders to Adult Court.* Washington, DC: Justice Policy Institute.

————. 2002. *Reducing Disproportionate Minority Confinement: The Multnomah County, Oregon Success Story and its Implications.* Washington, DC: Justice Policy Institute. www.cjcj.org/portland/portland_main.html.

Juszkiewicz, J. 2000. *Youth Crime/Adult Time: Is Justice Served?* Washington, DC: Pretrial Service Resource Center.

Juvenile Justice Racial Disproportionality Work Group. 1994. *Report to the Washington State Legislature.* State of the Administrator for the Courts, Washington State.

Kempf, K. L., S. H. Decker, and R. L. Bing. 1990. *An Analysis of Apparent Disparities in the Handling of Black Youth within Missouri's Juvenile Justice System.* St. Louis: Department of Administration of Justice, University of Missouri—St. Louis.

Kempf-Leonard, K. 1992. *The Role of Race in Juvenile Justice Processing in Pennsylvania.* Prepared for the Center for Juvenile Justice Training and Research. Shippensburg, PA: Shippensburg University.

Kempf-Leonard, K., C. E. Pope, and W. Feyerherm. 1995. *Minorities in Juvenile Justice.* Thousand Oaks: Sage Publications.

Krisberg, B. 1988. Testimony before the House Subcommittee on Human Resources.

Krisberg, B., I. Schwartz, G. Fishman, Z. Eisikovits, E. Guttman, and K. Joe. 1987. "The Incarceration of Minority Youth." *Crime and Delinquency* 33 : 173 – 204.

Leiber, M. J. 1992a. *Juvenile Justice Decision Making in Iowa: An Analysis of the Influences of Race on Case Processing in Three Counties.* Technical report. Des Moines, IA: Iowa Office of Criminal and Juvenile Justice Planning.

———. 1992b. *Juvenile Justice Decision Making in Iowa: An Analysis of the Influences of Race on Case Processing in Scott County.* Technical report. Des Moines, IA: Iowa Office of Criminal and Juvenile Justice Planning.

———. 1993. "The Disproportionate Overrepresentation of Minority Youth in Secure Facilities: A Survey of Decision Makers and Delinquents." Paper presented for the State Juvenile Advisory Group of Iowa and the Office of Criminal and Juvenile Justice Planning, Des Moines, Iowa, and the Office of Juvenile Justice and Delinquency Prevention.

———. 1994. "A Comparison of Juvenile Court Outcomes for Native Americans, African Americans, and Whites." *Justice Quarterly* 11 : 257 – 279.

———. 1995. "Toward Clarification of the Concept of 'Minority' Status and Decision Making in Juvenile Court Proceedings." *Journal of Crime and Justice* 18 : 79 – 108.

———. 2002. "Disproportionate Minority Youth Confinement (DMC): An Analysis of the Mandate and State Responses." *Crime and Delinquency* 48, no. 1 : 3 – 45.

———. 2003. *The Contexts of Juvenile Justice Decision Making: When Race Matters.* SUNY Series in Deviance and Social Control. Albany: State University of New York Press, 2003.

Leiber, M. J., and K. C. Fox. 2005. "Race and the Impact of Detention on Juvenile Justice Decision Making." *Crime and Delinquency* 51, no. 4.

Leiber, M. J., and K. Jamieson. 1995. "Race and Decision-Making within Juvenile Justice: The Importance of Context." *Journal of Quantitative Criminology* 11 : 363 – 388.

Leiber, M. J., and K. Y. Mack. 2003a. "The Individual and Joint Effects of Race, Gender, and Family Status on Juvenile Justice Decision-Making." *Journal of Research in Crime and Delinquency* 40, no. 1 : 34 – 70.

Leiber, M. J., and K. Y. Mack. 2003b. "Race, Age and Juvenile Justice Processing." *Journal of Crime and Justice* 25, no. 2 : 23 – 47.

Leiber, M. J., and T. L. Mawhorr. 1995. "Evaluating the Use of Social Skills Training and Employment With Delinquent Youth." *Journal of Criminal Justice* 23 : 127 – 141.

Leiber, M. J., M. Nalla, and M. Farnworth. 1998. "Explaining Juveniles' Attitudes toward the Police." *Justice Quarterly* 15, no. 1 : 151 – 174.

Leiber, M. J., and J. Stairs. 1999. "Race, Contexts, and the Use of Intake Diversion." *Journal of Research in Crime and Delinquency* 36 : 56 – 86.

Lockhart, L. L., P. D. Kurtz, R. Stutphen, and K. Gauger. 1990. *Georgia's Juvenile Justice System: A Retrospective Investigation of Racial Disparity.* Research report submitted to the Georgia Juvenile Justice Coordinating Council: Part 1 of the Racial Disparity Investigation. Athens: School of Social Work, University of Georgia.

Males, M., and D. Macallair. 2000. *The Color of Justice: An Analysis of Juvenile Adult Court Transfers in California.* Washington, DC: Justice Policy Institute.

McGarrell, E. 1993. "Trends in Racial Disproportionality in Juvenile Court Processing, 1985 – 1989." *Crime and Delinquency* 39 : 29 – 48.

McHale, R. 2001. *Minority Youth in the Juvenile Justice System (DMC).* Governor's Juvenile Justice Advisor Committee, State of Washington.

Milhalic, S., K. Irwin, A. Fagan, D. Ballard, and D. Elliott. 2004. *Successful Program Imple-*

mentation: Lessons from Blueprints. Juvenile Justice Bulletin. Washington, DC: Office of Juvenile Justice and Delinquency Prevention.

Miller, J. 1996. *Search and Destroy.* Cambridge: Cambridge University Press.

Montgomery, I. M., P. M. Torbet, D. A. Malloy, L. P. Adamcik, M. J. Toner, and J. Andrews. 1994. *What Works: Promising Interventions in Juvenile Justice.* Washington, DC: Office of Juvenile Justice and Delinquency Prevention.

Oregon Youth Authority. 1999. *Addressing Disparity in Treatment of Youth and Its Effect on Disproportionate Minority Confinement.* Oregon Department of Justice.

Pennsylvania Commission on Crime and Delinquency. 1996. *Report to the National Criminal Justice Association: Initiatives in Pennsylvania-Encourage the Recruitment and Retention of Minority Criminal Justice Professionals.* Harrisburg, PA: Pennsylvania Commission on Crime and Delinquency.

Poe-Yamagata, E., and M. Jones. 2000. *And Justice for Some: Differential Treatment of Minority Youth in the Justice System.* Washington, DC: Youth Law Center.

Pope, C. E., and W. Feyerherm. 1992. *Minorities and the Juvenile Justice System: Full Report.* Rockville, MD: U.S. Department of Justice, Office of Juvenile Justice and Delinquency Prevention, Juvenile Justice Clearing House.

———. 1990a. "Minority Status and Juvenile Justice Processing: An Assessment of the Research Literature." Pt. 1. *Criminal Justice Abstracts* 22:327–385.

———. 1990b. "Minority Status and Juvenile Justice Processing: An Assessment of the Research Literature." Pt. 2. *Criminal Justice Abstracts* 22:527–542.

Pope, C. E., R. Lovell, and H. M. Hsia. 2002. *Synthesis of Disproportionate Minority Confinement (DMC) Research Literature (1989–1999).* Washington, DC: U.S. Department of Justice, Office of Juvenile Justice and Delinquency Prevention.

Pope, C. E., and H. Snyder. 2003. *Race as a Factor in Juvenile Arrests.* Washington, DC: U.S. Department of Justice, Office of Juvenile Justice and Delinquency Prevention.

Sayan, R., R. McHale, and G. Bridges. 2000. "Washington's Systemic and Legislative Approach to Reducing DMC." Paper presented at OJJDP's Conference Workshop for Reducing DMC, December 12.

Schwartz, I. 1986. Testimony before the House Subcommittee on Human Resource.

Sherman, L., D. Gottfredson, D. MacKenzie, J. Eck, P. Reuter, and S. Bushway. 1997. *Preventing Crime: What Works, What Doesn't, What's Promising.* Washington, DC: U.S. Department of Justice, Office of Juvenile Justice and Delinquency Prevention.

Snyder, H., and M. Sickmund. 1995. *Juvenile Offenders and Victims: A National Report.* Washington, DC: Office of Juvenile Justice and Delinquency Prevention.

———. 1999. *Juvenile Offenders and Victims: A National Report.* Washington, DC: Office of Juvenile Justice and Delinquency Prevention.

Tauke, T. 1987. Testimony before the House Subcommittee on Human Resources.

Tonry, M. 1995. *Malign Neglect: Race, Crime and Punishment in America.* NY: Oxford University Press.

Tracy, P. E. 2002. *Decision Making and Juvenile Justice: An Analysis of Bias in Case Processing.* Westport, CT: Praeger.

Villarruel, F., and N. Walker. 2002. *A Call to Action on Behalf of Latino and Latina Youth in the U.S. Justice System.* Washington, DC: Allied Printing. Available at Building Blocks for Youth (www.buildingblocksforyouth.org).

Welsh, W. N., P. W. Harris, and P. H. Jenkins. 1996. "Reducing Overrepresentation of Minorities in Juvenile Justice: Development of Community-Based Programs in Pennsylvania." *Crime and Delinquency* 42:76–98.

Welsh, W. N., P. H. Jenkins, and P. W. Harris. 1999. "Reducing Minority Overrepresentation in Juvenile Justice: Results of Community-Based Delinquency." *Journal of Research in Crime and Delinquency* 36:87–110.

12

Mental Health Issues among Minority Offenders in the Juvenile Justice System

Elizabeth Cauffman and Thomas Grisso

THE MENTAL health of juvenile offenders has been recognized as a topic of concern for many years. As we have seen from its inception, the juvenile justice system has emphasized a rehabilitative and treatment-oriented approach. Since mental health problems may lead to maladaptive behaviors that are self-destructive or self-defeating, the juvenile justice system has had the overwhelming task of addressing not only the delinquency of these youths but also the mental health problems that may be underlying their behavior. However, a new era of juvenile justice emerged in the 1990s that focuses less on the interests of the youths and more on the protection of the community. Yet this change in climate has only strengthened the need to address the mental health needs of juvenile offenders. Because they often do not manifest themselves directly, such mental health problems (especially among delinquent populations) are often labeled "behavior problems," with the result that the underlying causes of the behaviors in question go untreated. In order to address the needs of the significant population of youths with mental disorders entering the juvenile justice system, it is essential that juvenile justice facilities have a clear picture of the prevalence of mental health problems in their populations and how to treat them.

While the mandates for rehabilitation and treatment of youths in the juvenile justice system seem self-evident, what is less often discussed are the reasons why we should be concerned about the mental health problems of delinquent youths from different cultural or ethnic backgrounds. First, minority youths are not only overrepresented in the juvenile justice system but are also the most underserved population in the mental health system (Isaacs 1992; Satcher 2001). Second, the majority of research on the mental health of youths is based on psychiatric and psychological research with non-Hispanic white adolescents, ignoring a substantial proportion of youths from different

390

ethnic backgrounds who are incarcerated in the juvenile justice system. Finally, the role of the juvenile justice system in providing mental health services to ethnic minority youths may be greatly complicated by political perspectives within minority communities that do not necessarily agree with the state's efforts to psychiatrically label, medicate, and psychologically recondition their children (a perspective that is understandable in light of historical abuses like the Tuskegee experiment).

Despite the recognized importance of identifying and treating mental health disorders in delinquent populations, however, the bulk of research on the subject to date has focused on the more preliminary step of establishing the prevalence of different disorders, which has proven to be a complex issue in and of itself. Our growing understanding of the rates of mental illness among delinquent populations, while informative, leaves numerous questions unanswered. How (and how successfully) are such disorders detected? How do assessments affect the services received? How are mental health services and treatments administered? And, more specifically, how do the prevalence, assessment, and treatment of these disorders vary by ethnicity?

Disproportionate levels of minority confinement combined with high rates of mental health problems among confined youths have created negative images about the role of the juvenile justice system in meeting the rehabilitative needs of minority youth with mental health problems. (Throughout this chapter, we will use the term "ethnicity" or "minority" when referring to race and/or ethnicity.) The goal of the present chapter is to address the mental health issues among offenders in the juvenile justice system as well as examine mental disorders among minority offenders in particular. Our discussion will begin with a review of mental health definitions and move to issues of measurement and evidence of mental disorders among juvenile justice youths, examining issues of ethnicity at each turn. These sections will focus on

How we define mental disorders among adolescents

How we measure and identify mental disorders

What we know about the prevalence of mental disorders among youths in general and in the juvenile justice system, with a particular focus on ethnicity

What we know about the juvenile justice system's identification of youths' mental disorders, its methods of mental health service delivery to those youths, and what issues arise in identifying and responding to youths of various ethnic backgrounds

It will become apparent that what we do *not* know about ethnic differences in mental disorders among juvenile justice youths far outweighs what we *do* know about these matters. Thus, at the conclusion, we will summarize what information is known about mental health issues among minority youth in the juvenile justice system and point toward future research directions as well as practical needs in this area.

Defining Mental Disorder
What Is "Mental Disorder?"

As noted by the surgeon general's report on mental health, mental disorders are real health conditions that have the potential to be disabling (Satcher 2000). Yet, even in this report, there is no single definition of "mental disorder." How one defines it often depends, in part, on one's objectives. For some purposes, the term refers to *formal mental illnesses* as defined by the *Diagnostic and Statistical Manual of Mental Disorders*, 4th edition (DSM-IV; American Psychiatric Association 1994). For other purposes, mental disorder may refer to *symptoms of mental distress or behavioral dysfunction* that do not correspond specifically to DSM-IV mental illnesses but may represent problems in need of attention but not necessarily intensive treatment.

There are variations, however, even within these two definitions. For example, major depression, conduct disorder, and nicotine use disorder are all mental illnesses, to the extent that these terms are identified in the DSM-IV. But whether one would want to give these disorders the same weight in a research study as other mental illnesses or in the development of policy for mental health services in juvenile justice will depend on their perceived relevance in those social contexts. Similarly, some symptoms of mental distress may be included or excluded from consideration when studies of the mental health needs of youths are being developed, depending on their relevance for broader objectives. For example, if one's objective were to identify mental distress that is in need of emergency intervention, few would argue that depressed mood is important to include. However, there would be greater disagreement about whether or not to include attention problems or somatic complaints. As a result, researchers who begin with different interpretations of the relevant domain of mental illnesses or symptoms of mental distress will find different prevalences of mental disorders among youths.

Further complicating the study of mental disorders among adolescents are difficulties in diagnosis associated with adolescent development. Most textbooks on child psychopathology (e.g., Cicchetti and Cohen 1995; Mash and Barkley 1998) point out that mental conditions among adolescents do not fit as well into neat categories as do adult mental disorders. Often, adult diagnoses or concepts are applied to children and/or adolescents without taking into account important developmental factors that may affect the applicability or validity of these constructs (for a review, see Achenbach 1995). In addition, comorbidity, in which multiple disorders are present, is common among disordered adolescents and complicates the diagnostic process, as does the presence of transient states associated with the developmental transitions of adolescence, which can mimic disorders of adulthood. For these reasons, the diagnosis of mental disorders in adolescents inherently involves greater uncertainty and error than in adults.

Ethnicity and Definitions of Mental Disorder

How policy makers, researchers, and clinicians define mental disorder is of potentially great significance for studies of mental disorder among minority populations, both in and outside the juvenile justice system. History provides numerous examples of definitions of mental disorder that have differential effects for the definition of disorder across ethnic groups. For example, in the mid-nineteenth century, Dr. S. A. Cartwright diagnosed slaves who ran away as suffering from "drapatomania," a condition that referred to an uncontrollable impulse to wander (Poussaint 1990). It is not surprising that this "disorder" was reported to have a higher prevalence among "Negroes" than among "whites."

Less obvious, however, are the ways in which the development of diagnostic taxonomies to classify disorders in a predominantly white society may have less utility when applied to ethnic minorities within that society. It is not self-evident that the DSM-IV would contain the same syndromes as it does if it had been developed in a United States in which African-American and Latino citizens were represented throughout the twentieth century—both in the general population and in the medical profession—in proportions similar to those of non-Latino whites. The non-Western cultures of origin for many of those citizens contained somewhat different notions of "mental disorder," which may have come closer to identifying relevant syndromes associated with their ethos. For example, as compared to whites, African-Americans are more likely to receive a diagnosis of schizophrenia and less likely to receive a diagnosis of affective disorders (Mathura and Baer 1990; Worthington 1992). Whether this is due to ethnic bias in the diagnostic process or to a true difference in the prevalence of the disorder is unknown. It was not until the fourth edition of the DSM that the issue of cultural variation in the symptomatology of various disorders was formally presented (American Psychiatric Association 1994).

Moreover, ethnic cultural heritage may influence the way that individuals experience their emotional and behavioral dysfunctional conditions (McNeil and Kennedy 1997). Depending on individual differences within an ethnic group in terms of acculturation, a person's experience may not coincide with the definitions provided in Western-based categories and syndromes for mental disorders (Canino, Bird, and Canino 1997). It has been argued that the conceptualization of psychiatric symptoms needs to be approached from the cultural group's perspective and not imposed by the mainstream's conceptions (Kleinman 1988). For example, in a review of thirty studies that explored the relationship between acculturation and mental health among Hispanics, the standard measures and assessments used to report mental health problems are usually translated, verbatim, into Spanish without regard for the cultural meaning and interpretation of the symptom expressions (Rogler, Cortes, and Malgady 1991). This method may prove problematic, as cultural expression of psychiatric symptoms has been shown to improve the assessment of mental health problems among minority populations (Malgady, Rogler, and Cortes 1996).

Thus, before we even begin to consider the measurement or assessment of mental disorders in adolescents of diverse ethnic backgrounds in the juvenile justice system, we are faced with a bewildering set of problems regarding definition. These are not merely academic issues. One will have to return to them again and again when attempting to account for any significant differences observed between ethnic groups in the juvenile justice system regarding a particular diagnosis or symptom of mental distress.

Measurement of Mental Disorders

Once defined, mental disorders may be measured and identified in a number of ways. Typically these include two broad types of instruments: structured and standardized interview methods (e.g., *Diagnostic Interview Schedule for Children* [Shaffer et al. 1996]), and standardized psychological assessment tools (for example, the *Minnesota Multiphasic Personality Inventory—Adolescent* [Butcher et al. 1992] and the *Child Behavior Checklist: Youth Self Report* [CBCL; Achenbach and Edelbrock 1983]). Many things about these instruments as a class are relevant when examining mental disorders among youths of diverse ethnicity.

Instruments provide a practical way of measuring (that is, they "operationalize") the theoretical characteristics associated with a disorder. Any instrument thus embodies the definitions of mental disorders with which the developers of the instrument began. Thus, all that we have said earlier about definitions of mental disorders when applied to diverse ethnic groups applies here as well. In addition, instruments employ words and phrases as stimuli to which the individuals being assessed must respond, whether by making marks on paper or by verbally answering questions that are asked of them. While various ethnic groups in the United States tend to have a common language, lack of familiarity with the language is disproportionately distributed across ethnic groups because of differences in the proportions of people for whom English was the language of their more or less recent childhood.

This creates a source of differential error in measurement across ethnic groups.

Moreover, interviewing and testing are a social event. Most of the methods for assessing mental disorder require self-reporting of one's thoughts, emotions, and behaviors. No matter how standardized, and no matter how little the verbal interaction between examiner and examinee, examinees are aware that they are telling another person, usually a stranger, about themselves. This is constant across all examinees, but it does not necessarily have the same meaning across examinees. An interview experience will have a different meaning for youths talking to an adult examiner than for adults talking to an adult examiner. The interview experience will also have a different meaning for youths being examined in the juvenile justice system than for youths in the public school system. And this experience will have a different meaning for youths belonging to different ethnic groups, especially when the examiner is of different ethnicity from the examinee. These facts need not invalidate the use of the same measure across youths of different ethnic backgrounds. But they present an additional source of potential error when measuring mental disorders and interpreting interethnic group differences. At present, we do not have the information necessary to determine whether such differences are due to differences in the appropriateness of our definitions of disorder across ethnic groups, to differences in the precision of our instruments across ethnic groups or different adolescent populations, or to actual differences in the prevalence of the disorder.

Finally, the development of instruments to assess mental disorders among adolescents often has not given adequate attention to these possible differential sources of error across ethnic groups. The "norming" samples for some tests have sometimes included primarily non-Latino white youths, while other tests have employed ethnically diverse samples. Even in the latter case, however, test manuals for instruments assessing adolescent psychopathology rarely provide information concerning whether their psychometric properties (for example, scale alphas or item analyses) are equally acceptable for various ethnic minorities and for non-Latino white youths.

We will remind ourselves of these sources of error from time to time in the following discussions. But let us turn now to what is known about the prevalence of mental disorders among youths in general, and among juvenile justice samples in particular.

Mental Disorder among Adolescents

Prevalence of Mental Disorders among Adolescents

Since there have been no recent epidemiological studies using current DSM-IV, the majority of national estimates on the prevalence of mental disorders among adolescents are typically based on data using the DSM-III-R. For example, as found in the National Comorbidity Survey (NCS), major depression and alcohol dependence are the most common psychiatric disorders, while mental disorders during the past year were most prevalent among youth between 15 and 24 years of age (Kessler et al. 1994). In order to get a more recent picture of the prevalence of mental disorders among youth in the general population, we are reliant on piecing together information from various studies in the field. These estimates, however, are fraught with problems in that the assessment strategies used and differences among samples may influence the final estimation. Using these rough estimations, Kazdin (2000) summarized that the rates of mental disorders among youths in the general community are as follows:

Conduct disorder	2%–10%
Attention deficit disorder	2%–10%
Substance abuse and dependence	2%–5%
Mental retardation	1%–3%
Learning and academic disabilities	2%–10%
Mood disorders	2%–8%
Anxiety disorders	3%–13%
Posttraumatic stress disorder	1%–3%
Psychoses and autism	0.2%–2%
Any disorder present	18%–22%

The rates outlined above, however, do not reflect the true level of impairment that adolescents may experience. The National Comorbidity Survey has shown that among a representative sample of the general population, 56% of those presenting with one mental disorder are also likely to exhibit two or more disorders, a phenomenon commonly referred to as comorbidity (Kessler et al. 1994). Thus, the majority of serious mental illnesses are concentrated in a group of individuals who are highly comorbid.

Prevalence of Mental Disorders by Ethnicity

Ten years ago, Isaacs (1992) reported that there were no large-scale epidemiological surveys of the mental health problems of African-American, Latino, or Asian adolescents in the general population. To the best of our knowledge, this statement is still true today. The majority of research that reports rates of mental disorders does not present findings by ethnicity and rarely assesses or examines differences between ethnic groups. A few recent studies have examined mental health problems in certain ethnic groups (e.g., CBCL scores in a sample of African-American youth; Barbarin and Soler 1993). While these studies are helpful, they do not enable us to make confident estimates of the general prevalence of mental disorders among youths with various ethnic backgrounds.

This has serious implications for the interpretation of studies, which we describe later, that have examined differences in the prevalence of mental disorders for adolescents of various ethnic backgrounds in the juvenile justice system. For example, if those studies find differences between African-American and white youths in the prevalence of a particular disorder, we do not know whether this is due to differences in prevalences in the general adolescent population or specific to delinquent or incarcerated youths. Because youths in the juvenile justice system are not necessarily representative of youths in the general community, we cannot infer that any differences that are found between ethnic groups in the juvenile justice system represent ethnic differences in the general population. This is because the selective processes and circumstances that bring youths into the juvenile justice system may be quite different for youths of different ethnic backgrounds, as is discussed elsewhere in this volume (Lauritsen 2005) and as we will discuss in a later section.

Mental Disorder among Adolescents in the Juvenile Justice System

The most common and most investigated forms of mental disorders among youth in the justice system tend to be conduct disorder (CD), attention deficit hyperactivity disorder (ADHD), and substance use and abuse (SUA). While a few studies have begun to investigate more internalizing types of disorders (e.g., depression, anxiety, posttraumatic stress disorder [PTSD]), adolescents with internalizing disorders are often more difficult to identify unless they become overtly suicidal or are so irritable that they are aggressive toward others (Holinger et al. 1994). Numerous research studies have tried to identify the prevalence of mental disorders among youths in the juvenile justice system. Studies prior to the 1990s, however, were of extremely limited value in addressing this question. Estimates in those studies tended to vary so extremely that they offered little guidance. For example, Otto, Greenstein, Johnson, and Friedman (1992) provided the following summary of prevalences (from lowest to highest) among juvenile justice youths based on an exhaustive review of studies published prior to the 1990s:

Conduct disorder	50%–90%
Attention deficit disorder	19%–46%
Substance abuse and dependence	25%–50%
Personality disorders	02%–17%
Mental retardation	07%–15%
Learning and academic disabilities	17%–53%
Mood disorders	32%–78%

Anxiety disorders   06%–41%
Psychoses and autism   01%–06%

As noted above, there is wide variation in the reported prevalences among the different studies, which may be due to many different factors. They are worth identifying, because they must be considered in all future research on the question:

Studies varied in their *definitions* of "mental disorder," as well as in *their methods of measurement* (ranging from specific psychological tests to psychiatrists' diagnostic impressions based on clinical interviews).

Sample sizes often were quite small, increasing the likelihood of error in estimates.

Most individual studies examined youths in a *single site*—that is, one geographic locale or one juvenile justice facility—thus producing results that might be associated with arrest and referral patterns, community sociocultural characteristics, or other conditions that were specific to that particular locale.

The results of various studies of youths in the juvenile justice system often were not comparable because their samples were drawn from *different points in the juvenile justice process* (e.g., intake, probation, pretrial detention, postadjudication), resulting in samples that were very different in composition because of selective processes associated with deeper penetration into the system.

More recent studies have begun to correct some of these methodological deficiencies. However, only a few have examined the prevalence of disorders as a function of ethnic background.

In an extensive study among juvenile detainees Teplin, Abram, McClelland, and Dulcan (2002) used the Diagnostic Interview Schedule for Children (DISC; Shaffer et al. 1996) to screen 1,829 youths between the ages of 10 and 18 (mean age = 14.9) in the juvenile detention center in Cook County (Chicago). The version of the DISC used in this study assessed the presence of a disorder in the past six months using DSM-III-R criteria. Youths were recruited to participate within three days of their admission to the detention center, making this study one of the first to use a common assessment time within a facility. The sample was specifically stratified by ethnicity, gender, age, and legal status (i.e., processed in juvenile court vs. adult court) in order to ensure a more diversified picture of youths in the justice system. Approximately 55% of the sample was African-American, 29% Hispanic, and 16% white, with 64% of the sample being male.

Results indicate that 65% of the boys and 71% of the girls met diagnostic and functional impairment criteria for one or more psychiatric disorders.

Table 12.1: DSM-III e Diagnoses of Youths in the Juvenile Detention Center in Cook County, Illinois

	African-American (%)	White (%)	Hispanic (%)
Any disorder:			
Males	63	78	68
Females	68	82	72
Any affective disorder:			
Males	19	14	21
Females	26	23	29
Psychotic disorders:			
Males	1	3	1
Females	1	0	2
Any anxiety disorder:			
Males	21	14	25
Females	30	29	31
ADHD:			
Males	17	20	14
Females	20	22	29
Any disruptive behavior disorder:			
Males	40	57	42
Females	39	59	55
Any substance abuse disorder:			
Males	48	59	54
Females	42	60	49

Source: Teplin et al. 2002.

These findings have been broken down further by both gender and ethnicity in table 12.1. The general findings from this study indicate that white youths have significantly higher rates of many mental health disorders and African-Americans have the lowest rates. The only change in this pattern is with separation anxiety—African-American youths display higher rates than whites. In addition, these data also suggest that females, and white females in particular, present with more mental health problems than males.

In a screening study conducted by Dembo and his colleagues (1994), the Problem Oriented Screening Instrument for Teenagers (POSIT; Rahdert 1991) was used to identify potential problems in ten psychosocial functioning areas (substance use or abuse, physical health status, mental health status, family relationships, peer relations, educational status, vocational status, social skills, leisure and recreation, and aggressive behavior and delinquency). Among a sample of approximately three hundred juvenile offenders (mean age = 15.2 years) screened at the Juvenile Assessment Center in Tampa, Florida, 82% of the youths were identified as having a potential mental health problem and 51% were identified as having a potential substance use or abuse problem.

In an extension of this research, approximately four thousand juvenile offenders were screened using the POSIT with 42% white, 46% African-American, and 11% Hispanic youths (Dembo et al. 1998). Findings indicated that the white youth presented with more behavioral problems, African-American youth presented with more economically stressed households and had higher rates of neglect, and Hispanic youth were more likely to experience educational difficulties. While these differences between ethnic groups should be reflected in plans to meet their needs, they do not contribute to our knowledge of potential ethnic differences in mental disorders among youths in the juvenile justice system.

In a study of mental health symptoms among incarcerated youth, over one thousand juvenile detainees in Massachusetts and approximately four thousand serious juvenile offenders in California were assessed for possible mental health problems (Grisso et al. 2001). The Massachusetts Youth Screening Instrument—Second Version (MAYSI-2) was developed for use in juvenile justice settings in order to assess potential mental, emotional or behavioral problems at entry points in the juvenile justice system. This brief screen—fifty-two items—provides information on seven domains of functioning: "alcohol/drug use," "angry-irritable," "depressed-anxious," "somatic complaints," "suicide ideation," "thought disturbance," and "traumatic experiences." The findings of this assessment indicated not only a high prevalence rate of mental health symptoms among both detained and serious offending youth but also significant gender and ethnic differences. Specifically, females continued to present with more mental health symptoms than males. Among the males, non-Latino white males were more likely than African-American males to present with substance abuse and anger symptoms, whereas Latino males were more likely to exhibit signs of depressed-anxious mood than African-American males. Among the girls, non-Latino white females presented with more substance abuse and trauma than the African-American females, whereas the Latino females were more likely to endorse somatic complaints and suicidal ideations than African-American females.

In a more recent study of over eighteen thousand youths in Pennsylvania detention centers, we find similar prevalence rates of mental health symptomatology (Cauffman 2004). This study found that approximately 70% of the males and 81% of the females scored above the clinical cutoff on at least one of the following five MAYSI-2 scales: alcohol/drug use, angry-irritable, depressed-anxious, somatic complaints, and suicide ideation. In addition, girls were more likely than boys to exhibit internalizing as well as externalizing problems, and the mental health problems were most prevalent among white youths and least prevalent among African-American youths. Since previous research has demonstrated a relation between the MAYSI-2 and DSM-IV diagnoses via the DISC-IV, it suggests that scores that reach the clinical cutoff on any MAYSI-2 subscale may identify youths with diagnosed psychiatric disorders (Wasserman et al. 2004), but that there are often discrepancies between the disorder "suggested" by an elevated score on a MAYSI-2 sub-scale and the disorder diagnosed by the DISC. This may be a reflection of the high rates of comorbidity common in young offenders, as well as the lack of direct alignment between MAYSI-2 scales and diagnostic categories. Thus, it is appropriate that the MAYSI-2 is used as a triage tool for emergent risk (Wasserman et al. 2003).

Taking into consideration the results of these four studies, it would appear that the prevalence of mental disorders among juvenile offenders is approximately 40%–60%, substantially higher than the prevalence of mental disorders among community samples of adolescents (approximately 17%–22%). While there is some concern that these prevalence rates may be inflated based on the diagnosis of conduct disorder (which contains criteria that would warrant incarceration), youths with conduct disorder frequently meet criteria for one or more other mental disorders. In fact, Teplin and her colleagues (2002) reported that, excluding cases involving conduct disorder in the absence of any other disorder, the overall proportion of youths in their juvenile justice sample with mental disorders was reduced only from 66% to 61% for boys and from 74% to 70% for girls (with additional requirements for significant impairment: 59% for boys, 66% for girls). Thus excluding conduct disorder would only slightly lower our estimates of the proportion of youths in the juvenile justice system with mental disorders (for a review see Grisso 2004). As we have noted, however, little can be said about any observed ethnic differences, given the lack of reference data for the general population and the definitional and assessment-related uncertainties involved in comparing across ethnic groups. In fact, even the overall differences in the prevalence of mental disorders is colored by the fact that there is an overrepresentation of minority youth in the justice system in comparison with community samples.

Juvenile Justice System Responses to Youths with Mental Disorders

Given what evidence exists for the prevalence of mental disorders among youths in the juvenile justice system, there is reason to be concerned about the system's ability to identify those youths and to provide necessary mental health services. Questions associated with the ethnicity of youths loom large in this area, because (a) minority youths make up the majority of youths in the juvenile justice system, and (b) as noted earlier in this chapter, little is known about the cross-ethnic reliability and validity of many of the major instruments that have been developed for assessing psychopathology in adolescents.

In this section, we first examine what is known about the overlap between the population of youths served by the mental health system in the community and the population of youths who are referred to the juvenile justice system. Then we discuss what is known about the juvenile justice system's methods for identifying youths with mental health needs, and finally we consider their responses to those needs, both generally and with reference to ethnicity.

Adolescents can enter the juvenile justice system and the mental health system through a number of different avenues. Courts place many youths in correctional facilities, although court-directed referrals to community mental health services can result if the necessary assessments are available to affect the court's decision. Mental health professionals, family members, and others (e.g., school counselors) are the primary sources of referrals to mental health facilities. The overlap between the "client base" of the juvenile correctional system and that of community mental health agencies is increasing, although only a few studies have examined this trend.

We have already demonstrated that youths in the juvenile justice system exhibit high rates of mental health problems. What is not well understood is the converse: what fraction of youths in the mental health system are engaged in criminal activity? The fact that youths may have dual-system involvement is consistent with the notion that mental disorders and delinquency may have common antecedents. Only a handful of studies have examined the degree of overlap between juvenile justice involvement and mental health services involvement. In a study by Rosenblatt, Rosenblatt, and Biggs (2000), of the 4,924 youths who had either been arrested or received mental health services over a three-year period, 2,683 received mental health services only, 1,557 were arrested only, and 684 were members of both groups. Thus, 20% of mental health service recipients were arrested, while 30% of those arrested received mental health services, over the course of the study. In a study of 645 10–17-year-olds who entered community based public mental health programs, approximately 21% were also found to be involved with the juvenile justice system (Stoep, Evens, and Taub 1997). Over the course of one year, youths who were involved in a community-based public mental health system were three times more likely to come into contact with the juvenile justice system than youths of similar gender and ages in the general population. Specifically, the results indicated that the co-occurrence of youths in the mental health system between 14 and 16 years of age had the highest rates of overlap with the juvenile justice system. In addition, African-Americans, Native Americans, and Hispanics had higher incidence rates than whites in both the juvenile justice system setting and the mental health setting. African-American youth had high rates of criminal interaction, regardless of their mental health system involvement, and Asian-American youths had low rates of criminal interaction regardless of their mental health system involvement. Hispanic youths who were involved in the mental health system were at the greatest risk of criminal involvement. It was also found that youth who were referred to the juvenile justice system via the mental health system were more likely to receive harsher sanctions. While this study was able to examine the co-occurrence of the use of the two systems over a one-year period, it was not able to determine the temporal sequence of mental health and juvenile justice system involvement.

The risk factors for identifying which youth in the mental health system are more likely to come into contact with the juvenile justice system have also been assessed (Evens and Stoep 1997). The results indicated that parents with a history of incarceration, drug or alcohol abuse issues, and being physically abused were all more likely to influence interaction with the juvenile justice system versus the mental health system. In addition, juvenile justice contact among youths was disproportionately more likely to occur among African-American youth—even after taking into account possible differences in substance use, physical abuse, and family criminal history.

These studies demonstrate that a large proportion of youth who come into contact with the public mental health system are also likely to be involved with the juvenile justice system, especially if they are from minority backgrounds and/or present with substance abuse, physical abuse, and a history of family criminal behavior.

The System's Response to Youths' Mental Disorders

The high prevalence of mental disorders among youths in the juvenile justice system has led some to quip that our jails are serving as surrogate mental hospitals (Cocozza and Skowyra 2000), particularly for minority populations (Barnum and Keilitz 1992). The latter characterization is based on such observations as the disproportionate rates at which courts judge white juvenile offenders to be mentally disturbed, while African-American offenders are more often judged disorderly (Cohen et al. 1990). There is increasing evidence of such referral biases, with African-Americans more likely to be referred to corrections than to psychiatric hospitals. For example, Dembo and his colleagues (1994) found that of 243 youth assessed via the POSIT at the Juvenile Assessment Center in Tampa, Florida, 38% of whites with mental health problems received treatment, whereas only 19% of African-American youths with mental health problems received treatment. This difference was also observed among youths presenting with substance abuse problems, with 18% of the white youth receiving treatment for this problem as compared to 6% of African-American youth. In a study of six hundred youths from various ethnic backgrounds (mean age = 14.7 years) in state custody in Tennessee, 52% of the youths scored in the clinical range on both the *Child Behavior Checklist: Youth Self Report* and the *Teacher Rating Form,* and were identified as in need of treatment (Glisson 1996). However, only 14% of these youth were referred for clinical mental health services. The reasons cited for referral, however, showed no relationship to the youth's mental health status. The primary factors that influenced referral to mental health services were gender (with females more likely to be referred) and ethnicity (with whites more likely to be referred).

In a similar study by Thomas and Stubbe (1996), the four best predictors of whether a youth would be referred for a mental health evaluation were, in descending order of significance, ethnicity (with African-Americans less likely to be referred), whether the child was accused of a sex offense, age (with older youths less likely to be referred), and the severity of the offense. Upon further examination, the results indicated that while criminal offenses and sex offenses did not have differential referral rates by ethnicity, African-American youths charged with drug offenses were more likely than white youths charged with the same offenses to be referred to a correctional facility instead of a mental health facility.

While the referral process is fraught with problems, the ways in which services are administered to youths within the juvenile justice system are also unsystematic (Barnum and Keilitz 1992). This may be due, in part, to the lack of a reliable mechanism for identifying those in need of services, to the perceptions of juvenile justice personnel regarding appropriate responses to different types of mental illness, or to resource limitations that result in treatment of only the most disruptive cases. Research has shown that the presence of mental illness has a differential impact on service provision depending on the severity of the disorder (Grisso 1988). Juvenile courts tend to select the dramatic features of mental disturbance (e.g., bizarre behavior, explicit self-destructiveness) for assessment rather than less noticeable disorders (e.g., depression, anxiety); moreover, those youth with more extreme behaviors tend to receive more restrictive detention and disposition decisions.

When youths with mental disorders are detected, there are several points in the processing of delinquency cases at which the system can respond in various ways to provide clinical services. Among them are

Police diversion to community mental health services
Intake probation referral (e.g., to community and inpatient mental health and substance abuse services)
Pretrial detention preventive services (e.g., suicide watch, restraint of aggression)
Secure detention referral (e.g., to inpatient mental health services)
Dispositional decisions (e.g., inclusion of mental health services in conditions for sentencing and rehabilitation)
Juvenile posttrial probation and corrections provision of services or referral for mental health services

There are a substantial literature and many empirical studies on the effectiveness or ineffectiveness of juvenile justice system interventions in dealing with psychosocial problems of delinquent youths and thus reducing further delinquency. The services that are currently delivered to youth in the juvenile justice system vary widely and include a diverse range of interventions. In some districts, delinquent youths may be referred to outpatient mental health settings for individual psychodynamic or behavioral therapy (Mulvey, Arthur, and Reppucci 1993), they may receive counseling from a member of the juvenile court staff, or, in the most serious cases, they may be placed in a residential facility (e.g., group home, psychiatric hospital, or training school), where individual therapy is combined with other types of therapeutic interventions (Bourdin 1994). An increasing number of delinquent youths are referred to family therapy as part of their probation, as well (Roberts and Camasso 1991). But virtually nothing in this literature describes or evaluates the juvenile justice system's provision of emergency medical and psychiatric services for youths with mental disorders while they are being processed at the pretrial stage, its methods for treating youths whose mental disorders and related behaviors disqualify them for the system's usual rehabilitation interventions at the dispositional stage of the adjudicative process, or the effectiveness of interagency strategies involving juvenile justice and mental health systems in meeting the needs of youths with mental disorders. Until we obtain reliable information about these services, we cannot provide good answers to the important questions about ethnicity and treatment—for example, whether there are ethnic disparities in receipt of clinical services, and whether minority youths are more or less likely to receive mental health services in the juvenile justice system than in their own communities. Despite the fact that juvenile facilities provide a "captive audience" for mental health treatments that are not only in need, but also intimately related to successful rehabilitation, the assignment of such services and their ability to rehabilitate remains inadequate.

Future Research Directions

The presence of mental health problems among juvenile offenders is exceptionally high. Moreover, because minority youths are overrepresented in the juvenile justice system, we know more about the prevalences of mental disorders among minority offenders than we do about the prevalences of the same disorders among the general (nonoffender) minority population. While this chapter has identified numerous gaps in our understanding of issues relating to mental disorders, delinquency, and ethnicity, one of the biggest gaps is the lack of epidemiological data on mental health among different ethnicities. Filling such gaps will allow more meaningful interpretation of much of the raw data that is currently being collected on delinquent youths. Rather than reiterate all of the numerous knowledge gaps noted throughout the chapter, however, we focus here on three specific research opportunities that would inform our understanding in three key areas: assessment tools, service utilization and perception, and long-term outcomes.

The first and perhaps the most important area that needs to be addressed is that of measurement. Issues of cultural sensitivity in measurement, as we have pointed out throughout this chapter, are critical if we are to get a better understanding of mental disorders across and within ethnic groups. To assess the extent to which mental health instruments measure different things in different ethnic groups, advanced analytical techniques are required. New techniques, such as item response theory (IRT) allow much more rigorous testing of instruments among different groups than was previously possible. (For a more detailed review of statistical techniques that can be used to detect item bias, see Van de Vijver and Leung 1997). Observed differences in test scores may be the result of measurement bias, real group differences, or a combination of these two factors. IRT methods provide a formal psychometric model that allows groups to be matched on underlying latent traits. By focusing on latent variables rather than manifest variables, IRT makes it possible to distinguish between measurement bias and true group differences. The significant changes in the ethnic makeup of a number of states, as indicated by recent census data, highlight the importance of ensuring that the tools we use to assess mental health provide information that can be meaningfully interpreted.

A second area of study that we believe is underexplored involves determining the underlying causes of observed differences in utilization of mental health services among ethnic groups. The proportion of youths in the mental health system is predominantly white, while those who are referred to the juvenile justice system are disproportionately minorities. Moreover, among delinquent populations, despite overrepresentation of minorities, white youths remain most likely to receive mental health services. There is some evidence that minority youths are more likely to associate stigmas with mental health treatment. In fact, among adolescents, mental health treatment is viewed more negatively than juvenile justice placement (Mulvey and Pieffer 1993). This may provide a partial explanation for the lower frequencies with which minority youths seek out mental health services, whether inside or outside the juvenile justice system. How youths perceive mental disorders, how they seek help, and how we respond to them are important factors to understand if we are to improve service effectiveness. Previous research has shown that youths are most likely to seek out friends for help with most problems, and if the problem is serious, they often will seek out parents or teachers (Boldero and Fallon 1995). However, youths who get into trouble may be less likely to seek out authority figures, and when they do, their requests for help may not be as favorably received as those of their better-behaved peers. As previous research has shown, disturbed adolescents are more likely to seek out help from their peers rather than their parents (Offer et al. 1991), and these peers are often disturbed as well (Sarbornie and Kauffman 1985). Effectively responding to the mental health needs of young offenders, and of minority offenders in particular, requires an understanding of the ways that these youths' perceptions differ regarding mental health symptoms and treatments.

Finally, in addition to improving our measurement of mental health among different ethnic groups and understanding ethnic differences in service utilization and perceptions, it is important that we determine how adolescent development, mental health, juvenile justice system involvement, and ethnicity influence each other during the teenage years. How do interventions (including incarceration) affect adolescent development? Conversely, how does adolescent development influence youths' reactions to intervention programs? Does incarceration exacerbate mental health problems that were already present, or cause new ones? Are there ethnic differences in the ways that these factors influence each other? Such interwoven issues are complex, and difficult to unravel, but they are vital to understand if we are to improve the effectiveness of the juvenile justice system in curbing long-term offending. Recidivism rates are lower in the juvenile justice system than they are for youths placed in adult facilities (Bishop et al. 1996; Fagan 1995), but these rates remain significantly higher than one would hope from a system emphasizing rehabilitation. Given the high prevalence of mental health problems among juvenile offenders, effective rehabilitation requires, first, that such problems be accurately diagnosed; second, that those in need of mental health treatment receive it; and third, that the services provided be appropriate for the developmental and ethnic context in which they are received. We believe the areas of study that we have highlighted for future attention are critical in addressing these needs.

The Politics of Psychopathology and Treatment

It is important to be aware that political and economic factors also play a role in the dynamics of diagnosis and treatment of mental disorders among youths in the juvenile justice system, and ethnicity and culture are significant factors in these dynamics.

Federal block grants to the states have recently been providing greater resources for mental health treatment of youths in juvenile justice systems. This comes after a decade of concern about youth violence and the importance of developing programs that increase public protection. Ironically, it also comes after a decade in which mental health services for children in the general community have received decreasing support. It seems that society's willingness to fund mental health services in the interest of reducing violence has been somewhat greater than its willingness to fund mental health services for children in general.

Shifting the role of mental health services from the public mental health system to the juvenile justice system has several possible consequences, many of which are negative. Several of those potential consequences are worth noting, even if there are no data with which to substantiate their magnitude. For instance, in some lower-socioeconomic African-American and Latino communities where mental health services are scarce (and have been decreasing throughout the past decade), families have begun to believe that their children's chances of receiving necessary mental health services are better if they refer their children to the police for even minor offenses (leading to arrest and delinquency convictions) than if they seek mental health services in the community. This "backdoor approach" to mental health services for youths requires that society and parents collaborate to label their children "delinquent" in order to meet their children's basic mental health needs. A delinquency record, of course, has future consequences, both in terms of youths' perceptions of their own identity and in an official sense in a world of "three-strikes-and-you're-out." Moreover, that labeling cost is disproportionately borne by families and children of color and of poorer socioeconomic means.

The practice of funding mental health services through federal assistance to the juvenile justice system often requires that the states demonstrate a prevalence of mental disorder among youths in the system that meets a criterion level. This can produce a motivation for juvenile justice systems themselves to find prevalence rates that will satisfy federal criteria (which, as we noted earlier, is not difficult to do given the wide variance in estimates based on the measures, methods, and definitions of disorder that one decides to use). Although there is no empirical evidence, it is worth considering the degree to which this dynamic augments the reported prevalence rates by favoring measures and definitions of mental disorder that will maximize the perceived need. This augmentation of the prevalence rates runs the risk of "psychopathologizing" our youths, with whatever consequences that might have. In the extreme, a great deal of delinquency, its causes, and rehabilitation that will reduce it potentially become redefined as a problem of mental illness.

The potential consequences of redefining delinquency as a problem of mental illness are profound, especially for African-American and Latino youths, who disproportionately constitute the population of youth in the juvenile justice system. Taken to its extremes, rehabilitation begins to focus on psychoactive medication and patienthood, and it provides apparently beneficent reasons for confinement that might otherwise require the due process protections associated with the state's police powers to confine. Because of that, conditions are created for African-American and Latino communities to claim that the state's increasing efforts to psychiatrically label, medicate, and psychologically recondition their children constitute a "backdoor approach" to increased social control, not beneficent treatment.

These potential consequences do not, in our opinion, call for a halt in the trend toward greater attention to mental health services for youths in the juvenile justice system. Despite variations in definitions of mental disorder, there is no doubt that some youths who enter the juvenile justice system are suicide risks, some have major mental disorders, and some have disorders of more modest proportion that nevertheless have serious consequences for their future delinquency. In a system that has had inadequate methods and procedures for identifying these youths, the recent increase in attention to them should be encouraged. But we must be aware that the politics of this trend, as with all societal changes that have beneficent objectives, has the potential for harm if we do not carefully analyze its progress. That harm, if it arises, will disproportionately affect youths and families of color.

References

Achenbach, T. M. 1995. "Developmental Issues in Assessment, Taxonomy, and Diagnosis of Child and Adolescent Psychopathology." In *Developmental Psychopathology: Theory and Methods,* ed. D. Cicchetti and D. Cohen. New York: John Wiley and Sons.

Achenbach, T. M., and C. S. Edelbrock. 1983. *Manual for the Child Behavior Checklist and Profile.* Burlington: University of Vermont, Department of Psychiatry.

American Psychiatric Association. 1994. *Diagnostic and Statistical Manual of Mental Disorders.* 4th ed. Washington, DC.

Barbarin, O., and R. Soler. 1993. "Behavioral, Emotional, and Academic Adjustment in a National Probability Sample of African American Children: Effects of Age, Gender, and Family Structure." *Journal of Black Psychology* 19:423–446.

Barnum, R., and I. Keilitz. 1992. "Issues in Systems Interactions Affecting Mentally Disordered Juvenile Offenders." Pp. 49–90 in *Responding to the Mental Health Needs of Youth in the Juvenile Justice System,* ed. J. Cocozza. Seattle, WA: National Coalition for the Mentally Ill in the Criminal Justice System.

Bishop, D. B., C. E. Frazier, L. Lanza-Kaduce, and L. Winner. 1996. "The Transfer of Juveniles to Criminal Court: Does It Make a Difference?" *Crime and Delinquency* 42:171–191.

Boldero, J., and B. Fallon. 1995. "Adolescent Help-Seeking: What Do They Get Help for and from Whom?" *Journal of Adolescence* 18:193–209.

Bourdin, C. 1994. "Innovative Models of Treatment and Service Delivery in the Juvenile Justice System." *Journal of Clinical Child Psychology* 23:19–25.

Butcher, J. N., C. L. Williams, J. R. Graham, R. P. Archer, A. Tellegen, Y. S. Ben-Porath, and B. Kaemmer. 1992. *MMPI-A (Minnesota Multiphasic Personality Inventory—Adolescent): Manual for Administration, Scoring, and Interpretation.* Minneapolis, MN: University of Minnesota Press.

Canino, G., H. Bird, and I. Canino. 1997. "Methodological Challenges in Cross-Cultural Research of Childhood Psychopathlogy: Risk and Protective Factors." Pp. 259–276 in *Evaluating Mental Health Services: How Do Programs for Children Work in the Real World?* ed. C. Nixon and D. Northrup. Thousand Oaks, CA: Sage Publications.

Cauffman, E. 2004. "A Statewide Assessment of Mental Health Symptoms among Juvenile Offenders in Detention." *Journal of the American Academy of Child and Adolescent Psychiatry* 43:430–439.

Cicchetti, D., and D. Cohen. 1995. *Developmental Psychopathology: Risk, Disorder, and Adaption.* Vol. 2. New York: John Wiley and Sons.

Cocozza, J., and K Skowyra. 2000. "Youth with Mental Health Disorders: Issues and Emerging Responses." *OJJDP—Juvenile Justice* 7:3–13.

Cohen, P., D. Parmelee, L. Irwin, J. Weisz, P. Howard, P. Purcell, and A. Best. 1990. "Characteristics of Children and Adolescents in a Psychiatric Hospital and a Corrections Facility." *Journal of the American Academy of Child and Adolescent Psychiatry* 29:909–913.

Dembo, R., J. Schmeidler, C. Chin, P. Borden, D. Manning, and M. Rollie. 1998. "Psychosocial, Substance Use, and Delinquency Differences among Anglo, Hispanic White, and African-American Male Youths Entering a Juvenile Assessment Center." *Substance Use and Misuse* 33:1481–1510.

Dembo, R., G. Turner, P. Borden, and J. Schmeidler. 1994. "Screening High Risk Youths for Potential Problems: Field Application in the Use of the Problem Oriented Screening Instrument for Teenagers (POSIT)." *Journal of Child and Adolescent Substance Abuse* 3:69–93.

Evens, C., and A. Stoep. 1997. "Risk Factors for Juvenile Justice System Referral among Children in a Public Mental Health System." *Journal of Mental Health Administration* 24:443–455.

Fagan, J. 1995. "Separating the Men from the Boys: The Comparative Advantage of Juvenile versus Criminal Court Sanctions on Recidivism among Adolescent Felony Offenders." Pp. 238–260 in *A Sourcebook: Serious, Violent, and Chronic Juvenile Offenders,* ed. C. Howell, B. Krisberg, J. D. Hawkins, and J. Wilson. Thousand Oaks, CA: Sage Publications.

Glisson, C. 1996. "Judicial and Service Decisions for Children Entering State Custody: The Limited Role of Mental Health." *Social Service Review,* June, 257–281.

Grisso, T. 1988. "Improving Mental Health Evaluations to Juvenile Courts." Presentation at Workshop on Mental Health Services and the Juvenile Justice System, Williamsburg, VA.

———. 2004. *Double Jeopardy: Adolescent Offenders with Mental Disorders.* Chicago: University of Chicago Press.

Grisso, T., R. Barnum, K. Fletcher, E. Cauffman, and D. Peuschold. 2001. "Massachusetts Youth Screening Instrument for Mental Health Needs of Juvenile Justice Youths." *Journal of the American Academy of Child and Adolescent Psychiatry* 40:541–548.

Holinger, P., D. Offer, J. Barter, and C. Bell. 1994. *Suicide and Homicide among Adolescents.* New York: Guilford Press.

Isaacs, M. 1992. "Assessing the Mental Health Needs of Children and Adolescents of Color in the Juvenile Justice System: Overcoming Institutionalized Perceptions and Barriers." Pp. 49–90 in *Responding to the Mental Health Needs of Youth in the Juvenile*

Justice System, ed. J. Cocozza. Seattle, WA: National Coalition for the Mentally Ill in the Criminal Justice System.

Kazdin, A. 2000. "Adolescent Development, Mental Disorders, and Decision Making of Delinquent Youths." Pp. 33–65 in *Youth on Trial: A Developmental Perspective on Juvenile Justice,* ed. T. Grisso and R. Schwartz. Chicago: University of Chicago Press.

Kessler, R., K. McGonagle, S. Zhao, C. Nelson, M. Hughes, S. Eshleman, H. Wittchen, and K. Kendler. 1994. "Lifetime and 12-Month Prevalence of DSM-III-R Psychiatric Disorders in the United States: Results from the National Comorbidity Survey." *Archives of General Psychiatry* 51:8–19.

Kleinman, A. 1988. *Rethinking Psychiatry: From Cultural Category to Personal Experience.* New York: Free Press.

Lauritsen, Janet L. 2005. "Racial and Ethnic Differences in Juvenile Offending." In *Our Children, Their Children: Confronting Racial and Ethnic Differences in American Juvenile Justice,* ed. Darnell F. Hawkins and Kimberly Kempf-Leonard. Chicago: University of Chicago Press.

Malgady, R., L. Rogler, and D. Cortes. 1996. "Cultural Expression of Psychiatric Symptoms: Idioms of Anger among Puerto Ricans." *Psychological Assessment* 8:265–268.

Mash, E., and R. Barkley. 1998. *Treatment of Childhood Disorders.* 2nd ed. New York: Guilford Press.

Mathura, C., and M. Baer. 1990. "Social Factors in Diagnosis and Treatment." In *Handbook of Mental Health and Mental Disorder among Black Americans,* ed. D. Ruiz. Westport, CT: Greenwood.

McNeil, J., and R. Kennedy. 1997. "Mental Health Services to Minority Groups of Color." Pp. 235–257 in *Mental Health Policy and Practice Today,* ed. T. Watkins and J. Callicutt. Thousand Oaks, CA: Sage Publications.

Mulvey, E., M. Arthur, and N. D. Reppucci. 1993. "The Prevention and Treatment of Juvenile Delinquency." *Clinical Psychology Review* 13:133–167.

Mulvey, E., and M. Pieffer. 1993. "A Comparison of Perceptions regarding the Process of Institutional Placement." *Journal of Mental Health Administration* 20:254–263.

Offer, D., K. Howard, K. Schonert, and E. Ostrov. 1991. "To Whom do Adolescents Turn for Help? Differences between Disturbed and Nondisturbed Adolescents." *Journal of the American Academy of Child and Adolescent Psychiatry* 30:623–630.

Otto, R., J. Greenstein, M. Johnson, and R. Friedman. 1992. "Prevalence of Mental Disorders among Youth in the Juvenile Justice System." Pp. 7–48 in *Responding to the Mental Health Needs of Youth in the Juvenile Justice System,* ed. J. Cocozza. Seattle, WA: National Coalition for the Mentally Ill in the Criminal Justice System.

Poussaint, A. 1990. "The Mental Health Status of Black Americans, 1983." In *Handbook of Mental Health and Mental Disorder among Black Americans,* ed. D. S. Ruiz. Westport, CT: Greenwood.

Rahdert, E. 1991. *The Adolescent Assessment/Referral System.* Rockville, MD: National Institute on Drug Abuse.

Roberts, A., and M Camasso. 1991. "Juvenile Offender Treatment Programs and Cost-Benefit Analysis." *Juvenile and Family Court Journal* 42:37–47.

Rogler, L., D. Cortes, and R. Malgady. 1991. "Acculturation and Mental Health Status among Hispanics: Convergence and New Directions for Research." *American Psychologist* 46:585–597.

Rosenblatt, J., A. Rosenblatt, and E. Biggs. 2000. "Criminal Behavior and Emotional Disorder: Comparing Youth Served by Mental Health and Juvenile Justice Systems." *Journal of Behavioral Health Services and Research* 27:227–237.

Sarbornie, E., and J. Kauffman. 1985. "Regular Classroom Sociometric Status of Behaviorally Disordered Adolescents." *Behavioral Disorders* 12:268–274.

Satcher, D. 2000. "Mental Health: A Report of the Surgeon General: Executive Summary." *Professional Psychology: Research and Practice* 31:5–13.

———. 2001. *Mental Health: Culture, Race, and Ethnicity: A Supplement to Mental Health: A Report of the Surgeon General.* Rockville, MD: U.S. Department of Health and Human Services, Substance Abuse and Mental Health Services Administration, Center for Mental Health Services.

Shaffer D., P. Fisher, M. Dulcan, M. Davies, J. Piacentini, M. E. Schwab-Stone, B. B. Lahey, K. Bourdon, P. S. Jensen, H. R. Bird, G. Canino, and D. A. Regier. 1996. "The NIMH Diagnostic Interview Schedule for Children, Version 2.3 (DISC 2.3): Description, Acceptability, Prevalence Rates, and Performance in the MECA Study." *Journal of the American Academy of Child and Adolescent Psychiatry* 35:865–877.

Stoep, A., C. Evens, and J. Taub. 1997. "Risk of Juvenile Justice System Referral among Children in a Public Mental Health System." *Journal of Mental Health Administration* 24:428–442.

Teplin, L., K. Abram, G. McClelland, and M. Dulcan. 2002. "Psychiatric Disorders in Youth in Juvenile Detention." *Archives of General Psychiatry* 59:1133–1143.

Thomas, J., and D. Stubbe. 1996. "A Comparison of Correctional and Mental Health Referrals in the Juvenile Court." *Journal of Psychiatry and Law* 24 (Fall): 379–400.

Van de Vijver, F. J., and K. Leung. 1997. *Methods and Data Analysis for Cross-Cultural Research.* Thousand Oaks: Sage Publications.

Wasserman, G., P. Jensen, S. Ko, J. Cocozza, E. Trupin, A. Angold, E. Cauffman, T. Grisso, W. Arroyo, M. Bigley, J. Burrell, L. Faison, P. Fisher, G. Fricchione, L. Greenhill, W. Haxton, K. Hoagwood, R. Kelly, C. Koyanagi, E. Loughran, L. McReynolds, L. Mufson, D. Quintana, L. Shapiro, H. Snyder, T. Stokes, L. Underwood, R. Wahl, and B. Waslick. 2003. "Mental Health Assessments in Juvenile Justice: Report on the Consensus Conference." *Journal of the American Academy of Child and Adolescent Psychiatry* 42:751–761.

Wasserman, G., L. McReynolds, S. Ko, L. Katz, E. Cauffman, W. Haxton, and C. Lucas. 2004. "Screening for Emergent Risk and Psychiatric Disorder among Incarcerated Youth: Comparing MAYSI-2 and Voice DISC-IV." *Journal of the American Academy of Child and Adolescent Psychiatry* 43:629–639.

Worthington, C. 1992. "An Examination of Factors Influencing the Diagnosis and Treatment of Black Patients in the Mental Health System." *Archives of Psychiatric Nursing* 4:195–204.

13

Minimizing Harm from Minority Disproportion in American Juvenile Justice

Franklin E. Zimring

THE ISSUES we confront in trying to fix the damages of disproportion in juvenile justice are a mix of the obvious and the obscure. There can be no doubt that the handicaps imposed on youth by arrest, detention, adjudication, and incarceration fall disproportionately on males from disadvantaged minority groups in the United States. It is equally obvious that the hardships imposed on formally sanctioned youth are substantial by themselves and even worse when they aggravate the other by-products of social disadvantage. But this concluding note is about the not-so-obvious choices that we confront when attempting to reduce the harms that disproportionate minority concentration produces. There are a variety of different approaches that can be taken to reforming juvenile justice to protect minority youth, and not all of them are of equal effectiveness. How best to address the problems documented with passion and skill in previous chapters?

My ambition in these pages is to identify some of the key policy choices that must be made in reducing injustices found in American juvenile courts. A clear definition of goals and priorities is absolutely essential to intelligent policy planning. My argument is that reducing the hazards of juvenile court processing may be a better approach to protecting minority youth than just trying to reduce the proportion of juvenile court cases with minority defendants.

The essay is divided into two large segments and then subdivided into smaller units. Part 1 concerns the conceptual equipment necessary to assess the impact of legal policies on minority populations. A first section of part 1 discusses whether it is best to consider the minority concentrations in juvenile justice as a special problem in the juvenile justice system or as part of the generally higher-risk exposures found in criminal justice and other state control systems. A second section proposes harm reduction as the principal criterion by which policies designed to respond to minority disproportion should be judged. A third section contrasts two competing measures of disadvantage to minorities—relative and aggregate disadvantage—as the appropriate goal of reforms. A fourth section compares two overall approaches to minimize harm—cutting back on the harms that juvenile justice processing produces and cutting back on the number and proportion of minority youth who are pushed through the system.

Part 2 attempts to apply the apparatus developed in part 1 to discuss recent chapters in juvenile justice law reform—changes in transfer policy, the deinstitutionalization of status offenders, and the embrace of diversion programs. A final subsection of part 2 contrasts the harm to minority youth from exposure to juvenile courts with the harm from criminal courts. If the proper standard for judging the impact of institutions on minority kids is reducing the harms these kids suffer, the current juvenile justice system—warts and all—is vastly less dangerous to minorities than the machinery of criminal justice.

I. Policy Perspectives on the Phenomenon

A. Juvenile Justice in Context: A Special or General Case?

The first issue on my agenda is whether the kind and amount of minority overrepresentation is importantly different in the juvenile justice system. How does the African American and Hispanic overrepresentation we observe for delinquency cases in the juvenile system compare to the pattern of concentration of disadvantaged minorities found in the criminal justice system in the United States?

But why should a question about the generality of the pattern that produces minority disadvantage be a starting point for seeking remedial measures? The reason is that the data can be expected to reveal whether the special organizational and substantive provisions of juvenile justice should be regarded as the proximate causes of the problem, so that shifting the special provisions or procedures of juvenile courts could be expected to provide a remedy. If it does, the specific approaches of the juvenile court should be a high priority for reform. If, however, the extent of minority overrepresentation in juvenile justice is about the same as that found in criminal justice, it is less plausible that this pattern is the product of any special characteristics of the juvenile system.

One example of the usefulness of this type of analysis concerns the relative concentration of young girls in incarcerated populations in juvenile justice. Figure 13.1 turns back the clock to compare juvenile and adult incarcerations by gender for 1974, as a familiar example of looking for special patterns in juvenile justice. The 1974 vintage for these data is to summarize patterns at

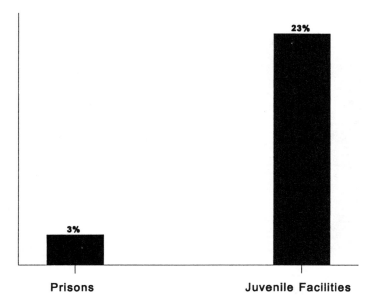

Figure 13.1. Percentage of incarcerated persons that were female in 1974. (Source: Bureau of Justice Statistics [Prisoners]; U.S. Department of Justice, Children in Custody [Juveniles].)

the time when federal legislation first mandated deinstitutionalizing status offenders.

The 23% of incarcerated juveniles who were female in 1974 constitute a proportion more than seven times that of females then found in prisons. The larger concentration of females in the juvenile distribution is an indication that different motives (including paternalism) and different substantive legal provisions (so-called status offenses) were producing different outcomes in juvenile justice. In such circumstances, reforming these special provisions should be an early priority of those concerned with the high traditional exposure of girls to juvenile incarceration. The juvenile system's rules and procedures have been clearly implicated in female incarceration.

Figure 13.2 contrasts the percentage of African Americans in juvenile and adult incarceration facilities in 1997. I dichotomize populations in prisons, jails, and juvenile facilities into African American and other groups to simplify the analysis. The other major minority group in criminal justice institutions—Hispanic populations—is more difficult to define and more uncertain in current measurements.

The 40% of incarcerated juveniles who are African American are grossly out of proportion to the African American percentage of the youth population (about 15%). Thus, overrepresentation is both obvious and substantial. But

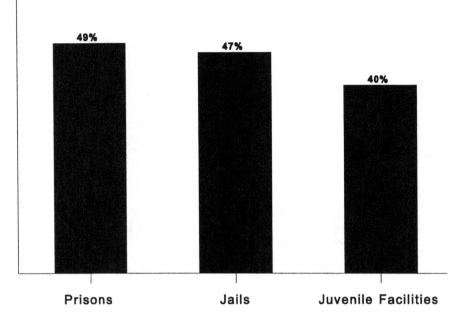

Figure 13.2. Percentage of incarcerated persons that were African American in 1997.

the concentration of African Americans incarcerated in adult criminal justice populations is even greater, with close to half of jail and prison populations so classified. If we could add in other minority populations, the size of the total minority shares would increase but the contrast between systems would remain close to that portrayed in figure 13.2.

The importance of finding this general pattern is not to minimize the problem of juvenile minority overrepresentation, but to alert policy analysts that the pattern extends beyond juvenile justice and is therefore less likely to have been generated by the peculiar rules and procedures that the juvenile system uses. The lower concentration in the juvenile system might actually suggest that shifting juvenile system priorities and procedures to what the criminal justice system does to older offenders would make things worse for minorities. This is the opposite of the likely impact of using adult rules and procedures for young girls that can be inferred from figure 13.1. So it appears that minorities are at a disadvantage in the juvenile system, but no more so than minority persons are in the rest of the criminal process. What disadvantages minority kids in delinquency cases is part of a broader pattern that probably should be addressed by multiple system approaches.

B. Equalize Disadvantage or Minimize Harm?

My friend and teacher Hans Zeisel once published a note showing that a peculiar kind of disproportion was evident in the death sentences accumulating in the state of Florida. Zeisel found that 95% of the death sentences in that state were imposed on defendants who were charged with killing white victims (Zeisel 1981). Zeisel showed that some Florida prosecutors believed that the solution to this problem was to add more murder cases with African American victims to Florida's burgeoning death row populations (Zeisel 1981, 464–466). The reason for Zeisel's anger at this tactic was that expanding a cruel and inhuman punishment was the last thing he wished to do, and moving closer to proportional representation by adding African American–victim cases to death row was a cynical manipulation of the system that again established its arbitrary cruelty. For Zeisel, much more than proportional overrepresentation was wrong with the death penalty system in Florida.

I wonder whether this story has exemplary value for many of us who worry about the overrepresentation of minorities in dead-end detention centers and training schools in 2005. The test question is this: imagine a prosecutor who responds to a finding of imbalance not by releasing minority youth but by trying to lock up many more Anglo-Saxon whites. Would this brand of affirmative action please or trouble the social critic? Why?

Many persons who justly worry about the burden of disproportionate impact on minority youth believe that the deep end of the juvenile justice system harms kids and they wish to minimize that harm. Expanding the number of kids harmed through an "affirmative action" plan that only adds nonminority targets is perverse from this perspective for two reasons. First, such an expansion of negative controls does not improve the life chances of any of the minority kids. They continue to suffer the same harms at the same rate. Second, the expansion of harms over a wider population hurts many new kids, placing them in positions of disadvantage close to those that troubled the critics about minority kids. Most of those active in addressing issues of minority overrepresentation care deeply about youth of all colors and backgrounds. This grisly form of affirmative action would be, in their view, a step backward.

My point here is that there are two problems that are rather different when addressing the impact of the system on minority kids: the disproportionate impact of sanctions on minorities and the negative effects that these sanctions have on the largely minority kids who are captured by the system. A critic of the system will have two goals—reducing the harm to kids and reducing the proportion of minority kids in the system. But which goal should have the larger priority?

In my view, the more pragmatic a system reformer becomes, the more she will choose measures that reduce the harms that minority kids suffer over programs of better proportional representation. If this is true, then harm reduction creates the opportunity to use concerns about the impact of the system on minority kids as a wedge to reduce the harmful impact of the system on all processed through it. The shift in emphasis from proportional concerns to harm reduction also means that there is no competition between minority and nonminority delinquents, but rather a natural community of interest across group boundaries to make the deep end of the juvenile system less hazardous.

There is also a dark side to the case for emphasizing harm reduction. The sharp edge of the blade in criminal justice almost always falls on disadvantaged minorities, and it is not clear that procedural reform can undo the damage. Some areas of criminal law (traffic and drugs) may respond to administrative controls that reduce the impact on minorities. Spreading traffic stops into nonminority areas can reduce the proportion of traffic arrests and fines that involve minorities. But other arenas, including violence, will remain problematic. Street crimes involve minority suspects more often than white kids for different reasons, and changes in law enforcement procedures will not end the overrepresentation of minority youth arrested for robbery and burglary. As long as minority crime victims are well served by city police, minority suspects will be a disproportionate segment of violence arrests in the United States.

C. Absolute versus Proportionate Standards of Harm in Choosing Reforms

The choice between harm reduction and proportional approaches to overrepresentation will lead to different judgments about which reforms work best. Assume that one reform will leave the proportion of incarcerated delinquents who are minorities the same but reduce the number of kids locked up by 10%. Another approach will lower the proportion of incarcerated minority kids by 10% but leave the number of minorities locked up the same. Which is better? The "least worst" outcome for minority kids in some settings will depend on what standard is selected as the most important measure of the problem. If a proportionate approach is most important, an observer will pick the outcome that results in the smallest percentage of total harm falling on the minority youth population. If a harm reduction standard is used, the observer will try to minimize the amount of harm the minority population suffers regardless of what share of total bad outcomes is absorbed by minority youth.

If highly selective styles of law enforcement concentrate bad outcomes on minorities, then the law enforcement approach that punishes minority kids in the highest percentage might still punish fewer minority kids than a system that spreads a much larger number of harmful outcomes somewhat more evenly across the youth population. The highly discretionary system may be more proportionally unjust than the system that spreads a larger level of punishment more evenly over the youth population, but the amount of harm the broader system does to vulnerable minorities is greater. A principled argument for preferring either outcome can be made. But more important than pointing to a particular preference is recognizing the potential conflict in standards.

My suspicion is that persons with backgrounds in child welfare will be more apt to choose the aggregate harm reduction standard and discount its distributive implications, while persons with strong legal orientations may be more likely to select higher aggregate harm if it is more evenly distributed.

Whatever might separate those who prefer harm reduction to reducing disproportion when hard choices have to be made, I do not think that different choices can be explained as a liberal-versus-conservative distinction. Instead, I think the conflict highlights the difference between two competing strains of opinion on the left side of the political spectrum that point to different priorities in some circumstances. I will briefly revisit this problem when discussing rules-versus-discretion competitions in reforming the law of transfer of juveniles to criminal court.

D. Evening Out versus Softening Consequences in Delinquency Cases

If minimizing the harm that falls on minority youth becomes the dominant standard for choosing policy in this area, there are many different policy levers available to seek this end. One contrast is between trying to reduce the number of minority kids subjected to harmful results without attempting to alter the consequences of a delinquency finding and trying to lower the amount of aggregate harm suffered by minority kids by reducing the harm produced by juvenile justice sanctions. The first approach tries to alter the distribution of sanctions but not the sanctions themselves. The second tries to take some of the sting out of the sanctions themselves.

Ultimately, which approach to take when choosing how to attempt reform is an empirical question that general statements cannot illuminate much. But there are some generalizations about such a choice that teach important lessons. The first point is that softening the bite of sanctions becomes a path to a priority reform only because harm reduction is selected as a priority. It is only when harm reduction is isolated as a goal that shifts in the content of sanctions rather than their distribution can compete with redistribution strategies on an equal footing in protecting minority kids.

A second point about taking some of the harm out of sanctions relates to its distributional advantage over reducing the number of minorities punished. The benefits of sanction reform reach all of those punished after the reform. All minorities who are sanctioned benefit, rather than just those who are spared the punishment as the result of a distributional reform. And all delinquents benefit, not merely the minority population. Further, since most youth held for serious acts of delinquency are at social disadvantage, the non-minority beneficiaries of the process are not all that different from the minority kids who are its core concern.

There is one potential problem with sanction-softening approaches that carries no practical weight in current conditions. A strategy that pushes for reducing the harm in sanctions would generate conflict where the youth advocate feels there are strong social and justice benefits in severe sanctions. However, most youth advocates dislike severe juvenile sanctions, so it seems safe to discount the prospects that youth advocates would be reluctant to reduce the negative impact of recent levels of sanction in American juvenile justice.

A third contrast between proportional reduction strategies and harm reduction strategies concerns the inferences about overrepresentation that justify the approach. A focus on reducing the share of sanctions absorbed by minorities may not require the assumption that some form of discrimination has produced the overrepresentation, but it is certainly much easier to justify proportional remedies when discrimination is suspected. But what if the large percentage of delinquents incarcerated for robbery and homicide from minority backgrounds is matched by arrest rates of minorities for robbery and homicide? By contrast, the question of proving discrimination is not implicated by attempts to reduce the negative impacts on sanctions for all delinquents.

I will not speculate here on the political circumstances that favor emphasis on reducing the concentration of minorities as opposed to reducing the harmful content of sanctions. These two strategies can complement each other in a coordinated program to reduce harm. Here I suspect is the reason that one rarely encounters hard-line policies toward criminal offenders in those interest groups that serve disadvantaged minorities. Minority interest groups become penal reform advocates by structural necessity.

A further implication of the close connection between concern about proportional disadvantage and concern about the harms of juvenile sanctions is that often our worry about disproportion reflects concern about the justice of the harshness of a penal measure. One reason for special concern about the overrepresentation of minorities on American death rows is the feeling that capital punishment is too degrading a sanction for a civilized nation. Our prison populations are just as skewed racially as our death rows, but ambivalence toward the death penalty makes the concentration in death cases a larger concern.

This pattern of larger distrust of more severe sanctions would predict that the expansion of sanctions in blended-jurisdiction juvenile systems, and the legislative trends toward more frequent transfer to criminal court, would exacerbate fears about minority overrepresentation in juvenile justice. Just as lowering the punitive stakes may take some of the bite out of disproportionate minority representation, raising the punitive stakes in the juvenile system can be expected to increase concerns about the extent to which this heavier burden falls on members of disadvantaged minorities.

II. Minority Disproportion and Modern Juvenile Justice Reforms

The first section of this chapter attempted to provide tools for policy analysis. The aim of this section is to apply the perspectives just outlined to consider the impact of three changes in juvenile justice policy over the past generation: (1) the proliferation of legislative transfer standards to supplement discretionary waiver by juvenile court judges, (2) the attempt to protect status offenders from secure confinement by creating separate legal categories with restricted dispositional options for status cases, and (3) diversion programs to resolve minor delinquency charges without formal juvenile court charges or adjudications. None of these three reform programs was centrally concerned with minority overrepresentation in delinquency cases; but each set of changes has an impact on minority presence in juvenile and criminal justice. Further, evaluating the impact of such changes on minority prospects is a critical task in contemporary policy analysis. A final part of this section views the substitution of juvenile court for the criminal process as a law reform that has had a positive long-range impact on minority youth in the United States.

A. Automatic Transfer Rules and Minority Harm

Almost all juvenile justice systems provide a method for transferring some accused delinquents close to aging out of the juvenile system who are charged with serious crimes into criminal court to face the much harsher sanctions that are available in the juvenile system (see Fagan and Zimring 2000). The traditional method of determining whether an older juvenile would be transferred was for a hearing to be held in the juvenile court and for the judge to decide whether he should "waive" the juvenile court's jurisdiction and therefore allow criminal prosecution (Dawson 2000). The issue before a juvenile judge in such a hearing is whether the youth is a fit subject for the juvenile court. This was always a discretionary decision, difficult to review and quite rarely reversed on appeal (Frost Clausel and Bonnie 2000).

   This type of discretion would seem an ideal breeding ground for attitudes that prejudice the prospects of African American and Hispanic juveniles. No precise studies have been done, but the track record of waiver for transferring high proportions of minority youth is not encouraging (Bortner, Zatz, and Hawkins 2000). At the same time, however, the signal virtue of traditional discretionary waiver was the low rate at which juveniles were transferred.

An almost universal addition to discretionary waiver provisions in recent years has been legislation that provides for automatic transfer of juveniles to criminal court if one from among a list of serious charges is brought against the juvenile. The charges frequently listed include murder, armed robbery, rape, and many other serious offenses (Feld 2000). The advantage of this legislative system is that it substitutes a clear rule for personal discretion. The disadvantage is that many more kids of all kinds, including many more minority kids, will be shipped to criminal court under mandatory transfer rules than under systems that transfer juveniles only after juvenile court waiver hearings. Even if the *proportion* of all kids transferred who are African American or Hispanic goes down with automatic transfer rules, the *number* of minority kids disadvantaged will increase. The rules-versus-discretion choice looks at this first impression like a competition between proportional representation and harm reduction. When automatic transfer replaces discretionary waiver, the number of minority kids harmed will increase even if the share of transferred kids from minority backgrounds declines.

A second look, however, suggests that "automatic transfer" standards have nothing to offer minority kids, not even the certainty of the application of a uniform set of rules. The only discretion less reviewable than a juvenile court judge's is that of a prosecutor, and the adoption of automatic transfer standards really substitutes a prosecutor's discretion for that of a judge. A prosecutor can select the charge to bring against a juvenile, and that charging decision will determine whether the case goes to juvenile or criminal court. No review can force a prosecutor to file more serious charges than he wants to file, or indeed to file any charges at all.

My guess is that the proportion of minorities transferred might go down somewhat in regimes of prosecutorial rather than judicial discretion, but not because prosecutors are more sensitive to minorities. Instead, as the number of juveniles transferred increased substantially, the population transferred would tend to become somewhat more like the general population of accused delinquents. By disadvantaging a much larger fraction of the youth population, the proportional share of minorities hurt by prosecutorial discretion systems might decline, but this is nobody's definition of youth welfare. The number of minority youth at risk of criminal sanctions would be expanded, and it would be small comfort that they had been joined in this vulnerability by larger numbers of nonminority youth.

Further, there is no enforceable legal principle behind this change, only the substitution of prosecutorial for judicial discretion, a shift that moves the locus of authority from a legal actor with a formal commitment to consider the welfare of the accused to a legal actor under no such obligation.

B. Deinstitutionalization of Status Offenders

Since the original juvenile court was presumed to be taking power only for the welfare of its youthful clients, that court was given power to order institutional placements including detention and training schools for young people who were truant or disobedient but had not behaved in ways that harmed others. Since juvenile court sanctions were not regarded as punishment, it was said that there was no need for proportionality limits on power assumed over delinquents, and thus no need to differentiate between burglars and runaways when distributing the juvenile court's helpful interventions.

From the start, this theory suffered from two linked problems. First, the detentions and commitments of juvenile courts were punitive in effect and often in intent, so that imposing them on kids who did not deserve punishment, or imposing much more punishment than disobedience would merit, was manifestly unjust. Second, there was no evidence that the punitive treatment of delinquents in twentieth-century juvenile justice was effective either as therapy or social control (Titlebaum 2002). The legal realism about juvenile justice that produced decisions like *In re Gault* also demanded that proportional limits be placed on the power exercised by the state over runaways, truants, and adolescents in conflict with parents. The particular target of the Federal Juvenile Justice and Delinquency Prevention Act of 1974 was to discourage the states from the practice of putting status offenders in secure confinement. While the effort to break status offenders out of juvenile jails was neither an instant nor an unqualified success, its core judgment that unlimited detention is unjust and ineffective for noncriminal misbehavior has stood the test of time, even with shifting sentiments about many other aspects of juvenile justice.

The shift in status offender policy is rarely considered as an important aspect of policies relating to minority group overrepresentation. The paternalistic excesses of juvenile justice were concentrated on girls, but the status offenders pushed into state processes were no more concentrated among minorities than were delinquents.

But did the emphasis on this policy goal help minority kids? Considering this question again raises the contrast between aggregate and proportional measures of minority disadvantage. The number of African American and Hispanic kids locked up in detention centers and training schools decreased as a direct result of successful deinstitutionalization. But the proportion of detained kids who were minorities may have increased as a result of the program. Although fewer African American kids were locked up, a greater proportion of the kids locked up might have been African American. Was this progress? I would suggest the answer to that question is yes.

But didn't the deinstitutionalization of status offenders strip the veneer of child welfare from the court and thus make harsher policy toward other classes of delinquency more acceptable (Empey 1979, 408–409)? After all, the intense pressure to crackdown on "juvenile superpredators" happened after the welfare facade of the court had been removed. So why not conclude that the latent function of status offender reforms was additional hardship for the largely minority residual of delinquents that stayed in juvenile court systems?

The first problem with such a spin on status offender reforms is that those who supported such reforms were skeptical about secure confinement for delinquents generally. There was no push to fill empty cells with burglars and joyriders from the policy analysts who had pushed the 1974 reforms on the public agenda. Nor did a juvenile court crime crackdown stem in any clear way from the status offender reforms. The get-tough rhetoric and punitive pressure that arrived in juvenile court policy debates in the 1980s were a spillover from crime policy changes in criminal justice that began in the late 1960s (Zimring, Hawkins, and Kamin 2001, chap. 9). The premises and the example of the status offender reforms probably worked against the push for punitive policy in juvenile justice and thus was consistent with the youth welfare interests of minority advocates. I will revisit this issue in the last section of this analysis.

C. Diversion and Minority Justice

What is the impact of reforms aiming to divert first-time and minor offenders from formal processing on the interests of minority offenders in juvenile justice? The policy thrust of diversion seems in harmony with lower levels of coercive controls and concern for youth welfare, but what are the results? Here again, the method of scorekeeping may determine the result. The aggregate impact of diversion on the number of minority youth in formal processing will be a benefit unless the diversion program is a complete sham. If substantial numbers of kids escape detention and adjudication, many of them will be African American and Hispanic. But even if the number of minority youth benefited is high, the proportion of those not diverted who are members of disadvantaged minorities will not go down, and it might increase. So a proportionate standard would not produce evidence that diversion had a positive impact on the problem of overrepresentation. Because I believe that harm reduction is the appropriate standard, my conclusion is that diversion programs benefit minority populations.

D. Juvenile versus Criminal Court

The last comparison that teaches us about harm reduction is between the current rate of minority incarceration from juvenile versus criminal courts. The comparison is instructive for two reasons. First, comparing the exposure

Table 13.1: Comparative Indicators of Minority Overrepresentation in the Juvenile and Criminal Justice Systems, 1995

	Juvenile Facilities	Jails	Prisons
Percentage African American in incarceration facilities	40	47	49
Incarceration rates	Ages 13–17	Ages 18–24	Ratio of 18–24-year-olds to 13–17-year-olds
African American incarceration rates	1,332 per 100,000	4,699 per 100,000	3.5

Sources: Bureau of Justice Statistics 1997a, 1997b (incarceration population); Bureau of the Census (U.S. populations).

to harm associated with these two systems is one way of forming a judgment about the aggregate impact of the juvenile court, itself a special reform in American law, on the welfare of minority populations. The second reason to compare aggregate juvenile and criminal court outcomes is to provide an indirect test of the effects that reforms like diversion and deinstitutionalization of status offenders have had on the welfare of minority youth. Comparing a system performing with these features against an alternative system for processing accused criminals might help us decide whether these major thrusts in juvenile justice over recent decades have made the system more or less sympathetic to the interests of minorities.

Table 13.1 repeats one measure of minority overrepresentation used in figure 13.2, the percentage of incarceration populations that is African American, but adds the rate (per 100,000 African American males) of incarceration in the mostly juvenile justice age brackets of 13–17 and the early criminal court age brackets of 18–24.

The juvenile versus adult data based on proportionate overrepresentation of African Americans show that 40% of all juveniles incarcerated are African American, a much higher proportion of the total incarcerated population than African American youth are of the total youth population. Still, the proportion of inmates that are African American is 20% higher for jails and prisons than for youth institutions.

But the important statistic for my argument is the rate of minority incarceration in juvenile and adult facilities. The incarceration rates for African American kids in the age 13–17 bracket is 1,332 per 100,000. The rate for African American males ages 18–24 is 3.5 times higher than for 13–17-year-olds. The adult system is not 20% more punitive than the juvenile system for African American youth; it is 250% more punitive! I suspect that the same juvenile-versus-criminal-court pattern would hold for other discrete and overrepresented minority male populations. The big difference in incarceration rates suggests that the aggregate protective impact of juvenile justice policy on minority youth is substantial when compared with criminal justice impact. To borrow a phrase from legal Latin, *res ipsa loquitur*.

Conclusions

The overrepresentation of disadvantaged minorities in the juvenile justice system is part of a broader pattern observed throughout law enforcement in the United States and in most other places. The particular doctrines and processes of juvenile courts do not appear to exacerbate overrepresentation when compared to criminal courts.

This analysis has contrasted two approaches to the problem of overrepresentation, a legalist view that emphasizes reducing disproportionate impact and a youth welfare view that attempts to reduce the harms suffered by minority youth.

The major positive reforms in juvenile justice over the past generation—deinstitutionalization of status offenders and diversion—have not had a dramatic impact on the disproportionate involvement of minority youth in the deep end of the juvenile system. But the lower levels of incarceration embraced by juvenile courts mean that the harms suffered within juvenile courts by all sorts of youth are much smaller than the harms imposed on young offenders in America's criminal courts. It turns out that the entire apparatus of juvenile justice is functioning as a substantial harm reduction program for minority delinquents.

What I have called a harm reduction perspective shows clearly that those concerned about the healthy development of minority youth must also be invested in the continued operation of the juvenile court as by far the lesser evil in modern crime control. That the institutions of juvenile justice need reform should not obscure the fact of their lesser harm or its policy implications.

References

Bortner, M. A., Marjorie S. Zatz, and Darnell F. Hawkins. 2000. "Race and Transfer: Empirical Research and Social Context." In *The Changing Borders of Juvenile Justice*, ed. Jeffery Fagan and Franklin E. Zimring. Chicago: University of Chicago Press.

Dawson, Robert O. 2000. "Judicial Waiver in Theory and Practice." In *The Changing Borders of Juvenile Justice*, ed. Jeffery Fagan and Franklin E. Zimring. Chicago: University of Chicago Press.

Empey, LaMar T. 1979. *The Future of Childhood and Juvenile Justice*. Charlottesville, VA: University Press of Virginia.

Fagan, Jeffrey, and Franklin E. Zimring, eds. 2000. *The Changing Borders of Juvenile Justice*. Chicago: University of Chicago Press.

Feld, Barry C. 2000. "Legislative Exclusion of Offenses from Juvenile Court Jurisdiction: A History and Critique." In *The Changing Borders of Juvenile Justice*, ed. Jeffery Fagan and Franklin E. Zimring. Chicago: University of Chicago Press.

Frost Clausel, Lynda E., and Richard J. Bonnie. 2000. *Juvenile Justice on Appeal*. In *The Changing Borders of Juvenile Justice*, ed. Jeffery Fagan and Franklin E. Zimring. Chicago: University of Chicago Press.

Moone, Joseph. 1993. *Children in Custody 1991: Private Facilities: Prevention Fact Sheet 2, 5*. Washington, DC: Office of Juvenile Justice and Delinquency Prevention.

National Criminal Justice Information and Statistics Service. 1974. *Children in Custody*. Washington, DC: National Criminal Justice Information and Statistics Service.

Titlebaum, Lee. 2002. "Status Offenders." In *A Century of Juvenile Justice*, ed. Margaret Rosenheim, Franklin E. Zimring, David S. Tanenhaus, and Bernardine Dohrn. Chicago: University of Chicago Press.

U.S. Department of Justice, Bureau of the Census. 1997. *Current Population Reports: Estimates of the Population of the United States by Age, Sex, and Race*. Washington DC: U.S. Government Printing Office.

U.S. Department of Justice, Bureau of Justice Statistics. 1974. *Correctional Populations in the United States*. Washington DC: U.S. Government Printing Office.

———. 1997a. *Correctional Populations in the United States*. Washington DC: U.S. Government Printing Office.

———. 1997b. *Children in Custody*. Washington DC: U.S. Government Printing Office.

Zeisel, Hans. 1981. "Race Bias in the Administration of the Death Penalty: The Florida Experience." *Harvard Law Review* 95:456.

Zimring, Franklin E., Gordon Hawkins, and Sam Kamin. 2001. *Punishment and Democracy: Three Strikes and You're Out in California*. New York: Oxford University Press. Washington, DC: National Criminal Justice Information and Statistics Service.

14

Conclusion: Our Children, Their Children

Kimberly Kempf-Leonard and
Darnell F. Hawkins

WE HAVE compiled this volume early in the twenty-first century, at a time of significant and unprecedented advances in science and technology. These breakthroughs allow many of us to communicate and work within an increasingly global economy, to live healthy and productive lives well beyond the ages of previous generations, and to offer our children the opportunity to experience a quality of life far superior to that of even the recent past. The discovery of DNA is only fifty years old, but already this knowledge has benefited health care, freed many wrongfully convicted of crimes, and raised the possibilities of therapeutic cloning. Nanotechnology is giving us access to the infinitesimal, and the vast frontier of space travel seems less remote, with satellites providing television and cellular phone programming, recording the locations of our cars, and even keeping track of some offenders serving sentences in the community. At the dawning of a new century, most of the United States has also recently experienced several years of unexpected declining rates of crime, particularly in those offenses involving juveniles. These declines have occurred despite dire predictions to the contrary during the late 1980s and early 1990s. This is also a historic period in many states during which there are centennial celebrations of the separate juvenile justice and welfare systems established to benefit and care for our children and assure their successful transition into adulthood. Progress is evident, and our lives have benefited in innumerable ways from both scientific achievements and unanticipated social change.

As in the past, periods of scientific advancement and social progress frequently lead to heightened and renewed interest in seeking solutions to longstanding social problems. The juvenile justice system reforms of the late nineteenth and early twentieth centuries also followed a period of enormous progress and change. Reflecting that impetus and precedent, the goal of this

428

volume has been to summarize what social scientists currently know about reasons for racial and ethnic disparities in juvenile offending and in the administration of justice in the United States, and about effective mechanisms to reduce those differences. As we noted in our introduction, this has been a vexing social and legal problem in American society for a long time. During the current period of otherwise rapid societal change, racial and ethnic disparities in American crime and justice persist and raise questions about how far the nation has come during the past half-century toward reaching its much-heralded goal of achieving fairness and equal opportunity in American society and in its systems of justice.

With the generous support of the John D. and Catherine T. MacArthur Foundation's Network on Adolescent Development and Juvenile Justice, we convened a stellar group of researchers who have previously pursued lines of inquiry related to this important social problem. Authors met and discussed substantive topics of interest and the state of scientific progress in this area of social and legal research, then commenced writing independent, but mutually reinforcing, chapters. Each chapter was subsequently reviewed by at least two external authorities that the editors chose and two reviewers selected by the publishers. The result is the book you have just read, the first volume devoted specifically to a comprehensive analysis and understanding of the extent and determinants of racial and ethnic differences in adolescent development in patterns and rates of offending, and in the administration of justice for American youths. Collectively, the authors review the current state of social scientific knowledge in this area of research and propose changes in law and public policy that may lead to more success for the nation's children, regardless of their ethnic or racial origins. In this concluding chapter we: (1) highlight the volume's major findings regarding racial and ethnic disparities in juvenile crime and in the administration of juvenile justice; (2) summarize what is known regarding the developmental, environmental, and broader social factors that contribute to these disparities, including a discussion of how community and neighborhood may factor into explanations related to behavioral differences and differential treatment; and (3) attempt to glean from the various chapters strategies to reduce unwarranted disparities and promote justice. We propose a strategy that emphasizes cooperation, competency, and accountability across the many legal and public policy arenas charged with the care of our children.

Identifying and Explaining Racial and Ethnic Disparities

Since its establishment as a nation, American society has been involved in frequently contentious efforts to reduce unwarranted disparities across the diverse racial, ethnic, religious, and cultural groupings that make up our population.[1] For more than a century, particular attention has been paid to assuring that law and governmental actions do not contribute to such disparity, which they had done during the two preceding centuries. As this legal and social movement has progressed, it has become clear that the realization of our now widely accepted national objective requires that we understand (1) where within the society and its institutions racial and ethnic disparities exist; (2) which racial, ethnic, or other groups are most affected; and (3) whether and why such disparities appear to be unwarranted and unacceptable. That is the social scientific task contributors to this volume were asked to undertake within the context of the nation's juvenile justice system. As several chapters in this volume have shown, our efforts to make such assessments within the nation's diverse, highly decentralized, and widely dispersed juvenile justice arena have been aided somewhat by federal legislation. With the reauthorization in 1990 of the Juvenile Justice and Delinquency Prevention Act, Congress provided a financial incentive for states to identify whether disproportionate minority confinement (DMC) was evident in their juvenile justice systems. The DMC component of the JJDP Act represents an important policy-relevant initiative; therefore, we begin our summary critique of the chapters in this volume and our own effort to identify future research needs and plausible interventions by revisiting the findings to date from that important initiative.

How Much Disparity? Which Groups Are Overrepresented within the Juvenile System?

It is often assumed, frequently on the basis of media accounts, that answers to the two straightforward questions of how much disparity there is and which groups are overrepresented in the juvenile justice system are easy to come by and that the data are unequivocal. Yet, while our review identified many frequently and uniformly reported findings in response to the questions we posed, there is also much yet to be learned. As Pope and Leiber report in chapter 11, the existence of racial disparity appears to have been documented with a high level of consistency in nearly every state of the United States since the DMC initiative began. While not focusing specifically on the DMC, Bishop reinforces their findings through her comprehensive review in chapter 2 of the broader scientific literature. Both the DMC research and Bishop's chapter reveal that the minority youths most often overrepresented in confinement are blacks, followed by Hispanics and Native Americans. Asian Americans, as a broad, undifferentiated grouping, tend to be somewhat underrepresented in juvenile justice system involvement. Beyond those general, often repeated observations much remains unknown. One unknown is the comprehensiveness and completeness of the sources of data used to reach these conclusions. Although they are the best nationwide data available, it is important to note that the observations and studies relied upon by Pope and Leiber are derived from voluntary and nonstandardized state responses to the DMC and may not document fully or accurately the extent of actual racial and ethnic disparities in the nation's elaborate and geographically dispersed juvenile justice system.

Beyond possible bias in reporting, current observations of disparity often reflect poorly specified race and ethnicity categories. Several authors in this volume argue that important distinctions of race and ethnicity cannot be observed across the broad categories currently available. Most information sources identify subjects as white, black, Hispanic, Asian, and Native American. In many studies researchers have reported levels of disparity across even broader, scientifically cruder categories, such as white and nonwhite youths. In addition, the measure of "disproportionality" used by the federal DMC initiative is based on a combined tally of individual cases of system processing for each state. This aggregation at the state level of disparities across broadly defined racial groups masks many meaningful local, regional or other subgroup differences that might be helpful in understanding the problem or suggesting a solution. For example, we cannot observe intraracial or interethnic differences such as those between Mexican Americans and Cuban Americans among Latinos, or between Asian Americans such as those of Chinese or Japanese descent, and so forth. Such intrarace comparisons, while not seen as politically and legally salient as white-versus-nonwhite comparisons, may nonetheless have much importance for understanding the causes of group differences in delinquency and for devising culturally sensitive intervention protocols within the juvenile justice system.

Such definitional problems and the politics surrounding them are hardly limited to this country. Both within and outside of the United States, how race and ethnicity are defined and enumerated (or not) largely reflects broader political and social contexts, and often very localized concerns. For example, in Canada public records allow for the specification of indigenous people but otherwise do not permit the recording of race and ethnicity, even in the form of self-identification, which the choices provided in the 2000 U.S. census allow. Many western European countries often fail to record the kinds of racial and ethnic distinctions in official records that we have grown accustomed to in this country. In parts of the United States, the use of specific racial categories is primarily a function of population size, rather than strict conformity to the broad racial categories typically used in the census and criminal justice record keeping. In those areas where certain racial or ethnic groups are represented in relatively large numbers, they are much more likely than groups of smaller population size to be "counted" as separate, identifiable groups in various public records. For example, until recently many areas of small town and rural America had so few persons of Latino descent that juvenile justice officials simply labeled them as "whites" or "nonwhites." In other areas where small numbers of Asian Americans, Latinos, and African Americans live, the composite group that is compared to European Americans becomes "nonwhites." Thus, the extent to which definitions of race and ethnicity are subjective and vary by time and location and how these affect findings of ethnic and racial disparity in the DMC and other studies are questions that merit additional inquiry.

In addition to identifying disparity, the federal DMC initiative also supports and encourages efforts to explain and reduce minority overrepresentation. That is, the federal initiative asked states to conduct research to help determine why racial and ethnic disparity exists across the widely used, albeit crude and ill-defined, racial/ethnic categories. Of course, the attempt to realize that goal has characterized much of social science research on crime and justice in both the adult and juvenile systems for nearly a century. To a large extent, most of the chapters in the volume attempt to probe this important question in some form or another. When compared to one another, the chapters in this volume clearly illuminate the state of the science in this area of research and public policy, including the current lack of consensus in response to the question of what causes observed race disparity. For instance, in their review of the progress of, and findings from, the federal DMC initiative, Pope and Leiber conclude that, as an explanation for racial and ethnic disparities in juvenile justice, most research points to differential official processing by race and ethnicity. In contrast, Tracy's critique (in chap. 10) of many of the same DMC studies leads him to believe that the results are much more equivocal. He argues that some contrary and inconclusive findings have been repeatedly mischaracterized as evidence of differential treatment and racial bias, in part to advance a political agenda of court reform. In his own analyses of juvenile cases in three Texas counties, Tracy identifies five of a possible thirty-six court stages of disparity that may negatively affect minorities and finds that differential rates of offending account for most of the disparity observed. In his view, "the problem is almost surely one of societal inequities rather than practitioner racism." As we later note, this tendency to contrast behavioral with system determinants of disparity permeates most of the literature on racial disparity for both juveniles and adults. It is an either-or contrast that is useful in some regards but that in the long run may not take us far toward truly understanding why racial and ethnic disparity exists and what can be done to reduce it. This is a point of view increasingly shared by both social scientists and decision makers (e.g., see McCord, Widom, and Crowell 2001).

Despite limitations, available data sources are sufficient for us to conclude that significant disparities for youths by race and ethnicity do indeed exist in the American justice systems and that these processing differences are not always easily or neatly explained in either-or terms. Furthermore, there is a persistent debate in this regard that can perhaps be traced to the origins of the juvenile court. It involves the question of whether racial and ethnic disparity within the juvenile justice is unexpected, is inherently unwarranted, and should always be avoided. Much of this debate has centered on the historic mission of juvenile justice as a kind of "safety net" or "intervener of first resort" for youth in distress. Both during the past and today, early intervention by juvenile justice has been seen as preferred to an "uncorrected" life of adult criminality. It has also been seen as the only viable source of help and support for many of the nation's most underprivileged youths. According to this line of reasoning, just as Irish, Italian, Polish and Jewish youths represented the underclass of an earlier era (Tanenhaus [chap. 4]), African-American, Latino, Native American, and some Asian youths represent today's underclass and have much the same needs (for correction) as their white ethnic predecessors vis-à-vis the juvenile justice and child welfare systems.

Using this logic, some would argue that the fact that some racial/ethnic minority groups are disproportionately represented within the justice system is as it "should be" given their economic standing and hence their "need" for the resources found within the juvenile system. There is some anecdotal evidence to suggest that many decision makers within the modern juvenile justice system refer greater numbers of minority youths, especially the most distressed among them, to "official processing" within the system (as opposed to various other alternatives) because they believe that these youths are more likely to get the help they need within the system than outside it. As during the past, this seemingly "noble" intention has both its pluses and minuses. Many of the assorted appendages that have come to be associated with the juvenile court were designed purposely to serve the "neediest among us." Along with the court itself, these agencies aimed to act as surrogate parents, state-appointed counselors, and psychologists or psychiatrists for at-risk youth. Given these avowed goals of juvenile justice and the fact that a disproportionate share of some racial and ethnic groups, such as African-Americans, Native Americans, and Latinos, are found among the "truly disadvantaged" (Wilson 1987), some argue that they will inevitably be disproportionately represented among the ranks of the youths that system serves. Of course, as earlier noted, whether the juvenile justice system actually rises to this challenge has been hotly debated. Similarly, and as is revealed in several chapters in the volume, the question of whether racial, ethnic, or social class bias or animus affect decisions regarding the choice of alternatives for "treatment" and "punishment" presumably available to the court is also widely debated.

Still other commentators argue that if decision makers within the juvenile justice system fail to take into account the comparative destitution of some groups of minorities in comparison to the majority of whites and more privileged minorities, they may be guilty of supporting a subtle form of "benign neglect." In 1970, Daniel Patrick Moynihan, then an adviser to Richard Nixon, called for a policy of "benign neglect" in response to the problems of the minority poor, especially those in the nation's inner cities. Viewing these blighted areas as potentially capable of "evolving" into more sustainable and economically viable communities on their own over time, the policy supported "benign neglect" as a way to push that transition more speedily forward. In the three decades since then, many social scientists, liberal politicians, and many minorities have used the term derisively to label and question the wisdom of numerous governmental policies that are said to ignore the plight of America's poor, especially poor people of color. In response to this seeming endorsement of the doctrine of *parens patriae,* other commentators have been quick to note that when governmental attention does turn to the minority community, "benign neglect" is often replaced with a sinister form of "malign neglect" or outright racial animus (Tonry 1995; Miller 1996; Cole 1999). In this regard, several contributors to this volume have noted the double-edged sword that is evident in the tendency to use the juvenile justice system to attempt to respond to such societal-level problems as poverty and racial discrimination. Even if this is well intended, one undesirable consequence of using the juvenile justice system as a surrogate parent or service agent is the accumulation of a juvenile "record." Once labeled as at-risk, even if perceived to be more in need of help than punishment, many minority youths often find themselves prime candidates for greater scrutiny and punishment as adults than they would have been in the absence of such early interventions. Ironically, the system that was designed to "save" youths from a life of adult criminality may actually increase the likelihood that this transition will occur. Those are the challenges we face today. They are also challenges and perceptions that have been confronted during the past, and, though perennial, they have much relevance for how we respond as a society to racial and ethnic disparity in juvenile justice and what we think can or should be done about it.

The Behavioral Difference versus Differential Treatment Debate

In 1935, Thorsten Sellin described and criticized "the marked influence of race and nationality prejudice in the administration of justice" (212). He characterized the racial disparity he observed in sentencing of adults during the 1920s and 1930s as follows: "It may be said, of course, that the statistics presented hide a number of possible variables, such as differences among these race and nativity groups in such factors as recidivism, aggravating circumstances, etc., which might produce differences in the length of sentences attributable to no prejudice on the part of the judge. While these factors may play a role, they are probably not responsible for the great and relatively constant variations observed. These we must largely attribute to the human equation in judicial administration and as evidence that equality before the law is a social fiction" (217). With the progress that has been made since then in scientific measurement and data analysis, today we recognize that Sellin's interpretation of the facts may have exceeded what his limited tabular analyses were capable of conveying. However, even with more sophisticated multivariate statistical techniques available now, social scientists continue to debate whether most race and ethnic disparity is best explained by differences in offending or by differential treatment by justice officials. As we noted, this lack of consensus on why disparity currently exists is evident among authors in this volume. On the other hand, we also think that their contributions point the way to moving beyond this etiological dilemma.

Following her critique of research on race, ethnicity, and juvenile justice processing in chapter 1, Bishop concludes that differential involvement in crime exists, but that differential treatment also exists independent of offending and at nearly every stage in juvenile justice. Her assessment, thus, offers support for each of the divergent views, including those of Pope and Lieber, as well as Tracy, which we discussed earlier. Further, Bishop highlights the complicated issues involved in understanding why disparities by race and ethnicity occur. Perhaps most important, she points out that most research on differential treatment has examined data measuring individual court cases.

From these court studies, Bishop reports that early stages of the juvenile justice process are very important. In particular, initial screening decisions enable white youths to be diverted from formal processing, while minority youths with similar offenses are more likely to be formally processed. However, within the formal process, where adjudication intuitively seems to be the most consequential, evidence of a direct race effect is much more contradictory and most often does not identify minority disadvantage. That is, once they have made their way into later stages of the justice process, white and minority youths appear to be treated relatively equally. This finding likely reflects selection bias, which occurs when researchers fail to consider "front end" effects, with white youths more often screened out of the system. As a result, these studies erroneously compare minority youths with a range of needs and offenses ("apples") to very needy and serious offending white youths ("oranges"). Sometimes the evidence is compelling that judges do not use race and ethnicity to sanction juveniles. A more common finding suggests system bias is an indirect race effect related to process. For example, minority youths are more likely than white youths with similar offenses to land in prehearing detention; and prehearing custody is often the best predictor of sentences with restrictive and longer dispositions.

Information on race and ethnic differences in offending is complicated in similar ways. Lauritsen and Tracy, in particular, both identify data that show an overrepresentation of black, and to a lesser extent, Latino, involvement in violent juvenile crimes. These differences are observed repeatedly in arrest data obtained from police agencies, although some categories are cross-validated by victim reports and other sources. For other types of offending, patterns of race and ethnic differences are observed less often or inconsistently across data sources. Most notable is the discrepancy across observations of drug offending; the race gap is large in police data but small or reversed in information obtained from self-reports on crime. This discrepancy suggests the need for caution in how we interpret race differences in some patterns of offending. In chapter 3, Lauritsen uses the "war on drugs" to highlight how police arrest practices can reflect race-linked policies and procedures and hence produce racially imbalanced "offense" data. Issues of reliability also exist in other sources of information about individual offending for nonviolent offenses among youth, but these other data are more limited in scope and availability and are less useful for reaching conclusions about the presence or absence of racial bias. Yet, if self-report data are accurate, many, less serious types of juvenile offending show much less ethnic/racial difference than the more serious categories of crime. Of course, serious crime is what elicits the greatest public concern.

Available information shows some variation in juvenile offending by race and ethnic groups but what we know about the differences is restricted to broad categories of crime and race within which important substantive variation is just beginning to be investigated. We know very little about subgroup differences found within broad racial and ethnic categories. Anecdotal data suggest that these differences may be significant in some instances. We do not know, for example, whether blacks of Jamaican, Haitian or African descent who have migrated to the United States have rates of offending different from those of native-born African Americans. Similarly, we do not know for certain how Puerto Ricans and Cubans differ from Mexican Americans or U.S. Latinos from South America. In addition, while it is well known that white southerners have different crime patterns than nonsouthern whites, we know little about other regional or ethnic group differences within the white population, including recent European immigrants.[2]

It is easy to become disheartened that social science has not yet resolved the question of whether and why racial and ethnic disparities in criminal conduct exist despite nearly a century of scientific investigation designed to do so. We have access to a plethora of data on offending and justice and increasingly robust techniques for analyzing them, but we still do not know why disparity exists. In the long-standing debate on whether racial disparity is chiefly attributable to race differences in behavior or case-processing decisions for the handling of individual cases, it is noteworthy that proponents on both sides now consider community and other multilevel social dimensions related to race and ethnicity the key to their argument. Given the increasing recognition of the importance of location for understanding and unraveling class, race, and ethnic differences in both conduct and system processing, let us now turn to that body of literature and examine its potential scientific and public policy relevance.

Race, Ethnicity, and Place: The Role of Community and Neighborhood

Several authors in this volume contend that lack of progress in explaining racial and ethnic disparities exists because researchers neglect community or other sociostructural differences and focus almost exclusively on directly observable (more or less) characteristics of individuals, such as skin color, ethnic heritage, nationality, social class "markers," or other descriptors of persons seen in arrest records and in records maintained by judicial and correctional entities. Similarly, while social context and environment would appear to have obvious relevance for understanding racial and ethnic differences in law enforcement and in the administration of justice, some contemporary researchers often have turned a blind eye. These failures to consider environment or location influences seem curious, given known connections between social conditions and crime, how these vary from place to place, and our country's history of segregation. Absent in these traditional analyses is the recognition that "poor" individuals often reside in "poor" communities; and in the United States racial and ethnic minorities inhabit communities that are often set apart from those of whites. This absence of an ecological perspective is at least partially the result of the now well-acknowledged limitations of traditional sources of data and analytical techniques, and of narrowly focused theories and research designs.

It is clear that to move beyond this impasse new inquiries must overcome these deficiencies by using multilevel theories and data and multidisciplinary approaches. Bishop suggests the following reciprocal connections: "differential offending and disparities in processing influence one another and are mutually affected by underlying structural conditions and the cultural contexts in which they occur" (p. 64). It also is clear that racial and ethnic disparity requires a multilevel explanatory model. Fortunately, some prior research does provide a good foundation on which to build new inquiries.

The critical first step is capturing the relevant risk and protective factors associated with varying locations. Poverty, as a risk factor, is the obvious first candidate on whose relevance many social scientists agree. As shown by Piquero, Moffitt, and Lawton (chap. 7), the deleterious effects on poor children, particularly African Americans, begin even before birth. In chapter 6,

Jargowsky, Desmond, and Crutchfield develop compelling arguments about the relationships between suburban sprawl and the concentration of poverty. The effect of this "spatial mismatch" is segregation by race and social class. The effects of this segregation are, in turn, poor schooling, lack of positive role models, parochial control, joblessness, and a subculture of poverty which increase the probability of juvenile offending in the area. According to Jargowsky and his colleagues, "The crime-conducive codes [of the streets] are products of street corner lifestyles, which are themselves products of joblessness in inner city neighborhoods, which isolate and concentrate poverty." Another result of living in poverty is that the juvenile justice system comes to serve as a surrogate mental and public health system, according to Cauffman and Grisso (chap. 12), who also suggest that the family-level effects of segregation are heightened risks of substance abuse, physical abuse, and mental health problems among residents. Piquero, Moffitt, and Lawton advance connections between such disadvantaged locations and environmental contaminants, such as lead poisoning, and developmental health problems, such as those that result from low birth weight, and conclude that these connections compound difficulties at the individual level.

Future research may find that the nexus of poverty and location is a necessary condition to explain varying levels in race and ethnic disparities, but it is unlikely to be completely sufficient. That is, other factors must also be considered. For example, Lauritsen reports on a study of five cities which found major differences in levels of juvenile homicide both by area and between black, white, and Latino males. To understand these location differences, she suggests looking within rather than across racial and ethnic groups and at the behavior of the police. Most prior research has treated police behavior as a constant, compared arrest rates only for black and white youths, and given no consideration to the spatial mismatch arguments.

The community-level argument from studies of juvenile justice processing also suggests that urban and rural systems respond to youths with different approaches. Rural and suburban systems generally serve smaller populations, so it is intuitive that they also have fewer cases and can use less formal, less hurried procedures to provide services. In contrast, busy urban systems are more bureaucratic and expedite case processing with criteria based on alleged offenses and the likelihood of a youth's guilt. If this relationship is true, the "criminalization" approach in urban systems may result in harsher sanctions, and it is urban locations where minority youths disproportionately reside. Bray, Sample, and Kempf-Leonard (chap. 9) use new techniques to examine this multilevel "justice by geography" issue. Consistent with the "criminalization" argument, urban courts make more use of "legal" offense factors than other courts. More important, courts do use race to decide case outcomes regardless of location.

The evidence thus far is compelling that race and ethnicity differences in behavior are real and are not simply an artifact of record-keeping practices or bias in the administration of justice alone. Official records of crime, in particular, show heightened rates for some minorities among offense categories that many consider serious and violent, but no difference or higher rates for white youths among minor offenses. The patterns are less evident in other sources of information, and some self-report data show reversed patterns for some drug offenses. There is room for improvement in the measurement of race, ethnicity, and crime in all sources. The evidence also is compelling that some officials within systems of justice for youths process cases differently based on race and ethnicity. Differential treatment may occur for many reasons, but all are made possible within a decision-making structure that allows considerable discretion. We discuss what is known about these more subjective influences next.

Do Subjective Decisions Perpetuate and Exacerbate Disparity?

In contrast to the adult system, juvenile justice officials are permitted to exercise considerably more discretion. This latitude is designed to provide individualized responses and assure the "best interests" of each child. Evidence suggests that children have not always benefited from the exercise of this discretion, and that minority youths may be even less well served by the unstructured decision making within traditional juvenile justice systems. In the absence of objective information and guidance, subjective decisions are more apt to reflect personal whim, intuition, or bias. They also are more likely than decisions guided by valid, relevant criteria to lack consistency across decision makers. Some degree of discretion is, of course, desirable and inevitable. Unfortunately, officials in both adult and juvenile justice systems must make many decisions, some quickly, in settings lacking information or knowledge about what is best (Gottfredson and Gottfredson 1980). Voters, teachers, neighbors, victims, and others in the community also make decisions that are not adequately informed, but few of these have the life-altering effects of decisions made in systems of justice. Decisions which lack competency, particularly when made by officials who are not held accountable for their actions, are another source of racial and ethnic disparity in juvenile crime rates and justice processing.

The negative impact for minority youths of subjectivity in diagnosing youth problems and developing appropriate treatments is documented in several chapters reported in this volume. Steen and her colleagues show in chapter 8 how the subjective interpretations in reports and recommendations made by probation officers negatively affect black youths. Officers more often blame external, family problems or suggest that the youth is failing to make constructive choices in cases involving white offenders. In contrast, for quite similar cases involving black offenders, officers more often disparage the youths' lack of goals, active pursuit of destructive choices, and their need to be held accountable for those choices. Personal attributes (extralegal factors) appear to outweigh purely legal factors in these subjective decisions of risk, and African Americans are disadvantaged in the process.

Similarly, Cauffman and Grisso identify subjectivity in mental health evaluations that interpret whites as mentally disturbed and in need of treatment, but similarly situated blacks as disorderly in their conduct and able to change on their own. They note the lack of epidemiological data on mental health by ethnicity and the widespread use of assessment instruments that are not sensitive to race and ethnic diversities. These authors also raise concerns about racial and ethnic differences in perceptions about the value of using mental health services and available access. Juvenile justice systems were implemented to serve the best interests of children, so it is easy to understand that systems should help those youths who need health care and other social services. To do otherwise would constitute neglect. Many child welfare advocates consider juvenile justice intervention an ideal option for youths without alternatives, but many also question the quality or comparability of treatment.

Given their role as initiators of much of the contact between youths and the justice system, the discretionary powers of the police play an important role in producing racial and ethnic disparity. Although there are fewer studies about police interaction with youths, Bishop found little evidence of overt bias by police. She speculates, however, that because of "typescripting" that implicitly includes negative stereotypes, law enforcement policies and practices appear racially neutral but are discriminatory in effect. There are several plausible scenarios. First, some areas are patrolled more heavily because of views about troubled neighborhoods that also extend to residents. Second, police-initiated stops and other forms of profiling reflect subjective interpretations, perhaps that youth suspects who are minorities tend to be insolent and uncooperative. Similar observations are made by Lauritsen. Clearly, the actions of law enforcement should be the target of much more research on racial and ethnic disparity in the future.

In addition, it is important to remember that subjectivity can flow both ways. Elevated arrest rates and hostile responses by minority youths to casual inquiries by police officers may also reflect stereotypes held by minority youths about police. These stereotypes may be a by-product of the aggressive patrol techniques used in minority neighborhoods. Much ongoing research suggests that such law enforcement practices, often in the form of racial profiling, have contributed to distrust of police and cynicism of the law and justice systems among minorities and are felt most acutely among youths.

Adding to the plight of minority youths, neighbors, including older minorities, may be more apt to fear them based only on distorted images from television and other media programming. Victims and others in the community might view minority youths as more deserving of custody and formal processing than white youths.

We need to understand how and where racial and ethnic biases in public perceptions and in perceptions of decision makers affect minority youths and their risk of being processed in the juvenile justice system. Some juvenile justice officials, neighbors, and residents of the community do consider youths of color more acutely in need of services, more of a risk to public safety, or both. Rather than impose custody or other restrictions, decision makers need to be better equipped to make the critical decisions in the community and in "official" justice systems. The important next step is to develop and disseminate information that can help improve the competence of these critical decisions so that all children benefit.

Reducing Disparity through Cooperation, Competency, and System Accountability

No children, whether generally perceived as "ours" or "theirs," will benefit if the attempted resolution of racial disparity in juvenile justice involves ignoring race and ethnicity or abolishing juvenile justice and returning to a single criminal justice system. Although either might be seen as a "quick fix" to problems related to discretionary decisions, experience has shown that both strategies fail. Actually, some, potentially more encouraging, steps to progress in overcoming problems of race and ethnic disparity in juvenile justice are pretty clear and have begun to be implemented in many jurisdictions, sometimes in response to the DMC. Nevertheless, because the causes of disparity are complex, and multilevel and interact to reinforce each other, these same traits must characterize our solutions if they are to be effective.

Some of the important next steps toward reducing racial and ethnic disparity require establishing a better setting for the decision-making process within the administration of justice. Researchers have suggested that competent decisions require (1) goals that are understood, (2) the existence of a well-defined structure within which decisions can occur, and (3) the availability to decision makers of the knowledge and information about the choices they have at their disposal, including an understanding of the circumstances in which each option is best (Gottfredson and Gottfredson 1980). Conceived correctly, a responsive and accountable juvenile justice framework will encourage a more responsive community environment, which will lead to a racially and ethnically more equitable distribution of youths who understand what is expected of them and who have the skills to fill the citizenship roles expected of them. It remains for us to encourage institutional reforms that can make competent decisions an integral part of routine procedures.

First, there must be agreement on the objectives of juvenile justice, and these must be the same goals for all children. We must overcome the view that public safety and individual empowerment are incompatible goals for a legal system of juvenile justice. This perceived mismatch is what Bernard (1992) calls "coercive social welfare" and what Feld (chap. 5) blames for the "transformation from a nominally rehabilitative welfare agency into a second-class criminal court." The current approach results in uncoordinated procedures which negatively affect minority youths. In this regard, Bishop says, "In sum, at both the individual and the community levels, it seems that the unique social welfare concerns of the juvenile court (based on real and perceived family, school, and other problems) combine with traditional social control concerns (focused on real and perceived culpability and danger to society) to produce greater minority involvement in the juvenile justice system" (chap. 2, p. 65).

Rather than sacrifice either the best interests of the child or public safety in favor of the other desired goal, competent procedures can achieve both. It is for this reason that Hirschi and Gottfredson (1993) favor expanding juvenile justice systems to serve adults too and Zimring (chap. 13) underscores the need to pursue procedures that minimize potential harm. This requires that the dual objectives of social welfare and public safety be retained, but structured within a system that makes it clear to administrators, juvenile offenders, victims, and the community that government accepts some responsibility and participates in the process of nurturing children. Juvenile justice systems should not be "the backdoor approach" to social services, as Cauffman and Grisso and others suggest now happens. The *parens patriae* doctrine needs to be reinterpreted to assure that it means legal responsibility *and* effective procedures for delivering adequate resources, attention, monitoring, and discipline to assure children become successful adults. Those who administer justice for juveniles need to recognize what parents of multiple children already know: no single method of parenting works for every child. To overcome the obstacles that now preclude an effective systematic approach for reducing race and ethnic disparity in juvenile crime and justice will require more cooperation, competency development, and accountability across many social arenas.

Second, we must provide a framework in which competent decisions can be made. This framework should be structured to encourage consistency and accountability of decision makers, but it should not be devoid of the power to deliberate effectively. Too often when procedures are standardized or mandated in an effort to be neutral on race, sex, class, or age, the unintended consequences of the reforms actually exacerbate existing inequities, create new problems, and institutionalize both. This happens because the social dimensions that interact with demographic traits are not considered. This is precisely the concern raised by Michael Tonry (1996) about current U.S. sentencing guideline policies. In sharp contrast to the "just deserts" reformers who blamed disparities on judicial discretion and indeterminate policies (e.g., von Hirsch 1976), Tonry advocates "guided discretion" to enable decision makers to consider the substantive differences among offenders in addition to their offenses. Others also argue that equal application of the law cannot exist in an unequal society (e.g., Simpson 1991). Although emphasis on uniform procedures is newer in juvenile justice, this trend is evident in recent waves of reforms, such as determinate sentencing, mandatory certification and detention provisions, and risk assessment and classification scores.

Many of these new policies rigidly define some children as ineligible for jurisdiction within juvenile justice systems. In some states, legislatures have lowered the age of criminal court jurisdiction, made certification more likely for certain types of allegations or at specific ages, and given responsibility to adult corrections agencies for supervision of some adjudicated youth. Without due consideration of meeting the needs of children, these changes may worsen disparities and reduce public safety because juvenile justice problems often pale in comparison to those in criminal justice (e.g., Rosenberg 1999; Zimring [chap. 13]). Moreover, when policies and procedures specifically for children are not available, experience has shown that citizens and justice system officials often will do nothing or opt for the minimum rather than subject youths to procedures intended for adults (Bernard 1992; see also Hamparian et al. 1982; Greenwood, Abrahamse, and Zimring 1984; Champion 1989; Clarke 1996). We also know that nonintervention typically does not serve the best interests of these children or enhance public safety.

Third, we must provide decision makers with choices and current knowledge about how each option relates to our objectives for children. Competency in this area also requires understanding racial and ethnic diversity. Rather than concerted efforts to make a homogeneous society or a one-size-fits-all system of justice, the role of government in preventing and responding to juvenile crime needs to reflect appreciation for diversity of all constituents. There also must be many resources, and from many domains.

Information and options must be coordinated across jurisdictional boundaries, not just between "adult" criminal justice and "kiddie" or "juvie" justice, but across social services, policing agencies, schools, health care providers, and private organizations that serve families and children. These entities now operate independently and routinely fail adequately to share relevant information about mutual clients or services, which diminishes the potential for any of them to be effective or efficient. In this volume Tanenhaus shows how the current independence, or lack of cooperation, evolved from early autonomy in juvenile justice systems. These early efforts to serve children within the narrow boundaries and resources of the new legal arena meant limited options, private facilities free of government oversight, and forced segregation by race, ethnicity, sex, and religion. Given recent centennial celebrations of juvenile courts, some of these difficulties appear to have been institutionalized for a very long time.

Fortunately, several authors in this volume identify concrete ways in which youths, including racial and ethnic minorities who are now overrepresented, can benefit from a cooperative and multifaceted approach in which government support helps other parts of society to nurture children and respond to crime. A competent system of justice for children requires a soup-to-nuts delivery of resources, attention, monitoring, and discipline. This integrated, cooperative system might best be viewed as a "public justice" model. An epidemiological approach has identified risk factors for juvenile crime, including those at the individual level, among families, and within communities, for which some minority youths are disproportionately at risk. Similarly, utilitarian policy solutions from which minority youths could benefit as much as or more than other youths might draw from successful multilevel models of public health responses (e.g., Rosenberg and Fenley 1991; Moore 1995; Gabor, Welsh, and Antonowicz 1996; Mercy et al. 2002).

As we explained in the introduction to this volume, nurturing children is a moral imperative in all societies. For that reason, efforts to assure that children have adequate resources and attention to promote successful development also contribute to justice in society. Jargowsky, Desmond, and Crutchfield discuss "ready to learn" issues, many of which apply more generally to the resources and attention to assure that children are ready to develop into successful adults. Many chapters in this volume also explain how necessary it is for beneficial services to be given to help some citizens overcome societal positions that are disadvantaged in exponential ways by their location, economic status, race, and ethnicity. Disparities cannot be overcome without adequate attention to inequalities in funding and quality of housing, schools, health care, and community development. Direct services that promote life skill development and self-esteem can reduce the likelihood of juvenile offending and are cost effective (Greenwood et al. 1996). To achieve justice in society, just as they are needed to achieve health in society, public and private partnerships are needed to address deficiencies that exist at the levels of individual infants and children, families, housing, and communities.

At the individual level, people must learn to behave responsibly and be held accountable for their actions. Teaching them to trust in themselves and to behave in such a way as to justify the trust of others generally is accepted as part of nurturing children to become productive citizens. Such nurturing also can promote desistance among chronic offenders, as those who accept responsibilities for their lives, try to help subsequent generations, and are optimistic about success are more likely succeed (e.g., Maruna 2001). Not only should offenders be held accountable for their actions, but active engagement in promoting justice should be a civic duty for which everyone is responsible (e.g., Braithwaite 1989).

When juveniles do offend, a competent system responds with monitoring, discipline, and services. Early intervention must be coordinated to include all three features and occur at the first signs of misconduct (e.g., Howell 2003); this is a critical aspect of effective nurturing for youths at risk of offending. Moreover, Steen and her colleagues show how important it is that attention be given to the process, not merely to system outcomes. Pope and Leiber also underscore the need for the process to involve community settings, and that minority youths are currently underserved in this way. It is clear that decisions from which confinement can result need to benefit more from relevant and accurate information that is shared by officials who are trained and sensitive to cultural differences. Officials, and the general public, must recognize that even well-intentioned institutionalization of youths now has negative consequences, too often especially for race and ethnic minorities. A competent system of justice for children works to minimize harm for all children.

Trust and accountability are essential elements in effective cooperation and thus need to be developed to reduce race and ethnic disparities in juvenile crime and justice. Like explanations for disparity and other aspects of the solution, accountability also requires commitment at multiple levels. Feld argues that those who make policy evade their obligations to all children with incompetent public policies because public policy discourse currently is inextricably intertwined with subjective ideas about race and ethnicity. At the level of justice systems, administrators should be held accountable for their decisions that fail to minimize harm for all children. Competent information and instruction, as well as monitoring and ongoing evaluation, can help to assure that accountability exist systemwide, which is important because it is clear that early decisions affect those that occur at subsequent stages.

In concluding, we recognize that although the reasons for disparity problems are complex, the solutions do not have to be. Applying the public health approach to develop a model of justice would underscore the cooperation necessary between prevention and intervention. Neither the needs of children nor the resources to address those needs are now, or perhaps ever will be, equally distributed. Effectiveness and efficiency are linked, however, so policy initiatives must target minimally acceptable levels and work toward achieving greater balance. Competency in knowledge and public policy go hand in hand. An effective system includes independent elements that work in unison to achieve a mutual goal or product. Race and ethnic disparity of youth in juvenile crime and justice exist partly because we do not have a society and justice system in which there are well-developed, cooperative, and well-funded institutional mechanisms to nurture children. Race and ethnicity differences in offending and system bias will be less problematic when society develops a cooperative, systematic approach in the United States to nurturing *our* children.

Notes

1. We use the term "unwarranted" to suggest that some level of racial, ethnic, and, particularly, social class disparity appears to be "built into" the logic of social reform that led to the establishment of the nation's juvenile court at the end of the nineteenth century. This is an observation we also make in our introduction. In addition, many chapters in this volume show that issues surrounding race and ethnicity within the juvenile justice system extend far beyond the question of whether disparity exists and whether or not it results from bias.

2. Scientifically speaking, these uninvestigated group differences are further compounded by the tendency of many researchers to consider "crime" as if it were a single entity and not a diverse assortment of offenses ranging from the very trivial to the very serious.

References

Bernard, Thomas J. 1992. *The Cycle of Juvenile Justice.* New York: Oxford University Press.

Braithwaite, John. 1989. *Crime, Shame and Reintegration.* Cambridge: Cambridge University Press.

Champion, Dean J. 1989. "Teenage Felons and Waiver Hearings: Some Recent Trends." *Crime and Delinquency* 35:577–585.

Clarke, Elizabeth E. 1996. "A Case for Reinventing Juvenile Transfer." *Juvenile and Family Court Journal* 47, no.4:3–21.

Cole, David. 1999. *No Equal Justice: Race and Class in the American Criminal Justice System.* New York: Free Press.

Gabor, T., B. C. Welsh, and D. H. Antonowicz. 1996. "The Role of the Health Community in the Prevention of Criminal Violence." *Canadian Journal of Criminology* 38:317–333.

Gottfredson, Michael R., and Don M. Gottfredson. 1980. *Decision Making in Criminal Justice: Toward the Rational Exercise of Discretion.* 2nd ed. New York: Plenum.

Greenwood, Peter W., Allan Abrahamse, and Franklin Zimring. 1984. *Factors Affecting Sentencing Severity for Young Adult Offenders.* Santa Monica, CA: RAND.

Greenwood, Peter, K. E. Model, C. P. Rydell, and J. Chiesa W. 1996. *Diverting Children from a Life of Crime: Measuring Costs and Benefits.* Santa Monica, CA: RAND.

Hamparian, Donna, Linda K. Estep, Susan M. Muntean, Ramon R. Priestino, Robert G. Swisher, Paul L. Wallace, Joseph L. White. 1982. *Major Issues in Juvenile Justice Information and Training, Youth in Adult Courts: Between Two Worlds.* U.S. Department of Justice: Office of Juvenile Justice and Delinquency Prevention.

Hirschi, Travis, and Michael R. Gottfredson. 1993. "Rethinking the Juvenile Justice System." *Crime and Delinquency* 39:262–271.

Howell, James C. 2003. *Preventing and Reducing Juvenile Delinquency: A Comprehensive Framework*. Thousand Oaks, CA: Sage.

Maruna, Shadd. 2001. *Making Good: How Ex-convicts Reform and Rebuild Their Lives*. Washington, DC: American Psychological Association.

McCord, Joan, Cathy S. Widom, and Nancy A. Crowell. 2001. *Juvenile Crime, Juvenile Justice*. Washington, DC: National Academy Press.

Mercy, J. A., A. Butchart, D. P. Farrington, and M. Cerda. 2002. "Youth Violence." Pp. 23–56 in *World Report on Violence and Health*, ed. E. G. Krig. L. L. Dahlberg, J. A. Mercy, A. B. Zwi, and R. Lozano. Geneva: World Health Organization.

Miller, Jerome. 1996. *Search and Destroy: African-American Males in the Criminal Justice System*. Cambridge: Cambridge University Press.

Moore, Mark H. 1995. "Public Health and Criminal Justice Approaches to Prevention." Pp. 237–262 in *Building a Safer Society: Strategic Approaches to Crime Prevention*, ed. Michael Tonry and David P. Farrington, Crime and Justice: A Review of Research, vol. 19. Chicago: University of Chicago Press.

Rosenberg, Irene Merker. 1999. "Leaving Bad Enough Alone: A Response to the Juvenile Court Abolitionists." Pp. 367–372 in *Readings in Juvenile Justice Administration*, ed. by Barry C. Feld. New York: Oxford University Press.

Rosenberg, M. L., and M. A. Fenley. 1991. *Violence in America: A Public Health Approach*. New York: Oxford University Press.

Sellin, Thorsten. 1935. "Race Prejudice in the Administration of Justice." *American Journal of Sociology* 41:212–217.

Simpson, Sally. 1991. "Caste, Class, and Violent Crime: Explaining Differences in Female Offending." *Criminology* 29:115–135.

Tonry, Michael. 1995. *Malign Neglect: Race, Crime and Punishment in America*. New York: Oxford University Press.

———. 1996. *Sentencing Matters*. New York: Oxford University Press.

Wilson, William Julius. 1987. *The Truly Disadvantaged: The Inner City, the Underclass, and Public Policy*. Chicago: University of Chicago Press.

Von Hirsch, Andrew. 1976. *Doing Justice*. New York: Hill and Wang.

Contributors

Donna M. Bishop, Northeastern University
Christine E. W. Bond, University of Queensland
Timothy M. Bray, University of Texas at Dallas
George S. Bridges, University of Washington
Elizabeth Cauffman, University of California—Irvine
Robert D. Crutchfield, University of Washington
Scott A. Desmond, Purdue University
Barry C. Feld, University of Minnesota
Thomas Grisso, University of Massachusetts Medical School
Darnell F. Hawkins, University of Illinois at Chicago
Paul A. Jargowsky, University of Texas at Dallas
Kimberly Kempf-Leonard, University of Texas at Dallas
Barry A. Krisberg, National Council on Crime and Delinquency
Charis E. Kubrin, George Washington University
Janet L. Lauritsen, University of Missouri—St. Louis
Brian Lawton, Temple University
Michael J. Leiber, University of Northern Iowa
Terrie E. Moffitt, University of Wisconsin at Madison
Alex R. Piquero, University of Florida
Carl Pope, University of Wisconsin at Milwaukee
Lisa L. Sample, University of Nebraska at Omaha
Sara Steen, University of Colorado at Boulder
David S. Tanenhaus, University of Nevada at Las Vegas
Paul E. Tracy, University of Texas at Dallas
Franklin E. Zimring, University of California at Berkeley

Subject Index